San Diego Christian College
2100 Greenfield Drive
El Cajon, CA 92019

DAVID JONES: MAN AND POET

DAVID JONES

NATIONAL
POETRY
FOUNDATION, INC.
UNIVERSITY OF MAINE

Man and Poet

Edited
with an introduction by
John Matthias

Published by

The National Poetry Foundation
University of Maine
Orono, Maine 04469

Printed by

The University of Maine
Printing Office

Library of Congress Number: 88-62931
ISBN: 0-943373-03-4 (cloth)
0-943373-04-2 (paper)

ACKNOWLEDGMENTS

This page represents a continuation of copyright information from the verso.

I

For permission to reproduce paintings, drawings, engravings and inscriptions by David Jones, acknowledgment is made to the following:

The Tate Gallery, London: for "Aphrodite in Aulis," "Sanctus Christus de Capel-y-ffin," "The Four Queens," and "Crucifixion";

The National Museum of Wales, Cardiff: for "Y Cyfarchiad I Fair," "Trystan Ac Essyllt," "Eric Gill," and "The Translator of 'The Chanson de Roland' ";

The National Library of Wales, Aberystwyth: for "Cara Wallia Derelicta" and "Pwy Yw R Gwr Piav R Goron";

Kettle's Yard, Cambridge: for "Vexilla Regis" and "Flora in Calix-Light";

Arthur Giardelli: for "Manawydan's Glass Door" and "Study for 'Trystan Ac Essylt' ";

The Victoria and Albert Museum, London (by courtesy of the Board of Trustees of the Victoria and Albert Museum): for "Dvm Medivm Silentivm";

The Trustees of the Imperial War Museum, London: for "Epiphany 1941: Britannia and Germania Embracing";

The Laing Art Gallery, Newcastle upon Tyne (reproduced by arrangement with Tyne and Wear Museum Service): "The Mother of the West";

The Anthony d'Offay Gallery, London: for "Tywysog Cariad";

Douglas Cleverdon and Clover Hill Editions, London: for "The Albatross" and "He Frees the Waters in Helyon";

Nicolete Gray: for "Vere Dignvm" (an inscription made by David Jones for Helen Sutherland for her eightieth birthday; private collection);

Mrs. T. S. Eliot: for "Nam Sybillam";

Paul Hills: for "Crucifixion" and "Lamentation";

Janet Stone: for "Petra Im Rosenhag."

II

For permission to reprint poems, memoirs, statements, essays and excerpts from essays or books, acknowledgment is made to the following:

Faber and Faber Ltd. for "From *Dai Greatcoat: A Self-Portrait of David Jones in His Letters*" (reprinted by permission of Faber and Faber Ltd. from *Dai Greatcoat* by René Hague) and "A Note on *In Parenthesis* and *The Anathemata*"

III

Several essays have been revised following their original publication. These include: Colin Hughes, "David Jones: The Man Who Was On The Field: *In Parenthesis* as Straight Reporting" (originally published as a David Jones Society pamphlet); Vincent Sherry, Jr., "The Ineluctible Monologuality of The Heroic" (originally published as "A New Boast for *In Parenthesis*: The Dramatic Monologue of David Jones" in *Notre Dame English Journal*, 14, 2 [Spring, 1982]; N. K. Sandars' "The Present Past in *The Anathemata* and Roman Poems" and Arthur Giardelli's "Four Related Works by David Jones" (both originally published in *David Jones: Eight Essays on His Work*, ed. Roland Mathias [Llandysul, Wales: Gomer Press, 1976]); Jeremy Hooker, "In the Labyrinth: An Exploration of *The Anathemata*" (originally published as part of his monograph *David Jones: An Exploratory Study of the Writings* [London: Enitharmon Press, 1975]); and Thomas Dilworth, "David Jones and Fascism" (originally published in the *Journal of Modern Literature*, 13, 1 [March, 1986]).

TABLE OF CONTENTS

THE POET

In Parenthesis

The Anathemata

LIST OF PLATES AND PHOTOGRAPHS

between pages 404 and 405

Hague's work, in part because it comes in for a certain amount of criticism in some of what follows. However much one may disagree with some of Hague's conclusions, or however much one may regret certain oversights or omissions, there is no question about his dedication or the significance of his work. If two of the main contributions of this generation were advocacy and elementary exegesis, Hague was the chief advocate and exegete.

The second generation of Jones criticism is characterized by the work of men like John H. Johnston, Bernard Bergonzi and Jon Silkin who sought to understand *In Parenthesis* in the context of the literature of World War I, and by both sharply focussed and generally introductory studies by David Blamires, William Blissett, Tony Stoneburner, N. K. Sandars, Nicolete Gray, Arthur Giardelli, Roland Mathias and (in France) Louis Bonnerot. Much of the work of this generation occurred during the period of Peter Orr's interviews with and recordings of David Jones (1964-1972), and some of the best of it was published in the two *Agenda* special issues on David Jones' work (1967 and 1974) and in Roland Mathias' *David Jones: Eight Essays on His Work as Writer and Artist* (1976). The most permanent contributions of this group are doubtless found in John H. Johnston's chapter "David Jones: The Heroic Vision" in *English Poetry of the First World War*, a study which Jones himself called in 1962 "the only decent analysis of *IP* that's ever appeared" (*DGC*, 188), David Blamires' *David Jones: Artist and Writer*, the first book-length study which considers Jones' work as a whole, the recordings made in association with the British Council and the Lamont Library edited by Peter Orr, *The Painted Inscriptions of David Jones*, edited and introduced by Nicolete Gray, along with the various critical essays by William Blissett and his booklength memoir called *The Long Conversation*.

Though the first two generations of David Jones critics are represented in this volume, the burden of work falls on the shoulders of a third. It is with this generation, I feel, that David Jones criticism comes fully of age. In the work of these critics--Thomas Dilworth, John Peck, Jeremy Hooker, Neil Corcoran, Paul Hills, Vincent Sherry, Kathleen Staudt, Patrick Deane, the somewhat senior Thomas Whitaker and Guy Davenport (and a few others whose work could not be represented here but which is taken account of in the bibliography)--criticism finally begins fully to recognize the poet and artist as a major figure who requires no special pleading, whether by Roman Catholics, Welshmen or historians of The War, but only a depth of understanding equal to his vision. Even the recent unsympathetic critics--Elizabeth Ward, for example, or Paul Fussell in *The Great War and Modern Memory*--are able to assume that they are writing about a very substantial figure indeed. Otherwise, their work implies, why bother? Some of the critics of this generation have been taught by members of the second generation (particularly by Blissett at the University of Toronto), and all have been instructed by the pioneering work of the first. While this group has not yet, of course, produced its final contributions to the study of David Jones, one can already single out for particular attention Paul Hills' excellent catalogue published on the occasion of the 1981 Tate Gallery retrospective exhibit, Elizabeth Ward's highly critical but important *David Jones Mythmaker*, and Neil Corcoran's monograph on *The Anathemata, The Song of Deeds*; and one may anticipate with pleasure the appearance, coincident with the publication of *David Jones: Man and Poet*, of Thomas Dilworth's massive study of all the writings, *The Shape of Meaning in the Poetry of David Jones*, and (in due course) his official biography. There are also booklength works now in progress (and in one case even at press) by Staudt, Gray, and Christine Pagnoulle. As Samuel Rees says in the introduction to his annotated bibliography, "the question of whether or not David Jones' work is merely the venerated object of a narrowly self-defined band of cultish admirers vexes some critics and commentators." Without arguing the question, he notes only--and this is answer enough--that his bibliography "includes criticism in five languages other than English . . . published in at least eight different countries on four continents . . . and by persons of a wide variety of religious and political persuasions." Though this book includes only British, Irish, Canadian and American contributors, the range of interests and the angles of engagement should help to dispel the misapprehension which Rees identifies.

3

This book, like others in the "Man and Poet" series, begins with a series of brief statements or tributes, poems dedicated to or inspired by David Jones, and several biographical studies. The focus of this part of the book, that is to say, is on the man. It seems to me that there are essentially four areas of the biography which remain in some sense controversial: the question of the causes, extent and effect of David Jones' neurosis; the question of his sexuality and his relationship to women; the question of his politics and its relationship both to the Catholic right in England and the rise of Fascism and Nazism abroad; and the question of the depth of his personal and poetic connection to Wales, not only with respect to the Welsh sources of "The Matter of Britain," but also with respect to contemporary Wales, the Welsh language, and the nationalism of firends like Saunders Lewis and Valerie Wynne-Williams. All four of these areas are discussed by various contributors to this book--especially by Thomas Dilworth, Neil Corcoran and John Peck--often with reference to the positions taken by René Hague in *Dai Greatcoat* and Elizabeth Ward in *David Jones Mythmaker*. Leaving the question of David Jones' politics (and the argument of Elizabeth Ward) pretty much in the hands of Thomas Dilworth, I want to say a few things about Jones' neurosis, his relationship with women, and the depth of his commitment to the things of Wales, by way of reference to *Dai Greatcoat*, the book which is likely to remain, until the publication of Dilworth's biography, the most authoritative biographical source.

I have included among the biographical essays and memoirs a selection of Jones' letters to H. S. Ede directly following the excerpt from *Dai Greatcoat*. One purpose for doing so, as I remark in my introduction to this corre-spondence, is to modify slightly the version of David Jones encountered in Hague. Most of the letters in *Dai Greatcoat* are addressed to Grisewood and Hague himself, and all of them, with the exception of one previously published letter to Saunders Lewis, are addressed to Englishmen; there are no letters to women and there are no letters to Jones' many Welsh friends and acquaintances. Hague's explanation of his sharp focus occurs early in the preface:

> What is printed concentrates on a single aspect of the man. He may well (indeed, I know that he does) speak in a different tone, and so present a different person, to others with whom he had a different relationship. I felt, however, that I could not bring myself to copy and print anything which I could not fully understand, could not fully get the feel of, because it went into intellectual, emotional, literary, historical or religious fields, and attitudes to those fields, that were in any degree foreign to me. I wished to print only what was said in a tone of voice that was completely familiar to me. I could feel sure of my ground only if I knew David's correspondent well enough to understand how what David wrote would be received and understood. Had I felt otherwise, a vast range of correspondence would no doubt have been open to me.... (*DGC*, 12-13).

This passage is candor itself, and yet I think we need to speculate for a moment about what might be missing from the point of view of a biographer or an editor of a hypothetical Collected Letters. Indeed Hague discusses these matters himself, referring his reader to Tony Stoneburner's *List of Letters by David Jones* (Granville, Ohio: Limekiln Press, 1977) which catalogues some seven hundred letters addressed to some seventy-five correspondents, an inventory which, though very useful, is by no means definitive or complete. A quick glance at Stoneburner shows many letters written to women--letters, for example, to Petra Tegetmeier (née Gill), to whom David Jones was briefly engaged, Nancy Sandars, Janet Stone, Kathleen Raine, and Helen Sutherland (the chief patron of David Jones' painting to whom there are 136 letters, more than to anyone else on the list). Surprisingly, there are no letters to Prudence Buhler (née Pelham), to whom David Jones must certainly have written many times. Hague calls this relationship "the most important in David's life." My point is that the chief omission in *Dai Greatcoat* is certainly of representative letters written to women, letters which would reveal, as Hague says, "a very different aspect of the writer" (*DGC*, 13). This is important both because Jones' notion of "the feminine" is of such central significance in his work, and because one of the foggy areas of the self-portrait in *Dai Greatcoat* has to do with Jones' relationships with women--both those with whom he was in love ("I believe in the reality of 'Romantic Love.' I always have" [*DGC*, 177]) and those with whom his relationship was of a different kind altogether--literary, artistic, scholarly, or what have you. It is not a question of Hague being too fastidious to print letters in which Jones writes of his emotional turmoil. Enough time seems to have passed, in fact, that he feels free to disregard Jim Ede's note "not for publication" written in the margin of the letter to him in which Jones expresses his great distress when Prudence Pelham decides to marry Guy Branch (*DGC*, 91). But the relationships with women friends, and especially the relationships with those Hague calls Jones' "cult figures," are necessarily pretty dimly outlined in the book in the absence of letters actually written to some of them.

Related to this matter is also the question of Hague's interpretation of David Jones' several psychological breakdowns and the severe psychological stress with which he had to deal throughout most of his life and which for long periods of time made work, particularly painting, a near impossibility. Hague's theory is surprising at first, but it would seem to be supported by most of the letters he prints which deal with what Jones usually calls simply "neurosis" or "neurasthenia," and what first Tom Burns, and later Jones himself, began to personify as "Rosy."

What surprises one is Hague's belief that David Jones' war experiences had virtually nothing to do with his breakdowns, and that the loss of Petra Gill and Prudence Pelham to other men figured only insofar as marriage was finally seen by Jones as necessarily incompatible with the practice of the artist's vocation in the civilizational phase in which he found himself. My guess is that the publication of further correspondence and other biographical studies will lead in time to certain qualifications of Hague's analysis and the evidence of the letters which he prints. Indeed, certain works cited in Samuel Rees' bibliography in this book, along with the biographical investigations of Thomas Dilworth, have already begun to do this.

For a long time now I think it has been assumed by readers of David Jones--and asserted by many--that Jones' war experiences were the central causal factor in the breakdowns and protracted illnesses. Douglas Cleverdon, for example, says in his essay on "David Jones and Broadcasting" (*Poetry Wales*, Winter 1972) that it was the "vivid externalisation of the horrors of trench warfare" brought about when Jones heard the November, 1946 BBC performance of the radio version of *In Parenthesis* that "precipitated an illness that lasted for several weeks" and led Jones eventually to Bowden House and the care of the sympathetic and gifted psychiatrist, Dr. Stevenson. And no doubt many of those who visited David Jones late in his life put to themselves the questions raised by Robert Craft after his visit to Jones at Harrow with Stravinsky: "At what point does the self-consciousness of the solitary man, and the pedantry and overdeveloped sensibilities which are his forms of hypochondria--at what point do they begin dangerously to shut him off from his 'super-ego' and the outside. . . ? Can one trace the malady to the war, to experiences and emotions that could not be shared afterward with women, and that therefore in some cases resulted in a withdrawal from women?" (*Themes and Episodes*, New York: Alfred A. Knopf, 1967, p. 258). But Hague is adamant. "David enjoyed the war," he writes in one of the passages reprinted here from his book. "He loved soldiering and comradeship. . . . *In Parenthesis* . . . is not an exposition or condemnation of the horrors of war, even if

it is concerned with them. A careful reading of the *Preface*
shows a pride and delight in the type of war that, by David's
reckoning, ended in 1916; and the core of the book is the
goodness of 'the intimate, continuing, domestic life of small
contingents of men, within whose structure Roland could
find, and for a reasonable while, enjoy his Oliver' " (*DGC*,
58). Finding even stronger confirmation in Jones'
conversation and letters, he says: "There were no nightmares,
no horrors that could not be mentioned, no noises, smells,
scenes that made wounds bleed afresh. . . . On the other
hand, the difficulties he met in his work, and the
accompanying at times paralysing mental and spiritual
stress, will be patent to every reader of his letters and
published work" (*DGC*, 58).

Before Dr. Stevenson and Bowden House, Jones had
been treated in 1932 by a neurologist specializing in the
treatment of shell-shock who advised "masterly inactivity"--
in particular no painting if painting brought on the illness--
and a long sea voyage to Cairo and Jerusalem. Though the
voyage was temporarily helpful, the "masterly inactivity"
was ultimately an impossible prescription, for, as Jones later
recognized, "the unconscious demands a higher and higher
blackmail--less and less activity as a price, so that the *only*
way is to beat the unconscious in open war" (*DGC*, 140).
Stevenson, says Hague, understood when treating Jones after
his 1946 breakdown "what David meant when he spoke of
the difficulties that present themselves to the artist in this
'age of steel,' and made David himself see that they could
be solved only by frontal attack. After a first period of rest
and gentle recreation, he was ordered to paint. He obeyed,
and he won" (*DGC*, 132). Some of the most interesting
"letters" in *Dai Greatcoat* are not, properly speaking, letters
at all, but rather what remains of the series of notes which
Jones wrote to Dr. Stevenson during his treatment
acknowledging "the ramifications of the sexual impulse"
and "the findings [of the doctors] . . . about my fear etc.
with regard to sex," but going on beyond such an
acknowledgment to argue that the fundamental cause of his
illness was to be seen, as Hague says, "in the tension which
arises when the artist has to accommodate himself to
modern civilization" (*DGC*, 136). An aspect of the artist's
essential vocational problem presents itself in terms Jones
feels to be "completely defensible and reasonable" even
though they *may* be interpreted, in his own case, as a
"rationalization" of his inhibitions:

I do emphatically say that over and beyond those symptoms of imbalance in my own make-up, there is the concept of "not marriage" as a perfectly rational desire in order to pursue what appears to this or that person to be a greater good. Here it seems to me the whole of history bears witness. ... I should also like to mention that I feel that the "contemporary situation" has a real bearing here--it seems to me (and I have all my life been aware of it) that at the breakdown of a culture (bringing great abnormality at all levels and very great divergence of standards of every sort, and economic pressure--all detrimental to mating and normal marriage even for tough and resilient persons) many people who otherwise in a normal world would get married, quite logically avoid doing so if they feel they have some vital work to do, because the conditions of their time make it virtually impossible for them to marry and bring up a family without at the same time prostituting (or something like it) the work they do. ... I think perhaps psychology as such is less concerned than are religion and metaphysics with hierarchies of perfection. What may be an admirable and salutary thing at one level may be unsatisfactory at another level. Whatever our psychic make-up, we all desire perfection, even at the expense of great misery.--This gets one into difficulties ... "Why do you want the moon when you have the stars?" (*DGC*, 136-37)

If Yeats is right and "the intellect of man is forced to choose/ Perfection of the life, or of the work," David Jones, according to Hague's explanation and according to the notes to Dr. Stevenson, chose perfection of the work. Making that choice, he suffered out the consequences in his life with an ever increasing understanding of his predicament and an ever increasing ability to articulate his situation--a situation which he took to be representative--in letters, essays and sometimes poems. The struggle against the dominant pressures of the age, however, against the "utile infiltrations," the "root trouble," the internalized demands for "less and less activity" as an artist had to be fought out initially in the arena of his painting, the activity in which what he calls his "major conflict" first and most radically displayed itself. Furthermore, his understanding of his difficulties was sometimes thought out more fully in accordance with classical Freudian analysis of his "rationalization of inhibitions" than in accordance with religious or metaphysical analysis of hierarchies of perfection. Thomas Dilworth, in an unpublished manuscript which will doubtless find its way into his biography (and from which I quote with his permission), writes that "while undergoing therapy and probably on the advice of his psychiatrist . . . David Jones read and reread *Totem and Taboo*, in which Freud writes that he regards 'the Oedipus Complex . . . as the nuclear complex of neuroses.' " In spite of the arguments advanced in his notes to Dr. Stevenson,

Jones also came to believe "that Freud really had it right, this father/mother relationship" (*DGC*, 131). Persuing the question biographically through speculation about "an increase in his mother's affections for fifteen-year-old David when his only brother, Harold, died at the age of twenty-one in 1910," Dilworth concludes that during his treatment at Bowden House in 1947 Jones must have come to understand that his repression of sexual feelings towards his mother was "so intense that it became a generalized reaction characterizing his relationship with other women."

> He must also have realized how sexual feeling and its repression help to account for the centrality of idealized women in all of his best figurative pictures and for the powerfully moving appearance of the Queen of the Wood, a fertility goddess, at the conclusion of *In Parenthesis*. In 1955 he says that if a man writes a poem about his sweetheart,
>
> > Heaven knows what his poem will really be 'about'; for then the 'sacramental' will pile up by a positively geometric progression. So that what was Miss Flora Smith may turn out to be Flora Dea and Venus too and the First Eve and the second also and other and darker figures, among them no doubt, Jocasta. One thing at least the psychologists make plain: there is always a recalling, a representing again, anaphora, anamnesis. (*E&A*, 167)
>
> From reading *Totem and Taboo* and doubtless from conversation with Dr. Stevenson, he realized, furthermore, how the repression of the libido becomes automatic and shifts to other areas of subconscious release, such as painting and writing, which it attempts to inhibit. At the advice of Dr. Stevenson, Jones assaulted his neurosis head-on by resuming creative work. As a result, he was able to produce most of his visual art and poetry, beginning with the remarkable allegorical painting *Vexilla Regis* (1947), and including the great chalice paintings of the mid 1950s, the lettered inscriptions, *The Anathemata* and *The Sleeping Lord*. Taken all together, this is not only an artistic and literary achievement unsurpassed by any Englishman in the twentieth century, but also, psychologically, a remarkable personal achievement. He consistently beat back his neurosis in its primary manifestation.

Without trying in any way to reduce Jones' painting or poetry to an Oedipal fixation, Dilworth means to say only what Jones himself says, "that everything one does is conditioned by one's psychopathology" (*DGC*, 137). Citing the passage stressed by Hague in *Dai Greatcoat* in which Jones "protests to his psychiatrist that his celibate dedication to his art is not merely 'a rationalization of my inhibitions and fears of sex' " (*DGC*, 137), Dilworth adds: "Nevertheless, the frustration of sexual desire intensifies sexual desire. And the intensity of his desire conditions the art by which it is only partially sublimated. After 1947, he was aware of all this, and his awareness conditions his art." Several of the contributors to this volume pursue a line of argument, arrived at independently, that might have been suggested by Dilworth's central paragraph:

> Idealized, sometimes deified, female figures continue to appear throughout this later work. His awareness of why this should be so is signalled in *The Anathemata* by repeated allusions to the Oedipal complex. Not that these allusions are merely private in significance; he saw the Oedipal complex as receiving broad cultural expression in the widespread pagan-mythic identification of mother with consort, and in the symbolic identification of Christ's mother with the Church-as-bride, "he her groom that is his mother" (*A*, 235).

The other area of biographical interest about which something ought to be said at the outset has to do with Jones' identification with Wales and the things of Wales. Because René Hague is so insistent in a passage here reprinted that it is the *English* rather than the Welsh tradition which is fundamental to his work, I had hoped to include Roland Mathias' long rebuttal from his book *A Ride Through the Wood* (Poetry Wales Press, 1985) called "Towards the Holy Diversities." Mathias' essay, however, is over forty pages long, and it turned out that, much as I would have liked to have the piece, we were unable to take space from new work for such a substantial reprint. When Hague writes that "in spite of all David's attempts to Cambrianize his work, in spite of all he says with such pathos and eloquence, and in spite of his devotion to a great Welsh myth, it was the English tradition that was most completely assimilated, and everything in his work that is most convincing, sincere, and based on real knowledge and understanding is English," (*DGC*, 23) Roland Mathias responds in his essay with a powerful refutation which is half biographical and half literary-critical. Hague's verdict, he says,

> Is astonishing most of all from an Anglo-Irishman and an old friend, the more astonishing in its use of the word *sincere*. But then it has to be realized that *Dai Greatcoat* itself is a portrait based on letters to *English* friends and one from which the Welsh enthusiasms have been editorially shaded out. David Jones is on record himself, not once or twice but often, in an attempt to explain the yearning of the man for whom an English culture and education are the *data* and for whom Welsh comes as a written language and too late, but who nevertheless reaches out constantly in learning and imagination towards his Welsh inheritance and who uses part of the myth which shapes that to point the direction of his writing. There can hardly be a sterner test of sincerity than to spend a life largely in fronting difficulties that an

Englishman, in the spiritual sense, need never have bothered himself with.

I have only space enough in this introduction to record my own opinion that Roland Mathias makes his case powerfully and decisively, and to recommend his essay to all readers of this book who are interested in the question at issue, whether from a biographical or literary-critical point of view. Both Teresa Phelps and John Peck enter into dialogue with Mathias' argument in their own contributions to this book in readings of "The Hunt," "The Tutelar of The Place," and "The Sleeping Lord." As one might guess, it is finally with his own reading of "The Sleeping Lord" that Roland Mathias rests his case. "The movement towards Wales in the later poems in *The Sleeping Lord*," he says, "is unmistakable." Politically timid, Jones was not able, Mathias understands, to move towards Wales to the extent that his nationalist friends Saunders Lewis and Valerie Wynne-Williams might have wished. And yet it was nevertheless, Mathias contends, "Left-dominated, 'bloody democratic' Wales, the pitiable remnant of a tradition going back to Troy, the Wales of David's present" that warred with his notions of *necessity* and *imperium*. "The *imperium* had been the emblem of his own need for strength and reassurance: Wales spoke to him constantly of freedom and a separate tradition. In the later years of his better health Wales came, of the two, to seem the more desirable and he moved towards it as far as he was able." This, again, is simply the conclusion of an elegantly written, long, subtle, and powerfully argued essay. But in my opinion it is, in this matter of Wales, the correct conclusion. It would therefore be wrong of me to let the paragraphs in my excerpt from *Dai Greatcoat* stand without at least calling to the reader's attention the existence of the best response to them that I know.

4

It remains to say a few words about the contents and structure of the volume and to acknowledge the assistance of several individuals and institutions; without them *David Jones: Man and Poet* would have been impossible to produce. (Formal acknowledgments, with technical data and copyright information, appear on the acknowledgments page.)

The format of *David Jones: Man and Poet* conforms, on the whole, with that of other volumes in the

National Poetry Foundation series. The chief difference is the result of an initial decision that David Jones' work as a visual artist must be discussed in the book along with his poetry and, more than that, abundantly illustrated. Included in the volume, therefore, are both the long essays by Paul Hills and Arthur Giardelli and reprints of the brief appreciations by Eric Gill and Kenneth Clark, along with a number of reproductions, both in color and black and white, of Jones' paintings, drawings, engravings and inscriptions. I am particularly grateful to Paul Hills and the Tate Gallery for lending me the color separations and black and white transparencies that were used in printing the 1981 David Jones retrospective catalogue. This has meant that we have been able to include more reproductions than we had at first thought possible and, needless to say, that we have been able to produce this work at less expense. I also wish to thank the estate of David Jones and all owners of art works by David Jones, whether individuals, galleries or libraries, for permission to reproduce the paintings, drawings, engravings and inscriptions. This book naturally falls open in one's lap to the reproductions of these visual works. Before reading a word of it, one is therefore likely to take in a range of visual images which characterize the writing as much as the painting and drawing. This seems to me wholly appropriate and desirable. As David Jones always said, drawing and painting came first for him--both chronologically and, as it were, by desire.

Enough has been said about the biographical section of the book. Directly following the initial poems, statements, letters and biographical essays dealing, on the whole, with "the man," the section on "the poet" is subdivided to present four essays each on *In Parenthesis* and *The Anathemata,* three on *The Sleeping Lord,* and one on *The Roman Quarry* as the source for and a perspective on much of David Jones' later writing. Following the sound principle which David Jones often quoted from the scholastics--"we proceed from the known to the unknown"--I have tried to organize the essays in such a way that introductory studies come first in each subdivision and more complex or specialized essays come last, or at least later. The new reader of David Jones might well begin his study of the works with the aid of Colin Hughes' essay on *In Parenthesis* as straight reporting, N. K. Sandars' introductory appreciation of *The Anathemata* from the point of view of Jones' interest in the ancient world, and Teresa Phelps' study of the fundamental tension of opposites in

The Sleeping Lord before tackling, for example, Vincent Sherry's piece on the Boast of Dai Greatcoat in *In Parenthesis*, Patrick Deane's linguistically technical analysis of language and style in *The Anathemata*, or John Peck's dense and erudite reading of poems from *The Sleeping Lord*. William Blissett's sharply focussed essay on "The Syntax of Violence" in *In Parenthesis* makes a good pair with Neil Corcoran's more general consideration of that text under the three aspects of its contemporaneity, its sexuality and its politics in "Spilled Bitterness: *In Parenthesis* in History." Also complimentary are Jeremy Hooker's and Thomas Dilworth's contributions on *The Anathemata* with their differing analyses of the structure of that work. In the section on *The Sleeping Lord* and *The Roman Quarry*, Tony Stoneburner's "Notes Toward Performing *The Sleeping Lord*" anticipates several of the themes taken up at greater length in Peck's "Poems for Britian, Poems for Sons," and, like Sherry's essay, traces *The Sleeping Lord* back to its sources in *The Roman Quarry*. Following the section on "The Artist" and the reproductions of visual work are two essays on David Jones' thought as it manifests itself in the essays published in *Epoch and Artist* and *The Dying Gaul* and in his reading of Spengler's *The Decline of the West*. Kathleen Henderson Staudt's consideration of Jones and Spengler, based in part on her study of Jones' annotations in his copy of *The Decline of The West*, focusses on one central aspect of David Jones' thinking. Thomas Whitaker, on the other hand, ranges widely through the essays to produce, in my view, the most ambitious and comprehensive account of Jones' basic equation--"Homo Faber, Homo Sapiens"--yet to be published. Like other volumes in this series, *David Jones: Man and Poet* concludes with "The Testament": Samuel Rees' annotated bibliography and Paul Hills' list of art works by David Jones in public collections.

I wish, in conclusion, to acknowledge the help and cooperation of all contributors to this book, particularly Thomas Dilworth and Vincent Sherry. On behalf of all contributors, I thank Faber and Faber Ltd., Agenda Editions, and the Estate of David Jones for permission to quote from the published works and letters of David Jones as well as from certain unpublished letters and documents housed at Kettle's Yard, Cambridge, and the Jones archive at the National Library of Wales. I also thank the curators and professional staffs at Kettle's Yard, the Tate Gallery, and The National Museum of Wales for assistance and advice.

Among individuals who have offered assistance along the way, I thank H. S. Ede, William Cookson, Roland Mathias, Joseph Buttigieg, Romana Huk, David Blamires, Douglas Cleverdon, Rosemary Goad and Cary Archard. Thanks are due to Marie McCosh Alpert and Betsy Graves for simultaneously typesetting and copy-editing all the texts, an extremely difficult task which may have left certain minor inconsistencies in the book but which, for reasons I cannot consider here, was entirely necessary if we were to meet our publication date. For help with proofreading, my thanks to Robert Banning. And for checking the accuracy and lineation of all David Jones quotes, my thanks to Sylvester Pollet. For travel and research grants awarded in connection with this project, I acknowledge the National Endowment for the Humanities and the Institute for Scholarship in the Liberal Arts at the University of Notre Dame. Finally and most importantly, I want to express the gratitude of all involved with the making of *David Jones: Man and Poet* to Carroll F. Terrell, Burton Hatlen and the National Poetry Foundation.

John Matthias
University of Notre Dame

Abbreviations and a note on the lineation of David Jones quotes

All contributors have adopted the following system of abbreviations (followed by page references) in their essays:

A	*The Anathemata*
IP	*In Parenthesis*
RQ	*The Roman Quarry*
SL	*The Sleeping Lord*
DG	*The Dying Gaul*
DGC	*Dai Greatcoat*
E&A	*Epoch and Artist*
IN	*Inner Necessities*
LF	*Letters to a Friend*
LVW	*Letters to Vernon Watkins*
TC	*Tate Gallery Catalogue*
PI	*The Painted Inscriptions*

David Jones' works characteristically modulate from prose
to verse and back again to prose. Over the years certain
marginal terminations of the justified prose passages have
become familiar. For example, the beginning of *The
Anathemata*:

> We already and first of all discern him making this thing
> other. His groping syntax, if we attend, already shapes.

This particular passage, however, like hundreds more in *The
Anathemata, In Parenthesis, The Sleeping Lord* and *The
Roman Quarry*, is a passage printed in all editions as
justified prose. "Thing/other" does not constitute the end of
one verse line and the beginning of another. The first line
of the passage could just as well have ended on "this" or
"other" as on "thing" had the margins or the type size been
different. This book reproduces all passages of verse as
meticulously as possible, adhering with great care to
indentations and lineations of the Faber and Faber editions
of *The Anathemata, In Parenthesis* and *The Sleeping Lord*,
and the Agenda edition of *The Roman Quarry*. Passages of
justified prose, however, are printed as justified prose. Given
a typeface, type size, and margins different from those in
the Faber and Faber and Agenda editions, this means that
the end-words of the prose passages will not be the same as
those familiar to readers of David Jones' books. The rule
has been to print justified prose passages as justified prose
and not to worry about what word ends up at the margin on
the right. There is one exception to the rule. If a passage of
justified prose *begins* at any point further from the left
margin than the usual three ems of indentation used for
normative paragraph indentation in the Faber and Faber
editions, we have set the *first line* in such a way that it
ends with the same word that ends that line in the book
from which it is quoted.

CHRONOLOGY[1]

1895

1 November: born in Brockley, Kent, son of James Jones, printer's overseer, of Holywell, Flintshire, and Alice Bradshaw, daughter of a mast-and-block maker of Rotherhithe.

1901-2

Earliest surviving drawings, mostly of animals.

1910-14

Attended Camberwell School of Art; taught by A. S. Hartrick. His ambition to become an illustrator of Welsh history or an animal painter.

1915-18

Served on the Western Front with the Royal Welch Fusiliers; most of his trench drawings destroyed.

1919

2 January: "certificate of transfer to reserve on demobilization."

1919-21

Studied at Westminster School of Art under Walter Bayes and Bernard Meninsky; Sickert an occasional teacher.

1921

Received into the Roman Catholic Church. Went to live with Eric Gill and his family at Ditchling, becoming a postulant in the Guild of St. Joseph and St. Dominic. He learned wood-engraving, and illustrated publications of St. Dominic's Press.

1923

Admitted as Tertiary of the Order of St. Dominic, but remained active as such only for a short time.

---

1. Adapted, with permission, from Paul Hills' Tate Gallery retrospective catalogue with additions by Thomas Dilworth and John Matthias.

1924

August: Gill moved to Capel-y-ffin, in the valley of the Honddu, north of Abergavenny. Jones, who had become engaged to Gill's second daughter Petra, joined the family at Christmas.

1925

Painted landscapes at Capel and on Caldy Island (Ynys Byr) where he stayed in the Benedictine monastery.

Golden Cockerel Press published *Gulliver's Travels* with his wood-engravings.

1926

Painted watercolors at Brockley, Bristol and Capel.

1927

His engagement broken off. Painted on Caldy, at Brockley and at Portslade near Brighton, where his parents rented a villa on the sea front. Visited Blake Centenary Exhibition. Joined the Society of Wood-Engravers.

Publication of *The Chester Play of the Deluge*, Golden Cockerel Press. Joint exhibition with Eric Gill at St. George's Gallery.

1928

His friend Ben Nicholson successfully proposed him for election to The Seven and Five Society; he exhibited with the society until 1933 in the company of Ben and Winifred Nicholson, Henry Moore, Barbara Hepworth, Christopher Wood and John Piper.

Visited Lourdes and Salies-de-Béarn, country associated with Roman Gaul and *Le Chanson de Roland*. After his return he started to write an epic poem of the Great War, *In Parenthesis*.

Gill moved to Pigotts in Buckinghamshire.

1929

Joint exhibition with Eric Gill at the Goupil Gallery. Coleridge's *The Rime of the Ancient Mariner* with ten engravings on copper published by Douglas Cleverdon. First of several visits to Helen Sutherland's home, Rock Hall, near Alnwick, Northumberland.

Did many drawings of animals at London Zoo.

Became an active member of an informal discussion group meeting weekly at Tom and Charles Burns' house in Chelsea. The group included René Hague, Harman Grisewood, Fr. Martin D'Arcy and Christopher Dawson.

1929 or 1930

Read the Anna Livia chapter of Joyce's *Work in Progress*.

1930

Eye trouble forced him to give up engraving.

Saw Botticelli's "Birth of Venus" in the exhibition of Italian Art at the Royal Academy.

Joint exhibition with Ivon Hitchens at Heal's Mansard Gallery.

Met T. S. Eliot at Tom Burns' flat.

1930-2

Painted watercolors at Portslade, Brockley, Pigotts, Caldy and Rock Hall. Also made some informal painted inscriptions.

1932

Impressed by Fouquet in the exhibition of *French Art* at the Royal Academy.

18 August: first draft of *In Parenthesis* completed; soon afterwards a period of very fluent painting brought to an end by a nervous breakdown.

His friends in The Seven and Five turned more dogmatically in favor of abstract art.

1934

Crossed the Mediterranean to visit Cairo and Jerusalem: a sea voyage had been recommended to cure his chronic insomnia.

1935-9

Lived for most of the time within view of the sea in Fort Hotel, Sidmouth, Devon. Drew very little at first, more after 1938.

1937

Publication of *In Parenthesis*, Faber, with support from T. S. Eliot. Death of his mother.

1939-45

Returned to London, where he lived with friends or in lodgings for most of the war.

London in the Blitz released new energies: the first drafts of *The Kensington Mass, The Wall, The Dream of Private Clitus* and *The Narrows* were written. His first important inscriptions date from c. 1942. "Aphrodite in Aulis" and his large Arthurian drawings, "The Four Queens" and "Guenever," all subsequently acquired by the Tate Gallery.

Gill died in 1940. Jones wrote an increasing number of reviews and essays: *Religion and the Muses* 1941, *The Myth of Arthur* 1942, *Art in Relation to War* 1942-3.

1943

Death of his father.

1946

Stayed with Helen Sutherland, who had moved in 1939 to Cockley Moor in Matterdale, above Ullswater: painted Cumberland landscapes. *In Parenthesis* adapted for radio by Douglas Cleverdon, with Dylan Thomas and Richard Burton in the cast.

1947

"In 1947 I had a return of my 1932 breakdown, only much worse, and had to go to Dr C. M.'s nursing home for treatment, that's how I came to be in Harrow. I was there for six months and made incredibly better. And went to Mr Carlile's house so as to be near the nursing home for a while." In fact, Northwick Lodge became his home until 1964; here he enjoyed the friendship of the other lodgers--several were masters from Harrow--and found the peace to draw and write.

1947-8

Did many drawings of the trees outside his window, culminating in "Vexilla Regis" (1947). Also drew, in pencil, crayon and chalk, heads of girls observed at Mass.

1949

David Jones, by Robin Ironside, published in the Penguin Modern Painters series, edited by Kenneth Clark.

c. 1950

Watercolors of flowers in a glass chalice.

1952

The Anathemata, Faber.

1954-5

Retrospective exhibition at the National Museum of Wales, the Tate Gallery, and Aberystwyth, Swansea and Edinburgh.

During the 1950s he suffered from bouts of depression and ill health; visits to central London became rarer.

1956-61

Made many of his finest painted inscriptions.

1959

Epoch and Artist: Selected Writings, Faber, edited by Harman Grisewood.

1962

Painted "Trystan ac Essyllt."

1963-64

"Y Cyfarchiad i Fair" (The Annunciation in a Welsh Hill Setting), his last major drawing.

1964

Moved to Monksdene Residential Hotel, Harrow.

1965

The Fatigue printed at Rampant Lions Press, Cambridge, to mark his 70th birthday.

1966

Visited exhibition of Bonnard at Royal Academy: probably the last exhibition he saw.

1967

Agenda: David Jones Special Issue: includes essays by Kenneth Clark, H. S. Ede and Stuart Pigott.

1968

Painted his last inscription--for Kathleen Raine.

1969

Tribune's Visitation, Fulcrum Press.

1970

June: fell, breaking a bone in his hip. Moved to Calvary Nursing Home, where the Little Sisters of Mary looked after him until his death.

1972

Word and Image IV: exhibition at the National Book League, subsequently toured Wales.

1974

The Sleeping Lord and Other Fragments, Faber.

Made a Companion of Honour.

28th October: died at Calvary Nursing Home.

13th December: Solemn Requiem at Westminster Cathedral.

1975

The Kensington Mass, Agenda Editions.

Memorial exhibitions at Kettle's Yard, University of Cambridge and Anthony d'Offay Gallery, London.

1975-76

Forty-two works acquired by public collections.

1976

Exhibitions at the University of Stirling and Manchester Cathedral.

Letters to Vernon Watkins, University of Wales Press, edited by Ruth Pryor.

1978

The Dying Gaul and Other Writings, Faber, edited by Harman Grisewood.

1979

Exhibition shown at Anthony d'Offay Gallery and National Gallery of Modern Art, Edinburgh.

Letters to William Hayward, Agenda Editions, edited by Colin Wilcockson.

1980

Exhibition of Inscriptions at Anthony d'Offay Gallery.

Dai Greatcoat: A Self-Portrait of David Jones in His Letters, Faber, edited by René Hague.

Introducing David Jones, Faber, edited by John Matthias.

David Jones: Letters to a Friend, Christopher Davies Ltd., edited by Aneirin Talfan Davies.

1981

Tate Gallery retrospective exhibition, 21 July-6 September. Shown at the Graves Art Gallery, Sheffield, 19 September-18 October, and at the National Museum of Wales, 31 October-13 December. Catalogue by Paul Hills.

The Painted Inscriptions of David Jones, Gordon Fraser Ltd., edited by Nicolete Gray.

The Roman Quarry and Other Sequences, Agenda Editions and Sheep Meadow Press, edited by Harman Grisewood.

1984

Inner Necessities: The Letters of David Jones to Desmond Chute, Anson-Cartwright Editions, edited by Thomas Dilworth.

THE MAN

T. S. ELIOT

A *NOTE ON* IN PARENTHESIS *AND* THE ANATHEMATA

There are two questions which people are given to asking, often in a peremptory tone, about certain modern works of literature. The first is: "Is this poetry or prose?"--with the implication that it is neither. The second question is: "What is this book about?"--with the implication that it is not really about anything. A good deal of time, which one would prefer to spend otherwise, can be devoted to trying to explain to such people that the questions are unimportant, even if not meaningless. These questions were asked about David Jones' *In Parenthesis.*

But people like to classify: and *In Parenthesis* was not so difficult to classify as his second book, *The Anathemata. In Parenthesis* could be regarded as a "war book," a book about the first world war; even though the author had said "I did not intend this as a 'War Book'--it happens to be concerned with war." The distinction is important. But if *In Parenthesis* was a "War Book," then, people could say, it was probably intended to be prose, even though you could not take the typography as a reliable guide. But as for *The Anathemata*, it is certainly not a "War Book," so what *is* it about? Now, Mr. David Jones is exceptional amongst writers of works of imagination, in writing for his own books introductions which do introduce, which explain to the reader what he is doing--if the reader is prepared to study them carefully and to believe that the author means what he says. *The Anathemata*, he says, is "about one's own thing, which *res* is unavoidably part and parcel of the Western Christian *res*, as inherited by a person whose perceptions are totally conditioned and limited by and dependent upon his being indigenous to this island."

Now that the first generation of "obscure" writers, those who survive, is approaching old age, the accusation of "obscurity" can no longer be employed so effectively for dismissing the work of younger men. And it might at last be worth while for some critic to ask whether there may not have been some cause of obscurity other than willfulness or charlatanism. My own belief is that we, including David Jones, have all been desperately anxious to communicate, and maddened by the difficulty of finding a common language. May not the malady perhaps be in the reader, rather than in the writer, unless it is a malady of the world to-day from which we all suffer? In the preface to *The Anathemata* David Jones shows himself aware of this problem. "There have been culture phrases," he says, "in which the maker and the society in which he lived shared an enclosed and common background, where the terms of reference were common to all. It would be an affectation to pretend that such was our situation to-day."

He is, in this context, justifying his Notes. *The Anathemata* is unusual, in my experience of long poems with notes, in having notes which really do give useful information. I recommend reading the book three times: first, rapidly without reading the notes; second, slowly and reading the notes with great care; third, at a normal pace, having become so familiar with the notes as hardly to look at them. I am aware that very few books are worth so much trouble, and that very few readers are capable of taking so much trouble. There may still be, however, even amongst readers capable of such mental exertion, some who will say: "I don't think this book is meant for *me*; there's too much that's Welsh and too much that's Catholic--but I dare say it would mean a lot to a Welsh Roman Catholic!" Well, if I thought the book was only for Welsh Roman Catholics, I should not have the impudence to talk about it. The book is, as the author says, about his own *thing*. Every author of works of imagination is trying to tell us about the world as he sees it. Nowadays, the more such a writer has to communicate, the more difficulty he may have in communicating it. So he must endeavor to convey a sense of his own private world--the world *he* lives in--*the* world as he has experienced it; he must turn that world inside out for you to look at, as if he was emptying his pockets on the table in front of you. Would you be annoyed to find that the contents of his pocket differed from yours? I am thinking of several other writers of major importance, besides David Jones. It seems to me that if we approach these authors in the right way we shall find that in coming to understand the different worlds in which each of them lives, we shall, each of us, come to know more about his own. And this is, at least, a surcease of solitude.

W. H. AUDEN

ON IN PARENTHESIS,
ON THE ANATHEMATA

ON IN PARENTHESIS

In his preface, Mr. David Jones speaks of the change that took place in the character of World War I shortly after the period with which his epic deals:

> The wholesale slaughter of the later years, the conscripted levies filling the gaps in every file of four, knocked the bottom out of the intimate, continuing, domestic life of small contingents of men, within whose structure Roland could find, and, for a reasonable while, enjoy, his Oliver. In the earlier months there was a certain attractive amateurishness, and elbow-room for idiosyncrasy that connected one with a less exacting past. (*IP*, ix)

In World War II, the mechanization, depersonalization and, above all, specialization were much greater, which leads one to wonder if any great work of art will come out of it. "The work of art," wrote Wittgenstein in his *Note Books*, "is the object seen *sub specie aeternitatis*. The usual way of looking at things sees objects as it were from the midst of them, the view *sub specie aeternitatis* from outside, in such a way that they have the whole world as background. The object is seen together with space and time instead of in space and time." It was both the glory and the tragedy of the 1914-18 war that it was so recklessly prodigal with its human resources. It seems unlikely that, in the last war, a man with Mr. Jones' intelligence, sensibility and learning, with the capacity, that is, to see it *sub specie aeternitatis*, would have been allowed to become one of

> the rifle strength
> the essential foot-mob, the platoon wallahs, the small men who permanently are with their sections, who have no qualifications, who look out surprisedly from a confusion of gear, who endure all things .... (*IP*, 126)

The chances are, surely, that, on the results of psychological and intelligence tests, he would have found himself pound-

ing a typewriter and unable, therefore, to look straight and
closely into war's grim visage.

Mr. Jones' purpose in writing *In Parenthesis* was
not, he tells us, to write a "War Book," though it happens to
be concerned with war.

> We find ourselves privates in foot regiments. We search how we may
> see formal goodness in a life singularly inimical, hateful, to us. (*IP*,
> xiii)

> Two armies face and hold their crumbling limits intact. They're wor-
> thy of an intelligent song for all the stupidity of their contest. A
> boast for the dyke keepers, for the march wardens.

His problem, that is, was to present accurately certain historical and geographical events, yet in such a way that they
possess a timeless and universal significance, to do for the
British and the Germans what Homer did for the Greeks and
the Trojans. For a twentieth-century writer, this is infinitely
more difficult than it was for Homer. He cannot, for
instance, introduce supernatural beings. Mr. Jones happens
to be a Roman Catholic, but that does not permit him to
identify any particular event as an act of God. Then, for
Homer, war can still be seen as a series of personal combats
between aristocratic heroes whose sacred quality can be
demonstrated by giving their family genealogies and the
names of the cities they rule. But twentieth-century warfare
is mass warfare; the actual fighting is not done by the great
ones of this world, the generals or their staff-officers who,

> sometimes in quiet areas when the morning's aired, do appear--
> immaculate, bright-greaved ambassadors, to the spirits in prison; who
> sip their starry nectar from nickel flasks at noon.

but by those whose names are unknown in Society or to the
Press,

>   ... we are rash levied
> from Islington and Hackney
> and the purlieus of Walworth
> flashers from Surbiton
> men of the stock of Abraham
> from Bromley-by-Bow
> Anglo-Welsh from Queens Ferry
> rosary-wallahs from Pembrey Dock
> lighterman with a Norway darling
> from Greenland Stairs ....
> Dynamite Dawes the old 'un
> and Diamond Phelps his batty
> from Santiago del Estero
> and Bulawayo respectively .... (*IP*, 160-61)

Such people have no family trees; on the other hand, a modern poet like Mr. Jones knows much more general history, real or legendary, than Homer, and it must be frankly admitted that he makes considerable demands upon the reader. Though his notes are generous and explicit, fully to appreciate his epic calls for a fairly thorough knowledge of Malory, *The Mabinogian, Y Gododdin* and the Offices of the Catholic Church. His physical descriptions and images present no problem:

> ... people spoke lightly to each other as they do on fine mornings in England, when the prospect pleases them--and they will insist it's such a lovely day--and Evelyn's operation is next Wednesday at eleven; Alex reckons it's not so serious, but old Mrs. Pennyfather wags her ex-professional finger--she's seen too much of that sort of thing. (*IP*, 117)

But his use of proper names may at first bewilder. For example:

No one to care there for Aneirin Lewis spilled there
who worshipped his ancestors like a Chink
who sleeps in Arthur's lap
who saw Olwen-trefoils some moonlighted night
on precarious slats at Festubert,
on narrow foothold on le Plantin marsh--
more shaved he is to the bare bone than
Yspaddadan Penkawr.
    Properly organized chemists can let make more riving
power than ever Twrch Trwyth;
more blistered he is than painted Troy Towers
and unwholer, limb from limb, than any of them fallen at
Catraeth
or on the seaboard-down, by Salisbury,
and no maker to contrive his funerary song. (*IP*, 155)

I would advise the average reader to do as it is best to do when reading *The Divine Comedy*; read it first straight through without bothering about allusions which he does not "get," then a second time consulting the notes, after which, before a third reading, he might well do some homework on his own.
    Q. "But *The Divine Comedy* is a masterpiece."
    A. "Precisely. So is *In Parenthesis*."

On THE ANATHEMATA

When *In Parenthesis* came out in 1938, I thought it--I think so still--the greatest book about the First World War that I had read. But nobody seemed to notice or write about it. Having lived with *The Anathemata* for the last ten months, I

feel as certain as one can feel of anything that it is one of
the most important poems of our time. But where are the
bells? Where are the cannon? I have given it to friends
whose literary taste I have always found reliable (true, they
are Americans), and they seem to be completely baffled by
it. I cannot, therefore, write an evaluatory review, for that
presupposes, or should presuppose, that the public are well
acquainted with the text: I can only attempt to describe the
sort of poem it is, the sort of thing I believe Mr. Jones is
trying to do. Let us consider the style first.

Before the drift
       was over the lime-face.
Sometime between the final and the penultimate débâcle.
         (Already Arcturus deploys his reconnoitering
chills in greater strength: soon his last *Putsch* on any scale.) Before
this all but proto-historic transmogrification of the land-face.
Just before they rigged the half-lit stage for dim-eyed Clio to step
with some small confidence the measures of her brief and lachrymal
pavan. (*A*, 68)

*   *   *

         Plucked with his jack bucket from
the Punic foreshore b' a bollocky great Bocco procurer, or I weren't
christed Elen Monica in Papey Juxta Muram. 'V'a mind to sign him
Austin Gregorians in Thames-water, an' ransom him with m'own
woman's body. (*A*, 167)

*   *   *

Within, the lights brighted
       under the dressed beam
all can eat the barley-cake
and sisters dear
       may plait him bearded
for their hair
and all can sing:
       Fol the dol the didiay

but he
       he must be broken off at knee.
Within, in the lighted *sacellum*
as yet the *signum*
        shorn soon
        draggled at Black Fosse
        lopped at the *agger*
stands dressed--reg'mental
       and the binding *sacramentum*
is reaffirmed upon it.

> Down the traversed history-paths
>   his stumbling *Grenadiere*
> in the communication-ways
>   his burdened infants
> shall learn like vows to take. (*A,* 227-28)

Joyce certainly, and Dante probably, have had a hand in
Mr. Jones' development, but his style is in no sense an imitation. Nor is this verse as "free" as at a superficial glance
it looks. Mr. Jones is not a Welshman for nothing. Welsh
poetry is famous for its use of internal rhyme and assonance,
and a careful examination of the last quotation, for example, will disclose similar subtleties. Like Joyce, Mr. Jones
uses a very wide vocabulary; like Joyce and Dante his poem
is full of riddles which require considerable erudition to
solve: unlike Joyce and Dante, however, he accompanies his
text with his own commentary notes. . . .

While the riddle element has always existed in
poetry, the disappearance of a homogeneous society with a
common cult, a common myth, common terms of reference,
has created difficulties in communication for the poet
which are historically new and quite outside his control.
The poet--and each one of his readers--is a particular man;
none of them can become a generalized type. As Mr. Jones
says in his introduction:

> The poet may feel something with regard to Penda the Mercian and
> nothing with regard to Darius the Mede. In itself that is a limitation,
> it might be regarded as a disproportion; no matter, there is no help--
> he must work within the limits of his love. There must be no mugging-
> up, no "ought to know" or "try to feel"; for only what is actually loved
> and known can be seen *sub specie aeternitatis.* The muse herself is
> adamant about this: she is indifferent to what the poet may wish he
> could feel, she cares only for what he in fact feels. (*A,* 24)

The question then arises whether a reader is entitled
to retort: "It so happens that Darius means a lot to me and
Penda nothing. I can only read about what I love and
know."

If, as I believe, the reader is not entitled to this
retort, it is because of a fundamental difference between
the imaginative activity of making and that of reading. If
the poet can only make a living work out of what he knows
and loves, it is only a living work that the reader can, and
with much less difficulty than one might suppose, translate
and understand in terms of his own, different yet analogous,
love and knowledge. The Darius-loving reader is able to see
his hero in the poet's Penda because, and only because, the
latter is a creation of love.

This applies not only to the subject of a poem as a whole but also to every detail in it.

> The words "May they rest in peace" and the words "Whosoever will" might, by some feat of artistry, be so juxtaposed within a context as not only to translate the words "Requiescant in pace" and "Quincunque vult" but to evoke the *exact historic over-tones and under-tones* of those Latin words. But should some writer find himself unable by whatever ingenuity of formal arrangement or of contextual allusion to achieve this identity of content and identity of evocation, while changing the language, then he would have no alternative but to use the original form.... it is not a question of "translation" or even of "finding an equivalent word," it is something much more complex. "Tsar" will mean one thing and "Caesar" another to the end of time. (*A*, 11-13)

To return to my American friends who have such difficulty in "getting" *The Anathemata*, their problem is not, I think , the introduction of strange historical proper names or the employment of foreign words, but the fact that what Mr. Jones calls "The Break," which occurred in Europe towards the end of the nineteenth-century as a result of the technological revolution, occurred in America when the "Mayflower" landed on its shores. It would have made little difference if the first settlers had been Catholics instead of Protestants; they were faced with a continent with which the gods and goddesses of pre-Christian Europe had no relation, and too late in time for there to be any Christian absorption of whatever Indian myths there may have been. As an epigraph for his poem, Mr. Jones might have put "Behold, I make all things new"; i.e. his attitude is very different from that expressed by Milton in his Nativity Ode, in which one consequence of the Incarnation is that, somewhat to the poet's regret, the mythological gods, the household spirits, the local geniuses are once and for all abolished: for Mr. Jones the consequence is not their abolition but their redemption; when the Word is made Flesh a possibility of redemption is offered to all speech and to all bodies, to both the natural and the historical order (which is why the elements offered in the Mass are not corn and grape-juice but bread and wine, the product of human work). But on the North American continent there was neither a Nature nor a History to be redeemed from magic and idolatry; Nature in America was from the beginning what it had only lately become in Europe, naked, faceless, "unnuminous" Force, Henry Adams' Dynamo. The patron saint of the Italian island where I am writing this review is a lady whom I strongly suspect of having once had a tail and who is apt to send a sirocco whenever the Madonna has a feast; the

Madonna of an American Catholic has never had such a rival.

Communication between persons with "unshared Backgrounds" is always possible if they have had analogous experiences--Welsh mythology, for example, is not one of my own "deposits," but thanks to other mythologies which are, I have little difficulty in acquiring it from the poet: but I can see that, for someone to whom *all* myths are stories mugged up at school from Bullfinch, very serious difficulties must arise. Since, however, everyone has, at least in his childhood, inhabited a magic mythological universe, I do not believe that difficulty means impossibility; the problem for an American or for most young townspeople today anywhere is how they are to recognize their own private and contemporary signs for such a world in Mr. Jones' historic signs. . . .

Mr. Jones has set out to write a poem which should be at once epic, contemporary, and Christian. It would be interesting, on another occasion, to compare *The Anathemata* with another poem which is epic and contemporary, but religiously excludes any religious references whatsoever, St. John Perse's *Vents*. Something has already been said about the problems of a contemporary epic; the peculiar and paradoxical relation, for a poet who is a Christian, between his art and his faith raises all kinds of other fascinating questions. Is all "Christian" poetry, for example, necessarily and profoundly, a joke? Is it possible, in poetry, to speak of God the Father without making him indistinguishable from Zeus, or of God the Son without making him into another culture-hero like Dionysus or Hercules? If it is not possible, does it matter? But a review is not the place to discuss such matters. I can only conclude by reiterating my profound admiration for this work and expressing the hope that many others will come to share it.

STEPHEN SPENDER

DAVID JONES

I first met David Jones in the mid-1930s when he was one of a group of friends--nearly all of them Catholics--who would meet for lunch in the rooms of Tom Burns. He was small, boyish-looking, slight, nervous, easily laughing, gaily argumentative. He had the air of someone who had come to learn, and was never in the least arrogant or overbearing. He was greatly attached to Father D'Arcy who was always at these gatherings.

From his friends I learned that he suffered from terrible migraines and led for the most part a secluded life. I did not as yet know of his writings but after I had seen some of his watercolors I thought of him staying in a lodging house on the south coast in a room which had a bay window overlooking the sea. I imagined him sitting at a table with a bowl of flowers on it, and also a large sheet of paper on which he drew in pen or pencil and water-color the sea with its boats and the pale green hills beyond, or perhaps a harbor.

He gave the impression of Blakean innocence and his watercolors, more than his poems perhaps, recalled the lines:

> And I plucked a hollow reed
> And I made a rural pen,
> And I stained the water clear
> And I wrote my happy songs.

After this superficial impression followed the far deeper one that David Jones' real inner life was that of a poet who had been an infantryman in the trenches during the First World War. Nearly all survivors who were at the Western Front for any length of time (I think particularly of poets--Robert Graves, Siegfried Sassoon, Edmund Blunden, Ivor Gurney) were, I should say, men apart, in some way dedicated by that tragedy, afflicted by an inner wound from which they never wholly recovered (perhaps this is the true cause of the wound of the Fisher King in *The Waste Land*).

In the lives of these former soldiers this wound was sacred, tragic and singing.

Later, reading *In Parenthesis*, I felt that David Jones belonged to a company of men whom, through this poem, he had mythologized and made holy. His letters show that he thought constantly about the war, even up to the last week of his life. The war meant to him the Western Front and the Royal Welsh Fusiliers in which he was a private. In his poetry (or prose poetry) the men of his regiment, their words, deeds and accoutrements become absorbed into the "signs" of the Celtic culture, as also into the patterns of living of soldiers in Roman times and in Shakespeare's historical plays.

In his essays David Jones is greatly preoccupied with the idea that the past culture of local places is in the process of being irremediably destroyed by the irreversible "progress" of modern world civilization. This, of course, is a view that has been put forward by many writers, from Thomas Carlyle, Matthew Arnold and others in the last century to T. S. Eliot in this, but it has a special poignancy in the writing of David Jones, because whereas Arnold, Eliot and the other great critics seem to regard the destruction of the culture as a matter primarily of concern for the poet, Jones regards it as the fate of ordinary men who were, in the ancient local culture, all makers. Viewed in this light one can see that he also regards his Welsh fusiliers of *In Parenthesis* as makers, exalted by their courage, suffering, laughter and comradeship into the company of the people of the past culture. If the fate of the soldiers on the Western Front becomes a metaphor for the destruction of the Roman, Celtic and Shakespearean-historical culture, that culture also becomes a metaphor for the modern soldiers. David Jones is not just a highly conscious "rememberer" and "shower-forth" of the past, dragging it up precariously into the garish and ruinous light of the present, and giving the reader the feeling that he is one of the last for whom such a salvage operation is possible--all traces of the past culture being doomed to obliteration on the morrow: he is one of those, like Eliot and Joyce, his literary heroes, who attained in his work a fusion of his vision of the past with his vision of the particular anguish of the twentieth century.

As a man, and perhaps as a writer, he does not seem to fall into the category of literary man, man of letters, poet even. My wife and I once had occasion to take Igor Stravinsky to see him in the room where he lived towards the end of his life in a convent at Harrow. When we left, Stravinsky remarked that it had seemed to him like visiting a holy man in his cell. David Jones would sometimes fish out from under his bed a very old gramophone of the kind that winds up with a handle, and play on it a worn record of plain-song Gregorian chant, almost inaudible to us through the rasp of the steel needle, while with hands clasped across his knees and an expression of bliss on his face, he swayed to and fro to the imagined music.

He was doubtless an artist who entered into, almost obsessively, the suffering of a century which has produced the most terrible wars in history, yet the memory of him that remains in my mind is of a man loving and happy.

HUGH MacDIARMID

*AN IDENTITY OF PURPOSE**

What I am concerned with here, and have been mainly and
ever more intensively in all my writing and living, is, of
course, what David Jones in *In Parenthesis* calls "the
Celtic cycle that lies, a subterranean influence as a deep
water tumbling under every tump of this island, like Merlin
complaining under his big rock," while, in general, like
David Jones', my concern is with "the genuine tradition of
the Island of Britain, from Bendigeid Vran to Jingle and
Marie Lloyd"--the children of Doll Tearsheet, and those
before Caractacus was--that great company in which "every
man's speech and habit of mind were a perpetual showing,
now of Napier's expedition, now of the Legions at the Wall,
now of 'train-band captain,' now of Jack Cade, of John Bull,
of the commons in arms. Now of *High Germany*, of *Dolly
Grey*, of Bullcalf, Wart, and Poins; of Jingo largenesses, of
things as small as the Kingdom of Elmet; of Wellington's
raw shire recruits, of ancient border antipathies, of our
contemporary, less intimate, larger unities, of *John
Barleycorn*, of 'sweet Sally Frampton,' of Coel Hen . . . ."
But, above all, a "kinship with the more venerable culture
in that hotch-potch which is ourselves." That elder element
is integral to our tradition. From Layamon to Blake,
"Sabrina" would call up spirits rather than "Ypwines floet."
As Mr. Christopher Dawson has written: "And if Professor
Collingwood is right, and it is the conservatism and loyalty
to lost causes of Western Britain that has given our national
tradition its distinctive character, then perhaps the middle
ages were not far wrong in choosing Arthur rather than
Alfred or Edmund or Harold, as the central figure of the
national heroic legend."

Like David Jones, I have always "had in mind the
persistent Celtic theme of armed sleepers under the mounds,
whether they be the *fer sidhe* or the great Mac Og of

*From *Lucky Poet*.

Ireland, or Arthur sleeping in Craig-y-Ddinas or in Avalon or
among the Eildons in Roxburghshire; or Owen of the Red
Hand, or the Sleepers in Cumberland." Plutarch says of our
islands: "An Island in which Cronus is imprisoned with
Briareus keeping guard near him as he sleeps; for, as they
put it, sleep is the bond of Cronus. They add that around
him are many deities, his henchmen and attendants"
(Plutarch's *De Defecta Oraculorum*). Compare also Blake's
description of his picture, "The Ancient Britons": "In the last
battle of King Arthur, only three Britons escaped; these
were the Strongest Man, the Beautifullest Man, and the
Ugliest Man; these three marched through the field
unsubdued, as Gods, and the Sun of Britain set, but shall
arise again with tenfold splendour when Arthur shall awake
from sleep and resume his dominion over Earth and
Ocean. . . . Arthur was the name for the Constellation of
Arcturus, or Bootes, the Keeper of the North Pole. And all
the fables of Arthur and his Round Table; of the warlike
naked Britons; of Merlin; of Arthur's Conquest of the whole
world; of his death or sleep, and promise to return again; of
the Druid monuments or temples; of the pavement of
Watling-street; of London Stone; of the Caverns in Cornwall,
Wales, Derbyshire, and Scotland; of the Giants of Ireland and
Britain; of the elemental beings called by us by the general
name of Fairies; of those three who escaped, namely Beauty,
Strength, and Ugliness"; this is indeed the abiding myth of
our people. (The beautifullest *and* the ugliest, i.e., the
Caledonian Antisysygy. Many of the leading ideas in this
book, as in my life and work generally, are announced in
these paragraphs--e.g. the idea of a Celtic Front; my love of
the North; the Synthesis of East and West. The reader is
asked to remember the boast of Taliessin at the court of
Maelgwn: "I was with my lord in the highest sphere, on the
fall of Lucifer into the depth of hell. I have borne a banner
before Alexander. I know the names of the stars from north
to south," etc., and the boast of Glewlwyd, Arthur's porter, on
every first day of May. "I was heretofore in Caer Se and
Asse, in Sach and Salach, in Lotur and Fotor, I have been
hitherto in India the great and India the lesser, and I was in
the battle of Dau Ynyr," etc., and the boast of the
Englishman, Widsith: "Widsith spoke, unlocked his store of
words, he who of all men had wandered through most tribes
and most peoples throughout the earth. . . . He began then
to speak many words . . . so are the singers of men destined
to go wandering throughout many lands . . . till all
departeth, life and light together; he gaineth glory, and hath

under the heavens an honor which passeth not away"
(translation from R. W. Chambers, *Widsith*). Just as I show
in the passage about King Arthur and the armed sleepers
above, here again many of the leading ideas in this book, as
in my life and work generally, are announced and seen to
be part and parcel of the very care of the abiding myth of
our people--e.g. the synthesis of East and West, multi-
linguistic interests, internationalism, world-consciousness,
etc. My aims and achievements, my boasts, are simply
repetitions, in the circumstances of the world of today, of
those of Taliessin, Glewlwyd, and Widsith again. The
essence of my luck as a poet is simply that I "chance" to re-
embody all these master ideas in a dynamic--an existential
--way today. If I advance a claim to any personal credit it
is simply because I have succeeded, by long-sustained and
desperately hard work, in becoming completely conscious of
these matters and all their inter-relationships and
ramifications--receiving them into my very blood and bone
and reliving them--and applying them anew to the crucial
issues of the present and the future.

II**

. . . a poetry the quality of which
Is a stand made against intellectual apathy,
Is material founded, like Gray's, on difficult knowledge,
And its metres those of a poet
Who has studied Pindar and Welsh poetry,
But, more than that, its words coming from a mind
Which has experienced the sifted layers on layers
Of human lives--aware of the innumerable dead
And the innumerable to-be-born,
The voice of the centuries, of Shakespeare's history plays
Concentrated and deepened,
'The breath and finer spirit of all knowledge,
The impassioned expression
Which is in the countenance of all science.' . . .

And above all a learned poetry, knowing how
Taliessin received the hazel rod
From the dying hand of Virgil
Who in turn got it from Homer

**From "The Kind of Poetry I Want"

--a poetry full of milk
'Milk rising in breasts of Gaul,
Trigonometrical milk of doctrine,'
In which it is more than fancy
That brings together the heroes of Arthur,
The founders of Rome and of New Rome,
Moslem and Manichaen,
Joseph of Nazareth and Joseph of Arimathea,
Lupercalian and Lateran rites,
The pagan and the Christian,
And groups them kaleidoscopically
Around Taliesin, our 'fullest throat of song'
--A poetry covering 'the years and the miles'
And talking 'one style's dialects
To London and Omsk.'

KATHLEEN RAINE

FROM "DAVID JONES AND THE ACTUALLY LOVED AND KNOWN"

I first met David at the house of our mutual friend Helen Sutherland, whose collection of his work is the best there is; now in the possession of Mrs. Nicolete Gray. I had of course seen some of his paintings before this closer familiarity; for he was always appreciated by his fellow-artists in both arts, although even now scarcely known to "the general public," for whom he is too subtle, too delicately gentle a spirit for those who see in gentleness weakness and in violence strength. In Helen Sutherland's house, Cockley Moor, near Ullswater, there were many of his works, some painted in Helen's former house, Rock Hall in Northumberland, and some at Cockley Moor; some indeed during periods when both David and I were staying in the house, where Helen loved to have her painters and writers come to work. David was less happy painting at Cockley Moor than he had been at Rock; not because the fell-side and the birch-trees from the windows were less beautiful, but because history had not moved over that landscape. The Romans had not come nearer than the ridge of High Street, on the horizon; no holy well or burial site or ancient battle had consecrated the landscape. In physical appearance the Lake District scenery is not unlike the Welsh hills he had painted in earlier years when he was a member of Eric Gill's community at Capel-y-ffin; but, lacking the consecration of sites by mankind's story, it lacked, for David, a necessary dimension. Wordsworth could enjoy "nature" untouched by man; but for David, as for Blake, "nature without man is barren." At Rock Hall he painted the little church and named it *Chapel Perilous*; *Rolands Tree* was a tall pine like any other, and certainly not the tree under which the hero of the *Chanson de Roland* actually died; but it was rooted in soil enriched by the blood of the armies of Charlemagne and by their stories. He loved painting animals; but it mattered to him that these too had significance not only in the natural world but in human history. His first preserved drawing, made as a child, of a dancing bear on its rope, may already have meant the more to him because the name of King Arthur derives from *artus*--the bear. The Welsh ponies he often painted might have descended from the cavalry horses of Arthur's Romano-British cavalry; the freeing of their horses by knights who survived the last battle of Arthur, and who, many of them, ended their days in religious houses, is an episode he lovingly describes in an essay on the Legend of Arthur. David's little horses have all chivalry behind them. The consecration of Chivalry as conceived in Arthurian romance, and especially by the holy latter-days of the knights, in consequence of which their horses were freed, consecrates the horses too, many generations after. This is not explicitly communicated in the painting; they are in no way laden with visible symbols of the past that for David they may recall; they are obviously not "symbolic" horses, but real Welsh ponies; and yet it is there as a quality which any sensitive person can feel, unable perhaps to give a name to that sense of romance and mystery which belongs to David's horses. In the same way the petals of the daffodils David so exquisitely painted in a radiant glass chalice are altogether real, down to that subtle spiral twist of the outer perianth petals that the Welsh daffodils have. But as David himself has written:

> If one is making a painting of daffodils what is *not* instantly involved? Will it make any difference whether or no we have heard of Persephone or Flora or Blodeuedd?
> I am of the opinion that it will make a difference, but would immediately make this reservation: Just as Christians assert that baptism by water "makes a difference," but that many by desire and without water achieve the benefits of that "difference," so, without having heard of Flora Dea, there are many who would paint daffodils as though they had invoked her by name. (*E&A*, 108)

I do not know what associations David had in mind as he painted an elegant Victorian teapot, or a pair of scissors--his mother's I believe they were--but the point is that, beyond that thrice-distilled quality of delicate line and luminosity of color, the associations were always there as an intrinsic part of the experience of painting a perfectly real flower or tree or teapot. They were for him "signs"--symbols--of many recessions; and for him every such "sign" was in its degree sacramental. "Ars knows only a sacred activity," he wrote in an essay entitled "Art and Sacrament" since "the notion of 'sign' cannot be separated from this activity of art" (*E&A*, 157). His symbols have nothing to do with the unconscious; David was a Thomist and an Aristotelian; he was not concerned with a mythological inner landscape (as for example that of Cecil Collins): the real is for him always incarnate. But incarnation is itself a sacramental meeting of heaven and earth. Nothing in "the unconscious" could ever have for David a mystery comparable in dignity with the actually seen and known. But for him, as for Blake, seeing and knowing were no mere matter of the senses. Like Blake, David could have said, "I see Everything I paint In This World . . . You certainly Mistake, when you say that the Visions of Fancy are not to be found in This World. To Me This World is all One continued Vision of Fancy or Imagination."

The phrase "actually loved and known" occurs in the wonderful introduction to *The Anathemata*, and leads us to the heart of the secret of that "difference" we find in David Jones' work, to which it is so hard to put a name. The artist, he constantly insists, is a "sign-maker"; that is to say, he presents us with images, pictorial or verbal, that stir in us those associations, those overtones of meaning, that enrich and deepen the experience of the senses by speaking also to other levels of our being. And David wrestled in bitterness of heart with the difficulty in our time, of discovering valid signs--signs that would speak to a generation forgetful of tradition and taught to look no further than the senses--still able to stir in us the rich complex of association that he wishes to communicate. . . .

* * *

One very beautiful aspect of David Jones' "actually loved and known" is the natural creation; above all the animals "who praised God with growl and cry" (*E&A*, 254) but also the kingdom of Flora Dea, and indeed the rock strata themselves, the forms of hill and mountain, the "creature of water"or "hearthstone creature of fire." For him man is not dissolved into the cosmic but the cosmos subsumed into the human. I remember his once remarking, about a picture he was painting at the time, on the difficulty of raising every element in a painting to the same degree of transmutation. His sense of the sacred extended to *all* the elements of the real world. It was a cow, I seem to remember, that was giving him trouble. Unless he could transubstantiate, consecrate, "make over" every flower, bird and beast as at once itself and significant of the sacred (and for David as for Blake everything that lives is holy because it is the signature of God) he would not be satisfied. He loved the words of St. Irenaeus, *nihil vacuum reque sine signum apud deus*. We are "at one with that creaturely world inherited from our remote beginnings" (*E&A*, 37). Others have pointed out the great delicacy of the extremities of the limbs of animal or human in his work; paw, or hoof, or the slender fingers of the Blessed Virgin in her Welsh wattle enclosure. It is as if he wishes to indicate to us that every creature is filled to its very claws and finger-tips with its essential being. Although the animals cannot know God they in a sense "are God." Those fine finger-tips of the Mother of God are akin to the innocent paws and claws and hooves he painted with no less reverence and delicacy for they are her kindred, her ancestors, she their flower. Of the animals he writes always with a wonderful perceptive warmth. From *In Parenthesis* (after a reveille and the departure of troops on their way to the front): "Only some animal's hoof against her wooden stall made a muted knocking, breaking from time to time upon the kindly creature's breathing" (*IP*, 16). Or the unloved rat:

> you can hear the rat of no-man's-land
> rut-out intricacies,
> weasel-out his patient workings,
> scrut, scrut, sscrut,
> harrow-out earthly, trowel his cunning paw;
> redeem the time of our uncharity, to sap his own amphibious
> paradise. (*IP*, 54)

"Creaturely" was one of David's favorite words; nature even at its most despoiled and bare is "creaturely"; in contrast to machines of destruction:

> Field-battery flashing showed the nature of the place the kindlier
> night had hid: the tufted avenue denuded, lopt, deprived of height;
> stripped stumps for flowering limbs--this discontent makes winter's
> rasure creaturely and kind. (*IP*, 30)

Man too is "creaturely," sharing with the animals our bodily being and earth as our home. David would have liked to, but could not, find the machines and chemicals typical of our present culture "creaturely and kind." These perhaps bear too clearly the signature not of God but of man's destructive will to seem any longer part of nature. In the Introduction to *In Parenthesis* he writes:

> We who are of the same world of sense with hairy ass and furry wolf
> and who presume to other and more radiant affinities, are finding it
> difficult, as yet, to recognise these creatures of chemicals as true
> extensions of ourselves, that we may feel for them a native affection,
> which alone can make them magical for us. (*IP*, xiv)

Knowledge without love cannot make them ours. Yet man makes himself somehow at home even in the trenches, finding there creatures, however humble, to which his love can hold.

> A man, seemingly native to the place, a little thick man, swathed with sacking, a limp, saturated bandolier thrown over one shoulder and with no other accoutrements, gorgeted in woollen Balaclava, groped out from between two tottering corrugated uprights, his great moustaches beaded with condensation under his nose. Thickly greaved with mud so that his boots and puttees and sandbag tie-ons were become one whole of trickling ochre. His minute pipe had its smoking bowl turned inversely. He spoke slowly. He told the corporal that this was where shovels were usually drawn for any fatigue in the supports. He slipped back quickly, with a certain animal caution, into his hole; to almost immediately poke out his wool-work head, to ask if anyone had the time of day or could spare him some dark shag or a picture-paper. Further, should they meet a white dog in the trench her name was Belle, and he would like to catch any bastard giving this Belle the boot.

> John Ball told him the time of day.
> No one had any dark shag.
> No one had a picture-paper.

> They certainly would be kind to the bitch, Belle. They'd give her half their iron rations--Jesus--they'd let her bite their backsides without a murmur. (*IP*, 89-90)

Among those treasured things David kept in his room--his mother's scissors, a postcard of the New Grange spirals, certain china teacups and a silver teaspoon, a nail in a glass chalice (signifying for him the nails of the Cross) there was a photograph of the little dog, Leica, sent up by the Russians in their first *sputnik*; a relation of Belle's.

And so with Flora Dea's kingdom, kindly to the dead who return to Mother Earth at the end of the story:

> The Queen of the Woods has cut bright boughs of various flowering.
> These knew her influential eyes. Her awarding hands can pluck for each their fragile prize.
> . . .
> Some she gives white berries
>   some she gives brown
> Emil has a curious crown it's
>   made of golden saxifrage.
> Fatty wears sweet-briar,
> he will reign with her for a thousand years.
> For Balder she reaches high to fetch his.
> Ulrich smiles for his myrtle wand.
> That swine Lillywhite has daisies to his chain--you'd hardly credit it.
> She plaits torques of equal splendour for Mr. Jenkins and Billy Crower.

Hansel with Gronwy share dog-violets for a palm, where they lie
in serious embrace beneath the twisted tripod. (*IP*, 185)

In this sleep of the dead the Mother is still the kindly
guardian, not an indifferent cosmic principle. Her
"influential eyes" give her a human face, and surely suggest
the Blessed Virgin Mary as the "gracious advocate" who
turns her "merciful eyes" towards mankind. As the Tutelar
of the Place she is "but one mother of us all . . . Gathering
all things in, twining each bruised stem to the swaying
trellis of the dance, the dance about the sawn lode-stake on
the hill where the hidden stillness is at the core of struggle"
(*SL*, 61). The Blessed Virgin in David's painting *The
Annunciation in a Welsh Hill Setting* carries a foxglove for
her lily and is enthroned surrounded with animals, birds and
flowers. The painter would indicate that in the Incarnation
all these are humanized, all become participants in the
consubstantiality of Heaven and Earth. While so many
moderns re-dissolve man into the cosmos, with David Jones
it is quite the contrary; for him the whole cosmos is "made
man" when God puts on our human flesh, which is of one
substance with the bear and the "thick-felled cave fauna"
and the older and less creaturely dinosaur and "unabiding
rock" and the "terra-marl" from all which we are made.
"Incarnational" was perhaps for David the most significant
word of all. What is "capable of being loved and known" is
God incarnate.

MICHAEL ALEXANDER

FROM "DAVID JONES" AND "THE DREAM OF THE ROOD"

FROM "DAVID JONES"

Unlike Joyce, Pound and Eliot, David Jones was a modest man, who did not suffer from the hubris of the modern artist. He aspired neither to be great nor clever. Although he was clearly a modernist, searching for an expressive style to trap our fragmentary and extreme experience in profound perspective, he was not an academic writer in an age where critics have increasingly become academic. He had a deep interest in common experience. He was not principally interested in high culture but in common culture and religion. Not that he was anti-intellectual: he was deeply versed in all sorts of tradition--in archaeology and in the liturgy, for example, but also in popular song, folk-song and music-hall song, and in the more popular parts of Chaucer, Shakespeare and Milton. He also knew the ways of ordinary people, their ways of thought and speech, and in his humility and sense of humor, I repeat, he lacked the hubris of the Wagnerian artist. He had a feeling for the deep popular tradition of the island of Britain, and for its long history--especially the contributions made by the Romans, the Cockneys and the Welsh: he was a Londoner of Welsh descent.

All this might recommend him in a democratic age. Less agreeable to the spirit of the times is the Christian viewpoint under which he considers these traditions--although it is the most inclusive kind of Christianity. *The Anathemata* is the center of his work, celebrating the origins of Britain--physical and anthropological as well as human and mythical. In *In Parenthesis* and again in *The Sleeping Lord* at the end of his career, this humane quality found in the earliest works of art and beliefs of mankind is confronted with an unsympathetic modern world: imperial, technocratic, utilitarian, commercial, megalopolitan, international and lacking in any local piety--not "rooted in one

dear perpetual place." In David Jones' work the Roman
Empire, which crucified Christ--and rolled out the map of
the West--is seen as an image of modern corporate civilization. In some ways this conflict between modern civilization and common humanity gives the early and later work a
drama lacking in *The Anathemata*. I hope I make it clear
that David Jones is not a writer only for the highbrow: he
was a common man, a humble man without pretension. He
reasserts the common humanity and the common traditions
of the British people. He became a Roman Catholic, but he
remained a catholic with a small c.

Before coming to David Jones' life and examples
from his work, I might say something about his remarkable
way of life in his later years. When I first read *In Parenthesis* I found it moving but also a little lacking in the
sophistication I had learned to associate with modern poetry
of the experimental sort. I later attended W. H. Auden's
Oxford lectures on *The Hero in Modern Poetry*. The Professor of Poetry used to make himself available to under-
graduates by taking coffee at the Cadena Cafe in Cornmar-
ket Street, and one day I went up and asked him why in
these lectures he had made no mention of my hero Ezra
Pound; I suspected some political antipathy. "One can't fit
everyone in," he replied. Questioning me further, he recommended me to read *The Anathemata*. A couple of years
later, in 1963, I found myself in the editorial office of a
publishing firm (Collins), which was reprinting Edmund
Blunden's prose memoir, *Undertones of War*, first published
in 1928, and I wrote to Robert Graves and David Jones as
fellow war writers to ask them for opinions of Blunden's
book which might be used for promotional purposes. David
Jones wrote a generous reply to this enquiry--all about the
trench war, and how faithful Blunden's impressions of it
were--a letter full of details of, for example, the names
given to local places by the British infantry, quite regardless of French or Flemish pronunciation--Wipers and
Armenteers and so forth. He discussed this at some length,
adding afterthoughts at right angles in the margins in different colored inks. I was struck by the contrast between
this flourishing communication and Robert Graves' briefer
response. I later wrote a piece on David Jones for the
London poetry magazine, *Agenda*, whose editor, William
Cookson, was printing some new work by the poet, by now
elderly and rather infirm. Soon afterwards, Jones invited me
to visit him as he particularly wanted to discuss a passage
in an Anglo-Saxon poem I had translated, *The Battle of*

Maldon. I paid my one and only visit to him in the later 1960s. He then lived at the Monksdene Hotel in Harrow on the Hill, a northwestern suburb of London, on the Metropolitan Line. I had never visited anyone who actually lived in a hotel, and was curious. The Monksdene was by no means a luxurious establishment--a large Victorian house turned into a small private hotel. At the desk of the rather cramped hall I waited for some time, looking at the heavy red-and-gold embossed wallpaper that used to be universal in the Indian restaurants, until I was shown along the corridor to Mr. Jones' room, where he made me very welcome and offered tea. He was then about three times my age, yet we got along very well. He was an easy charming person, utterly lacking in self-importance. We discussed the passage about the hawk in *The Battle of Maldon*--he didn't know any Anglo-Saxon, he explained apologetically. In his *In Parenthesis* he refers to "the speckled kite of Maldon. . . ." The only thing, I remember, he spoke about with any asperity was the vernacular liturgy now used in the Catholic Church. He thought that they had "buggered up the Mass."

It was only gradually that I took in the room. It was medium sized--perhaps 15 foot by 12--and dark; it was evening, but I did not notice any window. The room was dimly lit and quite brown with old books. It had one or two of his watercolors on the walls and on the desk a homely hand-made knife with an incised handle. It was the effort to make tea which revealed the simplicity of the arrangements. There was a gas ring and a tin tray. It was clear that meals also were served in the room on a tray. Eventually I realized that something I had been looking at for an hour was in fact a bed--*the* bed. This was the bedroom as well as the living-room. This bed was so covered in layers of books that I had presumed, in the dim light, that it was a long low table or chest. The books and papers had accumulated so thickly and in such disorder that it was hard to believe that it was ever slept in. David Jones lived in this humble room or another like it in a nearby house, for twenty years, and rarely went out. In the earlier house he had been able to paint, but there was not enough light at the Monksdene. He had blinked at the light in the corridor. I was, then, in the presence of a hermit--not a recluse, for he welcomed company--but a real Celtic hermit, such as in the age of the Saints lived in cells in the deserts of Britain's Celtic borderlands; like the Englishman St. Cuthbert on Lindisfarne, who spent days in water up to his neck so as to admire heaven with less distraction.

Apart from the electric light and the gas ring and the number of the books, it was indeed a hermit's cell: the implements were made by hand, and the hermit passed his time in poring over ancient religious texts, preserving, illustrating and interpreting them for posterity. The interwoven and circling nature of David Jones' literary style is very Celtic, and so is the tendency to allegory, fantasy and retrospection in his work, and his feeling for landscape and for animals is Celtic too. The Monksdene Hotel at Harrow on the Hill was thus a suitable place for David Jones: *harrow* in Old English denotes a sacred temple, and *dene* a wooded vale. David Jones referred to his monastic cell as his *dugout*. The trenches of the Great War remained vividly present to him throughout his life, and the experience as a private soldier in the infantry set him apart from the world, and not only from the world of what *Time* magazine called "swinging London." For, despite my Celtic analogy, and his father's Welsh ancestry, David Jones was a Londoner, a Cockney if you like, but of the Edwardian period, who spoke in the old way that can now sound genteel, pronouncing for example the world "laundry" *laandry*. He was thus at least as much English as he was Welsh. He was truly a British writer; which is not to say he was not European in culture.

"THE DREAM OF THE ROOD"

--a translation for David Jones

Hwaet!
A dream came to me
    at deep midnight
when humankind
    kept their beds
--the dream of dreams!
    I shall declare it.

It seemed I saw the Tree itself
borne on the air, light wound about it,
--a beam of brightest wood, a beacon clad
in overlapping gold, glancing gems
fair at its foot, and five stones
set in a crux flashed from the crosstree.

Around angels of God
    all gazed upon it,

since first fashioning fair.
      It was not a felon's gallows,
for holy ghosts beheld it there,
and men on mould, and the whole Making shone for it
--*signum* of victory!
        Stained and marred,
stricken with shame, I saw the glory-tree
shine out gaily, sheathed in yellow
decorous gold; and gemstones made
for their Maker's Tree a right mail-coat.

Yet through the masking gold I might perceive
what terrible sufferings were once sustained thereon:
it bled from the right side.
      Ruth in the heart.

Afraid I saw that unstill brightness
change raiment and colour
        --again clad in gold
or again slicked with sweat,
        spangled with spilling blood.

Yet lying there a long while
I beheld, sorrowing, the Healer's Tree
till it seemed that I heard how it broke silence,
best of wood, and began to speak:
"Over that long remove my mind ranges
back to the holt where I was hewn down;
from my own stem I was struck away,
    dragged off by strong enemies,
wrought into a roadside scaffold.
    They made me a hoist for wrongdoers.

The soldiers on their shoulders bore me,
    until on a hill-top they set me up;
many enemies made me fast there.
    Then I saw, marching toward me,
mankind's brave King;
    He came to climb upon me.

I dared not break or bend aside
against God's will, though the ground itself
shook at my feet. Fast I stood,
who falling could have felled them all.

Almighty God ungirded Him,
    eager to mount the gallows,
unafraid in the sight of many:
    He would set free mankind.
I shook when His arms embraced me
    but I durst not bow to ground,
stoop to Earth's surface.
    Stand fast I must.

I was reared up, a rood.
    I raised the great King,
liege lord of the heavens,
    dared not lean from the true.
They drove me through with dark nails:
    on me are the deep wounds manifest,
wide-mouthed hate-dents.
        I durst not harm any of them.
How they mocked at us both!
        I was all moist with blood
sprung from the Man's side
        after He sent forth His soul.

Wry wierds a many I underwent
up on that hill-top; saw the Lord of Hosts
stretched out stark. Darkness shrouded
the King's corse. Clouds wrapped
its clear shining. A shade went out
wan under cloud-pall. All creation wept,
keened the King's death. Christ was on the Cross.

But there quickly came from far
earls to the One there. All that I beheld;
had grown weak with grief,
        yet with glad will bent then
meek to those men's hands,
        yielded Almighty God.

They lifted Him down from the leaden pain,
        left me, the commanders,
standing in a sweat of blood.
        I was all wounded with shafts.

They straightened out His strained limbs,
        stood at His body's head,
looked down on the Lord of Heaven
        --for a while He lay there resting--

set to contrive Him a tomb
      in the sight of the Tree of Death,
carved it of bright stone,
      laid in it the Bringer of victory,
spent from the great struggle.
      They began to speak the grief-song,
sad in the sinking light,
      then thought to set out homeward;
their hearts were sick to death,
      their most high Prince
they left to rest there with scant retinue.

Yet we three, weeping, a good while
stood in that place after the song had gone up
from the captains' throats. Cold grew the corse,
fair soul-house.
      They felled us all.
We crashed to ground, cruel Wierd,
and they delved for us a deep pit.

The Lord's men learnt of it,
His friends found me . . .
it was they who girt me with gold and silver. . . ."

                [lines 1-77]

GUY DAVENPORT

IN LOVE WITH ALL THINGS MADE

Of the storms spawned by inhumanity that have darkened the history of our century--wars, the internal combustion engine that is the destroyer of cities, fouler of air and gratuitous slayer, and the fusion of fanaticism and religion into genocidal hatred--World War I has been most articulately shown in three transcendentally great works of art: Sir Stanley Spencer's murals in the Sandham Memorial Chapel in Burghclere, Hampshire; T.E. Lawrence's *The Seven Pillars of Wisdom*; and David Jones' *In Parenthesis*.

David Jones, poet, painter, calligrapher, engraver, managed with a stubborn dedication to give shape and a high finish to two books--*In Parenthesis*, a powerful meditation on trench warfare and the plight of the common soldier, and *The Anathemata*, a long poem about the Christian meaning of history. Both these works are fragmentary. *The Anathemata* (the accent falls on the third syllable, and the word means votive offerings, such as those the three Wise Men brought to the infant Jesus) is subtitled "fragments of an attempted writing." Aside from his essays (good reading, all) and graphic work, Jones' other small books, like *The Roman Quarry*, are collections of passages worthy of the two longer works; in fact, these passages were at one time parts of the major books but were removed by Jones in his final shaping of the texts. Scholars are right to publish these fragments, for they make evident the richness and painstaking care of Jones' fertile talent. All artifacts are fashioned, he believed, to the glory of God. The singularity of Jones' vision was a saint-like love and respect for all made things, from prehistoric paintings and tools to a page of *Finnegans Wake* or a Welsh miner's well-turned expletive.

Jones was Catholic in both senses, a man of gifted piety and an artist seeking comprehensive symbols for the unity of Creation. Not since Bernardus Silvestris' 12th-century Latin poem, "De Mundi Universitate," with its intellectual and sensual delight in the material world, has there

been a poem like *The Anathemata*. Speaking of the difficulties of reading his work and of the difficulties of modern
poetry in general, Jones told William Blissett: "There are
casualties." The matter has never been put less apologetically.

For David Jones art was a sacred act and he expected the reading of his work to be as much a rite as he performed in the composing of it. To those who have never
opened his books, one might say, as enticement or warning,
that he is conscious of reviving very old traditions of narrative and verse from Welsh, Irish and British sources; there is
something of Pound and something of Joyce in him. He
likes to range, frequently in one line, from a beautifully
formal Latinate diction to the saltiest of vulgar speech. To
read him properly requires learning a whole new sensibility
--for words, for the historical resonance of Roman army
terms, for the flavor of phrases in Welsh and for all sorts of
things that we may know in other contexts (such as those of
geology, archaeology and theology) but that we must
relearn in Jones' context. Like Joyce, he has made a total
anachronism of all history, so that the crucifixion is both an
event in time, upon which all perspectives converge, and an
event throughout time: The purpose of the evolution of the
world was to raise the hill Golgotha, grow the wood for the
cross, form the iron for the nails and develop the primate
species Homo sapiens for God to be born a member of. The
paleolithic Willendorf "Venus" is therefore as valid and eloquent a Madonna as one by Botticelli, and all soldiers
belong to the Roman legion that detailed a work group to
execute, by slow torture, the Galilean visionary trouble-
maker.

To make a Gospel of history, Jones brings into play
a complex, metaphysical poetry. His leaps of imagination
are daring, and many readers find the dense texture alluring
before they begin to find its meaning. His readers are
always going to be few but well rewarded, for Jones' Celtic
love of convolution and compacted images is always in the
service of his love of things and people; and judging from
the amount of commentary and elucidation that has been
published over the past decade, it would seem that he is
emerging as one of the great poets of our time.

What makes him so special? The answer will have
to be "tradition." Jones, I think, changed the meaning of this
word that has figured so much in modern criticism. He does
not use the word quite like Eliot or Pound, though he is at
one with them in knowing that tradition is maintained by

invention and innovation. Wendell Berry, the poet, has recently defined culture as the means by which dull people can be smart and successful. He was talking about the long tradition of agriculture, but he was applying the principle to all culture--to language, to the arts, to all skills that we inherit rather than re-invent generation by generation.

Every so often there comes along a poet or scientist who can realize for us the new configuration, which only our time can see, into which culture seems to be shaped and the historical processes that shaped it. Jones is one of these.

R. S. THOMAS

REMEMBERING DAVID JONES

Because you had been in the dark wood
and heard doom's nightingales sing,
men listened to you when you told
them how death is many but life
one. The shell's trumpet sounded
over the fallen, but there was no
resurrection. You learned your lettering
from bones, the propped capitals which described
how once they were human beings.

Men march because they are alive,
and their quest is the Grail, garrisoned
by the old furies so it is blood
wets their lips. Europe gave you
your words, but your hand practised
an earlier language, weaving time's branches
together to form the thicket the soldier
is caught in, who is love's sacrifice
to itself, with the virgin's smile poised
like a knife over it as over her first born.

JOHN TRIPP

A DAVID JONES MURAL AT LLANTHONY

for Jeremy Hooker

I

Rain had turned the countryside
into a sump. From Capel-y-ffin
that constant, dripping screen obscured the hills,
drowning a file of ramblers
and swallowing two sad pony-treks.
I sheltered under sopping oaks,
then lifted a latch into a long
monk's larder, with boxes of bad apples, oranges,
mouldy biscuits and cake,
a mysterious pyramid of fresh eggs.
On the stone lay a splintered carafe
crusting a sediment of wine at the base.

Then I saw it . . .

Delighted, I remember thinking:
if the dealers receive wind of this
they'll climb here with mallet and chisel.
It was a signed
original, flaking fast on a cracked wall--
the dark buff and faded red of his fine
leaning script, the numerals of Rome,
a Christian head and a believer's praise embedded in the text.
Time and neglect were chipping at beauty, scraping a
            masterpiece.

(He had walked this corridor,
studied the portraits of Tudor martyrs,
put his brushes on the floor beside me,

and gazed at the Black Mountains.
A few days, fifty years before,
occupied his mind and hand
to leave us a lost symbol
like some flourish of hope.
     Feeling, wondering, testing, watching,
     seeing clues in fragments--
     'For it is easy to miss Him at the turn of a
     civilisation.')

2

Six winters from the Flanders mud
he came here, looking for a slot
of peace, some method to preserve sanity.
Deep reticence after misadventure
informed his plan; the chronicles that unlocked his horror
were yet to be written.
                    All that complexity,
the full bulging yield of myth
was growing as he painted on a monastery wall--
history to be sacked, language to be made,
the honours far off, and the life
continuing, aimed at the past.
Its price brought the long
loneliness, to be lived through in a Harrow room,
for one soldier of goodness and truth.

JOHN MONTAGUE

FROM THE GREAT BELL
(CONVERSATIONS WITH DAVID JONES, 1969-1975)

Sleigh bells of Christmas
        a bourgeois torpor
while the great bell
        of Ireland's tragedy
knells again, unendingly.
        I find it hard to
think of anything else
        German & Iberian troops
dispatched from Rome
        to quell the Gauls
harsh as the Second Paras
        in the Ardoyne
or below the Hag's Bed
        in little Crossmaglen:
when will poor
        Ulster's sorrow end?
Or is it cursed,
        as it says in *The Tain?*
said the last British poet
        on his last bed
slowed by pain.

                *

Most of the nuns here
        are from Ireland
the nicest from Tipperary
        our old marching song
strange Dai & George
        dreaming of a valley
in a sister country
        they had never seen
some poor swaddy, maybe
        from Carrick on Suir,

like the Shakespeare song
        hail or shine, they
laughed and sang, even
        under the big guns
everyone liked them
        they kept our spirits
up, good natured but liable
        to flare at the least
hint of an insult
        to the old sod &
who could blame 'em?
        --poor blighters!

        *

After the Easter Rising
        I came home on leave
they asked me what
        did the Loyal Irish
in France think o' that
        I said the most of
them I knew are dead
        I helped to bury
a fearsome number
        of those Irish chaps,
scapulars & medals mixed.
        Poor old Paddy,
always passed over,
        they were the real
Empire builders
        fighting in India
fighting in Africa
        fighting in Europe
slogging footsoldiers
        Northern *and* Southern
united only in death
        Ledwidge lost in Flanders
a blackbird slain
        for Pax Britannica
& the Tower of Belfast
        glooming over the Somme
& don't forget the boys
        who mutinied in India
they got a bit excited
        when they heard of
Easter Week in Dublin

so let's arrange
another firing squad!

*

I *was* in Ireland
                before the Troubles
and after the War
                we had the privilege
of marching with
                our bayonets bared
through Limerick city
                a triumphal march
you might call it
                an old shawlie tried
to cross straight between
                the two battalions
slowly as a hen
                but our sergeant major
just knocked her aside
                with a single swipe
into the wet gutter
                & not one of our well bred
officers said a word
                kept marching on while
she lay there, all
                crumpled up, only
an inch from our boots.

*

Then I thought
                no wonder they hate us!
In England, of course
                you would *never* be
permitted to cross
                the road at parade time
and no one would
                even think of it!
It would be breaking
                the rules of the game
but it certainly showed me
                the difference between
soldiers at home
                & in a hostile country.
It must seem strange

to be Irish these days
when this blessed plot
            this earth of majesty
this sceptred isle
            has been interfered with
we can butcher & plunder
            to our heart's content
but let any ruffian
            lay rough hands upon
this other Eden
            and there's a terrible fuss
maybe England does need
            to be conquered & humbled
for a few centuries
            we've never knelt down
to kiss the jackboot
            but by God, we've made
older nations lick ours,
            from India to Ireland.

                    *

*a slow beating drum
            from the Fort of Gold
above Smerwick Bay
            the Spaniards march
in solemn procession
            under the white flag
the courteous Sir Walter
            receives their submission
ransoms the officers
            slaughters all others
orders the two priests
            to be crucified with
knee joints splintered.
            His fellow worshipper
of the Faerie Queene
            ledgers the victims
unnumbered in those Cantos
            lamenting his exile
in darkest Ireland.
            By evening the strand
is churned with blood
            renewed by a ghostly tide
commemorated in Gaelic
            as, the Wine Strand,
Treá an Fhiona.*

ANNE BERESFORD

THOMAS

In Memoriam David Jones

Yes, I remember the stifling room
where we huddled together
afraid to go out in the street
or open a window even.
The others swear that you came.
They believed all right.
But the circumstances were out of the ordinary
our minds were confused.
At that moment I would have believed anything--
anything that would bring relief.
Now, I still doubt.
I doubt that my fingers felt the wet flesh
that my eyes saw the marks on your feet and hands.
And yet I praise you.
Standing on arid ground
dying of thirst I continue to question.
My luggage is heavy.
At times my feet touch the pavement.
My body does not magnify you
but I feel your presence.
To speak the name of the dead
makes them live again,
restores the breath of life to him who has vanished.
The way is opened
and I have entered without understanding.

Blessed are they that have not seen.

RENÉ HAGUE

FROM DAI GREATCOAT: A SELF-PORTRAIT OF DAVID JONES IN HIS LETTERS

1895-1925

Fortunately we have, thanks to [David's] friend Peter Orr, at least the short autobiographical piece "In Illo Tempore" (*DG*, 19-29), which was written, or rather recorded, between 1966 and 1973. It covers the years up to 1917, and is the beginning of what would have been not a chronological account but a rambling contemplation of his life. In 1935 David had written for the Tate Gallery, at Jim Ede's request, the less decorative but more factual account of his earlier life from which I quote below.[1] This can be supplemented by information from David's nieces, Stella Wright and Mollie Elkin, and his nephew Tony Hyne, children of his sister, Alice Mary ("Cissie") Hyne, born in 1891. The following account was written, it should be noted, two years before the publication of *In Parenthesis*, and there is therefore no mention of the writings which were to become as important as, if not (because they necessarily reach a wider audience) even more important than, his painting.

Father: James Jones [1860-1943] printer's manager on the staff of Christian Herald Publishing Company Ltd., resident in London since 1883; worked previously on *The Flintshire Observer*; a native of Holywell; of the family of John Jones, master plasterer, of farming stock from Ysceifiog, below the Clwydian Hills, North Wales.

Mother: Alice Ann Bradshaw [1856-1937], daughter of Ebenezer Bradshaw, mast- and block-maker of Rotherhithe in Surrey, of an English family of Thames-side shipbuilders, of Italian extraction on her mother's side.

1895: Born on 1 November 1895, at Brockley in Kent.

---

1. Printed in the catalogue of the Memorial Exhibition of David's work held at Kettle's Yard, Cambridge, in February 1975, not long after his death.

Childhood: Backward at any kind of lesson and physically feeble. No enthusiasms other than drawing. Received from parents every possible encouragement within their power to foster this inclination. One of my earliest recollections is of looking at three crayon drawings of my mother's, one of Tintern Abbey, another a Donkey's Head, and the third of a Gladiator with curly hair. She drew extremely well in the tradition of Victorian drawing masters. Among other childhood things are remembrances of my father singing a Welsh song--(and I have always cherished, through him, a sense of belonging to the Welsh people)--and of his reading the *Pilgrim's Progress* to us on Sunday evening, which impressed me a good bit.

1903: The first drawing I can positively remember making was of a dancing bear seen in the street at Brockley (drawing still extant). Exhibited with the Royal Drawing Society; work confined to animals--lions, tigers, wolves, bears, cats, deer, mostly in conflict. Only the *very earliest* of these show any sensitivity, or any interest whatsoever....

1909-14: Became a student at Camberwell School of Art under Mr. A. S. Hartrick, Mr. Reginald Savage, and the late Mr. Herbert Cole. Owe debt of gratitude to A. S. Hartrick (he had known Van Gogh and Gauguin in Paris, and from him I first heard of the French movement--felt very proud to know a man who had studied in Paris) for counteracting the baleful, vulgarian influences of magazines, etc., and the current conventions of the schools--in short, for reviving and fanning to enthusiasm the latent sense of drawing for its own sake manifest earlier. Also to Mr. Reginald Savage for a certain civilizing influence, and for his introducing me to the great English illustrators of the nineteenth century: Pinwell, Sandys, Beardsley, etc.; and the work of the Pre-Raphaelites and the Frenchman, Boutet de Monvel. *Sad result*--ambition to illustrate historical subjects--preferably for Welsh history and legend--alternatively to become an animal painter. Remained completely muddle-headed as to the function of the arts in general.

1914-18: Enlisted in the Royal Welsh Fusiliers in London on 2 January 1915. Served as a private soldier with them on the West Front from December 1915 to February 1918. Demobilized in December 1918.[2]

During this period did small drawings in pocket-book in trenches and billets.... They are without *any sense of form and display no imagination.* But the *War landscape*--the *"Waste Land" motif--has remained with me,* I think as a potent influence, to assert itself later.

1919: Obtained Government grant to attend Westminster School of Art under Mr. Walter Bayes.... Interested in the ideas and work of the various English artists associated with the movements theorized in Paris.... Enthusiastic about Blake and the English watercolourists. Was profoundly moved by the first appearance of the El Greco *Agony [in the Garden]* on the walls of the National Gallery in 1919.... Mr. Bernard Meninsky, whose life class I attended, was also of great help and encouragement.

1921-24: Received into the Roman Church on 7 September 1921.... Attempted to learn the trade of carpentry under Mr. George

---

2. David's Certificate of Transfer to Reserve on Demobilization is dated 15 January 1919.

Maxwell, carpenter and builder. At the same time I learned the use of
the engraver's tools from Fr. Desmond Chute and Mr. Eric Gill.
Discovered I was no use as a carpenter, and gradually became able to
engrave tolerably enough to do small jobs for Mr. Hilary Pepler's
private [St. Dominic's] Press. Did a small watercolour drawing from
time to time....
       1925: Went to live with Mr. Eric Gill and his family, now
removed to Capel-y-ffin.

Looking back at the above we may make some additions
and corrections:
       The address with which one associates David and his
family in Brockley is 115 Howson Road, S.E.4. David, in
fact, was born in Arabin Road, near by, and the family
moved a couple of times before they settled in 115. He
would always emphasize his frailty as a child and lament
the lack of formal education. In both these matters, I
believe, he exaggerates. His sister used to say that, being
the youngest child, he was spoilt and that if he missed
school the reason, as often as not, was that his mother
yielded to his complaint of one of those mysterious pains
that often afflict indolent children as the hour for school
approaches. If I say that to the end of his days he was to be
similarly spoilt by his friends, I do not mean either that his
friends ever grudged the special treatment he called for--far
from it--or that he did not, for reasons that will be apparent
later, suffer from a real spiritual distress for which there
were good reasons, and which required affectionate
protection. Physically, however, he was always robust; but
he hoarded his store of well-being, rather as, in later years,
he hoarded many pictures the sale of which would have
relieved him from financial worry. (I should, in fairness, add
that he had a further reason, and a good one, for refusing to
sell anything. He believed that a man's work made one
whole and that it should remain intact, both the good and
the relatively bad. What was not so good must be seen with
and in the light of the better, but must on no account be
isolated.)
       In the matter of formal education, what David says
is an example of how much greener is the grass on the other
side of the hedge. He probably exaggerates when he says
that he learnt practically nothing at school, for he did win
at least one prize: a book called *Birds I have Known*.
Inside we read, "Brockley Road School. Awarded to Walter
Jones for Grammar, July 1907. Alfred Garside." To which
David has added, "Always known as David by his family and,
subsequently, David Jones the only signature"--which is not

quite true, since his earliest published drawing is signed "W. David Jones" (as were his cheques, to avoid confusion), and there were occasions after he was received into the Roman Catholic Church when he signed himself "David Michael" or "David Michael Jones."

It is remarkable and admirable that David was able to go, and that his parents were willing that he should go, to the Camberwell School of Art at such an early age as fourteen, "in knickerbockers and Eton collar"; and what he learnt from the teachers of whom he speaks with such gratitude must surely have been of more value to him in later years than learning Greek irregular verbs: not as "art school" training but as an introduction to all sorts of literary and historical studies that he was to pursue until the end of his life and which were to provide the material for his poetry.

David had an older brother, the eldest of the three children. He died young, and David seldom spoke of him. It was of his sister that he would speak, and although in his middle years he moved in a world that was separated from the world of his family, he and his sister remained close and came even closer in their old age--Alice died in February of the year in which David himself died, 1974.

His father and his mother both had an enduring influence on his way of thinking and working, drawing him in different directions. The former was Welsh, the latter very English: and it was James, the father, who won when it came to choosing a Welsh or an English name for David. The elder brother was given the Saxon name of Harold, and so he remained, for his second name, Peart, was a family name and not a Christian name. Though David started with the Teutonic name of Walter, the Welsh pressure was constant and Walter, as we have seen, was abandoned for David. On the other hand it was the mother who won in determining the character of David's writing--and of his painting, if we consider its essential quality and not the introduction at times of Welsh themes and subject matter. In spite of all David's attempts to Cambrianize his work, in spite of all he says with such pathos and eloquence, and in spite of his devotion to a great Welsh myth, it was the English tradition that was most completely assimilated, and everything in his work that is most convincing, sincere, and based on real knowledge and understanding is English. And the core of that English tradition, lying in the riverside and city of London, came to him from his mother and her memories of her youth in Rotherhithe. Even his father, in spite of his love of Wales, helped by first turning David towards the main current of English literature.

The conflict could be seen when James Jones' Welsh relatives came to visit Brockley. Alice would behave like Mrs. Joe Gargery in reverse. Mrs. Joe, you will remember, would, when deeply moved, turn Joe and Pip out of the room and busy herself vigorously with bucket and mop, broom and duster. Alice Jones would leave the others in the "front room" and make a great clatter in the kitchen, banging saucepans and slamming doors.

It was a great sorrow to David that he was cut off from Wales, but he was cut off from a Wales for which he had no more than a sentimental love. He was widely read in Welsh history, but the Wales he loved ended with the death of Llywelyn ap Gruffyd on 11 December 1282 (one date in Welsh history that none of David's friends could fail to memorize) and reached back into a Wales of myth and not of fact. This statement would, I fear, have brought from David the ultimate and most damning reproach of Nominalism. He held fast to the reality of universals, and among his universals was "Welshness." Of modern Wales he had little or no knowledge. He was seldom in the country except at Caldey Island and Capel-y-ffin, which are almost completely anglicized, and he could never have lived there; and he had few Welsh friends (fond though he was of those he had). Worst of all, in spite of years of application, he could never learn the language; and this was the cause of the most serious blemishes in his poetry. His ingenuous use of Welsh words as though they had some magical quality reminds one of the Saxon invader in *The Anathemata* (112) who will "latin-runes tellan," and very often such words or corresponding Welsh references are introduced with a crudity that he would not tolerate when using English. (The same applies to Latin and German.)

When James Jones married Alice Ann Bradshaw of 11 Princes Street, Rotherhithe, on 20 September 1888, in Christ Church, Rotherhithe (this is taken from a copy of the marriage certificate), he was twenty-eight and she was thirty-two. He describes himself as a compositor and she describes herself as a governess. Quite apart from schooling, David grew up in an environment of persons who were well read and well educated in an old-fashioned way--Bunyan on Sunday evenings, and Milton's "Hymn on the Morning of Christ's Nativity" at Christmastime. His father would bring home many papers and magazines from the printing office at the end of the week. His mother, later, reproved David for his letters from the Western Front: "The spelling is a disgrace to the family." His father was promoted to overseer or foreman, and later became production manager of the *Christian Herald.*

Most readers will be familiar with, or will easily be able to picture to themselves, the domestic circumstances of the suburban class in which David grew up: frugal, careful, but by no means poor in the sense that attached to poverty in those days. This is admirably illustrated in such pictures as David's *The Sitting Room*, in the group of Brockley back gardens, interiors and exteriors, *The Suburban Order*, or in *The Maid at No. 37*, even though the date of that watercolor (1926) is considerably later. At Mrs. Jones', across the road from No. 37, there was a servant who came in every day, all day, another who "did the rough," a woman who came on Thursdays to do the washing, and--a phrase that captures the whole climate and atmosphere--"the Saturday step-girl." In those years not long after the Great War, David was already looking at such scenes as an outsider. The comment contained in his work is such as would never have come into his mind in the years before the war when he himself was native to the scene.

In thinking of that society I am always reminded of the Grossmiths' *Diary of a Nobody*: not that there was anything ridiculous about Mr. and Mrs. Jones, but the type of house, the period, the way of living, the relationships with friends, the word with the parson--here Jim Jones as a lay reader was well ahead of Charles Pooter--the emphasis on the gentlemanly, the attitude to tradesmen, the biscuit barrel, the nightly rice pudding, all these bring the house in Holloway and the house in Brockley very close to one another. David had a special affection for that book, and must have understood perfectly the target at which its kindly humor is directed.

Two virtues in David's parents should, in view of what has just been said, be emphasized: their great dignity, and their humor, tolerant in his father, caustic in his mother--and the absence of anything that could be called "cockney." The cockney accent, habit, humor, tradition, became well known to David but only as to one who stands apart from it. He learnt that from some of the Londoners with whom he served in the London Welsh, but his two close friends in the army, Reggie Allen and Leslie Poulter, were, as he tells us himself, middle class, from the society in which he himself had originally been at home. Both his mother and his father would have been horrified by anything incorrect or "common" in his speech or behavior.

From Camberwell to the army. In his autobiographical fragments David speaks very briefly of the war years. *In Parenthesis* gives a close and, subject to the qualifications imposed by the nature of the writing, accurate account of his experiences from his departure for France until he was wounded in the small hours of the night of 11-12 July 1916. This can be checked and very much amplified by his later letters, and, from the point of view of the military historian, by A. C. Hughes' *Mametz, Lloyd George's "Welsh Army" at the Battle of the Somme, 1916.*[3] If David's letters can be regarded as providing a life of the poet (I always include the painter in the word), the life they provide is, it will be found, written almost in reverse. As the memory grows older it concentrates more and more on the past, and overlooks today and yesterday. Most of the memories of the war and of childhood appear in David's later years and letters; the picture, which starts a little tentatively, is then filled in and rounded off as it returns almost to its beginning.

It may be useful to summarize the chronology of the war years. First, enlistment. David must have decided to join up very soon after the outbreak of the war, for in September 1914 his father wrote to Lloyd George's Private Secretary asking about the formation of a London Welsh battalion of the Royal Welsh Fusiliers.[4] David writes of the "illusions" that he shared with others of his generation, and spoke of being influenced by the posters that read "Remember Louvain!" The following is taken from an undated draft or copy of a letter:

> It was now getting towards 1914 and I was seriously concerned with what I should do, for I was determined if possible to avoid becoming a "commercial artist," and as I refused to do the exams necessary to qualify as an art master, that occupation was closed, but I obviously could not go on indefinitely living on my parents and allowing them to pay the fees required by the art school. But my difficulties were solved by the outbreak of World War I. I tried to enlist in the Artists' Rifles, but was rejected as deficient in expansion of chest--they kept up the Regular Army standard very strictly and to the letter in the early months of the war.[5]

3. See also Hughes' shorter essay, "David Jones: The Man Who Was on the Field. *In Parenthesis* as Straight Reporting" in the present volume, pp. 163-92. Ed.
4. For the change, in 1919, to the spelling "Welch" Fusiliers, see Robert Graves, *Goodbye to All That* (London: Jonathan Cape, 1929), p. 121.
5. In conversation David would describe how he used to trot through the streets of Brockley and Lewisham, in running shorts, in order to build up his slight but resilient physique. Though no athlete--I doubt whether he played any game at all until 1947, when his doctors introduced him to medicine ball and badminton--he was in later years a

Actually I had wanted to join a Welsh regiment of some sort. And there was being raised a unit called "The Welsh Horse," and I think it might amuse you to hear of my attempt to join them. It had always been my ambition to ride a horse--preferably a cavalry horse-- and I thought here was my chance, so I went to some place in the Inns of Court, I think, where I was taken before a perfectly round man wearing an eye-glass, and this followed: "Can you ride?" "No, sir." "Do you know anything about horses?" "Well, not really, sir." "But y'r a Welshman, I take it?" "My father is a North Welshman, my mother English." "I see, that's all right, Welsh enough, and we'd like to have you, but between ourselves, if you'll take my advice, you'll enlist in some infantry mob--Welsh, by all means, but if you know nothing about horses this set-up is no place for you. We see to the care of mounts first and men second. You can please yourself, but I think you'll find it pretty tough--there'll be plenty of time and opportunity to join up, I assure you, and my advice to you is the infantry."

On 2 January 1915 David enlisted in the 15th (London Welsh) Battalion of the Royal Welsh Fusiliers.[6] Nearly the whole of 1915 was spent in training, first in billets at Llandudno and later at Winnol Down near Winchester. The battalion crossed over to France on 1 December 1915. From 5 to 19 December they trained at Warne, some eight miles south-east of St. Omer, and had their first spell in the trenches, in the La Bassée sector, from 19 to 30 December.

With so much detail available elsewhere and in later letters, it is sufficient here to say that after six months in the trenches the Division marched south through the hills of Artois towards the Somme. This was from 11 to 25 June 1916. Then followed the attack on Mametz Wood in which David was wounded. This is the end of *In Parenthesis* as a source. He was taken to hospital in Birmingham, and then to a nursing home to convalesce, near Shipston-on-Stour. He was back in France just before his twenty-first birthday, i.e., at the end of October, but found himself posted from his own company, B, to D Company. The battalion was then in the Boesinghe sector, north of Ypres, and David would have been involved in the attack on Pilckem Ridge which opened the Passchendaele offensive, had he not been kept back in "battalion nucleus"--a posting he tried, unsuccessfully, to get out of. The eleven months spent in that area and the next five months in the more southerly Bois Grenier area are referred to in letters. In February 1918 David had a severe attack of trench fever. He was sent back

great, and a swift, walker, and after the 1914-18 war made what was then still called a "walking tour," leaving Brockley to join the pilgrims' road from Winchester to Canterbury.

6. Llewelyn Wyn Griffith was for a time a company officer in the same battalion, and his *Up to Mametz* (London: Faber and Faber, 1931) covers exactly the same period, in the same areas, as *In Parenthesis*.

to England, and I have not been able to learn where he was
in hospital or for how long. He speaks of "some months,"
after which he was posted to Limerick, and of a "couple of
months" in Limerick. Since he was in Limerick until the
beginning of January 1919, the "couple" of months must have
been more like six. He says little in his letters about this
period, and nothing, for example, about his relationship with
or view of the Irish--and it was on the eve of the very
troubled years. From his conversation I have myself only a
vague recollection of David's speaking of going to tea at a
Church of Ireland Rectory (I think) and a still vaguer one of
the unpleasantness of being jeered at by women when on
guard duty at the barrack gates. One of his memories is
among the most beautifully contrived of his marginal
annotations.

From Limerick David went to Dublin, to be
demobilized in mid-January 1919. I may anticipate now
what I shall emphasize later, that his four years in the army,
the months in the trenches and the bloody battle of the
Wood left him spiritually and psychologically unscarred and
even invigorated: and for a short time at least ready for
more soldiering. After demobilization he wished at first--
until dissuaded by his father--to join the British forces in
Russia.

The years 1919-21, at the Westminster School of Art,
were to lead to an important change in David's life and
thought. In the trenches, he says, he had been a Catholic at
heart, and he had from early childhood been drawn, without
knowing it, towards the sacramental teaching of the Church.
He speaks highly of the R.C. chaplain to his battalion, Fr.
Daniel Hughes, S.J., M.C. (the Fr. Martin Larkin of *In
Parenthesis*), and hints that Fr. Hughes may have
influenced him in this direction; and he describes at some
length the deep impression that was made on him when by
chance he saw Mass being celebrated by candlelight in an
old building close to the front line. At the Westminster he
had some Catholic friends, and although they failed to
understand what David meant when he said that post-
Impressionist theory in the arts fitted in with what he saw in
the Church's teaching about the Mass as a making of a real
thing, of the liturgy as an artifact, of the sacraments as
effectual signs, I cannot help suspecting that it was one of
those friends who introduced him to Fr. John O'Connor of
Bradford. We know that it was Fr. O'Connor who suggested
that David should go to Eric Gill at Ditchling Common, and
that he first went there in January 1921. He spent some time

with Fr. O'Connor in Bradford, and, as the Certificate of
Baptism shows, was received by him into the Catholic
Church on 7 September 1921. It was then that he took the
further Christian name of Michael, his use of which
depended upon his varying attitudes to pious practices.

Eric Gill writes rather ominously to Fr. O'Connor on
13 September 1921: "We are delighted about David and hope
he'll come back afore long (then we'll have to keep him up
to the mark and knock some corners off him D.V.)."[7] This, I
believe, shows that David visited Ditchling Common more
than once during 1921 and finally went to live there soon
after his reception into the Catholic Church. I have not
found it possible to determine the exact date. Keeping
David "up to the mark" meant cutting him off from all art-
school tradition and habits and trying to make him a
"workman." He was put to work at first with George
Maxwell, the carpenter and builder, and it is hardly
surprising that this was a complete failure. On the other
hand, he learnt from Eric Gill and from Desmond Chute
how to engrave on wood, and he gradually and at first
almost surreptitiously went back to watercolors.

Philip Hagreen, who was very close to David at
Ditchling, writes:

> My main memory of David at Ditchling is of his utter goodness. He
> had an awful lot to put up with and he never blamed anyone or
> complained; the discomfort amounted almost to torment. He was lodged
> in a stable that was one brick thick and had a sloping brick floor. Around
> and under it clay--the dregs of Noe's flood not yet drained off. David's
> mattress grew mildew and I don't know why he did not get rheumatic
> fever. Our workshop was a hut without lining or ceiling. The wind blew
> between the weatherboards and the floorboards. David pulled his belt
> tight to make his clothes hug him and kept on working. At that time
> he produced an astonishing quantity of engravings, drawings and
> carvings. He followed Eric in working old blocks into reliefs. He made a
> *Mater Castissima*, a tiny thing of monumental majesty. But when he
> wanted to make a base he was flummoxed. To fasten two pieces of wood
> together was almost carpentry. I had to do that.
>
> Eric used to come into our shop and remonstrate with David
> about his methods--or want of method. Eric told him that his table
> was the altar on which he offered his work to God. As the priest he
> should have nothing on the table but the tools for the job in hand and
> they should be in a regular order. Also David should keep accounts. He
> should know how many hours he spent on each job and what the
> materials cost. David did not rebel. He would have obeyed if he could,
> but his table continued to bear a mound of books, tools, brushes, papers
> and paint box with cigarette-ends in it.

7. Walter Shewring, ed., *Letters of Eric Gill* (London: Jonathan Cape, 1947), p. 148.

The stable--though "barn" might be a better word--in which David lived, was in the grounds of a house called Woodbarton which had been built for Desmond Chute. David shared this with Reggie Lawson (now a Dominican lay brother in Rome), who taught the three Gill girls to sing; and at times with others. They provided and cooked their own rations. A rough billet. Joan Gill, golden-haired milkmaid, would deliver their milk every afternoon. "The term 'Sorrowful Mysteries' was used," writes Philip Hagreen, though he is not speaking of David and Reggie, "for the misfits and rolling stones that drifted to Ditchling. Mostly they had been sent by Fr. Vincent McNabb. Some were broken men and some were cracked. Eric was invariably kind, but there was little he could do. Some were given shelter in the stable, which thus got its name." It was on the wall of that building that David painted his *Entry into Jerusalem.*[8] Later the building was made into a dwelling house, with an upper floor, and the wall painting was obliterated.

There were two separate but allied organizations at Ditchling Common, the Guild of craftsmen (printer, stone-carvers, carpenter and builder, engravers) and the association of members of the Third Order of St. Dominic. David was a Dominican tertiary and attended the Little Office that was sung or recited at regular hours in the chapel. It was this that introduced him to many of the psalms in the Vulgate version that were important to his work. He was never at the heart of the endless Guild discussions and internal politics, and never, so far as I can ascertain, a full member of the Guild. A minute of 2 March 1924 in the then current Guild minute-book says, "It is agreed that David Michael Jones, T.O.S.D., is eligible as a postulant if he should desire membership," and then on 6 April 1924, "David Michael Jones is elected as a postulant of the Guild, to be received at the next convenient occasion"--such an occasion being the holding of a ceremony of reception in the chapel. Qualifications for Guild membership included earning one's living by creative manual work, owning one's tools and one's work. As regards work David's status was that of a learner; and at the meeting on 2 March they would have been discussing whether by that time he possessed the above qualifications. There is no record of his having advanced beyond postulancy, and he is

8. Reproduced in Robin Ironside's *David Jones* (London: Penguin Books, 1949), in the Penguin Modern Painters Series.

not mentioned again in the minute-book after his presence
was recorded at a Guild meeting on 1 May 1924.[9]

Ditchling provided David with a period of rest and
reorientation. It will be noticed that he often speaks of
"direction." If his work is going well it is "in the right
direction," if it is going badly he has lost his "sense of
direction." Direction implies a starting-point, and he found
a starting-point at Ditchling in Eric Gill's views on
industrialism, in the Scholastic philosophy of art as
presented by Jacques Maritain--in particular in Maritain's
treatment of the artifact as sign or symbol, the other half of
Gill's view of the artifact as a thing made "according to
right reason"--and above all in what David took most to
heart, the notion of the gratuitousness of the Creation and
the analogical gratuitousness of the work of man-the-artist:
the theme of much of his later writing.

In June 1924 David became engaged to Eric Gill's
second daughter, Petra, the first and undoubtedly the most
beautiful of his cult figures. Two months later, after a split
in the Ditchling Guild, Gill and his family moved to the
monastery at Capel-y-ffin in the Black Mountains on the
Monmouthshire-Breconshire border. With them went the
Hagreens (who did not stay long); the Attwaters were
already living in one part of the monastery. At the time the
Gills arrived, most of the monastery was empty and partly
derelict. It belonged to the Benedictine community of
Caldey, from whom Gill rented his part of the buildings and
the land that went with them.[10] He repaired the place with
the particular skill he had for such work.

I was living then in a house about three or four
hundred yards away, built by Fr. Ignatius for his mother,
which we called Plas Geneviève or, more often, the Grange.
My companions were two Caldey monks, Fr. Joseph
Woodford, who lived there for the sake of his health, and
Brother (later Dom) Raphael Davies, pattern of all
masculine and monastic virtues, who cared for Fr. Joseph
and was supposed to profit in some way from such little
knowledge as I possessed. I had been eagerly awaiting the
arrival of the Gills, because I knew that there were three

9. I am indebted to Valentine Kilbride, the present secretary of the Guild, for this
information. A fairly, but not completely, accurate account of Ditchling, the ideals and
the manner of life, and David's position in that group, may be found in Robert Speaight's
Life of Eric Gill (London: Methuen, 1966) and in Donald Attwater's *A Cell of Good
Living* (London: Geoffrey Chapman, 1969).
10. Donald Attwater gives an excellent description of the building and the valley at the
head of which it lay, in his *A Cell of Good Living*; anyone interested in the founder of
the community that once lived there should read his *Father Ignatius of Llanthony*
(London: Cassell & Co., Ltd., 1931).

girls; the heart of the eldest, Betty, had already been given to David Pepler, son of Hilary; Petra was engaged to David Jones; but the youngest? . . . my memory therefore of Capel-y-ffin is a golden glow of Arcady. It did not take me long to infiltrate the Gill household, although all I could bring to it was a readiness to learn from Eric. And if Eric had an enduring influence on David's thought--if little or none on his work--he determined my life.

David himself did not come to Capel until just before Christmas 1924. It was then that I first met him, and I found, as others of his friends have found, that friendship was immediate. This was because, if he was going to be bothered with a person at all (and he knew at once whether there would be anything of value to share with any particular person), he immediately established a direct relationship. This, I believe, explains how it was that, even more than most of us, he would keep different friends or different circles of friends, in different compartments. I do not mean that he in any deliberate way kept his friends separated from one another--indeed, one of his greatest joys lay in the sharing of friendships--but to each individual he communicated, as though for that person alone, one particular segment of his own self.

It was at Capel on Christmas Eve 1924 that, as he was to remember for so many years, the two of us "released the waters," as David describes in *The Anathemata* (238). I have a clear memory of him sitting, trench-coated, at a high, deep window sill, engraving; of long conversations in the evenings; of discussing Malory (the Waste Land theme had been with him for years); of taking tea up to his cell or cubicle in the early morning ("Ah, gunfire! Thank you, china!")--for I was then working for a local sheep farmer, and Laurie Cribb, the stone mason, Eric's assistant, and I would be the first to rise in the mornings; and I could take tea up to the youngest Gill daughter, Joan, only by the excuse of taking it to all the others.

That first winter at Capel was a hard one. David did a great deal of work, muffled against the cold in scarf and tightly lashed trench-coat. He was engraving and making small boxwood carvings; he painted the large crucifix and long inscription in what was at first the chapel and was later Eric's workshop, and the metal tabernacle still in the present chapel. He returned seriously to watercolors. One, I was astonished to see as I looked at our collection of photographs of his pictures, was painted out of doors in February: a tribute to his hardiness. At Capel, where this

first emancipated flowering began, he moved out of doors in
two senses: literally, in that he was working in the open air,
and metaphorically, in that, after taking many fundamental
principles from Eric Gill, he was beginning to develop and
express them in his own way and, more particularly, in his
own vocabulary.

At Capel David might have realized his ambition to
ride a horse or--what, indeed, he might have thought even
more romantic--a Welsh hill pony of the type he was later
to associate with the mobile striking force of Romano-
Britons under the leadership of an Arthur. Such ponies,
ridden or drawing a float, were the only means of transport,
apart from Dom Raphael's 1913 Austro-Daimler, which was
frowned on by the purity of our elders. The nearest that
David came to horse-management was to drive the float the
eleven miles to Llanvihangel to meet Petra. He found it
difficult to force the obstinate pony, Jessie, into a smart
trot, even though he stood up like an ancient charioteer and
urged her on with loud cries and sharp blows from the slack
of the reins.

David had no contact with the inhabitants of the
valley. It is true that in that very much anglicized borderland no Welsh is spoken--or was then--but the people of the
valley were very Welsh in their intonation and very different in their ways, in much of their vocabulary, in their
domestic economy and social habits, from the corresponding
English country people. The Englishman, Donald Attwater,
came to know them well. So to some degree did I, the
Irishman, in the year or more I worked for the sheep farmer.
David can hardly have even spoken to any of them. He
found them strange and frightening--just as he says later
that he found the English working class frightening.

David was at Capel until March 1925, when he paid
his first visit to Caldey Island. He went there at the
suggestion of Philip Hagreen who, having enlisted on the
very first day of the war and been discharged in 1916 on
medical grounds, had gone to Caldey to recover his health.
David stayed in the monastery, where he knew a number of
the monks, including the Prior, Dom Wilfrid Upson (later
Abbot), and, more particularly, Dom Theodore Bailey. He
had seen a good deal of the latter at Capel, knew his work
(even if he had no great admiration for it) and loved his
gentle and sensitive nature. Some of Dom Theodore's
painted lettering can still be seen in the chapel at Capel.

1925-1935

David had been working with increasing intensity and, in spite of what he says himself, success, up to a peak in the summer and early autumn of 1933. He was then at Pigotts, still living with us in our cottage; and it was there that he had his first "nervous breakdown," to use for convenience the term that was then commonly applied to such attacks. One spoke also of "neurosis" and "neurasthenia." (With Tom Burns it was personified as "Rosy," with us it was "the old misrubbs.") The form it took was an increasing quietness, a brooding, outward signs (in language and behavior) of an exasperated bafflement: "I can't work: it's a fair sod: the whole thing's a monumental bollux, a first-class buggeration." From this time dates his last engraving, *He frees the waters* (1932), that one of which he thought the most highly; and as, later, the first version of his *Tristan and Iseult* watercolor was to be savagely mauled, so that engraving shows the marks of angry jabs with a tool that refused to express his intention. Gaiety fled, but a wry and rueful humor remained. Joan and I were young at the time --not that David, at the age of thirty-seven, was even beginning to be middle-aged--and took his distress more lightly, perhaps, than we should have done. "Goodnight, Dai," one of us might say, passing through his bedroom, "for God's sake don't gnaw your blanket--there's enough mending as it is." He did not, I am sure, think that we were heartless, and understood that had the three of us succumbed to united wailing and lamentation his life would have been even more difficult to endure.

The misery of enforced and frustrating idleness increased until Tom Burns was called in. Tom took decisions. "You know, David, and you have often said, that the chief act of art is to *judge*. Remember now that the chief act of prudence is to *command*!" Tom took him to London, where his brother Dr. Charles Burns sent him to Dr. Woods, a neurologist who had specialized in the treatment of what was then called "shell-shock."

Meanwhile Tom had been in touch with Ralph and Manya Harari in Cairo and arranged that David should go and stay with them for some weeks. The journey would be made by sea, and Tom would accompany him. Tom saw to all the business of providing money, packing, arranging dates, times, tickets, cabins, transport to Tilbury. Dr. Woods believed that such a voyage and holiday would be of much more benefit to David than any treatment in London. And so it proved. At the very last moment there was nearly a tragic peripeteia: David refused to move, because he had no "little coat" to wear in place of his tweed jacket when the weather should become warmer: "No, Tom, it's no good--no little coat . . . I can't face it without a little coat; it's too late, too difficult . . . drop the whole thing." Tom swept this aside, and carried David off, with a promise of a little coat at Gibraltar: a promise which he kept, and I used the little unlined light jacket for many years afterwards.

Dr. Woods was right. Tom says that no sooner was the ship in calm and sunny waters--for the Bay was kindly-- than David was leaping about the deck playing deck tennis, all his misery gone. Always careful to keep in store a safe margin of ill-health as a protection against outside interference, he would be loath to admit this himself. "The sea trip," he wrote many years later to Saunders Lewis, "had done me a great deal of good, but I was still not up to much." "Not up to much" would, in fact, rank fairly high in a less cautious person's scale of well-being.

In the same letter, of April 1971, to Saunders Lewis (quoted here from a copy David retained), David described his visit to Jerusalem, where he went after Cairo to stay with Eric Gill and Thomas Hodgkin in the Austrian Hospice; they were joined later by Eric's wife Mary and by Joan. The weather was extremely hot and that in itself was enough to confine David to his quarters. The indefatigable Eric, who would have marched uncomplainingly with Lucan's Cato through the North African desert, was greatly annoyed that David should stay indoors reading *Barchester Towers*.

> ... In 1934 I went, or was taken, to Cairo to stay a few weeks with Ralph and Manya Harari, because the sea trip was considered good for my blasted breakdown, and from Egypt I went by air to Lydda and by car to Jerusalem, where it so happened I had two friends staying. Eric Gill was making some sculptures for I think the Hebrew Library or museum [assisted by Laurie Cribb]--can't remember, and Tommy Hodgkin was on the staff of the Governor of Palestine, then British mandated territory--so there were two familiar faces to meet me.... I hardly moved out of the Holy City, but used to watch from my window which faced south, with the Mount of Olives on my left and east, and the "Mosque of Omar" in the middle distance and the tangle of meandering streets from immediately below and stretching away to the west; and I used also to meander about the densely crowded and incredibly noisy streets and the Suq--chaps on donkeys or mules--Palestinian Arabs in ceaseless argument over the price of anything and everything from a melon to a tin kettle--(the colour of brass but seemingly most skilfully contrived out of discarded petrol tins)--then suddenly I caught sight of a figure who carried me back a couple of decades or

thereabouts, the very familiar stance of the figure, rather bored, indifferent glance towards a closely grouped fiercely gesticulating half-dozen Palestinians.

Or, may be, one chanced to come close upon a couple off duty: "Gotta gasper, mate? ... Christ, what a sod of a place." It might have been a rain-soaked Givenchy duck-board trackway instead of a sweltering Hierosolyma by-street.

But occasionally I saw either from my window or in mooching around, a squad of these figures that seen singly evoked comparisons of twenty years back, in the Nord or the Pas de Calais or the Somme. But now in their full parade rig, the light khaki drill shirts, the bronzed arms bare from above the elbow to the wrist and pale khaki shorts leaving the equally bronzed legs bare from above the knee to the brief ankle socks, the feet in heavy field-service hob-nailed boots, but above all the riot shields aligned to cover the left side and in each right fist the haft-grip of a stout baton, evoked not the familiar things of less than two decades back, but rather of two millennia close on, and the ring of the hob-nailed service boots on the stone sets and the sharp commands--so they were a section from the Antonia, up for duties in Hierosolyma after all!

And as the days and weeks passed this analogy I would say increased, but became established--there was a good deal else to think on. I did go to Bethlehem, which is, or *then was*, very beautiful.

David's letter to Saunders Lewis then goes on to say that "not only *The Anathemata*, but best part of" all his various later separate pieces, such as "The Wall," "The Tribune's Visitation," "The Fatigue," and even in roundabout ways "The Dream of Private Clitus" and "The Tutelar of the Place," derived from this "forced" visit to Jerusalem in 1934: " 'Forced' because of illness, for it is certain I should never have gone to Palestine off my own bat," he wrote; "for I hate what our American friends call 'going places.' "

It has often been said that David's breakdown in 1933 was caused by his war experiences. For my own part, I believe this to be completely untrue. David enjoyed the war. He loved soldiering and comradeship. (What he says about being "a knocker-over of piles, a parade's despair" is all nonsense: he was somewhat offended when a young friend of his took this too seriously--which of us, indeed, has known, or could tolerate, a serviceman who claimed efficiency? Good form dictates a certain ineptitude.)

His happiness in the ranks was largely due, I believe, to the absence of responsibility and of any need to make decisions. What the private soldier has to do is always the easiest thing: even if he has to overcome fear, he can only stay where he is and do what he is told to do. Discomfort, however great, is relative and has the consolation that the smallest alleviation, negligible in normal conditions, is exaggerated into a luxury. I find confirmation for this view

in *In Parenthesis*. This is not an exposition or
condemnation of the horrors of war, even if it is concerned
with them. A careful reading of the Preface shows a pride
and delight in the type of war that, by David's reckoning,
ended in 1916; and the core of the book is the goodness of
"the intimate, continuing, domestic life of small contingents
of men, within whose structure Roland could find, and for a
reasonable while, enjoy his Oliver."

Stronger confirmation comes from David's
conversation and letters. In neither was there ever any
attempt to avoid any aspect of his war experiences. There
were no nightmares, no horrors that could not be mentioned,
no noises, smells, scenes that made wounds bleed afresh.
There was only pleasure in the searchlight of memory, the
recapture of half-forgotten detail, the link with tradition,
the re-creation of personality, the analogy with the
problems of ordinary social and domestic life--and above
all humor.

On the other hand, the difficulties he met in his
work, and the accompanying at times paralyzing mental and
spiritual stress, will be patent to every reader of his letters
and published work. Of those difficulties there were three
aspects or stages. First, there was the initial problem
encountered by every person who seriously tries to make
any thing in the way most fitted to its end: a problem that
becomes more grave as the definition of the end becomes
more elusive, so that it is much more serious for the painter
than it is for the carpenter. In philosophic mood, David
would speak of the imposition of form upon matter, or the
wedding of form and content; more colloquially, this would
simply be a matter of "getting the bloody thing right." This
in itself can "give you," as he might say, "a right twisting."

The second stage was the enlargement of the
content. This entailed the introduction of every sort of
allusion, belief, tradition, hope, love, on top of, or
incorporated in, the subject-matter of his work. At first this
could be done in a simple way by a suggestion conveyed in
the title. Thus four very similar pictures dating from these
years (1927, 1929 and 1931), all drawn from the sea-lapped
bungalow at Hove, and all in content pure seascapes, are
entitled *Terrace Overlooking the Sea, Portslade, Eisteddfa
Calupso* and *Manawyddan's Glass Door*. The evangelist--
and I use the word in no derogatory sense--is already at
work. The next step was to incorporate in the picture itself
all that David felt to be contained in a "live" as opposed to
a "dead" title. (He notes, incidentally, of a title such as

Violin with Flowers, "a dead title.") The greater
complexity brought infinitely more work, as will be seen in
the long letter of 1949 to Mrs. Ede about that great
historical essay and statement of belief, *Vexilla Regis*
(1947). As he struggled to include more and more and yet
retain the fluidity of his earlier work--"fluid," as the
opposite of "tight," is his own word of praise--the tension
increased. He took *Aphrodite in Aulis* (1941) more or less in
his stride, relatively speaking, but was driven nearly to
distraction by the preliminary attempts at, and final version
of, *Tristan and Iseult* and, even more, by *A latere dextro.*
The reader will know for himself how this development is
paralleled in David's writing.

The final stage was the attempt to find an historical
and philosophical justification for his view of the function
of the artist in every society; to explain it to countless
correspondents; and, what caused him endless worry and
disappointment, to present it to a wider audience in his
published essays. In spite of, or perhaps partly because of,
his piratical raids on antiquity, which he looted for key
words that he adapted to his own purpose (*poiesis,
anamnesis, signum, gens, res*) and used as unreliable props
for what was basically a sound structure, he ended his days
with a bitter feeling that few had understood what he meant
in "Art and Sacrament," "Use and Sign" and other such
papers. To my mind, there can be little doubt but that this
accumulation of problems was an almost intolerable burden
and a sufficient explanation of his neurosis.

DAVID JONES

LETTERS TO H. S. EDE

Selected and Edited by John Matthias

The following selections from David Jones' letters to H. S.
Ede originally appeared in the English journal *PN Review*
(Volume 8, Number 2). In the same issue of that publication, I reviewed at some length René Hague's *Dai Greatcoat*,
the volume of Jones' letters to four correspondents with
linking commentary by Hague from which the immediately
preceding excerpts (mostly from the commentary) have
been drawn. My review of *Dai Greatcoat* was intended in
part to function as an introduction to the letters of H. S.
Ede now reprinted below. Hague tells us in his preface that
his early plan for *Dai Greatcoat* "changed as it was being
put together." He had at first intended something more in
the nature of a proper biography which was to have been
generously illustrated by the letters. As he worked away at
the mass of correspondence, "the material itself took control
and determined the form. It very soon became clear that,
left to himself, David would both record the progress of his
life . . . and at the same time portray his character and
personality."[1] What we have in *Dai Greatcoat* is, therefore,
very much "a self-portrait" with some considerable stress on
the article. The letters, with several exceptions, are
addressed to Hague himself, to Harman Grisewood, to Tom
Burns, and to H. S. Ede. The letters to Hague and to Grisewood dominate the selection: there are forty-six letters to
Grisewood and thirty to Hague, where there are only thirteen letters to Ede and twelve to Burns. Reading through
the one hundred letters of the Ede correspondence at the
same time I was reading Hague's book, it seemed to me that
even a slight adjustment in the volume of the proportion of
letters to these four old friends--forty-six to Ede, for example, and thirteen to Grisewood--would alter the features of

1. René Hague, *Dai Greatcoat* (London: Faber and Faber, 1980), p. 12.

the self-portrait to some subtle degree. *Dai Greatcoat* is not *just* a matter of leaving David Jones to himself to "both record the progress of his life . . . and . . . portray his character and personality." That would be the achievement of a Collected Letters. Hague's shaping hand--and not *just* "the material itself"--is very much at work in this book, and, though Hague is not quite a biographer, he is perhaps a kind of artist. The purpose of publishing further material from the Ede correspondence in *PN Review* was two-fold: first, simply to make available more letters from what I found to be a fascinating correspondence; second, to modify slightly the version of David Jones which one encounters in *Dai Greatcoat*. The letters are republished now in order to establish them in the more permanent context of *David Jones: Man and Poet*.[2]

H. S. (Jim) Ede was an early collector of David Jones' visual work and an enthusiastic and selfless supporter of Jones' work in various media from the time of the first letter (in 1927), and doubtless before, to the end of Jones' life. In his introduction to *Kettle's Yard: an Illustrated Guide* (reprinted from the 1970 Kettle's Yard *Handlist*), Ede says that Jones "brought shape to the ephemeral in me" and that "his profound vision of essential truth supported me. He had a tolerance not usual in artists and this enlarged my vision."[3] Writing more recently about his old friend in the 1975 Kettle's Yard memorial exhibition catalogue, Ede expands on his remarks in the *Illustrated Guide*:

> An outstanding quality of David Jones was his humaneness, his ability to be at one with human beings, and when he came to paint a picture from himself, he called it "Human being." There is in it a great feeling of a personality, of someone sensitive to an outside world, material and spiritual; of someone with a strange force which comes, not out of the strength of his body, but from the strength of his intentions; eyes which collect things inwardly, a body, still yet alert, and fingers which are sensitive instruments at his commanding. An ear too, it also is receptive, and David Jones' more than most.
>   With all this he became the greatest water-colorist and engraver of his day--one of the outstanding poets too, and one rightly

2. Thanks are due to *PN Review*, the Kettle's Yard Committee and the Trustees of the estate of David Jones for permission to reproduce letters from this correspondence which now resides at Kettle's Yard, Cambridge (and which was initially catalogued there by Diana Matthias in 1977). Though David Jones' handwriting is usually fairly clear, I am sometimes unable to make out certain words, especially when he writes in pencil or green ink. Where I am in doubt about a particular word or group of words I have bracketed two bars of space [ ]. This typographical convention must also serve when it comes to editorial additions, such as surnames. Ellipses indicate where cuts have been made in the text. Some of the letters, in fact, are quite long.
3. Jim Ede, Introduction to Jeremy Lewison, ed., *Kettle's Yard: An Illustrated Guide* (Cambridge: Kettle's Yard, 1980), pp. 2-3.

compared to Blake. Like him, he is essentially an artist and every thought which goes through him must turn to art. He has a great appreciation of concrete things, and in seeing the actual world he sees more than the actual world. His touch with reality, as much as that of any living artist I know, goes back to a well of essential life, that grand unchanging reality which underlies the changing actuality of the world, which at clear moments our quickest apprehensions see.[4]

Jim Ede himself, like David Jones, served in the First World War. Following the war, he was first at the Slade School and then (as "photographer's boy") at the National Gallery. Between 1922 and 1935 he was an Assistant at the Tate Gallery where he attempted to kindle interest in the work of Ben and Winifred Nicholson, Kit Wood, Henri Gaudier-Brzeska (whose biography he wrote), and David Jones. In 1936 Ede left England to live in Morocco and later, between 1952 and 1956, in France. During these years he also travelled widely in America lecturing on art. In 1956 he was awarded the Légion d'Honneur. Returning to England he founded Kettle's Yard in Cambridge in 1957, realizing his dream "of somehow creating *a living place* where works of art could be enjoyed, inherent to the domestic setting, where young people could be at home unhampered by the greater austerity of the museum or public art gallery and where an informality might infuse an underlying formality."[5] In *Introducing David Jones* I have called Kettle's Yard "a visual, tactile equivalent for David Jones' accumulating written works" where the stones, pictures, sculptures and objects which Ede "has assembled in his house [become his] *anathemata*."[6] Though I do not think I am alone in feeling that this correspondence exists between the walled off spaces of the house and the bounded, wattled areas of David Jones' books, evidently no one had mentioned this connection before to Ede himself, for he wrote to me in some surprise upon receiving a copy of the book to say: "Yes, it *is* my *Anathemata!*" Regretting deeply that David Jones was never able to "see it all" he adds--"I know it was his house, & wished he could come, but by 1970 he hardly ever stirred abroad."

The 1970 Kettle's Yard *Handlist* catalogues thirteen works by David Jones owned by Kettle's Yard, while the new *Illustrated Guide* lists five works presently on display, including the important *Vexilla Regis* purchased by Jim Ede's mother in 1949 to whom Jones writes one of the most

4. Jim Ede, "David Jones, 1895-1974," in Paul Clough, ed., *A Memorial Exhibition, Kettle's Yard Gallery* (Cambridge: Kettle's Yard, 1975).
5. *Kettle's Yard: An Illustrated Guide*, p. 4.
6. John Matthias, ed., *Introducing David Jones* (London: Faber and Faber, 1980), p. 13.

interesting letters in René Hague's collection elucidating
the work. It is natural, given Ede's orientation and interests,
that much of this correspondence should concern itself with
the visual arts. Hague's initial selection in *Dai Greatcoat* is
taken from the first half of the formal "Life" that Jones
wrote for Ede in 1935. Hague does not, however, print the
three paragraphs which conclude this chronology and commentary. Though they have been published before (in the
memorial exhibition catalogue), they constitute a sufficiently general statement of certain constants in David
Jones' work and thought that I feel it will be useful to begin
this selection by printing them once more.

I should like to speak of the quality which I rather associate with
the folk-tales of Welsh or other Celtic derivation, a quality congenial
and significant to me which in some oblique way has some connection
with what I want in painting. I find it impossible to define, but it has
to do with a certain affection for the intimate creatureliness of
things--a care for, and appreciation of, the particular genius of places,
men, trees, animals, and yet withal a pervading sense of metamorphosis and mutability. That trees are men walking. That words "bind and
loose material things." I think Carroll's Alice Books and *The Hunting
of the Snark* inherit, through what channel I do not know, something
akin to this particular quality of the Celtic tales. The Snark is
always a Boojum in Celtic legend, and tragically so in much Celtic
history. *The Hunting of the Snark* has for me an affinity to the
Gododdin of Aneirin and the Hunting of the boar Trwyth in the Olwen
tale, and the Grael Quest also. Interestingly enough, the English Folk-
Song commencing "There were three jovial Welshmen" seems to pay
tribute to this thing. In any typical English hunting song the hunts-
men meet to hunt the fox, they hunt a fox, and they kill a fox. But the
three jovial Welshmen meet to hunt a mortal creature: but at the
"view" the thing hunted turns out to be a "ship a-sailing" which turns
out to be the moon, which turns out to be made of cheese--I forget the
sequence, and the detail, but it is interesting in this connection. I know
nothing of the antiquity of this song or its history.

If you would draw a smith's arm think of the twisted black-
thorn bough--get at some remove from your subject. If you would paint
a wedding group concern your mind with the Marriage supper of the
Lamb. If you would draw a bruiser don't neglect to remember the
fragility of "this flesh" or you will be liable to make only a vulgar
tour-de-force and to obscure the essential humanity of your gross man.
There should be always a bit of lion in your lamb. The successful art
work is one where no ingredient of creation is lost, where no item on the
list in the Benedicite Omnia Opera Dominum is denied or forgotten.
This is not easy.

It was, I believe, the greatest Welsh poet of the 14th century
who remarked of the falling snow, that the angels were at their white
joinery in heaven, that the saints were plucking their geese. It is
important to be anthropomorphic, to deal through and in the things we
understand as men--to be incarnational. To know that a beef-steak is
neither more nor less "mystical" than a diaphanous cloud. God loves
both. The painter more than any man must know that the green grass on

the hill and the fairy ring are both equally real. He must deny nothing, he must integrate everything. But he must only deal with what he loves, and therefore knows, at any given time. He will come a cropper if he tries to be more understanding or inspired than he really is. Let him love more and more things. "It is better to love than to know" is his golden rule. He does not experiment like a man of science. As Picasso says, "He does not seek, he finds."

A little more than a year and a half before Jones outlined his "Life" for Ede, he discussed at some length, evidently at Ede's request, what he regarded to be the essentially British constituents of British art. He remarks that "there is *something* in [Ede's] idea about Englishmen--Doing this stuff in private & attics & all that. They make love in the same fashion, as compared with Frogs and Mediterranean basin chappies, perhaps--but how vague." He continues (in part):

Of all the complex affairs this takes the cake. I've only just tried to call to mind the bits of things that seem to me the high spots of what *I* feel characteristic in the arts of this complex island--it's to me always a *"loving handled texture"* free-flowing affair with a bit of thunder-storm-behind-an-apple-tree--linear--tentative--not large--*packed* with life, a bit of a joke--speckled--like a large thrush's breast & spear points in a garden. All this again is obviously futile but yet you would not, I think, be able to make this list fit say German--French--Italian Art--would you? It's the work of a motley race with Kent gardens and Capel-y-Ffin darknesses within a day's walk. Perhaps--it's a patchwork quilt, in a way, on the bed of a princess, with a dead dog on the mat. In scarlet town where I was born & the Cruel Ship's Carpenter, & all that. No less than this battle fares like to the morning's war--I rather fancy that the Bros Adams get a *kind* of English thing in the how-ever-so-much-derived-from-Europe classicism (like Dick Wilson) & I think that our Ben [Nicholson] even when he thinks he's most "Paris" & what not, has it very markedly--I think that the great 18th c Eng. paintings--that is to say what is reckoned "English art" & what I suppose floods Burlington House--is the counterpart to the same English-bible-Milton business.... The Eng. Bible, Milton, the Puritan Revolution, the Jacobeans, Pope--anything you like--"Ann" civilization, the whole 18th Cent business, God knows are England enough--but a great foreign influence seems to have all but strangled the particular quality we seem to all recognize electric from the remote past--Celtic-Anglo-Saxon--to make you weep in the early middle age--Still there in parts, later, but heavier or something (in eg. the *Morte Arthur*) & then [happy,] [prouder,] conscious, & having a regular fine old fling in our William & Co., Donne a bit--& the Stuart needle work. ... Kit Smart, Coleridge, the Romantic Revival picked it up by half--Blake with both hands & feet & so violently as to remould it into some quite other thing--immensely great & alone-- but it was "all British" raw material. I think some of the Pre-Raphaelites "recognized" the thing but for some reason or other & many reasons, just got every cart before all the wrong horses & so-- bloody pathetic affair....

Jones characteristically qualifies his observations--especially those regarding the English Bible, Milton, and eighteenth-century art--by calling them "ill-put, open to every wrong interpretation . . . & not to be taken at all literally." But *for him,* he says, there is a "truth lurking" here.

On Friday, 20 March 1936 Jones writes to Ede from the Fort Hotel in Sidmouth about the European political situation and the typescript of *In Parenthesis.* He has not been feeling well lately, he says, having caught a bad cold from Eric Gill who had recently been visiting.

> I agree about the European situation. Pray God it may turn out to be a "good thing."--I fear the French--& French pressure--if only we could talk fairly, calmly, & generously to the Germans*--it's what *everybody one meets desires*--from illiterate men one meets in pubs, to men of position, to men of intelligence--almost without exception--it's the only sane thing. But the devious ways of politicians--how can one tell what they will do? or what "interests" are behind it all. However one does hope & hope for the best. God grant we shan't be disappointed. (Left and right margin: *I thought Von Ribbentrop's speech at the League assembly most awfully good & convincing--*absolutely* reasonable. Are people you meet in London taking this view??--*Damn* this legalistic attitude of the Frogs & some of our people--why can't we make a great & generous gesture without "terms" of any sort--it's *always* the best thing.) . . .
>
> I'm working on the typescript of my book--it's got so far-- the stages seem endless--& now with all this trouble brewing it seems a foolish book--but perhaps we shall have a breather of peace & then it can be published--it seems terribly bad in places--in most places in fact--but I'm incapable now of forming a judgment. I would like to write a long letter but can't, must catch post & write two other letters as well. . . .

Jones writes again from the Fort Hotel on St. David's Day, 1937. After his characteristic apologies about not having written often enough, he turns to the subject of his painting, "Rock Sheep," about which Ede had inquired. Alluding to the "neurasthenia" which had resulted in a severe breakdown in 1932 and would result in another in 1946, he wonders if he will *"ever* get really well."

> Of course I should love you to have the Rock Sheep. I left it in charge of Prudence [Pelham] & will write to her & ask her where it is & to send it to you.--I think she is in Sussex at the moment & the picture, I expect, is in London. It is awfully nice of you to want to have it. That will be nice to think of you having it. I do wish I could see you. Do you know it is a *monstrous thing* but it was only last week I sent your brother the Am. alternate set of engravings & the extra ones I promised him last year.--I did feel an awful swine for not doing this before. Have you seen Faber's spring list with my book announced in it? I did not send you one because I thought you would be sure to see it. It has an embarrassing "blurb" but there it is. There will also be a prospectus for it later on & I will send you one of those. Dick de la Mare would

send you a spring list if you wanted to see it--it comes on p. 55 & René [Hague]'s translation of "Roland" is announced too on p. 58.

The printing arrangements are taking a *terrible* time & I've only just got the proofs of the first two parts & sent them back corrected. It may sound incredible but I've been still working on it quite a lot one way or another--while waiting for proofs etc. There seems no end to what one can do to a thing--& you shudder to think how bad it must have been before you made these necessary corrections & rearrangements, deletions, additions,--*tiny* things--but terribly *important*.

It is St. David's Day to-day & I ate leeks for lunch & walked on a snow capped hill above the sea.--It was a bloody cold wind but the snow was nice in patches with grass and brambles in between & the sea like a leaden plain, now it is sunny. I have been fairly depressed & distracted actually--but no matter. I'm better than I used to be but wonder often if I shall *ever* get really well. All right if nothing happens to stir the old stuff up again, or frighten me, or exhaust me--a pretty poor lookout in so rocky a world! Yes--London must be awful--I hate to think of it....

Glad the Rock thing went off alright. Helen S[utherland] wrote just before you went & was very pleased you were going. No news for you, I think.--let me see--Eric [Gill] fell off his great scaffold & broke his rib, & lay in pain on his stone floor--but he's better now & up & about. It is ages & ages since I wrote to you--& now it's March--& King Edward is gone--*God, I was angry about all that*--I thought he might have *done something*--but the Lord knows what! When do you prepare to return to Tangier?--I hope I see you before you go. I wonder when I shall paint again. Well Dearest Jim I must stop. & thanks so much for wanting [the] picture. I will write to Prudence, at once, now in fact.

At the time of his letter to Ede of 29-30 August 1942, Jones is living at 12 Sheffield Terrace in London and trying to finish *The Book of Balaam's Ass,* the work he finally abandoned. The letter is sufficiently rich and interesting to be worth printing almost entire. Ede himself is at this time living in Tangier, and has evidently recently returned from one of his American lecture tours.

I do hope you get this letter. That's one thing that strikes one writing perhaps--one feels the letter will take so long & may never get there at all. But I've always had that thing about chaps far off. It's much easier to write to a chap when he lives in the next street than when he lives far off. I don't know why. Unless of course one writes *regularly* once a month--that might be easier. Something to continue so to say. Well, I'm alrightish all rightish you know. Such a lot has happened. I think I'm really just the same. I expect if we met in the street tomorrow it would seem as if we'd never been separated. I had to leave Glebe Place* (that was a ghastly blow) last year & came to this boarding house meaning to stay for a few weeks but here I am still--a year has past. (Left margin: *Tom [Burns] had to give it up because of being abroad & I could not afford to run it & it seemed the best arrangement as things were then.) Yes, still trying to write the same book--it was going on pretty well a few months ago--but lately no good. No painting alas--it still brings on my old trouble if I do that. It is awful. One gets

little nearer understanding this nerve thing really. I mean one may
understand it a bit better--but there seems no cure really--God it's ten
years now since I started that breakdown--it seems impossible. But I'm
all right. & certainly a lot better than I used to be, a lot better. I am
about as worried about a lot of things as anyone could be, but I mean the
actual neurasthenia in most of its manifestations is better, but I can't
go into ramifications for that deplorable complaint. It does seem to be
able to immobilise as soldiers say, a person indeffinately, even when
the more violent & obvious & more outward symptoms have receded. It
certainly reduces all one's hopes as to creative work to a bare & shadowy minimum. Not least of its traits is that few people even now have
much conception of it & put down a good bit of one's inability to get
things done to a kind of inertia of the will, a kind of slackness which is,
in part reprehensible--none of which is even remotely true. Well
damn, I did not mean to write all this stuff--a pretty fine start after
two or three years of silence!
    Harman [Grisewood] got married in the midst of the London
Air blitz in 1940. I was half living with him then in King's Road &
half the time at Glebe. It was a strange period. Like all immediate
things (e.g. the front-line in the last war) it had its points. We had
some nice times in those hectic months. His wife is *heavenly* & they
are *very* happy & live at Richmond in a lovely little 18th (early
18th) century cottage bang on the riverside. I go there for the night
sometimes--it reminds me in some ways of your house at Elm Row--
only because it's 18th c I suppose--it's minute really & a proper
building that ambles & is contrived--not a damned standardized lifeless
construction like our modern stuff mostly is. Harman works very hard,
but has an interesting job, still at BBC. We often speak of you. Tom
[Burns] is still in Spain, he was home for a few days last autumn. Have
not heard from him for two months or so. But I expect he's O.K. Prudence [Branch, née Pelham] is very ill. She has, alas, Disseminated
sclerosis--which is incurable--it's so awful, it is intermittent, but
from all accounts is incurable--the [toxine] of it is not yet [filterable]
--& causes paralysis in different parts of the body for a certain time,
& then lifts for a bit--but in the end it kills one. She is *just the same*
--superbly cheerful & brave & defiant in spite of it all. I do wish it
was possible to think that this disease was curable.
    My father lives permanently in a Nursing Home in Syden-
ham. He had to give up his little house at Brockley because he got too
ill. Had to have a trained nurse always ready to inject stuff, because of
his heart being very bad. He is happy & cheerful & they are very kind
to him & he was allowed to take some of his belongings so he feels
more at home. But there he is a [prisoner] in the nursing home. Fortunately he's always had the most amazingly Xtian & resigned nature so
he's really astonishingly contented. The war bombed very badly where
he lived for weeks on end, but did not turn a hair! But probably the night
after night of no rest & getting up etc. etc. told on his health at his age
(82) & made his heart worse. He also often asks if I've heard from you
& wonders how you are. He's very alive to everything & reads a lot.
More than he ever did. I go and see him once a week and spend the day
there or part of the day. This is one of the reasons why I have stayed
in London. I feel I must be near him & traveling is a bit of a curse these
days. Actually I've not been out of London at all for two years except
quite recently (last week in fact). I went to Pigotts for Petra
[Tegetmeier]'s birthday & stayed a week! I went for two days but stayed

on, it was very nice there--but strange with dear Eric [Gill] no longer at
the helm. They go on fairly well--but of course things are a bit tricky
in many ways. Joan [Hague] works like a medieval peasant on the land--
she's really astounding & is just as she ever was. Looks jolly nice. René
[Hague] is an Officer in the Air Force, & he was home on leave. It was
heavenly seeing him again & cracking some old jokes & having a drink.
They also enquired after you both.

Was interested about the Pittsburgh professor having heard
of my work. I do wish there was *more* of it. The Tate purchased my
Mort D'Arthur picture (Guenever) & another one called "The Four
Queens," of Lancelot asleep under an apple tree & Morgan le Fay & the
other girls finding him--I did it last year & got ill again trying to do
another one which is still unfinished. But which I still hope to get
done sooner or later. O, one piece of nice news. I think the Penguin are
going to do a little monograph about me with coloured illustrations &
uncoloured ones (they are proposing to do a small series of a few
artists). I hope it all comes off.* (Margin: *It's all at present only
getting planned so don't talk about it, as sometimes these things fall
through.) Robin Ironside is writing my thing. He's a nice chap. He's
using the "life" I did for you to help him with the biographical stuff.
I suppose you know him. He's the Contemporary Art Society chap &
it seems has been interested in my work. It is a bit of a business getting
the ones for coloured photography, because I've got none left of my own
& the others are a bit scattered, but I think it will be done all right. I
don't know of course what kind of thing R.I. will write. I believe he's
more interested in my Morte D'Arthur kind of picture than some of
my others but I expect it will be all right.

Petra is just the same--still beautiful & with her very
beautiful children growing up into yellow-haired girls--the eldest is
fourteen or thirteen I suppose. I met Teddy Wolfe one day in June. He
was looking well & unaltered, with a beard, & he, of course, talked a lot
of you. Also had lunch with "Freddie" Graham in Kensington in the
winter & said I would go again but never have, I must. Saw Ben
[Nicholson] also a month or so ago--up from Cornwall. He still works
on his abstracts etc.--he's done some jolly good ones. I liked seeing him
again & found him very nice, &, I think, a bit more "human"--not that I
think he was ever "inhuman"--but somehow more tolerant or friendly
or something--it's difficult to express.

(Margins: Henry Moore has done some superb drawings of
chaps in air-raid shelters--the *best* things he's ever done. God be
praised! They are somehow "romantic" in the true sense. English
artists are "Romantic" or nothing--I'm sure of that. Even old Ben is
really romantic, in spite of the appearance of [Bosh] "intelligence"--
the old Frogs are really intelligent when they paint--we can't do it
that way--what *awful* generalizations one goes in for--sorry. ... I've
been seeing Kenneth Clark once or twice lately in connection with the
Penguin thing--I do find him most awfully nice. He is doing a *great*
work in England under war conditions for the arts, I do think. He's so
awfully understanding & able at the same time.)

... I liked your description of the scenery of San Francisco--
it's fascinating about all that primaeval shifting etc. of land--I like to
think of these slow-moving mutations & the great slow deep stuff
under the transitory things we see & live among.

During the 1940s Jones suffered considerably from financial worries, and in 1944 Ede proposed a scheme of support which would help to make him more secure. There are several letters going into considerable detail about various gifts and contributions from Jones' friends and patrons. In a letter written on 9 August 1944, when he was staying as a guest of the Hagues at Pigotts, he concludes:

> I think that is all there is to tell you about my means of subsistence-- apart from the odd sums from sale of older pictures etc. which, with Helen [Sutherland]'s and Tom [Burns]'s contributions have, so far, kept me going. I feel my words must sound exceedingly flat & ungrateful & taking-things-for-granted. But it is not really like that & I do indeed thank you & all of them for all the great kindness. I wish I could see you in person & talk--but that does not seem possible at present. If in some way, you could thank yourself, & those concerned, for me, I should be most grateful....
>
> I hoped I might do some drawing during the month I've been here but I can't seem to concentrate on much but my book & I get on with, or try to get on with that, as there is such an enormous lot to do to it. God knows if it's any good or not. Dear Harman and Margaret [Grisewood] came down for a week and Harman digged all the time in the garden & was very pleased to get a breather from his exacting work in London. They've gone now and I miss him most awfully.... Jim, I don't know what else to say about this: I hope I do right in accepting what you've planned--I feel very ungenerous & careless in the face of this generosity.
>
> The Normandy war seems to be going O.K. Perhaps, who knows, we may be getting somewhere near toward the close.

By 1946 Jones has abandoned *The Book of Balaam's Ass* and is working on *The Anathemata*. A letter written to Ede on 23 August of that year from Cockley Moor, Helen Sutherland's home, records an early private reading from the new work-in-progress at which Kathleen Raine was present.

> Vera [Moore] is here & is giving a special music thing tonight & Kathleen Raine is here & her two children--it's a very nice party. I do wish I could do some better paintings. I'm jolly rusty I suppose or it may be I shan't be able to do the old kind again--this writing may have done something to me. I'd much rather paint than write if only I could. I hope you are right about this new writing. I do indeed. I read some of it to Kathleen Raine & Helen & Vera (by special request!) last night. They seem to like it quite a bit, but I'm afraid it's damned obscure. Helen has made this place inside very lovely & Ben [Nicholson]'s pictures look good here--outside it's wild & remote but within it has all Helen's civilized feeling just as Rock had. I go back to London in the second week of September & then I think I shall go to Pigotts for a little while all being well. This is my first time right away from London for seven years--jolly odd thought. But it does not seem to matter awfully where one is--but still, in some ways it does. ... I went to dinner at the Clark's a few weeks back & saw again my big picture of Petra [Tegetmeier]. They were awfully nice & a jolly nice house, & he has some lovely pictures.

Jones' second major breakdown occurred at Cockley Moor at about the same time as the letter of 23 August. By spring, 1947 he had entered Bowden House in Harrow. It was not until May of 1948, however, that Jones wrote to Ede explaining what had happened.

I'm terribly sorry for this *intolerable* delay in answering your letter & for not writing at all for so long--but it is only during the last few months that I've been able to write. I don't know *when* you last heard from Tom [Burns], but what happened was that last spring (1947) I got a lot worse & went to a Nursing Home here in Harrow & was there all the summer & autumn until Xmas time. I received treatment, psychotherapy, & they did me a great deal of good & got me painting again. I came to this house which is kept by an ex-master of Harrow school in January & have been drawing etc. & am having a show of a few things at the Redfern Gallery commencing on May 24th, until June 26.

I still have to see the doctor as yet once a week but I'm infinitely better than I was last year. I was very sad to hear you may have to give up your house--I am indeed & *terribly* sorry that you won't be coming to England this summer. Gosh! How difficult all this money thing is getting now for everybody. I don't believe I could design a textile at all--I have not got enough sense of the "abstract" to do that. My thing is different from that. I suppose I might mess about with a complicated theme & get bits of feeling into it here & there with chalk & paint & pencil & spit & rubbings out etc.--but I can't imagine myself being able to get anything with a straight clear pattern which could be interpreted in textile. . . . no.

I do wish I had written to you before--I feel *very* guilty about that--I think of you both so often.--I wish you lived in England--but there it is--I do hope I get a bit of money out of this show.--but I don't imagine it can be much what with the 33 1/3 to Gallery & the mounting & framing & the income tax--[ ] it is wonderful to have been even well enough to paint at all after this long long long unwellness. I'm also trying to get on with my book but it is very difficult & complicated & won't get fixed or finished. I had hoped to have a publishable bit really fixed & right long before this. Lately I've done none of it because of this attempt to get some painting done for this show. We decided to have this show in October--but quite suddenly decided to have it *now* instead--so you can imagine the last minute scamper! I've been writing out invitation cards & stamping them until I pretty much hate the sight of them--one can never find anyone's address. Anyway, most of that is done now. I would love to see you both. God bless you & I *do* thank you for all you are doing & have done. The Artists' Benevolent gave me some money round about the time I left the [actual] nursing home which was a great help as I had *huge* bills in that place--but it is wonderful that the doctors have been able to do what good they have. I was fortunate in being under awfully understanding & good man called Dr Stevenson & it is he to whom I still go at present once a week. I must stop--I simply *must* try & write to you more regularly now I'm better than I was--much & much love to you & to dear Helen & the girls--where are they? let me know how all things go with you.

In December of 1949 Jones wrote from Northwick Lodge in Harow-on-the-Hill where he lived from the time

he left Bowden House in 1947 until he moved to the Monksdene Hotel in 1964. He has not been too bad, he tells Ede--
"ups & downs."

> Done very little painting I fear--been trying hard to get my writing
> nearer completion though it's still a long way off. Been doing a good bit
> of sorting out etc. & getting room a bit more ship-shape--had some
> shelves made (with great difficulty) & got my books in them & vari-
> ous bits & pieces. A mug & glass or two as for instance the 18th cent.
> German glass you gave me once & a few other oddments about the room--
> it looks a lot nicer & I'm glad to have them & be able to look at them.--
> Possible inducement to "still-life" drawings--I hope--& some of my
> old pictures on the walls. ... Glad you've been reading Hopkins*--I
> think he's superb & more interesting to me than almost any poet for
> centuries. He really understood what poetry was all about & how it is a
> made thing with a shape--He really "makes" his poems in a way that
> can be said of few poets. (Margin: *He had a very great influence on me
> --however unworthily & feebly employed in my stuff.)
>
> Glad you had the [playing] & Vera [Moore] & also seen Bran-
> cusi, & that Helen has been able to do some [playing]. It was good seeing
> you both again & Elizabeth that day--sorry it was not for longer--it
> was quite like old times, as they say & you all seemed just the same--
> thank God. They are plowing the fields that you could see from my
> window--it is an illusion of real country almost. I don't know what they
> are going to grow, corn, I hope. That will be very nice later on & I shall
> be able to sing "John Barley Corn" to myself. ... Glad, so glad, you like
> some of the pictures--I feared you would think them pretty mouldy. I
> wish I could do some I *really* like--one seldom seems to turn the corner
> one wants to turn. Some of the old ones did--or so I feel in retrospect but
> it's hard to know. ...
>
> No news really; not seen anybody for some time nor been to
> London. Dear Harman I see once a week if possible but lately either I've
> not been well or some other hitch has occurred [so] our sequence of
> lunches has been interrupted--but probably next week I'll see him--
> which I always look forward to more than anything. How old we are all
> getting--I was thinking the other day that I've known you for over 20
> years & Harman for just about the same time & Tom [Burns] for a few
> years longer (1923). I've not seen Tom either for a few weeks but he was
> all right & his family when last I saw him but very busy & rushed--
> business & the home etc. etc. How bloody lucky one is to have such nice
> friends.
>
> I see that they've made Gerald Kelly the successor to
> [Munnings] at the R.A. What a lot [of] balls all that stuff is. But I
> imagine G.K. is a more *cultivated* person than [Munnings], for what it's
> worth. It *is* a rum world that so-called "academic" painting world.*
> (Margin: *it seems to be fundamentally bogus--a vast misapprehension
> of the nature of the arts & [a] thing that has outlived its meaning &
> use.)

Ede received his copy of *The Anathemata* immediately upon its publication and wrote to Jones that he was
struggling with it. In his letter from Northwick Lodge of 16
November 1952 Jones writes about his use of "Leir" and

"Lear" in the text of *The Anathemata,* and about what sort of use Ede should make of the notes.

> Leir and Lear are the same. Leir is the form used by Geoffrey of Monmouth & others from whom Shakespeare got his stuff. In fact it *may* be spelt Leir in Shakespeare's First Folio, but I *don't know* & have no means of checking it as I now write. But Leir it is in Geoffrey of Monmouth, or at least in the first English translation of Geoffrey's Latin text made in 1718 by Aaron Thompson, a first edition copy of which I happen to possess. "Leir's river" may mean the Thames just as "Lear-sea" means the seas round this island. The Welsh is Llyr & the Irish *Lir.* He was a Celtic God of the elements--sea etc. So Shakespeare was continuing a very ancient tradition in associating "King Lear" with the tempest & storm. (Margin: I used the two forms deliberately to convey the successive layers of tradition that cling to the name. Though as the work is meant to be *said* the difference in spelling doesn't mean much. But it does do something when you see it printed on the same page.)
>
> I suggest in reading *Ana* that the best way is to take no notice of the notes except in the case of *pronunciation of Welsh words.* Read it once just as you would the Book of Isaias or, for that matter, *Tit-Bits,* or the Nicene Creed. The notes are best consulted separately. They are not intended to bolster up the text. That would be artistically indefensible. They are a quite separate commentary & are only added for the reasons explained in the preface.

At the Midsummer Banquet of 1968 David Jones was officially awarded the first Midsummer Prize of £1500 by the Lord Mayor of London. Looking back at the day he was notified about his award, Jones charmingly describes the surprise visit of the Lord Mayor's men to his room at the Monksdene Hotel in his penultimate letter to Ede of 21 February 1970.

> I was amused that you imagined I had gone to that Mansion House Banquet--No, I wasn't up to that, they most kindly sent me the prize and indeed were extremely understanding about my not being there to receive it in person--though I felt pretty awful about not being able to go. I was also absolutely astounded when they told me I was to be the recipient of it, for I'd never heard of it, it being the first occasion of it being given. They also did it in a very civilized manner. Not by letter, but two nice chaps on the Lord Mayor's staff came one day, out of the blue, & handed me a letter asking me if I was willing to receive the award. When I saw the arms of the City of London on the seal of a very large envelope, I thought & said Good God, what can this be. & the young man said, Don't be alarmed, open it and see.

On 31 December 1971, Jones wrote his last letter to Ede in response to some questions he had raised about the *Vexilla Regis,* the large watercolor-drawing which Jones completed at Bowden House and which Ede's mother had bought in 1949 following its exhibition at the Redfern Gallery in May and June of the previous year. The letter should be read as an extension of certain points made in the

letter to Mrs. Ede of 28 August 1949 which René Hague
publishes in *Dai Greatcoat*. It was sent from the Calvary
Nursing Home in Sudbury Hill, Harrow, where Jones had
gone following his stroke and fall of March 1970. On 30
December Jones had drafted a very long letter to Ede
which attempted to answer the questions he raised. Finding
the next morning that "it meanders on about all sorts of
stuff but fails to answer the questions," he begins again.

> I have with me here only a much reduced reproduction of *Vexilla
> Regis* in half-tone, plate VI in David Blamires book *David Jones
> Artist & Writer* published this summer by the Manchester Univer-
> sity Press. Have you read it? I cannot see much of the details at all
> plainly--naturally, using the necessary reduction. But I can make out in
> top right hand corner a descending bird with outstretched wings & a
> rising bird to meet and salute it--presumably a kind of *pleni sunt
> coeli et terra gloria tua motif*. There appears to be another bird in
> flight emerging from the *extreme* right corner flying more or less
> laterally, & I don't know about him, perhaps an attendant of the *mili-
> tia coelestis* or just a bird. No, no employment of the crowing cock
> motif--though I know that at one period in the iconography of the
> church it played a very important part. The tree on the right (that of
> the "bad thing") terminates with the legionary *Aquila* & down its
> length some of those disk-like forms called phalarae that Roman
> standards carried as battle honours--*not* a very good idea, sorry that the
> poor felon was executed by the state at the demands of the priests &
> rulers of the Sanhedrin. But I could not think of any other way & that's
> why that *stauros* is not a tree but stuck into the ground & held upright
> by wedges. The left hand tree ("good" thing) has in its branches a
> "pelican in her piety" on her nest & with her young & feeding them
> from her own flesh. The heap in the bottom left-hand order is meant
> to be a red *sagum* or cloak as worn by Roman soldiers & with a garment a
> *bucina** or *tuba**, a trumpet left by the guard of the fatigue-party at
> the place of execution. (Margin: *a *bucina* was, I understand, one of
> those large curved trumpets & a *tuba* more like a straight bugle.)
>   The whole conception is that the "Dreaming Rood" remains
> while the, so to say, "world-forest" whether of nature or culture rise[s]
> and fall[s]. (Margin: The A.S. poem "The Dream of the Rood" is now
> known to have been influenced by the Latin hymn *Vexilla Regis*.)
> There is, for instance, a classical statue on the left of the tree of the
> "good" thief on her plinth--perhaps the tutelar of the stream
> (Margin: which actually flows from a spring at the roots of the Cen-
> tral Tree) very near her & there is a "stonehenge" or sorts--The horses
> that cross the picture & hasten towards the hills was suggested by a
> line in Malory--after the death of Gwenhwyfar & the passing of
> Arthur & the general break-up.
>
> > "And there was none of those other knyghts but they redde in
> > bookes & holpe for to ssynge Mass & range bellys & dyd bodily al
> > maner of servyce, *And so their horses went where they would.*"
>
>   ...Sorry my tedious effort of yesterday turned out to be no
> bloody good--God bless you both. You say I owe you two letters, I
> expect I do but I spend all day about every day trying to cope with
> some work [ ] muddled with piles of correspondence. I feel so damned

tired. Two days before I had that bone-smasher of a fall I had a very slight stroke & the weariness may apparently be the result of that. This thing which I thought I'd be recovered from in about six months has in fact tied me up for about eighteen months. I too think of you both even I fail to write. . . .

WILLIAM BLISSETT

FROM THE LONG CONVERSATION

1959

15 January 1959

David Jones' letter in reply to my Christmas greeting had seemed rather weary, and I hesitated about telephoning him, not wishing to seem or be an exploiter: academic predators are my own breed and I understand their ways all too well; but he did write down his telephone number, twice. When he came to the telephone, I found his voice brisk (with a very slight English stammer) and cordial. "Why not this afternoon?" he said and told me how to reach Northwick Lodge.

The Lodge is halfway up the hill at Harrow, an oblong building, its white paint peeling, dead cold. Mr. Jones came downstairs to greet me, wearing his greatcoat and scarf. His room was warmer than the hall though still cold enough for our breath to steam. I was unused to being cold indoors, but this was cold even for England.

It is a large single room, untidy but not at all squalid, rather giving the impression of there being a great many things ready to hand. A fireplace, two chairs, a mantel with a number of objects arranged freely but not in a clutter--a small Calvary in wood, originally intended as a block for an engraving, an inscription in Welsh on dark greenish-grey stone; books everywhere, in bookcases and piled on shelves or on the floor; a large table with pens and brushes and engraving tools; pictures on the walls, on an easel, stacked against the wall. Profusion, not at all menacing--neither a bombardment of things nor a tightly clutched trove.

Mr. Jones himself is a rather small man, though his handshake on greeting me was larger and warmer than

mine; quiet, but with a good deal of nervous energy, so that
conversation may sometimes lapse but never sag. His face
can look tired and old in repose but has an almost boyish
animation when we are talking. There are glimpses of joy
and a certain radiance, no coercive power. Short, untidy
hair brushed down over his forehead. A man of the spirit but
not sacerdotal: too thin-skinned to be a priest, not methodi-
cal enough for a monk. More of an anchorite, a hermit, his
room a rather ample cell where he subtly compounds his
works of simples.

He was full of questions about Canada and the sort
of chaps I taught English to in Saskatoon, Saskatchewan. He
pronounced the name as if he had committed it to memory
as the last place in the world: we are used to that, and I was
able to convince him without much difficulty that my
native province is habitable, even civilized. As strangers
and pilgrims do, we exchanged perplexities about Americans, of whom he has come to know several in recent years,
servicemen, boarding at Northwick Lodge. The most surprising thing about them, apart from their general receptivity
and sudden chasms of blankness, was the way so many of the
hulking big bruisers turned out to their various churches on
Sunday mornings.

He kept thinking of new things to show me and so
the conversation was not very consecutive--and I'm not
much good at recalling what other people say. Before the
light failed I had a good look at a number of drawings,
including the large watercolor on an easel, *Aphrodite in
Aulis*, which has a depth and volume hardly to be guessed
from reproduction in reduced size. When it was first shown
in a gallery, a studious-looking man fell into talk with him
about it, said he took a professional interest in goddesses: it
was E. R. Dodds, author of *The Greeks and the Irrational*,
that splendid book. The title of the picture, by the way, has
no reference to George Moore's novel, which Mr. Jones says
he may have heard of but has certainly not read. The technical problem of the picture was so to dispose it as to make
Aphrodite dominant--blooming, buxom, but not heavy--and
the artist is satisfied on this score. The pencil line and the
coloring are laid on concurrently, not pencil first and then
color. This is not what one would expect, and I had the
sense that he often has to overrule the contrary assumption.

I had brought along my copy of *The Rime of the
Ancient Mariner*, and he inscribed it for me. It is the one of
his illustrated books that he thinks the most successful. He
said the Golden Cockerel Press people, like lunatics, called

in a bevy of girl art students to color the wood engravings for his *Gulliver's Travels.* Every single copy. He removed the color from his own. I was relieved to hear this, for I thought the coloring poisonous when I looked at the book in the British Museum. Contrary to orders, they used the wrong paper and didn't dampen it for *The Chester Play of the Deluge,* and so the black is not properly black: the reproduction in the Tate Gallery catalogue is superior to the book. As for *The Book of Jonah,* it is "pure Eric"--good, with that reservation.

I showed him *The Wounded Knight,* a copper engraving I had bought at the Redfern Gallery, but he thought it a pretty faint print that should not have been pulled and I could see that he preferred not to sign it. He didn't know that some watercolors of his were being shown there currently, and he wondered about their source of supply. His experience in trying to get money out of them has not always been happy, in spite of their calling him David to put him at his ease. He recalled that at his exhibition there some years ago he had wanted to show but not to sell *Vexilla Regis* ("The view from this window--that is the tree," he said, pointing),[1] and so had been persuaded to put an exorbitant price on it, but an old friend, a very nice chap from Cambridge [H.S. Ede], bought it for his mother, who was ill and had set her heart on it. It was the only high payment he had ever received, but he wishes he had kept the picture, as he needs his main "things" around him. "Serves me right for asking more than the just price." This he said with simple contrition, as if he were confessing to St. Thomas Aquinas.

When talking of *Gulliver's Travels,* he mentioned the great number of blocks to be engraved, conveying the sense of its having been a fatiguing commission, and this led to Aubrey Beardsley who at the outset of his career was given a huge commission to illustrate Malory, very gratifying no doubt but foreign to his temperament and crushing in its magnitude. Beardsley he admires highly; he did not know whether or not Canon John Gray had been in the Beardsley circle. He recalled Gray as a remarkable priest who, in his church in Edinburgh, was said to spend many hours regularly waiting in the confessional for anyone who might need him: a real mortification for one who started life as a minor poet of the 1890s and whose surname was appropriated, jocularly, by his famous friend Oscar Wilde in

1. But see René Hague, *Dai Greatcoat* (London: Faber and Faber, 1980), p. 151, for DJ's letter to Mrs. Ede of 28 August 1949, in which he traces the origin of the picture to trees outside the window of a nursing home.

The Picture of Dorian Gray. Canon Gray was a great walker and no matter how many miles he had covered in town or country always arrived fresh and unruffled, his shoes gleaming. He often talked of Wilde and others of that time but Mr. Jones does not recall his mentioning Beardsley.

Like Beardsley, David Jones does not work from sketches: the original drawing is revised and developed until it feels the way the first conception felt. I mentioned the signs of innumerable erasures in the Beardsley drawing of *Siegfried* now on display in the Victoria and Albert Museum, and that led to Wagner--as I had rather hoped than plotted. No, he doesn't like Wagner at all, thinks his style vulgar, doesn't enjoy opera: in fact, when his friends went to the opera years ago, he would sit on a bench in the Underground (or was it in the train itself, the Inner Circle Line?) and read a book until it was time to meet them. Any Wagnerism in his writing must come through as mediated by Joyce, of whom he never tires. Joyce is his writer, when he dares admit it.

He was curious to hear about T. S. Eliot's new play, *The Elder Statesman*, and was pleased when I said that I found it witty and wise. "Marriage has done wonders for Tom--filled him out, even physically. It's good to see him happy." Eliot he has known for a very long time; Edith Sitwell he has come to know in the past two years. He had feared she might be arty and brittle but instead found her warm-hearted and easy and quite without "side." He thought *she* would be a Spenserian, if I liked. He is himself put off mainly (not exclusively) by Spenser's fierceness in the matter of Ireland, and of course I didn't defend it except historically. I tried to persuade him to enter the heartland of *The Faerie Queene*, where he would find something like his own landscape. He gave me the look of a man who resolves to open his Spenser one of these days.

He showed me a little book on Bonnard. "Far superior to Degas. I can't understand how they have come to be so misjudged." "More heart?" I suggested, thinking of Degas' limiting sarcasm, and he agreed, or let it pass. He recalled that his old teacher at the Camberwell School of Art before the Great War, A. S. Hartrick, knew many French painters of that generation and always referred to Degas as Degaz, which he said was how the painter pronounced his name. Without ever being strenuously avant-garde, David Jones, from his earliest days, was aware of what belonged to "the Now," to use his phrase, and receptive to it. *Tachisme* he is out of sympathy with and says there is some fakery involved in claiming for accident what is (when it amounts to any-thing) skill. He admires Ben Nicholson in spite of his fanat-ical abstractionism. He was delighted with what I told him about the Canadian painter David Milne (whom I had men-tioned in my review): how he soldiered through the Depres-sion in the northern wilds, living in a shack and subsisting on pork and beans, how he avoided all commercial art or teaching (a vigorous nod of the head at this), and how, when he talked (not very much) about art, you could imagine a trustful chipmunk on his shoulder.

"What do you think of old Spengler?" he demanded, putting on a sort of Prussian bark very different from his usual quiet speech. I said I thought him a poet of ideas, obviously somebody--full of false analogies and true metaphors, I might have added, but didn't think of it until halfway home. He thinks Spengler underestimated and rather too easily forgotten when Toynbee and Mumford and Malraux come to mind. We talked about the tragedy of Germany, and he made the admission (rather, tore the admission out of himself) that he had been quite pro-Ger-man in the appeasement era, out of fellow-feeling for the "enemy front-fighters against whom we found ourselves by misadventure," having dismissed all earlier reports of Nazi cruelty and nihilism as propaganda, like the stories of sol-diers crucified on hay ricks in the Great War. The truth came as a terrible shock, and he has been pondering ever since on whether a new age of torment and outrage has opened or whether the old securities and decencies had been an illusion all the time. It was here that a lapse in conversation took place, for I had much the same sort of assent, to the opposite political evil, on my conscience.

We consumed two pots of Lapsang Souchong tea in the loose, mainly pleasant talk. When it was time for me to go, David Jones put on his scarf and coat and accompanied me to the front door, and I walked through the cold fog down to the station.

28 January 1959

"Don't knock. You know the way up," David Jones had said on the telephone. I walked up the hill from the station, the fog again obscuring all the view except the golden guinea of the sun.

Mr. Jones wanted to talk about Joyce. He had memorized "Anna Livia Plurabelle" from the record--one of the few things he had ever memorized since his childhood--

and it only gradually faded when the record along with a number of other things was stolen from his studio; now he has secured another copy. His experience is the same as mine: there are bits and islands in *Finnegans Wake* that he keeps going back to, venturing a little further from them every time. He has never been right through it but intends to make the effort soon with the help of the *Skeleton Key*, which he finds useful, modest, and therefore admirable.

The pictures were all in different places, with hardly an exception, and quite a few new ones appeared, including a large watercolor of a snow scene, done the winter before last. As a Canadian I talked rather a lot about snow as a substance and how it lies when fresh fallen or glazed by re-freezing, and the curious russet and blue shadows cast on it by street lights or moonlight, but I did give the picture some attention between remarks. Two of his pictures from the 1920s or early 1930s were there--a coastal scene, which might have been Lake Superior except for the vessel, and a nude, utterly unlike anything of his that I have seen, describable (I suggested) as by an anonymous master, school of Sickert. That turned out to be a good guess, for it was painted when he was studying with Sickert after the war. Artists paid their one-and-six a time at an old painting establishment in Kennington and painted away, and Sickert looked in on them occasionally. Nothing like that now: it's all formal and under the educational authority.

Those two pictures were done at the time that he was strongly tempted to go abstract. He is glad he didn't, even though he concedes that the best work of the present age may prove to be in that mode. Besides Ben Nicholson, he admires Victor Pasmore, whom he knew as an art master at Harrow, though he suspects that abstraction may have been the wrong turning for Pasmore. I threw out the notion that young painters may think they are being abstract when they are really representing modern buildings and kitchens and bathrooms. An amused look, no comment required: that finished our talk about art.

While he was inscribing and entering corrections in my copy of *In Parenthesis*, he let me read a portion of his new book of essays, in which he defended Pasmore against a particularly malignant critic. He recalled that only recently the *TLS* printed yet another (i.e., the same old) article on obscurity in poetry, apropos of Betjeman. As if any real poet produced easy or difficult poetry according to the fashion of the moment. Reviewers see everything in terms of their own preoccupation with the ephemeral.

Mr. Jones met W. B. Yeats once or twice, didn't like his pose, and thought that some at least of the beautiful women swarming about him might have employed themselves better in swarming about someone else. This he said with glee.

He had been through *Paradise Lost* twice in the past few years but had formed the impression, which I was at pains to correct, that Milton regarded sexuality as a consequence of the Fall. What he likes best is the impression of artillery fire in the war in heaven. He must be unique in singling this out for praise. (It is, as Samuel Johnson observes, "the favorite of children and gradually neglected as knowledge is increased.")

We were talking about *King Arthur's Avalon*, which he had seen but not read, and I told him of Geoffrey Ashe's surprising development from pacifism to a concurrent interest, while at Cambridge just after the war, in Marxism and Thomism. He joined the Karl Marx Club and the Thomas Aquinas Club, and the saint won the argument. Mention of the priory at Aylesford, Kent, near which the Ashe family lives, led to Sir Thomas Wyatt, who came into possession of it when it was secularized. Mr. Jones had quite forgotten that "stalk within yer chamber" at the opening of *In Parenthesis* was a phrase from Wyatt. Wyatt is a special poet of his, and Skelton, and Christopher Smart. He showed me an old article of his on Smart in the *Tablet* while he wrote something on the back of a sheet of stiff paper. This turned out to be a photostat of one of his inscriptions ("What Says His Mabinogi"), to which he had added in watercolor "Nid. Gorwaith. Moli. Mab. Mair" (It is not too much work to praise the Son of Mary); and on the back my name and his. Kindness of the best brand, quite incommensurate with the small chores my mobility enables me to do for him in London.

When it was time to go, he took my address and telephone number since he would like me to meet a friend of his who is a master at Harrow, in modern languages, and interested in my Wagner project.

26 February 1959

I telephoned Mr. Jones at a quarter to ten this morning after settling in at the British Museum--and got him out of bed. He claimed to have been awake. He had been up until three in the morning working on, I believe he said, an inscription for St. David's Day, which is this coming Sunday.

He sounded, as before on the telephone, rather down and I wasn't altogether reassured when he asked me out there, saying that he enjoyed my visits. He was full of solicitude about my recovery from the flu.

When I arrived, I found him looking tired and pinched, and we talked for a while about coffee and Irish whiskey (which he is allowed again, his ulcer having cleared up) and the danger of a cycle of drink and insomnia to a man living alone. He does not share my North American liking for milk (the big American bruisers at the Lodge like it)--any more than my love of early hours, he quietly intimated. The food is not good at Northwick, except for breakfast, which he prepares himself.

I had seen the film of *The Horse's Mouth* last week and gave my opinion of it, which is not high: it is full of every bohemian and pseudo-Dionysian cliché. Mr. Jones has known most of the modern painters in England, and only one--he didn't say which--he regarded as a bohemian. Most of them were direct, businesslike, and rather square. Even so flamboyant a character as Augustus John was pretty dependable.

He doesn't think anyone understood Wyndham Lewis, or could know what his heart's desire was. One installment of *The Human Age* on the wireless he had to switch off, it was so cruel, so harrowing, so much like hell. I spoke of the power and the falsity of *Self-Condemned*. The beer-parlor incident could not have taken place as related because in Canada women were not admitted to such places at all at the time of the novel, and later an escorted lady could not have been in the same room as single men. Lewis didn't take the trouble to get these things right. How much better the book would have been, too, if he had called Toronto by its own name instead of "Momaco"; it is as if he had attacked Birmingham as "Hirmingbam." Again, I could relate a curious incident in real life in which Lewis launched into a violent tirade in a Toronto street car addressed to a middle-aged lady whom he had met on some earlier occasion--all against the savagery of Canada, not knowing or caring that she, without leaving Canada, had known of his work as a painter and had been reading his books for twenty years. A typical story, Mr. Jones said. Eliot, who knew Lewis well, couldn't make him out--not that Eliot himself could be drawn on the subject. "Tom is the cagiest man alive--used to arrive at parties and leave at precise times, count his drinks, and disclose nothing." And yet we both find Eliot's writings, even when most "impersonal," revealing in the highest degree, just as he is most American when the American accent has almost disappeared.

Mr. Jones heard the recent broadcast discussion of a new theory of plainchant, which some experts think will undermine the old assumptions about style and performance which we associate with Solesmes Abbey. He is concerned because, if plainchant "line" and rhythm are more regular than had been thought, one of the chief precedents for his own poetry will disappear. Fortunately for him, he can't distinguish any great difference between examples of the old style and the new.

When he mentioned a "great controversy in the Catholic world," I had not expected the plainchant issue but the question of Newman's canonization. I told him of Geoffrey Ashe's touchstone: can you imagine an Irish washerwoman asking for his prayers? How like a convert, Mr. Jones said--the assumption that the woman must have a pure and simple, though altogether hidden piety because otherwise her existence would be too awful to contemplate. I said recklessly that the typical Catholic (if he existed) might be an Irish-American used-car salesman. At this he laughed and said that he enjoys the stories of J. F. Powers greatly, adding that a correspondent in "Kansass" asked him not to put "Esq." after his name on the envelope because it provoked mirth there.

We also talked (my cough making my throat raspy by this time) about Middle English poetry--Chaucer, Langland, Gower, and *Sir Gawain* (whose huge vocabulary he had struggled with, just as I had). Tolkien, the editor of *Sir Gawain*, he has never met. He read *The Hobbit* years ago but has not attempted the trilogy, and so there goes another chance for me to make a plea for Wagner and his *Ring*.

Before I left, he gave me a beautiful copy of *The Wounded Knight*. I had forgotten my disappointment with the copy I had bought, but he had remembered.

10 April 1959

Mr. Jones seemed frail and ashen today. He admitted to being very tired and said that he had been through a difficult time recently. He has the physique perhaps of the child of old parents: his mother, he said, would be over a hundred if she were alive; she was somewhat older than his father. He found this out when he looked after his father for a time after her death. His mother, he went on to say, had been taught the purest Catholic doctrine at her parish church in Rotherhithe by the old vicar who never wore anything more ritualistic than a surplice, but she had later conformed to her husband's fervent Evangelicalism. James Jones had been a lay reader and was staunchly Protestant; his son's going to Rome had been a heavy blow to him. David Jones, who was still an Anglican during and after his years in the trenches, wanted to make his confession before communion, and so he went to the rector of a likely-looking church and said, "I want to make my confession." The rector looked disconcerted and said, "Here, read this and come back in a week's time," but young David Jones said he didn't want to read things but to confess. They sparred a while and he left, but on the way out he met the curate, a much older man, and made the same request, and they were inside in half a minute, and very helpful the curate's counsel was.

Mr. Jones has no desire to go anywhere or to see anything unless it has some direct bearing on his work. He never was a good tourist: apart from the war and a voyage as a convalescent to the Holy Land, his only venture outside these islands was with the Gills once to the south of France. They inspected Chartres, and he enraged Eric Gill (who was enrageable) by preferring the old parish church of St.-Pierre to the cathedral. A little boy with them on the train, when asked by his parents, who met him, how he had slept, said that the lady was nice and quiet but the two gentlemen had argued all night. Mr. Jones laughed when I quoted D. H. Lawrence's review of *Art-Nonsense* (a very lively performance though Lawrence was dying when he wrote it) in which he said that Eric Gill argued like a man in a pub. "Just right, that's it exactly," he said. He also added that Eric and the old G. G. Coulton (the mediaevalist and anti-Catholic writer) were friendly foes and got along together hammer and tongs.

12 June 1959

My copy of *The Anathemata*, left with David Jones in April, was returned to me inscribed and corrected today; he also signed *Libellus Lapidum* and the new book, *Epoch and Artist*. My list of errata for the last he looked at but took no action on: the prospect of having to enter corrections in yet another book was probably not an agreeable one. What he did give full attention to was a little book of modern German watercolors I had brought him--not so much the drawings themselves as the technique of reproducing them on matt-finish paper comparable to watercolor paper, instead of the glossy paper (radically incompatible with watercolors) that English publishers use.

Now that I am getting to know Mr. Jones better, I have less clear-cut, more suffused impressions to record. That is one reason I find myself at a standstill now; the other is that I did most of the talking, as a returned traveller--about the Bonnards in the Musée de l'Art Moderne in Paris and the Tintorettos in Venice, about hearing Ildebrando Pizzetti's *Assassinio nella Cattedrale* at La Scala (very faithful to the Eliot play and musically best where the play is best, the scene of the Fourth Tempter), about seeing an unexpected sight in the streets of Rapallo. Having stayed a few days in Santa Margherita, I set out on my last morning to walk to near-by Rapallo. There, striding along the main street, shaking hands with passers-by and ducking in and out of shops for greetings and handshakes, was an old man wearing a very long scarf embroidered with Chinese characters, which he would periodically toss over his shoulder as he stared form side to side, looking like an owl in daylight. With him was a small woman, very English. When they came to an intersection, the rather glorious Italian traffic policeman, recognizing the old man, sprang to attention and saluted. The salute was gravely acknowledged. It could only be one person, but it took me some time to compose a question in Italian, to which the policeman replied, "*Il grande poeta Americano.*" I caught sight of the pair several more times, so that I was noticed, but although I was carrying my camera I did not steal a photograph on the day of the *grande poeta*'s return to Rapallo.

David Jones listened to all this with interest but had nothing to volunteer about Ezra Pound. About Tintoretto he spoke feelingly and acknowledged the specific influence of *The Rescue of Arsinoe* on his own composition. Somehow we got on to the subject of the cleaning or "restoration" of paintings--perhaps the Tintoretto had been restored, I don't remember. Anyway, a friend of his, "my melancholy friend," once telephoned and simply said, "It's gone," and he knew at once that he would never see Hogarth's *Shrimp Girl* again.

Stanley Spencer and Ben Nicholson he surprised me by naming as the two contemporaries he is nearest to. He acknowledged the same sort of surprise when an otherwise perceptive reviewer referred to him as earthy and Rabelaisian. This got us on to reviewers and the reception of *Epoch and Artist*. Kathleen Raine's review [in the *New Statesman*], very kind, perhaps too kind, is a model of informed friendliness, he said. He was not so much disappointed in Stevie Smith's review as in the journal for choosing a reviewer so completely out of touch with the concerns of the book: she doesn't like King Arthur and that's flat.

Mr. Jones had just poured the China black tea and I had helped myself to Bath Olivers when his doctor arrived on monthly rounds and I had to wait outside for a few minutes. Evidently the doctor's opinion of him was good--and he certainly looked years younger today than in the dead of winter. The doctor gives him only enough sleeping potion for a month at a time; this, I believe, is the usual practice, but I don't know from my own experience, being a famous sleeper.

The BBC people had been up to Harrow about a week before, to record an interview that will be broadcast on Thursday. He was ill at ease for the first few minutes, he said, but warmed as the conversation got on to old Spengler and the sense of cultural "lateness," which he feels very strongly. I have always been leery of this, some arts and sciences and sets of ideas being early in their development at the very time (and even in the very place) that others are late; but there is no getting away from the phenomenon in Venice. "I am so lated in the world that I have lost my way forever."

Mr. Jones didn't much like Geoffrey Ashe's book, *King Arthur's Avalon*, which I had left with him some time ago: said it was heavy and slow because it worked counter to the imagination. He suspected that the author was looking for a set of answers; this was before I told him of Ashe's cryptogrammatical cast of mind and his wartime work (as I guess, for he was sworn not to disclose) on ciphers. No riddles are solved, nothing is made easier by Catholic subscription, Mr. Jones said. By the way, he has not said anything about *Imitation and Design*,[2] a copy of which I gave him: I will not raise the subject.

8 July 1959

The hottest day since the creation of the world. I waited, sweating, twenty minutes in Charing Cross Road for a bus, which took forty minutes to mosey through shimmering heat to Baker Street. I arrived at Northwick Lodge a pulp. David Jones and his old friend René Hague were drinking lime

2. Reid MacCallum, *Imitation and Design*, ed. William Blissett (Toronto: University of Toronto Press, 1953).

and water--"Thank Christ for Rose's!" they exclaimed with astonishing vehemence, and I at once entered a swiftly flowing swim of conversation. Hague and Jones kept remembering old times and lapsing back into army talk, spoken in an exaggeratedly refined accent, such as they had used when living with the Gill family at Capel-y-ffin. "Biscuit?" "Neo, thenks very mach." "You mean you'll have fack-all?" "Fack-all, thenks very mach." Laughter flowing in from across the years. Hague radiates *brio* and wit, and I had never before seen David Jones in such high and boyish spirits.

I mentioned having read the biography of Dom Aelred Carlyle, *Abbot Extraordinary,* by Peter Anson, with great pleasure, in which Hague concurred. It would have been easy for the writer to make the whole story of the extravagant and finally bankrupt Anglican Benedictines of Caldey Island, who went over to Rome and became extravagant and finally bankrupt Roman Benedictines, a travesty and a romp, or to have gone all solemn and "but suriously," like a student debater who has told his joke. I was impressed by the story of Dom Aelred's later years as a missionary priest in the interior of British Columbia and as a waterfront missioner in Vancouver (what a distance from Walter Pater's priory where he began), and moved by the account of his return in old age to die an oblate in the monastery he had founded.

Both René Hague and "Dai" had been several times to Caldey Island, often spending more time than they had planned, for weather could maroon them there. Both had an eye for a fair dairymaid who, they said, must have been used by the Abbot, Dom Aelred's successor, to attach young laymen to the island! They remembered some old French monks who really went to work with toothpicks after a serious dinner--glorious, like something out of Belloc. It was a pretty hit-or-miss monastery in its Roman as it had been in its Anglican days, and they recall it with elation of spirit. They both like Anglicans (I felt they weren't just being nice to me), and Mr. Jones said always go to an ex-Anglican priest on any sexual matter if you want some human understanding and sympathy. The cradle Catholics just throw the book at you. Then, like naughty schoolboys, they added that the Dominicans understand because they have girl friends themselves, and the Jays (Jesuits) make a brave show of understanding but they never have. A Jay might shoot himself but would never run off and get married.

David Jones used to visit Graham Greene when he was living with his wife near Clapham Common. One day, on crossing the Common, he was accosted, twice, by prostitutes. Like something out of Graham Greene. When *The Anathemata* appeared, Greene wrote him a nice note, ending, "I've got a terrible cold and am very drunk, and so this is probably all balls."

Evelyn Waugh is always on stage creating a crusty character. Hague was with him near the London Library once when a little boy said, "Please, sir, can you tell me the time?" Waugh bristled and roared, "Time! Time! What has a child your age to do with time!" All very much for the legend and not at all the sort of thing a real Tory clubman would say. In spite of this act of his own, Waugh pretends to believe that all actors are cads. Once he said he saw an elderly gentleman coming towards him, obscured by the light, who looked exactly like Maurice Baring, "and so I called out to him, 'Speaight!' " Robert Speaight the actor is a great admirer of Baring and unconsciously has come to mimic him.

This was a short visit but frolicsome. The old friends of thirty years' standing enjoyed including me in their fun, but they doubtless had things to talk about and so I left early.

15 August 1959

David Jones telephoned me last night and we made arrangements for tea today. He was glad that I had met "old René" and that we had hit it off so well. A very remarkable chap, old René, astonishing how versatile he is: he can read and translate Greek and Latin with accuracy and grace-- French and Old French too, is a master printer and can do all kinds of lettering, including inscriptions in stone. As a boy he must have been a handful: the Benedictines were just at the point of expelling him from Ampleforth for a really shocking prank when he won a scholarship to Oxford. After coming down he tried his vocation with the Jesuits and lasted "about a week," then arrived at Ditchling in a thoroughly mixed-up state. It took Eric Gill and later Joan (Gill's daughter, whom Hague married), to settle him down. He was always dependable really, in spite of his high spirits and appearance of wildness. Irish, though brought up in England: that helps account for his beautiful speech.

David Jones himself considered trying his vocation at (I think he said) Caldey Island and was told to find some

nice Catholic girl. We laughed as we looked at the drawing
he had been at work on, a sort of Rokeby Venus with some
Courbet in it and a lot of Jones--including horses and ships
seen through a window and a crossbow and crucifix. *There's*
a nice Catholic girl. The wall by his work table is covered
with previous drawings relevant to this one in feeling,
theme, or detail.

In a man who, some months before, had expressed
the incredible sentiment of indifference to travel, even as
far as Wales, let alone the Continent, I detected today,
along with evidences of good health and lightness of spirits,
a great interest in the Prado, especially the Velázquez
paintings, and a willingness to consider the possibility of
actually going there. An old friend of his named Burns [T.
F. Burns, editor of the *Tablet*] has a Spanish wife, and her
family would be pleased if he would stay with them. I did
all I could to encourage this--without adding that I will not
myself enter Spain while Franco is head of government. It's
that, he said, or buy back his wood blocks for *Gulliver's
Travels* from Bertram Rota, the dealer in modern first editions.

We talked about holy places, how some churches
have a numinous "presence" and some have not. St. Paul's
has none at all, in his judgment: it might as well be a railway station, but some of the smaller Wren churches have a
great deal. I agreed, thinking of St. Magnus Martyr. The
Carmelite church in Kensington was the first such that he
knew. He went there as an art student, asked to see the
Father Superior, and borrowed a hood for a fancy-dress ball.
What cheek! And yet the place, which he was to know very
well later on, in the 1940s, made an immediate impression
on him. It was bombed out during the war, but its replace-
ment has the same quality, according to reports.

Then, rummaging about in his stacks of old papers,
he came up with the pencil sketches he had made in the
trenches--against standing military orders. "Bloody art-
school stuff, most of it," he said, and it is true that I can't
remember any detail. And photographs: of himself as a
"young soldier with his bag of salt," sharper in feature than
now and quite natty. Of a nurse and of an Irish girl, both
beautiful. Of himself, good-looking and well dressed, the
very day he met Yeats at Countess Somebody's (he remembered, I can't) and Yeats gushed over DJ's work and
"chuntered poems to himself at tea" and was, I gather, completely alien. A young chap at a Cambridge college had
recently written a very nice letter asking Mr. Jones to

come and speak to a literary group there and had referred to his tutor, T. R. Henn, as the author of "an important book on Yeats," as indeed he is, but the phrase struck us both as obscurely ludicrous (perhaps because *everybody* is the author of an important book on Yeats). And then there was a large photograph taken for Fabers at the time of *In Parenthesis* but not used--an impressive thing and very like. Another, agonized, at the time of his breakdown. And a couple taken recently when some friends came.

One of his most curious and memorable war experiences occurred when he was stationed in Ireland in late 1918 or early 1919, still not demobilized though with four years' service behind him. It was his only collision with the stone wall of army discipline. He had sprained his ankle rather badly, and when he was able to move about again, the Medical Officer told him to use a cane. He was crossing the parade ground when the Regimental Sergeant-Major, a huge man and a bully, with only a modest record of service in the trenches, shouted, "That man! drop that stick!" Private Jones hobbled nearer, said he had permission to use it. "Drop that cane!" "Sorry, sir, I have permission from the M.O." "Drop it!" "No, sir, I have permission." The R.S.M. thereupon summoned two soldiers, put the mutineer under arrest and marched him to the cells, ancient, dark, damp, crowded. One of the three nights was made hideous by Irishwomen screeching and jeering outside. The charge, originally "refusing to obey an order, using insulting language, and assuming a menacing posture to a senior non-commissioned officer," was somehow reduced by the sensible Colonel to one of unnecessary delay in obeying an order, and Private Jones was only confined to barracks. But the twist, the shame of which still makes him wince, was that, shortly afterwards, he met the M.O. in the street, who, instead of brazening it out or taking no notice, crossed over and apologized, saying officers have to stick together for the sake of discipline. Not exactly what Captain Fluellen meant by "the disciplines of the wars."

Unaccountably we got on to the subject of birth control, and how some young Catholic married people became callous by persistently going against their consciences and others, more sensitive, are terribly handicapped by large families. He thinks that the present rigid position will be modified, as the stand against usury was abandoned, and that a working arrangement with liberalism and even eventually with communism will have to be reached. I was much impressed by this deeply felt and reluctant expression of

misgiving--the first breach I had ever seen in that particular
Roman front. It made my agreement with the strict position
taste thin and sour.

We had a glass of Scotch, and Mr. Jones signed and
gave me his wood engraving, *The Bride*, which he said was
perhaps his best. Then, it being a very pleasant summer day,
he walked down to the station with me,[3] trying frequently
but without success to find a cigarette-vending machine
that would work. He has resumed smoking. I wish I could
find some tactful way to persuade him to buy sheets of
asbestos or other fireproof material. Everything in his room
is inflammable and everything is irreplaceable.[4]

On the train back to London I resolved to use some
of the money I have just inherited from an aunt to buy the
Gulliver blocks and make him a present of them.

28 August 1959

Out to Harrow bearing fardels--the forty-five blocks of *Gulliver's Travels* in one monstrous heavy bundle; in the other,
the two volumes of the book. Mr. Jones seemed almost
downcast with pleasure at seeing the blocks but was brought
to agree that he ought to have them. Last week he had lent
most of the money he had intended for the blocks (or for
Spain?) to a friend who was hard up, and he was apprehen-
sive lest some speculator get them.

At his suggestion I nipped out to Boots the Chemists
to get a bottle of "Milton," a gentle antiseptic mouthwash
ideal for removing watercolor, and he showed me how to
sponge and rinse the page without damaging the paper. He
is still indignant at the thought that the libraries of the
British Museum and the Victoria and Albert Museum have
copies embellished by lady art students, who seem to have
identified Gulliver in their mind with Malvolio in yellow
stockings. With a sigh he makes half a resolve to go up to
London and remove the color himself.

While sponging he asked me if I had seen the
Church Times or knew anything more about the outburst of

---

3. While it did not make much of an impression on me at the time, I now (1980) realize
how extraordinary it was for David Jones to leave his dugout and take an extended
brisk walk as if it were the most usual thing in the world. This was to be the only time I
ever saw him out of doors.
4. Some years later, in a review in the *Queen's Quarterly*, No. 71 (1965), of *The New
Orpheus: Essays Toward a Christian Poetic*, edited by Nathan A. Scott, I had occasion
to quote the great smell-a-rat passage from "Art and Sacrament" (*E&A*, 156-57) and
to make an important observation: David Jones' room was always fresh and though a
smoker who wore heavy clothes he was always well aired. No funkiness, no fug, no
smell-a-rat in his vicinity.

the Bishop of Southwark against a poor little Anglo-Catholic priest in his diocese who had said that he was "not interested in the Church of England" and had been removed from his parish. "Why, I might say that I am not the least bit interested in the Church of Rome and mean the same thing--that I am only interested in the Church of Christ." He had thought, as I had, that Catholicism was by now universally accepted as a possible Anglican position. Then, as if not even to appear to press an advantage in controversy, he went on to talk about (that is, against) the persecution of Protestants in Colombia.

Jacob Epstein has just died. David Jones knew him in his later years well enough to reverse completely an earlier dislike. What had seemed boastful bumptiousness seemed so no longer, or ceased to matter. As a modeller in clay he had hardly an equal for sheer excitement and skill of execution. The public has always concentrated its furious attention of course on the massive stone things. Mr. Jones likes among these the Madonna over the door of a convent in or near Wigmore Street. I remember seeing it once from a taxi and searching for it later without success. Once, when Epstein was hard up, he painted wallsful of the worst watercolors ever unloaded on to paper, and as they were sold he kept replacing them with more and more of the same.

Henry Moore Mr. Jones thinks of course a great sculptor, as everybody else does, but wonders whether he isn't at his best in his watercolor drawings (perhaps as everybody else wonders).

Abstraction again. Ben Nicholson is the best abstractionist: this said for the third time. Mr. Jones admires Nicholson's first or "real" wife, Winifred, and thinks little of the second one, Barbara Hepworth, who "hasn't the brains for abstract art: not that Ben is particularly brainy, but what brains he has are of the right kind." He laughed a little ruefully at the malice of that turn of phrase.

He has agreed to apply for a Bollingen award, and showed me the application form--a yard-long questionnaire. He thinks of the selection committee perusing it in their togas. "Quite a number of people have put in a word for me--there's Kathleen Raine and Bertie Read, who have some sort of connection with the Foundation, and Auden and Spender, Christopher Dawson, Father Martin D'Arcy, Kenneth Clark, and Tom Eliot." It is a measure of his tonnage that he is not swamped by such supercargo.

Talk about honors and awards. Stanley Spencer as a knight is a big joke, Spencer being physically the grubbiest of men. He thinks his own C. B. E. rather comical, "though it would have been a bit mouldy to refuse it." He liked the Court official in charge of arrangements, whom he telephoned a few days before the event to say that he had a terrible cold and might not be able to turn up. "Oh, that's all right," the official said. "Just drop us a postcard and we'll arrange to have you at the next do." But he did get there on the proper day and rather enjoyed it, especially the military chaps, who all had the look of the Crimean War about them. The Queen herself is a bit wooden, except with horses, and is getting the puffy cheeks of Queen Victoria. Princess Margaret's rather Jewish beauty, inherited perhaps from Prince Albert, is very much more to his taste. He showed me the C.B.E. cross and ribbon ("I wish they wouldn't, ever, put a crown on the point of a fleur-de-lys") and the citation. Unfortunately he can wear it only with full evening dress, and his habit as a third-order Dominican he can wear only in his coffin. And so I urged him to go to Bangor and pick up the honorary doctorate he was being given by the University of Wales, if only for his wardrobe's sake.

As I took my leave to return to Canada, he asked me if I liked being called William or Bill. The question is always coming up: though Bill can be a bit chummy, especially for former students and friends younger than myself, William is impossibly stiff, and so we settled on Bill. Since he did not ask me to call him David, I continued in my letters to address him as Mr. Jones until he settled the matter in 1967.

THOMAS DILWORTH

*DAVID JONES AND FASCISM**

More than any other important writer in English, David
Jones has relentlessly and intelligently tested traditional
values in the face of modern mechanized war, technological
pragmatism and political totalitarianism. In his two epic-
length poems and his sequence of middle-length poems, he
explores the crisis of modern civilization in the context of a
coherent cultural phenomenology which involves an original synthesis of Post-Impressionist aesthetics and Christian
metaphysics. Added to these is an elementary political
morality which may be summed up in his favorite words of
Augustine, "empire is robbery" (*A*, 85, n. 3; 88). Yet, in
David Jones Mythmaker, Elizabeth Ward repeatedly claims
that the poetry of David Jones has underlying affinities with
the basic attitudes of fascism. Like the fascists, she says,
Jones idealizes the past, dislikes modern rationalism and
materialism, and is critical of the capitalistic Western
democracies.[1] She also states that in the 1930s the poet was
probably pro-fascist in his sympathies. Some of her arguments might directly be disputed on strictly logical grounds,
but it seems more productive to explore the issue she has
raised.[2] I shall do so with reference to the poetry of David
Jones, to an unpublished essay by him entitled "Hitler," and
to information sent to me by Harman Grisewood, a close
friend of the poet from the mid 1920s.[3] We will see that the

*This is a revised and expanded version of an essay with the same title published in the
Journal of Modern Literature 13 (March, 1986), pp. 149-62.
1. (Manchester: University of Manchester, 1983), p. 190.
2. In "Recent Criticism on David Jones," *Contemporary Literature* XXVII (Fall,
1986), pp. 416-420, Kathleen Henderson Staudt deftly and convincingly refutes Ward's
contention that Jones' poetry is informed by a protofascist ideology.
3. I am grateful to Harman Grisewood for permission to quote from his letters to me.
In December 1952, David Jones writes about Grisewood: "He's an amazing person and
understands *everything*. He's almost the only person I can talk to absolutely properly
now, with complete understanding. I don't see him very often though because I live here
in Harrow, & am so often not awfully well & seldom go to London. But am in constant
touch, if only by telephone, and whenever I can & when he's not too busy--for he is very
busy in his job at the B.B.C.--I go up & see him" (*IN*, 28).
     For permission to include in his essay unpublished material by the poet, I am
grateful to the trustees of the estate of David Jones.

notion of David Jones as, at any time, pro-fascist is, to say
the least, problematic, and that at the deepest level of feeling and conviction, he was out of sympathy with fascist
political policy.

From the beginning, the poetry of David Jones is
anti-imperialist. He was never a pacifist; he believed in the
practical efficacy and occasional necessity of waging war.
But he also believed that, to be just, a war had to be defensive. That is why a prayer against "expeditionary war" is at
the center of *In Parenthesis*, which is based on seven
months of his own experience as an infantryman during the
First World War (*IP*, 83).

The poetry he wrote during and after the Second
World War is thoroughly and explicitly anti-totalitarian.
With reference to the politics of the twentieth century,
however, his attitudes are always implied through historic
analogies which reverse the Joycean mythic method.
Instead of the fictional present evoking the past, Jones' primary narrative or dramatic focus is the past, which parallels
the present. And it is not an idealized past. In "The Wall,"
for instance, a Roman soldier experiencing the moral and
existential "darkness" of his imperial service remembers a
triumphal march through the city of Rome in which ancient
empire evokes international capitalism but primarily the
state-capitalism of Italy and Germany in the first half of
the twentieth century. The "flat palm" of the legionary
standards recalls the fascist salute; the standards themselves,
complete with eagles, recall the fascist standards copied
from them; the march recalls the fascist parades and Nürn-
berg rallies; and the marchers' "extra fancy step" recalls the
Italian "Roman step" and its German counterpart, the goose
step (*SL*, 10). The soldier thinks back to earlier centuries
when "the hostile strong-points" on the Roman hills were
"one by one, made co-ordinate" (*SL*, 12)--a word synonymous
with *Gleichschaltung*, the Nazi term for ordering all aspects
of cultural and political life by party policy. In a later
poem, another of Jones' monologists prays to the Celtic
earth-goddess for protection "in all times of *Gleichschaltung*,
in the days of the central economies. . ." (*SL*, 63).

In *The Anathemata*, which is Jones' wide-ranging
critical analysis of Western civilization, the ancient Roman
analogue to fascism repeatedly emerges. During the decline
of republican Rome, "Tiberius Gracchus/wept for the waste-
land/and the end of the beginnings" (*A*, 89). Jones is
evoking the murder in 133 B.C. of Tiberius Gracchus by
senatorial capitalists for promoting land-reform. There are

many modern parallels but, when Jones was writing, the most striking of these was the murder in 1924 of the socialist Giacomo Matteotti by Italian fascists. Matteotti was a man of great integrity and vision. The ancient parallel, or one very close to it, did not go unnoticed at the time, for Filippo Turati, delivering Matteotti's eulogy, alluded to the last stand on the Aventine by Tiberius' brother, Gaius Gracchus, who was likewise murdered by opponents of reform.

The focus of *The Anathemata* later shifts to 30 A.D. and to the emperor Tiberius and his protege Sejanus. Like Augustus before him and in the manner of modern dictators, the emperor Tiberius made republican forms a vehicle for dictatorial power. And under Tiberius, for a while, Sejanus exercised power as "Co-ordinator of groupings" (*A*, 186)--a phrase evocative, again, of the Nazi policy of *Gleichschaltung*. Sejanus had "his weather-eye on the Diaspora," furthermore (*A*, 187): like the Nazis, he was ill-disposed to the Jews, and was probably responsible for the senatorial decree of 19 A.D. deporting four thousand of them from Rome to Sardinia and issuing the ultimatum to the remaining four thousand that they repudiate their religion or likewise be banished from Italy.

But, as Jones' poem recalls, Sejanus did not last long. Tiberius had him killed for plotting against the imperial line of descent, and "Tiber, by way of the Mamertine, has his broken body" (*A*, 187). A striking modern parallel is the murder of Ernst Röhm by Hitler in 1934. Just as the political power of Sejanus rested on his leadership of the Praetorian Guard, the power of Röhm rested on his leadership of the Nazi SA. To get at Sejanus, Tiberius circumvented the Praetorian Guard by using the City Watch. To get at Röhm, Hitler circumvented the SA by using the SS. Sejanus was executed in Mamertine Prison; Röhm was murdered in Stadelheim Prison. Each man died, ostensibly, for plotting a coup. Sejanus' death may also recall the numerous murders by Stalin of his political colleagues and generals, but here and in most of Jones' later poetry, the chief contemporary manifestation of political vice is fascism, particularly in Germany.[4]

Now to the matter of pre-war sympathies. Without a doubt, the poet was sympathetic to Germany. We shall see that this was largely in response to the unjust peace that

---

4. The one exception is "The Narrows," in which Roman military imperialism parallels Soviet imperialism (*RQ*, 59-63).

concluded the First World War, but it was also a result of his
feeling for "THE ENEMY FRONT-FIGHTERS" to whom he
partly dedicates *In Parenthesis*. On December 18, 1938,
David Jones sent a copy of *In Parenthesis* to Neville
Chamberlain and a letter thanking him for attempting "to
mend things in Europe & to save us from the worst," and
stating that

> When, during the war, we looked across to the other entrenchments, I
> know that at least for some of us, one thought was uppermost: we looked
> to the day when those opposite would be our friends again--indeed that
> perhaps that friendship might be the greater & more intimate
> because of our mutual hardship. It was an instinctive aspiration & one
> natural to soldiers--but since those days our hopes have been less than
> unfulfilled--no-man's-land has remained with us--our soldierly frat-
> ernization has not borne to us the common unity we wished.

The personal sympathy he felt for the enemy must
have extended, after the war, to Corporal Adolf Hitler. Both
men fought at the Somme and both suffered leg wounds in
Mametz Wood in 1916--though Jones was wounded in July;
Hitler, less seriously, in October. Furthermore, both men had
almost identical, deeply moving experiences soon after
being wounded. Jones regained consciousness behind the
lines in a hospital tent while being addressed, for the first
time in seven months, by a female English voice, that of a
nurse. In a letter to Harman Grisewood in 1958, he says that
the experience

> left an indelible mark on me, and, indeed, it may be, it may *well* be that
> that is why, in subsequent years, I've felt, to a rather exaggerated
> extent, the potency of hearing a certain sort of voice as if it were a
> *physical touch*--a healing thing it is almost, in a sense, or anyway
> jolly nice... (*DGC*, 175).

David Jones must have felt a certain empathy when reading
Hitler's account of a similar experience, also in a field hospital:

> I almost jumped from the shock when I suddenly heard the voice of a
> German woman--she was a nurse--speak to one of the men lying next to
> me.
>   For the first time, a sound like that after two years![5]

Hitler's other, extensive combat experience must also have
stirred sympathy in the poet, who had spent three years in
the trenches. In an unpublished letter to Grisewood dated 30
March 1935, Jones reacts to a newspaper photograph of
Hitler sitting stiffly upright beside a slouching Anthony

5. *Mein Kampf*, eds. Jay Chamberlain et al. (New York: Reynal & Hitchcock, 1939), p.
247.

_ıı.

ı_ıı.

Eden: "It's lovely how Hitler still looks the Eternal Corporal."

In the mounting pressure for war, Jones' sympathies for Germany and Hitler led him to write a long essay (twenty double-spaced, typed foolscap pages) dated May 11th, 1939, which was originally intended for *The Tablet* but was too long for publication in a newspaper. Moreover, as Grisewood remembers,

> he soon came to feel--we discussed the subject and the article a good deal at the time--that it was rash to write like this, even dangerous, because one would simply be thought of as pro-Nazi and the merit of the remarks would not be considered objectively. So we had the piece duplicated and circulated among a few friends.[6]

The essay is essentially a plea for peace, in which Jones sees Hitler's political ambitions as similar to those behind the first and second British Empires. He wants to avoid what would be, for England, another "expeditionary war."

I will summarize the first six pages, which are a sort of prelude. David Jones begins by regretting that while the British press did not support Chamberlain in his attempt to preserve the peace it now supports him when his policy has become more belligerent. Jones goes on to say that "the most questionable arguments are daily being put forward by those who regard war with the Dictators as inevitable and necessary" and that true patriotism lies in questioning these arguments if we are to avoid "the suicide of Europe." Admittedly the dominance of the world by force must be resisted, but, before going to war, we must first "know, beyond any shadow of doubt, that this feared domination" is "absolutely certain and absolutely the worst fate." Jones then complains that the press has characterized the Axis powers as the dragon and their opponents as "the Champion." But if the Champion includes "true defenders of liberty," it also includes "the instruments or creators of capitalist exploitation, of imperialist necessity, the unnamed forces that control commodities and gold and the instigators of world revolution."

6. A typed note dated 12 June 1975, attached to two copies of the typescript of the essay, which are deposited in the Burns Library of Rare Books and Special Collections at Boston College. Grisewood continues, "I considered including it in *Epoch and Artist* (1959) but on balance was against it. And so was David--for the same reasons as had caused one to feel at the time--six months before war broke out--that the observations in it would not get fair hearing ... perhaps it would not be so difficult now as it seemed in 1959 to attach an explanatory Note to show that the sentiments in the article do not imply any sympathy whatever with the Hitlerian methods."

I am grateful to Ralph J. Coffmann of Boston College for permission to publish excerpts from one of the copies of the "Hitler" typescript in the Burns Library. And I am especially indebted to Kathleen Henderson Staudt for letting me know of the existence of the essay and the location of these copies.

What follows is an edited version of the rest of the
typescript with elipses marking omissions, which shorten the
text without distorting its meaning. I also regularize punctuation.

In reading *Mein Kampf* I was often reminded of the problems I used to
hear discussed continuously by various groups of Catholic people concerning the recovery of social justice: how to break the "chain store,"
how to live uncorrupted by the "banking system," how to free men from
the many and great evils of "capitalist exploitation," how to effect
some real and just relationship between the price of things and the
labour expended. Sincere and idealistic men all had theories of how
best to resolve these problems because they said that if these problems were dealt with, men would live more justly and more fully as
men, and more responsibly as workmen, and much more besides. All took
it for granted that there existed powers inimical to a humane way of
life who were the enemy of any attempt at a solution, because of money
interest and one thing and another. The whole system was said to be corrupt, unChristian, intolerable. Now one did not have to be extra aware to
agree with most of this. But what to do? The solutions varied, especially in emphasis. In the main, however, there was the idea that
some sort of return to the Land was of great importance. Some hoped
that it might be possible for small units to live more humane, responsible lives as small-holders of one sort or another, or as independent
craftsmen of some kind. Some of this may be said to have partly succeeded by the efforts of heroic individuals, but in the main, I do not
think it unfair to say, in terms of a War Communique coming from
Enemy H.Q.: "The attempt to penetrate our system by infiltration
has failed."
 That there is something radically wrong, seems by now obvious to all. The cure, not so obvious. Now the writer of *Mein Kampf*
shared this conviction with so many of our friends, he even names the
same supposed evils. (He was also concerned with matters they hap-
pily have no conception of, a nation defeated and starving, not only, so to
say, accidentally exploited by the machinations of the "system" but
wilfully and purposely being punished by victorious enemies--but
that is another matter.) He too looked about and said "something must
be done," just as our best friends have said in one way or another. Just
like the ex-officer who "took a small farm" or the man who fled from
Brum, or even the typist who sang a folk-song on Saturday in Sussex, or
the art student who railed against Windsor and Newton and made his
own paints out of "earth" pigment even though they cracked and scaled,
not to mention the beloved originator, or rather the most notorious user,
of that phrase. The man whom our newspapers, with unspeakable vul-
garity and class-consciousness, talk of as "The Austrian ex-house
painter" also said something must be done about the exploitation of
the citizen, "chain-stores," alien financial control, lands going waste.
He came to the conclusion that only one thing was potent enough to deal
with these evils and that thing was the sword.
 He came to the conclusion that the intelligent goodwill of
artists, writers, land-reformers, poets, men of religion, was too frail an
instrument for such a brute task. Such a conclusion, if acted upon, meant
a rough house for most, and a hell on earth for many (whether innocent
or guilty could be of no consequence).

I am far from saying that he was right, but that was his conclusion; but ... to quote Joyce, his conclusion may only result in "Out of the paunschaup on to the pyre."

The necessary conditioning of a whole people for such a task means the temporary subordination of almost all the virtues to the virtue of courage. From most of our points of view this would simply mean that the sticky tyranny of Commercialism, money, etc., was replaced by the harsh and boring tyranny of the sword and all those new evils which as usual leap up where the old ones die--at all events temporarily. I think he shows an understanding of this.

He seems to cast his glance forward, even if it be eight hundred years; but, I admit, in the main his general conception of the destiny of the world is a pretty steely one....

At all events, those people who, in this country, have said strong things about the iniquities of the capitalist exploitation and money power ... must never forget that the conditions they find brutal and barbarous under Herr Hitler are largely the price paid for daring to deal arbitrarily, physically and directly with some of those very problems. I must say it is difficult to see how, other than by very severe and grim methods, various vested interests and organized and powerful controls can be shattered, if one thinks they need shattering. It is one thing to talk about this and that evil, but to do something about it always means, in practice, the letting loose of forces that are in themselves partly evil. It is a question of what you can stick and what is most intolerable to the human spirit.

....

What it boils down to is that there is much in both the Fascist and Nazi revolutions that demand our understanding and sympathy. They represent, for all their alarming characteristics, an heroic attempt to cope with certain admitted corruptions in our civilization. Even the terrible aspects of those regimes, the brutality and suppression of individual freedom, must at least be considered in relation to the nature and malignancy of the particular conditions and evils that those regimes set out to correct. We can, in this country, only vaguely imagine what happens when a person, regardless of consequences, actually does something to radically change the society for which he is responsible. We have to look back into our lost history to get some idea of the nature and necessities, the grimness and relentlessness of such struggles.

....

If some of us in this country, being of a certain kind or class, are "free" in so many ways, and enjoy a humane and tolerant existence, are able to pursue our individual preferences to a remarkable degree, it is largely because our ancestors so gathered the world's wealth, so established, by the application of armed and economic pressure, the British thing in the world, so set a bulwark of power round our pax-- that we, who can, live almost the lives of pure spirits and have almost forgotten the hard, brutal, realistic, unscrupulous, spade-work that has made our humane and tolerant virtues possible of growth. Within that established order it has been possible for the flowers of sophistication and refinement to grow. All this of the highest value, beauties otherwise unobtainable, and truths otherwise hidden have thus been discovered, but it would be extremely unintelligent of us (and a breach of the intelligence is the worst crime a sophisticated person can commit--intelligence is the one virtue such a person must possess, or lose all the purpose of his existence) not to see clearly that this "emancipated" world of ours has been historically made possible by acts of brutality and aggression, the destruction of cultures, the infliction of wrong. Impregnable defences have to be reared and brute force applied, it would seem, before the amiable, sensitized, individual, appreciative, humane type of human being we regard as normal to our society can begin to exist. It took a lot of gangster-work and breaking of heads and hearts to rear the stately homes of England, and you have to have a fairly large police force, I imagine, before it is possible for a neurotic aesthete, like myself, to exist at all. An incredible number of wolves heads have to be brought in tribute before the S.P.C.A. can begin to prosecute. This is all obvious I expect, but so obvious as to be forgotten, the forgetting tends to self-righteousness and that to indignation and that to interference and disastrous action.

    ....

Should this conflict come, it will not be an affair of morals, or the defence of civilization or the punishment of an aggressor, but rather an affair of supposed necessity and struggle for survival. That is why a sceptical attitude is necessary when any uplift is dragged into the argument. For any evil that war apologists can fling at the Axis Powers the Axis Powers can easily and justly retaliate.

If this catastrophe should occur with its miseries, and futilities, at least let us, sophisticated persons, not allow ourselves to suffer the final ignominy of being fooled as to the nature of it. ... It will no doubt be said that it would be more to the point to preach this kind of detachment in the dictator countries--and see where it landed one. But after all one can only properly understand the weaknesses of one's own group and is in any case only responsible to one's own group, and if free expression is as yet allowed us here, it is necessary to take advantage of it; moreover, the particular kind of attitude I am concerned with is, I think it is true to say, actually more evident in the democracies than elsewhere. Herr Hitler, for instance, in his writings, for all his contempt of the "intellectual," less often offends the intelligence by giving uplift reasons for his political actions than do his critics. His propaganda is easily recognizable as propaganda. His words constantly have an authentic ring, and correspond to the beastly actualities of this world and this world-order. Some say that that is because he is in league with the "cosmocrats of the dark aeon" and can make guile sound like the words of life. That apocalyptic view appears too partizan, too easy. I prefer: "Germany must export or die, Germany will not die" to "Honour is above peace"--if it comes to knowing why one must be blown up.

The dictators use their own brand of high-falutin', bombastic, speciously idealistic language when they are up to their propaganda-- but I think when they are seriously analysing a situation and formulating demands they are commonly more down to facts than is usually granted. Herr Hitler, certainly, in his last two important speeches has been very clear and intelligible, and considerate of historic realities (and also extremely interesting) in a way that is rarely known to our political leaders. For instance, his elucidation of the position of Teutonic-Celtic peoples of the East Mark, from which he springs, in relation to the dynastic division called Austria, was of great interest, and explains, at least to me, a lot of things concerning the Anschluss. Similarly his explanation of the incorporation of Moravia and Bohemia in the Reich seemed reasonable enough, taking a long view. If the Welsh, for instance, can be said to be geographically, historically, economically, and politically part of the English sphere of control, the Czechs can equally be said to be, by the same accidents, part of the German sphere of control. If this seems far-fetched, it is only because we choose to apply different standards over this "sacredness of small nationalities" principle according to how it suits us and according to all kinds of necessities and accidents. ... To continue the analogy, had the Welsh preserved their Catholic religion, and some vestige of political integrity, and had they established a contact with Ireland, and some sort of connection with a continental power, France for instance, then, even today it might be necessary for England to argue that this situation must be liquidated (especially if there was a Skoda munition works at Neath and turbulent and discontented minorities appealing for protection against the Cardiff Government, in the Lleyn Peninsula and Anglesay, as there certainly would be). Geographical, historical, cultural, economic, political arguments would soon be found by the London Administration to explain the necessity of incorporating the Welsh people within the English lebensraum and sphere of control, and no amount of talk about the sacredness of nationality, coming, let us say, from an Italian theorist, would stop the English Government from acting according to the political and strategic necessities of the situation, more especially would this be so if the Welsh State were being used by the Irish, backed by France, to undermine the prestige of England. It seems only by some such imaginary situation, in countries that we know as we know the palms of our hands, can we be fair to foreign governments dealing with a state of affairs that we can at best only guess at, for all the broadcast talks on what it feels like to be a Pole or a Ukrainian and for all the journalists who travel in, and report from, far countries, or for all the diplomats whose business it is to keep an eye on strategic positions, whether it be in Europe, Asia or the antipodes nor for all the leaderwriters who would drag in Owain Glyndwr as easily as they dragged in Wenceslaus, and forget them as easily as it suited their book. My point again is that it is unwise and irrelevant to raise the moral issue.

    ....

    The press reception of [Hitler's latest speech], and indeed the official reception of it, as far as one can judge from the remarks of ministers, has been profoundly disappointing. ... There was no attempt whatever, that I saw, to carefully consider the Fuhrer's arguments, or even to pay proper tribute to mastery of the thing as a thing. You may say that this is no time to appreciate art works, and that if it was, that would have no bearing on the contents. I think that is a great mistake, for where there is order and sequence and power of expression there is probably something worth expressing--even if it comes from an enemy, and in this instance so far from being an enemy, the artist in question protested and has always protested, as clearly as a man could, his desire to be our friend (unless, of course, words mean absolutely nothing and white *is* black, once you have determined to give your whitish dog a black name, then, even a streak of grey is hardly admitted). That is the tragedy now. By a sort of alchemy of prejudice and fear every word and every deed, good, bad or indifferent, coming from the supposed enemy, is transmuted into a base thing. To question and mistrust the works of such alchemists is surely our duty.

    ....

When reading this essay, it is difficult to retain a
pre-war perspective: we know so much now of which David
Jones was then ignorant. What he says about the Czechs is
ill-considered, and even in a world of *realpolitik*, surely,
intellectuals must never consider it "unwise and irrelevant
to raise the moral issue"--although Jones is certainly right
about our being quicker to raise it to blame an enemy than
to evaluate actions done in our own "national interest." Neither for imperial Britain nor for Nazi Germany do ends justify unethical means. In retrospect, he was wrong, moreover,
to think that "this feared domination was" not "absolutely
certain" and not "absolutely the worse fate." Yet his motives
for seeking to preserve the peace can hardly be considered
pro-Nazi, even though he sympathizes with Germany and
with Hitler.

Because of its rhetorical intention to counteract a
mounting public hostility toward "the enemy," the essay
does not fully express Jones' opinion on the subject. In private, he had his own reservations about the Nazis and maintained a critical distance from Hitler. After the Munich
Conference, Jones wrote to Harman Grisewood, "I *like* the
way Chamberlain treated Adolf as a truculent adolescent
who needed to be understood" (4 Oct. 1938). A month before
completing the Hitler essay, he records his impressions on
Mein Kampf in another letter to Grisewood:

> ... I'm reading the full edition of *Mein Kampf*, and it is *so* different
> from the miserable cut-about edition I read previously. I am deeply
> impressed by it, it is amazingly interesting in all kinds of ways--but
> pretty terrifying too. God, he's *nearly* right--but this *hate* thing mars
> his whole thing, I feel. I mean it just misses getting over the frontier
> into the saint thing--he won't stand any nonsense or illusions or talk--
> but, having got so far, the conception of the world in terms of race-
> struggle (that's what it boils down to) will hardly do. But I do like a
> lot of what he says--only I must admit he sees the world as just going
> on *for ever* in this steel grip. Compared with his opponents he is
> grand, but compared with the saint he is bloody. And I think I mean
> also by saints--lovers, and all kinds of unifying makers. Anyway, I back
> him still against all this currish, leftish, money thing, even though
> I'm a miserable specimen and dependent upon it. (*DGC*, 92-3)

The concluding statement is a reference to his own personal
poverty, which underlies his remark, a year later, that
" 'economics' are as important as Marx said--he merely
truncated the hierarchy of Being."[7]

As the passage above implies, Jones was not a racist.
Yet at this time he seems to have been influenced by the
antisemitism then prevalent in certain circles in England

7. Unpublished letter to Tom Burns, 28 August 1940.

for, on page ten of the "Hitler" typescript, he refers to "the iniquities . . . of international Jewry." By this he would have meant the unscrupulous scheming of financiers and armaments dealers--most of them, it was thought, Jews--who fueled the First World War and helped finance the Bolshevik Revolution. I include his remark about "international Jewry" for the record, which should, of course, be as complete as possible, but the effect of including it might be misleading since it is not characteristic. The unpublished manuscripts and correspondence of David Jones which I have seen--and this includes thousands of pages of letters to his closest friends--is free of antisemitism. And nowhere in his published writing is there anything which could be construed as racist.

Jones' attitude towards the Jews deserves further consideration, but that would take us off topic and must be left to his biography. For now it is enough to establish that he had always, from the outset, opposed the Nazi persecution of the Jews--which had, of course, begun long before the war. Stanley Honeyman, who became a friend of the poet at the end of the Second World War, remembers Jones telling him that he was visited by a senior German cultural attaché in 1937 or '38:

> Apparently there were just the two of them and as was to be expected of a German cultural attaché the man turned out to be courteous, interesting, erudite and a very enjoyable guest. David took the opportunity to protest at their treatment of Jews, whereupon the relaxed civilized visitor suffered an amazing transformation and, like a man possessed, rose to his feet and harangued an embarrassed David for a full five minutes on the iniquities of the Jews before lapsing into normality and resuming his seat.

There is good reason to believe this story, for, as Honeyman goes on to say, the poet told it not to exonerate or praise himself but to relate its interesting conclusion and to illustrate the schizophrenia of the German character which, for all its positive traits ("the best brains, splendid soldiers") had a hysterical streak that was apparent, he thought, in German art.[8]

In order to learn more about the poet's pre-war attitudes towards Germany and Hitler, I wrote to Harman Grisewood, who sent me, in a letter of 10 August 1984, an

---

8. Letter to Grisewood, 25 Sept. 1984. I am indebted to Stanley Honeyman for allowing me to quote from his letter. The conclusion of the German cultural attaché's tirade against the Jews was: "You throw them out the door, they come back through the window." This remark interested Jones and, at the time, amused him because it resembles a favorite saying of his which the British used in the First World War with reference to the Germans: "Shut the door, they're coming through the window, shut the window, they're coming through the floor."

extensive account which places Jones' "Hitler" typescript in
perspective. Because Grisewood's account is an important
biographical document, it is quoted here in full:

> ...before I try to summarize what I believe to have been his opinions I
> must insist upon an important distinction. His sympathy was with
> the portrayal of injustice in *Mein Kampf*, not with the brutal means
> taken to correct it. David's revulsion at the Nazi atrocities was as
> strong as anyone else's. It is often forgotten--even by those who lived
> through the war years--how slow the news of those atrocities was in
> coming to light. It was not until the last phase of the war that we in
> England knew anything of Belsen or Auschwitz. When I talked to David
> about those brutalities, he was as appalled as the most fervent anti-
> Nazi.
>   His natural sympathy was with the vanquished; that is
> obvious even to the most superficial reader of his work. And he was
> always quick to suspect a cry of self-righteousness among the victori-
> ous. Oppression of the conquered aroused not only pity but his disgust
> and anger. He was most eloquent, as is well-known, in his affection for
> the down-trodden Welsh. But it was the Welsh as a vanquished people
> which attracted his sympathy. The Welsh of our own day were his
> brethren through their historic derivations rather than through their
> contemporary characteristics. The Germans in *Mein Kampf* were
> also a vanquished people; and oppressed by exultant and tyrannous con-
> querors. David's affinities, you remember, are with Hector and Priam
> rather than with Achilles or Agamemnon.
>   There was another and different source from which his sym-
> pathy was nourished--the degeneracy of the European nations west of
> the Rhine. After the First World War the victorious seem to have
> been debased by victory rather than dignified by it. We in England were
> living in the afterglow of Edwardian prosperity. Imperial ideals were
> shrinking, and at home were being replaced by those of the salesman and
> the supermarket. When Hitler wrote about decadence, many of David's
> friends--myself included--agreed with his accusations. No one more
> positively than David himself.

Before resuming quotation, let me interject a
reminder that the reaction against Western pragmatic materialism was not a prerogative of fascism. Many Romantic
and Victorian writers and all the great modernists, including
Joyce in *Finnegans Wake* and, subsequently, Beckett, presume that the current condition of Western culture is
impoverished. Like the other modernists and, no doubt, like
Hitler too, David Jones is primarily indebted for his conceptualization of this awareness to Spengler's *The Decline of the
West*.
           Grisewood's letter continues:

> It was natural for David to represent historic change as the dramatic
> poet which he was. That Euripides and Shakespeare also presented
> history as poetry does not disqualify them from expressing percep-
> tions often deeper than those of academic historians. And so it is with
> David. He knew, better than the journalists or the professors, the
> peril of belittling the military virtues. He respected the force of

arms as a determinant in history; and he suspected our trust in the conference table as a substitute. Among the English such thoughts as these were heresy--but they were Hitlerian orthodoxy. You were regarded with contempt and derision if you said such things at the time. If you were found reading Hitler's prophetic book--as I was--you were suspected of traitorous inclinations. But David never shrank from speaking his mind through fear of disapproval. Now, in the light of subsequent events, we too should feel able to acknowledge the validity of military strength without being thought to condone the misuse of it.

Those interested in David's views will find it illuminating to consider his appreciation of the Roman Empire and of the imperial idea. Some would say he was inconsistent, sometimes presenting Rome as the provider of a culture of which we are the heirs; at other times Rome is the destroyer of local communities and of local loyalties. David was able to see the truth of both aspects. The truth of one did not invalidate the truth of the other. The strength and the delicacy of mind which enabled him to hold such a distinction are relevant both to his understanding of Nazi Germany in the thirties and of his view of the disastrous war which ensued. In the thirties he saw Hitler as a necessary rebuke to the debility of the Western world. His sympathy with that rebuke in no way diminished his eventual revulsion at the terrible chastisement which followed.

Fair enough. David Jones resisted generalizations and, just as he could with unerring perception, distinguish good things in bad paintings (and bad things in good paintings), he sought to be discriminating in historical and political matters.

But why, when it came to the Nazis, did he not discriminate more wisely? After all, in his typescript, he indicates an awareness of "the brutality and suppression of individual freedom" which were widely reported aspects of Nazi policy well before 1939. He was probably willing to tolerate the fascist gangsterism of the 1930s because for him, as for many others at the time, the alternative to fascism seemed to be international Communism--which, he knew from certain Ukrainian emigrees, surpassed pre-war fascism in brutality. The uncomfortable dilemma was made to seem more real than it actually was by the recent civil war in Spain, during which Jones and most of his Catholic friends had sided with Franco because of his opposition to Communism. (Through personal contacts, Jones was vividly aware of atrocities committed by Communists against priests, nuns and practicing Catholics.)

Immediately prior to and during the war, furthermore, Jones simply did not believe newspaper reports of Nazi brutalities. In this he was influenced by his experience during the First World War. Then, British newspapers regularly published accounts of German atrocities which he, as a soldier in the trenches, never witnessed and for which he could subsequently find no convincing verification. This experience of war-time propaganda made him sceptical of the new reports of German brutality, some of which were, in fact, mere propaganda. But of course, the worst reports were not and, at the end of the war, he realized and freely admitted, "I got that Nazi thing wrong."[9]

He may have got it wrong also because of a mythic, quasi-apocalyptic vision of history which reconciled him to the possibility of fascist political and military success. This vision is evident in his 1938 review of René Hague's translation of *The Song of Roland*. David Jones believed the West had begun to enter a new Dark Age and saw Hitler as a charismatic leader who might well forge the beginnings of a new order. As with the barbaric Germans of the original Dark Age, this new dominance of Europe would initially be catastrophic but not, ultimately, hopeless. As once the Germanic tribes had been baptized by the residually Christian Celts, so, in the distant future, there might be "a baptized Führership" (*DG*, 100). In the near future there could be only "a crude retrogression" from what remained of Christian spiritual ideals and morality.

> Yet there can be seen in this reorientation an aboriginal validity, and ... a kind of urgency ... which can only be tutored, like the wild unicorn, by a mistress with vision. It derives too much from the bowels to be amenable to ethical or legal arguments. (*DG*, 99)

He saw fascism as "a resurgence of the 'cult-hero' (in however ominous a form and with whatever violence of expression)"--a movement which might be transformed by an eventual emergence from the modern Dark Age into a new Christian dawn. This could occur "if ever (for it is permitted to us to dream dreams) the North is to make again a song as basically Christian as this Franco-Germanic epic. Or (to dream deeper) if Aachen is to become again pre-eminently the place of the chapel" (*DG*, 99). If it is difficult to imagine a "mistress" capable of taming the fascist unicorn, it is equally difficult to imagine fascism continuing forever unchanged. Jones' dream of the future is not, therefore, naive, as it may at first appear. It could have been a prophetic dream; fortunately, we shall never know. To fantasize at such a distance from the present and to provide distant consolation for immediate suffering may be politically irresponsible. But no Nazi would have endorsed his dream, which is really a Christian vision of a post-fascist future.

9. Quoted by Honeyman.

Apropos of David Jones and fascism, there is interesting bibliographical data in the surviving manuscript drafts of *The Anathemata* which might be construed as incriminating circumstantial evidence of an actual fascist connection. This intriguing material is the paper on which most of the early drafts of pages 176-178 of the poem are written.[10] In this section of *The Anathemata*, which is entitled "KEEL, RAM, STAUROS," Roman battering rams are described in a way that emphasizes the bare utilitarianism of late, dehumanized phases of civilization. Most of the drafts of these pages are written on the back of official fascist stationery, on which are printed the words: "*Il Ministro della Cultura Popolare. Appunto per il Duce.*"

When I wrote to Harman Grisewood, I asked him about this stationery and how David Jones might have acquired it. He replied, in a letter dated 29 July 1984:

> I had some once--I might have some still. So did Tom Burns. The origin of its possession by the three of us is theft. After dinner one evening [before the war] we were passing Bourdon Street--just as you go into Davies St off Berkley Square. For some reason that I now can't remember the Italian Consulate there seemed to be deserted yet accessible. We climbed over the railing--David, Tom and I--very daring because this is on the street--and broke into the Consulate which was deserted. Mussolini was unpopular with us by then (we had had some respect for early fascist theory as presented by e.g. Don Sturzo)--but Mussolini had become a somewhat absurd Opera Buffo character.[11] While going thro' the rooms of the Consulate we saw this stack of rather absurdly impressive writing paper. We thought it would entertain some of our friends and shock some others if we used this paper. So we took large quantities of it--and escaped with the loot without being imprisoned. I had quite forgotten this incident until you--kindly-- reminded me of it. It provides a wholesome correction to the picture of David lodged in the mind of some who didn't know him; and who would be surprised at him in the role of amateur burglar. He enjoyed the exploit as much as Tom and I.[12]

If the fascist stationery is not evidence of pro-fascist inclinations on Jones' part, it is nevertheless bibliographically important, for the stationery may have had a suggestive influence on the composition of this section of the poem. The influence may well have been conscious, since a few draft pages are written on the imprinted side of the paper. Moreover, in one of his early drafts of this material,

10. The drafts of *The Anathemata* are in the National Library of Wales.
11. Sturzo, a Catholic priest, was not a fascist. He was the founder of the Christian Democratic Party. While some of his early writing was approved of by the fascists, he was subsequently blacklisted by Mussolini and, before the war, fled for his life to England.
12. Tom Burns remembers taking the stationery but indistinctly and thinks it must have been from a refuse bin on the street in front of the consulate.

the analogy between antiquity and contemporary history is politicized by a reference to "the battery-führer's fancy piece"--a phrase subsequently omitted, possibly because the association is strained between "the Führer" and an ancient Roman führer who would be equivalent in rank to a lieutenant. But even in its final form, the sequence of siege engines is preceded by a reference to policy determining whether a ship is cargoed with "Kegged butter or, cradled *tormenta*" (*A*, 174), an allusion to the Nazi policy of "guns before butter." This passage is one of the many in *The Anathemata* which identify the Nazis with the pragmatism and political expansionism that threatens vital culture. Here and in his later poetry, the frequent allusions to fascism as representative of inhuman, totalitarian politics is doubtless partly compensation for his own early failure to see in fascism a potential for the appalling evils which were revealed to the world during and after the Second World War.

In the pre-war years, David Jones objected, as the fascists did, to the kind of democracy which is really the rule of the wealthy because they alone can afford to run for office or influence those who do. But his differences with fascist ideology are enormous, both in what he disapproved of--he was never a racist--and in what he proposed by way of remedy. For him, the solution to the spiritual bankruptcy of modern civilization is not political but cultural and religious. Only a widespread appreciation of symbolic activity which communicates spiritual values can, he thought, fill the vacuum at the heart of technological civilization. That is why the siege-engines in *The Anathemata* are juxtaposed to a series of cult objects, including the cross, in what is clearly an antithesis more profound than that which Goebbels first enunciated, between guns and butter.

David Jones was a man of broad sympathies, and before the war these extended to Nazi Germany. But he was never an active fascist-sympathizer as was Ezra Pound or even, for a time, W. B. Yeats--who, when Jones first met him in the late 1930s, was wearing the blue shirt of the Irish fascist party. (Because Jones' interest in party politics was never very great, he was unaware of the political significance of the color of Yeats' shirt, and thought it merely an aesthetic affectation.[13]) Yeats' support for fascism does not

13. At least this was my impression when, in August 1972, David Jones reminisced: "I met the man twice or so--once at Lady Chichester's house. He was lionized. I remember his shirt--it was blue!--and flowing silver hair. All the pretty girls gathered around

explicitly affect his poetry and seems not to have decreased the number of his readers. But Pound's outspoken fascist sympathies are apparent in his poems and have diminished the size of his audience. There may be some justification for avoiding a man's poetry on moral and political grounds, since we read literature for wisdom as well as beauty. But, on this score, the poetry of David Jones is unassailable. As we have seen, it is explicitly anti-fascist. And there is nothing in it like the quasi-fascist imaginative tendencies which critics detect in D. H. Lawrence or which seem so strongly evident in Ted Hughes' exclusive devotion to the brutal energy of the life-force.

Nor does Jones' early sympathy with pre-war Germany indicate an essential or enduring, implicit affinity with fascism. In fact, his basic convictions are not political, and, as he implies everywhere in his poetry and painting, his deepest affinities are with "saints--lovers, and all kinds of unifying makers." The clarity and consistency with which David Jones, in his later poetry, sees all totalitarian and dictatorial regimes as hostile to human life and authentic culture is morally and intellectually consistent with his early opposition to the political oppression and economic hardship that gave rise to fascism.

him. He chanted poetry throughout--but that's uncharitable of me. Maybe it was *him*. He said nice things about *In Parenthesis*."

THE POET

COLIN HUGHES

DAVID JONES: THE MAN WHO WAS ON THE FIELD. IN PARENTHESIS AS STRAIGHT REPORTING.[1]

I was fortunate, as a young man, to hear Douglas Cleverdon's 1946 radio production of *In Parenthesis*. Like the poet Vernon Watkins, I was "bowled over" by it. I can see now in my mind's eye the straight road leading to the front line; the working party trudging to its non-existent task and gazing wistfully across the open landscape towards the back areas; the long march south in the June sun; and, of course, the tragic assault upon the unnamed Somme woodland. I was attracted then to the idea of attempting to retrace the steps of that doomed unit but did nothing about it for more than twenty years when, by chance, I found myself working in the old War Office Building in London with ample opportunity to consult books and maps of the First World War. Armed with the appropriate information, I made a hastily arranged visit to Mametz Wood where, with little difficulty, I was able to identify and photograph many of the features mentioned in *In Parenthesis*: The Nullah, Acid (Drop) Copse, Line VYO & K and so on. These photographs were of little merit but, because the viewpoints were chosen to show the features as they would have been seen by the troops in 1915 and 1916, they drew an immediate response from David Jones and from Wyn Griffith, the author of another book about the same battle. Encouraged by this response, and spurred on by Wyn Griffith, I wrote a straightforward account of the capture of Mametz Wood[2] on which the present essay is based.

For much of the 1914-1918 war, 22579 Jones, Private Walter David, served in No 6 Platoon, B Company, 15th (London Welsh) Battalion of the Royal Welsh Fusiliers

---

1. "There is little in *In Parenthesis* that is not straight reporting": David Jones in conversation, 17 March 1973.
2. *Mametz: Lloyd George's "Welsh Army" at the Battle of the Somme* (Gerrards Cross: Orion Press, 1982).

which was one of twelve infantry battalions in the 38th
(Welsh) Division raised by Lloyd George and other promi-
nent Welshmen in the early months of the war. The commanding officer of the battalion during the period covered
by *In Parenthesis* was Lt Col R. C. Bell who had recently
returned from service in India--the Colonel Dell of *In
Parenthesis* who could reminisce calmly about Poona minutes before going into battle. He was one of the few regular
officers in the division and possibly the only one in the battalion. The second-in-command was a Major Jack Edwards
who, David Jones once told me, looked magnificent on a
horse:

> The body of the high figure in front of the head of the column seemed
> to change his position however so slightly. It rains on the transparent
> talc of his map-case.
>   The Major's horse rubs noses with the horse of the superior officer.
> (*IP*, 5)

The adjutant, as others have pointed out, was Captain Tom
Elias who, one morning in July, came to bid them all do
battle, as did Elias the Captain to King Mark in Malory's *Le
Morte d'Arthur*. Another of the young officers in the battalion was Wyn Griffith, whose moving account of the capture
of Mametz Wood, *Up to Mametz*, describes exactly the
same historical sequence as *In Parenthesis*, beginning and
ending with the same events. *Up to Mametz* was published
some years before *In Parenthesis* and there are signs that
David Jones made some use of it to fill gaps in his knowledge of the battalion's movements in 1916.[3]

At the beginning of the war the British Army con-
sisted of an expeditionary force of six regular infantry divisions and one cavalry division, and 14 divisions of the part-
time Territorial Force for home defense. In addition there
was the equivalent of six divisions on garrison duty throughout the British Empire. This was a tiny army compared to
the armies of France and Germany and when Lord Kitchener became Secretary of State for War in August 1914 he
complained that he was expected to fight a great war without any army. He therefore set about creating New Armies
by adding what were called "Service" battalions to the Regiments of the Line. He launched a recruiting campaign with
great success. By the first week in September recruits were
pouring in at the rate of 30,000 a day, swamping an organization designed to cope with as many in a year. The

3. Ll Wyn Griffith, *Up to Mametz*, 2nd. ed. (1930; rpt. London: Severn House
Publishers, 1981).

recruiting was necessarily indiscriminate and no attempt
was made to harness individual skills--hence the reference
in *In Parenthesis* to:

> Dynamite Dawes the old 'un
> and Diamond Phelps his batty
> ...
> both learned in ballistics
> and wasted on a line-mob. (*IP*, 161)

Lord Derby came to the War Office's rescue by offering to
clothe and administer locally raised battalions in the Liverpool area until the War Office was ready to take them over.
The offer was gratefully accepted and other politicians soon
followed Lord Derby's example, Lloyd George among them.
At first Lloyd George had taken little interest in these
affairs, busying himself, as Chancellor of the Exchequer, in
economic matters and he was anxious lest his favorite son
Gwilym should be persuaded to volunteer for service overseas. But now his mood changed and on 19 September at the
Queen's Hall London he launched his own recruiting campaign. Linking "little Wales" to "little Belgium" and Russia's
"little brother" Serbia, he said:

> I should like to see a Welsh Army in the field. I should like to see the
> race who faced the Normans for hundreds of years in their struggle for
> freedom, the race that helped to win the battle of Crecy, the race that
> fought for a generation under Glendower against the greatest captain in
> Europe--I should like to see that race give a good taste of its quality in
> this struggle. And they are going to do it.

A few days later the newspapers announced that Kitchener
had approved a plan for a Welsh Army Corps and that a
committee had been formed to carry out the project. Lloyd
George went to Cardiff to raise support for an Army Corps
of two divisions:

> It is important (he told his audience) that we should secure the cream
> of the youth of this country for this army. If we can get the right
> type of man to join we will have one of the most magnificent little
> armies ever turned out of this country.

Unfortunately, Lloyd George's campaign came too late for
instant success. By the middle of September the recruiting
boom--in which Welshmen had joined as enthusiastically as
others--was over, though it picked up again when Antwerp
fell to the Germans and when the War Office agreed to
lower the minimum height for recruitment in recognition of
the short stature of Welshmen. By the end of 1914, 10,000
had been recruited to the Welsh Army and the first division
was taking shape. Later on, however, recruits proved increasingly difficult to attract and replacements were desperately

needed for the mounting casualties in existing units in France. The idea of a second division was therefore abandoned, and with it Lloyd George's dream of a Welsh Army. The creation of one complete division was, however, no mean feat for a politician and the 38th (Welsh) Division--as the first division was officially called--carried with it something of the aura of Lloyd George's Welsh Army. Whether, as Lloyd George had hoped, it would be "one of the most magnificent armies ever turned out," remained to be seen.

The war establishment of an infantry division in 1914 was nearly 20,000 officers and men; 5,000 horses; 72 field guns in four artillery brigades of 18 guns each; and all the supporting services--supply train, engineers, ambulance brigades and so on--needed to make it self-supporting. The infantry, about 12,000 strong, was made up of twelve battalions (from a variety of Regiments of the Line) organized in three infantry brigades of four battalions each. A division was commanded by a Major-General; each infantry brigade by a Brigadier-General and a battalion--1000 strong--by a Lieutenant Colonel. An infantry division on the move occupied about 15 miles of road space. The Welsh Division looked like this:

38th (WELSH) DIVISION
(Maj-Gen. Ivor Philipps M.P.)

113 INF. BDE. (Brig-Gen Price-Davies V.C.)	114 INF. BDE. (Brig-Gen Marden)	115 INF. BDE. (Brig-Gen Evans)	ARTILLERY, SUPPLY TRAIN ETC.
13th RWF (1st North Wales)	10th Welsh (1st Rhondda)	10th SWB (1st Gwent)	
14th RWF (Caernarvon & Anglesey)	13th Welsh (2nd Rhondda)	11th SWB (2nd Gwent)	
15th RWF (London Welsh)	14th Welsh (Swansea)	16th Welsh (Cardiff City)	
16th RWF (2nd North Wales)	15th Welsh (Carmarthen)	17th RWF	

The division had more than its fair share of Liberal Members of Parliament. Ivor Philipps, the divisional commander, had retired from the Army in about 1904 as a relatively junior officer. He was MP for Southampton and his appointment as divisional commander had been engineered by Lloyd George on condition that Philipps made young Gwilym Lloyd George his aide-de-camp. David Davies MP, later Lord Davies of Llandinam (whose sisters established the Gregynog Press for which David Jones was subsequently to make some book engravings), commanded the 14th Royal Welsh Fusiliers and Sir Hamar Greenwood MP, later Lord Greenwood, the last Secretary for Ireland, commanded for a while the 10th South Wales Borderers. One of the Brigadiers, Price-Davies, was a young man who had won the VC in South Africa. He was rather prim and Wyn Griffith says that he was known to his fellow officers as "Jane." He is Auntie Bembridge "with her Mafeking VC." He had a weakness for chocolate and there is a reference to this in *In Parenthesis*:

> I say Calthrop, have a bite of this perfectly good chocolate you can eat
> the stuff with your beaver up, this Jackerie knows quite well that
> organising brains must be adequately nourished. (*IP*, 173)

For the first half of 1915 the Welsh Division was billeted in the sea-side resorts of North Wales, drilling on the sea-front and making dummy attacks on places like the Little Orme at Llandudno. Here David Jones first made the acquaintance of a Jew from the East-end of London who was to be wounded, in the backside, in Queen's Nullah, below Mametz Wood. He appears in *In Parenthesis*, in that setting, crying out, in his delirium, for Deborah his bride. In North Wales the battalions had sub-standard rifles and wooden bullets, and the artillery practiced with telegraph poles mounted on old bus wheels. On only one day in seven months did the division as a whole train together and that was more a picnic in the hills than a serious exercise. In August, however, the division moved to better training ground near Winchester but the shortage of rifles persisted until November, when the division was told to prepare to move to France. In the last, few, frantic weeks before embarcation each man was put through a hurried firing course on Salisbury Plain and on 29 November 1915 the division was reviewed by the Queen who drove past in the pouring rain on an inspection which signaled the imminent departure of the division for France. The troops by now were fairly smart and full of confidence though the War Office, conscious of the late start which had been made and the lack of experience of those officers appointed by Lloyd George and his committee, thought it less efficient than other divisions bound for the continent and suggested further training in France if conditions there allowed.

Early on the morning of 1 December 1915 the leading battalions of the 38th Division marched through Winchester en route for Southampton, Le Havre and the British
Expeditionary Force in France, and it is here that *In Parenthesis* begins. Between Winchester and Southampton, Lt Col
Bell lost his way--a difficult thing to do on a straight road--
an incident fastened on by David Jones with some delight:
"The bastard's lost his way already," says someone in *In
Parenthesis* (*IP*, 5).

This move to France at the end of 1915 was part of a
massive buildup for an offensive in 1916 by the French and
British on the Western Front, by the Russians in the East and
by the Italians on the southern flank. The division crossed
to Le Havre in rough weather and made its way to a billet-
ing area ten miles south of St. Omer where it joined XI
Corps commanded by Lt Gen Haking. Map 1 shows the front
line in December 1915 with XI Corps centered on Neuve
Chapelle. The 38th Division had its headquarters close to
St. Omer and the 15 RWF were at Warne where they trained
for two weeks from 5 December. This is described accurately and in some detail at the beginning of *In Parenthesis*. Divisional orders, for example, required each battalion
to select and train about 150 men as grenadiers. Each was
to throw ten bombs. *In Parenthesis* says:

> They did platoon-drill and arm-drill in soggy fields behind their bil-
> lets.... They were given lectures on very wet days in the barn ... lec-
> tures by the Bombing Officer... [who] predicted an important future
> for the new Mills Mk. IV grenade [actually the Mills bomb, Mk. V
> grenade].... He took the names of all those men who professed effi-
> ciency on the cricket field--more particularly those who claimed to
> bowl effectively--and brushing away with his hand pieces of straw
> from his breeches, he sauntered off with his sections of grenades and
> fuses ... like a departing commercial traveller. (*IP* 13)

5 December, incidentally, was the London Welsh
Battalion's third day in France, and it was a Sunday. So the
phrase on page 9 of *In Parenthesis* "on the third day, which
was a Sunday," with its biblical overtones, is also a plain
statement of fact. On 19 December, very early in the morning, the battalion made its way to the front line where it
was to come under the wing of the experienced Guards
Division. The unbroken arrows on Map 2 show the route
taken. The battalion left Warne in motor buses after an
inspection by the Brigade Commander (exactly as described
on page 18 of *In Parenthesis*) and rested part of the day in
Riez Bailleul, before marching to the front line. Riez
Bailleul is a hamlet of small farms, each with a small

courtyard flanked by barns, and it is in one of these that the extra-ordinary scene of the exploding shells is set: "out of the vortex, rifling the air it came--bright, brass-shod, Pandoran; with all-filling screaming the howling crescendo's up-piling snapt" (*IP*, 24).

The London Welsh served its apprenticeship with the Guards over Christmas 1915. B Company went in with the Grenadiers not "in wiv the Coldstreams" as suggested by Sergeant Snell in *In Parenthesis* (36), although C Company (in which Wyn Griffith served) did, and there is a reference to the Coldstream in *Up to Mametz*. This could have led David Jones into making one of his rare mistakes. On the other hand, he may have made the transposition deliberately, knowing that sergeants and corporals, for all their confident airs, were not always well informed.

In mid-January, apprenticeships over, the Welsh Division took over the line at Neuve Chapelle. Map 3, which shows the divisional frontage, is almost identical to the sketch map in *In Parenthesis* and is taken from the same source--a trench map of the Richebourg area--the main difference being the exclusion by David Jones of Biez Wood. This is surprising because the image of Biez Wood "looming out of the morning mist or delineated for a moment by a gun-flash or the moon"[4] dominates this part of *In Parenthesis* and remained with Jones for the rest of his life. Plate 1 shows Biez Wood as it is now, looking from the Neb, crops growing in no-man's-land, the trees no longer leafless and torn. Unfortunately, I could not photograph it in mist or moonlight but with a little imagination it can be seen as a "remote and forbidden domain" behind the enemy line.

For the next five months the Welsh Division occupied various stretches of the XI Corps line from Cuinchy in the south--on the La Bassée canal--to Fauquissart in the north, not far from Laventie. The Corps Commander--who was very pleased with the Welsh Division--was a particularly enthusiastic proponent of offensive action as "an effective way of breaking the enemy's morale." "Ascendancy over the enemy" was to be the aim and this phrase was used frequently by him in conferences with divisional commanders. Junior officers were skeptical and the troops would have preferred a quieter life. David Jones captures the mood nicely in his ironic description of the

4. Printed notes accompanying recorded readings by David Jones of excerpts from *In Parenthesis* and other works (Argo PLP 1093).

chaos that ensues when a party of Royal Welsh Fusiliers runs unwittingly into a German patrol at night:

> The thudding and breath to breath you don't know which way, what way, you count eight of him in a flare-space, you can't find the lane--the one way--you rabbit to and fro, you could cry....
> We maintain ascendancy in no-man's-land. (*IP*, 71)

As July approached--the chosen date for the combined Anglo-French attack astride the River Somme--there was a heightening of activity all along the British Front Line. A number of battalions of the Welsh division made raids on the German trenches, the most ambitious and successful of which was carried out by the London Welsh in May, when two raiding parties entered and occupied a considerable length of German line, inflicting heavy casualties without loss. As they withdrew, however, they were swept by enemy machine-gun fire and the young officers in charge of the parties were hit and fell. One of them, referred to in *In Parenthesis* as Mr. Rhys (though that was not his name) was one model for Piers Dorian Isambard Jenkins--the subaltern in charge of 01 Ball's platoon, of whom David Jones paints such a sympathetic portrait. He was not the only model, however, for the subsequent death of Mr. P. D. I. Jenkins in front of Mametz Wood was based on a real incident during that attack. The officer killed in the raid just described was, according to Jones, "an attractive man, very absentminded, and also fair headed like the squire for the Rout of San Romano" but without the " 'elegance' intended to be implied by my choice of the names Piers, Dorian, Isambard."[5]

The flurry of raids in May and early June marked the Welsh Division's farewell to XI Corps, and after six months in the trenches the battalions marched south through the hills of Artois towards the Somme. The broken arrowed lines in Map 2 (which is constructed from the London Welsh battalion's records) show how accurately *In Parenthesis* records these events:

> And so from Riez Bailleul they came, and the place called Paradis they left on the left; and through Lestrem, to a large uncomfortable town [Merville], and away in the morning. (*IP*, 116)

and later

---

5. Letter to the author dated 4 January 1971. (Between 1969 and 1972 I received from David Jones six long letters, covering in all 20 closely written sides of foolscap, dealing mainly, but not exclusively, with his experiences in the war. These letters are now in the National Library of Wales, Aberystwyth.)

Where tiny hills begin at last to bring you from the Flaundrish flats,
they rested, two days [Floringhem]. (*IP*, 117)

The subsequent part of the journey is telescoped into
a few days and a period of ten days in the vicinity of St.
Pol is ignored. Here the division carried out large scale
maneuvers on specially constructed training grounds which
simulated, as far as possible, the German defenses on the
Somme. David Jones seems to have forgotten this entirely
(as had some of the other survivors with whom I corresponded): "not a single bloody thing remained in my mind
when I was writing *In Parenthesis* nor can I now recall
anything at all of this extensive rehearsal," he wrote to
René Hague after reading an early account of my
researches.[6] This is, perhaps, not very surprising, for
compared to the joyous release from the trenches a few
days earlier and the tragedy that was to befall them later, a
divisional exercise, with trenches to be dug and with
inevitable spells of inactivity and boredom, is hardly likely
to stir the memory.

However the maneuvers did take place, with platoons and companies going into the attack over open ground
in extended lines or waves, each wave carrying the action
forward as the wave in front supposed itself in check. As a
climax, infantry brigades, artillery, machine-gun companies,
signalers, engineers and so on, joined in a mass attack,
assisted by aircraft from the Royal Flying Corps. But the
offensive techniques practiced diligently at St. Pol were to
prove less than effective on the field of battle. On 26 June,
the division marched west of Doullens where it came under
the command of II Corps, in GHQ reserve, and then south-
eastwards to Toutencourt, which it reached on 30 June--the
eve of the Battle of the Somme (see Map 4). Here the division waited for orders, prepared to move at very short
notice.

We shall leave the division at Toutencourt for a
moment and look at the opening stages of the Battle of the
Somme. Map 5 shows the objectives for Rawlinson's Fourth
Army on the first day. This was a very ambitious plan given
the strength of the German position and the limited range
of the British field guns. Since 1915, the Germans had been
improving their defenses along the length of their line,
building a second defensive line two miles behind the front
and then a third line two miles to the rear again. The front
line itself was considerably strengthened and barbed wire

6. René Hague, *Dai Greatcoat* (London: Faber and Faber, 1980), p. 258.

was massed into two great belts each 30 yards deep, inter-
laced with trestles and iron stakes. In this hilly country the
whole system of defense, traversed by interconnecting
trenches and provided with an excellent deep-laid telephone network, rose "tier upon tier" on the hillside to a distance of four to six miles.

The reality of the attack was very different from the
plan. At 7:30 am on 1 July, after seven days of heavy bombardment which was confidently expected to obliterate the
German wire and all defenders in the German trenches, the
British infantry rose from its trenches as the guns lifted
from the German line and, in brilliant sunshine, stumbled
under a heavy load across the broken ground of no-man's-
land into a hail of machine-gun fire. Thousands were mown
down near their own trenches; others were held up on the
German wire which in many places the guns had failed to
breach. Only in the south was there any lasting success, the
18th and 30th Divisions capturing their objectives around
Montauban; and the 7th and 21st Divisions of XV Corps partially doing so by capturing Mametz village and breaching
the German front line west of Fricourt. Elsewhere it was
total failure, though the 36th (Ulster) Division of X Corps
broke right through the German second position near Thiepval only to be beaten back, with heavy casualties, to the
German front line.

On the evening of the first day, Rawlinson decided
to concentrate his attack south of the River Ancre, the next
big objective being to capture the German second line at
its nearest point on the ridge between the Bazentins and
Longueval. Map 6 shows the position on the 3rd and the 5th
of July. Rawlinson planned a frontal attack uphill between
Mametz Wood and Trones Wood. The Commander-in-Chief,
Haig, was a little uneasy and stressed the importance of first
capturing Mametz Wood, without which, he insisted, the left
flank of the attack would be very insecure. Rawlinson was
not wholly convinced of the desirability of waiting for the
capture of Mametz Wood but he did as he was told. On 6
July he wrote in his journal: "the attacks by the III Corps
and XV Corps against Contalmaison and Mametz Wood will
be carried out as arranged. They have fresh divisions and I
hope all will go well."

One of the fresh divisions was the 38th Welsh and it
was thus committed to battle.

We left the Welsh Division at Toutencourt on 30
June waiting for orders. On the night of 1/2 July the battalions marched to Achieux about five miles behind the front

at Thiepval where they were to join in the expected break-
through. When the attack on this part of the front failed,
they partly retraced their steps before marching south to
Albert:

> It roused your apprehension that the third halt should so exceed the
> allowed five minutes; and what with the word passed down for the adju-
> tant, and with Brigade cyclists about at this hour, you gathered they
> were up to their antics--you weren't surprised when you found yourself
> facing the way you'd come:
> The brave old Duke of York--up it and down it again. (*IP*, 123-4)

On 5 July, the division was ordered to take over the
front between Bottom Wood and Caterpillar Wood from 7th
Division. Units of the division moved into the area below
Mametz Wood that evening, footsore and weary, to begin the
relief which was completed in the early hours of 6 July.
Siegfried Sassoon, who was in the 1st Battalion of the Royal
Welsh Fusiliers in 7th Division, watched some of them
arrive in Bottom Wood:

> The incoming battalion numbered more than double our own strength (we
> were less than 400) and they were unseasoned New Army troops. Our
> little trench under the trees was inundated by a jostling company of
> exclamatory Welshmen. Kinjack would have called them a panicky
> rabble.... Visualizing that forlorn crowd of khaki figures under the
> twilight of the trees, I can believe that I saw then, for the first time,
> how blindly war destroys its victims. The sun had gone down on my own
> reckless brandishings, and I understood the doomed condition of these
> half trained civilians who had been sent up to attack the wood.[7]

North of the road from Mametz village to Montauban, the ground falls away, gently at first and then more
steeply, until it reaches Willow Stream (see Map 7). The
final descent is down a steep chalk bank (called the "cliff")
varying in height from about 30 to 50 feet. From Willow
Stream the ground rises northwards for more than a mile to
the ridge, on which lay the fortified trenches of the German
second line. Mametz Wood, "a menacing wall of gloom,"
according to Sassoon, lay on a slight spur on this rising
ground, flanked by gentle re-entrant valleys rising up to the
ridge. Because of these undulations, an attack on the wood,
from whatever direction, would involve the movement of
troops down a slope and then up rising ground, exposed all
the while to fire from the wood itself and from nearby
copses. The wood, as Map 7 shows, was (and still is) very
large, being about a mile long, three-quarters of a mile
wide at the widest point, and covering an area of about 220

---

7. Siegfried Sassoon, *Memoirs of an Infantry Officer* (London: Faber and Faber, 1930),
p. 69.

acres. The northern edge was only 300 yards from the German second line from which the wood, overgrown by neglect, could easily be reinforced.

XV Corps' first plan was for an assault, on 7 July, by two divisions: one, 17th (Northern) Division, commanded by Maj-Gen Pilcher, attacking from the west; the other, the Welsh division, attacking from the east. There is a fine, accurate account of the events of that day in *Up to Mametz* and there is little point in dwelling on it here because David Jones was not involved--the Welsh Division's contribution being made by Brig-Gen Evans' 115th Brigade. Suffice it to say that the attack was a total disaster, neither division reaching the wood. The reason for the Welsh Division's failure can be seen from Map 7: the direction of the attack was almost parallel to the German second line thus exposing the troops to enfilade fire from Sabot and Flat Iron Copses. As a result of this failure, Generals Pilcher and Philipps were instantly sacked, though neither was responsible for the plan of attack. The Welsh Division was placed under the command of Maj-Gen Watts of the 7th Division, then resting.

Shortly before his dismissal, General Philipps had been working on plans for another attack on the wood, this time from the south, starting from White Trench. The attack was to take place on the afternoon of 9 July and the troops were moved forward in readiness. But when Philipps was relieved of his command, XV Corps ordered a postponement until 4:15 am. the following morning. "God knows what it was all about," says David Jones, "but they moved you back again that evening to another field of bivouac" (*IP*, 148).

The operations on 10 July were to be much weightier than before. The 38th Division was to make the main attack on the wood using two brigades, the 113th on the left and the 114th on the right, while 17th Division, which by now was in a state of exhaustion, was to assist by attacking Quadrangle Support Trench. The Welsh Division's plan had little subtlety, being a frontal attack across unpromising ground--that is down the cliff, then across the rising ground in the face of machine-gun and artillery fire. There was to be no support on the right and no attempt to outflank the wood--just a crude onslaught, relying on a three to one superiority in numbers. While this attack was taking place the rest of the British Army was to be at a standstill and the eyes of the Commander-in-Chief were therefore focused on the Welsh Division. XV Corps sent the following message:

> The Commander-in-Chief has just visited the Corps Commander and
> impressed upon him the great importance of the occupation by us of
> Mametz Wood. The Corps Commander requests that the Division and
> Brigade Commanders will point out to the troops of the Welsh divi-
> sion the opportunity offered them of serving their King and Country
> at a critical period and earning for themselves great glory and distinc-
> tion.

The troops were to attack in parallel lines, or waves,
as they had practiced at St. Pol, with bayonets fixed, rifles
at the high-port position, four paces between each man, 100
yards between each line, the 16th Royal Welsh Fusiliers
leading for the 113th Brigade with 14th Royal Welsh Fusiliers behind. They were attacking the narrow part of the
wood between the central ride and Strip Trench (see Map 8)
but had to have enough men to deal with the wider part of
the wood where it opens out from point J to point K. The
114th Brigade on the right had a wider frontage and so put
two battalions side by side into the attack--the Swansea
Battalion in the center and the 2nd Rhondda on the far
right. Facing them were very experienced German troops,
the Lehr Regiment of the Prussian 3rd Guards Division
holding the edge of the wood, with other units of the
division close at hand. Further back in the wood were units
of the 16th Bavarian and 122nd Wurtemberg Regiments.

The troops assembled at 3 am and waited for zero
hour to arrive. The London Welsh were in close support in
Queen's Nullah, David Jones among them. The 16th RWF,
forward of them and to their right, sang hymns before the
attack and received a little sermon from their commanding
officer about making their peace with God, as, he said,
"some would not come back." The hymn singing could be
heard in the Nullah as David Jones records:

and the Royal Welsh sing:
Jesu
        lover of me soul ... to *Aberystwyth.*
But that was on the right with
the genuine Taffies
        but we are rash levied
from Islington and Hackney
and the purlieus of Walworth
flashers from Surbiton
men of the stock of Abraham
from Bromley-by-Bow.... (*IP*, 160)

At 3:30 am. the artillery began a heavy bombardment of the southern edge of the wood; twenty minutes later
a smoke screen laid just south of Strip Trench drifted effectively north-eastward and shortly before 4:15 the troops

moved off. Captain Glynn Jones with the 14th RWF
described his approach to the wood thus:

> Machine-guns and rifles began to rattle and there was a general state of
> pandemonium, little of which I can remember exactly except that I
> myself was moving down the slope at a rapid rate with bullet-holes in
> my pocket and yelling a certain amount.... I noticed also that there
> was no appearance of waves about the movement at this time... there
> appeared to be no one ahead of us and no one following us ... the ridge
> behind us was being subjected to the most terrible machine-gun and
> artillery fire.... Meanwhile men were crawling in from shell-holes
> to our front with reports of nothing less than a terrible massacre and
> the names of most of our officers and nco's lying dead in front.

On the far right, the 13th Welsh were caught in the
flank by fire from German machine-guns skillfully placed
on the underside of the "Hammerhead," along line A to B.
Recalling his experiences some years ago, Sgt T. J. Price
of the 13th Welsh (2nd Rhondda) Battalion gave me a
graphic description of the approach to the wood which
brings to mind Sgt Quilter of *In Parenthesis*:

> As the barrage started we moved off in an orderly fashion. ... The ten-
> sion and noise cannot be described, what with the traction of shells
> through the air and the noise of explosions all around us, it was impos-
> sible to give verbal orders and we had to rely on hand signals for direct-
> ing any move. Men were falling in all directions due to intense
> machine-gun fire coming against us. How we got to the wood I do not
> know... but we got there.

Sgt Price's "It was impossible to give verbal orders
and we had to rely on hand signals" echoes David Jones'
striking description of the difficulties of command:
"Sergeant Quilter is shouting his encouragements, you can
almost hear him, he opens his mouth so wide" (*IP*, 166).

In the center, the Swansea battalion had the advantage of being protected by others from machine-gun fire on
the flanks and crossed the open ground in perfect formation
arriving at the wood just as the barrage was lifting back.
Once in the wood the men found it difficult to make
progress because of the thickness of the undergrowth and the
lack of any sense of direction. On the left, the 16th RWF
also entered the wood and was soon joined by the 15th RWF
from Queen's Nullah, which can be seen, as it is today, in
Plate 2. There was less grass in 1916 and much of the chalk
sub-soil was exposed. The Nullah is quite deep, having the
appearance of a blanked-off railway cutting. In the photograph, the left hand side of the Nullah is the face on which
01 Ball and his companions waited on that sunny morning,
with Mametz Wood to the left out of picture:

And the place of their waiting a long burrow,
in the chalk a cutting, and steep clift--
but all but too shallow against his violence. (*IP*, 155)

Plate 3 shows the view they had when they rose dry-mouthed out of the Nullah:

and to your front, stretched long laterally,
and receded deeply,
the dark wood. (*IP*, 165)

The "flat roof of the world" where "sweet sister death has gone debauched today" is in the immediate foreground. It is here, not many yards from the Nullah, that David Jones' platoon commander was killed, not on the open ground rising to the wood where Mr. P. D. I. Jenkins is placed at the moment of death. As they crossed the open ground, Jones will have seen the enemy's observation posts in the high trees shown in Plate 4, for he says, as his section breaks line to find a passage through the shell holes:

but high-perched Brandenburgers
from their leafy vantage-tops observe
that kind of folly. (*IP*, 167)

And as they entered the now crowded part of the wood between Strip Trench and the central ride the confusion was such that it was difficult to find anyone to give orders:

You wished you could see people you knew better than the "C" Company man on your right or the bloke from "A" on your left. (*IP*, 171)

They met strong opposition at Wood Support Trench and at the corner of the wood, point J, where the Germans had a well-defended redoubt, and they were held up for some time. Price-Davies went into the wood to sort things out and made his way up Strip Trench where he was distressed to see a party of men "running back in panic."

and Jesus Christ--they're coming through the floor,
endthwart and overlong:
Jerry's through on the flank...and: Beat it!--
that's what that one said as he ran past:
Bosches back in Strip Trench--it's a
monumental bollocks every time.... (*IP*, 180)

David Jones, who witnessed this incident, put it down to lack of supervision. "Something must have developed, if not into a panic, at least into a disorderly falling back--simply because of not having precise directions" he wrote in 1971.[8] "As we worked our way into the deeper parts of the

8. Letter dated 24 March 1971.

wood there was a mix-up not only of sections and platoons
and companies, but of battalions also--hence the difficulty
of getting exact orders. Even if one found an officer, he
would be desperately trying to find men of his own platoon
or company and could do little more than tell one to press
on. The Mr. Trevor (*IP*, 170) stood for a B Company
Lieutenant, but that does not mean that I did not change his
name." In the same letter, Jones goes on to describe how
the "green-gilled corporal" (*IP*, 172) did good work by
getting a number of them who were firing blindly and
individually into the thick tangle of trees to form a line
and fire from the "prone position."

The "thick tangle of trees" can be seen in Plate 5
which is a photograph taken in the wood about two days
after its capture. The officers in the picture are not from
the Welsh Division: they are engaged in the later, bloody
battle for the second line, in spite of their neat turn out.
One is a Brigadier and the photograph matches perfectly
the scene in *In Parenthesis* where:

> ... the Brigadier's up with ... Conduit Street bandboxed shirtings, to
> flash beige and vermilion at the lapels' turn and neat sartorial niceties
> down among the dead men .... (*IP*, 173)

In spite of the confusion the battle was going well
and Haig was pleased. By 9 a.m. the Welsh Division had
reached the first cross-ride and was pushing on--though now
more slowly as the troops tired. By about 11 a.m. all the
units of the 113th and 114th Brigades were involved in the
fighting and General Watts sent in the two battalions of
115th Brigade that had suffered least on 7 July. These
arrived in the middle of the afternoon and revived a flag-
ging attack. The battle swayed to and fro for some time,
but by half past six in the evening the division had reached
to within 30 or 40 yards of the northern edge of the wood
and was very close to the German second line. As this
exposed the troops to heavy fire they were drawn back some
200 to 300 yards into the interior where they dug in for the
night. Jones describes these fluctuating fortunes by quoting
from Malory:

> And then he might see sometime the battle was driven a bow draught
> from the castle and sometime it was at the gates of the castle. (*IP*,
> 181)

The following morning, Brigadier Evans took command in the wood, relieved the battalions that were the
most exhausted, and straightened the line before launching
another attack. This again took the division near the edge

of the wood but again it was forced to withdraw a little way to safety. That night, however, the German high command ordered a complete evacuation of the wood and a few hours later the Welsh Division itself was relieved. It had achieved much--as much indeed as any division on the Somme-- though with heavy casualties. But it did not live down the poor reputation it had gained in the eyes of higher command for its failure on 7 July. Glory and distinction were certainly not showered upon it. Instead, the division was bundled unceremoniously away and took no further part in the battle of the Somme. By this time, however, *In Parenthesis* has drawn to a close, David Jones having been wounded in the leg at the end of the first day. He crawled from the battle before being carried by stretcher to Mametz village and thence by ambulance to a field hospital behind the line.

It is clear from the above that in writing *In Parenthesis* David Jones used a strictly accurate account of the capture of Mametz Wood and of events leading up to it as a frame on which to weave his poetry, using as raw material his own observations and experiences. Sometimes the experiences are transposed from other periods of the war but only if they are typical of what would have been happening in the period to which they are assigned. "One of my rules," he wrote in 1971,[9] "is that when one uses some quotation or even a name that evokes some past author or event or historical or legendary association one must have an experiential, concrete, contactual matter in the narrative that corresponds in some way or other with the quoted situation or name." And when he is describing an event about which he would have heard, but could not possibly have seen, he arranges for 01 Ball to receive the information in an indirect way. Thus the scene of consternation in Aunty Bembridge's tent is relayed to Ball by a runner who could plausibly have witnessed it. One scene which does not seem at first sight to follow this pattern is that at HQ Company office just before the battle. Here, it will be remembered, Private W. Map is the observer; neither 01 Ball nor 79 Jones is present, and there is no mention of any third party relating the story. David Blamires has pointed out that the allusion here is to Walter Map, whose position at the court of Henry II enabled him to write an entertaining and informative account of court life. David Jones was for a time attached to the battalion's HQ Company (though not until

9. Letter dated 4 January 1971.

1917) and there can be little doubt that his own entertaining and informative account of office life--including such amusing touches as the swish of a soda syphon, and the clink of an officer's glass on the table--is based on that experience. His task in the office was to copy maps; his first name was Walter. So the reference to Walter Map is doubly appropriate and the "rule" of composition is strictly observed.

Plate 6 is a photograph of the interior of Mametz Wood, showing what remained of Strip Trench more than 50 years after the battle. "It is clear from the photographs" wrote David Jones in 1969,[10] remembering the wood only as a shell-torn waste-land, "that the Queen of the Woods has revivified her groves." "It reminds me," he added, "of the line from the folk song *John Barleycorn*:

And Barleycorn stood up again and that surprised them all."

10. Letter dated 18 November 1969.

Plate 1. Biez Wood, as it is now, looking from the "Neb."

Plate 2. Queen's Nullah, today.

Plate 3. Mametz Wood from the "cliff."

Plate 4. German observation post in Mametz Wood.
(Imperial War Museum photograph)

Plate 5. Mametz Wood, July 1916, showing undergrowth.
(Imperial War Museum photograph)

Plate 6. Strip Trench, more than fifty years after the battle.

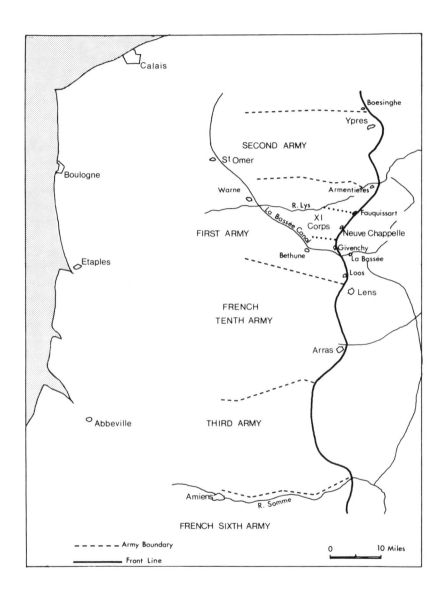

Map 1. The Western Front, December 1915

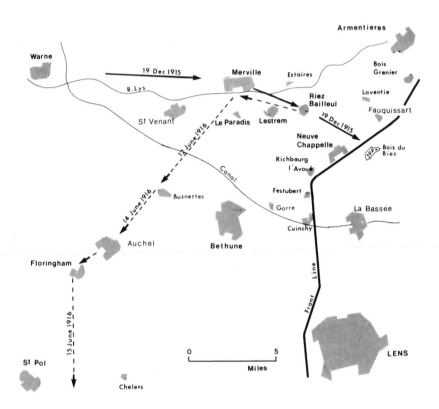

Map 2. Movements of the 15th (London Welsh) Battalion.

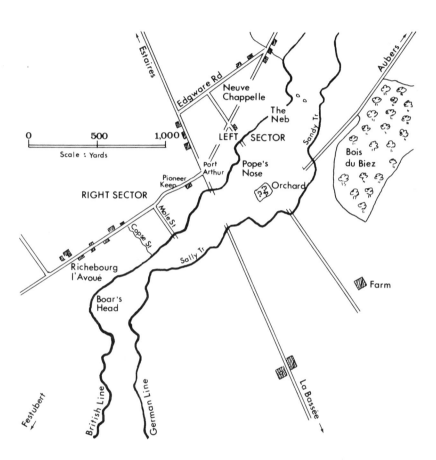

Map 3. Front line sectors held by 38th Division, December 1916.

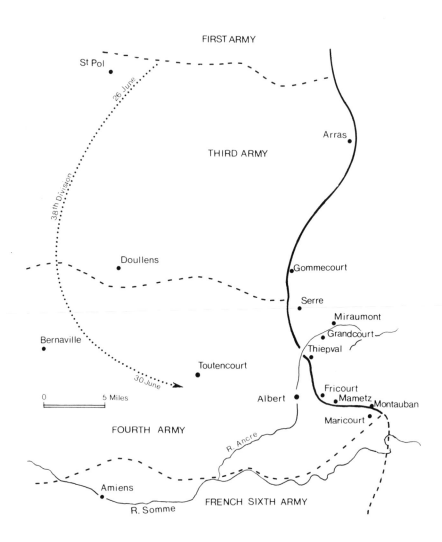

Map 4. Route from St. Pol to the Somme battlefield.

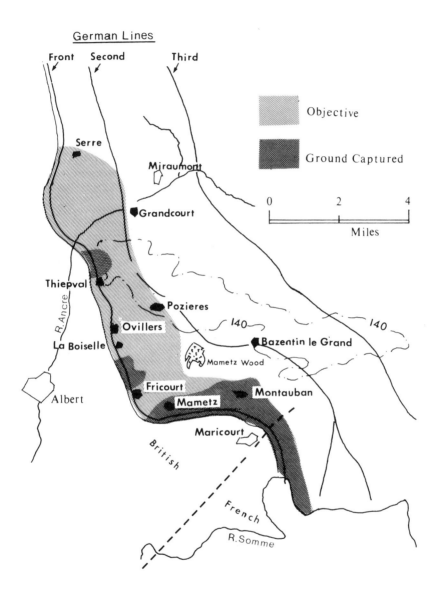

Map 5. Objectives and Achievements, 1 July 1916.

Map 6. Position on 3rd and 5th July.

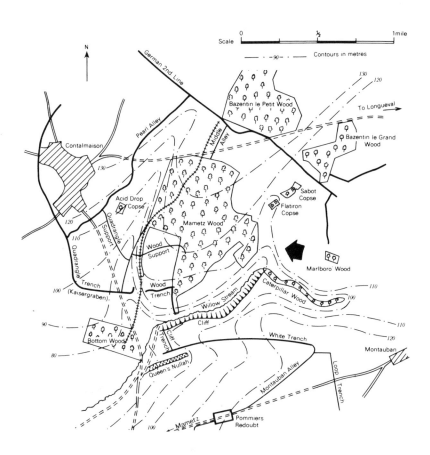

Map 7. Mametz Wood and surroundings, showing direction of attack
on 7 July.

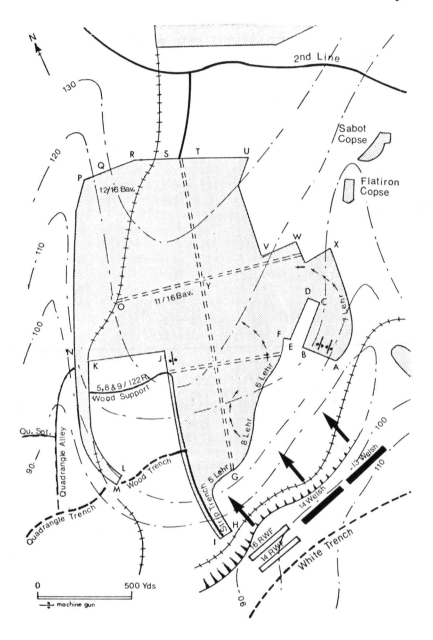

Map 8. Mametz Wood, 10 July 1916.

WILLIAM BLISSETT

THE SYNTAX OF VIOLENCE

I

Should an experience at the limits of human endurance call forth a corresponding testing of the limits of language? Must the literature of violence do violence to language? The Great War was unexampled in history; it was also a war like other wars. It was not the first modern war, nor is its literature the first to be faced with the inapplicability of the heroic tradition.[1] High explosives are new but explosives are not, the machine-gun is new but firearms are not. The whole list of the battle-honors of the Royal Welch Fusiliers (the regiment of Robert Graves, Siegfried Sassoon, Llewelyn Wyn Griffith, Frank Richards, and David Jones) belongs to the age of the grenade, and *The British Grenadiers*, "the march proper to them" (*IP*, 6), celebrates a new thing, unknown to Hector and Lysander: "Those heroes of antiquity ne'er saw a cannon ball/Or knew the force of powder to slay their foes withal." But the stationary mechanized "exchange of insults" by massed citizen armies year after year on a front stretching from the Alps to the sea was without example. New weapons brought with them new tensions, new rhythms, and new discontinuities with the past, discontinuities reflected in a failure of language and the blank dismay entailed in that. Soldiers always expect to fight the last (that is, the previous, and a final) war, but warfare is always technologically ahead of its age and therefore unimaginable and unnerving beyond its expected dan-

---

1. What is by now a commonplace was stated by Herbert Read in 1928 when writing of *Seven Pillars of Wisdom*: "In France and Belgium men of infinitely finer quality than these Arabs were enduring day after day, without the inspiration of the open horizon and all that conveys of adventure and surprise, the dull and dispiriting agony of trench warfare. No one will be fool enough to make out of that horror an epic story, or to see in our armies a race of self-reliant heroes; but this Arabian adventure was no more than a dance in the air beside the magnitude of that terrific earthy conflict." (Included in *A Coat of Many Colours* [London: Routledge, 1956], pp. 25-6).

gers and deprivations and ambuscades. That accounts for
the death-grip on whatever can still be imagined in the old
terms.

      Consider the bayonet. The bayonet is horrible
enough in all conscience, the more effective as a psychological weapon because its horror is well within the compass of anyone's imagination. Over and over again we hear
sickening accounts of the "inculcation of the offensive
spirit" by bayonet drill in training centers, especially the
infamous "Eetaps." Siegfried Sassoon, in a no-man's-land
between his early poetry of celebration of war and his later
poetry of protest, wrote of a bullet and bayonet in "The
Kiss":

> To these I turn, in these I trust--
> Brother Lead and Sister Steel.
> To his blind power I make appeal,
> I guard her beauty clean from rust.
>
> He spins and burns and loves the air,
> And splits a skull to win my praise;
> But up the nobly marching days
> She glitters naked, cold and fair.
>
> Sweet Sister, grant your soldier this:
> That in good fury he may feel
> The body where he sets his heel
> Quail from your downward darting kiss.

That was from early in the War; from late in the War comes
"The Happy Warrior." Fascination in Sassoon becomes revulsion in Herbert Read; there is something equally factitious
about both:

> His wild heart beats with painful sobs,
> His strain'd hands clench an ice-cold rifle,
> His aching jaws grip a hot parch'd tongue,
> His wide eyes search unconsciously.
>
> He cannot shriek.
> Bloody saliva
> Dribbles down his shapeless jacket.
>
> I saw him stab
> And stab again
> A well-killed Boche.
>
> This is the happy warrior,
> This is he....[2]

2. Siegfried Sassoon, *Collected Poems* (London: Faber and Faber, 1961), pp. 15-16;
Herbert Read, *Collected Poems* (London: Faber and Faber, 1946), p. 47. John H.
Johnston, *English Poetry of the First World War* (Princeton: Princeton University
Press, 1964), p. 257, praises this poem for its cold observation of hysteria. Herbert

One would never surmise from these and countless other writings that the real toll of death and injury was run up by bombardment, by rifle fire, by the machine-gun--bayonet wounds amounting to less than one percent of casualties.[3] The bayonet thrusts itself into literature because it wounds the imagination like a sword or a pike.

If the obtrusion of the bayonet is an example of distortion of observation and language, there are major successes in this most written-up of wars, as are witnessed by the survival of its vocabulary and the persistence of its tone of feeling in modern memory.[4] Many literary experiments, most of them failures (experiments in the arts, as in science, must be expected to have mainly negative results) were made to render the new stress and violence by violence of language and dislocation of syntax, to match the impact of high explosives and machine-gun fire, not forgetting the hardly less wearing, but opposite, experience of fatigue, boredom, attrition. Concurrently, the old conception of style as choice was being challenged by a new theory of style as deviation.[5]

Use of onomatopoeic devices is universal in war-*parole*, to a degree markedly higher than in ordinary speech and writing. When in the Great War, language at its limit was sought for experience at its limit, the first impulse of the unskilled was to drum up a hubbub of sound-effects in combination with the loose, "modernistic" license of the then-new free verse. Listen to the widely applauded soldier poet, Robert Nichols:

> I hear my whistle shriek,
> Between teeth set;
> I fling an arm up,
> Scramble up the grime
> Over the parapet!
> I'm up. Go on.

Read himself writes, "one and only one of my war poems has been extensively quoted in anthologies and reviews--a simple but very bitter and horrible poem called 'The Happy Warrior.' From a literary point of view I am sure it is by no means the best of my war poems, but it has had a terrible fascination for many people. It expresses in an extreme degree the horror of war, and it, and other poems and stories of the same kind, should have been an effective warning. As it is, the suspicion now grows upon me that such writing was fuel to the inner flames of the war spirit." *A Coat of Many Colours*, pp. 74-5.

3. See John U. Nef, *War and Human Progress* (London: Routledge, 1950), pp. 251-2; Jon Silkin, *Out of Battle* (London: Oxford University Press, 1972), p. 136 n; John Keegan, *The Face of Battle* (New York: Viking Press, 1976), p. 264, who gives the bayonet statistics.

4. The thesis, well sustained, of Paul Fussell, *The Great War and Modern Memory* (New York: Oxford University Press, 1975). For my serious reservations about the chapter on David Jones in this otherwise good book, see *U.T.Q.* 45 (1976), pp. 68-74.

5. Inger Rosengren, "Style as Choice and Deviation," *Style*, vi (1972), pp. 3-18, with bibliography.

Something meets us.
Head down into the storm that greets us.
A wail.
Lights. Blurr.
Gone.
On. On. Lead. Lead. Hail.
Spatter. Whirr! Whirr!
"Toward that patch of brown;
Direction left." Bullets a stream.
Devouring thought crying in a dream.
Men, crumpled, going down. . . .

Douglas Goldring speaks for everyone: "It was characteristic
of our war-time criticism that this masterpiece of drivel,
instead of exciting derision, was hailed as a work of genius
and read with avidity."[6]

Isaac Rosenberg, however, with similar impulse but
greater skill, broke through to a sense of the modern as true
as Nichols' was bogus. He dares in a sort of free blank verse
to rival the thunder of Milton's War in Heaven; respeaking
earthly thunder:

Maniac Earth! howling and flying, your bowel
Seared by the jagged fire, the iron love.
Dark Earth! dark Heavens! swinging in chemic smoke,
What dead are born when you kiss each soundless soul
With lightning and thunder from your mined heart,
Which man's self dug, and his blind fingers loosed?[7]

I may say in passing that Jon Silkin's reading of Rosenberg,
where the sound is fully in service of the sense, comes home
to its auditors as the best criticism of the poet.

Experiments in violent dislocated prose--expression-
ism in Germany, vorticism in England--were likewise seized
upon and applied to the War emergency. The cultivated
aristocratic staff-officer, Fritz von Unruh, knew both the
avant-garde literary welter and the *Front-Erlebnis* at first
hand. He overwrites deafeningly and is himself quite deaf
to the soldier's peculiar tone of deadpan irony, but his stac-
cato, explosive style and rapid pace capture something of
the movement of the war machine as it speeds glum anti-
heroes up the line to death.[8] Wyndham Lewis, an artillery
man (what else could the deviser of BLAST be?), had his
big chance in the autobiographical *Blasting and Bom-*
bardiering (1937), but apart from his recognition of the war

6. Poem and comment are quoted by Bernard Bergonzi, *Heroes' Twilight* (London: Constable, 1965), p. 64. See also J. H. Johnston, p. 50.
7. Isaac Rosenberg, *Collected Poems*, ed. Gordon Bottomley and Denys Harding (London: Chatto & Windus, 1962), p. 82.
8. Fritz von Unruh, *Opfergang* (Frankfurt a.m., 1925). See especially pp. 103-4.
(Translated by C. A. Macartney as *Way of Sacrifice* [New York: Knopf, 1928]. See
especially pp. 128-9.)

landscape as romantic I find in it mainly duds and back-fires. If style is choice, the options close in as context and habit are established; if style is deviation, the same is the case, as twentieth-century writers in the wake of expression-ism have found, to their exasperation.

Perhaps the prose that best catches the rhythm of the machine-gun, as T. S. Eliot and Stravinsky sought to catch the rhythm of the internal combustion engine, is that of Ernest Hemingway, a stylist who will be remembered as long as Ronald Firbank. "Perhaps," I say, for here is David Jones on a hidden machine-gunner at work:

> he finds you everywhere.
> Where his fiery sickle garners you:
> fanged-flash and darkt-fire thrring and thrrung athwart thdrill a Wimshurst pandemonium drill with dynamo druv staccato bark at you like Berthe Krupp's terrier bitch and rattlesnakes for bare legs; sweat you on the sudden like masher Bimp's back-firing No. 3 model for Granny Bodger at 1.30 a.m. rrattle a chatter you like a Vitus neurotic, harrow your vertebrae, bore your brain-pan before you can say Fanny-- and comfortably over open sights:
> the gentleman must be mowed. (*IP*, 182)

II

"Language is the armoury of the human mind; and at once contains the trophies of its past, and the weapons of its future conquests."[9] Coleridge's dictum has peculiar force for the readers of David Jones who have kept *In Parenthesis* in print for half a century. "First we have naming of parts," and only then, when the process of exploring its full working vocabulary is well under way does one notice that there is a corresponding range and accuracy of stylistic devices enlisted in support of the poem. Like an artilleryman (shall I say?) David Jones keeps "bracketing," changing his stylis-tic "register"; or, better, like the poor bloody infantry he belonged to, he finds himself detailed to do all sorts of things all at once, using his full though compact "stylistic tool-kit."[10]

Though explaining much of the literary and histori-cal background of the writing, his introduction has only a few words to say about style, mainly about strong and improper language. Rather surprisingly, the remainder is concerned with punctuation and the layout of type on the page. These matters were probably uppermost in his mind

9. S. T. Coleridge, *Biographia Literaria*, ed. J. Shawcross (Oxford: Clarendon Press, 1907), II 22 (Chapter XVI).
10. Graham Hough's phrase, *Style and Stylistics* (London: Routledge, 1969), p. 33.

at the last because his expert typist had the one fault of
inserting normal punctuation and because he and René
Hague took the printing very seriously--in fact formally
proposing to Faber (and printing a specimen) that the book
be a "crown folio, 10 by 15 inches, with two columns of 12 pt
Joanna, and a headline (just PART 4) in Gill Sans Bold
caps." Hague says that "it looked grand, but not very practical. [Richard] de la Mare thought we were out of our
minds."[11]

This is what David Jones himself wrote:

> It may be well to say something of the punctuation. I frequently rely
> on a pause at the end of a line to aid the sense and form. A new line,
> which the typography would not otherwise demand, is used to indicate
> some change, inflection, or emphasis. I have tried to indicate the sound
> of certain sentences by giving a bare hint of who is speaking, of the
> influences operating to make the particular sound I want in a particular
> instance, by perhaps altering a single vowel in one word. I have only
> used the notes of exclamation, interrogation, etc., when the omission of
> such signs would completely obscure the sense. I hope the stresses and
> changes intended will convey themselves to the reader. (*IP*, xi-xii)

It is thus, by the author's admission, a style of "stresses and
changes," of what the old rhetoricians called *energeia*.[12]
Clearly he intended the alternation of prose and verse to
stand in audible and visible counterpoint, and that both
should be shaped and imaginatively rendered as a guide to
pace, attack, and phrasing. The reader is required to be
exceptionally alert and active. One has the sense of
patrolling the no-man's-land between the regularities of
parallelism and pattern[13]--a danger zone fraught with sudden
breaks in syntax, prickly hyphenations, explosive verbal
nouns, deceptive underpunctuation, and other risky devices
we shall be noticing.

Here is an unpunctuated paragraph (there is one
comma) only slightly more experimental than the normal
indirect reporting of an Edmund Blunden or a Wyn Griffith.
It is not "stream-of-consciousness," being as-if-spoken, not as-
if-thought. The effect of this rigmarole is of surface
loquacity and deep dread--the perfect embodiment of the
"breeze-up" or near-panic of its concluding phrase:

> Well you couldn't go far afield because of the stand-by but blokes came
> across from "A" and the other companies to see their friends and peo-
> ple talked a good bit about what the Show was going to be like and were

---

11. From a letter to me by René Hague.
12. See Gerald L. Bruns, *Modern Poetry and the Idea of Language* (New Haven: Yale
University Press, 1974), pp. 44-5.
13. See G. N. Leech's distinction (*Guide*, 73-4) between obtrusive regularity (parallelism)
and obtrusive irregularity (deviation), between *schemes* as foregrounded repetition of
expression, and *tropes* as foregrounded irregularities of content.

all agog but no one seemed to know anything much as to anything and you got the same served up again garnished with a different twist and emphasis maybe and some would say such and such and others would say the matter stood quite otherwise and there would be a division among them and lily-livered blokes looked awfully unhappy, people you never would expect it of and same the other way the oddest types seemed itching for a set-to quite genuine it would appear but after all who can read or search out the secret places you get a real eye-opener now and then and any subsequent revealing seldom conforms and you misconstrue his apparent noble bearing and grope about in continued misapprehension or can it by any manner of means be that everyone is interiorly in as great misery and unstably set as you are and is the essential unity of mankind chiefly monstrated in this faint-heartness and breeze-right-up aptitude. (*IP*, 144)

In contrast to this incoherent interior commotion, the official language of war, snatches of which are overheard from time to time, deliberately tries to be the style of nobody: balefully influenced by the twin jargons of science and bureaucracy, it is value-free, impersonal, and bent on death. It appears only in an ironic light in the book, and to my mind carries as much weight of moral criticism as would many pages of overtly anti-war vehemence or pity or contrivance of atrocity: as, for example, when the decent young Lt. Jenkins reads to his men the precis of the official text:

Received from extract from issued G.H.Q. of the 2nd to be communicated to all ranks. With transport on the paved other road you missed half the good news ... and have carried his trenches on a wide front ... in the south subsector ... our advanced troops have penetrated to his third system. He raises his voice against the crying of the drivers and there is noise of stress at the bend to disrupt the tale of: his full retirement--the number of his elite gone to Divisional Cage--and other ranks like the sea-sand taken--field-howitzers and seventy-sevens running to three figures.
... of all calibre in our hands ... have everywhere been reached according to plan ... and are in readiness to co-operate with the infantry. The G.O.C. 444th Corps would take the occasion--but the four-ton changing gear by the traffic-wallah obliterated altogether his expressions of hearty appreciation.
They were permitted to cheer.
You are dismissed, to clean up billets. (*IP*, 122-3)

Technical language, of course, is a very different thing from official language, and David Jones recalls with approval a passage in Conrad praising its accuracy and beauty. It would require another essay as long as this one to demonstrate the strict accuracy of his vocabulary, a very rare thing among war writers.

War has always been the occasion of technological changes great and small; in the sphere of the mechanics of

writing this is evidenced, in the Second War in the acronym,
in the First in the piling up of nouns as adjectives and in
the omnipresent hyphen. Partly perhaps a German influence, the English answer to the compounding of words, it is
partly a fresh response to the necessity of conceiving thing
and function as one. Here is a splendid example--the inventory of the contents of a disused fire-bay (demonstrating the
epic love of catalogue), the whole requiring thirteen
hyphens:

> Picks, shovels, dredging-ladles, carriers, containers, gas-rattles, two of
> Mrs. Thingumajig's patent gas-dispersing flappers, emptied S. A. A.
> boxes, grenade boxes, two bales of revetting-wire, pine stakes; rusted-to-
> bright-orange barbed wire of curious design--three coils of it; fine good
> new dark efficient corkscrew staples, splayed-out all ways; three
> drums of whale oil, the splintered stock of a Mauser rifle, two
> unexploded yellow-ochre toffee-apples, their strong rods unrusted;
> three left-leg gum-boots; a Scotch officer's fine bright bonnet; some
> type of broken pump, its rubber slack punctured, coiled like a dead
> slime-beast, reared its brass nozzle out from under rum-jar and picket-
> maul. (*IP*, 90)

Writing doesn't come thingier than that, the union of function and substance being consummated by the hyphen.

A complementary passage, dominated by the verbal
noun to convey progressive action, establishes from the very
first page one of David Jones' characteristic turns of style:

> Heavily jolting and sideway jostling, the noise of liquid shaken in a
> small vessel by a regular jogging movement, a certain clinking ending in
> a shuffling of the feet sidelong--all clear and distinct in that silence
> peculiar to parade grounds and to refectories. The silence of a high
> order, full of peril in the breaking of it, like the coming on parade of
> John Ball. (*IP*, 1)

The "coming on parade" is closely similar to another pervasive habit of expression, again in the interest of uniting verb
and noun in a single process[14]--the combination of the verbal with the post positive preposition, as in "the letting in of
the beginnings of morning, an icy filtering through, with the
drawing back of bolts" (*IP*, 16).

Some other stylistic devices may be drawn from
stores for brief mention: they might easily escape notice,
but they add to the effectiveness of the passages in which
they occur. Like many epic writers, including the composers
of the Old Norse Sagas and the Song of Roland and in our
own century C. M. Doughty in *The Dawn in Britain*, David
Jones permits himself a rapid alternation or uncertainty of

---

14. See Angus McIntosh, "Linguistics and English Studies," in A. McIntosh and M. A.
K. Halliday, eds., *Patterns of Language* (London: Longmans, 1966), p. 54.

tenses.[15] On the march to the front, John Ball must drop his gaze from the stars to watch where he is going:

> Saturate, littered, rusted coilings, metallic rustlings, thin ribbon-metal chafing--rasp low for some tension freed; by rat, or wind, disturbed. Smooth-rippled discs gleamed, where gaping craters, their brimming waters, made mirror for the sky procession--bear up before the moon incongruous souvenirs. Margarine tins sail derelict, where little eddies quivered, wind caught, their sharp-jagged twisted lids wrenched back. (*IP*, 39)

Again, a very personal thing in this writing, David Jones modulates from the third person to the second, "they" to "you,"[16] or has John Ball think of himself as "you," as in "The last candle was snuffed out and thrust still warm at the wick and pliable into your tunic pocket" (*IP*, 16). Or, of the man immediately next in front,

> his dark silhouette sways a moment above you--he drops away into the night and your feet follow where he seemed to be. Each in turn labours over whatever it is--this piled brokenness--dragged over and a scared hurrying on--the slobber was ankle-deep where you found the road again. (*IP*, 33)

The two devices may be combined, as here:

> That one went up at an unexpected nearness. The faraway dancing barrier surprisingly much nearer; you even hear the dull report quickly upon the uprising light; and now, right where they walked, at sudden riot against your unsuspecting ear-drums, a Vicker's team discovers its position, by low builded walls of sacks; and men worked with muffled hammerings of wood on wood; and the front files pause again. (*IP*, 40)

He gains a measure of foregrounding, ironically of rhetorical "strength," by the avoidance of the expected strong verb form--lighted (30), shined (59), swimmed (117), builded (138)--and, conversely, by the use of the contracted "t" for "ed" in the past tense for effects of suddenness--"fall of trench dampt the fire, fall of fire spilt the water'; (74, also 85 stopt, shockt, 112 tipt, 163 snapt, 179 shockt).

In the matter of syntax, two contrasting techniques are used, corresponding roughly to two aspects of a war of attrition--the discontinuous and the continuous, the unpredictable and the predictable. Consider the service of a

---

15. See J. H. Johnston, p. 293; Turner, p. 92; Barker Fairley, "The Historic Present in *The Dawn in Britain*," *U. T. Q.*, xli (1972), pp. 256-62; René Hague's translation (used by David Jones) of *The Song of Roland* (London: Faber, 1930), sections 20, 153, 165, 251; George Johnston's translation of *The Gisli Saga* (London: Dent, 1963), p. xi and passim.

16. J. H. Johnston, p. 292; Roland Bouyssou, *Les Poètes combatants anglais de la Grande Guerre* (Université de Toulouse, 1974), p. 294, equates "you" with the French "on." An interesting possibility that I have not been able to explore is suggested by Geoffrey Wagner, *On the Wisdom of Words* (Princeton: Van Nostrand, 1968), pp. 155-6: "Gaelic literature, one of the last with an intimate animism, made of man's environment such a living force that a Gaelic writer could think of himself as 'You,' thus retaining a rich residue of psychic control."

periodic and asymmetrical syntax in this passage having to
do with the fragmentation of labor in modern war and modern architecture:

> You aren't supported as you spend yourself in this blind doubling on
> your bleedin' tracks by the bright reason for it, they know about back
> there.
> You know no more than do those hands who squirt cement till siren
> screams, who are indifferent that they rear an architect's folly; read
> in the press perhaps the grandeur of the scheme. (*IP*, 87)

Consider in contrast the use of isocolon, phrases of equal
length, in rendering the effect of a creeping bombardment
at specific intervals of time:

> Besides which there was the heavy battery operating just beneath the
> ridge, at a kept interval of minutes, with unnerving inevitability, as a
> malign chronometer, ticking off with each discharge an exactly mea-
> sured progress toward a certain and prearranged hour of apocalypse.
> (*IP*, 135)

III

A sentence from *Moby-Dick* is often cited as an example of
stylistic richness: "And heaved and heaved, still unrestingly
heaved the black sea, as if its vast tides were a conscience."[17] I should like to set beside it, from *In Parenthesis*, some treatments of the outward movement of marching
and the inward experience of life on the march. First
embarkation, a stepping from the familiar world to the
unfamiliar:

> Sometime between midnight and 2 a.m. they were paraded. Slowly, and
> with every sort of hitch, platoon upon platoon formed single file and
> moved toward an invisible gangway. Each separate man found his own
> feet stepping in the darkness on an inclined plane, the smell and taste
> of salt and machinery, the texture of rope, and the glimmer of
> shielded light about him. (*IP*, 8)

Now, approaching the front, the rhythm of an hour's marching being caught in a single phrase:

> For half an hour they pushed on; an occasional voice--an N.C.O. check-
> ing some minor fault, someone asking a simple question of his fellow,
> someone's personal sense of irksomeness becoming audible in grumbled
> oaths. But for the most part it was a silent half hour, *except for the
> regular beat of the feet on the stone sets*; the outside men of each four
> slithering now and again on the too acute camber. (*IP*, 19, italics mine)

---

17. Cited first by Michael Riffaterre in his influential article, "Criteria for Style
Analysis," *Word*, 15 (1959), pp. 154-74.

And finally this longer passage, the soldiers first seeing themselves like marionettes illuminated from without by flares, then feeling their humanity deep within:

> Wired dolls sideway inclining, up and down nodding, fantastic troll-steppers in and out the uncertain cool radiance, amazed crook-back miming, where sudden chemical flare, low-flashed between the crazy flats, flood-lit their sack-bodies, hung with rigid properties--
> the drop falls,
> you can only hear their stumbling off, across the dark proscenium.
>
> So they would go a long while in solid dark, nor moon, nor battery dispelled.
> Feet plodding in each other's unseen tread. They said no word but to direct their immediate next coming, so close behind to blunder, toe by heel tripping, file-mates, blind on-following, moving with a singular identity.
> Half-minds, far away, divergent, own-thought thinking, tucked away unknown thoughts; feet following file friends, each his own thought-maze alone treading; intricate, twist about, own thoughts, all unknown thoughts, to the next so close following on. (*IP*, 37)

Stylistic devices such as the ones we have been considering are established in the early sections of *In Parenthesis* and are capable of a great variety of effects in themselves and in combination. As the soldiers march away by night from the hated training center toward the line, the paroxysms of militaristic vainglory of the instructors left behind in safety are recalled, with a scorn equal to anything in Sassoon, as a blob of noun phrases heavily hyphenated: two of them are enough to give the flavor--"drum-majors knashing in their Blancoed paradises" and "buttocked lance-jacks crawling for the second chevron" (*IP*, 27-8). Great effects of violence are likewise achievable. The harsh galvanizing description of machine-gun fire has already been quoted; we may recall also the first, unexpected, explosion of a shell, so overwhelming that it is almost still:

> Out of the vortex, rifling the air it came--bright, brass-shod, Pandoran; with all-filling screaming the howling crescendo's up-piling snapt. The universal world, breath held, one half second, a bludgeoned stillness. Then the pent violence released a consummation of all burstings out; all sudden up-rendings and rivings-through--all taking-out of vents--all barrier-breaking--all unmaking. Pernitric begetting--the dissolving and splitting of solid things. In which unearthing aftermath, John Ball picked up his mess-tin and hurried within; ashen, huddled, waited in the dismal straw.

The description ends with an effective detail of foregrounding, something to set beside the metaphor of Blunden's bloodstained potatoes or the blood and brains staining the cheese in Adam Mickiewicz's epic, *Pan Tadeusz*[18]:

> Behind 'E' Battery, fifty yards down the road, a great many mangolds, uprooted, pulped, congealed with chemical earth, spattered and made slippery the rigid boards leading to the emplacement. The sap of vegetables slobbered the spotless breech-block of No. 3 gun. (*IP*, 24)

Before concluding, I should like to look more closely at the part in *In Parenthesis* called "King Pellam's Launde," evocative of a full day in the trenches from stand-to in the morning until the return of a patrol at midnight-- most especially at its beginning and end. A comparison with Stephen Crane is instructive. The opening paragraph of *The Red Badge of Courage* is most beautiful and evocative:

> The cold passed reluctantly from the earth, and the retiring fogs revealed an army stretched out on the hills, resting. As the landscape changed from brown to green, the army awakened, and began to tremble with eagerness at the noise of rumours. It cast its eyes upon the roads, which were growing from long troughs of liquid mud to proper thoroughfares. A river, amber-tinted in the shadow of its banks, purled at the army's feet; and at night, when the stream had become of a sorrowful blackness, one could see across it the red, eye-like gleam of hostile camp-fires set in the low brown of distant hills.[19]

At the beginning of "King Pellam's Launde" three things are happening: night is being replaced by the uncertain shifting light of a foggy dawn, consciousness returns to the soldiers after sleep, and (reflecting both) the syntax gropes toward its meaning while still encumbered by obscurity. (I'll wager that Auden learned from this in his poem "Prime".)

> Stealthy, imperceptibly stript back, thinning
> night wraps
> unshrouding, unsheafing--
> and insubstantial barriers dissolve. (*IP*, 59)

Are you lost? The reading eye seizes upon "wraps" as a verb to organize a sentence, but is frustrated; "wraps" must then be a noun and the object of a lurking, unexpressed subject and verb. In plain discourse what is said is that dawn has gradually stripped back and now thins the vesture ("wraps") by which night has concealed the world. Try it again, and proceed. As the passage continues, we soon come to realize that "she" is the earth and "he" the sun:

18. Edmund Blunden, *Undertones of War* (London: Cobden-Sanderson, 1928), p. 62; Adam Mickiewicz, *Pan Tadeusz*, tr. Kenneth Mackenzie (London: Dent, 1966), p. 206.
19. Stephen Crane, *The Red Badge of Courage*, ed. John T. Winterich (London: Folio Society, 1951), p. 27, also p. 104.

Stealthy, imperceptibly stript back, thinning
night wraps
unshrouding, unsheafing--
and insubstantial barriers dissolve.
This blind night-negative yields uncertain flux.
At your wrist the phosphorescent dial describes the equal seconds.
  The flux yields up a measurable body; bleached forms emerge and
stand.
  Where their faces turned, grey wealed earth bared almost of last
clung weeds of night-weft--
              behind them the stars still shined.
  Her fractured contours dun where soon his ray would show more clear
her dereliction.
  Already before him low atmospheres harbingered his bright
influence.
  The filtering irradiance spread, you could begin to know that thing
from this; this nearer from that away over. (*IP*, 59)

The men awake, and then, with clearer words of command,
comes the bright December sun:

Keep on that fire-step.
Keep a sharp look out.
Sights down--watch the wire.
Keep your eyes skinned--it's a likely morning.
  Behind them, beyond the brumous piling the last stars paled and
twinkled fitfully, then faded altogether; knowing the mastery and
their visitation; this beautiful one, his cloud garments dyed, ruddy-
flecked, fleecy stoled; the bright healer, climbing certainly the exact
degrees to his meridian. (*IP*, 61-62)

Many of the incidental devices we have been noticing are
exemplified here--mixture of tenses, the use of the second
person, "shined" for "shone." Invertebrate, ambiguous and
shifty at the beginning, the return of consciousness (with its
accompanying word of command and discourse) reopens the
book of creatures--earth and sun and clouds--and the book of
the Word to the discerning--"garments dyed," "bright healer."

  The conclusion of the section, from stand-down to
midnight, contrasts markedly with this beginning. To the
registering mind at the end of the long day, fully awake and
lucid though dog-tired, the world impinges in a series of
discrete one-sentence paragraphs. It ends thus:

The N.C.O. at the Gas Post looked to his apparatus, and placed in a
convenient sequence his ready rocket-gear.
But it peters out; and with the lull they speak to each other.
The sentries stand more erect.
They whistle, softly.
Solitary star-shells toss as the dark deepens.
Mr. Prys-Picton's patrol came in, well before midnight. (*IP*, 99)

  The immediate readability of *In Parenthesis*, as the
many readers who have persevered all attest, is impeded

because it does not deliver the expected and does deliver a great deal more; its re-readability is vastly greater than most war books. If one's initial impression is that David Jones' style is "a bit thick," one returns to the other war writers, especially the very loud ones, and finds many of them "a bit thin." The narrative line depends in large measure on expectation fulfilled, but the style in sharp contrast uses impediment, roughening, foreshortening, whereby the reader is put in the thick of things, a bombardment or an attrition of impressions. The surface of the writing often seethes with business. Depth, recession, coherence are given partly by the known narrative line, partly by an intricate technique of allusion, partly by the interplay of voices.[20] Not that any page of *In Parenthesis*, except a few ironically intended passages, is a "bombast circumstance horribly stuff'd with epithets of war." Nor can it be called a "formalistic" piece of writing, as being simply a compendium of distorting devices, for in it only such devices are deployed as are necessary for the achievement of ends; and not all these devices are explosive, there being a great deal of needed silence in the margins. David Jones' tact, his desire to be understood, and his theology of the Logos, put a limit to syntactical license.[21]

Here I insert an observation that may seem more of a digression than it really is. David Jones' second piece of imaginative writing, *The Anathemata*, I have described, tentatively, as "an epic in the interrogative mood"; the constant succession of questions (together with the alternation of verse and prose that it shares with *In Parenthesis*) is perhaps the most characteristic feature of its style. It is genuinely, ingenuously interrogative, with no flavor of the rhetorical question. When Milton asks "Who first seduc'd them to that foul revolt?" he answers explicitly and right away; there is nothing like that in David Jones. If one returns to *In Parenthesis* from *The Anathemata* (perhaps

---

20. This discussion might well be carried much further: *In Parenthesis* could be read aloud and its oral qualities observed, using the features of linguistic description outlined by David Crystal and Derek Davy in their *Investigating English Style* (London: Longman, 1969), p. 39, where they list the categories of pitch, range, loudness, speed, rhythmicality, tension, and paralinguistic features. Having taken part in several readings in the classroom and outside, I can attest that *In Parenthesis* reads aloud remarkably well.

21. David Crystal, *Linguistics* (Pelican, 1971), p. 51: Plato's "conception of speech (*logos*) as being basically composed of the logically determined categories of noun and verb (the thing predicated and its predicator) produced a dichotomous sentence-analysis which has fathered most grammatical analysis since, whether the parentage has been acknowledged or not." This being fully as true of the Thomistic philosophy to which David Jones assented, a tension is undoubtedly generated: friends of similar convictions to his were disturbed by the fact that *In Parenthesis* was "not written in sentences."

only if one takes that route), one notices the beginnings of this questioning, wondering, cast of discourse. It is a barrage of questions--a quiet barrage, as David Jones the painter is a *fauve* but a gentle *fauve*: it is a wonderfully open and receptive book, comparable in this to *Undertones of War* and *Her Privates We*, because it does not assert or accuse or threaten or warn or preach.

David Jones told me as he told many of his friends that one night as a very small child he heard a strange sound in the street and remembers getting out of bed and peeking through the slats of a venetian blind and seeing a most marvelous sight--a parade of mounted soldiers, the City Imperial Volunteers recruiting for the South African War. He wondered if they were messengers from another world and, if so, could he join them, but his mother came and firmly sent him back to bed. He didn't quite ask if they were angels but just asked what they were, receiving the unconsciously ironic answer, "You'll know soon enough."[22] The echoes and contrasts with the story of the child Peredur in *The Mabinogion*, the Welsh version of the Parsifal story, are eerie, as if David Jones were living a life of allegory. "22579 Jones Walter David, trade or calling, art student" was as a soldier, by his own humorously exaggerated account, "grotesquely incompetent, a knocker-over of piles, a parade's despair" (*IP*, xv) and so was John Ball, the central figure of *In Parenthesis*; but John Ball's farcical character is only a passing incident, and his real role is to keep asking, in his land of enchantment, a liberating question. When David Jones was confirmed as a Roman Catholic in 1921, he took, as is customary, a second Christian name and chose that of the warrior archangel Michael. Thereafter he had the strength to ask, as he could not before, the grail-question that pervades his book--in the words of St. James the Apostle, "Whence come wars and whence come fightings?" Suffused through the book is the answer: it is "because ye ask amiss"[23] that "in one another you will hate your own flesh" (*IP*, 121).

22. See *The Long Conversation* (London: Oxford University Press, 1981), p. 121. Robert Graves' mother "kept off the subject of war as much as possible; she always had difficulty in explaining to us how it was that God permitted wars." *Good-bye to All That* (London: Cape, 1929), p. 53.
23. James 4:1-3, Authorized Version.

NEIL CORCORAN

SPILLED BITTERNESS: IN PARENTHESIS
IN HISTORY

When David Jones published, as an addendum or coda to *The Sleeping Lord* in 1974, a fragment of his never-completed long poem, *The Book of Balaam's Ass*, he defined it as "a link of sorts between the two widely separated books: *In Parenthesis* and *The Anathemata*" (*SL*, 97). *Balaam's Ass* was actually begun, he tells us, during the period (1934-7) in which the completion and publication of *In Parenthesis* was delayed by "illness"; and, like the earlier work, it takes as (at least part of) its material Jones' experience during the First World War. The fragment he chose to publish just before his death contains a remarkable passage which has never, so far as I know, been particularly noticed:

> Tilly-vally Mr Pistol that's a petty tale of y'r Gallia wars. Gauffer it well and troupe it fine, pad it out to impressive proportions, grace it from the ancients. Gee! I do like a bloody lie turned gallantly romantical, fantastical, glossed by the old gang from the foundations of the world. Press every allusion into your Ambrosian racket, ransack the sacred canon and have by heart the sweet Tudor magician, gather your sanctions and weave your allegories, roseate your lenses, serve up the bitter dregs in silver-gilt, bless it before and behind and swamp it with baptismal and continual dew.
> No, Livinia, won't wash, and that you know well enough. To adopt the initial formula, 'Ladies and gentlemen, I will remove the hat.' You will observe the golden lily-flowers powdered to drape a million and a half disembowelled yeanlings.
> There's a sight for you that is in our genuine European tradition.
> Lime-wash over the tar-brush?
> No, but rather, cistern the waters of Camelot to lave your lousy linen. The salient is Broceliande, these twain indeed are one. (*SL*, 99-100)

Perhaps because of the unfinished and, presumably, unrevised state of the fragment, it is impossible to say who is "speaking" here: does that "Gee!," for instance, suggest an American voice, and therefore that "Cook's tourist to the Devastated Areas" envisaged at the end of *In Parenthesis*?

The passage seems to irrupt more or less of its own accord
into a text apparently reporting conversations about the
experience of war, and it is impossible to decide what kinds
of irony may eventually have been made to play over these
lines. As they stand, however, it is at least possible to regard
them as something quite extraordinary: as a savagely hostile
criticism of the procedures of *In Parenthesis* composed by
the author himself prior to the work's completion.

The "petty tale" described here is, after all, graced
from the same ancients as *In Parenthesis*: the "sacred
canon" of bible and liturgy; Shakespeare, and particularly
Henry V, with its "Mr Pistol"; the Arthurian material of
Malory and the Mabinogion, which may be thought to wash
the war's dirty linen in the "waters of Camelot," to identify
the Ypres salient with Merlin's forest of Broceliande.[1] The
passage knows that this "gracing" with literary and mythological referents and allusions is not morally or ideologi-
cally neutral. Morally, the procedure may be a "gauffering"
or "trouping" of an unbearably squalid and hideous reality.
"Gauffer," a variant of "goffer," is a technical term from
dressmaking (where it means to flute, crimp or frill) or from
bookbinding (where it means to "emboss or impress with
ornamental figures"). "Troupe," not in *O.E.D.* as a verb, is, I
imagine, a Jonesian mis-spelling or variant of "trope"
(neologized into a verb) which along with its customary
rhetorical sense of figurative language has also a liturgical
sense--"a phrase, sentence or verse introduced as an embellishment into some part of the text of the mass or the bre-
viary office that is sung by the choir."

Fluting, crimping, frilling, embossing, impressing,
figuring, embellishing; and, of course, padding, gracing, turning romantical and fantastical, pressing with allusions,
weaving with allegories, roseating, serving in silver-gilt,
blessing and swamping with baptismal dew: a formidable
array of ways in which a "bloody lie" might be told about
the First World War. This is a bloody lie which "won't wash,"
however, not even in the waters of Camelot: when the
magician's fluted hat is removed the gilded lilies cannot
hide "a million and a half disembowelled yeanlings." And it
is this sight, not the mythical embellishment, which is, as
the passage scathingly and rebukingly puts it, "in our genuine European tradition." "Tradition" there is stripped of its

---

1. I am unsure whether "the sweet Tudor magician" is Malory or Shakespeare. If the
former, it is historically inaccurate, but Jones could be thinking rather of the period of
Malory's greatest influence, in the court of Henry VII, than of the period of his existence. If the latter, it seems inappropriate: Shakespeare is more than Prospero.

Eliotic grandeur, demythologized and demystified: the sentence implies that what is carried on and handed over in European art and sacred canon--in the Bible, in Malory and in Shakespeare--is, below the magic of the literary practice, the practice of disembowelling the young. It is a moment in David Jones which brings strikingly to mind Walter Benjamin's dictum that "There is no document of civilisation which is not at the same time a document of barbarism."

David Jones' apocalypticism during the thirties shares, of course, very little else in common with Benjamin's great Marxist gloom, and he was led by it, indeed, close to political alignments--"for however brief a time and in whatever wilderness"--which are inexcusable and disgusting. The apocalypticism is also, however, coterminous with his insight into the realities of power in his own historical moment or "epoch." In the essay "The Arthurian Legend" of 1948 he refers to the "convulsions and stress which have characterized fairly continuously the lives of all of us living today," and observes that these bring with them "a corresponding responsibility; for we cannot plead that the conditions are unfavourable to an understanding; we have been forced to live history as Tennyson's generation was not" (*E&A*, 205). The remark is made in the context of a discussion of the place of an historical myth in a "late" civilization, about which, with reference to the Arthurianism of Tennyson and Charles Williams, Jones is judiciously clear-eyed and sensitively discriminating. What he says there may usefully gloss the passage from *Balaam's Ass*, since it suggests the intimacy of Jones' understanding of the ways in which myth may be appropriated to serve a particular reading of history: he understands, that is to say (Barthesian long *avant la lettre*), the collusion between myth and power, how myth is an element of ideology.

In the *Balaam's Ass* passage the clearest witness to this understanding is also one of its points of greatest pressure: "I do like a bloody lie turned gallantly romantical, fantastical, glossed by the old gang from the foundations of the world." This is itself surprisingly and perhaps doubly allusive: the "bloody lie" may recall Wilfred Owen's Horatian lie that "Dulce et decorum est pro patria mori"; and the phrase "the old gang" is Auden's in one of his most apocalyptic and minatory early poems, the fourth section of "It was Easter as I walked in the public gardens" in his *Poems* (1930). What Auden calls "love" in that poem (a term coded partly for the Marxian future)

Needs death, death of the grain, our death,
Death of the old gang; would leave them
In sullen valley where is made no friend,
The old gang to be forgotten in the spring,
The hard bitch and the riding-master,
Stiff underground; deep in clear lake
The lolling bridegroom, beautiful, there.

The communist future--"beautiful, there"--needs death, is
dependent on the necessary murder of "the old gang," the
ruling classes who have, at present, the power. This is the
"gang" or the class which glosses the reality of war with the
ideology of myth in the passage from *Balaam's Ass*; and
the passage may therefore be read as an acknowledgement,
by the author himself, of the complicity of the allusive and
mythologizing strategies of *In Parenthesis* in the mainte-
nance of an English ruling class ideology.

I am aware of course that there are obvious objections to my own "gloss on the book" here; and I shall spell
them out. The passage could have been intended ultimately
to resonate with the most straightforward irony: the voice
speaking here could have been insensitively uncomprehend-
ing. If the "bloody lie" does bear any relation to Owen's old
lie, then it is likely to be a modifying relation, since a letter from Jones to René Hague explicitly says that had Owen
"survived to consider 'in tranquility' he *might* have hesitated
and seen that there was no 'old lie,' but something more
akin to Isaias' *non est species ei neque decor, et vidimus eum
et non erat aspectus*" (*DGC*, 246)--one of the biblical
inscriptions at the end of *In Parenthesis* which presumably
establishes an analogy between the suffering, or dying, soldier and Isaias' suffering servant, and thereby implies that
the historical agony of the War has some kind of redemptive meaning. Finally, when a critic, John H. Johnston,
writes approvingly of Jones' allusive procedures, maintaining that they constitute the epic achievement of an "heroic
vision," Jones describes this (in 1962, of course) as "the only
decent analysis of *I.P.* that's ever appeared" (*DGC*, 188).

These are indeed formidable obstacles to reading
the *Balaam's Ass* passage as in any sense Jones' own
account of *In Parenthesis*, and I have no intention in what
follows of appearing so naive or myopic. Nevertheless it is
quite remarkable that at such an early stage in the work's
history its author should display himself so articulately alert
to its potential to attract a particular kind of derogatory
criticism. The passage is certainly consonant, for instance,
with Paul Fussell's well-known account of the "honourable

miscarriage" of *In Parenthesis*: he considers it "a deeply
conservative work" which seeks "to rationalize and even to
validate the war by implying that it somehow recovers
many of the motifs and values of medieval chivalric
romance," but that it is saved from this intention by "the
vigor and pathos of its own brilliant details."[2] It would be
easy enough to show how Fussell's account of the poem is
insufficiently awake to its complexities, but it is revealing
how many of the best critics of the work have also felt
compelled to address a sensed tension between material and
manner, subject and procedure, experience and myth. I want
to look again at some of the "details" themselves, some of
those elements of the poem which may be thought to exist
independently of its mythical incorporations, since Fussell's
"deeply conservative" has always seemed wrong to me; and I
want what I say to be shadowed by the quotation from *The
Book of Balaam's Ass* which I have discussed here, and by
the interpretative issues it raises, since I shall return to it
and to them at the end of my essay.

* * *

I shall consider these elements of the text under three
aspects: its contemporaneity; its sexuality; its politics of
class.
        David Jones began *In Parenthesis* in 1928, and the
drafts of the work in the National Library of Wales give his
holograph original completion date as 18 August 1932.[3] The
intervention of "illness" (the first of his nervous breakdowns)
delayed completion--including the titling of parts and the
preface--until 1937. The poem was begun, therefore, thirteen
years after the experiences it describes (December 1915 to
July 1916) and completed twenty-two years after; and the
preface is explicit about the opportunity to recollect emotion in tranquillity: "I have attempted to appreciate some
things, which, at the time of suffering, the flesh was too
weak to appraise" (*IP*, x). Much of the critical writing
about *In Parenthesis* has, correctly, emphasized the way
this "appraisal" takes the form of allusive and mythical
integration; but there are also, I think, other more muted but
modifying forms of appraisal at work in the poem: it con-
fesses the selectivity, even the exclusiveness of its account,

2. See *The Great War and Modern Memory* (New York and London: Oxford University
Press, 1975), pp. 144-54.
3. I am grateful to the Research Fund of Sheffield University for a grant which
enabled me to visit the National Library of Wales at Aberystwyth.

and it offers itself or insinuates itself as an element of
intervention, even of propaganda, in the political life of
Britain in the thirties. It becomes thereby a contemporary
poem, a poem of the moment of its own publication--1937--
rather than a poem definable by the period (1915-16) which
it describes.

The admission of selectivity is of course clear in the
preface where Jones famously explains why he isolates the
period he does for the poem's chronology; but the text is
itself explicit towards its close:

> The memory lets escape what is over and above--
> as spilled bitterness, unmeasured, poured-out,
> and again drenched down--demoniac-pouring:
> who grins who pours to fill flood and super-flow insensately,
> pint-pot--from milliard-quart measure. (*IP*, 153)

This is the opening (after a biblical-liturgical epigraph) of
the great climactic Part 7 of the poem, in which the men
meet their deaths, and it seems to act as an almost decon-
structive index of the incapacity of this writing to convey
this reality. "This writing," we remember from the opening
words of the dedication, "is for my friends *in mind of* all
common & hidden men . . . and *to the memory of* those
with me in the covert . . . " (my italics); and yet Part 7
insists that "The memory lets escape what is over and
above": what constitutes this writing is only a fraction of
what constituted the event, a "pint-pot" filled from a potentially "milliard-quart measure" (a "milliard" is a thousand
million). What is left over and above, as "super-flow," as
surplus, as the ungovernable and unmeasurable, as everything that puts its pressure on the text but is not itself text,
is "spilled bitterness." "Spilled" there draws its richness and
its terror from an intimately apprehended etymology: only a
page or two further into the poem and there is "No one to
care there for Aneirin Lewis spilled there." This deathly bitterness is the demon ("demoniac-pouring") which the text's
strategies of suasion and control attempt to discipline but
which (deconstructively) erupts here as gremlin, goblin, gar-
goyle. The lines therefore also throw attention onto the act
of making itself, onto the perilously fragmented individual
memory which is the poem's sole authority, and onto the
particular process of imaginative reconstruction (for
Mnemosyne is the mother of the muses) which is its behavior. This seems to me a significant and saving lapse from
the assumptions of impersonality and "troupe" which the
poem's allusions have been thought to make: *In Parenthesis*
acknowledges here that its material is not the War but a

War, one man's war, and only a part of that, and only what
he can remember of it years later as he tries to make sense
of it in a fractured and difficult life.

What the poem also articulates as appraisal, however, is the desire for peace between English and Germans.
In the England of 1937, when "peace" was likely to undergo
a sullying slippage into "appeasement," this was not, unfortunately, a neutral or innocent desire. The final images of
In Parenthesis are images of an Anglo-German fraternity
in death: interleaved and awarded their prizes without distinction of nationality, Emil lies down with Fatty, Balder
and Ulrich with Lillywhite and Billy Crower, Hansel with
Gronwy. The near-finale is reinforced by the later pun
which invites John Ball to "Lie still under the oak / next to
Jerry / and Sergeant Jerry Coke" (*IP*, 187). These lines are
immensely appropriate and moving, and they are consonant
with the dedication to "the enemy front-fighters who shared
our pains against whom we found ourselves by misadventure," and they are consonant too with Jones' drawing of
1941, *Britannia and Germania Embracing*, which, provoked
by the bombing of Coventry, depicts a longed-for reconciliation between the two powers, envisaged as the "sisters two"
of the Coventry Carol, but nevertheless wearing the helmets
of British and German soldiers of the First (not the Second)
World War. These emblematic relationships clearly have
the force of yearning and desperation, feelings which perhaps cry out to be articulated at the end of a poem about
war; but they can too easily blanch out and sentimentalize
those political realities which, in the late thirties, so obviously divided England and Germany. There is plenty of
evidence--always disheartening and occasionally scan-
dalous--in Jones' letters and essays of the period of his lack
of appreciation of these realities, and the critic of the work
should not blanch out or sentimentalize this. In a letter of
24 September 1938 Chamberlain is extravagantly praised
("simply the real goods . . . the only bright spot") and on 11
April 1939 Jones tells his correspondent, "I sent my book to
Chamberlain and had a nice letter from him" (*DGC*, 88 &
92).[4] The final phase of Chamberlain's career clearly
seemed an appropriate point at which to send him *In
Parenthesis.*

4. Since writing this I have seen Thomas Dilworth's "David Jones and Fascism," *Journal
of Modern Literature*, 13:1 (March 1986), pp. 149-62, a revised and expanded version of
which appears in the present book. He publishes a fragment of Jones' letter to Chamberlain and discusses this and related matters. Mr. Dilworth lets Jones off more
lightly than I would, but I am grateful to him for sending me an offprint of his piece.

In the light of this contextual evidence, it is possible
to scrutinize again the word "misadventure" in the preface:
another war would, in the opinion of the writer of that preface, under whatever provocation, also be "misadventure." It
is also possible to read part of Dai's Boast more clearly:

> O Brân confound the counsel of the councillors, O blessèd head, hold the
> striplings from the narrow sea.
>   In the baized chamber confuse his tongue:
> that Lord Agravaine.
> He urges with repulsive lips, he counsels: he nets us into expedi-
> tionary war.
> O blessèd head hold the striplings from the narrow sea. (*IP*, 83)

This now invites an allegorical reading: the baized chamber
is the House of Commons; Agravaine is the representative of
those who urged a stronger line against Hitler (Churchill
himself?); the expeditionary war is the envisaged war in
Europe. My confidence in reading such an allegory is confirmed by discovering, in the National Library drafts, that an
earlier version of the preface ended with a reference to "the
disturbances which now threaten us" and an obliquely
phrased hope that "there remains a residue of formal goodness."

What I have done here is to derive an inherent contemporary politics from *In Parenthesis*; and, although the
politics is neither, in my view, credible or honorable (my
view and, of course, history's view), extrapolating it in this
way does plunge the poem back out of myth into history,
out of any replete permanence into the confusions of its
own moment. The poem's parentheses are not sealed off
from, but osmotic to, the claims of "epoch"; and *In Parenthesis* must be judged accordingly.

I want to turn now to an altogether more credible
and honorable aspect of the poem's behavior, what I have
already characterized as its sexuality. The original edition
of *In Parenthesis* opened with Jones' frontispiece drawing
of a soldier surrounded by the paraphernalia and detritus of
war. The soldier is helmeted and almost naked (one foot is
booted or socked, and one arm jacketed). His left arm is
bent outwards from his body, the open palm of his hand
warding off the military impedimenta around him. Standing
under a blasted tree which branches about his helmet, his
figure draws on the iconology of Crucifixion, and the image
has a great tenderness of isolate, unaccommodated vulnerability. This impression is most profoundly sustained by the
naked genitalia which are positioned just to the left of center, and are therefore made to seem the point around which

the contingent clutter of warfare revolves. They are encroached upon by a tangle of barbed wire; they are almost prepubescently tiny; and, in a drawing which has, of course, its non-realistic elements, they hurt the viewer with their sudden punctilious realism. It is difficult to say what I want to say next with tact, and since it has never, so far as I know, been said before, perhaps it is mere lack of taste to say it; but I cannot believe that it has never been thought. With this compelling image of vulnerable male genitalia in mind, the reader of *In Parenthesis* moves to the opening lines of a poem whose central character is named there as "Ball." "How very singular," Thomas Beecham said to a cellist with the name; and that David Jones intends the onomastic pun is confirmed by the extraordinarily unlikely name of the soldier who precedes Ball in the roll-call: "Private Leg." The body of this battalion has at least two of its members accounted for.

The pun here works in a Joycean or Rabelaisian way appropriate enough to the carnival element undermining the "silence of a high order" represented by Ball's late, improperly dressed coming-on-parade. This element brushes against the mood and tone of the poem's first allusion, which is also its first line: the opening name on the roll is "Wyatt," to whom the sergeant addresses his unlikely reference, "I'll stalk within yer chamber." Wyatt's "They flee from me" is one of the most tenderly erotic poems in the language: the sergeant's gruff threat disrupts its sexual intimacy, while at the same time reminding us that sexual intimacy is what happens in this "chamber":

They flee from me that sometime did me seek
With naked foot stalking in my chamber.

The tommy of the frontispiece drawing also has a naked foot, and it is he who has stalked into the chamber of the reader's head before the opening of the poem. The Renaissance tenderness and the Rabelaisian indecorum are the poles of the erotic in *In Parenthesis*; established here at its opening, they remain its ambience. It is difficult to find the right word for this. "Homosexual" will not do, although the poem unperturbedly includes and is serenely unembarrassed by homosexuality ("lighterman with a Norway darling / from Greenland Stairs / and two lovers from Ebury Bridge, / Bates and Coldpepper / that men called the Lily-white boys" [*IP*, 160-1]), and will not do especially since we know in Wilfred Owen what a homosexual poetry of the War is like. And "homoerotic" seems weasel and forensic. Lacking a proper word, however, is not to lack the thing: happening between the vulnerable human nude of its opening and the Song of Songs citation of its epilogue ("This is my beloved and this is my friend"), *In Parenthesis*, if it is not a "war book," is a kind of love poem.

The preface is clear enough on the point, with its reference to "the intimate, continuing, domestic life of small contingents of men, within whose structure Roland could find, and, for a reasonable while, enjoy, his Oliver" (*IP*, ix) which sets, in the *Chanson de Roland*, the literary paradigm for the companionable, "intimate" relationships of the poem, for the poignance of its womenless, largely adolescent, death-directed sexuality. This is, first of all, a matter of casual reference and address: "O there couldn't be a colder place for my love to wander in"; "don't take on so Honey"; "me slumberin' lovelies"; "be a kind virgin"; "and Roland blows a kiss"; "Jonathan my lovely one"; and the constant litany of the affectionate "mate," "batty" and "china." It can veer from the solemn dignity of "These three loved each other" (139) to the suggestiveness of "He swayed his pelvis like a corner boy" (103) and the flirtatiousness of "Sergeant Charming's coming through your thorny slumbers, who bends over sweet Robin's rose cheek. / Morning sergeant--kiss me sergeant" (60).

This orientation of the work establishes a painful sense of the fragile, transient materiality of "this flesh": whatever implications of transcendence other elements of the poem's form may be thought to carry, *In Parenthesis* is informed by a desperate sense of loss. This is apparent in two of the poem's most striking passages about death, both of which link it to sexuality. The first links it also to that imagery of vegetation which supplies one of the poem's primary symbolic and mythical dimensions:

> from digged pits and chosen embushments
> they could quite easily train dark muzzles
> to fiery circuit
> and run with flame stabs to and fro among
> stammer a level traversing
> and get a woeful cross-section on
> stamen-twined and bruised pistilline
> steel-shorn of style and ovary
> leaf and blossoming
> with flora-spangled khaki pelvises
> and where rustling, where limbs thrust--
> from nurturing sun hidden,
> late-flowering dog-rose spray let fly like bowyer's ash,
> disturbed for the movement

for the pressing forward, bodies in the bower
where adolescence walks the shrieking wood. (*IP*, 170-1)

Those "limbs" cannot with certainty be classed as metonymic or literal: they would be the former if we could be sure their possessors were alive, the latter if we knew they were dead. The undecidability is the meaning of the passage: in this wood cherished, live limbs become discarded, dead objects; and the shifting perspective is located finally in the horrifying but restrained transferred epithet, "shrieking," of the climactic Dantean last line.

The way the whole poem has cherished the bodies of the young puts its pressure on these lines, and it is not only their "limbs" which are so poignantly evoked here. Those "flora-spangled khaki pelvises" are also in the enemy's sights, and the poem already knows what damage can be done there: several pages earlier "Wastebottom married a wife on his Draft-leave but the whinnying splinter razored diagonal and mess-tin fragments drove inward and toxined underwear" (*IP*, 157-8). The genitalia of the frontispiece drawing foreshadow these moments in the text which insist that the amatory, sexual and generative possibilities of these "yeanlings," any satisfactory bodily future, are all atrophied in this combat: "adolescence" is the sexual term of those who walk this wood. These lines beautifully, tactfully and obliquely figure this meaning in their vegetable correlative. This does not propose an analogy or offer a simile or metaphor; it simply holds the vegetation in a kind of suggestive apposition with the men--for it is, of course, the sexual and reproductive parts of the plants which are caught in the muzzle-fire, their most intimate and vulnerable parts.

The second passage is one of the best known in the poem:

> But sweet sister death has gone debauched today and stalks on this high ground with strumpet confidence, makes no coy veiling of her appetite but leers from you to me with all her parts discovered.
>
> By one and one the line gaps, where her fancy will--howsoever they may howl for their virginity
> she holds them--who impinge less on space.... (*IP*, 162)

Death is figured here as a hideous perversion of sexuality: it is whorish and incestuous, with its savagely parodistic-Franciscan sting. It also reverses the customary sexuality of a rape: here it is the much more powerful woman who rapes the man (or, more horribly, the men), and it is the men who howl for their virginity. The sexuality, in all of these respects, runs flagrantly counter to, is an appalling irruption

into, the established sexuality of the work: the female, whorish, incestuous and violent, confronts the male, fraternal and
affectionate. The woman of death is out of some Bosch
nightmare, and her "parts discovered" are the polar antithesis of those young discovered male parts in the frontispiece.
If this "sister" is subsumed ultimately in the poem by that
beneficent female presence and tutelary deity, the Queen of
the Woods, she is nevertheless crucially present as everything oppositional, antagonistic and other. The love poem
contained within the parentheses of the text encounters the
utterly alien of what is not "love": the material male virgin
body is "held" by what is not material and not male and not
virgin. The sexuality of *In Parenthesis* has conjured per-
suasively into presence what must always remain absent, but
what is the truest reality in a poem about war, death. And
the passage's final limping reductiveness--death as what
makes these bodies "impinge less on space"--has the stun of
recoil and incomprehension.

These moments of *In Parenthesis* seem to me not
deeply conservative at all, but subversive: they insist on
what will always remain outside any human effort of order
and control. "Subversive" also seems to me the correct word
for the poem's account of, and attitude to, class. All of
David Jones' poetry, and therefore his history, is written
from the perspective of the private soldier, not the officer,
from the perspective of the man who receives, not the man
who gives, the orders. The opening of *The Wall*, where
Jones' Roman soldiers also derive in part from the First
World War, defines the perspective and suggests the continuity:

> We don't know the ins and outs
> how should we? how could we?
> It's not for the likes of you and me to cogitate high policy or to guess
> the inscrutable economy of the pontifex
> from the circuit of the agger
> from the traverse of the wall.
> But you see a thing or two
> in our walk of life.... (*SL*, 10)

Lack of secure knowledge of the forces directly controlling
their lives (*In Parenthesis* is full of rumor), together with
what is nevertheless a kind of privileged insight, constitutes
the character of the lives Jones describes in the poem. The
men are the underdogs, the long-suffering, the put-upon, the
"doggo," the workers (*In Parenthesis* is a great poem about
work), "these other" of Part 5:

the rifle strength
the essential foot-mob, the platoon wallahs, the small men who permanently are with their sections, who have no qualifications, who look
out surprisedly from a confusion of gear, who endure all things....
(IP, 126)

These are, ultimately in the economy of the poem, the
"secret princes" of its final benediction. When, however, the
Queen of the Woods "speaks to them according to precedence" this is a precedence without precedent, cutting
across distinctions of class and rank. But it is immensely
significant that the issue of true rank should be the issue
with which the poem closes, since much of its matter is,
precisely, the fact of being "other ranks," and the tone in
which this matter is handled can be far from assuaging; it
can be sardonic and embittered. Jones' soldiers may "endure
all things," but his text does not; at specific points it appor-
tions blame: endurance becomes final retaliation.

In Part 4 the Staff officers appear from Whitehall,
viewed as an unimaginably remote Arcadian location.
"Starred, gold-faced, wreathed with silver-bay," they "talk
through interpreters" and are figured as angels of the
empyrean: "immaculate, bright-greaved ambassadors, to the
spirits in prison" (*IP*, 93). The polar opposition between
angel and prisoner is given a further binary, oppositional
figure in Part 7. Deriving, perhaps, from the implied politics of "talk through interpreters," the image comes in a
sudden, richly realized ironic epiphany about "talk":

Immediately behind where Private 25201 Ball pressed his body to the
earth and the white chalk womb to mother him,
        Colonel Dell presumed to welcome
some other, come out of the brumous morning
at leisure and well-dressed and all at ease
as thriving on the nitrous air.
Well Dell!
    and into it they slide ... of the admirable salads of Mrs. Curtis-
Smythe: they fall for her in Poona, and its worth one's while--but the
comrade close next you screamed so after the last salvo that it was
impossible to catch any more the burthen of this white-man talk.
(*IP*, 154-5)

That "white-man talk" makes the opposition between Dell
and Ball, commanding officer and private soldier, the opposition between colonizer and colonized. The officers "slide"
into their colonial niceties, and the verb is telling in its
conjuration of a smooth, well-oiled, efficient and impersonal social machine, as perfectly pivoted around its class
encodings as the double-barrel of Mrs. Curtis-Smythe's name
is pivoted around its hyphen. Assured, privileged and exclu-

sive, the "talk" glancingly registers a world of social (and
sexual) possibility utterly alien to Ball. What it audibly
excludes here is "the screams of the comrade close next
you." "Comrade" is as kind as it is in the Hopkins poem
which gives Part 3 its title: "March, kind comrade, abreast
him." It points up how much Dell's language refuses to
accommodate the manifest and ultimate reality of the
world into which it arrogantly intrudes. Which is to say that
it is what the text says it is, the language of the colonial.

The figures of angel and prisoner, colonizer and colonized, are accompanied elsewhere by that of industrial
worker and boss. In Part 4 "the bright reason" is hard to find:

> You know no more than do those hands who squirt cement till siren
> screams, who are indifferent that they rear an architect's folly; read
> in the press perhaps the grandeur of the scheme. (*IP*, 87)

The force of this lies, again, in what I think of as a waver-
ing metonymn. "Those hands who" and not "those hands
which," and therefore "hands" as a metonymn for "workmen";
but "hands who squirt cement," not "hands which," and therefore a sudden restoration to the casual and conventional
metonymn of its subversive force: the soldiers, like the
workmen, are reified as a function of a scheme which the
press might know about, but which they do not. The figure
is complemented by a paragraph in Part 6 which offers the
generalized alienation an epiphanic, non-heroic simile:

> As one long acquainted with misadventure whose life is ordered to
> discomfort, conscious of his soiled coat's original meanness of cut and
> the marks of his servitude, who stands shyly in a lighted Board-room,
> who notes their admirable tailoring and their laundered shirts; who
> looking down observes his cobbled feet defined against their piled
> floors, who is relieved and breathes more freely as the noiseless door
> glides to. He is on the kerb again in the world he knows about. (*IP*, 137)

The factory worker has become the small clerk here; but
the literal image of exclusion, which is all the more telling
for its being a grateful self-exclusion, compellingly annotates the givenness of the soldier's world.

The pressure of that givenness is ultimately released
into the poem's major instances of simple, unalloyed bitterness. There is the sudden, savage surrealist cadenza in which
Ball, in Part 6, imagines, when the War is lost as a result of
Staff ineptitude, a "*hara-kiri* parade by Whitehall Gate--
with royal Mary in her ermine stole and all the king's
horses, and the Chaplain General," at which "rows of Field-
Marshals . . . will / fall on their dress swords" (*IP*, 142).
There are the Brigadier and Aunty Bembridge, with their
"neat sartorial niceties down among the dead men" and

their rejecting language ("I say Calthrop, have a bite of this perfectly good chocolate"), intruding into a scene of infinite pathos and pity:

> But O Dear God and suffering Jesus
> why dont they bring water from a well
> rooty and bully for a man on live
> and mollifying oil poured in
> and hands to bind with gentleness. (*IP*, 173)

And there is, finally, the dreadful prophecy of what will happen, after the war, to the injured:

> Nothing is impossible nowadays my dear if only we can get the poor bleeder through the barrage and they take just as much trouble with the ordinary soldiers you know and essential-service academicians can match the natural hue and everything extraordinarily well.
>   Give them glass eyes to see
> and synthetic spare parts to walk in the Triumphs, without anyone feeling awkward and O, O, O, its a lovely war with poppies on the up-platform for a perpetual memorial of his body. (*IP*, 176)

The bitterness of that knows that they do not take just as much trouble with the ordinary soldier; and it is profitably glossed by a passage from a letter Jones wrote during the Second World War:

> Death, mutilation, deprivation of every sort comes with a singular disparity on the "rich" and "poor." The very nature of their fear is of a subtly different character.... That is really what this war is about, a good bit. (*DGC*, 107)

Alert to the defining marks of caste and class, David Jones' poetry writes history from the perspective of those usually excluded from it. "Who built Thebes with its seven gates?" asked Brecht: "Books say it was kings." The book of *In Parenthesis* witnesses that it was not kings; and the man who does not know this has not understood anything.

* * *

I want to return now to the passage from *Balaam's Ass* with which I began. What it seems to me to indicate is that during the composition of *In Parenthesis* David Jones was self-critically alert to the dangers of assuagement and order, of grace and baptism, which the mythical method might perform on the material of the First World War. What Seamus Heaney has called the "opulence of Jones' imagining"[5] was clearly deeply compelled and satisfied by the attractions of his recovered and recuperated mythical material,

---

5. See my own *The Song of Deeds* (Cardiff: University of Wales Press, 1982), p. 112.

and *In Parenthesis* is of course a poem gratefully allusive
to literature, liturgy and myth. The elements I have been
tracing here, however, which are elements of a kind of
heightened realism, persistently brush against the grain of
the myths of *In Parenthesis*, insisting on the attritions of
memory on which the imagination perilously depends, on
the terrible poignant materiality of the human body, and on
the imprisoning social and political circumstances which
impel subjected individuals to their deaths.

Fussell's "deeply conservative" will not serve for this;
and neither will it serve for the fact that the saving grace
of anxiety and insecurity feeds back into the poem's mythical material itself. John Barnard has excellently shown how
the use made of *Henry V* in the poem is a countervailing
one, a *Henry V* without the king, of which Bardolph, Nym
and Pistol ("the essential foot-mob"?) are the (subversive)
heroes.[6] I think a similar case could be made for the work's
incorporation of other literature: for that hard irony in
which Coleridge's albatross merges with John Ball's rifle, for
instance ("With you going blindly on all fours, it slews its
whole length, to hang at your bowed neck like the Mariner's
white oblation" [*IP*, 184]) or for the carnivalesque naming of
Part 7 from *The Hunting of the Snark*, a name in which we
must read through the snark's identification marks the five
wounds of Christ--a lack of decorum perhaps not inappropriate to its occasion, as an uncontrollable laugh may be not
inappropriate to a funeral. The most mythical moments of
the poem might also be said to, as it were, withhold full
assent from themselves. Dai's Boast is at best equivocal
about the tradition it invokes, since it implicates that tradition in a history of repression, treachery and cruelty. Dai
"was the spear in Balin's hand / that made waste King Pellam's land"; he "was the adder in the little bush / whose
hibernation-end / undid, / unmade victorious toil"; he was
one of those who crucified Christ, and is therefore ambiguously both necessary and culpable, prefiguring the soldiers
of *The Fatigue*. In the Queen of the Woods passage this Dai
is missing: "she can't find him anywhere" and cannot therefore give him the bough which would, presumably, allow
him passage to the other world. His absence (presumably
because he has been blown unrecognizably to pieces) obdu-
rately insists on what will always remain outside the
assuaging and emollient reconciliations of myth. Not being

---

6. See "The Murder of Falstaff, David Jones and the 'Disciplines of war' " in Wellek
and Ribeiro, eds., *Evidence in Literary Scholarship: Essays in Memory of James Marshall Osborn* (Oxford: Oxford University Press, 1979), pp. 13-27.

available in his material body, Dai is not available to
benediction: which may have been, for David Jones, good
Catholicism; which is, for the reader of *In Parenthesis*,
good realism, good morality, and, calling the operations of
myth into question, good literary criticism. And *In Parenthesis* ends not with the absolving and consolatory gesture,
but with the continuity of violence, not with the Queen of
the Woods, but with "these latest succours: / green Kim-
merii to bear up the war" (*IP*, 187)--new yeanlings for dis-
embowellment.

In Part 3 of *In Parenthesis* John Ball dozes while
marching and intermittently dreams of being back at art
school:

> Hurdles on jerks-course all hard-edged for inefficient will not obtain
> the prize ones, who beat the air; wooden donkeys for the shins of nervous
> newcomer to the crowded night-class, step over to get your place beside
> Mirita; it's a winding mile between hostile matter from the swing-
> door, in and out the easel forest in and out barging, all of 'em annoyed
> with the past-pushing with clumsy furniture. Stepping over Miss
> Weston's thrown about belongings. Across his night dream the
> nightmare awaking:
> Move on--get a move on--step over--up over. (*IP*, 32-3)

"Miss Weston" there is slyly knowing, in the way that naming in *In Parenthesis* can be (when there is a canceled
boxing match between "Mr. Hague" and "Taffy Hopkins," for
instance): since Jones' indebtedness for some of the mythical material of his poem is, of course, to Jessie Weston's
From Ritual to Romance. In Parenthesis therefore steps
over Miss Weston's thrown about belongings too: they are
part of the work's own "dream stuff" which can "juxtapose,
dovetail, web up, any number of concepts, and bovine lunar
tricks" (*IP*, 32). But always across the dream of *In Parenthesis*, its long "deep-sleep" dream of history and pre-history,
of myth and liturgy and literature, comes the nightmare
awaking to unaccommodated and irreducible human fact.
In Parenthesis is a poem, a great poem, in which the First
World War dreams itself newly, terrifyingly and pitifully
awake as personal and historical nightmare.

VINCENT SHERRY

THE INELUCTIBLE MONOLOGUALITY
OF THE HEROIC

David Jones' *In Parenthesis* was hailed by T. S. Eliot as a
"work of genius," as "literary art that uses the language in a
new way."[1] What indeed impresses one about the work is its
extraordinary verbal texture, the extreme variety and particularity of its poetic voices. Perhaps most distinctive is
the one lengthy passage of sustained single voice, the
"Boast" of the infantryman "Dai Greatcoat" (*IP*, 79-84).
Occurring as the middle part of the middle section, the
heroic Boast is of central importance to the war book. It is
also the focal point of that widely working traditional
imagination which Eliot likewise praised in Jones (*IP*,
viii). Dai's set of adventures includes the major conflicts of
Western history, legend, and myth: Cain's murder of Abel,
the battles of the biblical and classical worlds, the heroic
era of Arthurian Britain, the Roman guard at the crucifixion
of Christ. Ultimately, one feels, Dai speaks as a kind of
Universal Soldier, viewing life through the metaphor of war
and managing to condense aeons of human experience into
his own timeless present.

This literary journey has its precedent in the Boasts
of the Welsh bard Taliessin and the Old English poet *Widsith* "Far-Traveler," models acknowledged in one of Jones'
own expository notes (*IP*, 207, n.37). Thirty-four pages of
such annotation demonstrate Jones' formidable rooting in
the heroic literature of other ages: *Y Gododdin, Le Morte
d'Arthur, Le Chanson de Roland*. Despite these well developed medieval interests, however, Jones, like his friend
Eliot, held strongly to the idea that an artist be of his own
time and place.[2] And he succeeds in restoring the ancient
form of the heroic Boast by adapting to his modern purpose

---

1. Eliot's remark appears in his "Note of Introduction" to the 1963 edition (*IP*, vi).
2. The problems and tasks of the historical imagination urged themselves increasingly
on Jones during his career. See his statements on a required "nowness" in the Preface
to *The Anathemata* (15, 24).

the special methods and effects of the modern dramatic monologue.

The traditional Boast occurs in a semi-theatrical setting, and its speaker resembles the dramatic, combative character of several other, equally antique literary forms: the flyting and the riddle. These modes appear as influences in Dai's Boast, and together will suggest some specific points of correspondence with the modern dramatic monologue. Once I have adduced the substance of this connection, I will apply and test it in an overview of the Boast. An active reading of its verbal and allusive complexities will then proceed through a close analysis of the character-in-voice, the speaker of a modern dramatic monologue, who provides the center and controlling consciousness of this fascinating central place.

I

The Boaster, "This Dai," emerges from a medley of soldiers' voices, who introduce as well one "Nobby Clark":

> Not the only bugger--there's Nobby Clark
> back at the Transport
> reckons he snobbed for 'em at Bloemfontein,
> reckons he's a Balaclava baby,
> reckons his old par drilled the rookies for
> bleedin' Oudenarde,
> reckons he'll simply fade away.
> They're a milintary house the Clarks...
> Vittoria Ramillies Namur,
> thet's the Nobby type o'
> battle-honour.

> This Dai adjusts his slipping shoulder straps, wraps close his misfit outsize greatcoat--he articulates his English with an alien care.
> My fathers were with the Black Prinse of Wales.... (*IP*, 78-79)

Nobby's exploits are recorded in the same style of formulaic repetition that prevails in the catalogues of the Boast ("reckon" originally means to itemize in a list). He stands as an alter-Boaster. Jones' casting this double for Dai follows upon his reading *Widsith*, the study by R. W. Chambers, who argues from several allusions in that poem that the scop would be paired with another poet while reciting in hall.[3] Jones also adapts this dramatic situation in a special way. He sets up the dramatic format of the flyting or poetic con-

---

3. Raymond W. Chambers, *Widsith: A Study in Old English Heroic Legend* (Cambridge: Cambridge University Press, 1912), p. 176. Jones cites Chambers' work, including his text and translation, p. 207, n. 37.

test; Dai squares his shoulders as though to confront this rivalling Nobby; the poetic altercation is certainly the appropriate form for the voluble mind and irascible speech of the agonistic character.[4] This agonistic temper is further highlighted by Dai's "misfit outsize greatcoat." This token of old combat is modelled on the hand-me-down coat of Dai de la Cote Male Taile in Malory's *Le Morte d'Arthur*, whose "over-garment," similarly, "sat over-thwartly"; when questioned by Arthur, he explains its martial record:

> I had a father, a noble knight, and as he rode a-hunting... there came a knight that... all to hewed him; and this same coat had my father on the same time; and that maketh this coat to sit so evil upon me, for the strokes be on it as I found it, and never shall be amended for me. Thus to have my father's death in remembrance I wear this coat till I be revenged.[5]

The modern Dai's opening words, "My fathers," clearly evoke his namesake's duty of memory and revenge. His agonistic nerve, equally, touches his whole imaginative act of historical memory.

Such a quarrelsome poetic contestant is commonly regarded as a descendant of the ancient Norse, Welsh, and Anglo-Saxon riddlers: the riddler's taunting of his audience matches the challenge in the poets' duel. Further, the dramatic riddle expresses strife both formally and substantively: the antagonistic game with the listener and the clashing opposites in the imagery (often portraying seasons at war in the annual cycle) show conflict as the formative principle of the riddle.[6]

Dai, too, aims riddles at his reader, and, as is usually the case, the speaker is the subject. Recurring throughout the Boast, these enigmas of the soldier's character are a major source of unity in it. Each is projected as though teasing, "What am I?":

a)   I was the spear in Balin's hand
      that made waste King Pellam's land

b)   I the fox-run fire
      consuming in the wheat-lands

---

4. The flyting and its descent from the ancient agon are discussed by W. Mackay Mackenzie, ed., *The Poems of William Dunbar* (1932; rpt. London: Faber, 1950), p. xxxii. An allusion to Dunbar's marriage song, *In Honour of the City of London*, occurs midway in the Boast (*IP*, pp. 81, 209, n. J).
5. Sir Thomas Malory, *Le Morte d'Arthur*, intro. Sir John Rhys (Everyman's Library, Nos. 45 & 46, 2 vols., 1906; rpt. London: Dent, 1972), 1, IX, i. Subsequent references will be given in the essay. I cite the volume in arabic numerals, the book and chapter in the roman numerals of this edition (used by Jones).
6. The agonistic vision of nature in the typical folk-riddle is summarized by Frederick Tupper, Jr., ed., *The Riddles of the Exeter Book* (Boston: Ginn, 1910), p. xv. He also lists many versions of the agonistic taunt and risk-taking, p. xix.

c)   And I the south air, tossed from high projections

d)   I the adder in the little bush
     whose hibernation-end
     undid,
     unmade victorious toil

e)   I am the Single Horn thrusting.... (*IP*, 79-84)

Dai, having entered the poetic altercation, turns from the contestant Nobby and confronts us in equally dramatic form, challenging us with his riddle and involving us in the problem of his agonistic character. We find now the rhetorical situation of the dramatic monologue: an implied exchange between the dramatic speaker and the listener.

The connection between the modern dramatic monologue and the ancient riddle will find its content and depth once we consider the moral element in Dai's puzzles. Although the riddles of, say, the Tarot or the I Ching always supply provocative imagery, we would rarely find a moral ingredient in the problem. But to recognize it here we need only consider the conventional representation of the soldier in the Great War: the figure of the passive and innocent victim that recurs in the lyric poetry.[7] Dai disguises himself as an unmotivated object or instinctual animal; he confounds our ideas of human agency and passivity in war; this paradox of active passivity performs a sharp twist on the vision of soldier as passive victim. Dai converts that conventional moralistic sentiment into a moral riddle.

The importance of such moral ambiguity in the modern dramatic monologue has been established convincingly by Robert Langbaum, in *The Poetry of Experience: The Dramatic Monologue in Modern Literary Tradition*.[8] Indeed, the "impossible moral case" forms the basis of his now classic argument concerning the effects of the genre. Moral paradox frustrates an attempt to classify the speaker. Forced to set aside such moral categories and "external" systems of judgment, we must, instead, project ourselves sympathetically into the speaker to grasp the meaning of the poem. Likewise in Dai's Boast. The sympathetic response to the speaker of the dramatic monologue is required to penetrate and solve the insistent riddle of the soldier's state.

7. The best appraisal of this conventional lyric sentiment of the passive victim is made by John H. Johnston, *English Poetry of the First World War: A Study in the Evolution of Lyric and Narrative Form* (Princeton: Princeton University Press, 1964), pp. 15-16.
8. Robert Langbaum, *The Poetry of Experience: The Dramatic Monologue in Modern Literary Tradition* (1957; rpt. New York: Norton, 1971), passim. See esp. pp. 192-99, where Langbaum treats the initial moral ambiguities of Browning's *Childe Roland to the Dark Tower Came*.

Dai Jones, certainly an adept of intertextual sleight of hand, adapts his allusive techniques perfectly in fashioning these puzzles. Dai voices many of his riddles in literary allusions and so hides the answer from view. Our primary assumption, then, is that these allusions are fully intentional (the author has given us suggestive notes) and, further, consciously and poetically shaped in this text; our method will be close scrutiny of this active intertextuality.[9]

It is also important to realize at the outset that answers to riddles can be either simple or sophisticated.[10] The solution can be a concrete object; or the answer can be an abstract philosophical or religious idea, which may explain the puzzling imagery. Conceptual solutions of this kind occur in context for Dai's first and last riddles, important points in the structure of the Boast and, as such, suited for an overview and for a test of our formula of sympathetic response.

Here is riddle (a) in the context of the opening passage:

> My fathers were with the Black Prinse of Wales
> at the passion of
> the blind Bohemian king....
> I was the spear in Balin's hand
>   that made waste King Pellam's land. (*IP*, 79)

Dai first refers to the battle fought at Crécy by Edward the Black Prince;[11] he then identifies himself with the spear used by Balin in *Le Morte d'Arthur* (1, II, xv-xvi) to wound King Pellam, to devastate his domain and to leave him awaiting the restoration of his lands and health (the typical narrative pattern of medieval Grail romances). Thus, from the panorama of the Crécy battle, Dai recalls the semi-legendary "blind Bohemian king," the defeated and nearly blind King John of Luxembourg, as a type of the maimed king in the romance. The restoration of the invalid king depends on a knight's asking the meaning of the

9. One of the strongest advocates of intentionality in literary significance is E. D. Hirsch, Jr., *Validity in Interpretation* (New Haven: Yale University Press, 1967). See pp. 51-57, where Hirsch develops the idea of "willed" significance to include both conscious and unconscious meanings, especially p. 52; "Will can extend into unknown and unnoticed regions as far as it likes, but it cannot relinquish its connection with that aspect of itself which is conscious." The opposing view was set out earlier by William K. Wimsatt, Jr., with Monroe C. Beardsley, "The Intentional Fallacy," in *The Verbal Icon: Studies in the Meaning of Poetry* (Louisville: University of Kentucky Press, 1954), pp. 3-18.
10. Riddles are divided along these lines into the simple folk-riddle and the sophisticated literary riddle by Arthur Taylor, *The Literary Riddle Before 1600* (Berkeley: University of California Press, 1948), p. 4.
11. The battle is described and the subsequent legends are recounted by John Cammidge, *The Black Prince: An Historical Pageant* (London: Eyre and Spottiswoode, 1943), pp. 69-70.

objects carried in the Grail Procession. This mysterious
procession itself is a type of riddle (witnessed again by its
frequent appearance below in Dai's enigmas). The answer to
this Grail riddle is the Eucharistic sacrament, which will
heal the king both spiritually and physically (*Le Morte
d'Arthur*: 2, XVII, xx-xxii).[12] Thus the word "passion" above,
besides recalling King John's valiant stand against superior
forces and the suffering of King Pellam, surely evokes
Christ's passion, reenacted in the eucharistic body and blood
of his death. This sacramental Grail, as cure for the crippled king and as answer to the Grail riddle, offers itself also
as the remedy for the old King John's agonistic suffering
and as the solution to the soldier's problem, too.

This answer is evoked and not claimed and is important as such. Patient intertextual analysis reveals a clear
and consistent solution to the problem, but we must *read in*
that answer. Our doing so depends on an act of intellectual
and emotional sympathy characteristic of the modern dramatic monologue.

This proof of this intricate artistry lies in its
repeated patterns, and the same themes and techniques and
effects occur again at the end of the Boast. The last riddle
(e) of the series pictures a Unicorn: "I am the Single Horn
thrusting / by night-stream margin / in Helyon" (*IP*, 84).
The imagery is drawn from the *Itinerarium Joannis de
Hese* (and is depicted in Jones' later etching *He frees the
waters*),[13] where the magical animal acts like the questing
knight in the Waste Land romances, attempting to purify the
deadly waters of Helyon. There the "venomous animals poi-
son that water at the setting sun, so that good animals cannot drink of it, but in the morning, after sunrise, comes the
Unicorn, and dips his horn into the stream, driving the
Venom from it, so that the good animals can drink there
during the day." This restoration is only partial, however,
and as such is related essentially to the agonistic character's
plight. The division into a nightly poisoning and a daily
cleansing matches that *Sturm und Drang* of seasonal
cycles which appears frequently in the imagery of riddles
and, as mentioned earlier, stands as a source for their deeply
agonistic structure. Dai thus seems to seal his Boast with

12. I refer to the later versions of the romances in Malory, whose Christianization of
folk-lore and of primitive ritual is taken by Jones to perfect this tradition. See his
essay "The Arthurian Legend," in *The Tablet*, 25 Dec. 1948, rpt. *E&A*, p. 203. For the
subsequent point concerning Christ's death and the Eucharistic sacrament, see Jones'
remarks in the Preface to *The Anathemata*, p. 37, and p. 37, n. 1.
13. The text is provided by Jones (*IP*, p. 210, n. N); his wood engraving is reproduced in
The Anathemata, facing p. 213.

the emblem of his soldiery, the signature of his problematic
state.

In the preceding episode, however, he hints at both
the solution for the riddle and the special method of
achieving it. Here he refers to the enigmatic procession of
Lance (and Cup and Dish) in the legend of the Grail, his
companion riddle. He gives the knight's task of asking the
question to "you." We as readers recognize ourselves being
addressed here, who are as well the audience for his riddles:

> You ought to ask: Why,
> what is this,
> what's the meaning of this.
> Because you don't ask,
> although the spear-shaft
> drips,
> there's neither steading--not a roof-tree. (*IP*, 84)

We, modern questers so to speak, ought to ask the meaning
of Dai's riddle, and to do so we must take his part: "you"
includes both speaker and reader. Responding to the speaker
of the dramatic monologue with this sympathetic identification, we may thus envision and apply the answer to his
problem. Here, as earlier, the answer is the vision of Christ's
saving sacramental life.

2

Following his allusion to the battle of Crécy, Dai refers to
several figures in the Old Testament, relives an episode in
the British campaign of Caesar's *Gallic Wars*, recalls the
heroic death of Roland at Roncesvalles, and presents the
legendary battles of Arthur in a detailed poetic catalogue.
Four of the lyric riddles of the soldier's character occur in
these lines. The concentration is in fact so dense that the
paradox of active passivity touches nearly all the material.
This problematic riddle can be solved, however, according
to the guidelines set earlier. By the end of this section, we
will see further connections between the riddle and the
Christian solution, through the methods of the dramatic
monologue.

In the first of the Old Testament episodes,

> I was with Abel when his brother found him,
> under the green tree (*IP*, 79),

Dai voices his riddle through a complex poetic allusion.
The tree image is taken from Malory's version of the murder (2, XVII, v). There, Eve takes a branch from the Garden-
tree which, when planted, grows to be white; she and Adam

beget Abel beneath it, whereupon it becomes green; when
Abel is slain beneath this green tree, it is stained red forever. The incident involving Dai thus occurs at the precise
moment of Cain's attack. The timing of the action all too
clearly points up the problem of the passive agent: being
"with Abel when his brother found him," should Dai stop
Cain's hand by force or let the murder occur?

    Following the intertextual pattern, however, the allu-
sion to Malory's version of the story also evokes a solution
to Dai's problem. Biblical typology customarily identifies
the first victim Abel with Christ, and the tree image here,
prophetic of Christ's cross, substantiates that connection.
The green tree of innocence and the tree of redemption
from sin discover a further correspondence.

    The liberty taken to achieve this religious vision is
the most complex and important part of our response. We
must set aside conventional religious morality--morality,
like his stance at the murder, being ambiguous--in order to
solve Dai's dilemma in the way we have found opened to
us. Once we cut across external systems and enter sympathetically into the character, we are free to see and to
employ the vision hidden within the images here. The sympathetic response of the modern dramatic monologue is the
condition of our finding the solution to the problem.

    A series of episodes unfolds rapidly in the following
lines, where Dai recounts battles of the medieval and biblical and classical eras and projects three riddles of passive
activity (a, b, c):

    I was the spear in Balin's hand
                    that made waste King Pellam's land.
    I took the smooth stones of the brook,
    I was with Saul
    playing before him.
    I saw him armed like Derfel Gatheren.
    I the fox-run fire
                    consuming in the wheat-lands;
    and in the standing wheat in Cantium made some attempt to form--
    (between dun August oaks their pied bodies darting) And I the south air,
    tossed from high projections by his Oliphant; (the arid marcher-
    slopes echoing--
    should they lose
    Clere Espaigne la bele). (*IP*, 79-80)

    After likening himself to Balin's spear, Dai high-
lights that riddle of passive agency in playing David.
Though he takes the brook-stones for his fight with Goliath,
he does not mention his acting to sling them, and his passiv-

ity in war is illustrated further in his role as harper-bard to the chieftain Saul (1 Samuel 17: 1-18, 30).

Dai then speaks as David the poet, praising his lord Saul arrayed for battle: "I saw him armed like Derfel Gatheren."

> *Derfel Gatheren. Derfel Gadarn*, 'Derfel the Mighty,' whose wonder-working effigy, mounted and in arms, stood in the church of Llanderfel in Merionethshire.... The Welsh ... maintained that Derfel's suffrages could fetch souls from their proper place. In the iconoclasm under T. Cromwell this image was used at Smithfield as fuel for the martyrdom of John Forest, the Greenwich Franciscan. The English made this rhyme of him:
>
> > 'Davy Derfel Gatheren
> > As sayeth the Welshmen
> > Brought him outlawes out of hell
> > Now is com with spear and shield
> > For to bren in Smithfield
> > For in Wales he may not dwell.'
>
> I quote from memory, and may be inaccurate, but it explains my use of the form 'Gatheren' in text. (*IP*, 207-8, n.B.)

Mark the emphasis here on the intercessory powers of the figure and the repetition of the fire motif: Jones' verse and expository note make an especially fine example of intertextual art. Thus the poet's renaming the figure as "Gatheren" represents the legend of Derfel's gathering souls from hell, a feat whose associations with Christ's legendary Harrowing of Hades is very strong and which, in conjunction with the fire of the friar's martyrdom, establishes the positive idea of delivery from the flames. Certainly the blaze here is designed to reflect the fire image, "I the fox-run fire / consuming in the wheat-lands," the riddle in which Dai, like the foxes firebranded and loosed by Samson (Judges 5: 4 ff.), is both an active instrument and a passive victim of destruction. The intertextual art of verse and note weaves together inextricably the riddle and the solution, the problem of the soldier's state and a suggested delivery. But the efficacy of the answer depends entirely on our desire to project it for the speaker. This scheme, as noted before, represents Jones' unique combination of the ancient riddle and the sympathetic response of the modern dramatic monologue.

Similar imagery prompts the same response in the prose paragraph which follows, where Dai adapts Caesar's account of his expedition into Cantium (Kent) in the *Gallic Wars*. There the seventh legion, lured out of camp to cut a

field of wheat, is ambushed by the local tribe of Britons.[14]
The soldier, seen in the biblical wheat-fields as "the fox-run
fire consuming," now in his volatile fear threatens "the
standing wheat in Cantium." Although his "attempt to form"
might counter the destruction of rampaging flame, his
endeavor is purely intentional and incomplete; as such, it is
compelling and important. The reader must again take the
speaker's part and complete the task through an act of
imaginative sympathy--and Jones again provides us with the
material to do so. We may fulfill that "attempt to form" by
envisioning for him the formed "steading" and stable "roof-
tree," images seen in our overview as the goal of his quest
and as the solution to his problem, remedies depending
likewise on our act of sympathetic projection.

This idea of sympathetic completion deserves special stress, since the speaker's helplessness is central to the
whole dilemma of passive agency. "I the south air, tossed,"
an image derived from the horn call sounded by Roland
before his death at Roncesvalles, expresses the problem
quintessentially. The riddle presents Dai as helpless as air
tossed from that trumpet. Further, to the horn blast he adds
the phrase "should they lose . . .," spoken by the Moor Blancandrin at the opening of the geste to instigate this treachery on Roland.[15] Dai undercuts the heroic trumpet call by
impersonating that insidious speech and calling up its disastrous consequences. Such wan fatalism epitomizes the
dilemma of the powerless speaker, who relies again and
again on our imaginative sympathy and support.

The opening suite in the Boast concludes as Jones
presents the legendary victories of King Arthur in the traditional catalogue of the Anglo-Latin chronicler Nennius.[16]
Preceding this list is an image drawn from Malory's account
of Arthur's last battle at Camlann. There, while Arthur and
Mordred are engaged in council for peace, an adder startles
a soldier who lifts his sword, alarms the enemy, and opens
the conflict in which Arthur dies (2, XXI, lv). Dai thus converts Nennius' list into a catalogue of loss, making himself
the cause in the riddling identification with that serpent:

> I the adder in the little bush
> whose hibernation-end

14. Caesar, *Gallic Wars*, Classic Interlinear Translations (1893; rpt. New York: David McKay, 1952), Book IV, ch. 32.
15. Blancandrin's speech is made in laisse 4 of *The Song of Roland*, trans. René Hague (London: Faber, 1937), p. 3. Hague, Jones' friend of many years, made this translation available to him before its publication.
16. Nennius, *History of the Britons*, trans. Rev. W. Gunn, in *Six Old English Chronicles*, ed. and trans. J. A. Giles (London: Bell and Daldy, 1848), pp. 408-09.

undid,
unmade victorious toil:
In ostium fluminis.
At the four actions in regione Linnuis
                    by the black waters.
At Bassas in the shallows.
At Cat Coit Celidon.
At Guinnion redoubt, where he carried the Image.
In urbe Legionis.
By the vallum Antonini, at the place of boundaries, at the toiling
estuary and strong flow called Tribruit.
By Agned mountain.
On Badon hill, where he bore the Tree. (*IP*, 80)

The "hibernation-end" is a significant addition to Malory's account of the snake. Reptiles tend to shed their skins just after emerging from hibernation; undoing his skin at his "hibernation-end," Dai thus "undid" the glories of Arthur. His action, however, is merely a passive compliance with the cycles of nature--a familiar riddle.

Posing the soldier's problem involved adding a preface to Nennius' catalogue, and solving it entails a change in the conclusion. To Nennius' account of the battle of Badon Hill, Dai adds the words "where he bore the Tree," taken from the Welsh *Annales Cambriae*, where Arthur's martial action is identified with Christ's carrying the cross (his shield probably bore a cross image).[17] The intertextual weave again reveals an answer to the riddle, providing for agon both the supreme example of Christ's passion and a potent symbol of spiritual transcendence. We may thus resolve Dai's dilemma, according to our pattern, by sympathetically reading in the positive image of Christ's redemptive suffering.

Now at the end of this section, we may see the special internal connection between Dai's riddle and the Christian solution. The idea of Christ's willing victimage solves the riddle of active passivity. Christ is indeed the analogue and archetype of the agent-victim Dai. Through an act of radical sympathy with the speaker of the dramatic monologue we can make this identification and read in the solution. Dai's account of his presence at Christ's passion--to be examined next--unmistakably tells us to do so.

17. This alternate account is quoted and its origins explained by Rhys, intro., *Le Morte d'Arthur*, 1, pp. xi-xii.

3

In the narrative of the crucifixion, Dai records his presence as passive witness: "I watched . . . I heard . . . I saw . . . I heard . . . I saw." "But," as he admits, "I held the tunics of these"--of the soldiers who drove in the nails. The riddle of the passive agent is both conspicuous and finely shaded in this episode; the problem and its answer will engage us at some length:

> I served Longinus that Dux bat-blind and bent;
> the Dandy Xth are my regiment;
> who diced
> Crown and Mud-hook
> under the Tree,
> whose Five Sufficient Blossoms
> yield for us.
>   I kept the boding raven
>   from the Dish.
> With my long pilum
> I beat the crow
> from that heavy bough.
>   But I held the tunics of these--
> I watched them work the terrible embroidery that He put on.
> I heard there, sighing for the Feet so shod.
> I saw cock-robin gain
>   his rosy breast.
> I heard Him cry:
>   *Apples ben ripe in my gardayne*
> I saw Him die. (*IP*, 83)

The witness' statements contain allusions to literature and legend stemming from the passion. Explaining their original significance will allow us to see their intrinsic significance in the Boast.

      Three images are taken from the medieval poem *Quia Amore Langueo* or "I for Love Languished," a lyrical version of the medieval allegory of divine and physical love. Christ speaks as a suitor and relates his passion and redemption to his listening lover. The image of his wounded hands, "embroidered" with blood like red trothing gloves (ll.43-45), is reflected in Dai's picture of the "terrible embroidery that He put on." The "Feet so shod" recall the shoes buckled on, like a lover's bond, with the piercing of his feet (ll.50-52). Dai at the end hears Christ invite his lover to the recovered Garden, proclaiming the redemption from sin:

> Fair love, let us go play!
> Apples ben ripe in my gardayne.
> I shall thee clothe in a new array. (ll.73-75)

Dai also alludes to the legend of "cock-robin": that bird "gained his rosy breast" when, attending Christ on the cross, he was sprinkled with his blood.[18]

The passage provides perhaps the most striking and important instance of intertextuality in the Boast. The first text is an experiential account of the historical event (see also the next paragraph below). However, Dai illustrates the meaning of this event, the redemption achieved by Christ's death, from secondary texts and from a perspective greatly distanced from the historical scene. The characteristic device of anachronism in the Boast, here in its most sustained and obvious form, makes clear that our sympathetic response to the speaker of the monologue is the intended effect. The second perspective is our cultural point of view as an audience; we take the speaker's part because he speaks our cultural language (the famous examples of this are the historical characters in Browning's and Pound's dramatic monologues).[19] We hold both the perspective and the material for solving Dai's problem, for reading his experience in terms of our cultural experience, thus supplying the meanings of redemption and spiritual transcendence.

Not surprisingly, cultural traditions of Dai's own time and martial station inform his view on the event, and yet in this milieu, too, he enacts the plight of soldiery. He views the crucifixion as a sacrifice to a pagan war-god, specifically to Odin, the northern Mars (Dai is true soldier of Rome's world-empire). The rites to Odin as war-god involved the hanging of captives as propitiatory meals for the raven, the war-god being embodied in the traditional beast of battle and called "the raven god," "the raven tempter," "the priest of the raven sacrifice."[20] Appearing in the Boast as "the boding raven," Odin would approach "the Dish" proffered to him. Dai, however, interrupts the consummation of this rite: "I kept the boding raven / from the Dish"--a problematic action. His inner debate about what he does is voiced in the antithetical arguing "But," in the following line, where the comma adds to the sense of hesitation. Why has the author devised this dilemma in the mind of his character?

18. *Quia Amore Langueo*, in *The Oxford Book of English Verse 1250-1900*, ed. Arthur Quiller-Couch (Oxford: Clarendon Press, 1904), pp. 53-59. The legend of cock-robin and its derivations are given in *Popular Superstitions*, ed. George Gomme, *The Gentlemen's Magazine Library*, vol. 3 (London: Eliot Stock, 1884), p. 210.
19. Langbaum, p. 94, makes the same point concerning anachronisms in the modern dramatic monologue.
20. E. O. G. Turville-Petre, *Myth and Religion of the North* (London: Weidenfeld and Nicolson, 1964), pp. 46, 48.

Like the problematic riddles met throughout the
Boast, the dilemma encountered in performing the pagan
rite prompts a sympathetic projection on our part, induces
our desire to read in the Christian mystery (evoked in the
next lines by the imagery of *Quia Amore Langueo*). There
is indeed a firm and specific precedent for our projecting
the Christian text onto the pagan context here. The northern martial rites were modelled on Odin's own mythical
sacrifice upon the world-tree Yggdrasil, which, as related in
the skaldic poem *The Havamal*, has traditionally invited
comparison with Christ's immolation. The axial beam of
the northern cosmos reflects the central tree of the Christian universe, while the phrase "myself to myself" has
always echoed the Christian conception of the second
divine person's sacrifice to the first:

> I know that I hung on a windswept tree for nine whole nights, wounded
> with a spear and given to Odin, myself to myself, on a tree about which
> no one knows the roots from which it springs.[21]

Another analogue, a probable source for this passage
and of the problem Dai experiences as a martial character
here, lies in the Old English poem on the passion, *The
Dream of the Rood*.[22] It is usually held that the poem has
two authors, though both speak as the personified Cross. The
first recounts the death and experiences what is, according
to the conventions of heroic poetry, an unsolvable paradox:
he is obliged as thane to serve his lord by assisting in his
death. However, the poet of the second part--probably a
Benedictine monk--takes the part of the venerated crucifix
and overcomes the Rood's dilemma of divided obligations
in the war-band. Speaking from the spiritual community of
a monastery, he envisions Christ his lord enthroned in heavenly glory and expresses trust in his personal salvation.

Dai articulates a problem, like that of the Rood-
thane, in the grammar of northern ritual-myth. And, like the
second speaker in the Old English poem, he represents the
salvation achieved by Christ's sacrifice: the fruit and blossom imagery from *Quia Amore Langueo*. But, unlike the

21. *The Havamal*, trans. D. E. Martin Clarke (Cambridge: Cambridge University Press,
1923), p. 179. Jones alludes earlier (*IP*, 67) to these same skaldic verses. When explaining
a reference in his later poem on Christ's passion, *The Fatigue* (*SL*, 32-33, n.7), he
employs the traditional Christian interpretation of the northern myth. This tradition
is also mentioned by Turville-Petre, p. 279.
22. *The Dream of the Rood*, in *The Vercelli Book*, ed. George Krapp, *The Anglo-Saxon
Poetic Records* (New York: Columbia University Press, 1932), II, pp. 61-65. Jones'
early knowledge of the poem is revealed in "The Roland Epic and Ourselves," *The
Tablet*, 24 Dec. 1938, rpt. *DG*, p. 98. My points on the poem's two speakers follow the
argument of John V. Fleming, "*The Dream of the Rood* and Anglo Saxon Monasticism,"
Traditio, 22 (1966), pp. 43-72.

beatified Rood and monastic author of the second part, Dai cannot maintain the character or the perspective to claim such spiritual meanings. Indeed, the last line, "I saw him die," which is taken from the nursery rhyme on cock-robin, is spoken there by the fly.[23] Only by sympathetic projection, an action which cuts across conventional religious personalities and any normative morality, may we reach the spiritual meaning and apply its significance to the speaker. This channel is opened to us clearly once we examine the recurring actions and themes here; indeed, the idea of unconditional acceptance will emerge as the religious substance of this passage and of the Boast as a whole.

Dai's keeping the raven from the Dish, besides disrupting the ritual, tempts us to ask his intention for doing so--that inward motive is the point that attracts our sympathetic projection (as earlier with Caesar at Cantium). Correspondingly, his own action seems to spring from a feeling of sympathy for the victim's plight. This sense of his action clarifies a double allusion here: related to the legend of cock-robin is the story of the cross-bill, who, trying to draw out one of the nails, gained his ruddy plumage from Christ's spattered blood.[24] Just as that attempt shares the sympathetic motive of Dai, Dai, like the bird, might partake of Christ's saving blood in an equally gratuitous way. Surely the gift-love of the passion is the central idea in *Quia Amore Langueo*: it stands out now as the most important theme in our passage, too. In responding sympathetically to the speaker of the dramatic monologue, we enact the meaning of the divine event for him. It is a gratuitous salvation for the dilemma of agon, achieved on all levels through profound acts of sympathy.

The Boast at the center of *In Parenthesis* may be considered now, in conclusion, to repeat and to perfect a prevalent method in the book. The leading experiential character, John Ball, speaks usually as "you," where the identification of speaker and reader in the pronoun includes that sympathetic identification essential to the modern dramatic monologue, and required, we may now say, to comprehend the full significance of the narrative experience. This method of response has led us repeatedly to the center of coherence in the Boast. Dai Jones' Boast includes things old and new, peripheral and central, parenthetical and major.

23. *The Oxford Dictionary of Nursery Rhymes*, ed. Iona and Peter Opie (1951; rpt. Oxford: Clarendon Press, 1962), pp. 130-31.
24. *Popular Superstitions*, p. 210.

N. K. SANDARS

THE PRESENT PAST IN THE ANATHEMATA *AND ROMAN POEMS*

When I was asked to write about David Jones from the point of view of his interest in the ancient world, I had not at all realized how difficult this was going to be. For an archaeologist, a student of ancient literatures, and one who loves language and has an inordinate admiration for the writings of David Jones, it should not surely be too difficult? After all archaeologists have found in David Jones *their* poet.

Stuart Piggott puts this very well in his *Agenda* article, when he says of David Jones that he "explores the deposits with the anxious care of a good excavator . . . the simple-seeming syllables . . . explode in a radiant and beneficent blast of highly charged meanings, associations and . . . correspondences" (*Agenda* 5, 1-3, 1967, p. 76). This is very true; but how in this is David Jones so different from all the other poets who write about our common past, for they are all doing it now?

There is of course David Jones' almost fanatical insistence on "getting it right." You have it in his drawings too: the artifacts, be it a ship's tackle, or suburban parlor furnishings, are real and understood in all their capabilities. So too in the writings. His use of the special terms of geology and archaeology is never pedantic because he is driven to use them by the necessity to understand and to show. Here is a passage from *The Anathemata*:

> Before the microgranites and the clay-bonded erratics wrenched from the diorites of Aldasa, or off the Goat Height in the firth-way, or from the Clota-sides or torn from either Dalriada, with what was harrowed-out *in via*, up, from the long drowned out-crops, under, coalesced and southed by the North Channel.
>   As though the sea itself were sea-borne
> and under weigh ... (A, 72-73)

What a marvelous description of the ice-sheet advancing from the polar regions.

And from *The Sleeping Lord*:

> Millenniums on millennia since
> this cold scoria dyked up molten
> when the sedimented, slowly layered strata
> (so great the slow heaped labour of their conditor
> the patient creature of water) said each to each other:
> 'There's no resisting here:
>   the Word is made Fire.' (*SL*, 72)

And men too, the "tundra-wanderers," "wearing the amulets
of ivory and signed with the life-giving ochre." The men of
the last glaciation did indeed cover their dead with life-
simulating red-ochre, and we have seen and handled the
"amulets of ivory."

In our lifetime the limits of the knowable world
have expanded through astronomy, physics, geology,
anthropology, and archaeology. This new, this larger and
infinitely more complicated world is intellectually known,
but hardly yet *felt* at all. Or if it is felt it is in its more
frightening and alienating aspects. Into this new territory
the feeling mass of human-kind is moving fast, and in the
forefront are the poets. Some have colonized the tiny world
of the microscope, some have sent spies into the great
galaxies and interstellar spaces; but more still are exploring
the language of anthropology and reconstructions of the
preliterate past.

This is right, this *is* our world; and just as soon as
scientific knowledge has apprehended new territory it is
proper that the poets should appropriate it; as long before
Schliemann, they appropriated Troy-Town; and Geoffrey's
Britain before General Pitt-Rivers and the scientific
archaeologists got at it. But now we have gone far beyond
those frontiers, and again I come back to this question. How
is it that David Jones is so different in his whole manner of
handling past time? And what is this difference that makes
prehistorians claim him as their particular poet, above other
poets, even where the subject-matter may be the same
distant past?

It might help to compare another contemporary
poet, and a very fine one, who has been much concerned
with the past. Robert Lowell in a volume called *History*
(1973) begins a long series of sonnet-length poems with the
same geological deposits as David Jones explores in *The
Anathemata*. The same dinosaurs sway onto the scene.
There is a poem called "Our Fathers":

> That cloud of witnesses has flown like nightdew
> leaving a bundle of debts to the widow and orphan--

the virus crawling on its belly like a blot,
an inch an aeon; the tyrannosaur,
first carnivore to stand on his two feet,
the neanderthal, first anthropoid to laugh--
we lack staying power, though we will to live.
Abel learned this falling among the jellied
creepers and morning-glories of the saurian sunset.
But was there some shining, grasping hand to guide
me when I breathed through gills, and walked on fins
through Eden, plucking the law of retribution from the tree?
Was the snake in the garden, an agent provocateur?
Is the Lord increased by desolation?

This is fine stuff but it is pretty frightening too. Between ourselves and this past there is a deep gulf and if "guiding hand" there is, there is nothing comforting about it. Another poem called "Northmen" has these lines:

These people were provincials with the wind
behind them, and a gently swelling birthrate,
scattering galleys and their thin crews
of pirates from Greenland to the lung of Thames ...
The Skyfleets hover coolly in mirage;
our bombers are clean-edged as Viking craft,
to pin the Third World to its burning house ...
Charlemagne loved his three R's, and feared the future
when he saw the first Northmen row out on the Rhine:
we are begotten in sorrow to die in joy--

How dazzling this is, making its points with wit and concentration, but am I wrong, I wonder, in feeling a touch of self-consciousness? Today and the past don't really cohere; these bombers don't really belong with the Viking craft. It's all so intellectual and we are spectators outside it and aloof. This is mankind's history, therefore *our* history; and we read it as mankind's representatives.

But David Jones takes this great heap of the past and tells it not as history, but as something we have experienced in our own flesh; it is closer to direct memory than anything else. Collected memories, recollected experience of things that once happened, either to ourselves, or our parents, half-forgotten stories of a mother or grandmother. It is his, and through him *our family* story that David Jones is writing down.

Other people have tried to do this with bits of the past, but who else would ever have conceived of doing it with the *prehistoric* past? In *The Anathemata* those terrifying distances, "the humid paradises of the Third Age" and "an older Great Cold . . . Before the drift was over the lime-face," (*A*, 65, 62, 68) are become at once local, colloquial and friendly, and somehow they cease to terrify

because they belong to the *family* story. Our forefathers of
40,000 years ago are treated with the same courtesy as the
"men of Bronze" in the Aegean a mere four thousand.

The tundra hunters on the glaciated plain where the
fineblown loess settled under the long arctic winds of the
last glaciation are also among those

> that follow the Lamb
> from the Quaternary dawn.
> Numbered among his flock
> that no man may number
> but whose works follow them. (A, 78)

The succession exists, unbeknownst:

> An aureole here
> for Europa's tundra-*beata*
> who of duck's bone had made her needle-case.
> And where the carboniferous floor
> yields from among the elk-bones and the breccia
> this separated one
> the data of whose cause is known alone to *him*. (*A*, 77)

The needle-case *was* made of duck's bone, and it is
necessary that we should know it, for the flights of duck
from the glacier-dammed lakes were the stuff of life, and
the needle meant clothes, safety from frost-bite in the near
arctic cold, the ability to hunt and to survive.

> Himself at the cave mouth
> the last of the father-figures
> to take the diriment stroke
> of the last gigantic leader of
> thick-felled cave-fauna?
> Whoever he was
> *Dona ei requiem*
> *sempiternam.* (*A*, 66)

Again this is true. There must have been just such a
moment when the incredible, last, three-yard-high, cave-
bear was killed at the cave mouth by some collateral of
ours.

David Jones' Dedications are always important. The
Dedication of *In Parenthesis* tells us that it was written for
his friends, his companions in the war, men of the Royal
Welch Fusiliers, and certain others, unnamed infantry, and
last the "enemy front-fighters who shared our pains." This
tells us a great deal about the whole writing; and the
dedication of *The Anathemata* also tells us something
important about that poem:

> *Parentibus meis et prioribus eorum et omnibus*
> *indigenis omnis candidae insulae Brittonum*
> *gentis.*

All the men of the islands of Britain, yes, but first his parents and those in line before *them*. Everything follows from this.

In this dedication the whole matter is collected together, or rather recollected: the parents, the forebears, and all the people of the island, and through his parents and grandparents, David had it all: the Welsh, the English, the Mediterranean, for all sorts of nations came to the Pool of London in the great days of the last century and the early ones of this; and all sorts of crafts were practiced, but especially ship-building and fitting-out. How he used this multiple inheritance he explains in a note to *The Anathemata*:

> I use these terms: *gens, Volk, cenedl* as symbols of the three elements which compose us. Together, these three elements, broadly speaking, compose 'the West': we are Germans, Latins, Celts and can apprehend only in a Latin, Germanic and Celtic fashion. *What* we so apprehend, lay hold of--sciences, principles, wisdoms, evangels from, e.g. Hellas at some remove, from Judaea at a greater remove--that is another matter.

He also continues with the warning:

> *Gentes* other from us, of other culture-groups, of other bloods and environments, have no doubt equally significant and warm images. But even if I knew and could pronounce those alien crucial-words, my list could not here extend beyond the three I have found myself using, because they serve sufficiently, within the context, to cover what is historically 'ours'. (*A*, 242)

It is the "warmth" of the images that is so revealing here, "large as life and twice as natural" as he says himself for that "simple person"

> ...reared up by Redriff mast-pond; swaddled, crawled and found my walking legs in a keel-haw, did know a sheaved block from a dead-eye before I were gunwhale high, knowed the lily i' the shipman's card before any water-boy made for to know me.
>
> Learned much of the dear God's created orbis from such as navigate and circumnavigate
>
> from tarpaulins and salts, clerks of nautics
> that thither from the known to the knowable
> and hither again to haven
> whose first premiss, main-stay and Last Gospel is: That the Lode be constant
>
> yet dealing much
> in the peregrinations of Venus.
> Much have I learned of them. (*A*, 135)

In a fragment of autobiography first published in *Agenda* and now collected in *The Dying Gaul* ("In illo tempore," *DG*, 19-29), David tells us about his maternal grandmother, with her Italian good looks, who married Eb

Bradshaw, the very English master mast and block-maker of
Prince's Stair, Rotherhithe, by the Pool of London: and when
he speaks through the Lady of the Pool, behind her
transformations, impersonations and figurations--territorial
goddess, Tutelar of the Place, the Virgin Mary, the seller of
lavenders--unnamed but nonetheless among them, is also
that maternal grandmother, Italian-looking, of Latin blood.
Again, David Jones, glancing back over his shoulder, saw his
forebears, certainly, "among the rising contours of the hills
and far beyond them in the morning light the misted
heights, now lost, now found, away to the fastnesses of
Gwynedd Uchaf . . ." as he describes his first sight of his
father's home in northeast Wales (*Poetry Wales*, 8, 3, 1972,
p. 8). But he also saw over his shoulder Rome, his *Flora
Dea*, and, at a "greater remove," Jerusalem and Troy Town;
the "warmth of the image" was because of the
acknowledgment of kindred,

> the living, dying, or dead traditions in which one has oneself
> participated or heard of with one's own ears from one's own parents or
> near relatives or immediate forebears. These things received in
> childhood are of course fragments or concomitants only of the whole
> above-mentioned complex. I am thinking only of the means whereby
> those concomitants and fragments reached me. I am speaking of
> channels only, but of immediate channels and such as condition all that
> passes through them, and which condition also one's subsequent
> attitude to all the rest. These I judge to be of the most primary
> importance. It is through them that 'all the rest' is already half
> sensed long before it is known. If ever it is known. You smell a rat or two
> pretty early on. (*A*, 40-41)

If it comes to smelling rats there is a case in point
in that same piece of autobiographical writing. In it he
tells the story of his memory, as a little boy, of hearing a
column of troopers clattering through the street outside his
bedroom to the sound of bugles.

> I suppose my first remembered thing was in 1900, or about 1900. I was
> tucked up in a cot next to my mother's bed, but an unfamiliar sound from
> the roadway outside impelled me to creep out as cautiously as I could
> and make for the window, to look between the slats of the venetian
> blinds; and what I saw and heard was a thing of great marvel--a troop of
> horse, moving in column to the *taratantara* of bugles. It was in fact a
> detachment of the City Imperial Volunteers on a recruitment ride
> through the outer suburbs, for the war in South Africa of which I was,
> as yet, in blissful ignorance. But to me, those mounted men were a sight
> of exceeding wonder, and I said to myself, 'Some day I shall ride on
> horseback,' a desire never to be realized, to my continued regret to this
> day. Anyway, I had but very brief joy of the equestrian column and the
> inimitable sound of steel-shod horse hooves, and the sight of white
> dust rising, and the metallic sound of bugles; though I thought I had
> been very careful, those damned venetian blind slats had evidently

betrayed me, for in an instant my mother appeared and without a word swiftly lifted me back to the cot, covering me with an extra blanket.

Then comes this conversation. His mother, having scolded young David with "Cot's best for you at this hour, now go to sleep," is quickly questioned.

'But mother, what are those men on those beautiful horses, and why did they blow those trumpets?'

'Go to sleep, you'll know soon enough, but for now be off to sleep.'

'But mother, are there Guardian Angels like Miss Best says, but which Daddy says can't be proved from the Bible, but that someone called Dr. Pusey got it from what he calls Papists?'

His mother was able to deal with that one too:

'Now goodnight and don't let me hear another sound, you understand?'

'Yes, mother.'

And he continues:

After her leaving me with the gentle command to sleep, I lay some time wondering who, in fact, were those strange horsemen .... Why had mother been so guarded in answer to my question about angels? Before I fell asleep I heard, much farther off, the bugles renewing *taratantara*, but from very far off indeed, and beneficent, I thought, as from a detachment of the heavenly armies--so they were angels after all. (*DG* 19, 20)

David then goes on to explain the roundabout and complex ways in which this childhood memory, long slept on, played itself through his life and later writings, particularly *In Parenthesis*; what he calls the "tricky" business of "sources" and "influences" with equally mysterious things said by a sister concerning *Luna Vatis* of Rome. All this is very much the way that the world's remembered childhood plays through *The Anathemata* and other writings.

I don't think it can be chance that in the same paragraph David refers to Peredur, for when he first read in the *Mabinogion* that particular story he must have smelt a sizable rat. His own question "But mother, what are those men on those beautiful horses, and why did they blow those trumpets?" and his mother's enigmatic reply, "Go to sleep, you'll know soon enough" echo, in a way that is quite peculiar to his own methods the *Mabinogion* conversation between Peredur and *his* mother. It is from the passage near the beginning which tells how after his father was killed, and six sons, his mother fled with him to the wilderness.

Never a one took she in her company, save women and boys, and meek
contented folk who were incapable of combat or wars. ... Never a one
would dare mention arms in a place where her son might over-hear, lest
he set his heart upon them. And every day the boy would go to the long
forest to play and to throw holly darts ... and one day they saw three
knights coming along a bridle-path beside the forest. ... "Mother",
said he, "What are those yonder?" "Angels, my son", said she. "I will
go as an angel along with them" said Peredur; and he came to the path to
meet the knights.[1]

And thereafter follows the whole story with its other
and more famous question. This passage was certainly in
David's mind when he wrote of Peredur near the end of *The
Anathemata*:

> His woodland play is done, he has seen the questing
> *milites*, he would be a *miles* too. (*A*, 225)

If there is any rightness in my suggestion that in
David's hands the earth's past is not so much impersonal
history as a personal shared memory, then I think it follows
that just as we ourselves, when we come to a certain
vantage point of years and begin to look *back* on our lives
rather than forward, generally, most of us, try to make sense
out of the muddle, the incoherent backwards and forwards of
it all, we try, probably quite futilely, to see some pattern, to
make out a direction. This, I think, is what David Jones did
with our common life of man-on-earth; and even before
man, with the ages of the beasts; and before that again, he
finds those "eternal clarities" in the foretimes. For him
prehistory makes sense in quite other terms than the cold
dogmas of evolution and survival:

> From before all time
>   the New Light beams for them
>   .....
>   species, sub-species, genera, families, order.
> Piercing the eskered silt, discovering every stria, each score and
> macula, lighting all the fragile laminae of the shales.
> However Calypso has shuffled the marked pack, veiling with early
> the late.
> Through all unconformities and the sills without sequence, glorying
> all the under-dapple.
> Lighting the Cretaceous and the Trias, for Tyrannosaurus must
> somehow lie down with herbivores, or, the poet lied, which is not
> allowed.
> However violent the contortion or whatever the inversion of the
> folding.
> Oblique through the fire-wrought cold rock dyked from convulsions
> under.

1. "Peredur Son of Efrawg," *The Mabinogion,* trans., Gwyn and Thomas Jones (London:
1949), pp. 183-84.

Through the slow sedimentations laid by his patient creature of water.
(*A*, 73-74)

The long ramshackle story has a center-point, the Passion and Crucifixion of our Lord, and the once-and-for-ever enactment of the Mass. The Roman poems all revolve around, and illuminate, that center. The past is a whole, and is comprehensible, wholly improbable as this may appear.

Between the desolate beginning of *The Anathemata* and its triumphant end on Sherthursday and Venus Day, something extraordinary happens, the poem *does* the thing it describes, and life runs again into "the failing *numina*." David was always looking for new beginnings, though with increasing despondency; but in this great poem, for a while at least, the sap years are restored. How this comes about is a matter of many new beginnings and returnings. But also it works for one especial reason, because in telling the history of the world David Jones is tapping a very ancient source of power. It is a fact that can be illustrated from many civilizations and from literatures as different and distant in time and space as Anglo-Saxon and ancient Sumerian, that when there is a matter of crucial importance to be taken in hand--confirming the king on his throne, or assuring the succession of the seasons and the crops, or even curing a bad toothache--then the rites to be performed are made effective by a deliberate recitation of the story of the Creation. Each New Year in Babylon, when the political order was established afresh, at one point in the twelve-day ceremonial the long poem was recited that tells of the creation and ordering of the world in the beginning and the defeat of the powers of chaos by a hero god. It was itself an act in the battle for order, symmetry and good sense, and as such an effective protection against the powers of destruction and misrule. This is the special purpose behind the digression, that is no digression, in *Beowulf*, when the minstrel sings God's creation of the world (in Michael Alexander's translation):

> It was with pain that the powerful spirit
> dwelling in darkness endured that time,
> hearing daily the hall filled
> with loud amusement; there was the music of the harp,
> the clear song of the poet, perfect in his telling
> of the remote first making of man's race.

Then there was Caedmon's lost poem, and many many more. To tell the tale of Creation is to set in motion a great spell, and David Jones' telling of the story of the world, and the sense that he makes of the world, do this too in another manner. His method is, of course, sharply contemporary. It employs many levels, many voices; three voices in especial, a point to which I shall return. There is much use of symbol and of sign. "Calypso has shuffled the marked pack, veiling with early the late" (*A*, 74). It may be Calypso, or it may be David, but it is shuffled with a purpose.

Let me return to something I said at the beginning. An essential of David's writings, as of his paintings, is that things are *made to work*. He seems to have thought of the seen and the heard in much the same way, for he writes that "The problems that confront the poet . . . though they concern only such elusive matters as the validity of a word, are themselves as objective as is the development of an aero-engine" (*A*, 22). This is part and parcel of that complete harmony between the mysterious and the everyday. In the picture called *Major Hall's Bothy*, under the tall tree and against the airy diaphanous distances is the workmanlike tent-tackle--stay and guy-ropes, that would not let you down in a storm. It is the same in the "window pictures": the background is crisscrossed with luminosity, ivory lights are held in the folds of the napkin, but the growing things have the tensile power of gossamers. And in all these pictures, down there in the foreground is something very forthright like a window-catch; the pepper-pot is as weighty as the chalice.

This is what David says about the ship in the Trystan ac Esyllt picture: ". . . how can one begin to juggle with the form and content of chaps messing about with cordage, canvas, tackle, unless one has a fairly clear notion of how in fact these things work?" And again: "I have to know *exactly* what are the details *a propos* of such and such, before I can use the word I want . . . Generalisations are useless." This applies equally to the boat in the *Ancient Mariner* illustrations and to the "ship from Aleppo" in *The Anathemata*. Whatever manner of ship it may be (and the possible manners are many), and however many its meanings, it is vitally important *how* the mizzen mast is raked. Under the symbols and the many significances the corporeal artifacts are supreme and words are artifacts.

That ship "over-due a nine month, writ-off for lost" . . . no matter what else she was, or whether she was named as "sweet Christ's dear Tree" . . . make what you like of the "water coming from the right side, about mid-ships" . . . leave all that aside and you still could trust your life to that vessel:

                                Coming up on a spring tide
with her Rotherhithe mate and her Limehouse skipper and a
Sittingbourne bred pilot in her conning-house
                                        his flag in the blow
in the morning.
Her main top-mast by the board, a stick of a jury for fore-
mast, her mizzen-mast raked more nor natural and canted
somewhat athwartships, sprung, woolded, but entire.
                                Her yards and sprits
and all her spars, all woolded; what you could see of her clewed-up
maincourse were patched as a Welshman's quilt.
We wont speak of her top-hamper nor the aspect of her dear,
gay garnishings
                                                        but
sweet Christ's dear Tree!
                                her cordage!!
how does it stand
                        to stay?
how does it run
                        to brace or lift or hale?
can the wraith of a laniard extend the ghost of a shroud?
                        render or freshen, p'r'aps
but how take-up or belay
                        a hemp o' gossamer?
                        But, a cloth of buntin'
at her damaged main cap, another to pennon her jury
                                        and
bended to the fretted halliers--not all that tattered and bleached but
what to gaudy yet her after-castle--
                                her native ensign:
as proper to her as is the dog-rose to a' English beggar's hat, abaft the
weathered rags that served her for mizzen.
                                There was no sign at all
of her bonadventure.
                                She seemed but dressed for
Breaker's Yard. (*A*, 137-139)

I wonder if it is not possible that some of the
interpretations of David Jones' use of symbolism (or "sign"
as he prefers to call it, with a more tactile emphasis on the
act, fact and thing) and the explanations of his complex
meanings within meaning, allusion and counter allusion,
may not for some people actually put up more barriers to
straight enjoyment than they remove. David was well aware
of the dangers of this, and I think always rather unhappy
about the long, necessary, notes which he added to his
writings. He would so much have rather that we all had his
amazing knowledge, and were all able to take the allusions
without help from him; but he accepted that we cannot.
"Most of all," he says, "I could wish of my 'mystery,'
misterium or *ministerium*, that it should give some sort of
pleasure" (*A*, 33-34).

There is something very down to earth in his own comments, a dislike of solemnity, and he is often so funny. Who on earth but David would have put a really ghastly pun into the middle of the *Dies Irae* (*A*, 208)? Or he'd use the echo of a music hall song, as well as a latin versicle. In "The Dream of Private Clitus" the "man on the flying trapeze" is a nice (if undercover) companion to musings on the nature of dreaming:

> Heavy bodies sail the air with the greatest of ease in these dreams, there's no end to the unions these sleep-dreams can lend to things separate enough in wake-a-day. (*SL*, 18)

I would like to set down here what David said in a letter (31.viii.71) about his "jokes." It was in connection with *The Tribune's Visitation*, and he said,

> I can't make my stuff except out of recalling of things read, half- or ill-remembered from sources of all sorts, and over the years, and to me jokes are so much a part of the fabric that it depresses me to realise how few chaps, far more informed than am I, or can ever now be, show no glimmer of having even partially seen the joke, while expressing enthusiasm for the confounded stuff as 'literature' or what not.

He goes on to describe the visit of a solemn admirer to whom he played one of his recordings and whose face, he says, reminded him of that jingle of "the Lady-killing Cowboy" who was visited in the death cell by the sheriff and the chaplain:

> And the parson he did come
> he did come
> and he looked so goddam glum
> goddam glum
> as he talked of kingdom come
> blast his eyes!

Jeremy Hooker in an essay, which appeared first in *The Anglo-Welsh Review* (22:50, Autumn 1973, later part of *David Jones*, Enitharmon Press, 1975), and which has been revised for the present volume, has said that it is the rich humor as well as the rhythms and the language that above all he finds exciting in David Jones' writings. The greater part of the essay is taken up with an exploration of the more difficult side of the writings but, he says, fairly and squarely, that "none but a pedant is going to make this particular voyage 'from the known to the knowable' unless the movement of the poem and the quality of its language carry him forward." A prominent review of "The Kensington Mass," for its total incomprehension, makes this sadly clear. "The Kensington Mass" is not the best point from which to begin reading David Jones, but the fact that any reader can miss the point so completely is strange and depressing.

Why on earth, it seems to be asked, should we bother with so dense and difficult a poem as this, or as *The Anathemata*? If I am neither a Christian nor a Celt what do all these names and liturgical symbols have to do with me? One has heard this said and perhaps the answer *is* "nothing at all." When David writes, in the Introduction to *The Anathemata*, that "if a requisite now-ness is not present, the sign, valid in itself, is apt to suffer a kind of invalidation" (*A*, 15), he shows himself very alive to the possibility. If you come from David's Wales, or from the Pool of London, Rotherhithe or thereabouts, the allusions and textures of his writings will be the richer for you; but these are far from being necessary to the enjoyment. With them or without it is there for anyone who cares.

So much has been written, and so well, about those profounder meanings that I shall not apologize for dwelling rather on the plain enjoyment that is here:

Six centuries
        and the second Spring
and a new wonder under heaven:
       man-limb stirs
           in the god-stones
and the kouroi
       are gay and stepping it
but stanced solemn. (*A*, 91)

And a little later:

Down we come
     quick, but far
to the splendours
     to the skill-years
and the signed and fine grandeurs.
O yes, technique--but much more:
the god still is balanced
         in the man-stones
   but its a nice thing
as near a thing as ever you saw. (*A*, 93-94)

Not even Keats in the "Ode to Maia" came closer to Greece than that. Or there's the haunting picture:

... run and fetch Calypso
        out for to see
she 'ill be only moping
        over an old tale
        in the half-light
        on the back balcony
that gives towards the sea.

> She's sibylline enough
>   she too knows dendrite beauties. (*A*, 191)

Perhaps it's the dance name that does it, but I seem to see a
shack in the West Indies somewhere and the blowsy old
woman looking out to sea with her memories, more than
any sibylline portents. Or again, there are the greater set-
pieces, as here, with the succession of sea-scenes:

> Backings, veerings
>   dead calm
>   becalms.
>   Shifts of unshaping mist.
>   Thicked shapeless hours by muffle of grey fog
>   grey hauls of wind
>   more wind
>   strong head-wind walls of wind
>   half-a-gale o' wind.
>   Thicks of rain
>   Gale!
>   The weather 'gins to clear?
> Then loom 'em red-tawnies!
>   vancurrers of snow
>   and thunder-noons of yallery night
>   and the dark night's
>   night-drench of white spindrift.
>   Scend by send of the sea.
>   Hove down of back-wash--
>   into the wind
>   careened to leeward--
>   of the wind.
>   Green arcing darks
>   that thud inboard green-white, fore-castle and after-castle
>   fretted and veronica'd of marrying falls of foam.
>   (The conflux midships
>   were sea-boots high and well over.)
>   All her sheer
>   the entire trembling keel-length of her vessel of burden
>   silvered of
>   driven rain
>   gilted of
>   bends of paly light
>   white as the Housel of spume.
>   The tilted heavers
>   her oblation-stone
>   immēnser hovers dark-ápse her.
>   Over where
>   unfathomed under her
>   in the under-stills
>   the washed-white margaron'd relics lie, where the pearl is,
>   as was the weather-eye of Ben Backstay
>   *lux perpetua luceat ei*

and upon all the precursors--as knowed their ropes--that have gone before us under the regimen of the ship-star and sleep the sleep with father Ulysses. (*A*, 139-141)

This is marvelous physical description with its "walls of wind" and "thicks of rain," while at the same time it is imperceptibly lifted and removed to a quite other height. I think "silvered" in "silvered of/driven rain" starts it, until, quite naturally, the liturgical Latin

lux perpetua luceat ei

from the canon of the Mass falls into place--where those gone before us are remembered, among whom is father Ulysses. Ulysses it *had* to be, for, to quote from a letter of David's to another friend, he says,

When I first read that Clement of Alexandria, Gregory Nazianus, Gregory of Nyssa and others of the fathers took it for granted that Odysseus self-bound to the mast ... was typic of our Lord made fast to the tree of the cross, and that the barque of the ecclesia was safe thereby, I was pleased that this heritage of the Greco-Roman deposits was used along with the deposits of the canonical Scriptures to assert, 'Though his Barke cannot be lost/Yet it shall be Tempest-tost.'

The Anathemata passage conveys us, by some method peculiar to David himself, imperceptibly from the shallows of our own experience of wind and weather onto quite different levels.

And old Nestor
                    fetch him
bad blind old man
he'll like not know
                    another spring. (*A*, 192)

Here's the past evoked, here's what it really tastes like, immediate and tangy, our own property and met with a gleam of mutual recognition. There is no effort of the imagination, for "one is trying to make a shape out of the very things of which one is oneself made," he says. The things of the past are introduced with the affectionate familiarity of some much loved and caressed object, a worn bone knife-handle, for instance, or a charming elderly tea-pot. This is what makes the difference. The poet, as he has said again, "must work within the limits of his love. There must be no 'mugging up,' no 'ought to know' or 'try to feel'; for only what is actually loved and known can be seen *sub specie aeternitatis*" (*A*, 24). So there it is again: iron integrity which was his own skin, the total innocence of pretension, even mockery of it, for he could be quite sharp at spotting pretension.

I am not at all sure how far one can, or should, treat the so-called "Roman" writings separately. There is not very much of Rome in *In Parenthesis*, but in *The Anathemata* it pervades the whole poem--because of the accident, that is no accident, of the Roman occupation of Judaea, and certain events in that province around 5 B.C. and 30 A.D. David Jones himself employs "accident" in "The Fatigue," "a chance numbering off by a corporal's whim" (*SL*, 41) in a like manner, for his choice of a mixed body of recruits who "happen" to be serving in Jerusalem at the time of the Passion and Crucifixion. He admits "taking liberties with history" when he brings representatives of many nations, and among them Celts from "farside the Gaulish strait," to the walls of Jerusalem. But these are no more than the liberties that reveal the flow, and uncover the real sense of history. Their truth may lie ahead in future time; only then will the border province be found to have been the center of the world.

I remember an old friend telling with delight that she had met someone she used to know well, and at one time saw much of in London, but had not seen for a number of years. She asked him where he was living now. "In the Levant." "Why there?" "Because it is *so central*," came the answer.   And why not? The Levant is as central in the latitudes of world geography as Rome and Jerusalem are in the longitudes of history. Caesar's legionaries talk like Great War tommies because what they are talking about has not changed.

In a letter of David's (31.viii.71) about *The Tribune's Visitation*, he says that its topicality, the contemporary thing, was the intention but "it had to be stated in terms that were not out of place with the 1st Century A.D., and not so to say 'dragged in.' "

> I have a word to say to you as men and as a man speaking to men, but, and a necessary but, as a special sort of man speaking to a special sort of men at a specific but recurring moment in *urbs*-time. (*SL*, 49-50)

In the letter the words "*at a specific and recurring moment in urbs-time*" are under-lined, and David goes on,

> I believe that to be true. The 'setting' and *dramatis personae* might well be some civilian milieu--a department of the state, civil servants, politicians, pressure-groups, or what you will, but I have had no day-by-day contactual experience of all that world. I know of it only from various friends, but my experience, contactual, and day-by-day, was only of the military sources of a world-imperium which, by the chance of the 1914-18 war, I found myself necessarily involved in from the inside as a private of one of the 'Kitchener Armies', so any

attempt of mine indicative of the Tribune as a man speaking to men, and
a special sort of man ... etc. had of necessity to be drawn from the
attitude, slang, complaints, responses etc. of those I lived among for
those three years or so. I had no other way but to see the machine of
Caesar's armed forces through the eyes of the only armed forces I had
any experience of. No doubt in actual historic fact the differences were
very considerable, but in other ways much the same, in *some* ways
astonishingly the same, from what I've gathered in reading of details
of organisation.

He gives as an example of this the soldier "with the
Etruscan look" 330099 Elbius (there's a quite nastily erudite
joke here), of whom the Tribune says,

But with a taste for the Boards eh? We must remember that at the
reg'mental binge... (*SL*, 47)

This refers to a regulation whereby each Roman soldier had
a fixed amount of his wretched pay docked to provide for
an annual carousal of some sort--what we would call a
"Regimental Dinner."

How totally different this is from any deliberate up-
dating! Still less is it a matter of using past events self-
consciously and didactically to illustrate the present
situation. Certain facts about the Roman Empire are facts
about *Empire*, permanent, "specific and recurring": the
flattening, the conditioning of an imposed world order. So a
private in the Royal Welch Fusiliers would slip easily under
the skin of the Roman soldier and still feel himself at
home. It is possible to push these recurring likenesses
further back still. The note to *The Tribune's Visitation*
begins with an explanation of the inscription that forms the
cover and frontispiece to the poem, and especially of the
words "*idem in me*"--"the same (holds good) for me." This is
the soldier's oath that was taken by every enlisted man in
the Roman service, at first individually, and later by drafts.
The words committed the individual personally to Caesar,
both as Pontifex Maximus and Imperator, head of the state
religion and of the state war-machine.

The Tribune near the end of his charge calls it "the
sacramentum that binds us all" (*SL*, 56). I think David
Jones would have been glad to know (regretfully I don't
think he ever did) that, a thousand years before Rome was
founded, the Hittite Empire, the great power established on
the central plateau of what is now Turkey, also had a
standing army in which the recruits on enlisting took an
oath as part of an extended ceremony, each man repeating,
"Be it thus." The point is that the Hittite Empire, with its
gifts of administration, its elaborate system of road-building,

its frontier posts, garrison forts and long *limes*, and with all
its military virtues, was a forerunner of Rome.

Already when he wrote the Preface to *The
Anathemata* David had foreseen these distant analogies. He
wrote then "that an extension of state control characterizes
the period in which we now live, [and] that something
analogous to that extension is remarked by students of the
period of Valens and Valentinian, and that like effects may
possibly have like causes" (*A*, 22). The germ of the idea of
The Tribune's Visitation is already sketched in this Preface:

> When rulers seek to impose a new order upon any such group belonging
> to one or other of those more primitive culture-phases, it is necessary
> for those rulers to take into account the influence of the poets as
> recalling something loved and as embodying an ethos inimical to the
> imposition of that new order. Whether the policy adopted is one of
> suppression or of some kind of patronage, a recognition of possible
> danger dictates the policy in either case. Leaving aside such political
> considerations as may cause such recognition under such circumstances,
> we may still recognize the 'dangerous' element. Poetry is to be
> diagnosed as 'dangerous' because it evokes and recalls, is a kind of
> *anamnesis* of, i.e. is an effective recalling of, something loved. (*A*, 21)

"The times are late and get later" (*A*, 15). Nothing is
so out of date as the language of our immediate prede-
cessors. David's Rome is full of a "requisite nowness" (*A*, 15),
and completely lacking in the theatrical falsities of a
pedantically "correct' consistency to period. How does he do
it? He does it, I think, by stretching our own memories
further than we would ourselves have believed possible, so
that what we find is what we already know, and have always
known. One does not find oneself saying, "That's how a
Celtic recruit in the Roman service overseas would have
spoken," or "a Roman from Rome," for that matter; one
catches oneself rather saying, "That's what *we* said"--or
"that's how it seemed then." Nor is it any superior
transcending "we" who spy on the event. In "The Fatigue"
and "The Tribune's Visitation" and the other "Roman"
poems, as in *The Anathemata*, we are inside time though
"late in time" (*A*, 50). "These things are happening round
me and to me," we say: "I don't altogether understand, but
here I am and perhaps one day I *shall* understand."

The language of the poem shifts comfortably, as a
guard "at ease" shifts his weight from one foot to the other,
between cockney colloquialism, the formal rhetoric of
command and empire, and the poetic leaps of intuition and
"mystery." The changes of voice, or key, or, as David says of
"The Fatigue," the "change of gear," intensify what is being
said in each. In "The Fatigue" the changes are more than

usually distinct. First is the everyday soldier's talk that ends
with "keep that regulation step" (*SL*, 31). In the second a
poetic leap is made and the "ordinary chaps" of the first
part have become "instruments/to hang the gleaming
Trophy/on the dreaming Tree" (*SL*, 31-32) and the richer
textures of Northern, Celtic and old Israelite mythology are
brought into the language. This part ends at "The Tumulus"
(*SL*, 38). Then follows the third and last change of gear,
and the same events are now viewed from the "most interior
room" (*SL*, 39) of a sinister officialdom, through whose
minute devolutions the "accident" is decided of exactly who
"in this relief of all" will "furnish/that Fatigue" (*SL*, 41).

There are interlockings and overlappings, of course,
but broadly speaking the threefold distinction holds. These
three voices are in fact present in most of David Jones'
writings in some manner. Of the first, the "Cockney" voice,
the voice of the tommies and legionaries, David writes in
the Preface to *In Parenthesis*:

> I am surprised to find how much Cockney influences have determined
> the form; but as Latin is to the Church, so is Cockney to the Army, no
> matter what name the regiment bears. It is difficult to dissociate any
> word of command, any monosyllable remembered, coming at you on a
> dark duck-board track, from the Great Bell of Bow. If the language of
> England passed and all we know dissolved, some squad of savages,
> speaking a new tongue, might yet respond to a sharp formula,
> remembered, fossilised: 'Kipt thet dressin cahncher', might well be
> for them what *Kyrie Eleison* is, breaking the Latin crust, for Father
> O'Connor's boy. (*IP*, xii)

After this, when we come to *reflect* on the same
things, we hear a different voice again, and this voice
speaks often in the Celtic and Arthurian language, whereas
the formal voice of command and empire speaks in the
tones of the Tribune or Sejanus or some nameless N.C.O.
The changings and interlockings are just one of the ways in
which David's wizardry works, easing us into the skins of
individuals, and suddenly stepping back to show what it all
means in other terms, under another allegiance.

The Anathemata is, I believe, a very great poem. It
does triumphantly what it sets out to do. As David says in
the Preface, "I mean by my title as much as it can be made
to mean, or can evoke or suggest, however obliquely: the
blessed things that have taken on what is cursed and the
profane things that somehow are redeemed." And again,
"Our final condition or last end is not yet, whereas our
artifacts have their completion now or never" (*A*, 28-29). In
this sense too *The Anathemata* is a complete artifact.

JEREMY HOOKER

IN THE LABYRINTH: AN EXPLORATION OF THE ANATHEMATA[1]

> "I am the child of earth and starry
> heaven; but of the heaven is my
> lineage.... I am withered by thirst....
> Give me cool water quick from the Lake
> of Memory."[2]

1

There is, I believe, one fact which we must be aware of in order to gain a reasonable understanding both of the themes and of the pattern and structure of *The Anathemata*: it is set "in the time of the Mass," and is therefore not confined to a specific temporal or spatial dimension. As David Jones says in the Preface:

In a sense the fragments that compose this book are about, or around and about, matters of all sorts which, by a kind of quasi-free association, are apt to stir in my mind at any time and as often as not 'in the time of the Mass'. The mental associations, liaisons, meanderings to and fro, 'ambivalences', asides, sprawl of the pattern, if pattern there is ... have been as often as not initially set in motion, ... by some action or word, something seen or heard, during the liturgy.... You can go around the world and back again, in and out the meanders, down the his- tory-paths, survey *religio* and *superstitio*, call back many yesterdays, but yesterday week ago, or long, long ago, ... during those few seconds taken by the presbyter to move from the Epistle to the Gospel side, or while he leans to kiss the board or stone (where are the tokens of the

1. This essay derives from my book, *David Jones: An Exploratory Study of the Writings* (London: Enitharmon Press, 1975). While following the argument advanced there, and in large part identical with it, it also represents a substantial reorganization of the material, with significant revisions, additions, and omissions, which are intended both to clarify the argument and to modify certain points in accordance with my subsequent thinking.
2. From an Orphic fragment giving directions to the dead initiate entering Hades. Quoted by W. F. Jackson Knight in *Cumaean Gates* (1936), which is included together with *Vergil's Troy* (1932) and 'The Holy City of the East' (1939) in W. F. Jackson Knight, *Vergil: Epic and Anthropology*, ed. John D. Christie (London: Allen and Unwin, 1967), p. 179.

departed) or when he turns to incite the living *plebs* to assist him. (*A*, 31-32)

He further explains his meaning in this passage in a letter to Saunders Lewis: "When I say somewhere in Preface that one can think of a lot of things in the brief moment it takes the celebrant of the Mass to move the missal from the Epistle to the Gospel side of the mensa domini, I literally meant that. The action of the Mass was meant to be the central theme of the work for as you once said to me 'the Mass *makes sense* of everything.' "[3] The previous quotation with its references to "fragments" and "a kind of quasi-free association" is typical of the attractive modesty with which David Jones comments on his own work. It is potentially misleading, however. I believe *The Anathemata* is initially a difficult work, not because it is loose or fragmentary in structure, but because its unifying pattern is extremely complex, and that to understand what is meant by the Mass making sense of everything is to go some way towards discovering how David Jones creates unity from his richly diverse materials in the poem.

To say that the time of *The Anathemata* is "the time of the Mass" means, in effect, that it is "now" and "always," since the Mass was instituted by an act in time, but is for all time, bringing eternity into time and setting time in the context of eternity. Thus, the time of the poem is both historical time ("now") and sacred time ("always"). Christ is "the Lamb, slain / *ab origine mundi*" (*A*, 208).[4] He is the eternal Redeemer, constant through all the time scales that man finds both frightening and exhilarating to contemplate:

From before all time
            the New Light beams for them
and with eternal clarities
            infulsit and athwart
the fore-times:
            era, period, epoch, hemera.
Through all orogeny:
            group, system, series, zone.
Brighting at the five life-layers
            species, sub-species, genera, families, order.
Piercing the eskered silt, discovering every stria, each score and macula, lighting all the fragile laminae of the shales. (*A*, 73-74)

For David Jones the Cross is "the Axile Tree" (*A*, 243) of the universe, and it is the act of Redemption occurring in time

3. "Two Letters from David Jones," introduced by Saunders Lewis, *Mabon* 5, ed. Alun R. Jones and Gwyn Thomas (Bangor: 1972), p. 18.
4. David Jones' note on this refers us to Apocalypse, V, 12 and XIII, 8, the second of which speaks of "the Lamb slain from the foundation of the world."

which makes sense of time so that *The Anathemata* relates
all historical, prehistorical, and geological events to the
time of the Crucifixion. Yet if I were rashly to attempt to
sum up, in a few words, what *The Anathemata* is about, they
would be, first, "interdependence" and "adaptation": the
interdependence of Creator and Creation, man and woman,
order and diversity; the adaptation of culture to culture,
people to place. I would then want to add "diversification,"
and would soon have several weighty abstractions which the
poem, sensuous and precise in detail, mysterious and rhyth-
mically exciting, would continue to mock.

For all that, such words may still point to the unity
which is not an abstract system. "Interdependence," for
instance. In the Preface David Jones writes: "Something has
to be made by us before it can become for us his sign who
made us. This point he settled in the upper room. No arte-
facture no Christian religion" (*A*, 31). Thus the form of the
Mass, although celebrating an act deliberated "out of time,"
and valid for all time, occurred in time and was prepared
for--and prefigured--from his beginnings, by what man made:

In the prepared high-room
he implements inside time and late in time under forms indelibly
marked by locale and incidence, deliberations made out of time, before
all oreogenesis

        on this hill
    at a time's turn
        not on any hill
but on this hill. (*A*, 53)

In one sense, then, the institution of the Sacraments was
dependent on man since he prepared the "forms indelibly
marked by locale and incidence" under which it occurred,
but this dependence rested upon man's fundamental ground-
ing on the sacred, since he is only truly man when his activities are sacramental.

The opening passage of the poem reveals the same
interdependence:

We already and first of all discern him making this thing other. His
groping syntax, if we attend, already shapes:
    ADSCRIPTAM, RATAM, RATIONABILEM... and by pre-
application and for *them*, under modes and patterns altogether theirs,
the holy and venerable hands lift up an efficacious sign. (*A*, 49)

At once, the poem's temporal and spatial dimensions ("now"
and "always," "here" and "everywhere") are established by
the interpenetration of sacred time and historical time.
"Adscriptam, Ratam, Rationabilem," words from the Prayer
of Consecration, set the poem "in the time of the Mass."

The pronouns refer both to the priest and to man, and the time is the present and man's beginnings. It is man who, from his outset, prepares the form of the Mass: he makes "this thing other," and "shapes" with "his groping syntax" the sacred words--for example, the Prayer of Consecration. But since the Mass centers time upon eternity, and applies to all time, man partakes of its benefits even in the process of preparing its form. Although the Redemption was "from the foundation of the world," it was not imposed upon time, reducing all to a uniform system, but occurred "under modes and patterns altogether theirs," so that, for David Jones, Christianity is the form of universal order which requires diversity, "forms indelibly marked by locale and incidence," for its expression, and which therefore establishes the great value of different things belonging to particular times and places. This belief both guarantees the integrity of history-- by observing the ways in which "man makes himself," and the processes by which what goes before conditions what comes after--and apprehends all time as eternally present in the Mass. But a belief which is perfectly coherent may also sometimes produce, in an experience of time or place, deeply perplexing results. For example:

> I do not know what time is at
> or whether before or after
>   was it when--
> but when *is* when? (*A*, 170)

and

> Levites! the new rite holds
>   is here
> before your older rites begin.
> Here.
> Where?
>   Here when? (*A*, 230-231)

However, "the time of the Mass" gives the recalling of pre-historical, historical, and geological events in *The Anathemata* its special quality of recession *and* immediacy.

The Mass is an "anamnesis," a term which David Jones uses, as he tells us in a note (*A*, 205), according to the following definition by Gregory Dix in *The Shape of the Liturgy*:

> It (anamnesis) is not quite easy to represent accurately in English, words like "remembrance" or "memorial" having for us a connotation of something *absent* which is only mentally recollected. But in the scriptures of both the Old and New Testament *anamnesis* and the cognate verb have a sense of "recalling" or "re-presenting" before God an

event in the past so that it becomes *here and now operative by its effects*.

In another note we are told that "in the rite of the fourth-century Egyptian bishop, Serapion, the eucharist is regarded as a recalling of all the dead" (*A*, 76). However, David Jones continues, "no institution can, in its public formulas, presume the membership of any except those who have professed such membership. But over and above these few there are those many, of all times and places, whose lives and deaths have been made acceptable by the same Death on the Hill of which every Christian breaking of bread is an epiphany and a recalling" (*A*, 76). Poetry, too, "is a kind of *anamnesis* of, i.e. is an effective recalling of, something loved" (*A*, 21). Thus, if the Mass is an universal anamnesis, "a recalling of all the dead," "of all times and places"--indeed, David Jones says that, "in some sense," the Mass is offered on behalf "of all sentient being, and, perhaps, of insentient too" (*A*, 106)--*The Anathemata* is a partial anamnesis, a recalling of the loved things which have gone to the making of the poet. Not only as an individual, of course, but as a product of his culture. As David Jones says, in words that are the most succinct expression of his whole endeavor: "one is trying to make a shape out of the very things of which one is oneself made" (A, 10). Since this is so, we need to understand the process by which the action of the Mass and the poet's mythus (his "very things") are conjoined in the poem. How, in other words, *The Anathemata* is at once a meditation on the action of the Mass and a meditation on the geological and cultural formation of Britain.

In approaching an answer to this question, I want initially to establish two important points. First, *The Anathemata* is a commemorative poem, but the belief that anamnesis recalls or re-presents "before God an event in the past so that it becomes *here and now operative by its effects*" ensures that the poem is not an elegy for the dead, but a re-presentation, here and now, of the living past. A brief comparison should help to clarify this.

Formally, David Jones and Thomas Hardy have too little in common to justify an evaluative comparison of their work; nor would I want to make one under any circumstances, since their work represents, for me, the two most vital, different but complementary, channels of modern British poetry. There are, however, certain affinities between their preoccupations. For example, they have a common feeling for the oneness of all life, and both are fascinated by geological time. But Hardy is primarily elegiac and David Jones is not. The feeling of Hardy's poetry is dominated by his nostalgia for an irrecoverable past and his belief that memory of the dead is only coextensive with the consciousness of the living. Certainly this is a feeling which ascribes supreme value to the living moment; but Hardy's churchyards are green with the evidence of decay and the unconscious forces of nature feeding on the dead-- only the living haunt such places. For Hardy, living in the age of Lyell and Darwin, the discovery of geological time opened up a terrible vista before the mind: a vista of measureless ages in which nature, directed by no benign intelligence, may be seen operating according to laws which benefit the strong, the cunning, the adaptable, and destroy those not motivated by ruthless self-interest, and to which man when he eventually appears is of no more account than the trilobite. It is a vista which, for Hardy, concentrates the human span into an infinitely small, infinitely precious, moment, and projects its extreme vulnerability.

The discovery of geological time occurred very recently in the history of man, and the poetry that registers its impact and makes sense of it is not extensive. Hardy responded to the discovery in one way, which ascribes supreme value to the human world by locating it in an indifferent universe. More often, as in the case of Robinson Jeffers, or of Hugh MacDiarmid in "On a Raised Beach," the response has supported a kind of mysticism of brute powers and of the material world. David Jones, on the other hand, is a sacramental materialist. For him, the universe is the Creation, disclosing "from before all time / the New Light" shining in every life-form and form of matter. In *The Anathemata* he takes the biological and geological sciences which struck an icy awe into the minds and hearts of Thomas Hardy and numerous fellow Victorians, and were a major influence in undermining religious faith and establishing a secular view of the world, and transfigures them by the light of the original and all-pervasive creative order. The past is eternally present, and "the Axile Tree" stands immovable through all the cataclysms and slow sedimentations of geological metamorphosis. The Cross does not foreshorten the vistas which prehistory and geology open before the mind, but is the center to which all events in time and space are related. Consequently *The Anathemata* is not elegiac, but a poem of "birthday and anniversary," of "continuity" and "a new beginning" (*A*, 51).

The second point I want to establish concerns the relation between priest and poet in David Jones' thinking.

Of the poet, he says in the Preface: "Rather than being a seer or endowed with the gift of prophecy he is something of a vicar whose job is legatine--a kind of Servus Servorum to deliver what has been delivered to him, who can neither add to nor take from the deposits" (*A*, 35). The poet is a sign-maker whose "specific task" is, "somehow or other, to lift up valid signs" (*A*, 23). Accordingly, the poet's role is analogous to the priest's: each depends wholly on the fact that man is a sacramental creature, a sign-maker. In the modern world, therefore, they confront the same crisis. For although what their signs signify is eternally valid, the signs themselves have undergone a process of partial invalidation. For example, "bread" and "wood" and "water" can no longer be assumed to carry the symbolic import for a technological age which they bore in previous ages. Thus, for David Jones, a Christian poet committed to the notion of sign, the problem is how to make the signs valid for the present, for "the works of man, unless they are of 'now' and of 'this place,' can have no 'for ever' " (*A*, 24). He is concerned with symbols which reach far back into prehistory, but he has to renew them in the language and forms of the twentieth century.

2

As *In Parenthesis* presents the First World War as a phase of the crisis of the West, so *The Anathemata* presents the worsening crisis in the context of the Second World War:

> I speak of before the whale-roads or the keel-paths were from Orcades
> to the fiord-havens, or the greyed green wastes that they strictly grid
> quadrate and number on the sea-green *Quadratkarte*
>   one eight six one G
>   for the fratricides
> of the latter-day, from east-shore of Iceland
> *bis Norwegen*
> (O Balin O Balan!
>   how blood you both
> the *Brudersee*
>   toward the last phàse
> of our dear West.)   (*A*, 115)

The chart issued by the German Naval Command in 1940, which grids the "*Brudersee*" and imposes its formulae on the "whale-roads" and "keel-paths" named by earlier Germanic invaders, belongs to the same order of reality as the "Draughtsman at Army" in Part 4 of *In Parenthesis*, who "made note on a blue-print of the significance of that grove as one of his strong-points" (*IP*, 66). The pattern of *In*

Parenthesis opposes the "culture" of the trenches, in which
the men recover the "corporate inheritance" (*IP*, 192) of the
Island of Britain, and the military order which turns the
men into an efficient fighting machine. The opposition is
embodied in two kinds of language: technical jargon and
the language of command and of numbers, on one hand, and
a "creaturely" and "kindly" language, with historical and
mythological depth, on the other. The two kinds of order do
not represent a simple opposition, however, because David
Jones' attitude towards the army is as complex and ambivalent as it is later to the Roman Empire. The opposition, as
it develops in his writings, is rather a division within man,
between sacramental and utilitarian principles, than a
direct confrontation between different powers. Nevertheless,
there is confrontation, and an additional difficulty of David
Jones' writings arises from the complicated movements
between an idea of external opposition and an idea of
internal division in his thinking. Thus, *The Anathemata* has
a more heightened sense of the crisis of the West, and treats
it on a broader front, than *In Parenthesis,* and its more
detailed presentation of the opposing forms of order is even
more complex, but with strains which the largely celebratory nature of the work tends rather to obscure. *The Anathemata* is also more elaborate than *In Parenthesis* in its portrayal of the West as a Waste Land, and its use of the associated symbols is more sustained. Similarly, the pattern of
initiation through which the men in *In Parenthesis* enter
into the two forms of order is developed with more conscious deliberation and with universal significance in *The
Anathemata.*

The opening of the poem depicts the present as a
time when "dead symbols litter to the base of the cult-
stone" (*A*, 50). As the poet at Mass perceives: "The cult-man
stands alone in Pellam's land: more precariously than he
knows he guards the *signa*" (*A*, 50). In Pellam's land, the
Waste Land, the task of "the cult-man" is to guard the
"*signa,*" but the poet's role is not merely defensive. The
word "cult-man" combines four related meanings: he is the
priest, and he is the poet in his role analogous to that of the
priest; he is also, in a way reminiscent of Oswald Spengler's
"culture man,"[5] the man of a living, organic culture; and he
is the hero of the Grail quest, and therefore, like the priest,
a representative of Christ. Thus the poet as cult-man is one

---

5. Oswald Spengler, *The Decline of the West,* abridged edition by Helmut Werner
(London: Allen and Unwin, 1961), p. 51.

who seeks to restore the wasted land by renewing the signs: his task is to "free the waters" by releasing the life locked in the "dead symbols." Poet and priest both "intend life" (*A*, 49).

If the figure of the cult-man is associated with the "culture man," Pontius Pilate, "the fact-man," who takes his siesta "within the conditioned room" (*A*, 239) at the hour of the Crucifixion, recalls Spengler's description of Caesar as "a pure man of fact."[6] In "Mabinog's Liturgy" the unifying principle of Christianity, incarnate in Christ, is contrasted with the organization of Tiberius and Sejanus, the "cosmocrat" (*A*, 187). The contrast between the imperialists' world-ordering system and the Christ-child placed in a Welsh setting looks forward to "The Tribune's Visitation" and "The Tutelar of the Place," in which the conflict and interaction between the two powers and forms of order is most fully developed. "The Tribune's Visitation" is also-- among other things--an acute psychological portrait of a man like Spengler, who indulged a nostalgia for the "Cultures" while asserting the necessity of Caesarism. Nevertheless, the understanding of the type evidently owes something to tensions David Jones felt in himself. Thus, although he sees that for "the men of rule, whose *religio* is rule," "robbery is conterminous with empire" (*A*, 85), his attitude towards the Roman Empire remains ambivalent.

David Jones' horrified fascination with what, on the face of it, one might have expected simply to repel him, had, no doubt, complex causes. It may be part of the truth that his mind, which was the least "protestant" of minds, inclined naturally to authority, and another part, that his attitude towards the Roman Empire was strongly colored by his complicated feelings for the British Empire, which was in fact the main historical shaping force of the kind of Britishness he espoused. In my view, his imaginative experience of Empire, both in its ideals and in its negative and positive consequences, makes him a peculiarly Virgilian figure among modern poets, with the result that it will take us some time to realize all the implications and contradictions in what he shows, since we are still to some degree suffering the history he lived and from which he wrote. All the same, it may be asserted with some confidence that he recognized in Empire a "*religio*," which was both a terrible parody of the Christian religion, and in some respects one of its necessary conditions. In allowing Christ to be crucified

6. Ibid., p. 52.

the Roman Empire unwittingly sowed the seeds of its own destruction; it unconsciously assisted in the spread of Christianity, and it supplied the language as well as some of the forms (the *sacramentum*, for instance) of the Roman Catholic Church. So "cult-man" and "fact-man" are fundamentally opposed, yet also related. I would suggest tentatively, as all my suggestions are tentative where they touch on matters of religious provenance, that the true irony of the relationship is implicit in the word "conditioned": the *religio* of rule which conditions men to act in a certain way is itself a condition of the divine plan.

Speaking of Roman Britain in "Rite and Fore-Time," David Jones describes "crux-signed / old Roma" as "the yet efficient mid-wife of us" (*A*, 72). *The Anathemata*, like *In Parenthesis*, pays tribute to the Roman occupation as a principal unifying factor in Britain and as contributing a great deal to the Island's "deposits." Imperial Rome also provides a parallel to the mid-twentieth century situation-- not merely to "the last pháse / of our dear West," but to "our Engle-raum in this Brut's Albion." This phrase is put in the mouth of the Lady of the Pool, but it speaks David Jones' mind. It is a startling phrase to hear applied to England in the context of the Second World War, and is the strongest possible condemnation of what England has done, and is still doing, to the diverse cultures of the British Isles. The use of Welsh material in the poem, and of Welsh words to "incant" the Welsh deposits, is correspondingly a subtle subversion of the general English assumption that Britain is synonymous with England. In particular, the use of Welsh words is part of the process of naming which opposes the language of uniform, mechanical organization. Similarly, the poet's English, especially in the mouth of The Lady of the Pool, is often at variance with standard middle-class usage. In this respect David Jones was one of the very few British poets of this century who could tap rich resources of dialect without self-consciousness. Unlike T. S. Eliot in *The Waste Land*, he never used it as if from a great height. After all, Cockney was just as much a part of him as his Welshness.

3

In his fine essay "David Jones: A Reconnaissance," Rene Hague says that the ship is "the dominating symbol that rules the whole poem."[7] While I do not disagree with this, I prefer to say that there are in fact three dominant symbols, at least two of which are, as it were, important components of the ship symbol. In "Rite and Fore-Time" David Jones refers "the stone / the fonted water / the fronded wood" to Vergil's description of the palace of Priam in the *Aeneid* and says: "By whatever means of fusion he (Vergil) hands down three of the permanent symbols for us to make use of" (*A*, 56). These are the symbols that rule *The Anathemata*.

"The stone" is the altar: it is the stone at which man has offered up "anathemata" to the gods since his advent on the world-stage as man the sign-maker, millennia before the Incarnation, yet in the light of "the Lamb slain from the foundation of the world." Anathemata are "the blessed things that have taken on what is cursed and the profane things that somehow are redeemed. . . . Things set up, lifted up, or in whatever manner made over to the gods" (*A*, 28-29). The word signifies, above all, Christ himself, as the following texts make clear: "And I, if I be lifted up from the earth, will draw all *men* unto me" (John 12:32). "For he hath made him *to be* sin for us, who knew no sin; that we might be made the righteousness of God in him" (2 Corinthians 5:21). "Christ hath redeemed us from the curse of the law, being made a curse for us: for it is written, Cursed *is* everyone that hangeth on a tree" (Galatians 3:13). It is typical of his method that David Jones, when discussing the meanings of "anathemata," does not allude to this primary significance, although these texts--and others--must surely have been to the forefront of his mind when explaining his choice of title. Nevertheless the stone is where the sacrifice is offered--"Himself to himself" (*A*, 225)--now and from the foundation of the world. It is where man partakes of the benefits of the sacred meal even as he prepares its form. The stone is the altar of the Mass.

Stone is equally the material which man handles, carving it into images of man and woman, god and goddess, and so, in the course of his long development, making himself according to the image of God which he is:

Who were his *gens*-men or had he no *Hausname* yet
no *nomen* for his *fecit*-mark
     the Master of the Venus?
whose man-hands god-handled the Willendorf stone

7. *Agenda*, David Jones Special Issue, Vol. 5, Nos. 1-3 (London: 1967), p. 67. David Jones' fullest prose exploration of the ship symbol is, of course, his great essay, "An Introduction to *The Rime of the Ancient Mariner*" (*DG*, 186-225), which is, of all his writings, the best introduction to the symbolism of his own poem too.

                           before they unbound the last glaciation
           for the Uhland Father to be-ribbon *die blaue Donau*
                       with his Vanabride blue.
O long before they lateen'd her Ister
or Romanitas manned her gender'd stream.

O Europa!
                                        how long and long and long and
very long again, before you'll maze the waltz-forms in gay Vindobona in
the ramshackle last phases; or god-shape the modal rhythms for nocturns in Melk in the young-time; or plot the Rhaetian limits in the
Years of the City.
             But already he's at it
the form-making proto-maker
busy at the fecund image of her.
             Chthonic? why yes
but mother of us.
      Then it is these abundant *ubera*, here, under the species of worked
lime-rock, that gave suck to the lord? She that they already venerate
(what other could they?)
             her we declare?
Who else?   (*A*, 59-60)

There is much more in this passage than I need for the
immediate purpose of illustration; but I could not write on
David Jones at length without quoting it, and it is relevant
to much else in this essay besides the stone symbol. Here,
early man is recalled as maker of images of the forces on
which his life depends. At first, he apprehends the divine
presence as the creative principle in nature, which he
shapes under the form of the Great Mother. In course of
time and a long process of artistic and cultural differentiation the image of Venus Genetrix, the Aurignacian "Venus
of Willendorf" is refined into separate aspects of the female
principle--as in "the Delectable Korê" (*A*, 92), for example--
which men worship or which drive men mad. All are re-
integrated and purified in the figure of the Queen of
Heaven whose images, in the Middle Ages, embody all
man's yearning for creaturely and divine love. Venus Genetrix, carved in stone, is "fecund" in two senses. She is an
image of the chthonic powers which give birth to man and
nature alike, and her image generates a long line of developing images of the female principle. Although it is an
image of fecundity which early man shapes, she is truly
"mother of us": matrix of Western culture. So *The Anathemata* recalls man in the process of creating his culture by
making signs for the forces which move him to the depths
of his being, because they express his true nature. His signs
are images by which he grows, and to which he adapts himself: forms which develop in complexity with the rise of the

West which they partially bring about. Hence the impor-
tance of Troy for the West, and of the legendary founding of
Troy Novant by the Trojans on the site of London for
Britain. Troy, with the figures of Hector and Helen, is

> matrix for West-*oppida*
> for West-technic
> for West-saga (*A*, 57)

Similarly, David Jones traces Western culture back into the
matrix of stone. It was "these abundant *ubera*, here, under
the species of worked lime-rock, that gave suck to the lord."
Even the Madonna is dependent on the forms which man
made, preceding her, and preparing her image, from the
dawn of prehistory. Yet she is pre-eminently the mother
which the early signs shadowed in the stone. Troy, on the
other hand, symbolizes man's divided nature: "while our civilization remains the word 'Troy' will equate automatically
with 'love and war' " (*A*, 57). But without that division, that
"fault" in the very seams of being, there would have been no
need of a sacrificial Death to engender life.

Stone in *The Anathemata*, as in the history of man, is
both an unchanging substance and infinitely adaptable to
human use, both material and sign. Wood, likewise. Under
the form of the sacred tree, wood is a sign for the Cross; as a
material, it is the stuff from which the ship is made. The
ship is the vessel of culture, no less adaptable than stone
and always voyaging laden with the commodities and raw
materials, the ideas and beliefs which fuse with, modify or
transform native traditions and draw "Brut's Albion" into the
culture of the West. In "Keel, Ram, Stauros" wood is
recalled as the primary material of armaments as well as of
Cross and ship, and thus, in these differentiated forms, signifies the division--yet also the interaction--between commerce, warfare, and religion in the development of the
West. The ship links wood and water, and is fused with the
symbolic vessel of Christ's "voyage," as it is described in a
keynote: "What is pleaded in the Mass is precisely the
argosy or voyage of the Redeemer, consisting of his entire
sufferings and his death, his conquest of hades, his resurrection and his return in triumph to heaven" (*A*, 106). The argonauts or prospectors are described as "the precursors at the
steer-trees" (*A*, 158), and the steer-tree is a sign for the
Cross. It is they who, from long before historical times, carried "the Mediterranean thing" (*A*, 105) westward, and so
opened up "the history-paths" by which Christianity, in the
wake of cults of the Great Mother, reached the shores of

Britain. Thus steer-tree and Cross, the argonauts and Christ
the argonaut, are united without loss of identity in the symbol of the ship, which is, of course, a traditional symbol of
the Church, elaborately re-fitted and deep-laden. The voyage symbolizes both an Otherworld Voyage, described in
specifically Christian terms but drawing on the provenance
of this theme in Celtic legend, and countless voyages
through the seas of this world. It is able, therefore, to assim-
ilate other figures--including Arthur and Odysseus--to its
symbolic pattern, and to combine elements of history and
myth. The ship symbol is launched early on in "Rite and
Fore-Time" when the seats at the Last Supper are described
as the "thwart-boards" (*A*, 53)--which, incidentally, is a nice
example of David Jones' common practice of marrying a
technical term and a term with theological significance.
The ship then proceeds, without ever losing its primary religious meaning, to become the vessel bearing innumerable
voyagers, from the prospectors of prehistory to "the fratri-
cides of the latter-day," and hence commerce, warfare, and
cult: the main elements formative of Britain within the
West. It is a deep, extremely complex symbol, protean in its
metamorphoses, flexible in its fusions and adaptations, and
at once physical and metaphysical, calling to mind David
Jones' note on the English Metaphysicals, "who wrote a
poetry that was counter-Renaissant, creaturely yet other-
world-ordered, ecstatical yet technically severe and inge-
nious, concerned with conditions of the psyche, but its
images very much of the soma; metaphysical, but not un-
intrigued by the physics of the period; English, but well represented by names hardly English" (*A*, 17)--which, with certain slight modifications to make it, so to speak, more nautical, applies admirably to *The Anathemata*. The brief
sketch I have given here barely indicates the symbol's depth
of meaning; and the conjunction of ship and water remains
to be considered.

A note on "the sign-stream" in "Sherthursday and
Venus Day" helps to disclose the complex unity of David
Jones' imaginative world:

> The references are: to the term "valid matter" used by theologians of
> the material water in the Sacrament of Water; to the material water
> essential to the Sacrament of Bread and Wine; to the water-metaphor
> used of all the seven signs; to the entire sign-world to which the
> metaphor of water flowing from a common source could apply; to the
> actual streams, our rivers, which are themselves signs of conveyance
> and themselves physically convey, which not only provide the
> metaphors but the material stuff without which the sacraments could
> not be. (*A*, 236)

Since the implications of this note for *The Anathemata* would require a book to draw out, I shall confine myself to stating the aspects of water as material and sign which I believe to be of principal importance in the poem. First, material water is essential to the Sacraments, and the Sacraments are fundamental "to the entire sign-world to which the metaphor of water flowing from a common source could apply." Secondly, water is a primary symbol of woman, especially of woman as mother. Thirdly, "in Britain, 'water' is unavoidably very much part of the *materia poetica*" (*A*, 17)--for the reasons stated above and because Britain is an island, historically dependent upon water for contact with and defense against other peoples, and a place where, from ancient times, streams and rivers, springs and pools, have been sacred to female tutelary spirits. Indeed, a large part of its Celtic mythology, including "The Mothers" and the close link between women and the otherworld, belongs to the same domain as the latter. Fourthly, water is integral to the Waste Land theme. The Grail Castle is usually located in a semi-aquatic area, and whether the object of the quest is interpreted in Christian or pagan terms, as spiritual renewal or the renewal of fertility, it is bound up with "the freeing of the waters." Moreover, in "death by water" and similar themes water symbolizes the element of rebirth and is an organic part of the pattern of initiation. Further, "crossing the water" is often a rite of passage between two worlds or states of being, and the semi-aquatic area of the Grail Castle is a semi-magical locality or borderland[8] between this world and the otherworld. Although all these meanings of the Water-sign are fused in *The Anathemata*, I cannot deal with them as a whole or with each separately here. There are however two aspects of the symbolism that I must discuss in more detail.

The Lady of the Pool, native to the place where the inland waters flow into the sea and the culture-streams flow into the river, is tutelar of the Pool of London. Constant through all her metamorphoses she guards "the foundational things" of Brut's Albion and keeps the sign-stream of "this Matriarch's Isle" (*A*, 145). The Pool is both the historical Pool of London and the common source of all our island

8. David Jones' fullest discussion of the symbolic borderland of Celtic myth and legend occurs in "The Myth of Arthur" (*E&A*), although it appears as an important "location" in his work as early as *IP*. I have discussed his use of the borderland in *John Cowper Powys and David Jones: A Comparative Study* (London: Enitharmon Press, 1979), especially pp. 29-30. Alwyn and Brinley Rees' *Celtic Heritage* (London: Thames and Hudson, 1961), has much of interest to say on this theme, as well as on other Celtic matters which play an important part in the work of David Jones.

signs. It is where "the old Jason" (*A*, 121) calls for repairs to
the ship on "Eb Bradshaw, Princes Stair" (*A*, 118), and thus
combines the poet's personal memories and ancestral
waterside past, through his maternal grandfather, with the
older deposits of the Island. It is the Lady who speaks for
the protective powers that lie at the sacred foundations of
the city--"chthonic *matres* under the croft" (*A*, 127) and
"slumberers" like Arthur (*A*, 164)--powers opposed to the
destructive forces which, even now, in the period of the
poem's composition, have devastated the city and are
continuing to reduce the diverse traditions of Britain to an
uniform "Engle-raum." It is she who represents the creative
female principle in its human and elemental forms, "the
mother" whose "deep fluvial doings" have caused "a deal of
subsidence hereabouts" and whose regenerative power
represents the hope, both for Britain and for the individual
mind cut off from deep sources of renewal, that "what's
under works up" (*A*, 164). Yet through all her changes she is
one person, a cockney lavender-seller, credulous, tender, and
humorous, aware of her own charms and susceptible to the
attraction of men. Rooted deep in time, her language is
richly sensuous from the long contact of people with place.
It is principally through her, at the center of the poem, that
British history and mythology are reborn as a living
national past. But she too, like many of the female figures
in *The Anathemata*, is but one aspect of the female presence
who shares with the central male figure sovereignty of the
whole. In order to take this point further I shall have first to
say more about the pattern of initiation referred to earlier.

4

The archetypal pattern of initiation is the form of many
myths and legends--including the Grail legends and their
integral Waste Land theme--as well as of much of the Christian religion and of many, often formally and thematically
diverse, literary works. It is a pattern with many associated
symbols, and I believe that almost all David Jones' writings
embody it, in varying degrees of completeness, as a unifying
structural principle. In general, the initiation, the rebirth,
the change of state or the passage from one world or dimension of reality to another, can take many forms. It is not
procrustean, though it will be conditioned by the writer's
beliefs. It should also be said that, although the idea of
archetypes in its modern form obviously owes a lot to Jung,
there is no reason why the truth of the archetype should be

considered to be only psychological, instead of a universal truth in which the psyche recognizes its deepest needs. This should be borne in mind together with the fact that David Jones saw myth not as fiction, but as a vessel of reality, which to him was "sacred and religious" (*E&A*, 158), according to his specific belief.

According to the writings[9] of W. F. Jackson Knight, the labyrinth is intimately connected with the ritual pattern of initiation as the place, often a tomb or cave, where in ancient times the initiate participated in the cosmic marriage between earth mother and sacred king. In fact, the labyrinth was both the body of the earth mother and the tomb of the sacred king, thus in some sense uniting the opposites of male and female, life and death, heaven and earth. This is not the place to tread out the fascinating pattern of Jackson Knight's ideas; I merely wish to make three steps relevant to the subject of this essay. First, this ancient pattern, of entry into the labyrinth for the purpose of rebirth, is still a potent metaphor capable of recovering some of its primal significance or of embodying more sophisticated religious or psychic meanings. Secondly, labyrinths or mazes are boundaries, or symbolic boundaries, between different worlds or realities or forms of order, and may permit or withhold entry under certain circumstances. Thirdly, they are closely associated with earth and water--above all, with the apprehension of earth as the Great Mother and of water as the element of rebirth.

Writing to Harman Grisewood on 13 April 1940, David Jones recorded his enthusiastic response to *Cumaean Gates*, which he was then reading or had recently read for the first time, and commented that, "of course it all bears very much on the thing I'm trying to write" (*DGC*, 95). He remarked in the same letter that, "if there were one or two more Jackson Knights who combined real slap-up scholarship with a nose for the pattern and eternal correspondence of this with that, it would be jolly nice and helpful." In the Preface to *The Anathemata* he singles out Jackson Knight for special mention of his indebtedness to him, second only to Christopher Dawson: "Then there is Mr. W. F. Jackson Knight whose particular *numen* or sprite is something of an Ariadne, who pays out more than one length of thread" (*A*, 36). But what exactly was the nature of David Jones' debt to Jackson Knight? In my view, it was for confirming and

---

9. The principal writings in this context are *Cumaean Gates* and *Vergil's Troy*, referred to in note 2 above.

clarifying what he already half-knew, and deeply felt, even
more than for exciting scholarly information. What he
found elaborated and illumined by Jackson Knight was "the
pattern and eternal correspondence of this with that" which
he had already discovered for himself.

Indeed, a writer may learn about archetypal patterns
from his reading, but the force of his use of them will
depend upon the extent to which he is *their* discovery; and
in the work the pattern will be discovered in the material,
not imposed upon it. This is the case with David Jones. The
conscious use of symbol and symbolic pattern, which on one
level reveals the scope and depth of his reading, is primarily dependent on his discovery of their significance from
within, from experience of chaos and order, and on his
capacity to keep the lines of communication open between
child and man, and past and present. *In Parenthesis*, written before David Jones had read Jackson Knight, already
embodies the pattern of initiation, into two opposed but
inter-related forms of order, and even makes fragmentary
use of the labyrinth to symbolize the trenches and the
thoughts of the men. There, in the labyrinth of the mind,
boundaries between past and present crumble, and the
trenches are a boundary between the familiar, civilized
world and a primeval state of existence. They are
labyrinthine, subterranean, and a watery, earthen grave. As
in the ritual pattern of initiation labyrinth and cave, womb
and tomb, are virtually identical as symbols of the earth
mother's body, so *In Parenthesis* describes the trenches, at
various times, in images of all of these. The effectiveness
of the depiction of the Western Front as a Waste Land is due
largely to its consonance with the realistic portrayal of the
trenches as a wasted, labyrinthine area of mud and water,
and to the Arthurian material mediated by the Welshmen
and the allusions to Malory. The Grail quest is a form of
the archetypal pattern of initiation, and the men, as
sacrificial victims and as restorers of order, are related to
protagonists of the quest on two levels. *In Parenthesis*
shows that the place in which David Jones experienced
chaos was also where he perceived the form of a great
order.

In *The Anathemata* birth and rebirth are major
themes, united by the common element of water and the
archetypal pattern of initiation. Both themes are inseparable from the central figures of Christ and Mary--rarely mentioned by name, and never in a devotional context in this
great devotional poem. David Jones emphasizes Christ's

physical birth. He "is called He-with-us / because he did
not abhor the uterus" (*A*, 75). He "was hers / that laboured
with him that laboured long for us at the wine-press" (*A*,
156). Labor has, of course, two meanings in this context: it
signifies the labors of Christ, by analogy with the labors of
Hercules, and the travail of his mother. These meanings are
fused in the voyage which symbolizes, in yet another pattern
of associations, the birth of Christ the argonaut. In the
imagery of an allied symbolic pattern, which draws on
David Jones' favorite Celtic myth, Christ is for nine months
the sleeping lord:

> Marquis of demarking waters
> > Warden of the Four Lands
> from her salined deeps
> from the cavern'd waters
> > (where she ark'd him) come.
> > His members in-folded
> like the hidden lords in the West-tumuli
> for the nine dark calends gone.
> Grown in stature
> > he frees the waters. (*A*, 224-225)

Characteristically, the passage combines the waters of the
world with the waters of the womb and the sacramental,
restorative waters, which themselves have several meanings.
Water therefore unites the historical, biological, mythological and religious meanings of the voyage; it is life-giving
under all these forms and as both element and sign it carries a complex but unified significance: "one man, by water,
restores to us our state" (*A*, 238). Christ, "the *fons*-head," the
original and continuous source of the sign-stream, who
uttered the terrible, "desiderate cry: / SITIO" (I thirst) (*A*,
237), chose the waters of the womb. The poem insists on
this fact more than on any other except the fact of the
Cross, and it insists on the regenerative, life-giving nature of
the Death on the Cross. Thus, as a meditation "in the time
of the Mass," *The Anathemata* contemplates, above all, the
Redemption. It insists upon Mary's Fiat and upon the fact
that Christ was born of woman though engendered by no
mortal man. Its symbols and images stress the union of
nature and divinity in the Incarnation, and its depiction of
cosmic order centers on this fact. As one of the sisters in
"Mabinog's Liturgy" says: "Begetters of all huge endevour we
are. The Lord God may well do all without the aid of man,
but even in the things of god a woman is medial--it stands
to reason" (*A*, 214). Again at the heart of the poem, the ship
symbol is intimately associated with Mary, its tutelar, when
the Lady of the Pool says:

> her fiat is our fortune, sir: like Helen's face
> 'twas that as launched the ship.
>
> (*A*, 128)

Mary is "the Mistress of Lodemanage," Christ is her "storm-quelling son" (*A*, 167). When the poem ends at the Cross, which is where it began, in presence of the sacrifice on the altar, it is "the voyage-end" (*A*, 242).

The poem celebrates a birth which is at once the birth of Christ, the birth of the West, and the rebirth of man through the Redemption. But it simultaneously celebrates a marriage too, since "He that was her son / is now her lover" (*A*, 224). Or, more drily, as David Jones puts it in a note, because, "to use a mythologer's terms, she (Mary) is both bride and mother of the cult-hero" (*A*, 234). Consequently, with more subtle fusions than I can describe, the protean "he" and "she" of the poem are united in the relation of son and mother, groom and bride, lover and beloved--and of captain and ship, sun and moon, diversity and universal order. Christ, the principle of universal order, is wedded to Mary, the tutelar of all creaturely and culturally diverse forms. Thus *The Anathemata* celebrates, on a cosmic scale, both a rebirth, and a birth and marriage. But these are not separate: they are figures in a single archetypal pattern, which is fulfilled in David Jones' Christian belief.

This, then, is what I mean by the complex unity of the poem, and it is in accordance with this interpretation that I apprehend its form. David Jones says that "if it has a shape it is chiefly that it returns to its beginning" (*A*, 33). Gwyn Williams has suggested that both *In Parenthesis* and *The Anathemata* are "constructed on an inter-weaving pattern" similar to that used in certain early Welsh poems such as *Y Gododdin*, and has likened the pattern, evocatively, to the form of "stone circles or the contour-following rings of the forts from which they (the Celts) fought."[10] With regard to the fusion of symbols in the poem, Jacobsthal's description of the characteristic "ambiguity" of Celtic art and of "the mechanism of dreams, where things have floating contours and pass into other things"[11] is suggestive. This is relevant to David Jones' paintings too, and recalls the working of dreams as described by his Private Clitus, with their endless "recessions" and "superimpositions," "precision and exac-

---

10. Gwyn Williams, *Welsh Poems: Sixth Century to 1600* (London: Faber, 1973), p. 11. Originally *The Burning Tree*, with Welsh texts. David Jones' article on the latter, "Welsh Poetry," was reprinted in *E&A*, and includes the comment on Joyce and the Book of Kells quoted above.

11. Quoted in Myles Dillon and Nora Chadwick, *The Celtic Realms* (London: Cardinal edition, 1973), p. 32.

titude" of "dream-data," "comings together" and "unions,"
"possibilities" and "metamorphoses" (*SL*, 17-21), which is sin-
gularly revealing of his methods as artist and writer. Not
surprisingly, David Jones' comments on Celtic visual and
aural art are no less apposite to his own work. For example:
"In that visual art questions of the formal and the contential
hardly arise because what we see is the visible image of
their union. It was just this total oneness of form and content that the unflinching integrity of Joyce was determined
to achieve in literary form; it was not for nothing that he
looked steadfastly at a page from Kells" (*E & A*, 63-64).
All these descriptions have imaginative appeal, yet, when
applied to *The Anathemata*, do little more than suggest
metaphors for its method and form. That is the danger when
writing about this subject, and I offer the following idea
tentatively, conscious that it may not avoid it.

I believe that in celebrating a cosmic birth and
marriage in *The Anathemata* David Jones discovers the form
proper to his themes. That is to say, it has the form of a
labyrinth or circular maze. The poet himself virtually says
as much in the Preface. He refers, in a modest but significant image, to "the meanderings that comprise this book."
He observes that "making a work is not thinking thoughts
but accomplishing an actual journey." It is particularly
revealing when he writes: "there is indeed an intention to
'uncover'; which is what a 'mystery' does, for though at root
'mystery' implies a closing, all 'mysteries' are meant to disclose, to show forth something." (*A*, 33). *The Anathemata*
does indeed accomplish a journey, a journey of intricate
and by no means aimless "meanderings" that "returns to its
beginnings," and it leads the reader through the maze in
order "to disclose, to show forth something." The journey is
based on two principal quest motifs--the Grail Quest and the
Otherworld Voyage--together with the historical voyages of
the argonauts. Each of these is sufficiently complex in
itself but all are united by the common element or symbol
of water, by the fact that each is a quest which involves
crossing the water, and by the comprehensive archetypal
pattern of initiation to which each belongs. Each journey
entails facing dangers and even death with the object of
winning new life or a new beginning; each is associated
with a union of the male and female principles; each either
starts from the same center, to which it returns, or, in the
case of the argonauts, helps to prepare or propagate the center, which is, of course, the Cross; symbolically, each begins
from and returns to the same place. The Cross represents

the life-engendering Death and is inseparable from the cosmic marriage. Consequently the poem has the form of a labyrinth or circular maze; but it is a circle whose center is everywhere. This, too, is what the poem "uncovers": the omnipresence of the Cross. Jackson Knight has described this elaborate pattern in its primal form and argued that the rebirth derives from participation in a sacred marriage of heaven and earth in the tomb or cave that is also the place of generation. David Jones uses it to disclose the cosmic union, within the primeval cave, of forces which reason polarizes, and to show forth the Christian union which it prefigures, in a sophisticated, deeply devotional, unified Catholic vision of the relation of man to God, man to woman, creator to creation. The cosmic dimension is achieved, then, partly by setting the action celebrated by the Mass in the context of the primeval initiation in which the neophyte was reborn through his participation in a union of natural and divine forces; partly by the elemental symbolism of water, wood, and stone; and partly by the prevalence in the poem of the language and rhythms of the liturgy. The liturgy of the Church echoes the rhythms and imagery of the changing seasons, but David Jones apprehends a cosmic liturgy in the vast movements of geological time:

> Now, from the draughty flats
>   the ageless cherubs
> pout the Southerlies.
> Now, Januarius brings in the millennial snow that makes the antlered mummers glow for many a hemera.
>   The *Vorzeit*-masque is on
> that moves to the cosmic introit.
> *Col canto* the piping for this turn.
> Unmeasured, irregular in stress and interval, of interior rhythm, modal.
>   If tonic and final are fire
> the dominant is ice
>   if fifth the fire
> the cadence ice.
> At these Nocturns the hebdomadary is apt to be vested for five hundred thousand weeks. (*A*, 63)

The awe generated by these vast temporal and spatial movements is matched by the tenderness with which he perceives the same harmonies in all creative human and natural activities. All the movements, represented by rhythms that modulate between the excitingly dynamic and the subtle and delicate, and by the language and symbolism, are embodied in a form which is probably the most elaborate enactment of the ritual pattern of initiation in all literature.

THOMAS DILWORTH

THE SHAPE OF TIME IN
THE ANATHEMATA

The form of a literary work is related to, but not the same as, its meaning. A work must generate its own form and--to the extent that its subject matter is not already given significance by tradition or convention--it must also discover significant pattern or relationships in its content. For a work of large scope, and for the long poem especially, the subject matter in which meaning must be sought is always, to some extent, time. The greater the time-span, the more urgent the need for significance. The temporal scope of *The Anathemata* encompases prehistory and the whole of ancient and modern Western history. In the poem, a complex and original structure does interpret this expanse of time.[1] So does a thoroughgoing symbolic resonance which, in various ways, interrelates most of the work's images, figures and speaking personae.[2] But aesthetic form is limited in its ability to discover significance in so vast a subject. To thoroughly interpret Western history, therefore, David Jones also employs a theory of culture to govern selection and emphasis. This theory allows him to delineate the changing status through time of spiritual values within phases of civilization, and enables *The Anathemata* to discern in history a distinctive inscape. Jones' theory of culture is not only a

---

1. The complex symbolic structure of the poem is discussed in my article "The Anagogical Form of *The Anathemata*," *Mosaic* XII (Winter, 1979), pp. 183-95, and in my recent book, *The Shape of Meaning in the Poetry of David Jones* (Toronto: University of Toronto, 1988), pp. 156-74. I am grateful to the trustees of the estate of David Jones for permission to quote from the poet's unpublished letters and manuscript drafts in the present essay, a version of which also appears in *The Shape of Meaning*, pp. 181-200.
2. These unifying symbolic interreverberations were first considered in Jeremy Hooker's *David Jones an Exploratory Study* (London: Enitharmon Press, 1975), pp. 40-8; and have been examined more recently in Neil Corcoran's *The Song of Deeds* (Cardiff: University of Wales Press, 1982), pp. 78-91; in Vincent B. Sherry Jr.'s "Current Critical Models of the Long Poem and David Jones' *The Anathemata*," *ELH* 52 (Spring, 1985), pp. 244-9, and in chapters five and six of *The Shape of Meaning in the Poetry of David Jones*.

means to ordering the content of the poem but also an original and important contribution to modern thought.

By impressionistic time-shifting, the meditative consciousness of *The Anathemata* zigzags back and forth through Western history. The result of this fracturing of chronology is to imply a temporal structure more significant than mere diachronic sequence. Similarities between various culture-phases gradually emerge which initially suggest Spengler's morphology of cultural life-cycles. Here David Jones is indebted to *The Decline of the West,* which he read shortly after the First World War and reread in the 1940s while working on *The Anathemata.*[3] In a Spenglerian sense, parallel phases are contemporary. They occupy identical sections of time's morphological curve. But Spengler's conceptualization of time is modelled on the biological cycle, whereas David Jones' conceptualization is modelled on the seasonal and mythic cycle of birth-maturity-death-and-rebirth, which he derives, partly at least, from *The Golden Bough.* In *The Anathemata,* declining civilizations become matrices for cultural vitality that eventually transforms collapse into renewal. This schema extenuates the cultural mortality of Spengler's closed circles, therefore, by breaking them, connecting them to each other in sequence, and extending them into a spiral.[4] In this way, the poet retains the conventional continuity of ancient, medieval and modern culture-phases which Spengler intends to do away with by separating 'Classical' culture from 'modern' culture. The spiral of time is initially suggested by the poem's epigraph, a folk-fragment suggestive of an infinite regression of circles connected by narrative continuity so that they form a spiral:

> IT WAS A DARK AND STORMY NIGHT, WE SAT BY THE CALCINED WALL; IT WAS SAID TO THE TALE-TELLER, TELL US A TALE, AND THE TALE RAN THUS: IT WAS A DARK AND STORMY NIGHT...

By assimilating the audience, moreover, this aural fragment implies the trans-fictional aspect of the poem as concerning the historico-cultural reality "WE" inhabit.

The meaning of time's continuous helix is not merely progression--as, for example, with the Hegelian dialectic; the spiral remains Spenglerian to the extent that

---

3. According to his note on its front end-papers, Jones acquired his own copy of the book on "Aug. 19th, 1941." We know he was "immersed in Spengler" in February 1942 (*DGC*, 115).
4. In his copy of Patricia Hutchins' *James Joyce's World* (London: Methuen, 1957), David Jones underlines her contention that time is "a spiral, not a straight line" and writes in the margin, "concedo" (81).

it retains morphological repetition. In this respect, Jones' temporal schema resembles that of Yeats. For both poets, morphological repetition makes possible, through significant similarities and differences, the psychological illumination of historically separate culture-phases. But Yeats' long view of time is limited to meaningless movement back and forth within interpenetrating gyres. The centre of Jones' spiral is, by contrast, a continuous forward movement which is teleological and, as we shall see, gives time a cosmic significance. But the initial difference between the morphologies of Yeats and Jones is in the psychological principle by which each discriminates between culture-phases.

For David Jones, the principle of discrimination is the general balance in a culture-phase between utility and gratuity--utility being the technological motive; gratuity the quality essential to religion and art. Derived originally from Aristotle, the distinction between utility and gratuity "is the only rubicon" Jones acknowledges as "dividing the activities of man" (*E&A*, 275). A culture-phase predominantly on one side or the other of this rubicon produces anathemata, or special things, by which its character may be distinguished. Jones' idea of anathemata partly derives from Spengler's conception of symptoms of "the physiognomic of world happening":

> Poems and battles, Isis and Cybele, festivals and Roman Catholic masses, blast furnaces and gladiatorial games, dervishes and Darwinians, railways and Roman roads, "Progress" and Nirvana, newspapers, mass-slavery, money, machinery--all these are equally signs and symbols in the world-picture of the past that the soul presents to itself and would interpret.

David Jones brackets this passage in the copy of *The Decline of the West* that he was reading in the 1940s (I, 160). For the poet, the physiognomic symbols, or anathemata, on one side of the rubicon contrast with those on the other side. Jones intends the title of his poem to connote this contrast: he writes in his Preface that the word "anathemata," which originally means "holy things," means just the opposite in the New Testament, and he continues, "this duality exactly fitted my requirements," serving "my double purpose, even if it did so only by means of a pun" on the English "anathema" (*A*, 28). The duality of Jones' title deserves stressing, since critics habitually interpret the word "anathemata" only in its positive sense.[5] Positive anathemata symbolically

---

5. See most recently Corcoran, p. 10; and Rosenthal and Gall, *The Modern Poetic Sequence* (New York and Oxford: Oxford University Press), p. 299. The only critics who explicitly recognize the antithetical meaning of "anathemata" are William Noon SJ,

express positive spiritual values; negative anathemata imply the displacement of such values by pragmatism and expediency. Positive anathemata are primarily symbolic; negative anathemata are only secondarily, and inadvertently, symbolic. Between these two extremes are anathemata which combine the gratuitous with the utile in equal or inverse proportions. The proportion or disproportion of this combination is the primary indicator of the spiritual and cultural condition of a historical phase. Another, parallel indicator, in this poem, is the presence or absence of imperialism.

The exploration of time in *The Anathemata* extends back into prehistoric fore-time, but only during the three millennia of Western history does a spiralling shape clearly emerge. This shape is that of a continual metamorphosis which formally evokes and extends through history the geological and evolutionary mutations which are the subjects of the poem's opening section, *Rite and Foretime.* During the historical millennia, culture-phases rhyme to form a pattern centering at the time of Christ. In this respect David Jones shapes his Spenglerian-Frazerian synthesis to traditional patristic historiography.

In *The Anathemata*, the phases preceding the incarnation rhyme with corresponding phases that follow it. The aftermath of the Dorian invasion rhymes with the Dark Ages, sixth-century Greece rhymes with the high Middle Ages, fifth-century Greece rhymes with the late Middle Ages, and the period of Roman World-dominance rhymes with the modern commercial and industrial age which extends from the Renaissance to the present. While consistent in sequence, these chronological parallels involve no relative correspondence between dates or durations of phases. There are, furthermore, internal rhymes cutting across the regular rhyme-pattern which preclude simplistic schematization, and which have, till now, obscured the poem's cultural *cynghanedd* of historical phases.

The Dark Ages that follow the fall of Rome rhyme with the wake of Mycenaean civilization, which is destroyed by Dorian "storm-groups" (*A*, 90). As the evocation of Nazi *blitzkriegs* suggests, David Jones believes we are now entering a new Dark Age.[6] But the correspondence is primarily between the Dorian invasion and the barbarian destruction of classical Roman civilization.

Poetry and Prayer (New Jersey: Rutgers University Press, 1966), pp. 228-9; and Ann Carson Daley, "The Amphibolic Title of *The Anathemata*," *Renascence* XXXV (Autumn 1982), p. 49 ff.
6. In a letter to Desmond Chute, Jones writes, "we are in the 6th . . . Cent." (*IN*, 57).

The Dorian warriors "fractured the archaic pattern," and their rule from the end of the Bronze Age into the Iron Age is distinguished by no enduring cultural achievement. The voice of the poem asks, however,

> Within the hoop
> of the iron years
> the age is obscure--
> and is the age dark? (*A*, 90)

Darkness, as distinct from obscurity, may be no more applicable here than it is to the period glibly called the Dark Ages by historians of the Enlightenment. If Greek artisans under Dorian rule "beat out utile spares," they also shape "amulets" to signify the "new god-fears" of raiding Dorian captains. Here, as in the recent Dark Ages, gratuity is eventually restored to balance utility, and this makes possible a renewal of cultural vitality: "From the tomb of the strife-years the new-born shapes begin already to look uncommonly like the brats of mother Europa" (*A*, 91). The tomb of Mycenae is the womb of the ancient West--at parturition, "the West-wind on our cheek-bones." If this age is dark, it is the darkness of dawn, "very grey and early in our morning" (*A*, 91).

The corresponding gestation of the modern West during the more recent Dark Age is the subject of the poem's third section, *Angle-Land*, and is touched on during the description of Gwenhwyfar in the seventh section, *Mabinog's Liturgy*. In the latter, in Britain at the start of the Dark Age, "the situation is obscure" (*A*, 204) and so recalls that of post-Mycenaean Greece. A century or more later, in what is now Angle-land, barbarian invaders have fractured the archaic pattern of Roman city-life. Once-civilized Roman Britons are forced to flee

> from the *fora*
> to the forests
> Out from *gens Romulum*
> into the *Weal*-kin
> *dinas*-man gone *aethwlad*
> *cives* gone wold-men... (*A*, 113)

The cultural mix-up of Latin, Celtic, and Teutonic elements is figured in the language--fractured and fused, halting, broken (though musically assonant), Babel-like. Concerning the start of the current Dark Age, when post-Roman Britons fight a guerrilla war, it is asked,

> has toga'd Rhufon
> (gone Actaeon)
> come away to the Wake...? (*A*, 112)

"The Wake" is the funeral watch and eddying aftermath of
Roman Britain, and it also recalls the Saxon outlaw Here-
ward the Wake, or "the alert," who, centuries later, will resist
the Norman invaders, and so re-enact the present resistance.
"The Wake" evokes *Finnegans Wake*, furthermore, which is
concerned, like *Angle-Land*, with metamorphoses of language and culture, and, like *The Anathemata* as a whole,
with cyclic time. The evocation of Joyce's *Wake* implies
imminent cultural revival.

The nature of this revival is hinted at by reference
to Irish "Nials gathering hostages" (*A*, 204), who include St.
Patrick. He is one of the Celtic saints, many of whom will
enter England and appeal to the "god-fears" of the barbarians who dread the apparition of a Roman-British ghost
announcing "IAM REDIT ROMA" (*A*, 112). The Latin is from
Virgil's Fourth Eclogue, which was interpreted in the early
Church as prophesying the coming of Christ. Here it also
recalls the prophecy about Arthur, who led the Roman-
British resistance, a prophecy which has affinity with the
words of MacArthur, "I shall return."[7] Christian culture will
return, and it will be Roman.

Cultural renewal is the primary difference between
Jones' historical schema and that of Spengler, for whom a
culture dies and remains dead at the end of its life cycle.
Because Elizabeth Ward thinks Jones merely borrows Spengler's morphology, without transforming it into something
new, she insists repeatedly and at length on the poet's
"historical pessimism" and "private [sic] cultural despair."[8]
Neither pessimistic nor optimistic, unless by turns, Jones'
spiralling schema anticipates more than a new Dark Age,
which in any event is not dark with the darkness of despair
but with the obscurity of gestation which will issue in
rebirth.

In historical sequence, the next correspondence
between culture-phases is between Greece in the sixth century B.C. and Europe in the thirteenth century A.D.

In Hellas it is now, since the Dorian takeover,

7. Arthur's epitaph, *Rex quondam Rexque futurus*, is quoted on p. 164. In 1952 Jones
writes, " 'Arthur' has become as historically feasible as MacArthur, and as congruent
with a given situation" (*E&A*, 201).
8. *David Jones Mythmaker*, pp. 141, 153. Jones' "despair," which is only for our particular phase of culture, can hardly be considered private when it is shared by many of the
great writers and thinkers since the inception of the Industrial Revolution and by the
most important modern writers, including Joyce--if Earwicker's impotence means anything in *Finnegans Wake*--and Beckett. In his Preface to *The Anathemata*, Jones
writes that cultural decline has "been evident in various ways to various people for
perhaps a century; it is now, I suppose, apparent to most" (*A*, 15).

```
Six centuries
          and the second Spring
and a new wonder under heaven:
          man-limb stirs
                    in the god-stones .... (A, 91)
```

This wonder, which contradicts the cynicism of Ecclesiastes, is both aesthetic and spiritual. Greece experiences a "second Spring"--words that combine Spengler's term for cultural vitality with Newman's term for a general renewal of religious life. Before this, cult-statues are almost entirely chthonic, "god-handled" like the Venus of Willendorf (A, 59), but now for the first time sculpted kouroi capture human nature in balance with the divinity they symbolize. This balance is analogous to the hypostatic union of humanity and divinity in Jesus. The analogy is underlined by the statue of the "Delectable Kore," which seems "all parthenai made stone" (A, 92), and is therefore an aesthetic approximation to the Incarnation, in which "the Word was made flesh."

This Kore also evokes famous women--one who helps shape the ancient culture-phase which the Kore represents, and two at least who help shape the modern culture-phase to which the ancient phase corresponds:

```
by the radial flutes for her chiton, the lineal, chiselled hair
the contained rhythm of her
                    is she Elenê Argive
or is she transalpine Eleanore
or our Gwenhwyfar
                    the Selenê of Thulê
                    West-Helen? (A, 92)
```

The career of "transalpine Eleanore" of Aquitaine (transalpine from the Greek point of view) has marked affinities with the story of Helen Argive. Moreover, Eleanore commissioned the Arthurian romances. As the heroine of these romances Gwenhwyfar is "West-Helen"--the counterpart to the heroine of the Homeric epics, which, at this time in Greece, are about a hundred years old in written form. The ancient epics and the modern romances are anathemata with a great deal in common: they are concerned with love, war, and the end of civilizations, and are redactions of centuries-old oral traditions. Regarding this correspondence, the poet writes in an early, pre-foliation draft of the description of Gwenhwyfar in *Mabinog's Liturgy* that she is as

```
Helenê too, for some bitter
tides flooded & neaped to
her lunulations, and over our
```

> New Hissarlik the fires
> > because of her
> & neo-Hectors dead
> > because of her
> and over all the West a New Song
> > to this day
> because of her.

For "transalpine Eleanore," Jones may also have in mind the Eleanore who married Llywelyn, the last Welsh prince, whose death in 1282 is the final reverberation of Arthur's fall, and therefore a near-contemporary historical enactment of the written romances. Jones calls Llywelyn "the living 'Arthur' " (letter to Grisewood, 11 Dec. 1970).

The numinous Kore of sixth-century Greece radiates the profound paradox of feminine humanity. She is "Agelastos Petra," the chthonic Laughless Rock of Eleusis, but as the poem says, addressing her, "you smile from your stone" (*A*, 92). The paradox has to do with Kore Persephone being a dying and rising goddess. Sculpture approximating the Kore in quality, and such a smile, will occur "not again, not now again" until a nameless queen smiles from the *Portail Royal* of Chartres Cathedral, one of the "west-portals / in Gallia Lugdunensis" (*A*, 92), or central France, which David Jones visited in 1933 with Eric Gill. (Together, in fact, they visited Chartres Cathedral.) At Chartres, the lady's smile represents a new, post-Romanesque humanism, and it expresses the belief that she, like the smiling Kore, will rise from the dead. Near the medieval smiler, at the center of the west *portail*, is a statue of Christ in which "the word is made stone" (*A*, 93)--words that echo the description of the sculpted Kore of the earlier, parallel phase.

Now, as then, personal resurrection has its analogue in cultural renewal:

> ... West-wood springs new
> > (and Christ the thrust of it!)
> and loud sings West-cuckoo
> > (Polymnia, how shrill!) (*A*, 92)

In the spirit of the smile, men of the Middle Ages are singing,

> Summer is i-cumen in
> > Lhude sing, cuccu!
> Groweth sed and bloweth med
> > And springth the wude nu.
> > > Sing, cuccu!

From Polymnia, the veiled and solemn muse of stately hymns, this eleventh-century song is surprising. Shrill especially is the word "cuccu," the highest part of the madrigal, sung by the highest voice. It is the high Gothic period, and the high proportion of gratuity and symbolism in its anathemata make this, like sixth-century Greece, a "second Spring."

The spiral of time next turns to the late-classical culture of fifth-century Athens, which corresponds in spirit to the late Middle Ages:

> Down we come
>   quick, but far
> to the splendours
>   to the skill-years
> and the signed and fine grandeurs.
> O yes, technique--but much more:
> the god still is balanced
>   in the man-stones
>   but it's a nice thing
> as near a thing as ever you saw. (*A*, 93-94)

Sculptured figures, now no longer predominantly "god stones," still symbolize divinity, although the balance between god and man is precarious. Examples of such sculpture in this period are the colossal statue of Athena the Champion towering beside the Parthenon and, within, the chryselephantine statue of the Parthenos by Phidias. Athena personifies classical wisdom and evokes the Hellenic devotion to the arts that informs Western culture. The "grandeurs" of Athena are "enough and to snare: / West-academic / West-hearts" (*A*, 94). As everyone knows, the Renaissance seeks to be, and to some extent is, a rebirth of the spirit and ideals of classical Greece. But the correspondence here is to the Middle Ages, which is when this rebirth really begins--with the monastic preservation of classical texts, with the practice of rhetoric and the other classical arts, and with the influence of Aristotle and Plato on scholastic philosophy and theology.

In the fifth section of the poem, Elen Monica--"the Lady of the Pool" of London in the late fifteenth century-- imagines a theological dispute consisting of the interplay of the liberal arts inherited from classical Greece:

> ... does the Trivium curtsy and does each take
> hand and to the Quadrivium call: Music! for a saraband?
>   And does serene Astronomy carry the tonic *Ave* to the
> created spheres, does old Averroes show a leg? (*A*, 129)

If the music of the spheres accompanies an *Ave Maria*, it is because the debate concerns the dignity and theological status of the Virgin Mary, the Christian counterpart of Athena. The Greek goddess in her fifth-century "Maiden's chamber" is a "tower of ivory" and "house of gold" and, towering above the Acropolis outside, a "Virgo Potens" (*A*, 94)-- all titles of Mary in her litany. Like Athena, who personifies wisdom, Mary is liturgically identified with wisdom (see 234 n 1), and "the budged owls" or scholars of Oriel College who argue about her recall the totemic night-birds of Athena-Minerva. On a medieval Christmas Eve in *Mabinog's Liturgy*, the witch Marged says of academics in their ornate universities, "more surely on this night the white owls of Britain, seeking their Lady Wisdom where the columned Purbeck gleams, would find her under Pales' thack, *ad praesepem*"--at the stable (*A*, 215-16). The classical allusion to Pales and the Latin of the medieval nativity hymn concisely evoke the Spenglerean contemporaneity of the late classical and late medieval cultures.

Medieval disputation aesthetically corresponds, moreover, to classical sculpture by maintaining, but only barely, a balance between technique and gratuity--because the elaborate technique of disputation serves the gratuitous purpose implied by the root meaning of the word "philosophy," love-of-wisdom. The ultimate "uselessness" of medieval disputation is underlined by the chaplain of a medieval ship posing the question, "Sirs, consider nautics, is it in itself a good?" and by the vehement cursing this elicits from one of the sailors (*A*, 149).

The balance between "technique" and utility reflects a cultural harmony between what Augustine calls the earthly city and the city of God--"the twin-*urbes*" (*A*, 50) which all men inhabit. Elen Monica indicates this balance in the late Middle Ages when, at the start of *The Lady of the Pool*, she marks time "by tax-chandler's Black Exchecky Book" and also by "Archie's piscopal *Ordo*" (*A*, 127). The imagery here recalls Christ's remark about taxes: "Render to Caesar the things that are Caesar's and to God the things that are God's" (Mark 12:17). Late classical Greece and late medieval Europe have in common, then, this exact cultural balance, "as near a thing as ever you saw."

Time's spiral turns, finally, to the period of Roman World-dominance, which corresponds to the military and commercial imperialism that begins in the Renaissance and reaches its height in the mid-twentieth century. Of all the poem's temporal parallels, this one receives by far the

greatest emphasis, and it demands, therefore, special attention. One of the criticisms of *The Anathemata* that irked
David Jones is the complaint that the poem is not contemporary in its content, that it "draws mainly on the last few
millenniums *exclusive of the last few decades*" (*E&A*, 138).
Recent decades are not absent from the poem but present
by implication through analogues in Roman history which
presume the reader's knowledge of contemporary history.
This is a reversal of what Eliot calls "the mythic method,"
for the implied parallel works from the past to the present.
In this poem, moreover, the twentieth century is an extension of the previous century, which receives a great deal of
explicit attention.

The correspondence between imperial Rome and the
present age is established at the start of the poem by the
"Cult-man" who is at once, metaphorically or by double
exposure, an ancient Roman pontifex and a modern
Catholic priest (*A*, 50). Both priests live in phases of civilization in which aesthetic and spiritual balance has been
lost, though neither priest may realize "that dead symbols
litter to the base of the cult-stone, that the stem by the
palled stone is thirsty, that the stream is very low" (*A*, 50).
(The stone table, the tree and the pool of the Roman
Atrium are also the altar, the cross and the font of a modern church.) The images here evoke those of Eliot's *The
Waste Land*, in which

> ... you know only
> A heap of broken images, where the sun beats,
> And the dead tree gives no shelter, ...
> And the dry stone no sound of water. (lines 21-24)

As the surviving cult implies, for early Rome there
were once "wonder years" (*A*, 85). But numinous myth has
been displaced by imperialism and pragmatism. This
change is captured in the metamorphosis of the god Mars
implied in the recollection of him by the earth-figure Ilia,
on whom he fathered Romulus and Remus. In words
evocative of the coming of the Holy Spirit at Pentecost, she
remembers "how his glory filled the whole place where we
were together" (85, see Acts II, 1-2). He is "of the
Clarissimi"--a member of the highest social rank but also, as
one of "the bright ones" of heaven, a god and a planet. But
he approaches Mother Earth like a technocrat. First he
surveys the site, locating the position of the market place
on the Palatine where the "sacred commerce" is to take
place. Then he proceeds, without gratuitous foreplay, "nor
had he gratitude to unlace the mired greaves of surly iron"

(*A*, 87). In retrospect, Ilia realizes that "his aquila over me
was robbery," in contrast to the banner of love in the Song
of Songs (2:4). Their intercourse typifies its fruition. Ilia is
the first to know: " 'T's a great robbery / --is empire" (*A*,
88).

For Ilia and for the earth, "departed myth / left rav-
ished fact" (*A*, 86), but the diminution occurs first of all in
the god Mars. He is originally an agricultural deity, as Ilia
can still tell "b' the clod smell on him." She calls him a
"Georgie," punning on Virgil's agricultural *Georgics*, and on
"Geordie," which is slang for a Newcastle coal pit-man who,
in pre-industrial times, would have been a farmer, and who
remains as a miner the farmer's industrial counterpart, reap-
ing even if he does not sow. Like the modern Geordie, Mars
has left the farm and has undergone metamorphosis. No
longer a fertility god, he wears armor and a Bronze-Age
Greek helmet to signify his recent identification with Ares,
the god of war. His ancient liturgical text--which originally
may have meant "Be thou sower, Sower Mars, sow the soil"--
is now interpreted, as Jones notes, "Be satiated fierce Mars,
leap the threshold" (*A*, 176). He retains his elemental sexuality, but in brutalized form.

The modern transformation of vital culture to imperialistic civilization is projected in a siren whom Elen Monica imagines as tempting a late medieval ship, the *Mary*,
to its doom. As with Mars and with all mermaids, her
approach is sexual. But she promises another kind of commerce as well, for she asks of sailors "a trident," a shield
("Aegis"), a helmet, and somewhere to sit (*A*, 145-6). In short,
she--the siren, that is, not Elen Monica who impersonates
her--wants to be Britannia, symbol of the British Empire.
And, from the Renaissance on, she will be Britannia--a
debased Athena, goddess not of wisdom but of pragmatic
greed. She is the female counterpart to imperial Mars, with
whom she is linked symbolically by her deadly sexuality
and iconographically by her helmet. He is her true
archetype, and that suggests a trans-sexual dimension to her
perverse, aggressive femininity. Britannia is Mars in drag.

The brutal sexuality of Roman Mars is expressed in
a series of ancient weapons with sexually suggestive nick-
names. These include "Bumping Hecate," "Long Doris," and
"Lysistrata No. 2," which recalls the play by Aristophanes
that has as its dominant image the erect phallus. By operating such siege engines, a British recruit in the Roman army
earns his reputation as "the layer, from Londinium" (*A*, 177).
In one of the twenty-three pre-foliation drafts of the passage

about siege engines, they are called "piercers of the esche-
lon'd veils of cities." Cities in this poem are feminine.

Roman war-machines symbolize dehumanization in
imperial Rome and evoke the same condition in the modern world. They are offensive weapons and therefore essentially imperialistic. Their chief significance is not their
use, however, but the restriction of their meaning to their
usefulness. One of the rams mentioned visually emerges as
a hieroglyph on the page:

Off the secret list?

> maximum impact
> penetrative power
> bias, rebound
> > effect of 'X' releases

on propulsion-gear, deficiencies
serious defects
listed in detail for the coded files
summarized for circulation to affected departments
metamorphosed for general release?   (*A*, 178)

The bare technological language suits its subject. In an
essay published in 1947, David Jones writes that weapons are
quintessentially utile, owing "their existence and meaning
to what they *effect* rather than what they *are*." If they are
beautiful, that is an accidental by-product of function and
without intentional significance. Theirs is what the poet
calls "the beauty of a mathematical formula 'made flesh,'
given material projection." He adds, "the gods of the power-
age are best symbolized by those objects which are themselves power-devices. In the weapons, pure function stands
naked" (*E&A*, 104 n 2). Weapons of this sort are anathemata
in the negative sense of the word.

Republican Rome has experienced a decline of cultural vitality by the time "Tiberius Gracchus / wept for the
waste-land / and the end of the beginnings" (*A*, 89). In 133
B.C., the senatorial capitalists murder Tiberius Gracchus for
promoting land-reform legislation. In a passage Jones marks
in his copy of *The Decline of the West*, Spengler sees this
murder as an indication of the end of Classical culture (II,
50). There are a number of modern parallels, perhaps the
most striking being the murder by Italian Fascists in 1924 of
the socialist Giacomo Matteotti, a man of extraordinary
integrity and vision. The parallel, or one very like it, does
not go unnoticed at the time, for Filippo Turati, delivering
Matteotti's eulogy, alludes to the last stand on the Aventine
by the brother of Tiberius, Gaius Gracchus, who is likewise
murdered by opponents of reform.

There are further evocations of the politics of the
twentieth century. A hundred years after Tiberius' murder,
Augustus builds the *Ara Pacis* or Altar of Peace to com-
memorate a senatorial decree of "Peace in Our Time" (*A*,
186). The words are those of Neville Chamberlain's famous
reassurance after meeting with Hitler at Munich in 1938.
Concerning the Ara Pacis David Jones notes, "there have
been Temples of Peace built in our time also." He has in
mind the Peace Palace at the Hague and the Assembly
Hall of the League of Nations at Geneva, with its large
wall-sculpture by Eric Gill.

Like Augustus before him and in the manner of the
modern dictators, the emperor Tiberius makes republican
forms a vehicle for dictatorial power. Under Tiberius for a
while, moreover, Sejanus exercises power as "Co-ordinator of
groupings" (*A*, 186), a phrase evocative of the Nazi policy of
Gleichschaltung or co-ordination, whereby every aspect of
social and cultural life is brought under the control of the
Party. Sejanus has "his weather-eye on the Diaspora" (*A*,
187), furthermore: like the Nazis, he is ill-disposed to the
Jews, and is probably responsible for the senatorial decree
of 19 A.D. deporting four thousand of them from Rome to
Sardinia, and issuing the ultimatum to the remaining four
thousand that they repudiate "their unholy practices by a
given date" or likewise be banished from Italy.[9]

But Sejanus does not last long. Tiberius has him
killed for plotting against the imperial line of descent, and
"Tiber, by way of the Mamertine, has his broken body" (*A*,
187). A striking modern parallel is the murder of Ernst
Röhm by Hitler in 1934. Just as the political power of
Sejanus rests on his leadership of the Praetorian Guard, the
power of Röhm rests on his leadership of the Nazi SA. To
get at Sejanus, Tiberius circumvents the Praetorian Guard
by using the City Watch. To get at Röhm, Hitler circumvents the SA by using the SS. Sejanus is executed in
Mamertine Prison; Rohm is murdered in Stadelheim Prison.
Each man dies, ostensibly, for plotting a coup. Sejanus'
death may also recall the numerous murders by Stalin of his
political colleagues and generals, but here and later, in *The
Sleeping Lord*, the chief contemporary manifestation of
imperialism is fascism, particularly in Germany.[10]

9. Tacitus, *Annals* II, 85; and E. Schurer, *The History of the Jewish People in the
Times of Jesus Christ* (Edinburgh: T. & T. Clark, 1886-90) II, ii, p. 236; I, ii, p. 86 n.
René Hague is wrong, in his *Commentary on The Anathemata*, in saying that the reference here to a "Diaspora" is an anachronism.
10. Elizabeth Ward argues fallaciously (in a technical, logical sense) that Jones' anti-
totalitarian "bias" is irreconcilable with his criticism of the non-totalitarian West

For ancient Rome, "the waxing of the megalopolis and the acute coarsening of the forms" (*A*, 90) becomes generally symptomatic of cultural decline from about the time Augustus establishes the Principate. The corresponding phase in the modern era is the nineteenth century, when "Western Man moved across a rubicon" (*A*, 15) to an exaggerated emphasis on utility at the expense of gratuity and symbolism. In the poem's fourth section, *Redriff*, the Victorian shipwright Eb Bradshaw holds to the integrity of his craft and resists utilitarian pressures from potential clients, but he fights a losing battle. His own work may transcend expediency, certainly his language is elaborately symbolic, but he exemplifies the isolation of the artist in the modern world. For David Jones, a contemporary type of the alienated artist was Eric Gill who, as a passionate arguer on behalf of good craftsmanship, probably underlies the characterization of Eb Bradshaw. (If Bradshaw is named for the poet's maternal grandfather, Eric Gill was also, for the poet, a father figure, and very nearly his father-in-law.) Shortly after Eric Gill's death in 1940, David Jones writes about the isolation of the artist that "we are all very like men forced into guerrilla tactics--we operate in a terrain over-run by the enemy" (*E&A*, 106) or, putting it a little less metaphorically,

> Today we live in a world where the symbolic life (the life of the true cultures, of 'institutional' religion, and of *all artists*, in the last resort--however much we may disavow the association) is progressively eliminated--the technician is master. In a manner of speaking the priest and the artist are already in the catacombs, but separate catacombs--for the technician divides to rule. (*E&A*, 103)

Cultural fragmentation, with priest and artist in separate catacombs, accounts for the Mass at the opening of the

because, like the fascists, he dislikes Western rationalism and materialism and idealizes the past. Op. cit., p. 190. The differences between his perceptions and fascist ideology are enormous, both in what he disapproves of (Jones was never a racist) and in what he proposes as a remedy, which is cultural and religious, not political (and this is why he idealizes the early Middle Ages and not, like the fascists, imperial Rome). Ward insinuates, furthermore, that in the '30's the poet himself was pro-fascist. Certainly he was sympathetic to Germany, but his sympathy was moral rather than ideological. In a letter to me dated 10 August 1984, Harman Grisewood writes about the poet, "His sympathy was with the portrayal of injustice in *Mein Kampf*, not with the brutal means taken to correct it .... It was not until the last phase of the war that we in England knew anything of Belsen or Auschwitz. When I talked to David about those brutalities, he was as appalled as the most fervent anti-Nazi." Grisewood goes on to explain that his friend's pre-war sympathies were with the Germans as "a vanquished people ... oppressed by exultant and tyrranous conquerors." Even before the war, the poet was critical of *Mein Kampf*, which he says is wholely marred by "this *hate* thing" and by "the conception of the world in terms of race-struggle" (*DGC*, 93). The pre-war, pro-German sympathies of David Jones should not, I think, arouse scepticism about, or require qualification of, the clear evidence in his later poetry that, when he wrote it, he was profoundly unsympathetic to fascism. For more on this subject see above "David Jones and Fascism."

poem being celebrated in a neo-Gothic church, bastardized
with elements of classical and baroque styles:

> between the sterile ornaments
> under the pasteboard baldachins
> as, in the young-time, in the sap-years:
> between the living floriations
> under the leaping arches
>
> (Ossific, trussed with ferric rods, the failing numina of column and
> entablature, the genii of spire and triforium, like great rivals met
> when all is done, nod recognition across the cramped repeats of their
> dead selves.) (A, 49)

In contrast to the Gothic architecture of the Middle Ages,
when "West-wood springs new," this product of the nineteenth-century Gothic Revival signifies cultural decline.
The poem's passage reflects Spengler's contention that cultural decline in our own age, and in every modern period, is
characterized by eclectic revival of archaic, "dead
forms . . . put into the pot anyhow, and recast into wholly
inorganic forms. Every modern age . . . puts revivals and
fusions of old styles in the place of real becoming" (I, 207,
294).[11]

While Eb Bradshaw resists expediency in Victorian
London, Austrian ladies and gentlemen dance to Strauss'
Die blaue Donau. They "maze the waltz-forms" in gay
Vienna (A, 59) in unconscious imitation of the Roman Troia
or maze-dance which, according to the poet's friend Jackson
Knight, was "intended to create a magical field of exclusive force, and abstract defensive entanglement."[12] But the
bourgeois culture of these dancers cannot stave off the
decline of the West. Strauss' lovely waltz lacks explicit
transcendent significance, in contrast to its musical prede-
cessor "in the young-time," when, in Gregorian chant, monks
"god-shape the modal rhythms for nocturns in Melk" near
Vienna (A, 59). The waltz's evocation of the Troia has its
primary meaning, therefore, in the Troia's funerary association: the Troia was danced at funerals and is part of the
funeral games of Anchises in the *Aeneid* (V, 545-603). Vien-
nese waltzers "in the ramshackle last phases" of the Austro-
Hungarian Empire dance at the funeral games of the West.

---

11. In his own copy of *The Decline of the West*, David Jones marks with marginal lines
the paragraphs in which Spengler argues his point. The passage from *The Anathemata*
quoted here also reflects Spengler's comparison of Gothic architecture with living vegetation (I, 396), which in his copy Jones marks with marginal lines and glosses with the
comment "good." See also the architectural criticism of Eric Gill, *Autobiography*
(London: J. Cape, 1940), p. 102.
12. *Cumaean Gates* (Oxford: Basil Blackwell, 1936), p. 78. See also p. 76. David Jones
acquired his copy of this book in 1940.

Imperialism, along with utilitarianism, waxes at the waning of vital culture. The Austro-Hungarian Empire will be torn apart only to be swallowed, eventually, by the Third Reich. And the British Empire enjoys a dominion whose range is implied by Eb Bradshaw's catalogue of wood, which includes West Indies lignum vitae and "cis- or trans-Gangem-land teak" (*A*, 118, 120). The Latin for Ganges, and the echo of "cis- and trans- alpine Gaul" suggests the correspondence with Roman imperialism. This correspondence also underlies a reference in the final section of the poem to Pontius Pilate as "the fact-man, Europa's vicar," taking his nap "under the tiffany" (mosquito-netting) "after tiffin," which is British Indian-army for "lunch" (*A*, 239). The poet derives the term "fact-man" from Spengler's "civilization-man" or "pure man of fact" who is "strong minded, completely non-metaphysical man, and in the hands of this type lies the intellectual and material destiny of each and every 'late' period" (I, 38, 32).[13]

The poem's earliest and most striking representative of British imperialism is Sir Clowdisley Shovell, commander of several war ships sunk off the Scillies in 1707. The voice of the poem asks, "what Caliban's Lamia / rung him for his hand of Glory?" (*A*, 100). His drowned body is robbed, but Sir Clowdisley too is a thief. A "hand of glory" is the greased hand of a corpse used as a candle by a thief to render himself invisible and to keep his victims asleep.[14] The phrase "hand of Glory" refers as well to Shovell's expensive rings, and is capitalized to evoke the nationalistic song of imperial England, "Land of Hope and Glory." Such songs, and the propaganda they comprise, are likewise used to render robbery, or imperialism, invisible.

Imperialism always wraps itself in ideological myth, which usually involves bogus eschatology. Goebbels is a modern master of this ultimate debasement of art, and there are others whose political myths are less malign than his, though no less futile. The ancient counterpart to such modern political propagandists is Augustus, who promoted "the conscious revivals, the electic grandeur / . . . the grand years / since we began our / Good Time Coming" (*A*, 90).

13. Jones marks these words in his copy of Spengler, and first uses his own expression, "fact-man," in a marginal comment on II, p. 220. Ward accuses the poet of regarding "Nazi and British imperialism" as "indistinguishable" because he allows Roman imperialism to evoke them both, whereas he merely identifies them as the same species of vice (i.e. robbery) without specifying--as it hardly seems necessary to do--the degree to which mass murder and repression differentiate them. Op. cit, p. 190.
14. John A. MacCulloch, "Celtic Mythology," *The Mythology of All Races* (Boston: Marshall Jones, 1919), p. 107.

Not now the valid myth and mystery of the "wonder-years";
instead, Augustus announces a bright secular future to the
tune of Stephen Foster's "There's a Good Time Coming,"
which was written, ironically, shortly before the start of the
American Civil War. Augustus' good time turns out to be
the materialism and general corruption of the Empire.
Despite his programmes and propaganda, "the branded
numerals: *sexcenti sexaginta sex*" already appear "on every
commodity and on the souls of men" (*A*, 90). The failure of
secular eschatology becomes the target of authentic
prophecy in the Book of Revelation (13:16-18), where the
number of the Beast is the sum of the numerical equiva-
lents of the Greek letters spelling "Caesar God" and also of
the Hebrew letters spelling "Caesar Nero."

Augustus' political myth fails to bring about the
society it advertises, but it does give prophetic expression to
a fulfillment greater than, and altogether different from,
anything expected by Roman propagandists. It is Virgil, the
greatest of these latter, who to please Augustus, foretells the
passing of the iron age and the commencement of a new
circuit of time when "IAM REDIT . . . VIRGO / . . . IAM
REGNAT APOLLO" (*A*, 219).[15] We saw that, for the early
Church, Christ fulfills the prophecy of the Fourth Eclogue.
He infuses the Roman world with spiritual vitality and
benign gratuity enough to balance and outlast imperial utility.

This then is the diachronic rhyme-scheme of *The
Anathemata*, culminating in the rhyming of the Roman
Empire and modern civilization. The Incarnation is the
hinge and center of the spiralling historical schema, uniting
the ancient West with the modern West. The coming of
Christ during the cultural decline of Rome suggests either
that the current decline of Western culture will coincide
with a revival of Christianity like that which began during
the Dark Ages, or that the current decline will end in
Christ's second coming. In any event, time's poem is not
complete within the bounds of history. Fore-time must yet
find its rhyme in the end-time, when the spiral of chronology collapses into an eschatological circle.

In *Rite and Fore-Time*, this circle is implied by the
coincidence of the actual beginning of the world with its
symbolic ending, but the cataclysm symbolized is one of

---

15. P. 219. When the eclogue was written, Octavius was not yet Augustus, and Virgil's
patron was the consul Pollio, a supporter of Anthony; nevertheless, the poem seems to
celebrate the policies of Octavius, who is favorably referred to throughout the
Eclogues as a special devotee of Apollo.

ice, not fire (see *A*, 58 n 1). Just as once, in fore-time, the
world is covered with the great, Permocarboniferous glacial
sea, so, in the future, it is possible that "there shall be yet
more / storm-dark sea" (*A*, 58). The image recalls and
reverses that of the Book of Revelation, where "there was
not more sea" (21:1). The end may not be far off: "Already
Arcturus deploys his reconnoitering chills in greater
strength: soon his last *Putsch* on any scale" (*A*, 68). The
northern constellation here evokes Arthur, who will come
again to set things right, but whom Elen Monica consigns,
with other Celtic warriors, to the earth "till the Sejunction
Day" (*A*, 164).

The first forecast of time's end occurs in brackets
during the telescoped account of oreogenesis and the Permocarboniferous glaciation, which is also an elaborate catalogue of place-names (*A*, 55-58). Early in the poem, this
poetically powerful catalogue establishes civilizational
catastrophe as a general counterpart to individual mortality
which together, but in different ways, express the human
need for the renewal or resurrection that can only come
through religion. Although it is too long to quote, the catalogue deserves thorough explication.

Most of its apocalyptic images acquire rich historical associations by evoking the endings of the "worlds" constitutive of the West, present here before the West began.
These worlds are evoked by the names of heights listed in
an abbreviated, catastrophic history of the past five millennia. All the famous West-sites lie, with "Ark-hill," under a
world-ending flood of ice, including Parnassus, which is the
Mt. Ararat of the classical flood-story. The major, central
portion of the catalogue is devoted to Troy's Hissarlik, the
site of the West's ur-catastrophe which resonates in the
West's subsequent catastrophies. Also under ice are the
Cyclades, which together with Troy's hill, recall the great
mercantile powers formative of Aegean culture from the
third to the first millennia B.C. Mentioned too is Mycenae
which will fall to invading Dorians despite the defensive
magic of its famous "Leo-Gate" (*A*, 57).[16] ·Thebes is also
under ice, and a name to conjure with, especially when
evoked in association with its tutelar love-goddess. It is the
site of the Oedipal tragedies which history seems almost to
imitate on a larger scale when the city, previously the pos-
sessor of a Boeotian empire, is utterly destroyed in 336 B.C.

16. Concerning the aptropaic intent of the Lion Gate, see Jackson Knight's *Vergil's*
Troy (Oxford: Blackwell, 1932), p.131. According to a note on the flyleaf of his own
copy, Jones had this book out of the library "in 1949 or 1950."

under Alexander for rebelling against Macedonian rule.
Rome's "montes" and Mount Sinai lie under, alone with
"hautes eagle-heights," which evoke the death of Roland by
way of the *Chanson*'s *"hautes montagnes."* Low lies Bredon
hill where the Belgae, expanding under Cunobelin
(Cymbeline) in the first century A.D., will massacre
defenders of the hill's fortress, though Rome, before the end
of the century, will snatch their 'British Empire' from them.
Low too lies Lambourn Down, site of "The Seven Barrows" or
mass graves and one of the "West horse-hills" associated
with the last victory of Arthur and the battles of Alfred.
And where, asks the poem, are the hills of Wales, "All the
efficacious asylums / *in Wallia vel in Marchia Walliae*?"
The word "asylums" recalls the first Asylum on the Capito-
line that will have fallen long before these outermost
extensions of Rome cease to give aid. The fall of Wales,
which completes Rome's fall, also reenacts Troy's fall
because *"Terra Walliae"* is the "Enclosure of the Children of
Troy" (*A*, 55). All these high places lie under,

> obedient to the fiery stress
> *und* icy counter-drag
> down... (*A*, 57)

This is the geological equivalent to German *Sturm und
Drang*, the pre-Romantic political and literary movement
to sweep away all established institutions and conventions.
The symbolically charged catalogue of heights implies the
violent fall of empires as a repeated image and reminder of
the ultimate world-ending.

Among the catalogue's depressed heights are "crag-
carneddau," which include Carnarvon's mountains and, chief
among them though not specified here, Snowdon. The highest peak in Wales has special apocalyptic connotations (see
A, 68 n 2). Elsewhere in *Fore-Time* it is called "the gestato-
rial couch of Camber the eponym" (*A*, 67), whose bed of
Precambrian bedrock "the muses" keep for as long as time
lasts (*A*, 68). There, sleeping Camber will dream the dream
of history

> ...till the thick rotundi-
> ties give, and the bent flanks of space itself give way
> and the whitest of the Wanderers
> falters in her transit
> at the Sibyl's *in favilla*-day. (*A*, 68)

Then Camber will be rudely awakened by the collapse of
Einstein's curved space and by the "shaking thunder" that
will "smite flat the thick rotundity o' the world" in answer

to Lear's call for an end to things. This will be the *Dies Irae*'s "day of ashes." "Lord! what a morning," writes David Jones at the conclusion of his catalogue of submerged heights (*A,* 58). The words belong to the Negro spiritual that anticipates the day "when the stars begin to fall."

Because of its eschatological boundary, which is beyond time's inscape, the spiralling diachronic content of *The Anathemata* symbolically collapses into circular synchronism. If this is suggested by the symbolic presence of the world's end in the world's beginning, it is insisted upon by the poem's narrative context being the Consecration of the Mass, which establishes the poem's meditative time as nearly instantaneous.[17] We saw that the birth of Christ marks the midpoint of history's spiralling duration. Because the sacrament is correlative to and theologically includes the Incarnation, the poem's diachronic spiral has the Incarnation as its meditative circumference as well as its center of meditated duration. Without losing its extension in time, history is consequently, and paradoxically, coextensive with the synchronic circle of the Christian eschaton, which is also the circle of the Eucharist. Without this coincidence of time's spiral and eternity's circle, the helix of history would have only the aesthetic sense of its own repeated pattern. But since the spiral and the circle do coincide, aesthesis passes beyond itself to metaphysics, and relative form symbolizes ultimate meaning.

17. See "The Anagogical Form of *The Anathemeta*," pp. 185-6.

PATRICK DEANE

THE TEXT AS "VALID MATTER": LANGUAGE AND STYLE IN THE ANATHEMATA

That a work of art "must be a *thing* and not the impression of something" (*DGC*, 232) is an idea that may have entered David Jones' aesthetics by way of Post-Impressionism, but in some form at least it was an inevitable consequence of his conviction that "man is unavoidably a sacramentalist and . . . his works are sacramental in character" (*E&A*, 155). One of Jones' notes to *The Anathemata* reminds us that sacramental signs are first and foremost "material stuff" (*A*, 236), and without this "valid" materiality, "could not be." The "thingness," the materiality of *The Anathemata*, he drew attention to in the work's subtitle, "Fragments of an Attempted Writing," and throughout the text there are obvious signs posted to remind us that what we are contemplating is artifice. Principal among these are self-reflexive comments ("If this, though sure, is but allegory"); direct revelations of the composing presence ("speaking most factually/ and, as the fashion now requires, from observed data" [*A*, 216]); and frequent play with narrative formulae, versions of the usual "Once upon a time" ("Once there was . . ." [*A*, 85]; ". . . once/ Upon a time" [*A*, 231]). Our sense that what we are reading has been made, is not spontaneously present, is cultivated from the start by the epigraph "*IT WAS A DARK AND STORMY NIGHT* . . . ," which invokes the idea of tale-telling and in its circularity provides an analogue for aesthetic self-reflexivity.

Such signs make the objectivity of the text apparent. But they also draw attention to a real and intractible materiality that is asserted by the work at the elemental level of lexis, grammar and syntax. This fundamental resistance to effacement of the verbal object is the subject of what follows. My aim is to demonstrate that the objectivity of *The Anathemata* can be discerned at a level deeper than the apparent "presence" of its maker and its discursive self-consciousness. The materiality of the text is asserted in the atomic and molecular elements of discourse itself--not only sentence structure, but clauses, phrases and words as well-- and, in a discussion of representative samples, the following pages will attempt to indicate precisely how this is so.

Although Jones' primary motive in quoting Latin, Welsh and German phrases was, he tells us in the preface, to import into his text their *"exact historical over-tones and under-tones"* (*A*, 11-12), an important subsidiary effect was to make the text more emphatically a verbal morphology, what he calls in his introduction to *In Parenthesis* "a shape in words" (*IP*, x). Jones knew what any reader knows: that as a text runs into foreign languages it becomes, at least to some extent, opaque. Writing to Helen Sutherland, he remarks that "Latin has the . . . advantage of presenting one with a sort of pattern first and then slowly (if at all!) the meaning of all (or some!) of the words" (*PI*, 106-7). In one's own language there is always the possibility that meaning may eclipse the physicality of language, but when confronted by a phrase such as "REDDITOR LVCIS AETER- NAE" (*A*, 134), even a proficient Latinist must, in some measure, first see it as a "shape in words." Such phrases force the verbal medium upon us with a resistant physicality suggestive of the art of inscription. Indeed, some *are* inscriptions-- "REDDITOR . . ." and "SENATUSPOPULUSQUE" (*A*, 89), for example--and they link up with other obvious and less obvious devices to emphasize the physicality of the text. Among these, the use of upper-case Roman letters as in "THIS BOROUGH WERE NEVER FORCED" (*A*, 163) and "BECAUSE OF THE CHILD" (*A*, 216) is most striking. Kathleen Staudt, discussing another capitalized passage, "VNVS HOMO NOBIS . . ." (*A*, 238), comments that "the use of V's in place of U's here deliberately recalls the form of ancient Roman inscriptions, once more stressing the *Anathemata*'s role as an artifact built out of words".[1]

These overtly inscriptional passages stress not just the "role" of the text, but its nature; they underline a morphological approach to language that pervades the whole work, and the manifestations of which are frequently very subtle and inconspicuous. There are clear hints of the approach in Jones' preface, where he writes that

> Each word is meant to do its own work, but each word cannot do its work unless it is given due attention. It was written to be read in that way. And, as I say above, the spacings are of functional importance; they are

---

1. Kathleen Staudt, "The Text as Material and Sign: Poetry and Incarnation in William Blake, Arthur Rimbaud and David Jones," *Modern Language Studies*, 14, No. 3 (Summer 1984), p. 25.

not there to make the page look attractive--though it would be a good thing should that result also. (*A*, 35-6)

Typographic spaces are, it seems, intended to focus the reader's attention upon the individual word "with deliberation," and it is only by realizing every word that he is able to "get the intended meaning" (*A*, 35). As we see in an earlier passage from the preface, meaning (or the apprehension of meaning) depends upon the reader's ability to recognize the physical attributes of certain words:

I have had occasion to use the word *mamau*. This key-word means "mothers" and can also mean 'fairies'. Now the Welsh diphthong *au* is pronounced very like the 'ei' diphthong in the English word 'height'. Hence *mamau* can be made to have assonance with the Latin word *nymphae* and the English words 'grey-eyed' and 'dryad', and I have employed these particular correspondences or near correspondences, on page 238; but to the reader unacquainted with the Welsh 'au' sound, the form of this passage would be lost. (*A*, 13)

Turning to page 238, we notice that it is not only the "form" of the passage that would be lost. The assonance intended underscores a real correspondence between the "barley-tressed" mothers and the "grey-eyed" nymphs, all of whom are joined together in consequence of the crucifixion. And furthermore, the recurring "ei" sound binds them to Christ himself, whose "desiderate cry" and "ninth hour outcry" (*A*, 237-8) frames the passage in question. Thus there is no possibility of "losing" the form and retaining the meaning. If we look a little closer we notice that assonance has replaced syntax as the agent of cohesion:

<pre>
                              What will the naiads
do now, poor things:
                         the lady of the *ffynnon*
Es Sitt that moves the *birket*, fays *del lac*, the donnas of the lyn, the
triad-*matres*, the barley-tressed *mamau* and the grey-eyed *nymphae* at
the dry *ffynhonnau* whose *silvae*-office is to sing:
                    VNVS HOMO NOBIS
                         (PER AQVAM)
                    RESTITVIS REM.
                              (*A*, 237-8)
</pre>

As occurs so frequently elsewhere in the text, the colon in the second line signals the suspension of syntax and the beginning of a paratactical parenthesis. The logical thrust forward gives way to lateral proliferation, and words, freed from grammatical subordination, seem to impress themselves upon us as things. We have, in fact, a kind of morphotaxis, a heaping-up of verbal objects. Our sense of the materiality of language is partly caused by the foreignness of so many words, and partly by the openness of the syntagmatic chain, the failure of individual verbal units to coalesce around a single point of grammatical resolution. The two compound adjectives ("barley-tressed," "grey-eyed") and two compound nouns ("triad-*matres*," "*silvae*-office") reinforce this sense because they reveal the way in which discourse is made by putting together a number of discrete verbal "objects." The passage that follows the first colon is full of such objects, mostly monosyllabic and frequently monomorphemic words. Only one, "*ffynhonnau*," has more than two syllables, all others are either mono- or bisyllabic: this is a discourse made up of discrete units and elementary verbal compounds.

The "objectivity" of words is further strengthened by a simple and assertive stress pattern. Although the passage is written as prose, it can be broken down into a paratactical arrangement of two-stress units: "the láardy of the *ffýnnon* / *És Sítt* / that móves the *bírket*, / fáys *del lác*, / the dónnas of the lýn, / the tríad-*mátres*, / the bárley-tressed *mámau* / and the gréy-eyed *nýmphae* / at the drý *ffynhónnau* . . ." It is interesting to notice that every foreign word or phrase is stressed, and furthermore that each occupies the salient position at the end or climax of a verbal unit. It is as if, within each unit, a number of smaller "objects" gather themselves into a word of almost lapidary objectivity. The process does indeed occur on the larger scale, as this series of what Jones would call "positive" words (*IN*, 42) culminates in an overt inscription: "VNVS HOMO NOBIS/ (PER AQVAM) / RESTITVIS REM."

In this brief passage we have been able to discern a number of strategies which combine to emphasize that the text is not a "transparent" vehicle for meaning, but a morphology of words. Almost any reading of *The Anathemata* will disclose other such devices, but the most obvious of these is word-play. In the following example, "We" are musing on the obscure early history of the Roman people:

Half a millennium or so
                    since
                    out went the Lucomos
since we became
                    abasileutos.
A good year?
                    But little more
(the Kalends are erased or never reckoned)
since those hidden years
when an armaments commission
                    (Tuscan at that)
        could and did

effectively proscribe us:
                        plant
                        operatives
                        raw metal.
That takes you back
                        and aback.
The Urbs without edged iron
                        can you credit it?
                        Nudge Clio
she's apt to be musing.
Slap her and make her extol
                        all or nothing. (*A,* 88)

In this passage there is a distinctive speaking "presence" which stimulates our sense of the "presence" of the text itself. Where a simple historic narrative would, in a sense, defer to the reader and objective fact, this text interrogates its reader ("A good year?") and draws attention to its verbal fabric.

"That takes you back/ and aback": there is an ingenuous wit in this, a frank revelation of how language *makes* meaning rather than simply conveys it. In a manner not unlike the compound nouns and adjectives in the passage discussed earlier, these two lines reveal the process by which individual verbal elements combine in the propagation of a text. "Back" is monomorphemic and part of the pleasure of this word-play is to see what new dimension of meaning is constituted by its amalgamation with another (free) morpheme, "a-". More simply put, the play on words draws attention to the text as a play *in* words, a "writing"; in that sense it functions as rhetorical questions do at the discursive level of the text, bringing home the constitutive power of language. More than anything else, however, it shows the real objectivity of words and of the linguistic system which recognizes as meaningful the distinction between "back" and "aback." That is to say it demonstrates the degree to which language (and discourse) is a thing and not the impression or expression of something else.

In the wider context of "Middle-Sea and Lear-Sea," one is bound to recognize a possible play on the nautical meaning of "aback"; a ship "taken aback" is one with its sails pressed against the mast by a headwind. That "we" (the readers?) should be "taken aback" by historical fact is not inappropriate, given our constant implication in *The Anathemata's* various voyages, and David Jones' suggestion that "making a work [and, *mutatis mutandis*, reading one] is not thinking thoughts but accomplishing an actual journey" (*A,* 33). Looking in the process of reading for an experience analogous to the nautical "taking aback," one immediately thinks of the way in which, in the pages of "Middle-Sea and Lear-Sea" and "Angle-Land," our forward progress is constantly impeded by explorations along a "vertical" axis (a mast?) of narrative possibility. For example, the voyage narrative begun after the mention of Athene Promachos (*A*, 94) repeatedly loses its momentum under the weight of speculation on the various courses which the story might take and on the background of its characters. This experience is at its most intense at the very moment that the voyagers must battle a headwind "telling fifty in the chops" (*A*, 101). Such reflections reveal how deeply-integrated with the whole the apparent afterthought "and aback" will prove to be.

From this line on, the passage under discussion sustains and extends itself through more word-play. Perhaps the question, "can you credit it?" puns on the idea of financial credit. This is not unlikely in view of the fact that the immediate context is the Etruscan imposition of sanctions on Rome, and the resultant industrial shortages: "plant/ operatives/ raw metal." The next sentence is a more obvious pun: "Nudge Clio/ she's apt to be musing." Rene Hague points out that there is a double word-play here,[2] since "apt" can mean both "likely" and "appropriate." In other words, the lines can be read to mean either "Nudge Clio, she's likely to be musing (cogitating)" or "Nudge Clio, her job is to do what muses do." Finally, as the digression ends, the speaker plays on the etymology of Clio's name: "Slap her and make her extol / all or nothing." A few pages earlier, *Kleio* is translated in the notes as "she that extols" (*A*, 86, n.3).

Word-play of this sort is a direct revelation of verbal artifice, and in that sense the digression conforms to a pattern which is repeated throughout *The Anathemata*. This passage is a kind of eddy in the mainstream of the text, in the "story" of Christian history, and on either side we are provided with temporal co-ordinates: "Half a millennium or so / since . . ." (*A*, 88) and "Five hundred and thirty-nine years since . . ." (*A*, 89). As in the later, and frequently interrupted, voyage narratives, continuity is here broken by a question, "A good year?" Similarly, the long digression involving St. Guthlac and his response to the speech of surviving Britons around his monastery at Crowland (*A*, 112-

2. Rene Hague, *A Commentary on "The Anathemata" of David Jones* (Toronto and Buffalo: University of Toronto Press, 1977), p. 100.

3) begins when the narrator starts to speculate on Guthlac's thoughts, and narrative gives way to questioning: "Is Marianus wild Meirion?/ is Sylvanus/ Urbigena's son?" (*A*, 112). The questions become gradually more tangential and gratuitous--"what's the cephalic index of the *morforynion*?" (*A*, 113)--and the digression culminates in a bold allusion to *The Tempest*: "the pearls that were Ned Mizzen's eyes, at the five fathom line off the Naze?" (*A*, 113). As the speculative imagination reaches its furthest extension, language declares itself as artifice. The allusion does less directly in the Guthlac passage what word-play accomplishes in the digression beginning "A good year?". In both passages, fissures in the sequential movement of the work, the reader probes downward toward the roots of discourse, finding himself confronted ultimately with the objectivity of words. Beyond this he cannot go, and so there is invariably a return to continuity.

Such digressions tend to describe a similar "shape": following the fracture of continuity, focus shifts from the extension of discourse to its component elements. Thus narrative frequently gives way to speculation on the various possible forms any given element might take: "Did he tie up across the water/ or did she toss at the Surrey shore?" (*A*, 118), for example. The St. Guthlac digression and the passage we have been discussing work in an analogous way, since they lay bare the atomic parts of which the text is built. In the latter, however, the view is particularly microscopic, since the text is revealed to be built, not out of just narrative phrases, but also words and even morphemes.

It must also be said that this "shape"--the characteristic movement, within a textual unit, towards the "thingness" of words--can often be discerned in fragments as small as a phrase. The passage beginning "What will the naiads / do now, poor things . . ." (*A*, 238) culminates, as we saw earlier, in an inscription. It may also, therefore, be said to trace the usual movement. But, as was revealed by my earlier analysis of its stress pattern and syntax, that movement is adumbrated in the "shape" of each of its component units, moving as they almost invariably do, towards a word of "positive" materiality. The careful positioning of a foreign word at the end of each unit is a manifestation of the same tendency that causes Jones' digression on the Etruscan embargo of Rome to resolve itself in word-play. The parallel is strengthened by the fact that the latter passage is also

succeeded by an inscription, indeed by a discussion of the
inscriber's art itself:

> How long since first we began to contrive
>   on the loose-grained tufas
> quarried about the place;
>   incise, spaced and clear
> on the carried marbles
>   impose on the emblems:
> S E N A T U S P O P U L U S Q U E...?
>   for all the world-nurseries
> to say: Roma knows great A. (*A*, 89)

A fuller version of this passage is to be found in one
sequence of *The Roman Quarry*, where a Roman is made to
say: "Our masons seem to have a genuine understanding of
the alphabet in a kind of physical way" (*RQ*, 181).[3] Given
Jones' view, expressed in the preface to *The Anathemata*,
that typographical spaces "are of functional importance" (*A*,
36), that they serve to realize each word, a similarly
"physical" type of understanding might be said to underlie
his own approach to words. This seems especially true in
light of the following lines from *The Roman Quarry*: "I'd
rather overlooked the inscriptions--we--are--aristocratic--
there. It's an extremely interesting thing--one detects a
streak of true refinement there--the spaces *between* the
incisions have such significance in the best examples" (*RQ*,
181). Of course one might see an analogy between these
spaces and the digressions that separate salient points in *The
Anathemata*'s narrative continuity. In any event, this
"physical" understanding of language and letters is regarded
very favorably. In *The Anathemata*, its exponents are
credited with a "perfected aesthetic" (*A*, 89), and in *The
Roman Quarry* the speaker comments that "If 'and in them
the Word is made stone' is what posterity will say of us, it is
some consolation." "The Word is made stone": the phrase
was omitted from *The Anathemata* at this point, but
introduced a few pages later where it is applied to Gothic
sculpture (*A*, 93). Nevertheless, it perfectly summarizes the
kind of morphological approach to individual words that we
have been examining in the preceding pages.

Word-play, then, asserts that the text is composed of
things, verbal "objects" brought into relation with one
another. In that sense, St. John Chrysostom's definition of
the word *anathemata* applies quite literally to Jones'

---

3. In his *Commentary*, p. 101, Hague is uncertain of whether the *Roman Quarry* passage is an expanded version of the lines from *The Anathemata*, or a version from which
the latter were condensed.

"attempted writing": "things . . . laid up from other things" (*A*, 28). It is to the process of "laying-up" that I now wish to turn, focusing on the way in which syntax compels the reader to an engagement with words *as words*.

There is an act of laying-up which dominates the whole work, and this is described in the very first sentence:

> We already and first of all discern him making this thing other. His groping syntax, if we attend, already shapes:
> ADSCRIPTAM, RATAM, RATIONABILEM ... and by preapplication and for *them*, under modes and patterns altogether theirs, the holy and venerable hands lift up an efficacious sign. (*A*, 49)

In the first three lines we have an almost paradigmatic version of what will become so common later on in the text: language "groping" towards a new verbal "shape," culminating in a boldly inscribed phrase. One's first impulse is to suggest that form is here imitating content. The clue given by allusion to the Roman Mass, combined perhaps with refractorily persistent assumptions about the "transparency" or referentiality of language, may well lead the reader to take more for granted here than the text will really allow. The "content" of the lines may thus be taken to be the actions of a man (unidentified), carried out in conformity with the customs of certain others (also unidentified), and involving an unknown "thing," which do, in some way, resemble the eucharistic rite of the Roman Catholic Church. The reader's first response is, in other words, to assume that the phrase "this thing" has a referent beyond the text: the process by which it is "made other," or "laid up from other things," is given priority, and the way in which syntax "gropes" towards an inscribed, "set apart" (*A*, 64) verbal "shape" is regarded as little more than an imitation of that action.

This sort of reading is correct, of course, though only in part. It is bought at a certain cost to verbal and grammatical accuracy, for there are a number of ambiguities and other linguistic features which, if accorded the "due attention" Jones requested for each word (*A*, 35), must to some extent destabilize such an interpretation. To begin with, what we "already and first of all discern" is far from clear: the first sentence of the poem is a string of anaphoric deictics, words apparently referring to previous elements in the utterance, which are strikingly referent-less. The reader can have no way of knowing precisely what "this thing" is, or who is meant by "him" or "*them*." Some certainty is delivered if we take "this thing" to be the text, or language, itself. In fact, far fewer questions are raised if the phrase is

interpreted reflexively than if we take "this" as either a
limiting or demonstrative adjective. This reading would be
supported by the fact that the second sentence both narrates
and enacts the way in which language is gathered or
"shaped" into a verbal object. Thus two interpretative possibilities come to focus on the single word, "this": first, that
the text is a self-reflexive object, and second, that it is
"transparent," pointing beyond itself to a world of nonverbal
objects and actions. There is weighty evidence for the latter possibility, most notably the plethora, in these opening
lines, of demonstrative adjectives and relative pronouns.
But in fact these words merely serve to create the illusion
of referentiality, and because they force the reader to
engage with the text--to read on--in order to discover what
such apparently referent-less signs might signify, they participate in the text's self-reflexiveness, confronting the
reader with the objective reality of the text as surely
(though not as obviously) as the phrase "this thing."

Closer analysis thus reveals that form, in the opening
lines of *The Anathemata*, does not imitate content, but is
instead identified with it. What we "already and first of all
discern" is language, and the process by which a verbal
object takes "shape." In short, it is the material "otherness"
of the text which confronts us; its grammar ensures a high
degree of linguistic opaqueness, so there can be no effacement of the verbal object. This emerges particularly
clearly when we subject certain pronouns to the sort of
scrutiny just conferred on "this thing." Once again, a reader
who is keen to see "beyond" the text will likely not be "held
up," as Jones would say (*IN*, 42), by what seem to be superficial verbal difficulties. But the moment we concede that
"this thing" might refer to the linguistic object itself, the
subject of the enunciation (the speaker of the text) becomes
peculiarly de-centred.

At the root of this effect is the strong connection
which the opening "We" establishes between the speaker of
the text and its reader. One result of that connection is that
the speaker occupies, from the start, a spectatorial position
with regard to "this thing," and the man who makes it
"other." Now, if "this thing" is the text itself, the speaker's
own words, then the subject of the enunciation is signified
in both "We" and "him": he is both the one who discerns and
the one discerned. This is a further extension of the text's
self-reflexiveness, and one is reminded of the regressive epigraph, "*IT WAS A DARK AND STORMY NIGHT ....*"
In the present context, this de-centering of the speaking

subject is particularly important because of its effect on the reader, whose identification with the speaker must now leave him deprived of a stable interpretative center. And without that, "meaning" and "content" will remain perpetually unsettled, language and form resisting effacement. The reader is forced to grope for meaning in the "shape" of the text, a verbal object which holds him up with ambiguity, word-play, and the disruption of continuity. Denied the transcendent, coherent, hermeneutical position promised by the opening "We," he is committed to the linguistic "body and the embodied" (*DG*, 167).

It begins to seem as if the opening lines of *The Anathemata* marshall, if not for immediate then at least for later development, a full range of linguistic devices, all of which serve to assert the "opaque" materiality of the text. There is one that remains to be noticed--easily missed, as they all are, if we do not give each word "due attention"-- and this is found in the phrase "already and first of all." A first-time reader might not be held up by these words, for they seem little more that an overt sign that he is entering *in medias res*. As the second word in the work, "already" impresses in the reader's mind the idea that there is a world of action and event in existence anterior to the genesis of language, or of the text at least. The word therefore encourages expectations of verbal "transparency," as do the numerous anaphoric deictics which follow the text's first verb, "discern." But as we have seen, it very soon proves difficult to "see through" language; there is an inescapable murkiness to the picture we "already . . . discern." Some of the causes of this instability have already been discussed, but the problems begin with "already" and its apparently supporting phrase, "first of all."

The "and" which joins them suggests an identity of meaning, and the second phrase is to a large extent overshadowed in the reading by "already," so the fact that they do not exactly co-operate is very easily missed. But of course the two elements pull in opposite directions: "already" away from the textuality of the text and towards the continuity of the announced subject, "first of all" towards the text itself, the experience of the reader, and the genesis of enunciation. "Already and first of all" collocates continuity and origin in much the same way that the institution of the eucharist is later said to be "birthday and anniversary" (*A*, 51). The ambivalence of the phrase is aptly rendered in these words from the same context: "if there's continuity here, there's a new beginning" (*A*, 51).

It is obvious that the words "first of all" draw our
attention to the text as an object; they do this simply by
admitting that the beginning is a beginning, and in that
sense directly oppose the apparent plunge *in medias res*, "a
convention," in Edward Said's words, "that burdens the
beginning with the pretense that it is not one".[4] But that
opposition itself produces a real, not just apparent, linguistic
"opaqueness," as will become clear in a brief analysis.
"Already" and "first of all" are, in fact, competing candidates for the same syntagmatic position. According to the
Saussurean model, meaning becomes stabilized when all but
one of the possible occupants of each such position are
excluded. That is to say, in order for discourse to be coherent, contradictory and alternative elements, ranged on the
"associative" or paradigmatic (as opposed to syntagmatic)
linguistic axis, must be kept "outside" of discourse.[5] This is
to some extent common sense: saying something requires
that one not attempt to say everything. However, "already
and first of all" challenges the coherence of the syntagmatic axis by not only failing to exclude one of two contradictory elements, but also (by means of the powerful conjunction "and") insisting upon their equivalent significance.
Were the phrase "already *or* first of all," exclusion would be
the reader's prerogative, but as it stands he can omit neither
element. Thus, within a strongly coherent syntagmatic unit
("we . . . discern . . . him"), and threaded into that unit by
the binding "and," the paradoxical phrase is an agent of
decomposition, ensuring that the meaning of the work's
opening lines will not "settle."

This strategy, in which conventional grammar and
syntax are used to bind together a number of mutually fugitive elements, is used elsewhere in the text.[6] Here, as in
those other cases, the resultant hermeneutical difficulties
prevent the effacement of language by meaning. For a
reader to have the illusion of seeing "through" the text,
meaning must be recoverable as a coherent "object."
Strategies of this sort make that impossible, and compel the

4. Edward Said, *Beginnings: Intention and Method* (New York: Basic Books, 1975), p.43.
5. See Ferdinand de Saussure, *Course in General Linguistics*, trans. Wade Baskin (1959;
Glasgow: Fontana/ Collins, 1974), Ch. 5 *passim*, but particularly p. 123.
6. In the lines "from before long ago he / sailed ..." (*A*, 170), for example, Jones
"decomposes" time by linking terms of temporal relativity one to the other, without
reference to any specific time. "Long ago" is a vague point defined in relation to the
present, whenever that is on the scale of historic time; "before long ago" has hardly
any meaning in terms of that scale, and the confusion of sequence is completed by linking the word "from" (waiting for the implied "till ...", we assume that the voyage continues), with the past tense, "sailed" (which suggests it is over). This is conventional
syntax used to undermine the very idea of sequentiality.

reader into an engagement with the objectivity of the text itself.

This determination not to exclude antagonistic possibilities from the syntagmatic chain is clearly another form of what occurs in *The Anathemata* at the narrative level. There, the development of a coherent narrative line is constantly impeded by the speaker's inability (or his refusal) to choose from a large number of storytelling alternatives. The result is that, to a large extent, the horizontal movement of the text is an exploration of "vertical" possibilities, as if the syntagmatic axis were partly the paradigmatic one laid on its side. The tendency for syntax to give way to parataxis is an obvious effect of this curious congruency between what is "in" discourse, and what must usually, for the sake of coherence, be kept "outside." The inclusion of mutually fugitive elements subverts coherence and, as is obvious in the case of narrative, prevents the establishment of continuity. The effect is as disconcerting at the narrative level as open contradiction is at the grammatical, and both bind the reader into a world of words. This phenomenon-- the syntactical connection of alternative terms, epitomized by "already and first of all"--is iconically related to central elements in the work's content, and ultimately to its underlying ideology.

"Keel, Ram, Stauros," for example, might be described as a dialogue between the vertical and the horizontal. It is a meditation upon the wood of the cross, and until quite late in the typescript stage bore the title "The Adzed Wood." In comparison with this, and the other titles Jones considered,[7] "Keel, Ram, Stauros" emphasizes the linear configurations, rather than the qualities of the wood. As the section progresses, we consider its multiple functions and attributes, but particularly its disposition: as the keel, "prone for us / buffeted, barnacled / tholing the sea-shock / for us" (*A*, 174); as a battering ram, "horizontal'd" (*A*, 176); "set up" as a maypole "for the garlands" (*A*, 175), and as a cross, "gibbet / for the dented *spolia* (*A*, 175-6). The dialectic between vertical and horizontal is also carried on less obviously, as in the following lines:

7. See National Library of Wales David Jones 1978 Purchase, Folios A0.2 and A0.3, as at July 13, 1983. In A0.4, "The Adzed Wood" has been crossed out, and "Keel, Ram, Stauros" written in. Lower down on the same folio, Jones has toyed with other possibilities: "Barnacled or Garlanded," "Timber of Foundation," "The Keel," "The Adzed Beam," and "The Timbers." All are crossed out, and above "Timber of Foundation" has been written "Keel, Ram, Stauros." Quoted by kind permission of the trustees of David Jones' estate.

> Two-stranded marline
> > or straight-cored
> heart-of-hemp hawser
> > *altus* and hoist
> at the cathead or bowered to the fundus.
>
>
> > And the thewed bodies
> the true-hearted men so beautiful
> > between perpendiculars
> and over-all. (*A*, 175)

Hague tells us that "altus" (pronounced "awl-tus") refers to
the anchor in its raised position, "secured at the cathead,"
and "fundus" to the sea-bed. What joins the one to the other
is the bower-cable, standing as a vertical to the sea-bed's
horizontal. "Between perpendiculars" and "over-all," furthermore, "refer to the measurement of length of a ship, the
former being taken from the stemhead to a point perpen-
dicularly above the rudder head."[8]

Vertical and horizontal, therefore, come together in
the ship itself. The keel-beam, "the quivering elm on which
our salvation sways" (*A*, 73), is the vessel's foundation and
the principal symbol of its horizontal disposition. The main
vertical element is, of course, the mast, but what is most
important in the present (linguistic) context, is that "Keel,
Ram, Stauros" stresses that whether "horizontal'd" or
"vertical'd" (*A*, 178) it is the same wood. The ground of this
identity, the place where vertical and horizontal intersect, is
the salvific wood: "All wood else hangs on you" (*A*, 174).
The two axes come together in the image of the Holy Cross
standing: "Agios Stauros / *stans*?" (*A*, 180).

In *The Anathemata*, as we have seen, the ship invariably finds itself "taken aback" at precisely the moment the
narrative of its voyage stalls. Furthermore, we remember
Jones' assertion that "making a work is . . . accomplishing
an actual journey" (*A*, 33). Together, these ideas permit us
to see the verbal body of the text as a kind of vessel, and it
is not difficult to see a relationship between keel and mast
on the one hand, and the syntagmatic and paradigmatic
axes on the other. Of course by now those last two terms
must be understood in both their precise linguistic sense as
well as analogically, referring respectively to narrative
sequence and the (discontinuous) range of narrative
possibilities. In any case, the reconciliation between keel
and mast which occurs in "Keel, Ram, Stauros" presents
itself as a striking metaphor for what occurs in "already and

8. Hague, *Commentary*, pp. 198-9.

first of all" and *The Anathemata*'s many instances of
narrative failure, when the syntagmatic and paradigmatic
axes seem congruent if not identical. Failure to exclude
contradictory elements arrests the forward movement of the
text, will not allow meaning to settle, and therefore
impresses us with the morphological opaqueness of language. All of these effects are reflected in the lines "Agios
Stauros / *stans*?": verbal objectivity in the foreignness of
the words; stasis, obviously, in *"stans"*; and tentativity of
meaning in the final question mark.

When certain aspects of *The Anathemata* are anal-
ysed in terms of Saussure's axial metaphor, and that analysis
placed alongside elements in the work's subject matter, a
remarkable connection between form and content begins to
emerge. Jones called *The Anathemata* "a kind of 'dance
round the maypole' of the stauros" (*IN*, 75), and if the work
can be said to have a single subject, it is surely the reconciliation of time and timelessness effected by Christ's sacrifice and emblematized by his cross,[9] where horizontal and
vertical come together. The world transformed by the
Incarnation and Crucifixion is precisely the "thing" which
this verbal "shape," *The Anathemata*, seeks to render, and so
it is not surprising to find the origins of its resistant textuality in a strategy which reconciles the syntagmatic and
paradigmatic linguistic axes, syntax and parataxis, diachronic and synchronic time.

"Already and first of all" is a manifestation of this
tendency at its most radical, for not only does it not
exclude alternative candidates for a single position in the
syntagmatic, chain, but it *includes* an opposite. At the level
of narrative, the equivalent moment--when the "decomposition" of meaning is at its most acute--is the end of "Angle-
Land" and the beginning of "Redriff," where the speaker
undermines the established narrative by raising a fundamentally opposed narrative possibility. But for the most
part, at the linguistic as well as the narrative level, this
tendency involves the incorporation in the syntagmatic
chain of alternatives rather than opposites, and though this
does unsettle meaning it does not preclude it. In the narrative, as we saw, it is common for the speaker to turn aside
from his sequential tale and meditate upon what seems a

9. In an unpublished essay, "Stat Crux dum Volvitur Orbis," William Blissett argues
that "the order and movement of the poem is an invention and exaltation of the Cross":
"The earlier sections are congruent with the vernal festival of the Invention of the
Cross (3 May, suppressed 1960), the later with the autumnal festival of the Exaltation
of the Cross (14 September)."

potentially ever-extending range of associative possibilities:
failing syntagmatic coherence typically coincides with a
foregrounding of the associative axis. In *The Anathemata*,
what is true of narrative is frequently true of the smaller
components of discourse, sentences in particular, and I now
wish to examine the relation of syntax to parataxis in a
number of specific passages.

Let us pick up the text again at the first page and
the beginning of the third sentence:

These, at the sagging end and chapter's close, standing humbly before
the tables spread, in the apsidal houses, who intend life:
> between the sterile ornaments
> under the pasteboard baldachins
> as, in the young-time, in the sap-years:
> > between the living floriations
> under the leaping arches.

(Ossific, trussed with ferric rods, the failing numina of
column and entablature, the genii of spire and triforium, like great
rivals met when all is done, nod recognition across the cramped repeats
of their dead selves.)

These rear-guard details in their quaint attire, heedless of incon-
gruity, unconscious that the flanks are turned and all connecting files
withdrawn or liquidated--that dead symbols litter to the base of the
cult-stone, that the stem by the palled stone is thirsty, that the
stream is very low.

> The utile infiltration nowhere held
> creeps vestibule
is already at the closed lattices, is coming through each door.

The cult-man stands alone in Pellam's land: more precariously than he
knows he guards the *signa*: the pontifex among his house-treasures,
(the twin-*urbes* his house is) he can fetch things new and old: the
tokens, the matrices, the institutes, the ancilia, the fertile ashes--
the palladic foreshadowings: the things come down from heaven
together with the kept memorials, the things lifted up and the venerated trinkets. (*A*, 49-50)

If language is here caught in a kind of syntactical stasis
with no insistent progression from subject to verb to object,
the reason is clear: there is an extraordinary preponderance
of nominal and adjectival terms over active verbs. Of the
five sentences that comprise the passage, only one has a
single principal verb. This is the parenthetical section
beginning "Ossific, trussed with ferric rods . . . ." But even
there we must wait a long time for the verb, which comes
only after the speaker has progressed through a number of
associations--"failing numina . . . genii . . . great rivals"--
which are related paratactically. Furthermore, "nod" is a
rather slight verb, so at best it can be said to keep alive,

though not assert, the power of syntax against parataxis. This is particularly true because it is the first principal verb in eleven lines of paratactical constructions. The previous sentence has a number of participles, of course ("sagging," "standing," "living," "leaping"), but its one verb occurs in an adjectival clause: "who intend life." In the absence of a principal verb and strong bonds of syntactical coherence, language is here ordered anaphorically. Thus, in the first line, "these" must be taken to be the implied subject of each of the clauses that follows it until the colon. In the succeeding five lines of verse anaphoric relations are more boldly indicated: the first and fourth (equally indented) both begin with "between," while the second and fifth (equally indented as well, but set off from "between") both begin with "under." Thus the same construction ("between . . . under") occurs on either side of the third line, which, significantly, is also an anaphora: "in the youngtime, in the sapyears." There is striking geometry to all this, and these five lines of verse make a very tight unity. But it is paratactical unity, an artifact built upon the principle of association rather than grammatical subordination; it is a paradigm, a "shape" of phrases, rather than a syntagma or sequence.

In the third sentence of the passage quoted there is again no principal verb, though there are several verbs. Interestingly, these do not challenge but instead serve the sort of anaphoric construction just described. The sentence begins as the first did, with the word "these," and so one observes in passing that there appears to be a kind of anaphora of sentences as well as of phrases. "These rearguard details in their quaint attire, heedless . . . unconscious" does indeed seem to pick up where "These, at the sagging end and chapter's close" left off, and the intervening lines are shown, as a whole, to have been tangential to the forward movement of the text--a digression. And it is interesting to notice that they culminate in a real parenthesis, for this seems not unrelated to the way in which, as we saw earlier, digressions in *The Anathemata* tend to conclude with a linguistic assertion of their objective nature. At any rate, this third sentence opens with the same kind of anaphoric construction as the first. But while the first moved into verse, something very different occurs here: the clause beginning "unconscious that the flanks are turned" both extends the opening construction (it is still descriptive of "these"), and inaugurates a new one, for "unconscious" is to become the referent for a new association of clauses, beginning "that." The transition from the one to the other is

marked by a dash, after which the anaphora becomes obvious: "that dead symbols litter to the base of the cult-stone,
that the stem by the palled stone is thirsty, that the stream
is very low." Here, as in the verse passage, the ground of
unity is not sequence but parallelism and repetition. The
binding recurrence of "that" is reinforced by powerful assonance (as in "dead" and "stem") and consonance, particularly
involving the sounds /l/, /s/, /t/, and combinations of
these. Three active verbs--"litter," "is," and "is"--occur at the
end of this sentence, but they function within the paratactical arrangement just described, serving rather than dominating the noun-world.

The fourth sentence appears to have a principal verb
in "creeps," but the promise of syntagmatic unity quickly
falls away when an alternative verb is introduced, this
becoming the hinge of yet another anaphoric construction:

> The utile infiltration nowhere held
> creeps vestibule
> is already at the closed lattices, is coming through each door.

The first two lines give us the essential elements of a conventional sentence, a subject and a predicate. "Creep" is
almost certainly used here in its transitive sense, as in
"creep the Cross," but it is usually intransitive, and with
"vestibule" lacking a preposition, Jones' reader is likely to
be held up on the predicate. Typically, this relatively weak
syntagmatic chain gives way to substitutions from the
paradigmatic axis, and so two clauses are introduced with
which "creep vestibule" must share its grammatical position. Anaphora stresses their equivalence, and so the claim
of "creeps" to be principal verb is cut by two thirds. In a
sense, what occurs in the third line is a distribution of the
predicate function through a group of parallel clauses: syntax gives way to parataxis.

In the fifth sentence the colon is used four times,
serving as it does in mathematics to indicate a proportion.
A:B:C suggests that all three elements are proportionally
equivalent, and it is interesting to compare with each other
the first three clauses separated by the colon:

> The cult-man stands alone in Pellam's land
> more precariously than he knows he guards the *signa*
> the pontifex ... he can fetch things new and old.

In each case the subject is the same and the verb in the
present tense, although in the last it differs slightly, being
subjunctive. And of course "stand" is intransitive, whereas
"guard" and "fetch" are not. Even admitting these factors, it

seems true to say that the three clauses are in fact varia-
tions on the same verbal "shape." In the voyage narratives,
the "shape" of the journey seems consistent while various
substitutions are made for the captain, the crew, and the
ship. Something similar seems to occur in this group of parallel clauses: the same syntagmatic form is repeated, only
with variation in certain of its component elements. The
process is neither mechanical nor uncomplicated, but there
is sufficient syntactical uniformity between the clauses to
shift the focus of meaning from words in their sequential
relations to the chains of association that bind a word in
one clause with its substitute in the next. This is another
version of what has been noticed in each of four sentences
discussed so far: a foregrounding of the paradigmatic axis
which coincides with the suspension of syntagmatic progression. Thomas Dilworth has argued that what Jones himself
called "association-perceptions" (*E&A*, 98) constitute "a new
aesthetic," and are the means by which Jones' poetry is
largely written.[10] In the clauses under discussion, meaning is
discovered in the exploration of three lines of association:
the first links "the cult-man" with "the pontifex"; the second
joins "stands," "knows," and "can fetch"; and the third connects "the *signa*" to "things new and old." These lines of
association bind the three clauses into a non-sequential
unity; they function not unlike assonance and consonance in
the third sentence, making connections without subordination.

    After the third colon, and after the paratactical
arrangement of the first three clauses has turned our attention to chains of association, the remainder of this fifth
sentence offers an unimpeded excursion along the paradigmatic axis. For "signa," the third clause had substituted
"things new and old." Now we are given a long list which
reveals the full associative "recession and thickness through"
(*A*, 24) of that phrase:

> the tokens, the matrices, the institutes, the ancilia, the fertile ashes
> --the palladic foreshadowings: the things come down from heaven
> together with the kept memorials, the things lifted up and the vener-
> ated trinkets.

We have seen the disregard of syntagmatic relations consis-
tently associated with anaphoric constructions of one sort or

---

10. Thomas Dilworth, "The Technique of Allusion in the Major Poems of David Jones,"
Diss. University of Toronto 1977, p. 1. Dilworth construes the term "association-
perceptions" quite widely to include "the analogues, parallels, evocations and
references usually grouped under the single heading of allusions." It is interesting to
discover that association prevails over sequence at the narrowest (linguistic) level as
well.

another; it is not surprising, therefore, to find anaphora pervasively used here where the text is at its most obviously paratactical.

I noted earlier that it is very common in *The Anathemata* for this kind of extreme exploration of paradigmatic possibilities to occur as the climax of a digression, and it is in conformity with that trend that in the very next paragraph there is an attempt to pick up the thread of sequential discourse by returning to the subject of the previous sentence, "this man, so late in time . . ." (*A*, 50). I also pointed out that, following the failure of syntagmatic continuity, such digressions move towards a revelation of the elemental components of discourse: morphemes, words, and phrases, for example. In this passage, something similar occurs. The three clauses which begin the fifth sentence maintain a dialogue between alternative modes of linguistic arrangement; they are discrete syntagmatic units arranged paratactically in relation to each other. Beyond the third colon, the units thus arranged are smaller--at first single words, conjoined only with the definite article. Other units involve a noun and adjective, or a noun and asyndetic relative clause. Thus the list of "things new and old" is in linguistic fact a heaping-up of verbal objects, of individual words or very simple clusters. It is a proliferation of substantives, and if these are not the *most* elemental matter of language, they are at least its "body." In this kind of paratactical arrangement each word or cluster commands the reader's due attention, confronts him as a "token," a thing set apart from other things. As in the art of inscription, the "spaces" between these letter objects are significant; on the paradigmatic axis, meaning resides in distinction rather than combination.

David Jones' pursuit of the associations, "*over-tones and under-tones*" (*A*, 12) of particular words has, in its two principal manifestations, the effect of impressing the reader with the "opaque" objectivity of the text. As we saw earlier, foreign words and phrases, though partly intended to enlarge the work's content by their powers of evocation, nevertheless draw attention to its inscriptional form. And as the preceding analysis has begun to make clear, paratactical constructions tend also to increase textual opaqueness. This is because digressions along the associative axis will not allow for the completion of coherent, extended, syntagmatic units --will not allow meaning to settle, in other words. In long passages such as the one discussed in the preceding pages, the reader waits in vain for the principal verb that will unite all of the text's fugitive elements, that will complete the text, thereby rendering it "transparent." But in *The Anathemata* the muse Clio is much abused; though syntax is constantly vying with parataxis, it rarely prevails completely. There is always the chance that association could begin to "play old Harry," in Jones' words, with the "more defined contours" of language (*A*, 89).

It can therefore be said that the resistant materiality of *The Anathemata* is, to a very great extent, the product of style. It is a style distinguished less by the particular character of its lexical and grammatical choices[11] (though of course these are significant) than by the writer's apparent reluctance to choose at all. Thus, while Saussure argues that in order for language to be coherent certain choices *must* be made, certain elements kept out of discourse, David Jones "participates in no excommunications . . . [and tends] to include rather than to exclude."[12] In a letter to H.S. Ede he writes that the artist "must deny nothing, . . . must integrate everything," and in those words we can see why the sequential movement of his text so frequently gives way to excursions along the paradigmatic axis. "The successful art work," he tells Ede, "is one where no ingredient of creation is lost, where no item on the list in the *Benedicite Omnia Opera Dominum* is denied or forgotten" (*HSE*, 11). It is in this spirit that the title of *The Anathemata* is intended to mean, as Jones' preface notes, "as much as it can be made to mean" (*A*, 28), and of course it can be made to mean everything. Or rather it is better to say that it can mean nothing in particular, for the word "anathemata" is an amphibole, a word with two contradictory meanings. As Carson Daly has pointed out, what the term stands for is "neither of its two opposite definitions, but the idea of contradiction itself."[13] And for David Jones, of course, contradiction is not an indication of meaninglessness, but rather of multiplicity. Thus "anathemata" means all things, accursed or devoted, "counter, parti, pied, several" (*SL*, 62).

---

11. Nils Erik Enkvist writes that stylistic choice "exists on a number of different levels, not only in the *lexis*. It may involve stylistic features (special voice quality, speech rate, etc.), phonemes (singing/ singin'), morphemes (sings/singeth), words, phrases, clauses, sentences and larger units." See "On Defining Style: an essay in applied linguistics," in *Linguistics and Style*, ed. John Spencer (London: Oxford University Press, 1964), p. 17. In "The Syntax of Violence," an essay which appears in this volume, William Blissett discusses the question of style as choice or deviation in the context of *In Parenthesis*.
12. Monroe K. Spears, "Shapes and Surfaces: David Jones with a glance at Charles Tomlinson," *Contemporary Literature*, 12, No. 4 (Autumn 1971), p. 403.
13. Carson Daly, "The Amphibolic Title of *The Anathemata*: A Key to the Structure of the Poem," *Renascence*, 35, No. 1 (Autumn 1982), p. 56.

It is appropriate to find this phenomenon repeated in
the text itself, where a contradiction such as "already and
first of all" effectively keeps the syntagmatic chain open to
multiple substitutions from the paradigmatic axis. An
amphibolic phrase, it excludes no possibilities, means nothing in particular. The tendency to actually include strings
of associated terms has already been amply illustrated, but
it is worth drawing attention to the fact that the last paratactical list mentioned--of "things new and old" (*A*, 50)--is
resolved, after running to a sixth term, in an essentially
amphibolic construction: "the things come down . . . the
things lifted up."

In these strategies, words make an anamnesis of the
Word. In a letter to Aneirin Talfan Davies, Jones elaborates
on his statement that each of his works was intended to be a
plenum, to contain "the entirety or totality in a little place
or space." He draws an analogy between the work and
Christ, "the *Baban* (Babe) in the Ventricle of Mair (Mary),"
proposing this sacred text as a motto for artists: *quem totus
non capit orbis, in tua se clausit viscera factus homo* (*LF*,
81). Given this, it is not surprising to find that amphibolic
constructions, which do in fact allow language to contain
usually uncontainable extensions of meaning,[14] find their
archetype in Christ:

> what does his Boast say?
> > *Al pha es et O*
> > > that which
> > the whole world cannot hold.

Because the Word is at once everything and nothing in
particular, it expresses itself as a contradiction. And this, as
so often in *The Anathemata*, allows the paradigmatic
possibilities to parade in:

> Atheling to the heaven-king.
> Shepherd of Greekland.
> Harrower of Annwn.
> Freer of the Waters.
> Chief Physician and
> *dux et pontifex.*
> Gwledig Nefoedd and
> Walda of *every* land
> *et vocabitur* WONDERFUL. (*A*, 207-8)

Here the Word has actually entered the text in a series of
words, and the passage repeats almost exactly the pattern
which we have noticed in numerous other examples. Syntactical connections are replaced by parataxis, and, as the

14. On the way in which amphibole "tries to express the inexpressible," see Daly, p. 56.

potentially endless list of divine names extends itself, language proclaims its materiality in inscribed capitals: "WONDERFUL." What is striking in this case is that in Christ's own words association asserts itself against syntax. This brings home the remarkable extent to which the most distinctive stylistic feature of *The Anathemata*--a linguistic materiality derived from the constant failure to exclude lexical, narrative, and other alternatives from the body of discourse--appears, in fact, to be a poetic response to the Incarnation.

TERESA GODWIN PHELPS

THE TRIBUNE AND THE TUTELAR:
THE TENSION OF OPPOSITES IN
THE SLEEPING LORD

"There is always a Virgo Potens to direct the *via*" (*E&A*, 195). Thus concluded David Jones in his 1955 broadcast "The Viae" in which he reflected on the building of the Roman roads in Britain. Its few words capture Jones' conviction about the "feminine principle" and its necessary centrality in all creative and spiritual undertakings: its presence is requisite to direct the way. In the same broadcast, he said "The truth is that whether we are Greeks or barbarians, Celts or Romans or whoever we are, we cannot, for long suppose a creativity without the female principle" (*E&A*, 195). All of David Jones' poems reveal these convictions in that feminine figures or images appear at crucial times to direct or to inspire creativity so that the actions of men may be transformed and sanctified. In *In Parenthesis*, the Queen of the Woods appears to transform the soldiers' seemingly meaningless deaths into a Celtic/Christian rite of sacrifice. In *The Anathemata*, Guinevere, the Lady of the Pool, and the three witches (to name but a few of the multifarious feminine figures in the poem) come together in the image of Mary by whose "fiat," Jones insists in the poem, Christ came to save all humankind.[1] In *The Sleeping Lord*, the Tutelar of the Place is invoked to correct the malign influence of the Roman Empire, to reinstate the creative and the spiritual that the Roman rule has attempted to obliterate. (If, in "The Viae," Jones implies the feminine is an instrument of Rome, he corrects this impression in *The Sleeping Lord*.) In other words, the femi-

---

1. Recall the witches in *The Anathemata* saying: "It all hangs on the fiat." One of Jones' notes in *The Anathemata* elaborates: "Though 'Minerva springs eternally from the head of Jove', the Eternally Begotten could not have become begotten on a creature except by a creature's compliant will .... Jesus leaves no doubt that the blessedness of his mother resides firstly in the compliancy of her will .... Which Irenaeus ... had expressed when he said 'She was constituted the cause of our salvation'" (*A*, p. 128, note 5).

nine principle "connects" the mundane with the holy, men
with God, and directs the way from earth to heaven. We see
in the poems a tension between "masculine" and "feminine,"
which seem to be conflicting modes of perception and ways
of being: the masculine representing qualities such as order,
utility, reason, conformity and secularity; the feminine representing imagination, creativity, intuition, diversity, and
spirituality.[2]

This essay is part of a larger descriptive study[3] that
analyzes the role of the feminine principle in David Jones'
poems. In it I argue, in part, that the tension between the
masculine and feminine animates much of Jones' work and
that Jones sees hope for a transformation of the maladies of
modernity and technocracy in the restoration of the feminine principle so that it can once more "direct the *via*."
The modern world is too "masculine": "it is to be hoped," he
wrote in 1940, "that this masculine emphasis is at all events
tempered by the saving scepticism of the female mind;
there is a danger of Juno being put into a concentration
camp, of her being liquidated" (*E&A*, 240-1). This essay's
purpose is to describe the poems of *The Sleeping Lord* and
to demonstrate the structural and thematic significance of
the feminine principle in *The Sleeping Lord* sequence.
This, David Jones' last published collection of poems, is
composed, in part, of fragments rejected from *The Anathemata* and taken from *The Roman Quarry*.[4] The work,
nonetheless, possesses a powerful symmetry that we have
come to anticipate in Jones' long pieces (despite his claims
that they are "fragments"). The poems that comprise *The
Sleeping Lord* evolve from despair to hope, beginning with
the artist lamenting the modern waste land's dearth of symbols and concluding, as Jones' earlier works do, with a vision
of faith and reconciliation.[5] After the cry of despair that is

2. In *David Jones: An Exploratory Study* (London: Enitharmon Press, 1975), Jeremy
Hooker focuses a considerable part of his discussion on Jones' perception and presentation of the feminine principle. He sees Jones as "a devotional poet who celebrates all
aspects of the female principle," and he defines Jones' "apprehension of it to
be ... tenderness ... all creaturely and kindly qualities ... chthonic powers, the primary
creative force in nature ..." (pp. 27-28).
3. Teresa Godwin Phelps, *The Empress of the Labyrinth: The Feminine in David
Jones' Poetry* (unpub. diss.) 1980.
4. For a discussion of *The Roman Quarry* sources of *The Sleeping Lord*, see Roland
Mathias' "David Jones: Towards the Holy Diversities," in *A Ride Through the Wood*
(Cardiff: Poetry Wales Press, 1985), pp. 13-56. Also see, in this volume, Stoneburner's
"Notes Toward Performing 'The Sleeping Lord'"; Sherry's "The Roman Quarry of
David Jones: Extraordinary Perspectives" (for a discussion of Jones' overall poetic
design); and Peck's "Poems for Britain, Poems for Sons" (particularly about the connection between "The Book of Balaam's Ass" and the rest of *The Sleeping Lord* poems,
which critics, including myself, have hitherto sought in vain).
5. *In Parenthesis* begins with a scene set on the military parade ground; *The Anathemata* with the "cult-man [who] stands alone in Pellam's land"; *The Sleeping Lord* with

"A, a, a, Domine Deus," the poems retrace the condition of the modern world to the Roman Empire, dominated by order, discipline, fact, expedience, uniformity, and the utile,[6] and evolve into a vision of the Celtic world, which allows, even encourages, diversity, attachment to locality, imagination, and creativity. The Roman Empire manifests those qualities that Jones tends to see as "masculine," and the Roman Tribune of "The Tribune's Visitation" is a synecdoche for the Empire and unmitigated masculinity. The Celtic world, on the other hand, manifests "feminine" qualities, and the Tutelar of the Place is the embodiment of these. The tension between these two, the masculine and the feminine, the Tribune and the Tutelar, give *The Sleeping Lord* its dynamic and integrated structure. Their differences collapse in and into the mystical androgynous vision of the sleeping lord, evoked in the final poem, who lies under the Welsh soil. The power and unified beauty of *The Sleeping Lord* are achieved because the reader too journeys from despair, through the Roman world and into the Celtic with its promise of renewal. "The Tutelar of the Place," the central and pivotal poem of the sequence, directs the way from one to the other.

Although it is clear from Jones' essays and poems that he attributes the modern waste land to the effects of the Roman Empire, it is important to remember that he had an embivalent attitude toward the Empire, an attitude which Jeremy Hooker describes in an essay revised for the present volume:

> [Jones] confronts the horror of Imperialism without prevarication; but he recognizes that the Roman Empire was in some respects a necessary condition of the Christian religion. In allowing Christ to be crucified it unwittingly sowed the seeds of its own destruction; it uncon-

the plaintive cry of the frustrated modern artist. Into these worlds, Jones integrates images, figures, characters, and voices representing the feminine principle, and he concludes each work with a mystical vision of a renewed cosmos in which both masculine and feminine elements coexist.

6. The word "utile" is one of Jones' key terms which, like "anathemata," "gratuitous," "anamnesis," etc. come up again and again in various contexts. He clearly lays out what he means by it in a gloss on "Art and Sacrament" called "The Utile": " 'Utile' seemed the best word to cover the wholly functional works of nature, whether animalic or insentient (e.g. nest-building or mountain-building) and such works of man as tend to approximate these processes of nature. For example, the characteristic works of our present technocracy *at its best and at its worst* seek the 'utile' " (*E&A*, 180-1). Art, on the other hand, is "extra-utile" and hence sacramental, in that it is a gratuitous making of something. The utile and sacramental were once united, but "technocracy . . . achieves the vacuity and deprivation apparent in the thousand-and-one utensils and impedimenta of our daily lives, domestic or public." Modern man is reduced to a "search in antique-dealers' shops for a single spoon that does not affront the senses . . . [which is] symptomatic of a general, if muddled, nostalgia for things which though serviceable and utile are not divorced from the extrautile . . ." (*E&A*, 181). See "Art and Sacrament" (*E&A*, 143-179), "The Utile" (*E&A*, 180-185), "Wales and Visual Form" (*DG*, 63-93), "Use and Sign" (*DG*, 177-186).

sciously assisted in the spread of Christianity and supplied the language as well as some of the forms (the sacramentum, for instance) of
the Roman Catholic Church.[7]

Despite acknowledging the benefits rendered by Rome,
Jones remained painfully cognizant of the costs, and the
Roman poems in *The Sleeping Lord* enumerate these costs,
which he saw as an obliteration of feminine values by
overweening masculinity. He wrote elsewhere that Rome:

> ... so imposed [its] shape upon the waking minds of men[,] so insinuated
> the male principle as to vulgarize & flatten out the subtle maze--so
> squared and mapped the meander of our intuitive origins.[8]

And on the insinuation of the male principle, he quotes
Jackson Knight:

> ... Juno is fiercely feminine. She was not among the principal early
> deities of Rome, and was never one of the greatest. Rome worshipped
> male gods first. Rome began because Juno acknowledged defeat. (*E&A*,
> 241)[9]

Juno's defeat brought about the deprivations of the modern
world: the loss of the feminine values of the united utile
and sacramental and of the diversity and particularity present in small localities, which have become swallowed up
by imperialism. "The loss of political independence," Jones
says, "means in the very long run the loss of most else" (*DG*,
84, note 13). The Roman Empire, and empire in general,
have certain intrinsic consequences, still discernible in the
modern world. Empire severs cultures from their pasts and
their heritages, their myths and their symbols. Since art can
effect connections between present and past in its use of
myth and symbol, Empire discourages art. The perpetrators
of Empire impose a kind of masculine order which demands
the uniformity that deprives nations of their histories and
eliminates cultural diversity. Those eliminated values are
feminine: creativity, inspiration, cultures connected to their
pasts, locality and diversity. In *The Sleeping Lord* Jones
shows the Roman Empire as dominated by the masculine
principle and seeking to obliterate any feminine influence.

In the four Roman poems, "The Wall," "The Dream
of Private Clitus," "The Fatigue," and "The Tribune's Visita-

7. Jeremy Hooker, *David Jones: An Exploratory Study of the Writings* (London:
Enitharmon Press, 1975), p. 39.
8. René Hague, *A Commentary on The Anathemata of David Jones* (Toronto: University of Toronto Press, 1977), p. 103. This is from a previously unpublished Jones
"fragment."
9. Jones has used this theme before. Consider the masculine personified as Rome over-
coming the intuitive feminine in *The Anathemata* in the scene in which Mars seduces
Ilia: "Though he was of the Clarissimi his aquila over/me was robbery. /'T's a great
robbery/--is empire" (*A*, 88).

tion," the feminine is present only in dream and memory. In order to show effectively a world dominated by masculine values, Jones turns again, as he did in *In Parenthesis*, to the military, which for him best exemplifies the masculine estranged from the feminine presence. In these poems, he personifies the masculine principle in the Roman officers: the Legatus of "The Wall," the centurian Brasso (recalling an N.C.O. on the way up) in "The Dream of Private Clitus," the *principalis* in "The Fatigue," and most prominently, the Tribune. These figures establish and perpetrate Empire, instigate war and death, and, most insidiously, manipulate language to convince the common soldiers that Empire and all it stands for are necessary: "Let the gnosis of necessity infuse our hearts, for we have/purged out the leaven of illusion." (*SL*, 58). Each poem is primarily dialogue or monologue through which Jones contrives to force the masculine to manifest itself in the words of the Roman officers and soldiers which promote masculine values at the expense of the feminine.

In "The Wall," the soldiers patrolling the Roman wall are estranged from the meaning of their task. They do not understand their role:

We don't know the ins and outs
        how should we? how could we?
It's not for the likes of you and me to cogitate high policy or to guess the inscrutable economy of the pontifex .... (*SL*, 10)

The *Legatus* and the other officers have told them the reasons for their military service and the soldiers reflect on the permutations and inconsistencies in the officers' rationale:

            ... they used to say we marched for Dea
Roma behind the wolf sign to eat up the world, they used to say we marched for the Strider, the common father of the Roman people, the father of all in our walk of life, by whose very name you're called ...
            but now they say the Quirinal Mars
turns out to be no god of war but of armed peace. Now they say we march for kind Irene, who crooks her rounded elbow for little Plutus, the gold-getter, and they say that sacred brat has a future .... (*SL*, 14)

The "sacred brat" Plutus has a future indeed, a future that extends even into the late twentieth century. Jones maintains that war and money "have now become so interlocked and confused as to be both now seen only as material-as-power--both implying domination and neither stopping at any degradation to both man as artist and man as moral being" (*DG*, 165). The soldiers in "The Wall" fit into this pattern; they are "warriors" caught, albeit unwillingly, in the

pursuit of war and money. The degradation of man as artist
and moral being has begun.

    Although the officers in "The Wall" and the other
Roman poems represent exclusive masculinity, the common
soldiers in these poems retain some vision and memory of
the feminine, although only in dream and reminiscence.
The soldiers differ from their officers in part because they
are not exclusively Roman: some are "drafted for service far
from their own green valley-ways" (*SL*, 25). Risking historical accuracy, always an important element in his work,
Jones has Romans, Celts, and Greeks serve in the same
Roman unit, doing so "with deliberation in order to convey
a far more important historical truth: the heterogeneous
composition of the forces of world-imperium" (*SL*, 24).

    The patrolling men in "The Wall," reluctant instru-
ments of Empire, intuit that knowledge of their origins and
reasons for their being derive not from their officers but
from the feminine, and yet "so cold it is, so numb the intelligence, / so chancy the intuition" (*SL*, 13), they cannot
clearly recall or properly make the needed connections:

> What did our mothers tell us? What did their mothers tell them?
> What the earth-mother told to them? But what did the queen of
> heaven tell *her*? (*SL*, 14)

This passage outlines a feminine chain of wisdom: men
learn from their mothers, who learn from their own mothers,
who, in turn, learn from nature, which is ultimately
informed by a divine feminine figure, "the queen of
heaven." Apparently Empire has successfully weakened the
mediation of the feminine principle that could link the soldiers to the wisdom of the queen of heaven. They are
required to follow orders, to suppress feelings, and "to subor-
dinate . . . personal rights and . . . family rights" (*E&A*,
93):

>   now all can face the dying god
>   the dying Gaul
>   without regret.
> But you and me, comrade, the darlings of Ares, who've helped a lot of
> Gauls and gods to die, we shall continue to march and to bear in our bodies
> the marks of the Marcher--by whatever name they call him .... (*SL*,
> 14)

Through this ironic acquiescence of the enlisted men in the
plan of Empire, Jones shows the dehumanization that occurs
with Empire. The common soldiers, so that they can bring
about the deaths of "a lot of Gauls and gods," cultures and
religions at variance with those of Rome, "without regret,"
are cut off from emotion and love. They become instru-

ments of Empire, degraded as moral beings. Their objective indifference can result only by suppressing feminine subjectivity and emotion, and the officers rightly fear the infiltration of the feminine principle into their order.

For example, Brasso, in "The Dream of Private Clitus," interrupts Clitus' dream of the Tellus Mater, the Roman Earth Mother, and the "parts where he was born" (*SL*, 20). Private Clitus relates to his companion Oenomaus a dream he once had of the "superb marble relief carving of the Tellus Mater[10] which formed one of the two panels on the east front of the Ara Pacis Augustae facing the Flaminian Way leading north from Rome" (*SL*, 15). In his dream, Clitus has a vision of reconciliation with the feminine and of restoration of its values:

> And so she herself gravely inclined herself and seemed to reach her sizable marble limbs toward me and my mate in our bivvy, him sleeping and I waking, and the large uncertain phantoms of my dream that leaned over me up there in the *Teutoburg* became concrete in the proportioned limbs of Tellus Our Mother, leaning living from the east wall below the cornice and all the world seemed at peace deep within the folds of her stola as she leaned over our bivvy and all but touched our bivvy-sheets with her strong marble fingers. (*SL*, 19)

Clitus and his mate Lugo clamber into her lap, and from that vantage point daily "watch the tyros/sweat . . . to exercise . . . I laughed right out/at that, a last dream laugh"[11] (*SL*, 20). Although Clitus the Roman dreams that he and the Celt Lugo climb together into the embrace of "the proper mother of us all, from whose/containing deeps we come, to whose embrace we turn . . ." (*SL*, 19), they retain their diversity. Lugo calls her "Modron" and Clitus calls her "Matrona"; Clitus recognizes that "his Modron and our Matrona are one" (*SL*, 20).

In these Roman poems, such healing and unifying visions occur only in dream and reverie and Clitus' dream ceases when Brasso wakens him to the realities of the Roman world plan. Brasso is a foil for Clitus and Lugo in that he is much like one of them, a common soldier, but one who has become a mere puppet for his officers. His dreams are unlike those of Clitus and Lugo: "For these fact/men, Oenomaus, have their/hallucinations, don't forget that, indeed their delusions would/beat a garret poet--only

10. Jones defines the Tellus Mater in "Art in Relation to War" as "the deity of Mother Earth; honoured, together with Ceres, as the goddess of fruitfulness, she was "both womb and grave" (DG, 142, note 15).
11. Clitus' "last dream laugh" echoes the "last laugh" of Mary and Sophia in the final pages of *The Anathemata*, and the reader is reminded that the Tellus Mater of *The Sleeping Lord* also prefigures the Virgin.

there's calculation in the very dreams of/a Brasso" (*SL*, 22).
He interrupts any dream of home or the feminine lest the
plan of Empire be undone by such reveries:

> Why, yes, of course, who else but Brasso? Who else should shake a man
> from such a dream? ... there's always a Brasso to shout the odds, a fact-
> man to knock sideways and fragmentate these dreamed unities and
> blessed conjugations .... (*SL*, 21)

Brasso, whose very name sounds of hardness and inflexibil-
ity,[12] is an indispensable tool in furthering Empire, and if
"the Urbs falls, you'll know that Brasso must have/fallen
previous" (*SL*, 23). Empire depends upon the continuance of
the masculine perspective personified by Brasso, the "fact-
man." Dreams and intuited unities, feminine visions capable
of melding the disparate, threaten the flattening-out uniformity required for Empire, and its survival mandates that
feminine visions be suppressed.

The *principalis* in "The Fatigue" displays a similar
insistence on world-order as he chastises the soldiers for letting their attention and their eyes wander while they patrol
the wall. As in "The Wall," the gods are invoked to justify
the intentions of Empire:

> A few like you can undo
>   and properly bitch
> all the world plan
>   though Jove himself
> direct our august ordering. (*SL*, 29)

The *principalis* accuses the recalcitrant soldiers of being
followers of Christ: "are you a Gallatic initiate/of this Ara-
maean cult, or what?" (*SL*, 30). Christianity, in which Jones
believes masculine and feminine values coalesce, threatens
Empire. The *principalis'* fear is both justified and
prophetic: his men are garrisoned in Palestine during the
Passion. What happens there will undo the Empire. The
poem ends with the dawning of Holy Thursday[13]--the beginning of the Christian sacrifice: "tomorrow is already/putting
on to-day" (*SL*, 41).

Jones most clearly and emphatically delineates the
masculine outlook requisite for world dominion and defines
the feminine values which threaten it in the lengthy speech

---

12. Brasso is also, appropriately enough, the name of a metal polish used on military
equipment.
13. Most Christians see the crucifixion on Good Friday as the beginning of the Christian sacrifice that culminates on Easter. David Jones, following Maurice de la Taille,
S.J., insistently makes the point that the sacrifice properly begins with Christ's Last
Supper on Holy Thursday. It was at that Supper that Christ "put himself in the order
of signs," thus becoming the apotheosis of man-the-artist. Christ "employ[ed] art-
forms and establish[ed] a tradition commanding the continued employment of those
forms" (*E&A*, 143-179).

delivered by the Military Tribune in "The Tribune's Visitation." The Tribune's rhetoric mirrors the modern attitude which devalues, disparages, and ridicules feminine qualities. His speech also reflects an attitude in contemporary society which Jones abhors--the refusal to face what we have lost as a result of progress. In "Art in Relation to War," Jones says:

> What we ask is that any loss shall not be glossed over, but faced. It is indeed no use crying over spilt milk... but it is equally no use, and worse than no use, to refuse to look at the empty milk jug, the wet stains on the tablecloth, and the expression of contentment on the cat's face, and worse still to pretend that we have no use for milk anyhow, that we always did think it useless stuff--those techniques of the 'optimist' that we know so well: those who refuse to call death by its terrible and exact name, but employ any euphemism which will disguise the reality of loss. (*DG*, 153)

This is precisely what the Tribune does; he instructs his men to forget their origins, to disallow allegiance and love for their homesites, saying: "Only the neurotic/look to their beginnings" (*SL*, 51) and "so is the honey-root of known-site/bitter fruit for world floor" (*SL*, 56). Attachment to home and origins is linked to the feminine principle, and the Tribune's attitude is antithetical to feminine values. The Tribune contends that such attachment is childlike and inappropriate for Roman soldiers:

> It's not the brotherhood of the field or the Lares of a remembered hearth, or the consecrated wands bending in the fertile light to transubstantiate for child-man the material vents and flows of nature into the breasts and milk of the goddess.
> >   Suchlike bumpkin sacraments
> > are for the young-time
> >   for the dream-watches
> > now we serve contemporary fact.
> >   It's the world-bounds
> > we're detailed to beat
> >   to discipline the world-floor
> > to a common level.
> >   till everything presuming difference
> > and all sweet remembered demarcations
> >   wither
> > to the touch of us
> >   and know the fact of empire. (*SL*, 50-1)

Since arts such as poetry, song, spells, and fantasy, which derive from the imaginative facility, only operative under the auspices of feminine powers, would remind the soldiers of their cultures and homes, these too must be discarded:

> Song? antique song
> >   from known-site

spells remembered from the breast?
    No! (*SL*, 51)

Personal memories menace the Roman order that seeks a "common level." The Tribune sets himself up as an example, using what Jones calls "the techniques of the 'optimist,' " claiming that he himself has dutifully discarded these "useless" arts. He demands that his men do likewise:

> But enough: analogies are wearisome and I could analogize to the end of time, my Transpadane gradma's friend taught me the tricks. I'd beat the rhetoric of Carnutic conjurors and out-poet ovates from druid bangors farside the Gaulish strait. But I'll be 'forthright Roman' as the saying goes... (*SL*, 48)
>
> ....
>
> Old rhyme, no doubt, makes beautiful
>   the older fantasies
> but leave the stuff
>   to the men in skirts
> who beat the bounds
>   of small localities
> all that's done with
>   for the likes of us
> in *Urbs*, throughout *orbis*. (*SL*, 50)
>
> ....
>
> Spurn the things of Saturn's Tellus?
> Yes, if memory of them
>   (some pruned and bearing tree
>   our sister's song)
> calls up some embodiment
>   of early loyalty
> raises some signum
>   which, by a subconscious trick
> softens the edge of our world intention. (*SL*, 52)

The Tribune ridicules the very things most valuable to Jones, most importantly, the ability of art to hold up a sign that recalls the past. Through the Tribune, Jones makes the reader aware of the insidious and self-righteous argument that labels feminine values weak and impotent.

    The Tribune goes on to emphasize the value of Empire over human compassion, explaining precisely the dangers of the feminine quality of attachment to home if it is allowed to infiltrate the Empire: "lest, thinking of our own, our bowels / turn when we are commanded to storm the palisades of others and / the world-plan be undone by plebian pity" (*SL*, 55). The Tribune becomes the very antithesis of all that is feminine, finally even the fertile, life-giving feminine aspect, whose exclusive province is

birth. The Tribune suggests a perversion of the act of birth
itself:

> The cultural obsequies must already be sung before empire can mas-
> querade a kind of life.
>
> ....
>
> What then?
> > Are we the ministers of death?
> > of life-in-death?
> do we but supervise the world-death
> > being dead ourselves
> long since?
>
> Do we but organize the extension of death whose organisms withered
> with the old economies behind the living fences of the small locali-
> ties? (*SL*, 56)
>
> ....
>
> Let the gnosis of necessity infuse our hearts, for we have
> purged out the leaven of illusion.
> If then we are dead to nature
> > yet we live
> > to Caesar
> > from Caesar's womb we issue
> by a second birth. (*SL*, 58)

For Jones, a poet whose images and metaphors honor physical realities, "Caesar's womb" is an unspeakable perversion.
Caesar, supreme Roman, replaces in the world the Tribune
evinces even the life-giving feminine. The physical impossibility of the Tribune's trope gives the lie to any second
birth. The Tribune cannot do what Jones insists on in "Art
in Relation to War": "We must call deaths, deaths, and admit
a real loss" (*DG*, 153).

Through the Roman officers, particularly the Tribune, Jones portrays the narrow, exclusive masculinity present in the Roman Empire and still manifest in the world
today. Empire seeks to disconnect a culture from its
deposits, abhors art which can effect such a connection,
brings about deaths of men, cultures, and religions, encourages uniformity and world-order at the cost of known-site
and locality, creates only the utile, and fears the feminine,
its antithesis. It therefore continually attempts to annihilate
the feminine principle in order to ensure its own continuance.

Yet in the Roman poems Jones suggests that the
feminine spirit is never completely absent, cannot be completely suppressed, by depicting the feminine in the dreams
and reveries of the soldiers. Hope for a renewal of feminine
values always exists, even in a world as predominantly mas-

culine as the Empire of these poems, if humankind can
reconnect with the feminine principle and reinstate its wisdom and influence.

   This principle becomes flesh in the next poem in
the Tutelar of Place, the Tribune's counterpart and antagonist: "She that loves place, time, demarcation, hearth, kin,
enclosure,/site, differentiated cult" (*SL*, 59). This feminine
Tutelar is invoked in hope and in defiance: "There is one
alternative: defiance towards the tragedy which is presented
to us . . . and in which we are compelled to act . . ." (*DG*,
155).

   "The Tutelar of the Place," the central and pivotal
poem of *The Sleeping Lord*, is essentially an invocation of
the feminine deity who guards and protects local habitats,
and a prayer for her mediation. Jones originally conceived
the speaker of this poem-prayer as a figure like one of the
common soldiers of the first four Roman poems--a "Gaulish
soldier on the wall of Hierosolyma telling his mate of the
homeland in Celtica."[14] He abandoned this idea and "The
Tutelar of the Place" has no designated speaker; it is spoken
by the poet, perhaps; in a way, by soldiers of the Roman
poems who retain dreams and memories of just such a feminine figure; and, I think, by the reader in profound relief
after the unmitigated despair (except in dream and memory) and seeming hopelessness of the first five poems of *The
Sleeping Lord*. The vision of Empire and its leaders is so
grim, so bereft of compassion, that the poet compels the
reader to participate in the prayer of the faithful that comprises "The Tutelar of the Place." He employs the
stratagem of contrast and tension, as he does in *The Anathemata*, for the purpose of conversion. Readers, consciously or
not, desire a resolution to the situation Jones presents in the
first part of this work, and are thus, perhaps, more easily persuaded than they would be otherwise that the resolution that
Jones presents is appropriate.

   This central poem which focuses on a potent feminine figure leads the way from one vision to another, and
directs the *via* as only the feminine can do in Jones' cosmos. By placing this poem, which celebrates the feminine,
in the middle and not at the end of the sequence, Jones
indicates that invocation of the feminine principle, however
magically beautiful the form, is not in itself the solution.
The Tutelar, like all of the feminine figures in Jones' work,

14. From a letter to Saunders Lewis published in *Agenda*, Vol. 11, No. 4, Vol. 12, No. 1
(Autumn-Winter, 1973-74), p. 24.

functions by mediating, connecting, and directing. Jones does not advocate merely the return of the feminine, but insists that the real remedy lies in those activities brought about by the presence of the feminine: its function is maieutic. In other words, in *The Sleeping Lord*, the renewal of the feminine may inspire all of humankind to engage in the kind of Celtic quest depicted in "The Hunt" and animates the hope and faith, the domain of the feminine in all of Jones' work, inherent in "The Sleeping Lord."

The poem petitions the Tutelar for many things, among them to build a new kind of wall "where all stones of demarcation/dance and interchange" (*SL*, 60), "demarked by a dynast or staked by consent" (*SL*, 61). The Tutelar's wall, like a Celtic wattle, clearly defies the intentions of Empire:

In all times of *Gleichschaltung*, in the days of the central economies set up the hedges of illusion round some remnant of us, twine the wattles of mist, white-web a Gwydion-hedge
    like fog on the *bryn iau*
    against the commissioners
and assessors bearing the writs of the Ram to square the world-floor and number the tribes and write down the secret things and take away the diversities by which we are.... (*SL*, 63)

Sweet Mair devise a mazy-guard
in and out and round about
double-dance defences
countermure and echelon meanders round
the holy mound
       fence within the fence
pile the dun ash for the bright seed
       (within the curtained wood the canister
within the canister the budding rod)
troia in depth the shifting wattles of illusion for the ancilia for the palladia for the kept memorials, because of the commissioners of the Ram and the Ram's decree concerning the utility of the hidden things. (*SL*, 64)

This wattled fence encloses, provides a wholeness that still accommodates differences, and thus effectively represents the vital synthesis of unity and diversity necessary in the figure of "Sweet Mair." Jones links the Tutelar to the earth-mother as well as to the Virgin by calling her "one mother of us all" and declaring that, "one earth brings us all forth, one womb receives us all, yet to each / she is other, named of some name other . . ." (*SL*, 59). The Tutelar is the apotheosis of the feminine principle, which is both unified *and* "a rare one for locality" (*SL*, 59).

Since she protects and nurtures diversity, she is the Tribune's opposite and can undo the work of Empire. The

poem petitions her to "confuse their reckonings," to "notch
their tallies false / disorder what they have collated" (*SL*,
62). Jones creates in the Tutelar a powerful feminine figure
under whose influence the diversity intrinsic to small localities might return. The Tutelar exemplifies those transub-
stantiating *numina*, which even in the early days of the
Roman Empire in Wales enabled the Celts of that region to
be "ironically, bizarrely un-Roman, and quickly reverting to
Celticity in all respects . . ." (*DG*, 115). For David Jones,
Celticity and Wales represent "not only the British Princi-
pality but also any small, self-conscious, oppressed and
oppositional historic group."[15] Jones portrays the "unique
vision of the Celts," with these connotations, in the final two
poems of *The Sleeping Lord*, "The Hunt" and "The Sleeping
Lord."

"The Hunt," the shorter of the two poems, describes
the legendary hunt for the great boar, Twrch Trwyth. The
hunters in the poem are a motley and diverse band of men--
"the men of proud spirit and the men of mean spirit, the /
named and the unnamed of the Island" (*SL*, 65)--and they
are led by "the diademed leader / who directs the toil /
whose face is furrowed / with the weight of the enterprise"
(*SL*, 67).

Jones describes their leader in such a way that he
seems to be both Christ and Arthur.[16] On the one hand, he
"directs the toil," words always associated with Arthur; on
the other hand, he has "priced tresses" and "scarred feet,"
words which describe Christ. The leader of the hunt is a
composite figure,[17] with attributes for David Jones of the
two greatest mythic leaders. Désirée Hirst points out that
Jones "sees Christ as a Welsh prince,"[18] and Jeremy Hooker
maintains that "for David Jones the Celtic foundations are
all of a piece with Christianity."[19] Interestingly, for the
poet, both Christ and Arthur (and thus the leader of "The
Hunt") incorporate the feminine principle, in sharp contrast

15. Harman Grisewood, Introduction to *The Dying Gaul and Other Writings* (London:
Faber & Faber, 1978), p. 11. But exactly how Wales figures in Jones' work and his life
are intensely-debated points. René Hague finds his use of Welsh material insincere and
sentimental (*DGC*, 23-24); Mathias argues that Jones' Welshness is more genuine,
"that Wales, after many vicissitudes, won a great battle for him." "David Jones:
Toward the Holy Diversities," p. 16. Peck newly enters this fray in this volume, pp.
367-392.
16. Peck quite accurately points out in "Poems for Britain, Poems for Sons" that Adonis is also invoked. See pp. 367-392.
17. Jones may well be "blur[ing] an essential distinction between pagan myth and Christian revelation" as René Hague feared (*CA*, 11), but its effect (which I think is pur-
poseful) creates a singular Celtic *and* Christian leader.
18. Désirée Hirst, "Particularity and Power," *Poetry Wales*, Vol. VIII, No. 3 (Winter,
1972), p. 51.
19. Jeremy Hooker, "The Poetry of David Jones," *Poetry Wales* (Winter, 1970), p. 35.

to the Roman leaders in the earlier poems, who disparage
and exclude it.

Arthur, according to Jones, has a curious partly feminine derivation. He writes of pre-historic Britain "when 'our
Arthur' was hardly the Bear, still less the *Dux*, was not yet a
Celtic battle-deity, let alone a Roman calvary leader, was
not even a male, but as yet, perhaps, some female goddess
of fruition--not the warrior, but the creatrix" (*DG*, 125). In
another essay, he notes that "The Bear of the Island [Arthur]
is inestimably old, its visage reflects millenniums of
change. It knows sextransmogrification, as it knows
ploughshares can become swords . . . " (*E&A*, 233). Moreover, Arthur, with his transsexual heritage, is closely allied
to Christ for Jones. The poet speculates that "sometimes
one seems to detect in his [Arthur's] attributes things
analagous to attributes of the Son in Christian theology . . ." (*E&A*, 236).

The Christ-Arthur figure, although austere, is filled
with love and compassion for his doomed men:

> if his forehead is radiant
> like the smooth hill in the lateral light
> it is corrugated
> like the defences of the hill
> because of his care for the land
> and for men of the land.
> If his eyes are narrowed for the stress of the hunt and because of the
> hog they are moist for the ruin and for love of the recumbent bodies
> that strew the ruin. (*SL*, 67)

This leader, unlike the Roman officers and particularly
unlike the Military Tribune with his showy sentimentality,
displays real emotion, and such feelings in this poetic,
Celtic world do not need to be suppressed. This leader
knows that death is death and does not try to sublimate the
feeling of loss.

The hunt itself is derived from an ancient Welsh
legend that first appears in Welsh literature in Nennius (c.
79).[20] Jones, however, uses the later redaction found in the
story of "Kilhwch and Olwen" in the *Mabinogion*. In this
story, Arthur embarks on his hunt for Twrch Trwyth so that
his cousin Kilhwch can win the hand of Olwen, daughter of
a cruel king. Twrch Trwyth "was once a king and God had
him transformed into a swine for his sins."[21] The boar
embodies the evils of death and destruction as he kills and

---

20. J.A. MacCullough, *The Religion of the Ancient Celts* (Edinburgh: T. & T. Clark, 1911), p. 211.
21. *The Mabinogion*, trans. Lady Charlotte Guest (New Amsterdam Book Co., 1902), p. 199.

maims men and ravages the land. In the story and in Jones'
poem, the boar is an evil preternatural force that functions
not unlike those social evils brought about by Empire as
described in the Roman poems. In "The Sleeping Lord,"
Jones describes the work of Twrch Trwyth with words evoking both the results of Empire and the battlefield of *In
Parenthesis*:

> It is the Boar Trwyth
> > that has pierced through
> the stout-fibred living wood
> > that bears the sacral bough of gold.
>
> It is the hog that has ravaged the fair *onnen* and the hornbeam and
> the Queen of the Woods. It is the hog that has tusk-riven the tendoned
> roots of the trees of the *llwyn* whereby are the tallest with the least
> levelled low and lie up-so-down.
>
> It is the great *ysgithrau* of the *porcus Troit* that have stove in the
> wattled walls of the white dwellings, it is he who has stamped out the
> seed of fire, shattered the *pentan*-stone within the dwellings; strewn
> the green leaf-bright limbs with the broken white limbs of the folk of
> the dwellings, so that the life-sap of the flowers of the forest min-
> gles the dark life-sap of the fair bodies of the men who stood in the
> trackway of the long tusked great hog, *y twrch dirfawr ysgithrog hir.*
> (*SL*, 89-90)

Jones portrays the possibilities for new leadership and vision
in the Christ-Arthur figure "who rode / for the healing of
the woods / and because of the hog" (*SL*, 68). As "The
Tutelar of the Place" reveals the potentiality of a renewed
feminine influence, this poem discloses the nature of the
figure who lies under the soil of Wales, who is, in fact, the
"sleeping lord." When he awakens he will lead again the
hunt for the force that destroys the land and the men of the
land.

"The Sleeping Lord," the last poem in this book, is
set in contemporary Wales and the poem's speaker begins by
asking a series of questions[22] about the sleeping lord:

> And is his bed wide
> > is his bed deep on the folded strata
> is his bed long
> > where is his bed and
> > where has he lain him.... (*SL*, 70-1)

---

22. This kind of questioning characterizes all of Jones' poetry and he explicates the
centrality (indeed, the spiritual necessity) of this stylistic mannerism in several essays:
"But you will recall how the hero in the ancient tale (Peredur, better known as Perceval) was blamed, not only for not 'asking the question' concerning the Waste Land, but
for actually causing the land to be waste by failing to ask the question" (*DG*, 184-5).
"Because the Land is Waste (or seems so to the writer) it seeks to do what the hero in
the myth was rebuked for not doing, i.e. it seeks to 'ask the Question'. Although, alas,
unlike the myth, it does not suppose that in asking the question the land can be
'restored'. Although if all the world asked the question perhaps there might be some
fructification--or some 'sea-change'." (*DG*, 123). Also see Peck, pp. 367-392 and
Stoneburner, pp. 351-366.

The speaker of the poem then asks about the sleeping lord's Foot-Holder. He queries: In what fashion does the Foot-Holder behave? Where is the sleeping lord's Candle-Bearer? He then reflects on the ancient tradition of candle-bearers at court, remembering a Priest saying Mass. The Priest at Mass, in turn, recalls and prays for those who have gone before him--hermits, priests of cities and rural areas, all others who have said Mass before him, lords and rulers of the land, and poets "who loved the things of the Island" (*SL*, 82). The Priest reflects on Mary's role in redemption and finally prays for all the dead, incorporating even those of pre-Christian times into the Christian mythos, echoing the theme of "Rite and Fore-Time" in *The Anathemata*. The speaker proceeds to wonder if the Candle-Bearer is inside or out, and considers the fallen trees that were felled by Twrch Trwyth. The poem concludes with more questions about the sleeping lord, and this discussion focuses on these questions.

The last few pages of "The Sleeping Lord" return to the theme of the beginning of *The Sleeping Lord* sequence in that the poet again laments the state of the modern world. In this last poem, however, it is not the condition of the modern artist that concerns him, it is the despoiling of the land and the dehumanization of the worker brought about by technology. The speaker of the poem asks if the lord knows of the polluted waters and the hard labors of the miners:

> Are his wounded ankles
> > lapped with the ferric waters
> that all through the night
> > hear the song
> from the night-dark seams
> > where the narrow-skulled *caethion*
> labour the changing shifts
> > for the cosmocrats of alien lips
> in all the fair lands.... (*SL*, 90)

The speaker asks whether the sleeping lord weeps for the land and whether he is angry at what has happened to it:

> Is the Usk a drain for his gleaming tears
> who weeps for the land
> ....
>
> > > Is his royal anger ferriaged
> where black-rimed Rhymni
> > > soils her Marcher-banks
> > > Do the bells of St. Mellon's
> toll his dolour
> > > are his sighs canalled
> where the mountain-ash

```
                              droops her bright head
        for the black pall of Merthyr?
        ....

            Or, is the dying gull
                              on her sea-hearse
            that drifts the oily bourne
                              to tomb at turn of tide
            her own stricken cantor? (SL, 91-3)
```

In these last few pages of the work, Jones most poignantly
depicts his own grief at the effects of technology and urban-
ization on rural Wales. Most despairingly, the speaker questions if even the lord's fight with the hog, which is here
analogous to Christ's own travails, is in vain:

```
                              when he dream-fights
        his nine-day's fight
                              which he fought alone
        with the hog in the Irish wilderness
                              when the eighteen twilights
                              and the ten midnights
        and the equal light of nine mid-mornings
        were equally lit
                              with the light of the saviour's fury
        and the dark fires of the hog's eye
        which encounter availed him nothing. (SL, 92)
```

The time of this poem is the present, and in it the poet
indicates that this is an ebb time in history and in civilization. He describes the times in "Art in Relation to War":

> The hour of the daemons of power that take possession of the Waste
> Land when true cultural life is at its lowest ebb and the 'young hero' has
> not yet restored 'the maimed king' and the time of resuscitation is not
> yet. When all is 'doing' and there is no 'making'. When there is no
> organic growth, but only organization and extension of dead forms. (DG,
> 129)

The hope, nonetheless, is in the theme of the Arthurian
myth and the Christian mythos. The myth of Christ and the
legend of Arthur share the theme of betrayal, defeat, and
subsequent resurrection. Both Christ and Arthur, on whom
the figure of the sleeping lord is based, overcome defeat
and death and come again to restore the world.

The Christ-Arthur figure that lies under the Welsh
soil offers hope for a new spirit and new leadership, since in
Welsh folklore Arthur is "the sleeping-hero-who-will-come-
again" (E&A, 218). In the stories, Arthur has no grave and
the Welsh peasants believed, and perhaps still believe, "that
in their hour of most need he would come again out of
annwfn, or . . .'out of Faerie' " (E&A, 224). Most impor-

tantly, a resuscitated Arthur means a renewal of Welsh tradition.

The feminine principle figures importantly in this vision of renewal for several reasons. First, Arthur was once a female creatrix, and then a god of agriculture. There was a time when "the god of war was the god of agriculture and the cities had no walls, and that Arthur might reverse his roles . . ." (*DG*, 166). This does not mean that the sleeping lord is a feminine figure, but it does imply that the new leader's nature might well have feminine attributes, in particular attachment to the land and respect for it. Second, the return of the sleeping lord means a renewal of Welsh traditions and customs. The Welsh deposits are linked with locality, terrain, and site; the Welsh are an imaginative people who once created intricate art forms; the Welsh have a "sense of the local, the physical, the love of the fenced-in and familiar, and affection for what is known" (*E&A*, 283); and, most importantly, in ancient Wales, the artist-craftsman was an esteemed member of society. All of these are "feminine" qualities or results of feminine influence, and indeed the feminine principle has always been important in Wales. In "Wales and the Crown," Jones points out that "in Wales, Y Mamau, the mothers, have always been influential, whether as mortal women or as fairies reflecting the cult of the Deae Matres of Antiquity" (*E&A*, 48). Jones never suggests that the feminine principle should supercede the masculine; instead, he argues for a renewed feminine spirit united with the masculine, which will once again connect cultures with their heritages, inspire the art capable of making this connection, mediate effectively between man and God, and thereby fructify the waste land. He identifies a "duality, a dichotomy perhaps, in the Celtic thing. The warrior aristocracy had its skygods but beneath it were peoples of earlier cultures . . . for whom the Mother Goddess and various chthonic deities were tutelar . . . [W]hat's under works up. Or is it that the Great Mother is coming into her own?" (*DG*, 57). The seeming polarities of masculine and feminine, which have been torn asunder, are united into a new, third thing, whose shape and face are as yet unknown.

Lastly, the feminine principle figures significantly in the vision of hope in "The Sleeping Lord" because the poet suggests that the lord might be the land itself:

Are the slumbering valleys
            him in slumber
            are the still undulations
the still limbs of him sleeping?

> Is the configuration of the land
> > the furrowed body of the lord
> are the scarred ridges
> > his dented greaves
> do the trickling gullies
> > yet drain his hog-wounds?
> Does the land wait the sleeping lord
> > or is the wasted land
> that very lord who sleeps? (*SL*, 96)

In his earlier works, particularly in *The Anathemata,* Jones developed the idea that primitive man worshipped the earth mother or great goddess in the topography of the land itself. In the hills and caves of the land, early man saw and worshipped the fertile belly and breasts of the numinous and fecund feminine principle. A resurgence of honor and respect for the feminine principle as embodied in the land by all of mankind would counterbalance the dire effects of technology depicted in "The Sleeping Lord."

Jones refrains from being simplistic and conclusive: ambiguity is intrinsic to his vision. He gives no specific answer to who the new leader might be nor concrete form the sleeping lord might take; he instead leaves us with a legacy of hope for Wales, for England, for all humankind, "whether we are Greeks or barbarians, Celts or Romans." In "The Myth of Arthur" he says: "If we are altogether impatient of what is seen darkly in a mirror we shall have little use for the myth of Arthur" (*E&A*, 237). In the same essay, he opens the way for any possibility: "From the machine-age the strayed machine-men may create a myth patient of baptism. Arthur may return from 'faerie' in the least expected of guises" (*E&A*, 259).

TONY STONEBURNER

NOTES TOWARD PERFORMING
"THE SLEEPING LORD"

The sounds the instruments of an orchestra make when it is
tuning up are not the sounds they make in performance, yet
the first (truing pitch and playing scales and runs of other
intervals) prepares for the last. I offer the following notes in
the hope that they advance a full performance of "The
Sleeping Lord."[1]

NOTE I

"The Sleeping Lord"
among his other works

"The Sleeping Lord" pairs itself with other works by David
Jones. Among his inscriptions, it pairs itself with "cara Wallia derelicta" (1959), both inasmuch as it too is a lament for
present Wales in its colonial or third-world status, its people
and natural resources exploited by the first world and many
of its citizens complicit with the first world, and inasmuch
as it too recalls an earlier moment of decisive damage to
independence, in its case political, economic, and cultural,
in the death of Llywelyn. "The Sleeping Lord" faces the
social and ecological consequences of colonial industrialization and recalls the legendary defense by Arthur against
the ravaging boar (a parallelism between devastation by
superhuman/supernatural evil beast and devastation of

---

1. I have made several previous attempts, either sustained or in passing, to offer
preparation for a reading of "The Sleeping Lord." They contribute to the present
essay; it corrects them.
1973 "So Primitive, So Civilized: The Eucharistic Vision of David Jones." *Anglican Theo-*
logical Review 55, pp. 484-491.
1977 "Making and Dwelling: The Finding and Making of Meaning in Three Recent Long
Poems." Pp. 1-48 in *Faith and Meaning in the Human Venture.* Chicago: Brent House
Ecumenical Ministry and Rockefeller Memorial Chapel.
1978 "Triad from Great Britain: Introduction to Three Recent Longer Poems and a
Trying-Out to Discover If Faith Coinheres There." *Semeia* 13, pp. 93-129.
1984 "The Poetry of David Jones." *The Kenyon Review* NS VI, 4, pp. 119-124.

human beings and nature by colonial industrialization
emerges).[2]

Among his paintings, "The Sleeping Lord" pairs itself,
if only partly, sketchingly, tentatively, with "The Four
Queens" (1941), in the sense that it too belongs to the Matter
of Britain. Even though he is Lancelot and not Arthur, there
is a sleeping warrior in a Welsh setting (indeed, the area
around Capel-y-ffin figures in detail in both painting and
poem) and as he dreams he combats or counters evil.

Among his prose-compositions, "The Sleeping Lord"
pairs itself with "The Myth of Arthur" (1940-1941: *E&A*, 212,
footnote 1 drastically exaggerates the degree of revision
between the first and second printed versions). The essay is
far-ranging but in several paragraphs it records an early
imagining of a vital component in the final version of "The
Sleeping Lord." We will consider them in Note IV.

Among his other poems, "The Sleeping Lord" obviously pairs itself with "The Hunt." In its early draft, it follows the passage that supplies the *ur*-text of "The Hunt" in
The Roman Quarry and it follows "The Hunt" in *The Sleeping Lord and Other Fragments*. Clearly it is a sequel or
tangent of the other poem. Pursuit of the mythological
beast and confrontation with it wear down, and worse, Arthur
and the men that he leads and the animals that they use. As
rest follows work, so "The Sleeping Lord" follows "The
Hunt."

Yet if "The Sleeping Lord" follows "The Hunt" in
narrative connection or plot, the former differs much from
the latter in manner of presentation. "The Hunt" is state-
mental and straightforward, the version of a fragment of the
virtuoso medieval prose-work, "Culhwch ac Olwen"; but "The
Sleeping Lord" keeps ambiguity fluid or in solution without
solidifying by the use of both questions and hemming-and-
hawing locutions. It is full of indirection (elaborations and
digessions). Plot links "The Hunt" and "The Sleeping Lord,"
but mode-of-being divides them.

---

2. We find a kind of rehearsal of the verbal dimension of the inscription in the prose of
David Jones: in "Welsh Poetry" (1957), he has incorporated phrases that he later combined much more compactly in the polyglot calligraphic masterpiece: *Ac yna i bwriwyd
holl Gymry y'r llawr* and *Venit summa dies* and *Nyt oes na chyngor na chlo nac egor* and
Penn Llywelyn dec and *a vraw byt bot pawl haern trwydaw.* (*E&A*, 61-63)

NOTE II

An Early Imagining of "The Sleeping Lord": The Roman Quarry

The Roman Quarry (published 1981 but written *c.* 1935 on) prints a major source of the final version of "The Sleeping Lord." It, asking if we can identify contemporary colonial Wales with legendary Arthur (or if there is any hope for wholeness for contemporary Wales), seems the primary imagining of the poem, particularly a passage (*RQ*, 27-37) whose opening and closing sections, interrogative and concerning landscape as either makeshift bed or recumbant figure, are almost identical with that of the final version, as the following quotations demonstrate.

> And is his bed wide
> > is his bed deep on the folded strata
> is his bed long
> > where is his bed.... (*RQ*, 27: see *SL*, 70-71)

And

> Does the land wait the sleeping lord or is the wasted land that very lord who sleeps? (*RQ*, 37: see *SL*, 96)

After about two solid pages of matter identical with, or similar to, sections of the final version, the passage in *The Roman Quarry* introduces subjects that the final version omits--Dylan and Manannan (about four pages), Nodens and Bright (about two pages)--yet each of these two sections offers a few lines which, revised, the final version includes:

> Wave is rough and
> cold is wind
> but
> bright is candela (*RQ*, 31: see *SL*, 90)

And

> ... where they sing their West *In Paradisum* and the Corposants toss for the dying flax-flames and West-world glory in transit is. (*RQ*, 36: see *SL*, 94)

Only about half of the original passage belongs to the final version (some of the omitted parts, those about Dylan and Manannan, for example, seem to undergo a seachange and appear in *The Anathemata*; in "The Sleeping Lord" divine beings give place to human beings). The final version, with human beings, members of the household of Arthur, to the fore, is much longer than the passage in *The Roman Quarry* and draws a large part of its remaining imagining primarily

from another source. Yet *The Roman Quarry*, in sections
outside the passage basic to "The Sleeping Lord," supplies
the final version several other bits and pieces:

> For all the gay eroders that lush the draining valley-troughs to
> Narberth, where the *palas* is
> and by the dark boundary-stream:
> where the prince who hunted, met
> the Jack of Hunters
> in the woof of grey
> and the pale dogs deep under earth-floor lit the dim chase. (*RQ*, 13-14:
> see *SL*, 91)

and

> ... before the Arya came, and the ministering sons who uncover the
> father's fires, whose charge is the bright seed under the piled ash
> which is the life of the people. (*RQ*, 22: see *SL*, 78)

and

> ... was the stench-track blighting the Iscoed oaks
> does the red spot pale on the high boned cheeks in Ceredigion because
> the cleft feet stamp out the seed of fire, is the fire-back stone split
> with the riving tusk in the white dwellings. (*RQ*, 27: see *SL*, 90)

Of course, modification, some minute and other enormous,
occurs between *ur*-text and ultimate version. The opening
passage of the latter, compared to its counterpart in the
former, exhibits modification of lineation (original prose-
paragraph converted to lines and hemistichs), language,
idea, and insertion. Compare the first form of the section

> where is his bed and where have they
> laid him from Buelt to Gower?
> Is the tump by Honddu his tilted pillow does the gritstone outcrop
> incommode him does the deep syncline sag beneath him...? (*RQ*, 27-
> 28)

with its last form (with words that alter, rather than add to,
the first form in capital letters)

> where is his bed and
> where HAS HE LAIN him
> from north of Llanfair-ym-Muallt
> (a name of double *gladius*-piercings)
> south to the carboniferous vaultings of Gŵyr
> (where in the sea-slope chamber
> they shovelled aside the shards & breccia
> the domestic litter and man-squalor
> of gnawed marrowbones and hearth-ash
> with utile shovels fashioned of clavicle-bones
> of warm-felled great fauna.
> Donated the life-signa:
> the crocked viatic meal
> the flint-worked ivory agalma
> the sacral sea-shell trinkets

> posited with care the vivific amulets
> of gleam-white rodded ivory
> and, with oxide of iron
> ochred life-red the cerements
> of the strong limbs
> of the young *nobilis*
> the first of the sleepers of
> Pritenia, *pars dextralis,* O! aeons & aeons
> before we were insular'd.)
> Is the tump by Honddu
> his LIFTED BOLSTER?
> does a gritstone outcrop
> incommode him?
> does a deep syncline
> sag beneath him? (*SL*, 71-72)

There is also big-scale modification. For example, a major insertion comes after the introduction of the one whom the original draft calls the "foot-chafer" (and the final version the "Foot-Holder"--*RQ*, 28: see *SL*, 72-73). In the first form the officer receives a single mention merely in passing; in the last form he receives much more sustained attention, as his setting, which is also that of the exhausted leader resting, receives more elaborate description of landform, flora, and weather. We see loyal service to leader by follower.

The long insertion continues, to become an extended section about the Candle-bearer, another faithful follower (*SL*, 74-77). There is a candle in the first form, as we have seen (*RQ*, 31: *candela*), but not a Candlebearer. He looms large in his own section and then reappears to declare a fine final word, or grace-note (*SL*, 87).

The long insertion adds a short passage that permits us to have a view of the lord when he is not directing a campaign, riding hard to engage the enemy or sleeping out overnight exposed to weather, but when he is in his dwelling with his retinue at table for a meal (his face shows the care of governing to be almost as deep-cutting into physiognomy as the conduct of warfare) (*SL*, 77-78).

The continuing insertion adds a long passage that presents the Priest of the Household: what takes place in his interior monologue during a silent moment at the end of the grace before the meal becomes the heart of the poem in the final version of "The Sleeping Lord" (*SL*, 78-86).

It is almost as though the original draft gave a frame and the final version filled it with lord-attending human figures.

NOTE III

"The Sleeping Lord" among the poems of the contemporaries of David Jones

"The Sleeping Lord" pairs itself with other poems of its period, if we designate its period the years of its first conception. According to the endnote or *subscript* that dates the final version, we see that it is the creation of an intense half-year, "*November 1966 to March 1967*" (*SL*, 96). Yet if we consult *The Roman Quarry*, we see that elements of it already existed as an integral part, if that is the accurate phrase, of the MS from which David Jones extracted starting-matter for both *The Anathemata* and the poems collected in *The Sleeping Lord and Other Fragments*. David Jones worked on this text from the mid-thirties on (*RQ*, xiii-xiv). It seems permissible then to associate the first conception with the period of international depression and the accumulating thunderhead of international war, the decade of economic and ideological and militarist/nationalistic chaos from the mid-thirties through WWII, almost a third of a century earlier than his completion of the poem.

"The Sleeping Lord" pairs itself with poems that announce the end of an epoch or of a civilization, like "Astronomical Changes" by D.H. Lawrence or "The Second Coming" by W.B. Yeats. It is as though David Jones answers the question of Yeats ("what rough beast?") with the invasive and devastating mythological boar Trwyth from "Culhwch ac Olwen" (*RQ*, 36).[3]

---

3. Six pages after the paragraph about the boar there is another end-of-the-world (and role-of-leader) passage.

> O man, this is but a beginning--we, who reckon we suffer so late in urbs-time, who come late in time, when times have gone to the bad, are but at the initiation days of megalopolitan time--Caesar is but a pallid prototype of what shall be, and what is shall pale for what is to come. Take a common instance, mate: A laureate--supposing him well lined, primed, dined, and well boosted, can yet, with a cheek full of tongue, sing In Praise of the World; but laureates shall need two tongues and double-bandaged eyes, and hemlock for the prescient faculties and counter-magic against the vengeance of disgusted Muses, who shall presume to sing in praise of the world yet to be.
>
> Our time is Strider's time--and what's world-time but Caesar's time. When Caesar's clock is wound it runs not down, but rather accelerates--fast and faster the wheels go round--till the Crixuses and Oenomauses, the you's and me's at the world-end, in the last milleniums, shall think of us as living in an Age of Gold, as almost human, as relatively free, as children playing at empire.
>
> What if the senate is Caesar as once was, or Caesar the senate as now is, or by some other name that Caesar, Caesar is, as in times yet to be? If the dictatorship is Caesar's, the dictated are the people, no less are the dictated the people if the people make themselves Caesar and the Dictatorship is of themselves--for still they can but dictate their own deaths as does our life-giving Caesar--no man--there's no end to it nor no way out, neither. (*RQ*, 42)

To establish some perspective on the period of the original draft from which David Jones made the final version of "The Sleeping Lord," I quote the conclusion of "May-June, 1940" by Robinson Jeffers, the self-denominated anti-humanist, who sees WWII not as a desired end-of-civilization event but merely as a power-struggle within our present civilization system.

> And why do you cry, my dear, why do you cry?
> It is all in the whirling circles of time.
> If millions are born millions must die,
> If England goes down and Germany up
> The stronger dog will still be on top,
> All in the turning of time.
> If civilization goes down, that
> Would be an event to contemplate.
> It will not be in our time, alas, my dear,
> It will not be in our time.

"The Sleeping Lord" also pairs itself with poems concerned with a central figure, the leader, the major man, crucial or essential to the excellence or well-being of society, counterer of economic chaos and political anarchy, like "Coriolan" by T.S. Eliot (see *E&A*, 241), the Malatesta sections and others of *The Cantos* by Ezra Pound, and "Examination of the Hero in a Time of War" by Wallace Stevens. The image of Arthur elaborated in "The Hunt," as the public person responsible, waking or sleeping, at whatever risk or cost to self, for the commonweal, recurs in "The Sleeping Lord." A society whose subsystems were contradictory among themselves and counterproductive (for example, overproduction of food and people hungry and starving within the same country) was desperate for solutions to its systematic problems and asked deeply how it could accomplish transformation toward being a consistent and productive system. Some people entertained the possibility that mass-movements offered the solution; other people entertained the romantic historical answer of individual greatness that unites a whole people to act sacrificially and accomplish transformation--the leader as the master of symbolization. Like others of his period, David Jones explored the second alternative when he meditated the figure of Arthur.

"The Sleeping Lord" also pairs itself with works that identify human beings and landforms, like *Finnegans Wake* by James Joyce, the Arthurian poems by Charles Williams,

---

The logic of processes already operative and negative guarantees regular worsening even unto utter dehumanization and alienation.

and *Paterson* by W.C. Williams. David Jones asks about
the dialectical relation between a people and a place,
about the spirit of the one and the spirit of the other, about
the person eventually given the title Once and Future King
and the terrain of southern Wales. Can place transmit the
spirit of past accomplishment there to an oppressed present
as a liberating and transforming spirit?

If David Jones initially formulated his questions in
the thirties and forties and they resembled the questions of
his elders and peers among the poets of that period, when he
returned to the original draft of "The Sleeping Lord," after
he had written and published *The Anathemata,* a third of a
lifetime or more later, he had other or additional questions
and the final version differs correspondingly.

NOTE IV

An Early Imagining of
"The Sleeping Lord":
"The Myth of Arthur"

As we promised in Note I, we come to consider the several
paragraphs of "The Myth of Arthur" (*E&A,* 212-259) that
offer evidence of an early imagining (1940-1941) of a vital
component in the final version of "The Sleeping Lord."

Let us consider first a passage that introduces the
Bard of the Household as a hyperbolic handler of traditional
lore; that joins with a passage in *The Roman Quarry* in
treating hearth with fire as the focus of the dwelling; that
names Arthur and that relates him to a lord of the land; and
that manifests realism within the enthusiasm of David Jones
for the things of Wales:

> 'Our conversation is in heaven' urges Paul on the proletarian Christ-
> ians in the tenements of Roman Philippi--'Our conversation is with
> Arthur' urges the Bard of the Household on his patron, the lord of a
> sheep-run hill and half a valley, seated by the central hearth-stone,
> where the life of the household smoulders, between the central sup-
> ports--the song of the lost living-space of empire adding zest to the
> more immediate project turning in his mind, of how best to fore-stall
> his detested kinsman over the hill, in the matter of grazing rights and
> the cutting of timber. (*E&A,* 217)

In the interior monologue of the moment of silent intercession of the Priest of the Household, the Priest refers to the
Bard of the Household with the ambivalence of rivalry and
respect (*SL,* 82; the Bard of the Household also appears
briefly in the section on the Candle-bearer as an example

of a pre-eminent officer within the retinue of the lord: *SL*, 76). The Priest sets his historical facts from scripture over against the Bard's fictions from traditional mythology and legend, and feels superior to the Bard in relation to truth; yet recognizes that they have in common a deep affection for the people and things of their Celtic culture (as the reader discerns a parallelism between destructiveness of mythological boar and colonial industrialization, so he or she discerns a parallelism between the Bard of the Household in his difficult time and David Jones in our difficult time).

The prose-paragraph offers a compact imagining of the dwelling of the lord with its focus the hearth with undying fire; the final version unfolds the compact imagining:

> and the Silentiary
> has struck the post for the *pared*[2]
> to hear
> and for all the men
> under the *gafl*-treed roof-tree
> of the *neuadd*, to hear
> whether they are seated or standing
> on either side of the wattle-twined *cancelli*
> below or above
> THE centred HEARTH-STONE
> (WHERE THE LIFE OF THE HOUSEHOLD SMOULDERS).

[2] *pared*: screen or partition....
   The hall (*neuadd*) of a Welsh chieftain was of wooden construction. Wooden pillars supported the roof-tree. It was partly divided into an 'upper' and a 'lower' hall by two half screens running from the side walls, rather as a church is divided into nave and chancel (*cancelli*). The fire (which must on no account go out, for it represented the life of the household) was placed centrally between the two half partitions. Each of the various officers of the court sat in order of precedence. The Silentiary (*Gostegwr*) struck with his rod one of the supporting pillars when silence was required. (*SL*, 78, with words that duplicate the language of the prose-paragraph in capital letters)

The prose-paragraph furnishes the starting-matter for what in the final version becomes the center of the poem, the house of the lord and its officers, the lord who dwells and governs as well as rides, defends, attacks, bivouacs, and slumbers. It also furnishes a corrective picture of the material and social circumstances of leadership in pre-Romance, pre-feudal, tribal Wales.

Some people accuse David Jones of idealizing Wales. Perhaps he does. But in the present passage we can see him making his claims small and realistic. He gives us the low-down. The lordship is small potatoes and the lord individualistic and divisive. Highfalutin phraseology flatters

him. If he likes elevated language, he has mean motives.
David Jones is closer to belittling than magnifying setting
and goals. He is closer to debunking than idealizing. Half a
paragraph just before the conclusion of the essay links with
our prose-paragraph in language ("over the hill") and in situation and confirms its impression.

> Everyman's hand was against everyman and men sat wondering
> what was brewing over the hill or across the neck of water. The apos-
> tles of the West did not bring to those so situated a message of freedom
> from encounter or lessening of tension; they were naive men, but not so
> naive as to suggest a 'better time coming'. On the contrary they pro-
> posed a more arduous warfare and more fearsome privations as necessary
> to the taking-on of Paul's adversaries and theirs, 'the prince of the
> power of the air' and the 'cosmocrats of the dark aeon', and as necessary
> incidentally to the living of a possible life in this world, for only
> within their enclosures was there normal order in that age. (*E&A*, 257-
> 258)

Arthur defends, making possible survival. Arthur governs,
establishing a humanizing measure of 'normal order' for his
people, even though the mythological boar threatens annihilation.

    In the first prose-passage from "The Myth of Arthur"
the lord whom David Jones characterizes is not Arthur. Yet
in large part he puts Arthur in the place of that lord. Even
so, such reductions and contractions do not diminish the
dimensions of the wholeheartedness of the leadership of
Arthur.[4]

    David Jones created the final version of "The Sleep-
ing Lord" at least a quarter of a century after his first imagining of the passage from *The Roman Quarry* and the scattered fantasizing paragraphs from "The Myth of Arthur."
What led him to wed the two? I think that it was an

---

4. One other passage of "The Myth of Arthur" seems to anticipate a passage of the
final version of "The Sleeping Lord," a passage in the interior monologue of the moment
of silent prayer of the Priest of the Household in which he directs his recalling of, and
intercession for, the dead to outstanding Welsh women among them.
> To proceed with our fantasy: There, far from the Plantagenet charade, maybe
> they could commune with Creirwy the daughter of the enchantress, and Tegau
> of the Golden Bosom, and Esyllt Slender-neck, and Bright Day (Arthur's aunt),
> and White Swan, and Creiddylad daughter of Lear .... (*E&A*, 229)
Here is the passage from "The Sleeping Lord" that it seems to have inspired:
> AND CREIDDYLAD the DAUGHTER OF LEAR than whom no maiden of
> the Island or of the isles in the waters that moat the Island could compare in
> majesty either in her life-time or in the ages before her or in the times yet to
> be; and Elen the daughter of Coil, lord of Stratha Clauda between the Vallum &
> the Wall and there was she whose agnomen was Aurfron[4] on account, it would
> appear, of her numinous & shining virtue, for the epithet 'GOLDEN' betokens
> what is not patient of tarnish ...
>   and there were SLENDERNECKs and Fairnecks and she that was called
> BRIGHT DAY, the daughter of the *gwledig*, Amlawdd ...
[4]Aurfron: GOLDEN Breast.
(*SL*, 85, with words that duplicate the language of the prose-passage in capital letters)

attempt to answer a question implicit in *The Anathemata* in its completed form.

NOTE V

"The Sleeping Lord" among his own works
or
The Final Imagining of
"The Sleeping Lord"

Among the poems by David Jones, "The Sleeping Lord" pairs itself with two other poems besides "The Hunt"; it pairs itself with "A, a, a, Domine Deus," the short (one-page) poem that opens *The Sleeping Lord and Other Fragments* ("c. 1938 and 1966," as the *subscript* says: *SL*, 9), because the two of them ask the same question, can one discover and enjoy divine immediacy in the next epoch, the alien and alienating darkness of unknown and perhaps evil things to come "at the turn of a civilization?" The short poem directly and overtly identifies what counts for divine immediacy in the next epoch as a manifestation of Jesus as crucified, risen, glorified, and eternal Life-fulfiller. "The Sleeping Lord" answers implicitly and indirectly by a recital of multiple Masses in polymorphous situations (for the Mass counts for divine immediacy). A synergism of which the Mass is agent also yields beneficent byproducts in an age past the end-of-an-age in which annihilation and even darker things threaten. There are epoch-transcending powers at work in the longer poem.

The Mass is central to "The Sleeping Lord," but by suggestion more than by explicit statement. As there is sleight of hand, so there is sleight of mind. There is no Mass celebrated for Arthur and his retinue in the poem, yet eucharistic action is at its heart. Sleight of mind enables the Mass both not to be and to be crucial to it.

The poem has the grammatical forms proper to the problematic character of the poem as a consideration of the future. The poet is not in a position to make unconditional declarations. Instead, he asks questions (even if leading ones), or balances matters between alternatives. The interrogative mood dominates the opening and close of the poem and erupts in the interval between them upon occasion. The poem sometimes also even formulates uncertainty: "But whatever may have been the cause of this phenomenon . . ." (*SL*, 76). At the juncture of the poem in

which the Priest of the Household is about to appear, we
have *whether/or* twice:

So whether his lord is in hall or on circuit of the land ... (*SL*, 77)

and

Whether seated
                at his board ...(*SL*, 77)

The second instance becomes virtuoso in a semi-Faulkner-
ian fashion, for what follows *whether* goes on and on for
pages (*SL*, 77-87) before reaching the long postponed *or*
that opens the options:

So then, whether seated
                at this board in his hall
or lying on his sleep-board
                in his lime whited *ystafell*
with his bed-coverlet over him to cover him
                a work of the Chief Stitching Maid
to Yr Arglwyddes (his, the Bear's wife)
of many vairs of stitched together
                marten-cat pelts
contrived without visible seam
                from the top throughout.

                Or, here, out
on the cold, open *moel ion*
                his only coverlet
his madder-dyed war-*sagum*
                where he slumbers awhile
from the hunt-toil .... (*SL*, 87: within the long *whether/or* passage,
shorter "whether"-ing occurs, once on 80 and thrice on 81)

We meet the Priest of the Household amid problematic or
uncertain statements. The poet rehearses typical behavior
of the Priest within larger routine patterns. When the company in the hall quiets at the wood-knocking noise by the
appointed official, the Priest, with proper ceremony (a bow;
the sign of the cross) and the formulaic expressions of ritual,
says the expected grace before the meal. After brief spoken
words, he also says silently a prayer for the dead. If the spoken words are brief, the silent words are many and excur-
sive. Whatever the actual duration of the silent speech
(only a moment?), the linguistic amplitude is page-taking
(*SL*, 79-86). As he recalls the dead with gratitude and prays
for them, he makes a rollcall of classes of people and
almost invariably links each class to its specific civilizational situation and correlate characteristic eucharistic celebration ("the White Oblation," 79; "the same Oblation," 80;
"they offered the Eternal Victim," 80; "solitary at the
mensa," 81; "the merits of the same Victim are pleaded at

the stone," 81; "the same anamnesis was made," 81; "the Oblation," 83; "the Oblation made at the lighted feast board," 83;
"the dyptycha of the Island" [ML *diptychum* list of the dead
for whom prayers were said at Mass], 85).

The Mass that is no Mass but only a moment of
silence after the brief food-and-drink-blessing finally
upgathers in its blessing the human dead of Wales, Celticity,
Christendom, and the whole planet. The moment, in reca-
pitulating human being in prehistory and history, is history-
transcending. "Every age stands in immediate relation to
God," Ranke says. If civilizational continuity fails, divine
immediacy is available. The Mass (or its approximations,
anticipations, and antitypes) transmits divine immediacy.

Human beings, victims of civilizational disconnec-
tions, with only fragments of previous human cultures, in
interaction with the Mass-communicated divine immediacy,
make things new, things appropriate to the conditions of the
emergent time. The fragments of the past (which the Priest
of the Household recollects in his silent prayer), present
urgency, and divine immediacy yield creativity after the
end of an epoch, even within the paw-press and claw-rake of
survival-threatening rivalries.

Although Arthur appears in the poem, he does not
appear by name but only in riddle-like anonymity. The
poet gives him identity-establishing titles, "The Bear of the
Island" (*SL*, 76, 81, 87) and "The Director of Toil" (*SL*, 78)
and describes him as the antagonist of the demonic mythological boar with burnt-earth policies.

But he is not the first among peers at the Round
Table or the Flower of Chivalry. His rank is less and his
time earlier. He lacks the later glamour. Yet he is the
starting-matter of the Matter of Britain and the Myth of
Arthur. He will undergo metamorphosis, and magnetically
attract other legends and lores to his associates and himself,
and fill the imagination of Europe with a glimpse of
grandeur. Another person himself, he supplies the makings,
after almost half a millenium, of the Once and Future King,
who has endured for a millenium and more.

If the leader is anonymous, his identity and future
create dramatic irony. The poet mentions neither name nor
future but the reader knows them. The unspoken speaks,
informing the further reaches of meaning. Leader and people have suffered loss. Defeat defines them better than victory, even if they have not given up. Dramatic irony counts
on our knowing that eventually they will undergo final
defeat--and yet, transmuted by imagination and art, their

destiny is widespread and longlasting triumph, international
and trans-epochal. Even today, Arthur shines in the mind.
Shapeshifting, he gathers new life in each subsequent period
that he enters. The defeated of one epoch, transfigured by
imagination, can become paradigmatic for the next epoch.
Whatever is deeply human undergoes transfer with integrity.

There is a definitive grace-note in "The Sleeping
Lord." The Priest ends his momentous silent summoning and
summing-up of the dead with the sign of the cross and
voiced sound just loud enough for hearing. The Candle-
bearer, alert but the lowest officer in the hierarchy of the
household, and one whom official etiquette requires to stand
mute in assembly, answers loud and clear the liturgical
words of the Priest with the customary closure-producing
(yet novelty-introducing) antiphon. Newness breaks out in
small matters as well as big ones.

Different circumstances evoke life-fulfilling novelty:
the Mass, the figure of Arthur radiant and regnant in the
imagination of the West for a thousand years, the spontaneous and gracious outburst of the irrepressible Candle-
bearer betoken that beyond the turn of a civilization a
valuable life is possible.

Among the poems of David Jones, "The Sleeping
Lord" also pairs itself with *The Anathemata*. Both are great
acts of recalling within a moment of deepest crisis. Dark-
ages annihilation threatens Arthur and his people in "The
Sleeping Lord," and colonial industrialization and incorporation (or swallowing) by empire threatens to replace all that
is distinctive and special about Wales with global uniformi-
ties and other deprivations for the poet meditating contemporary Wales. World War II threatens the end of Great
Britain, of Western civilization, and of being fully human to
the extent that fact and technology threaten to replace
symbol and ceremony. In *The Anathemata* David Jones can
see nothing good on earth beyond the looming darkness of
the threefold terminations. In a way, "The Sleeping Lord" is
a rerun of *The Anathemata* in epitome, but with one question added (what do we see if we look beyond the end?) and
with a manifold answer added (the recreative Mass, responsible Arthur, the inspired spontaneous Candlebearer; the possibility of efficacious counterparts within or beyond contemporary grim Wales--David Jones would not be surprised
by the logic of empire that leads the powers that be to
locate the most radioactivity-emitting atomic energy center in Great Britain in Wales).

"The Sleeping Lord" is the reply David Jones, wedding his two early imaginings, made to *The Anathemata*. If *The Anathemata* ackowledges the necessity of NO for the planetary human future beyond the triple threat, "The Sleeping Lord," despite its suspensions among problematics and uncertainties, considers the possibility of YES.

JOHN PECK

POEMS FOR BRITAIN, POEMS FOR SONS

(Several themes referred to in the following study appear in the argument of a previous section not printed here. These include David Jones' attention to naming in parallel with his handling of the divine incest symbolism in the Christian sacrifice of the Son, a handling that emphasizes the Son's return to the Mother as her spouse. Also with naming go Jones' treatments of memory and anamnesis, his reliance on paronomasia, and his view of the "secret marriage" in sited names (divine incest again, along with a glance towards James Joyce). Other themes are burial and embedding, distortion or "pseudomorphosis," the cultural and poetic defeat tradition, circlings around the type-idea behind modern revivals of the Leader, and human cries (including the "in-cry" and "out-cry" of section eight, *The Anathemata*). The "Irish introit" mentioned below refers to the end of section seven of that poem. The recurrent formula about imbalances between transmissibility and tradition is borrowed from Walter Benjamin.)

I

About "The Roman Quarry" René Hague noted in his preliminary editorial work that its "real point is to bring the pre-Roman, pre-Aryan indeed, myth and religion into line with what we already accept as a foreshadowing of the Christian, through the medium of Rome," and that "it is a comparatively simple piece," even with breaks imposed by the loss of ten and one-half pages of ms. at several points (not indicated, alas). By "simple" I guess Hague meant that the evolutionary sequence closely follows a grand design, with precedents in the Church Fathers to be sure, of "pre-application or . . . retroactive application" of non-Christian cultures to the Christian drama (*RQ*, 216-17).

Hague and Harman Grisewood can outline this on pages xv-xvi of their edition, but their sympathies won't let

them sense the great tension sprung into the design by its
function as a forcing-bed for "applications." Through the
voices of Roman legionary, the poet (at first shadowily), and
the soldier and Tribune of the poems reworked into *The
Sleeping Lord*, a curious thing takes place: a millennial
form rises from the prime matter of both earth and culture.
Evolutionary, it is also greatly disrupted. At first it is
ichthus "knowing the mutations and the silent metamorphoses," then a "palace prince," then buried chieftain and
"sacred body," then lord of the hunt and sleeping lord of
both megalithic tombs and Arthurian romance; a Roman
surveyor supervenes, then a Roman administrator, before the
crucified Lord presides over the split-off mystical bodies of
Church and Empire; finally a Roman Tribune inaugurates a
mock Last Supper to reinforce the military oath that levels
local cultures, including his own, to uniformity. This draft,
forming "Sections VIII-XII" of an unknown whole, moves
between geology and early Christian symbol even at its outset, with the primordial Ichthus "who kept slow amoeboid
vigils on world-bed," through the developing male form as I
have scoped it, with crucifixion circling to earth in incest-
return: "Back to the womb of Tellus drips the fertile flood."
Over this long curve the earth gets worked by the emerging
figure--fish over world-bed, Christ fertilizing Tellus, Romans
who "grid the green shadow-floor," sleeping lord who inhab-
its its contours, Tribune who bitterly serves "to discipline
the world-floor to a common level." Simple, yes--but the
design veers between subtle incantations and heavy-handed,
implausibly delegated, sometimes blatantly designing
monologues--an unworkable whole, whose disaster Jones'
editors do not address. Yet the disaster encodes or contains
many of Jones' better passages, and of course a number of
the later published poems *in nuce*: an art stuck in the prime
matter of the cultural matrix. The most privileged experience of Jones' form, and the most telling contact with his
treasures in their pristine state, comes from reading "The
Roman Quarry"--say, from the mixed "marches" of spirit and
matter (17) through the originals of "The Hunt" and "The
Sleeping Lord" (21-38)--most privileged because still
embedded in the uncertainties which dog old-soldier-and-
survivor's nerves, and therefore still struggling towards clarity and connection. His questions have not yet become
merely rhetorical, for vertigo still spins them as it does in
the battle zones of *In Parenthesis*, or in *The Anathemata*'s
notes of dislocation ("And when / where, how or ever
again? /. . . or again?" and "When (How? . . .)" and "but

when *is* when?" *A*, 93, 61, 170). With that anxiety intact, questions stay like Percival's and do not become polemical-rhetorical. Since the redeeming or Percivalian question is what his essays aim at, the embedding of it along with a gigantic half-emergent form gives greater effect to the clutter of "The Roman Quarry" than one finds in the geology of *The Anathemata*. What the essays show to be finely considered, the Mother-lode draft mires in the preconscious struggle between magic and anxiety, leading it even after a review of sleeping-hero legends and the Arthurian myths to a still-emergent gigantic male form, divine Son or still in the toils of the goddess-mother earth's wracked deposits. Consider a passage early in the curve which jumbles late and early traces (and shifts syntax):

> Are they Goidel marks for Pretani monolith or do the *mamau* with the adze of night incise the standing stones?
> Does the riding queen recede from the pursuer or does the unbridled pursuit recede from the still queen?
> In this place of questioning where you must ask the question and the answer questions you
> where race sleeps on dreaming race and under-myth and over-myth, like the leaf-layered forest floor, are the uncertain crust, which there has firm hold, but here the mildewed tod-roots trip you at the fungus-tread. (*RQ*, 18)

Then a later passage extending this vein:

> In this charged land of under-myth and over-myth where lord rests on greater lord and by lesser names the greater names are called; where the inversions are and the high anticlines are hid by newer valley ways. And the under-strike of the ultimate folds--how does it run? What ageless Mabon recollects, which long-winded Nestor knows the axile line of the first of the sleepers? and from what exertion was he fain to lie down? and what commotion faulted him through and through? (*RQ*, 38)

Conscious control over this unearthing sometimes veers into polemic, as in one question that inters a triad of Latin roots among megalithic tombs in order to deepen contemporary malaise: "does the stone mastaba cairn the negotiator? Does the false entry guard the mercator? Does the holed slab within the darkened passage keep the dark Promoter?" (*RQ*, 20) But these easier moves do not smooth the main action, a gigantic disinterment far more strenuous and unsettling than Mr. Hague felt it to be. Dreaming fish, embittered Tribune, divine Son--this curve of change frames a chaos within the mother's body, the discrimination of which occupies much of the poetry.[1] Alone among it, "The

---

1. The effort was "exacting" in Jones' phrase, in ways he tied to Celtic form sense-- which encourages "an inter-weaving that is freer but by no means less exacting, on the

Roman Quarry" throws out the whole curve of development while continuing to register chaotic pulls backward and down. The *figura* in it, from ichthus to Ichthus-Son, appears embedded and sleeping, stands embodied for sacrifice in reunion with Tellus, and then in medieval legend sleeps hidden, re-embedded once more. Sacrifice of the embodied Son would renew embodiments of local culture (the higher incest sacrifices embedded relations in order to secure embodied ones), but the perennial forces of imperial civilization push embodiments back into the chaos of embeddedness. Inversions, hidden under-strikes, pseudo-morphoses, transpositions of sequence, and recovery of the "greater names," become the spirit's manly tasks in this mess, where manliness splits along the lines of youth and age, Mabon and Nestor, in the recollective struggle. Midway in this effort falls an interval of suspension that cyclically returns (both megalithic and Arthurian): the phase of the sleeping lord. As "The Hunt" lays it out, this phase contains the head-on battle with evil (the destructive Hog), but "The Sleeping Lord" sets against this the *longue durée* of retrenched waiting for transformation, and a myth of the lord's deferred return, in the Celtic defeat-tradition. I believe that the Percival form of questioning, disoriented and genuinely inquiring, is most at home in this phase of Jones' understanding, for within his developmental sequence the sleeping lord hangs in two-way fashion between heroic struggle and dormancy, a tension played out in the figure-ground grammar-shifts of the formula ("Is A B, or is B A?"--riding queen and unbridled pursuit). In other words: it becomes a redeeming question, addressed to mythical knowing and to scientific knowledge alike, to ask about the shifting position each holds, and thereby to ask about thigh wounds left in the one body they both should serve:

> And does the tilted capstone, do the triliths, move in a space of mist,
> or does the veiling mist recede and come again, now closely wreathe and
> now disclose the fixed, positioned dolerites
>   that stone-drags dragged from augite-brighted dyke for love of his
> sacred body? (*RQ*, 19)

contrary exacting in the extreme," and in which unity is not "architectonic" (*David Jones: Letters to a Friend*, ed. Aneiran Talfan Davies [Swansea: Triskele Books, 1980], p. 89). His reluctance to disengage "fragments" from his accumulations is the negative side of this form sense, showing him caught by his material's ever-engendering embrace. A related sort of catch waits for those of us who with Jones prefer Skelton or the Scots ballads to most modern poetry ("there seems to me to be a power & urgency and conciseness and a closer touch with reality in the earlier stuff" [*LF*, 84]). There is, but more for the man who finds those masculine strengths in the maternal deposits, and so whose very rightness may leave him caught in a subtle way.

> Does the land wait the sleeping lord or is the wasted land that very
> lord who sleeps? (*RQ*, 37; cf. *SL*, 96)

This entangling perspective is what "two-cultures" discourse
foregoes, whether in Snow's hands or Kermode's (Kermode's
review of Jones refers more to Snow and Cassirer and "the
problem," etc., than to Jones). Here Jones' poetic language
works like Heidegger's advocacy of questioning, for it unset-
tles with both "shattering" and "cohering" force (unlike the
other side of Jones' rhetoric). To such polarities Jones
resupplies the mythology of a sleeping lord rebound to the
earth but ready to strike again.

Two points here, one literary and the other political.
First, Jones' preferred way of building an image--slowly
freeing it from broken strata of disclosure--nicely frustrates
received modern appetites for imagery. The ancra-man passage in *The Anathemata* provokes Elizabeth Ward to charge
Jones with "desperate esotericism" that leads him to obscure
"the single haunting image lost in the sheer verbal barrage"
of the passage itself.[2] Jones half agreed, as she easily shows.
A harder thing to admit, but useful, is that this kind of
emergent image withstands routine studious handling as
cussedly, and as gloriously, as its first cousins in Pound's
poetry, the swiftly rising vortex or the slowly surfacing
forma. None of these emergent disclosures is reproducible;
all the fine instances are rare; but together they post limits
in the sky, sea, and littered, discontinuous ground of undis-
missible writing.

The politics going along with such imagery in Jones
is patiently dual, poising itself among tugs either way.
Already here, the last stage of his *figura* is split within
itself: Roman administrator sacrificing the locality he loves,
against the Son crucified by him, whose sacrifice rejustifies
bonds to local maternal ground. More crudely but more
clearly than elsewhere, Jones found his elemental pattern.
For the splitting reflects our own dispositions to conflict--we
still divide among reductive handlings of the natural ground
and weaker but persistent homages to it which, in the
remarrying mode of myth, can at least imagine a willing
sacrifice. This split, crying out for a resolution that has not
yet appeared, grimly stays, to what ends no one can say.
That is why Jones' last three published poems, with intrinsic
plausibility, raise literal cries for rescue and transformation,
and why his bequest to poetry primitively expresses the

2. Elizabeth Ward, *David Jones Mythmaker* (Manchester: Manchester University
Press, 1983), pp. 146-48.

sophisticated thing. All of these cries anticipate, but none
defines, a figure yet to emerge from the discontinuous
embedded state into the unknown embodied one. And so,
too, they wail counterpoint to the 1930s impulse to baptize
as much of Führership as would take the chrism.

II

When questions turn rhetorical in Jones, they may support
raucous puns. "The Sleeping Lord" features one of these:

> ... is the dying gull
>> on her sea-hearse
> that drifts the oily bourne
>> to tomb at turn of tide
> her own stricken cantor? (*SL*, 93)

In 1959 Jones had written the talk focused on the Roman
bronze copy of a Greek "Dying Gaul," where battle horns lie
on the wounded man's shield. "When the Welsh attacked,"
Jones reports from Giraldus Cambrensis, "the sound of their
deep-toned trumpets mingled with their harsh cries" (*DG*,
51). His poem seven years later, filled with Welsh names
and crying his harsh pun, blows not the battle trumpet but
the horn of lament. From its beginnings, Welsh poetry sang
with "the sense of fighting a losing battle" in "a kind of
defeat-tradition" (*DG*, 53). From the perspective of English
poetry, this remained but an undercurrent. In his last work
Jones brought it to the surface, and through the gull's persistent note harmonized it with an afflicted natural environment. A main current it became, stronger than the initial
note of the last poems, the stammering claim to prophecy
in "A, a, a, Domine Deus." Jeremiah and Ezekiel he might
unabashedly echo, but not for long. It was the cry of
calamity which led him farther, and through which he came
to suspend the note of prophecy.

The earliest Welsh poetry enters "The Sleeping Lord"
with Princess Heledd's lament for her brother Cynddylan
and his court destroyed at Pengwern:

> *stafell* [hall] of the lord of the Cantref [tref: rural community]
>> *ys tywyll heno*
> shieling [hovel] of the *taeog* [peasant] from the bond-tref
>> *heb dan, heb wely.* (*SL*, 88)

In his note on this ruined hall which "is dark tonight, without fire without bed," Jones says that stanzaic repetitions of
the hall's name Stavell Gyndylan "burn themselves into the
mind, very much as certain great phrases that echo in a
Liturgy," and that the words he incorporates "evoke a whole

situation far beyond their immediate 'meaning' [so] that, in
my view, it is our duty to conserve them however little we
'know' the original languages" (*SL*, 88; for more on the
lament see *DG*, 111). Here it is, gull's harsh death-cry, and
poetry's memorious role as well, with a long gamble taken
on their transmissibility. Stricken, or no?

In his essay on Arthurian myth Jones called Malory's
prose an immense *liturgy* which ends, beyond its requiems,
with a "flattening-out after the power-drive" in the mode of
a "Dickensian 'conclusion' " (*E&A*, 250, 253). This reflected
history, he thought. The same period which "left a tradition
of successive and inevitable defeat" also produced a decisive Celtic renewal in monastic and wandering hermit life,
marked by "a love . . . of the animals who praised God with
growl and cry" in the sites of retreat (as in *The Anathemata*'s
ancra-man passage). Here Jones already enters the zone
probed by the last poems, where requiem shades into a
phase one can anticipate only along the lines of such former renewals. But the anticipation is not prophetic. Both
the essays and the late poems hold the prophetic impulse in
check, with their treatment of cultural seasons, animal cries,
Malory's heroes, hunt, burial, pursuit and enclosure, all
within the suspended phase of the sleeping lord.

Jones' intent here can be misread, especially by
Americans, as nostalgic,[3] when he marks the place for
prophecy while not leaping into it. In "The Roman Quarry,"
treating the "Gallic rooster's" cry at Peter's betrayal, he
tries, at first wordily, to hold together history's welter and
still tillable culture so as to set against certain destruction
what cock-crow brings: new light.

Down the meander and crooked labyrinth of time and maze of history,
or historia intermeddled with potent and light-giving, life-giving,
cult-making mythos
we hear as yet that third crow
dawn crow of dolour
as clear as we hear
        the echoing blast
from Roncesvalles
        and with it, of necessity
the straight, exact, rational and true
'Sirs, you are set for sorrow.' (*RQ*, 92)[4]

3. He heads off such misreadings of his attitude, *expressis verbis*, in "Wales and Visual
Form," 1944 (*DG*, 88 n17).
4. Turpin's line in *The Song of Roland* (in René Hague's translation) drew several
responses from Jones, in 1938--"almost, for us, too near the knuckle to be read without fear" (*DG*, 96)--and in 1942: "our text" (*E&A*, 259).

Certain prophecies are not difficult at all. More difficult is
the labyrinthine hearing of spiritual promise in ruin's
prospect.

The late poems dug out of "The Roman Quarry" listen for that cock-crow. Consequently the accent and pitch
are nearly everything. Myths themselves are part of the
sound because they change the stuff of past conflict to meet
present need (*E&A*, 243), and the choices are Romano-
British and Welsh because in these, notably in things
Arthurian, "prototype and type become one" (*E&A*, 45-6),
and because in the post-Malory defeat aftermath such fusion
continues to live.

> Whatever the hair-splitting, the severities, the taboos, the back-
> ground is the flora and fauna of Thule, where the contours are lost and
> found....
>   It was a complex of enthusiasms that blazed up from the ashes of
> the lost West. It is as though the strayed animals of the *milites*,
> going 'where they would' became mettlesome in their new freedom and
> neighed against the warriors from the woods, and from among the
> tumuli bid them remember [in the *Stanzas of the Graves*]:
>
>> After blows and bloodshed
>> And white steeds caparisoned
>> This grave holds Cynddylan (*E&A*, 255)[5]

In "Wales and the Crown" of 1953 Jones had stipulated, "Who
would re-present this Island must be clothed in a mantle of
variety" (*E&A*, 47). That is the attempt in "The Hunt,"
where the Arthur-type, evoking flower-decked Adonis and
thorn-scarred Christ but named as neither and unnamed as
Arthur, rides furiously "caparison'd in the flora / of the
woodlands of Britain":

> and like a stricken numen of the woods
>   he rode
> with the trophies of the woods
>   upon him
> who rode
>   for the healing of the woods
> and because of the hog.
>   Like the breast of the cock-thrush that is torn in the hedge-
> war ... so was his dappling and his dreadful variety .... (*SL*, 68)

Malory's riderless horses Jones had already etched,
friskily energetic, into his dry-point of 1930, *Wounded
Knight*, where the arrow-pierced man is cradled pietà-fash-
ion by a lady whom Jones' ms. notes identify as Arianrhod,
Queen of the Celtic Otherworld and Layamon's 'Argante
Queen of Avalon': "it is to her that Arthur is taken, after the

---

5. The same horses appear in *E&A*, 251.

battle of Camlan, to be healed of his death wound."[6] Forty
years later "The Sleeping Lord," aligned with the Island's
numerous mound-sleepers and the legend of Arthur's unlo-
catable dormancy, became a note on which to end while
looking ahead. Behind, more than fifty million dead in
Europe alone; ahead, prospects which gave Jones no reason
to set aside this myth of emergence, for which he had long
served as sentinel.

Into the mythical sleeping lord's phase--suspended,
two-way, embedded male in Tellus--maternal shapes may
still be read from history's page. If the *cynedd* or lord's hall
cannot protectively hedge things in such a time, measures
will be found through which spiritual change does come.
"The long toil and dark winter of the West, that was, in fact
a bright birth time," was "as ours threatens to become" an
age of armed camps and uprooted city dwellers "thrown
back among tribal and enduring rustic communities," given
to even fiercer combat and deprivation, "for only within
their enclosures was there normal order in that age" (*E&A*,
256-8). Retreat to these hedged and wattled enclosures
begins in Jones' work with *In Parenthesis* (e.g. 117), continues in *The Anathemata* (e.g. 89), and peaks in "The Tutelar
of the Place" ("the living fences of the small localities,"
SL, 56), so that feminine protection passes with his other
motifs into the suspended phase. "We do not yet know how
narrow our own choice may be, or what news our strayed
horses may bring" (*E&A*, 259).

We do seem to know that enclosures and their sanc-
tuary are no longer ours to claim. As coda to *The Sleeping
Lord* comes a section from "The Book of Balaam's Ass,"
chosen as coda though written in the late 1930s and early
1940s. With the Somme Offensive and litanies for the dead
and macabre notations of survivors' luck ("bloody funny,
though people don't usually find it so"--Blissett *LC*, 93),
Jones lays out the ground from Passchendaele to here, level
without a ripple to our elbows. Pte Squib "Pussy" Lucifer
and Pte Pick-em-up Shenkin and Pte Austin the Dodger are
the three to escape "from the diversion before the Mill," but
"for all the rest there was no help on that open plain." And
with this fact Jones does a remarkable thing. He reinstates
the shape of the great sixth-century lament at the beginning
of Welsh poetry, Aneirin's *Y Gododdin:* "Of all those who
charged, after too much drink, / But three won free through

6. Quoted in Paul Hills, "The Romantic Tradition in David Jones," *Malahat Review* 27
(July 1973), p. 63.

courage in strife, / Aeron's two war-hounds and tough Cynon, / And myself, soaked in blood, for my song's sake."[7] Remarkable, because only the shape is reinstated. Jones' three named comedians render human a nameless place familiar since World War I, which has destroyed the two things that gave Aneirin's culture its meaning: "Fellowship" among soldiers, and meaningful individual heroism. An unsheltered survivor, Jones alludes to Aneirin's trio because their world is gone forever, and with it every fence that might protect continuities of action between then and now. What it does leave is a song filled with names cried by the dying.

In the myths Jones chooses, hunt and vigil remain. His handling of them resists the seductive Spenglerian note (as do his essays: see *E&A*, 242) while keeping open the prospects to both ruin and "birth time." The winter-spring paradox of the Arthurian essays goes straight through the imagery of "The Hunt" and "The Sleeping Lord." There are wintry "gusts that do not slacken / but buffet stronger and more chill" (*SL*, 74) against new growth made possible by the incest transformation. "The Sleeping Lord" goes so far as to frame parallels between the dead Christ and Aphrodite's dead lover Adonis through the "delicate agalma" of Welsh spring foliage "made over to her," only to assault both renewals with recursive winter wind under Aquarius who "careens on his fixed and predetermined cursus" (it assaults leafy bough and "anemone," the flower that sprang from Adonis' boar-spilled blood).[8] This is the same "veering of the wind" that Jones found among most peoples, not Germany alone, in the slide towards "heroics," "masculine emphasis," and "fanatical devotion to the mystical body of the tribal *ecclesia*" (*E&A*, 240: 1942). It is not surprising then, that "The Sleeping Lord" couches masculine energy dormantly within the earth, or that Adonis and vegetation gods ride with the flower-decked lord of the hunt. As for the milder wind presiding over the end of "The Hunt," it gives us the measure of Jones' expectation, so let us turn to that.

The boar hunt in *Culhwch and Olwen*, the tenth-century tale from *The Mabinogion*, is led by Arthur, among the heroes and war-bands of all Britain, against Twrch Trwyth and a band of other hogs--from whom they secure the tokens which Culhwch needs in his quest to win Olwen, but whom

---

7. Stanza 21, trans. Joseph Clancy, in *The Oxford Book of Welsh Verse in English*, ed. Gwyn Jones (Oxford: Oxford University Press, 1977), p. 3.
8. *SL*, 73-75. Compare the wind here to "The Myth of Arthur," *E&A*, 248: "late frost blight bud and steel wind strip tree."

they cannot kill off. From references in "The Sleeping Lord" to the same struggle with the Hog, it is clear that Jones reads in this malign power the levelling forces of techno-cratic civilization. Yet this reading remarkably inverts the sense of the tale. Since Culhwch means "pig-trench" (his birth site), the boar denotes the untransformed fury of the matrilineal culture he leaves behind in winning his bride. Arthur, whom Jones often ties to ancient Artio or the Bear ("The Bear's Chapel" figures in "The Sleeping Lord"), brings with him another venerable animal symbol of the same maternal world. (Jones' hints of Adonis, victim of the boar, I have already noted.) First of all, then, Jones turns the story on its head, making the conquest of an outraged natural force into resistance against a masculine force on the ram-page. In the name of threatened local cultures and the ancient unities, Jones has utterly revalued the struggle. The tale's own refrain and Jones' clincher--"life for life"--don't mean the same thing.

His poem begins by listing the various warriors of the hunt, the massive fellowship of the legend: "to each *comitatus* / one Penteulu," Arthur as "first among equals." No regressive primal form, they represent Britain's original unity, which can be rebegun but to which one cannot return: *thus* the "change-wind" in the coda to "The Hunt." No less crucial, I believe, is the comitatus as carrier of precisely what modern warfare eradicated--both individual heroism and fellowship. For the "Following" was loosely federal and voluntary yet bound by loyal ties of friendship. What "The Book of Balaam's Ass" shows to have disappeared in fact in our century is resummoned in this manner, through the insti-tution specific to local settlement in England, by "the named and unnamed of the Island."

Jones had argued that the vision of Britain's unity, surviving in the Celtic fringe, was carried by the Romano-British figure of the war-chief, at first a vehicle "at the best shadowy, indeed the shadow of a shadow," but later taking on body in "the metamorphosis" of English kingship. Yet the magical boar hunt outbid even history, among "the older strata," in its "authenticity and urgency" (*E&A*, 220-26). With it emerge both Arthur and Artio, "the female bear-deity of pre-history" in medieval chain-mail "swaying under the last star-shell" of a modern battlefield. "Across the waste land the growl of the creature . . ." (*E&A*, 232-33). Since Arthur also carries the roles of conveyor of order, redeemer, consolidator, channel of power, protector, "and more significantly for us 'the Director of Toil' " (*E&A*, 237:

a phrase reused in "The Sleeping Lord"), whatever might still yield itself to baptism in a Charlemagne-rooted Führership rests for Jones within the whole of this unearthed figure. Through name and trait the last poems unearth most of it. But they also rebury it, and even before that in the coda to "The Hunt" they stop it in its tracks.

Nothing like this coda occurs in *Culhwch and Olwen*. It halts Arthur's chase with an exchange of looks, the response of an animal chorus, and the great alteration which then sets in:

> And if his eyes, from their scrutiny of the hog-track and from considering the hog, turned to consider the men of the host (so that the eyes of the men of the host met his eyes) it would be difficult to speak of so extreme a metamorphosis.
> When they paused at the check
> when they drew breath.
> And the sweat of the men of the host and of the horses salted the dew of the forest-floor and the hard-breathing of the many men and of the many dogs and of the horses woke the fauna-cry of the Great Forest and shook the silent flora.
> And the extremity of anger
> alternating with sorrow
> on the furrowed faces
> of the Arya
> transmogrified the calm face
> of the morning
> as when the change-wind stirs
> and the colours change in the boding thunder-calm
> because this was the Day
> of the Passion of the Men of Britain
> when they hunted the Hog
> life for life. (*SL*, 68-9)

You might say that nothing happens in this calm, in some nowhere Type of the Great Forest. But that name registers a Breconshire place (another Joycean secret marriage) and the time is a crisis still unfolding (the day of the Passion has its coming storm). This coda announces the spiritual change demanded by the West's unfinished struggle.

So its change-wind opposes the anemone-blasting wind soon to come in "The Sleeping Lord." How much of the spirit prior to such change, like the ancient Breconshire place name, enters this pause? The essays cue us to an answer: recall the flora and fauna of Thule, the Welsh legendary realm, together with Jones' ear for Malory's battle horses turned wild and neighing from the woods to admonish the warriors, and then the ear of Celtic Christianity for animal growl and cry. The entire aftermath of the great defeat, the springtime hidden in the first collapse of the West, sings in this coda. Its haunting occasion, the gaze,

summons what modern conflict has eradicated in the way of
"fellowship"--those bonds eulogized by Malory and spotlit by
Jones as the ones "in whose brightness 'either saw other . . .
fairer than ever they saw afore' " (*DG*, 103). So the metamorphosis within this exchange of looks marks self-recognition within the order of masculine spirit just when that
spirit must enter some new phase. The unity of a resummoned heroic type, matured by the West since Homer, hangs
there. On the wind float Jones' chime-notes, *transmogrified*
and *metamorphosis*--the harmonics of both his historical
view and his sense of expectation. Using just those words
and using them at extremes, "The Myth of Arthur" speaks of
nothing else: "so strangely," the accent falls, "does myth plus
legend plus history weave its meander" (*E&A*, 221).

The attitude Jones takes before this weave stands
within the maternal form sense. He refuses "to both isolate
a part and then to develop and embroider it," and he holds
on to "the whole weight of what lies hidden" (*E&A*, 234).
He bends poetry to this strain to keep the discontinuous
power of change, so alive within the stuff he would transmit,
and especially in its Thulic background, available to our
own attitudes. For continuous definition blinds one to that
disruptive but engendering force which Arthur, as an ectype
of the Son, carries as "binding and loosing power" (*E&A*,
236).

This sense of things, attuned to harmonics of change
within accumulations, can *check* the headlong tendency of
expectation to flee from defeat-under-way into either
despair or false hopes. "The Hunt" poises its recovered patterns on the cusp of forbearance rather than prophecy.
Within a supreme moment of cultural self-recognition,
mired in the struggle against civilizational dominants, the
coda calmly resists the besetting drives of our political
thinking in the interests of a far wider and also much
stranger voice. "The Myth of Arthur" prepared a way for
this:

> It is an idle question whether this change [our own descent] is a retro-
> gression or an advance, for man does not determine these things.... We
> do not know in what fashion a new synthesis will be effected, how the
> gains will be consolidated and the ills overcome--if either .... When
> the realm is 'wholly mischiefed' and all the armament is 'tobrast,'
> their tradition [the romance writers] drops a hint of where man would
> say the next wonder is to be felt, and suggests the nature of the recov-
> ery, no recovery at all in the immediate sense. (*E&A*, 241-2, 258)

Jones will presume to say only that "the culture-tangle" wounds a man innerly, in Hopkins' terms 'selfwrung' and

'shelterless,' with groans and cries (*DG*, 101). If "The Hunt" and "The Sleeping Lord" together lay out a mid-phase of suspension between struggle and dormancy, then "The Sleeping Lord" takes up the in-cry of this phase, lodged in the mothering hills.

This cry carries the hunt lord's battle wrath into the dream-time of buried change. So it is the West's frustrated heroism that smolders within its cultural deposits now.

> But yet he sleeps:
> >   when he shifts a little in his fitfull
> slumber does a covering stone dislodge
> >   and roll to Reynoldstone?
> When he fretfully turns
> >   crying out in a great voice
> >   in his fierce sleep-anger
> does the habergeon'd sentinel
> >   alert himself sudden...   (*SL*, 94)

He does, wakes his buddy, and this pair of English comedians proceed to pass the word topside, for even though they think the sound "but a wind-bluster" they also remain disconcerted by the residual magickings of "these whoreson March-lands / of this Welshry." If not the wind, it may be "stir of gramarye / or whatsomever of ferly--who should say?" (*SL*, 95-6) From within the cultural mound, the cry carries just that uncanny force which tradition also transmits, a grammar whose buried sense stays alive (*gramarye* is enchantment). "The Roman Quarry" called this business "the exchanges" in a Welsh setting: "is the wolf-cry from the grey stone the spell-changed voice of the palace prince under bondage of the beast-spell" (*RQ*, 17). Much later "The Tutelar of the Place" has Makers "seek hidden grammar to give back anathema its first benignity" (*SL*, 61). In both animal ferocity and anathema the wrath abides, yet the change that can be worked restores conscious devotion (anathema's older sense is *offering*) through hidden protection--the protection that lies in both ordered accumulation and in magic, grammar and gramarye.

All of this points to a conservative role for poets-- "rememberers" in Jones' phrase (*E&A*, 141)--who hear in the vowels of Heledd's lament "a whole situation beyond their immediate meaning." It also writes no tickets: "we do not know what songs may yet be possible or what shape our myth will take" (*E&A*, 242). Beyond that Jones finds our nervous clichés, which he caricatures in the poem itself. The sentinels who discount the cry read the winds of change with our mixed hermeneutics--their indecision reflects the

split between reductive no-nonsense measures and an inadequately irrational alertness to our fate.

Sentinels: one probably cannot over-stress Jones'
reliance on a self-correcting vigilance, something like the
proper sentinel's attitude, carried in his frequent reflections
on the "Two Marches" of matter and spirit. The uniform
pressures in modern life towards disembodiment, away from
life in a place and work on material, dissolve what holds
human duality in balance (*DG*, 88-90), and to this the adequate sentinel stays constantly alert, suspecting that the cry
will be for compensating embodiment even when that cannot be. Here the natures of out-cry and in-cry in the last
fragments will tell us most of the story.

The sleeping lord's buried cry revalues the poem's
earlier voices. An aged Household Priest mutters requiem
in the Bear's chapel after his swift mental litany of the
dead, then his Candle-Bearer responds ("he could not contain himself"), ET LUX PERPETUA LUCEAT EIS. Here the
rememberer whose memory has begun to fail (an oblique
self-portrait)[9] nonetheless offers an eight-page memento.
Though a mental wink, this litany of "the named and
unnamed of the Island" becomes the poem's central busi-
ness--a bulge of tradition *as* the transmissible. Of expectations about a sleeping lord one may say, *Affecting but meaningless*; about the litany, however, one says no such thing.
Its limited infinity, already decaying at the edges, holds the
vision of Britain's unity as surely as do the hunt chief's war-
bands, but now under the aspect of death. The effects of
some actual Celtic revival were not Jones' main concern at
the end, at least when he had poetry in view. As the keeper
of litany's flame, poetry can hold out for a long time, this
poem says magisterially. But it proposes something far
more interesting, because the in-cry running below litany,
the sleeping lord's muffled cry of anger, voices what must
yet change and what must itself work further changes,
unforeseeably. A litany moves fixedly. But though tribal
rememberers have been lionized of late even in popular
culture, their devotion to unvarying order and complex
naming is only part of poetry's task here. For Jones rekin-
dled myth and its persistent candle light without wholly
returning to prelogical mentality, and also without leaping
towards apocalyptic expectation. Earnest quibbles over
recapitulation (Hague's term) and anamnesis cued to its

9. William Blissett notes Jones' amusement in 1974 over his inability to recall the iden-
tities of several of the more than one hundred names in "The Book of Balaam's Ass"
fragment: *LC*, 138.

etymology (lodged between the memorious, the marriage-seeking, and the tomb), would lead nowhere unless they served Jones' actual practice in these fragments. His balancing act in "The Sleeping Lord" honors defeat through requiem, ends requiem decisively and confidently, and then holds back from nurturing prophecies--in order to frame the poetry of his bequest, a shelterless survivor's summa.

As the litany ends, it reaches beyond Britain, past "the Patriarchate of the West," to include the whole host of the dead. But in the unsheltered world of the Windmill Diversionary Attack, placed last in this last book, that universal comes in by way of the names cried out. The dying call not only on lovers, friends, relatives, mothers, Christ, the saints, and the founder of the Western Patriarchate--"On the key-man, the sword-bearer, because he lied to a nosey girl and warmed his hands at a corporal's brazier" (*SL*, 108)--but also on an older foundation.

> On all the devices of the peoples, on all anointed stones, on fertile goddesses, that covering arbours might spring up on that open plain for poor maimed men to make their couches there.
> On her that wept for a wounded palm that she got by a mortal spear --that she might salve a gaping groin that the race might not be without generation.
> On the unknown God.
> Each calling according to what breasts had fed them--for rite follows matriarchate when y'r brain-pan's stove in. (*SL*, 110)

The footnote reads, "Cf. the principle of the Xtian ecclesia: Rite follows Patriarchate." Paronomasia haloes not only Peter but also Venus, Aeneas' mother and healer on the field, and then by extension acknowledges the maternal principle as every dying soldier's bottom line. This amounts to more than assiduous inclusiveness. The impossibility of naming the key modern experience, which comes with a "fanned-flashing to the higher dislocations" (*IP*, 30), makes the re-calling of origins *in extremis*, of root-sources eradicated by that very experience, the last way of staying human. The secret marriage within a man's communicable source-names can, perhaps just only, countervail the marriages that stay secret (King Cophetua goes unnamed in the passage inset below) within his shattering new knowledge. The long litany in "The Book of Balaam's Ass," beginning as "a difficult breathing coming up from the earth, and intermittently the half-cries of those who would call strongly from their several lonely places," is framed by bloody funny escapes and ironies, yes, but also ends Jones' work in primi-

tive responsory to an unnamable union and metamorphosis.
Artillery rounds and intuitions explode in the same name:

> ...while there is breath it's only right to bear immemorial witness.
> There were breakings of thin ice I can tell you and incomings to
> transmute the whole dun envelope of this flesh.
> We have seen transfigurations on a plain, swiftly and slowing,
> unsheafing slow like beggar-shifts king's hands make fall from secret
> queens. (*SL*, 99)

The buried sleep-strangled lord's cry of wrath, the
modern soldier's invocations while dying, the thirsty in-cry
marking the crucifixion, the inly cry of the culture-tangle,
the harsh cry of the dying gull--these rise in chorus with
that Old-Testament note of *In Parenthesis*, the pouring out
of men's souls upon their mother's bosom.

Tallied with the change-wind chorus of animal cries
in "The Hunt" and the litany of "The Sleeping Lord,"
together the cries draw discipline from lament. This poetry
choruses the need for rescuing transformation without plung-
ing ahead towards answers to these cries. Beginning with
the Gallic Rooster, the chorus urgently announces a phase
change, but the voices stay on its verge or remain embedded in the transition. No student of alchemy, Jones did not
echo alchemy's burial of the king's cry within *mater*. But
Jones in fact did something very like that within his own
handling of Christian theology and Romance mythologies,
by lodging the transformative male-female relationship
within the mid-phase stasis of our culture-tangle's defeat
tradition.

Were we to stack the cries of his poetry vertically,
the ground level would be held by "The Tutelar of the
Place." There the sons of locality cry out to the mother
principle for magical protection and a return to her primal
unities. That return cannot be unconscious, for its object is
to win hidden grammar for the making of good anathema.
Beneath ground level sound the terrible cries of the Somme
battlefield; of the dying Lugobellinus in "The Dream of Private Clitus"; of the dying gull as a feminine spirit-version of
the Celtic defeat tradition; the cries of the lords of the hunt;
the indeterminate cry of the sleeping lord in the mythic
strata of the West; and finally the cries of thirst and abandonment by the Son in his spiritual incest union with the
Mother. Above ground level sing the Gallic rooster and
those eerie animal choruses, both marking the need for spiritual change; the Irish introit to the three Masses of Christmas; and the Island litany completed by the Candle-Bearer.
Through it all the Son's name (unless it is Mabon Son of the

Great Mother Modron) is never pronounced directly, but invoked only by paronomasia and type names; the principle that gives names their validity goes unnamed. Son joins Mother, then, in a secret marriage which describes for poetry the little that it can still do. The hedged and wattled enclosures of Welsh history and legend represent the connections to reality which names shelter, but which themselves must stay covered to survive. Demythologize as you will, you still won't touch the tendency of the memorious to abide--"regressively" or "magically"--within single names. Jones moves more and more towards litany, the gathering-in and chanting of names, while holding fast to the reticent, the awed, humorous, and apotropaic, and the matrilineally roundabout connections of periphrasis and paronomasia. Explicit litany, through its patronymics, fills out patriarchal rituals, while paronomasia seems, by the multiple ties of context and attribute, to stem from the more primal and participatory rites of matriarchate. In the first, the parent tradition speaks as if in order to identify all of its children, "brother by sister / under one *brethyn* [blanket]" (*SL*, 60). But in the second the scattered children, as it were ("we are all of the diaspora now"--*DG*, 88), speak as if they were the Son invoking *in extremis* what the mother tie has established. Their cries acknowledge the spiritual incest they require in order to pass through the great phase-change. And of course Jones' paronomasia invites his readers to supply the name while taking pleasure in recognizing context and attribute: that is, to take on the mother's role and so inhabit the transmissible. Double diagnosis is at work here, for in such not-naming or complex by-naming, either it is all "known" and need not be mentioned (security) or it has been forgotten and so would be "obscure" if simply named (the disembodied life of a diaspora). By either mode, the mother protects her child. But protection of the second kind goes hand in hand with prolonged trials whose outcome remains in doubt.

The cries actually released in the poetry carry overtones which the essays do not fully gloss. Which of course one expects; but Jones allows for it, too, by having some of these cries announce a synthesis that is unknowable, and by suspending it among incommunicable dislocations to which the other cries respond. Taken together, they restore a large margin of maternal refusion, indeterminacy, and primitive life to the present. And this goes on, I think, well below the wished-for *recapitulatio* in Christian Mystery.

The fullest example of this restoration happens to be glossable by Jones' prose, and comes in "The Dream of Private Clitus." Within the Italian legionary's dream, his Welsh buddy Lugobelinos and then Clitus himself identify the Mother Goddess carved into the Ara Pacis relief, each in his own local terms, Welsh or Latin. In the dream she lifts them into her arms as if they were the two marble boys carved there, but as Clitus laughs to think of their infantry drills on the Campus Martius, Lugo starts with a different recognition:

> Modron! he cries, and then,--but very low-voiced though: Porth-Annwfyn. Some numinous, arcane agnomen, but which to my dream cognition was lucid as moonshine and did plainly signify: Gate of Elysium.

Within days Lugo in fact dies in battle beside Clitus, "and he cried loud the same cult-name, but not the last bit, for he was done before he could utter it./ So, as I figure it, his Modron and our Matrona are one, and his *porth* that shadowy portal beyond which Proserpine abides, from fall till crocus-time" (*SL*, 20). Tellus Mater (as Roma of the Augustan Peace) also is the Death Mother, unambiguously claiming her sons. Roland Mathias sees Clitus' interpretation as the typical attitude of conqueror to provincial subject: the Latin homologizes each local otherworld and its goddess to his own. Mathias firmly believes that Jones' view of the Celtic Beyond, Annwfyn or Annwn, comes down on the side of a hell without benefits, or the gulf of death, which would align him with Procopius and John Davies' landmark lexicon of the 17th century.[10] Were this the view of most scholars, and plausibly Jones' view as well, Mathias' case would hold: Clitus' "fond belief" that Lugo fancies himself Roman and Trojan is belied, argues Mathias, by Lugo's terrible cry in Clitus' dream, for what this cry recognizes, and which Clitus ignores, represents "a potential *break* with the whole idea of empire" (*op.cit.* 50). But only a few of Jones' glosses on Annwn fit the Hades-Elysium mold, while the balance of his estimates of Welsh legend embrace the other readings of it as a blissful place, not for the dead but for the gods, which may not even be underground (the majority view in scholarship is summarized by R. S. Loomis in *Wales and the Arthurian Legend* of 1956). The *porth* of this region features in the early "Spoils of Annwn" (*ynys pybyrdor*, isle of

---

10. The *Antiquae Linguae Britannicae et Linguae Latinae, Dictionarium Duplex* (1632), where Annwn / Annwfyn is "Abyssus, profundum, orcus, antipodes." Mathias' discussion of the question appears in "David Jones: Towards the 'Holy Diversities,'" *A Ride Through the Wood: Essays on Anglo-Welsh Literature* (MidGlamorgan: Poetry Wales Press, 1985).

the strong door), and so of course would be as much a part
of Lugo's equipment as Elysium Gate is a part of Clitus'.
Therefore its appearance in Clitus' dream, though it augurs
Lugo's actual death, does not submit to reduction to ironies
on imperial consciousness. I am further convinced of this
because Clitus, our amalgamator, bears much the same witness that Mathias finds in Lugo. Clitus' dream changes the
marble Tellus into a rural *matrona*, and the stone sheep to
a lamb sacrificed at the Juno Feast in March, during a
game of Greeks and Trojans in his childhood, when he
recalls crying out as the lamb had been taken away, "and so
I seemed to bellow now, at my dream-ending," a cry that
turns out to come from the Sergeant as "fact-man," old
Brasso. Now, again these cries compose a chorus. Jones says
he chose the name *Lugobelinos* because it is the early form
of the royal name Llywelyn; but Lugobelinos is also the
Celtic Mars, assimilated into the Roman patheon, while
Mars Field is the dream ground, with a rural Juno Feast
exacting sacrifice to his mother (wrathful Juno, angry
because rejected as feminine, as Jones argues after Jackson-
Knight, was assimilated to Mars as mother by local cus-
tom). Without going further into background, one can see
that Clitus' bull-like bellowing (which brings to life the
companion animal on the relief) scopes the childhood loss
of a pet lamb to Juno with the grown man's total subjection
to the order of Mars, both the boy's cry and its adult ampli-
fication being swallowed up by the Sergeant's bark. Lugo's
cry had identified Tellus Mater with death; Clitus' double
bellowing suffers "metamorphosis" under the aspect of Tellus Mater as rural Juno *matrona*, carrying the whole Roman
rejection of the feminine, and the early transformation of
Mars as grain god often cited by Jones, with her as background.[11] The dream chorally differentiates recognitions
within *both* Celtic and Roman earths so as to cry out from
both margin and center the terrible cost with which empire
is built and then maintained. Since the differences among
these cries leave them in harmony, Mathias' point offers
only half the truth about them. They disclose some of that
hidden grammar which aims at benign anathema, sighting
here towards the Juno lost behind Tellus, and the Mars
buried within Mars. Such recognition cries out for incorporation, but remains half-conscious and can only bellow with

11. Jones' high estimate of W. F. Jackson-Knight's studies of Virgil seems to center in
such matters as much as in city-founding rituals. See Jones on Knight's Juno in *Dai
Greatcoat* as well as in "The Myth of Arthur:" "Rome began, because Juno acknowledged defeat" (*E&A*, 241).

animal pain as it is swallowed by Rome. A recultification
of Juno and Mars, as original Mother and Son, lies hidden
within the distinguished academic stone-cutting, of Earth
Mother and her sons, co-opted into the iconography of the
Augustan Settlement. Between the unrecoverable Mother
and Son, and the ambiguously established ones, die the men
and animals who blood that establishment. As with *In
Parenthesis,* so here: the not-unbloody sacrifice opens onto
a long history, still not played out, through recognitions not
wholly conscious to the victims.

Not being wholly conscious, the suffering voiced by
these several cries requires inclusiveness and patience. Thus
Jones' constant (and motherly) urging: do *not* throw out
blood-thirsty Jahweh or those disquieting Mystery cults or
the Greek *theotokos*--"we must be careful with our rejec-
tions or there will be a disintegration . . . no king then"
(*E&A,* 234). Revivals, though, are the last thing Jones had
in mind (*DG,* 86), because sleeping-lord ethics also say:
"There is no point in blurring the shape of the situation. It
is better to say that the culture is stone dead [as a "form-
creating way of life"] than to suggest something analogous
to . . . 'passing on' " (*DG,* 83). He reframed a myth of suspended potency, within the geology of Tellus, to shield the
historical sense from enthusiasm and deformation, whether
revivalist or apocalyptic. "Pseudo-morphosis . . . does not
mean false but rather that the form taken is the only form
possible given the circumstances and conditions." The
Methodist Revival was his case in point--an outbreak of
withheld energy, specifically Celtic in expression, that gave
voice to a "long-delayed, transmogrified and unconscious
Welsh vengenace for the Act of Union and the whole policy
of anglicization" (*DG,* 113). Should stifled energies break
out, their effect cannot be metamorphic, however satisfying
they may seem to the hunger or rage of what has been
pushed under. The myth of the sleeping lord guards against
that as dominant attitudes do not. "The people who 'believe
in progress' and the people who look back wistfully are
almost equally unreal" (*DG,* 153). So the real connection
has to be deliberately refashioned to re-enter the body of
the cultural mother--to skirt the dangerously concrete incest
situation of revivalism, yet still risk the spiritual rebirth
required by the *mise en scène.* Do our ubiquitous progres-
sivists and revivalists know themselves to have been long
possessed by the *mater seava cupidinum,* the savage mother
of desire? Hardly. And so even Jones' offhand figure of
speech constructs a lifeline with two strands, a handmade

umbilical cord but also the cord that conducts us back out of the maternal labyrinth: "No knots must be cut here but everything conscientiously untied. Each link must be tested to see what holds and what does not hold" (*DG*, 89).

To put it otherwise: the way in which a form sense works through cultural deposits, or the male re-enters the mothering hills, determines changes that remain possible. That re-entry, as burial, is no new proposal; it forms the heart of both the early Roman and Greek Orthodox Easter liturgies. Jones' innovation lies in his disposition of the chorus: the monitory and anticipatory animal cries around the estranged cry of the sleeping lord and the mortal cries of wounded sons. In that oratorio, animals rather than a tenor sing *Wachet auf*! and none of the soloists is allowed to smuggle in an *I John* (David) *saw*. It is *I Shenkin* (David) *scraped through*, to the unearthed tune of the ambiguously growling Bear.

Before one dismisses Jones' goddesses as fond confections of the Types, and his sleeping lord as a British version of *l'Action Francaise* patriarchalism, one should acknowledge his canniness about pseudomorphoses. And one could note that he did better by both of the slippery Great Parents than his engaged radical counterpart Simone Weil. For all of her Cartesian clarity, Weil's thought about Rome and the Great Beast seemed pressed into simple lines by Hitler and the fascist state. The Great Beast is not only Plato's, it is also Rome through the eyes of the first Christian apocalyptic generation. Later growths in this myth, real metamorphoses, were of no moment to Weil. Eusebius' collaborationist glorification of Constantine was the first of these, which nurtured expectations of a Last World emperor whose role in the end-time was positive; another was the medieval split within this figure, giving rise to end-time contentions between evil and good popes. The vitality of these notions gives one pause. Chief among them stands out Dante's overheated view of Henry VII: "Elect of God and Augustus Caesar," a second Moses, the apocalyptic Bridegroom, and a second Octavian restoring order to foreshadow "that Rome of which Christ is a Roman." Under the shock administered by Hitler and the spread of idolatrous nationalisms, Weil disregarded all such fantasies, tossing them out in the spirit of rejection that Jones feared. She rolled back the entire Western elaboration of the Father *figura*, as if it were corrupt and collaborationist, and reinstated Rome as the apocalyptic Great Beast, "the deadliest phenomenon to be found in history," as she wrote to Déodat Roché. Recoiling from tribalistic mass movements, she correspondingly redemonized their putative origins. Though jolted and sometimes seduced by the same forces, Jones used greater care in disinterring the carriers of order buried in the West. Though he demonized Rome and its *dux* ("through Caesar we have a second birth"--"The Wall"), the multifarious Christianization of Europe sufficiently counterbalanced Rome's crushing weight, and let him reclaim what he could of the *dux*, which he did by working only on its buried or embedded forms, and then only at the peripheries of empire. In effect he submitted the civic and quasi-spiritual father, the "cult-hero" whose mana Arthur and Charlemagne nearly divided between them, to a measured reincorporation, cultifying or ploughing him under so that tomb might stay prospective womb. His view resisted just that deformation by recoil, that pseudomorphic reversion to prophetic and apocalyptic tension, which marks the otherwise shrewd political thinking of Simone Weil.

Self-idolatrous nationalisms among the developed powers are not going away, so these distinctions are not academic. They draw meaning, too, from the convergence of Weil's radical concerns with Jones' conservative ones in several essentials. As with factory work in Weil, so with war in David Jones: neither was sheltered, and each really knew the Somme or the mines of St. Etienne. Both resisted progressivist thinking, and both knew that practice, exemplified in craft knowledge, had to return to the center of thinking.[12] No more than Jones' Wales did Weil's Languedoc constitute a nostalgic myth of return; both were constructions by historical thinkers at war with the progressivist assumptions fueling much Western thinking about history, morality, and spirituality. Both left places for tragedy in their constructions, with the sheer weight of "the power drive," and they insisted on scrupulously acknowledging the real losses going with suppressed directions of development. This broad kinship makes their separation, on pseudomorphic lines, all the more telling. Jones might still try to redeem a nationalism that Weil might demonize, as he would maintain an ambivalent perception of the Roman donation rather than chuck it out as wholly contaminated.

12. "The different trades would have occupied the place of honor," Weil contended about the civilization she saw in embryo in a Languedoc still continuous with pre-Roman spirituality. This Marxist ideal, salvaged from a Marxism hobbled by addictions to production and progress, she replanted in a local Gallic culture. The parallel with Jones' views, nourished by Maritain and fellow craft socialists at Ditchling, continues along French lines; the Descartes who advocated craft education became her Maritain-- more of a socialist than any Marxist, she said.

As for the Mother's murky zone, Jones could not stay with what the Church has made of it through unitary symbols of containment. "Elen-Monica" yokes the Romano-British goddess of the legions, "Elen of the Army Paths," with Augustine's visionary mother. His desire to secure the "couchant hills" for a myth of suspended ordering powers had long led him to distinguish and recombine opposing feminine tendencies--even to the extent of allying a militant, road-building Venus with the mystical mother of Christianity's first field marshal. But this symbol-making is not arbitrary. It refines a plausible intuition about the West--that we both experience the conflict of spiritual change, and also contain it, within the zone of the Mothers. Historical theologians admit that Augustine converted not so much to Christianity as to a greater mother, the Church; and before him, writing the myth of the Augustan Settlement, Virgil kept his hero within the divine mother's protection: Venus healed the wound of Aeneas. By concentrating on the mother-son relation, Jones was not advertising spiritual progress. But he was specifying the containing feminine power as much as the deposits allowed, while suspending inside it the chequered development of the wounded lord.

Meanwhile the Mothers at the Wake, fertile yet terrible, he heard singing about the bloody transformation ("He lets for her heaped belly") in the accents of pub women, each to each. They rehearse the Mystery, set outside the city's wall circle, in the clang of Joycean vulgate:

> My Ned he offered the reed.
> Her Larry was tarragon boy with his dope.
> Nell's Jerry won his tunicle, she says it's a gran' bit o' weave. Was high stakes, an' he called Mudhook in the nick o' time. She says he's luck's on at lune fête.
> Three on 'em yes--two were naut.
> A cock-shy for a priest's deliberate lob.
> A Sally without the alleys and lanes of our city he reigns from the stark post.
> A guy for a pronged plot to put all in a fine dilemma, hang each on a nice fork. (RQ, 130-31)

Language here gets refertilized, and grammar grows benign for anathemas. In it the highest embodiments bring the lowest elements into chorus. In it profanity rumbles with vast underlife: "A first clarst bollocks and murthering of Christen men" (IP, 138). This is the mother-tongue, which the wise argot of our elected fathers has left behind. " 'One adult should strive to do to another what will enhance the other's development (at his age, in his condition, and under his circumstances) while at the same time enhancing his, the doer's, own development (at his age, in his condition, and under his circumstances)' "--that is Erik Erikson's "developmental" version of the Golden Rule.[13]

At our age and in our condition, maybe it is inevitable that we find Yves Bonnefoy, Paul Valéry's successor at the Collège de France and poet of *présence*,[14] relying on developmental psychology in his inaugural address at the Collège. Behind his perspective looms the archaic world, while within it looms the infantile primary relation as the paradisal desire in need of transformation. The "maturation" growing out of these towards "presence" does not, however, have Bonnefoy leaving the primitive human community behind. Meanwhile his language smuggles the Mysteries back in--bread, wine, and "reality at last fully incarnate"--and poetry's role gets clarified through explicit anticipation of catastrophe. By telescoping a long paragraph I can suggest his intent.

> The horizon . . . , though devastated, though unfit for a long time to nurture our dreams, would *be*, also, would be as one had forgotten a thing could be . . . : the main features of the place, the tools of labor, later perhaps the materials of a first moment of rejoicing--one will say then the bread and the wine. (445-6)

This hypothetical rebirth of consciousness from the ground up, in "winter" and with a poetry able only to "keep the memory of itself," is either the consolidation or the collapse of poetry. How can I think that when the collapse, if that is what it is, comes so close to the terms of Jones' work? I cannot pretend to think my way through the welter of sophisticated reprimitivizations with which poets confront us in our century, among them Eliot, Pound, Charles Olson, Snyder, Jones, and Bonnefoy. But it is evident that David Jones did not invoke the Mysteries for the sake of poetics alone, and that he wrote a developmental agenda subtler and less prone than Bonnefoy's to the higher mystifications. Jones' poetry does not hypothetically remember itself; it actually litanizes the dead and gives memorious voice to the dying. Bonnefoy broadly invokes presence, eros, and the Other, but at a narrower moment (the birth of speech amid terrors) and at a deeper remove (the hypothetical primal separation, with no references to matriarchal and patriarchal forms). Jones' last published fragments distinguish and

---

13. "Reflections on Ethos and War," *The Yale Review* 73.4 (1984), pp. 484-5.
14. A friend reminds me that Bonnefoy's "plenitude without God" echoes the "Cantique des colonnes," and that the Paul, Barnabas, and Timothy of *présence* are Hegel, Blanchôt, and Lévinas. Bonnefoy's address has been translated by John Naughton as "Image and Presence," in *New Literary History* XV.3 (1984).

recombine those forms from the side of the crippled masculine (reflecting too, one must somehow say, his own crip-
pling dependencies and his uncertain social status). From
that side, "The Hunt" brings the patriarchate into a separation and heroic struggle, "The Sleeping Lord" names the
dead in litany and buries the leader in *tellus mater*, augur-
ing a latent marriage under conflicting signs of winter and
spring, and "The Book of Balaam's Ass" defeats the
immemorial patterns of heroic action and fellowship, but
with grim humor and a more primitive litany returns to the
earth. Some features of these poems are Homeric. Others
are romance. Still others reinvent litany. Among them falls
the chance to feel why what may be potent remains latent,
or why the unavailable early stages of human community
seem to draw their enclosures around poetry once again.
That *why* stirs in Bonnefoy nothing like Homer, but reissues
the *il y a*. In Jones it uncovers both tested cord and specific
labyrinth.

What Americans might make of all this remains, too,
a developmental question, for they are the children of
Europe who never submitted to a long, ambivalent, but ini-
tiating adolescence under the Roman mother. They are the
people without a middle, whose poetry now rehearses private family initiations. I wonder if a Yank can be thrown
back--as Jones surely is in the last poems--on the prelogical,
prediscursive, culturally primitive functions of memory,
because one's people have too many dead for whom to
account. *Back* is not what memorious necessity seems to us;
transcendently down or modishly deep is what it usually
becomes. But what it became in the Celtic defeat tradi-
tion--the crying of names in litany as if in defiance, evocation, succor, reinvigoration, and lament all at once--an
American can only imagine. Want to imagine it he often
does, with earnest moral stretching and apocalyptic *frisson*:
the latest instance of this known to me,[15] though eloquent
and tough-guy respectful ("Milosz and Kundera know what
they are talking about"), tumbles into the old mystical participation, this time with the great dispossessed poets of the
East, that nourishes the prophetic pseudomorphosis which
Jones resists but to which we remain temperamentally and
culturally disposed. If the cries in David Jones' poetry reach
us at all on these shores, we shall have heard the transmissible indeed.

---

15. Terence Des Pres, "Poetry and Politics," *Tri Quarterly* 65 (Winter 1986), "The
Writer in Our World: A Symposium."

VINCENT SHERRY

THE ROMAN QUARRY OF DAVID JONES: EXTRAORDINARY PERSPECTIVES

From about 1935 until his death in 1974, David Jones labored over several extended poetic sequences, published as *The Anathemata: fragments of an attempted writing* (1952) and *The Sleeping Lord and Other Fragments* (1974). Although these poems display a Modernist, mosaic-like organization of "fragments," most critics regard *The Anathemata* as a firmly unified poem, *The Sleeping Lord* as a dynamic sequence of complete poems. Readers of David Jones have realized that the pieces in the later volume emerged from a larger work-in-progress; few, however, could have known the extent and ambition of his poetic design. It was a wide-ranging scheme which he could not complete in his lifetime. The posthumous publication of *The Roman Quarry and other sequences*,[1] the collection of poetic manuscripts edited and annotated by René Hague and Harman Grisewood, makes intelligible the larger plan and significance of this work. *The Roman Quarry*, in effect, provides a Rosetta Stone for the poet's later writings.

David Jones evidently intended a single poem of great historical scope. Its focus is on Roman Jerusalem at the time of Christ's death, which is viewed historically against the backdrop of the Roman Empire in the first century. Poems published in *The Sleeping Lord* volume, printed here in manuscript versions and grouped with several important additional pieces, establish this broad backdrop: they range in locale from Roman and Celtic Britain to Roman Jerusalem in 30 A.D. Three poems in a newly discovered sequence, "The Old Quarry," narrow the scope, viewing the events of Holy Week within the political crucible of Roman Jerusalem. Just as the Catholic mass, as Jones emphasizes in his essays, reenacts these events of Holy

1. David Jones, *The Roman Quarry and other sequences*, ed. Harman Grisewood and René Hague (London: Agenda Editions, 1981); page references will be given parenthetically in the essay.

Week in symbolic form, a group of three mass poems repeats the motifs and images of "The Old Quarry" sequence. Completing the collection is the manuscript of "The Book of Balaam's Ass," which Jones began shortly after finishing his war-book *In Parenthesis* (1937). Earliest of the manuscripts, this is a sometimes delightful medley of voices and anecdotes in the free-wheeling style of soldiers' post-war conversations, but it does not seem to fit, at least at first sorting, into the coherent design comprised by the other three sequences.

"The Roman Quarry" sequence displays a strong internal coherence as well. Between the separate poems in the manuscript there are transitional passages, which make explicit the underlying continuity, only hinted at through subtle mirror- and echo-patterns in *The Sleeping Lord*. An important transitional device is the figure of the legionary sounding the bugle in a Roman garrison in Jerusalem, announcing the change of watch and signalling the shift between poems. Most important, the watch-change he signals also symbolizes "the turn of a civilisation,"[2] that historical change David Jones represents in *The Sleeping Lord* with beautifully double implications: the shift from classical to Christian culture in the time of the poems, from religious to technological culture in the time of the poet. Also sounding this theme of historical change is the newly published "Under Arcturus." Here an aging Celtic legionary recounts how the northern Votodoni tribe breached his sector of the Antonine Wall, symbolizing the end of Roman control and occurring, appropriately, while the bugler in that garrison was blowing the change of the guard. In this epoch of bitter endings and sometimes wondering, sometimes bewildering beginnings, each piece seems to look both forward and backward; Jones' speakers reach back to the symbols of ancient Roman and Celtic myth to prefigure the Christian faith already developing; there is a magical, mysterious sense of continuity and coherence within the feeling of change.

Unifying the poems in "The Old Quarry" sequence is a political perspective on Christ's crucifixion. "The Old Quarry, 1" opens in the scene of a modern mass and moves to the first liturgy of the Last Supper, but Jones quickly shifts the focus to the machinations of Judas' betrayal, the politics of the High Priesthood in Caiaphas, thence to the

2. The phrase occurs in the introductory lyric, "A, a, a, Domine Deus," in *The Sleeping Lord* (London: Faber, 1974), p. 9; the piece originates in the manuscript of "The Book of Balaam's Ass," in *The Roman Quarry*, pp. 209-11.

intrigue of the arrest and the subsequent crucifixion. The editors give the second piece the appropriately political title "The Agent"; it follows Judas' flight from the upper room of the supper to the High Priest; Judas' soliloquoy and conversation with Caiaphas reveal the political forces behind the betrayal with a condensed, bitter eloquence. The third piece, "The Old Quarry, 2," shifts to the chambers of an aging Roman administrator in Jerusalem, who speaks from a wizened political perspective to his daughter at the precise hour of the crucifixion.

Not as a unified sequence but as successive versions of a single work, three mass poems stand as the second section of *The Roman Quarry*. Begun around 1940 as "The Grail Mass" but subsequently lost, started anew in 1952 as "Caillech," then published in a fragmentary form as "The Kensington Mass"[3] in 1975, these three poems display parallel lines of movement. Opening in the midst of a modern liturgy, "The Grail Mass" moves toward a scene in Malory's *Le Morte d'Arthur*, where Lancelot, standing alone outside the Grail chapel, is prevented by his sin from entering and achieving the Grail sacrament. In "Caillech" an Irish woman's musings take her--in circumlocutions as wonderfully self-inquiring, self-responding, self-sustaining as Anna Livia's, Joyce's washerwoman--from a sermon on chastity, into the scene of the three washerwomen in Celtic myth, to converge on the same figure of Lancelot standing outside the Grail chapel. Similarly, in "The Kensington Mass," the associations move from the hem of the priest's garment to the mythic Elen of Britain, to her husband the Roman Emperor, thence to Roman Jerusalem where Peter, after betraying Christ, is left standing in Pilate's courtyard, as much an alien as Lancelot excluded from the mass in the Grail chapel. Why should this enigmatic "outsider" figure reappear in the different mass poems, and how is he significant to the other sequences?

An important discovery to be made from these manuscripts is that all three mass poems bear explicit dedications to Fr. John O'Connor,[4] the priest who received David Jones into the Catholic church. A scene in "Caillech," in fact, recalls specifically the church of St. Cuthbert in Brad-

3. Published as an unfinished draft, with manuscript continuations, as *The Kensington Mass* (London: Agenda Editions, 1975).
4. A paper wrapper around the script of "The Grail Mass" reads "written (in part) in memory of the late Monsignor J. O'C." (*The Roman Quarry*, p. xx); all the sheets of the "Caillech" manuscript are headed "Mass. Ken. m. J. O'C." (*The Roman Quarry*, p. xviii); and "The Kensington Mass" bears a beautiful inscriptional dedication to Fr. O'Connor (*The Roman Quarry*, p. 87).

ford, where O'Connor received Jones in 1921.[5] The outsider figure might reflect, in some profoundly imaginative way, Jones' own initial relation to the church as a type of outsider. Most compelling, the poet seems to be imaginatively reenacting his conversion through this figure. In relation to Lancelot, specifically, he emphasizes themes integral to the convert's experience: initiation, reception into the church. Thus, as in *Le Morte d'Arthur*,[6] Lancelot at "The Grail Mass" sees the priest at the interior altar elevating the host as though struggling with a great weight and desires to enter and help him. But to Malory's account Jones adds the image of a dog chained outside the chapel, as it were, "for a thousand quarantines" (*RQ*, 109), that is, forty day or Lenten periods. It was in Lent, of course, that converts traditionally trained for final reception into the church on Easter eve. Argos the dog is the counterpart of Lancelot standing outside, while the Lenten motifs of preparation and initiation emerge dramatically in his passion to be accepted within:

Lake-wave Lawnslot
     beats against that
varnished pine
     his quillon'd *cleddyf*-hilt
fractures the notices for the week
he would see
     right through that chamber door
he would be
     where the Cyrenean deacon
leans inward
     to relieve the weight
he too would aid the venerable man
     surcharged with that great weight.
In the south porch
     Argos the dog
howls outright. (*RQ*, 110)

The personal connection between David Jones and Lancelot becomes clearer through an episode in the poet's biography. In a letter to René Hague, he relates how, one day in Flanders during the war, he came upon a shattered, apparently abandoned farm building. Approaching more closely, he discovered a Catholic mass proceeding with full ritual appointments. He stood for a long time at the wall, gazing in from outside, much like Lancelot at the door of the Grail chapel. In this account, he emphasizes his status at that time as an uninitiated outsider; most important, he sug-

5. The point is made by the editors, p. xxi.
6. See Sir Thomas Malory, *Le Morte d'Arthur*, Everyman Edition, vol. 2, Book xvii, ch. 15 (1906; rpt. London: Dent, 1972), pp. 257-8.

gests that this occasion was a milestone, a turning point, the beginning of a conversion:

> I can't recall at what part of the Mass it was as I looked through that squint-hole and I didn't think I ought to stay long as it seemed rather like an uninitiated bloke prying on the Mysteries of a Cult. But it made a big impression on me. ... [F]or at that spying unintentionally on the Mass in Flanders in the Forward Zone I felt immediately that oneness between the Offerant and those toughs that clustered round him in the dim-lit byre--a thing I had never felt remotely as a Protestant at the Office of Holy Communion in spite of the insistence of Protestant theology on the "priesthood of the laity." (*DGC*, 249)

The outsider figure, it is important to note, reappears as different characters throughout David Jones' poetry and functions as a controlling perspective in the poet's historical vision. In "The Roman Quarry," soldiers in Roman Jerusalem observe the new Christian religion from outside, from before its time, groping toward an understanding of the nascent faith from the viewpoint of ancient Roman mythology. Similarly, the Roman administrator in "The Old Quarry, 2" regards the emerging faith from the crumbling institutions of Roman religion. Here, of course, conversion occurs as "the turn of a civilisation," as historical rather than personal experience. Still, the personal dimension of Jones' own conversion lends depth and drive to this historical process, and doubtless accounts, at least in part, for his life-long interest in this epoch of change.

The outsider provides David Jones with a perspective essential to his imaginative and artistic vision as well. Speaking for the artist in "The Old Quarry, 2," the Roman administrator observes: "to be a supreme artist one has got to know and yet be as one who knows nothing" (*RQ*, 180). Here is a prescription for the outsider's point of view. For, like an outsider, an artist must relinquish certainty for a sense of wonder, mastery for an aura of mystery and fascinated inquiry. (Look at David Jones' watercolors, which seem to touch their subjects in tentative wonder rather than represent them with objective certainty.) Thus, in the poetry, David Jones envisions the myths and symbols of Christianity from the extraordinary perspective of the outsider, from a viewpoint conducive to the qualities of wonder and strangeness he valued in art. Moreover, in a brilliant application of this principle, the outsider envisions symbols, like himself, outside the canon of received Christian tradition, symbols whose original, imaginative, and unusual nature conveys the wonder, aura, and numinous power of art.

Thus Peter, standing as the archetypal outsider in
Pilate's courtyard during "The Kensington Mass," uses the
death of Absalom as a symbol for the imminent crucifixion
of Christ. Both Absalom and Christ were "sons of David";
both were pierced and hung in death on trees; but David's
prodigal son is certainly an unusual, an arresting, an eccentric symbol of Christ.[7] An equally fresh, powerful, and
unorthodox symbol appears in the same passage in the figure of the fertility priest in the oak grove at Nemi. This
priest underwent a sacrificial death to renew the life of the
grove, represented in the perennial "Golden Bough"; here the
figure stands enigmatically for Christ's redemptive sacrifice. Feel the fabric of foreign words (Latin and Greek as
well as Old English) weaving the spell of strangeness and
wonder the poet sought to restore in his art:

> That great *lignum arbor una nobilis* within the inmost *nemeton* of
> this wild Ephraim *holt*, had for Golden Bough the pierced & hanging
> son of the Lord of Salem. (*RQ*, 96)

John Milton excluded such pagan prototypes from his hymn
"On the Morning of Christ's Nativity," but David Jones, echoing that poem in "The Grail Mass," reinstates these unorthodox symbols. Fabricating his own nativity crèche, he displays these ancient foretypes with the numinous radiance
and wonder felt most acutely by outsiders like Lancelot:

> Yes, brutish you
> 　　　　but you his forerunners
> each of you, his *figura*.
> ...
>
> So stay
> 　　　　but when they sing
> 　　　　QUI VENIT
> here all of you
> 　　　　kneel
> every Lar of you
> 　　　　numen or tutelar
> from *terra, pontus* and the air
> or from the strait bathysphere.
> 　　　　Now constellate
> are all your brights
> 　　　　of this lifted Lode.
> What light else
> 　　　　brighted you ever? (*RQ*, 107)

"The Book of Balaam's Ass," though unrelated in
most respects to the other sequences, provides a splendid
paradigm for this technique of imaginative perspective. In

---

7. Peter refers to the scribal traditions of biblical exegesis (pp. 94-5), pointing out that
he is unlettered, to sharpen this departure from normal biblical typology.

the biblical story of Balaam's ass, a donkey, unlike his master, is able to see the angel of God and thus to announce the divine message. Like Peter's and Lancelot's, the beast's perspective is certainly "extraordinary." And, as though to prove David Jones' use for this unique viewpoint, the beast itself becomes a correspondingly new, fresh, and unusual symbol of the God he praises:

> But look! where he stands to mock your anthropomorphic prejudice, see where he regards you, his grey beauty flaming, his strong pelt praising the Lord of all glistening hair on lion, on fox, on tunnelling badger. See him lurching his glory, see his loose limbs stretched familiar on the predella of the throne, with the nine choirs to stroke him. And hear his grim voice that his erect throat trumpets out among the flock of the elect; see him, the ravager of folds, redeemed and foldkeeper. (*RQ*, 202)

David Jones creates a fresh perspective on familiar themes by recreating and renewing the reader's experience of signs. Appropriately, he suggests an analogy between his artistry and the restoration quests of medieval romance. There, typically, a knight proceeds to a castle where, if he asks a question about the meaning of the mysterious Grail procession, he will cure the maimed king of the Waste Land and revive his wasted domain. In the earlier manuscript version of "The Sleeping Lord" poem, the lord recumbent beneath the land is identified several times with the ailing king of the Waste Land; also, like Joyce's Finnegan and Williams' Paterson, he represents the buried deposits of tradition which the poet seeks to revive. Thus, for the poet, as for the knight, to revive the king is to ask the question, in a larger sense, to approach the traditional deposits with a sense of mystery and wondering inquiry:

> In this charged land of under-myth and over-myth where lord rests on greater lord and by lesser names the greater named are called.... What ageless Mabon recollects, which long-winded Nestor knows the axile line of the first of the sleepers?...
> But in this place of myth on wonder-myth, in this place of questions.... (*RQ*, 38)

The analogy is sufficiently important to occur again in the manuscript of "The Hunt":

> In this place of questioning where you must ask the question and the answer questions you
> where race sleeps on dreaming race and under-myth and over-myth, like the leaf-layered forest-floor, are the uncertain crust.... (*RQ*, 18)

This principle of wondering inquiry shapes the rhetorical texture of David Jones' poetry. No other poet uses the form of the extended question with such consummate artistry; *The Anathemata*, for example, has been called "an epic . . . in the interrogative mood."[8] No mere stylistic mannerism, this questioning rhetoric, one may now realize, serves a calculated effect; it presents the forgotten materials with the wondering attitude required to revive them.

The means of poetic mystery are not only stylistic; there are structural methods, too, for which the manuscripts provide an important gloss. The Roman administrator in "The Old Quarry, 2" notes that "the mind of the insular peoples [Celts] is essentially asymmetric"; he continues: "It will be a new thing indeed for them to observe . . . how it is possible to establish contact between two points other than by proceeding in spirals" (*RQ*, 157). He is distinguishing between Roman and Celtic principles of organization, between rational Roman directness and imaginative Celtic obliquity, between, say, a Roman road system and a Celtic burial mound: the first is linear, rational, its design simultaneous and clear, the other is labyrinthine, mysterious, its order elliptical, inscrutable. Speaking against political expediency, he laments the process whereby the Roman road of reason paves over the Celtic maze of mystery:

> Or are we so potent and have so imposed our shape upon the waking minds of men, so insinuated the male principle as to vulgarize and flatten out the subtle maze, so mapped the meander of our intuitive origins (Aphrodite of the oblique approaches, pray for us, who gave us Aeneas).... (*RQ*, 181)

Since his own experience in the labyrinthine trenches of the Great War, recalled in *In Parenthesis*, David Jones has labored over labyrinths in his verse and painting. "The Old Quarry, 1" exhibits another version in this collection. Just as there is no focussed center in the maze, the central event of Christ's Passion recedes into the labyrinthine channels of Roman politics in Jerusalem, into a maze of pre-Christian foretypes as well.

Certainly the "oblique approach," the extraordinary perspective, the unique viewpoint, creates a wonder equal to that of the "subtle maze." Thus the Roman administrator identifies Lancelot with the Celtic labyrinth at New Grange; the outsider and his extraordinary perspective are a source of wonder like the labyrinth, the means of a renewing mystery like the magical cornucopia at the navel of the maze:

> No Lancelot no! you must be lost before you find the cornucopia, ... at the navel of the spiral at New Grange .... It's always from chamber to

8. William Blissett, "David Jones: Himself at the Cave-mouth," *University of Toronto Quarterly*, 36 (April 1967), p. 264; Blissett also remarks perceptively on the images of the labyrinth in *The Anathemata* and *In Parenthesis*.

chamber--in and out the creep-way as you have done before. ... [Y]ou'll feel like a motherless child before Rhea encloses you a second time, before you revive the maimed king before you find your margarite. You must be lost, and the Roman way is to be certain of one's bearings. (*RQ*, 182)

It seems appropriate that these manuscripts, which afford an unexpected perspective on familiar material, should demonstrate so well the poetic art of the unusual viewpoint. Through such perspectives, the poems David Jones already quarried from his deposits continue to exert wonder and fascination for his admirers. But unsympathetic readers may look through the same glass and see things more darkly: "density," "pedantry," and "willful obscurity" are catchwords in the detractor's vocabulary. These objections may be typical of an age which, paradoxically, regards intensely private experience as somehow accessible in poetry, historically public traditions as unpardonably recondite. In any case, *The Roman Quarry* will at least make it clear that David Jones designed the lithe labyrinth of his work with the conscious, dedicated skill of a master mason, and with the wondering inquiry of a life-long initiate.

THE ARTIST

1. The artist at work. (1965)

2. "Manawydan's Glass Door" (1931)

3. "Petra Im Rosenhag" (1931)

4. "Aphrodite in Aulis" (1941)

5. "Vexilla Regis" (1947)

6. "Flora in Calix-Light" (1950)

7. "Trystan Ac Essyllt" (1962)

8. "Y Cyfarchiad I Fair" (1963)

9. "Dvm Medivm Silentivm" (1952)

10. "Vere Dignvm" (1961)

11. "Crucifixion" (1920)

12. "Lamentation" (1925)

13. "Sanctus Christus De Capel-Y-Ffin" (1925)

14. "Crucifixion" (1926)

15. "Tywysog Cariad" (1929)

16. "The Albatross" (1929)

17. "Eric Gill" (1930)

"He Frees the Waters"

18. "He Frees the Waters in Helyon" (1932)

19. "Epiphany 1941: Britannia and Germania Embracing" (1941)

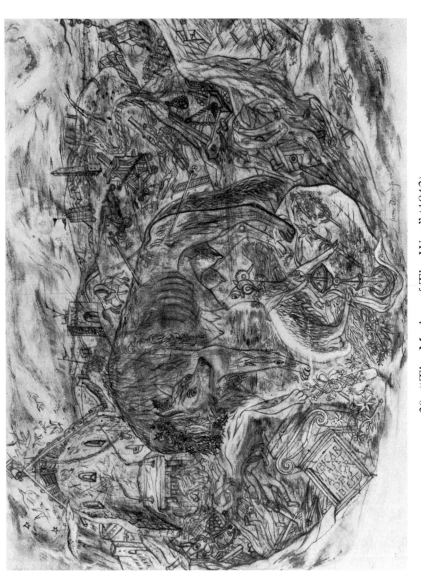

20. "The Mother of The West" (1942)

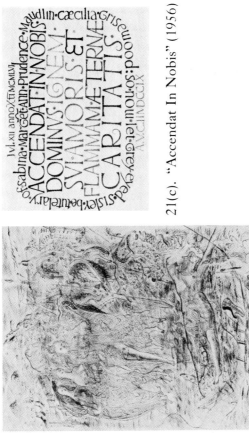

21(c). "Accendat In Nobis" (1956)

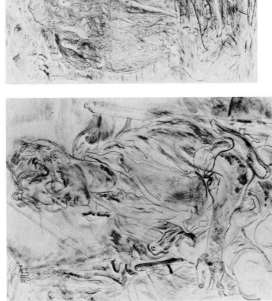

21(b). "The Four Queens" (1941)

21(a). "The Translator of
'The Chanson de Roland'" (1932)

22. "Study for Trystan Ac Essyllt" (1959-60)

NAM·SIBYLLAM
QVIDEM·CVMIS
EGO·IPSE·OCVLIS
MEIS·VIDI·IN
AMPVLLA·PENDERE
ET·CVM·ILLI·PVERI
DICERENT
ΣΙΒΥΛΛΑΤΙ·ΘΕΛΕΙΣ
RESPONDEBAT·ILLA
ΑΠΟΘΑΝΕΙΝ·ΘΕΛΩ.
LA·TERRE·GASTE·ETSOUTAINE
NAC·ANIVEIL·NA·MUIGNA·DYN
ne·in·the·watir·no·fyssh·DauidmefecitThomæ

AprilisthecruelstmthbreedīgLilacsoutofthedeadland

23. "Nam Sibyllam" (1958)

cara·Wallia·derelicta
ÐVGWYL·DAMASEVS
BAB·YRVNVED·DYÐAR
ÐEG·O·VIS·RAGFYR
DVW·GWENER✝
ACYNA·I·BWRIWYD
HOLL·GYMRY
Y'R·ILAWR.VENIT·SVMMA·DIES
ET·INELVCTABILE·TEMPVS
DARDANIÆ.PENN·DRAGON
PENN·DREIC·OED·ARNÄW
PENN·ILYWELYN·DEG
DYGYNA·VRAW·BYT·BOT
PAWL·HAEARN·TRWYDAW.
ab·hieme·añ·1282

NYT·OES·NA·XTN·GOR·NA·XLO·NAC·EGOR.

24. "Cara Wallia Derelicta" (1959)

25. The Jones family, with David on his mother's lap. Harold, the eldest child (who died at the age of 21), is standing next to his father. Alice Mary is in the middle.

26. Private Jones, Royal Welsh Fusilier, 1915.

27. The Royal Welsh Fusiliers somewhere in Wales, 1915. David Jones is in the center of the back row.

28. At Ditchling in the 1920s.

29. In August of 1927.

30. In the early 1930s.

31. A Joyceian pose. Perhaps at sea, on the way to Cairo in 1934.

32. At Harrow, 1965. One of the 70th birthday photographs taken by Mark Gerson.

ERIC GILL

FROM "DAVID JONES"

Mr. David Jones is a painter who sees the modern dilemma very clearly, and we should miss all the quality of his work if we did not see that it is a combination of two enthusiasms, that of the man who is enamored of the spiritual world and at the same time as much enamored of the material body in which he must clothe his vision. The difficulty of preserving a balance between representative felicities and those which are purely intellectual and aesthetic is perhaps greater for painters than any other kind of artist. Verisimilitude, though perhaps not easy in any art, is easier in painting than in most, especially when four centuries of concentration upon it by artists and the illustrated press have flooded the world with photographic representations. The imitation of natural appearance, if it ever was a difficulty, is difficulty no longer. Of course, it requires hard work and obedience to the rules to become proficient, but these are difficulties which determination can overcome. The real difficulty now lies in making a rebellion which shall be neither an affair of archaism nor of charlatanism. The painter must have a very clear idea as to what a picture really is, and as to why and what he really likes painting. And not only must the painter thus clear his head, but he who buys and he who criticizes are under the same obligation. The most clear-headed and enthusiastic painter may fail to win any support unless those who see his work are capable of sharing or sympathizing with his aims.

David Jones was born at Brockley in Kent in 1895. He was a student under A. S. Hartrick, at the Camberwell School of Art, from 1910 to 1914. He served throughout the war with the Royal Welch Fusiliers. From 1919 to 1921 he was a student, under Walter Bayes, at the Westminster School of Art. Apart from a few small sculptures in boxwood (things which alone would place him in the first rank of modern artists), his work has been chiefly wood and copper engraving, and water-color drawing. He has done engravings for the St. Dominic's Press, the Golden Cockerel Press (*Gulliver, Jonah, The Deluge*) and for Douglas Cleverdon, Bristol (*The Ancient Mariner*). Of the last it may be said that Coleridge's poem has for the first time found adequate pictorial accompaniment. As a water-colorist he has worked chiefly in Wales, the south of France, at Hove and at Brockley. Though in one place he may find more inspiration than another, it is not places that most concern him. What concerns him is the universal thing showing through the particular thing, and as a painter it is this showing through that he endeavors to capture. The eye sees particular things, but the man's delight in the physical vision is checked by the mind's apprehension of the universal informing it. Nevertheless, in spite of this idealistic attitude he never loses sight of the fact that it is a painting he is making--or a drawing, or an engraving; it is not merely an essay in Platonic research. Paper and paint, the brush, the graver all make their own proper demands and yield their own proper fruits. The difficulty, the job, is one of translation--how to translate this universal thing into terms of paint and paper.

What starts a man painting, why this physical concern for spiritual things? It must on no account be supposed that David Jones is that kind of "high-brow" whose essays in paint are a condescension. Paint, color, flowers, flesh, these are the things which delight him. But his is that kind of fastidiousness which is not content with simple reproductions of delightful things. Even "the particularly juicy bit" which starts him off he holds with a grasp which at any moment he is prepared to relinquish. And yet, and yet--even though the grasp be relinquished, the thing and its delightfulness still pervade and must pervade the painting.

To David Jones, a painting is neither simply a representation nor simply a painted pattern. He resists equally firmly the seduction in either direction. If he delights especially in the beauty of flowers and animals and young girls, his paintings are not therefore to be regarded simply as records of those things; there is nothing of the Pre-Raphaelite in him. If he delights in the purely aesthetic quality of paint on paper, the beauty of arabesque, of light and of color, his paintings are not therefore simply essays in abstraction. He is not an Impressionist, nor, except by accident of date, a Post-Impressionist. It is not for me to say simply that his work is good; my object is rather to make a clear statement of his point of view, so that those who see his work will at least be in the position to judge fairly, and will not be in the position of those unfortunate persons who, having paid to see a football match, find a cricket match inflicted upon them.

1930

KENNETH CLARK

SOME RECENT PAINTINGS BY DAVID JONES*

In this note I shall try to describe the impression made on
me by some recent paintings and drawings by David Jones.
The most fully worked-out is a large water-color of Trystan
and Essyllt (what we should call Tristan and Iseult) on
board their ship, drinking the love potion. For this watercolor there exists a large drawing, and to compare it with
the final version is to learn something of the thought and
invention that David Jones puts into all his work. In both
the foreground is occupied by the deck of the boat looking
aft; in both the masts rise into a sky full of seagulls and of
stars that tell us it is between day and night on St. Brigit's
Day, the first of February; and in both Tristan and Iseult
stand in the middle of the deck, with the disastrous cup held
between them. But although the subject is basically the
same, the two designs make a very different impression.
The original drawing is dominated by the diagonals of spars
and ropes that run down from the right hand corner and cut
across the lovers. Tristan's face, stricken and dismayed,
gains in intensity: but the forceful argument of those diagonal ropes annihilates Iseult, and her head is undefined. Yet
she must become the motive force of the picture, so the
ropes and spars must go, and leave her a space in which to
assert herself. She becomes a formidable figure. The line of
a stiff bow or steel spring, starts from a shadow on her face,
and runs through her whole body till it joins the curve of
the ship. She steps forward, one shoe off and one shoe on,
leg, toes, and instep all painfully clear and close to Tristan's
naked foot. She stares past him, triumphantly, defiantly, like
one who has shot the lights, but also with some of the
somnambulist's surrender of will. And from her tiny, vesti-
gial head her yellow hair envelopes the wretched Tristan in
a candy-floss whirlpool. Although embroidered with the

---

*Recent, that is, when Lord Clark first published this essay in *Agenda*, Vol. 5, Nos. 1-3,
1967. [Ed.]

emblems of chivalry, this is the same motive as Munch's Vampire.

Tristan and Iseult are not alone. Even in the first drawing a sailor is lying, half-hidden by the gunwale, his leg stretched out across the deck, and another comes up from below, his head emerging from a hatch, like a moon-calf witness. A cat walks towards him gingerly, its feet spread out to counter the movement of the ship, which in their state of ecstasy, Tristan and Iseult do not feel. To these original inhabitants of his imagination David Jones has added other figures, who, beautiful as they are, remain immigrants or settlers. Amongst them are a quantity of sailors, some on deck, others struggling with the top sheets, who heighten the tempo of the drawing: but they lack the inevitability of the single sailor's leg and the cat. Only one addition has this quality, the cockboat or dinghy, that floats beside the ship, containing a present for King Mark of two Irish wolf hounds. The gunwale is bound with a fender of rushes that make it look like some coracle from the golden age.

As in all David Jones' work the sharpness of focus with which the details are seen varies from inch to inch. I am reminded of the hours I used to spend fishing off the coast of Skye, when, on calm days, one could look down many fathoms to gently undulating streamers of weed, sea-urchins, sea-anemones and puffs of sand where the furtive flounder burrowed its way out of sight. Then a breeze would ruffle the surface and this garden of delights would be disturbed, but through a window of calm water one could still catch sight of certain man-defined objects, an old anchor or a discarded rowlock. So, in David Jones' drawing, the welter of clouds, seagulls and stars that surrounds Tristan's ship seems to be ruffled by the wind, but on the ship itself the mechanism of sail is made clear, with anchors, blocks and a contrivance known as a knight-head, drawn as sharply as Iseult's foot.

In spite of all that has been added to the final watercolor, it is possible to prefer the full-sized sketch. It has kept the vitality of rough weather; and, in the end, Tristan is more interesting than Iseult. He is elder brother to the private in the frontispiece of *In Parenthesis*, equally lost and vulnerable, the sacrificed man, the scapegoat conscious of his fate. How could he have been made to confront that triumphant doll? An artist as deeply personal as David Jones must be perpetually balanced between the needs of his inner world and the demands of his subject, with their influence on design. Behind all his apparent simplicity he has a strong conscious skill in the art of picture making; and yet it is the self-revealing moments of vision that count.

Next in importance to the Tristan and Iseult is a large watercolor, almost a monochrome, of the Annunciation. The scene is set in the Welsh mountains with stone circles and other signs of an earlier faith; and to some extent these old beliefs are continued, for the Virgin is also a nature goddess, surrounded by living creatures. Dozens of birds fly round her, providing almost the only positive color in the picture. But the most brilliant of them is the goldfinch, the long-accepted symbol of Christian sacrifice; and when we turn to the angel, we see that he holds in his right hand a sword to which clings a broken strand of thorns. With his other hand he points to the stars, where Jupiter is coming into conjunction with Libra and Virgo; but this promise of the Virgin's destiny hanging above Her head is less vivid than the scene of nature at Her feet and our eyes return gladly to the birds and to the workmanlike fence of withies which forms her *hortus conclusus*. This fence actually existed, woven while David Jones was staying with Eric Gill in Wales, and David Jones made a drawing of it, which he kept for over forty years till it should come in handy.

On re-reading what I have written about the Annunciation I see that it might just as well be a description of a Pre-Raphaelite picture. It is in the same vein as Ruskin's description of *The Light of the World* (although far less eloquent); and of course a David Jones watercolor does not look at all like a picture by Holman Hunt. The difference lies in the greater freedom with which, since 1910 or so, all artists have been able to treat appearance. Even David Jones, who like all visionary painters seldom takes a step outside the world of visible matter, selects as much or as little of an appearance as will fit in with his inner life or with (what is really the same thing) his peculiar calligraphy. Instead of his hand laboriously describing each object, it performs its own self-revealing movements in relation to the object, stopping and starting at the dictates of feeling, and sometimes seeming to break of in the middle of a phrase. I can well imagine someone unfamiliar with his work being puzzled because certain details (usually hands, arms and feet) are drawn with the skill and precision of a de Limbourg, while others seem almost childish. But these changes of focus come from a refusal to simulate intensity of vision where none exists. To an unusual degree David

Jones knows when he is recording a vivid experience, and can give it the maximum of precision, and when he feels no more than a general emotion, and must be content with suggestion. So, in his best paintings, there are none of those passages of dull description that dilute the work of the Pre-Raphaelites.

Some of the finest of David Jones' recent paintings are not of literary subjects, like Tristan and Isolde, but represent simply a vase of flowers on a table. A pleasant subject; but we are not for long under the illusion that this is an ordinary "still life." The vase, broad and capacious like a Byzantine chalice of the eighth century, stands facing us on a plain table. Although no exclusively Christian symbol is visible, we at once have the feeling that this is an altar, and that the flowers in some way represent parts of the eucharist. There are wine-colored carnations and ears of corn, thorny stems of roses and blood red petals, which drop onto the small white table cloth. Yet none of this is insisted on, and we are far from the closed world of symbolism. Every flower is there for a dozen reasons, visual, iconographical, or even on account of its name, and how far they can be interpreted as Christian imagery no one, perhaps not even the painter, can tell. All the great poets I have known have given very simple explanations of their most obscure passages; all the bad poets have given very profound explanations of their banal ones. David Jones is a great poet. He does not require obscure interpretations: although no doubt the alchemy which accompanies each stroke of his brush is infinitely recondite.

ARTHUR GIARDELLI

FOUR RELATED WORKS BY DAVID JONES

What if earth
Be but the shadow of heaven, and things therein
Each to each other like, more than on earth is thought.

In an essay on Nicolas Poussin André Gide wrote, "*Dans le grand naufrage du temps, c'est par la peau que les chefs-d'oeuvres flottent.*" The skin of a water color by David Jones consists of translucent layers of pigment flooded on, one over another, by a hand under the spell of an intense experience. Yet the result is strange. Sometimes the areas of the washes of pure color shining one through the other convey to the mind that ambiguous unnamable impression made by nature herself, as when one says: "Now whatever color would you call that?" The flooding colors give the effect of a day when the hidden sun is nevertheless bright. There is no hard edge of shadow. Light plays off the colored areas of things in a haze. Sometimes the painter makes a line in brilliant pigment or pencil--he uses pencil grey as he uses a water color pigment--to delineate a window ledge, a ship, a couple walking on the shore, or a door lock. Of a painting done in 1931 he wrote in a letter on 4 September, 1964:

> Wish I could do that kind still, but I can't. What you said about it took my mind back to when I made it. You were quite right, the 'glass door' jolly well had to shut, and even so the curtains flew about. It was an astonishing house, part of a line of houses called 'Hove Seaside Villas'. They were built simply bang on the beach, and at high tide or when it was at all rough spray burst over them.

Earlier in the same letter he talks of "that incomparable great master Turner" and his own watercolors of this period share with those of Turner the quality of being at one and the same time convincing records of a particular experience of nature, and yet strange. It seems as though the strangeness strikes him too because when he looks at the result of his work he sees that he has painted not only the view over the beach at Hove, but also that that wicker chair on the verandah has been transformed in the western light into a throne waiting for Ulysses. In another instance he finds that the door which doesn't keep out the winds blowing up the English Channel is also Manawydan's Glass Door which looks across the sea towards Cornwall from the island of Gwales, identified by contemporary scholars as Grassholm, where today gannets breed. Schumann records a similar experience. When he had finished his piano composition "In der Nacht" he found that he had told in music the story of Hero and Leander.

There is no doubt that if it is left to the skin of the paintings done at Hove they will float on and on. But what of the flesh, blood and bones? Does the title matter? What is Manawydan to us? The clue can be followed in Lady Charlotte Guest's translation of *The Mabinogion* where David Jones first read of Manawydan. What is recalled in this painting is told in the second portion of *The Mabinogion* entitled, "Branwen the daughter of Llyr." "Bendigeid Vran, the son of Llyr, was crowned king of this island and he was exalted from the crown of London." He was killed in a war in Ireland but, before he dies, he commands Manawydan and Pryderi that they shall take his head and bury it under the White Mount in London where it shall ensure that no invaders shall plague the island. It is when they are on their way to London with the head that they pass fourscore years in a royal hall in Gwales. The door in the picture is that of which Manawydan says, "See, yonder, is the door we may not open." So long as they do not open it they remain oblivious of every sorrow and loss and unaware of the passage of time. It was behind this very door in Hove that David Jones had escaped from time in making many works. Here he started writing *In Parenthesis*. Concerning the significance of the head of Brân (otherwise Bendigeid Vran) which remains uncorrupted with them in the royal hall in Gwales, David Jones has more to say in his essay "Wales and the Crown" in *Epoch and Artist*. In the essay this painter of English, Italian and Welsh descent gives, "some tentative reflections round and about what is called, in the *mabinogi* of Branwen, the 'Crown of London' " (*E&A*, 39).

Apart from these echoes which relate to David Jones' reading of Celtic mythology to be found in the painting *Manawydan's Glass Door*, there are matters of visual form and atmosphere which recall works by other painters. Turner has already been mentioned. There is a debt. There is also an evident debt to Sickert and David Jones' conversations with him and the insight this must have brought into the art of the Impressionists. Furthermore, he remembers Hartrick in a letter (4 September, 1964):

> ...dear old Hartrick... he was not a great artist but a real one... at his best he could be pretty marvellous... I think it was being sent off to Paris in the middle of that Bonnard, Degas, Toulouse-Lautrec, Van Gogh era that made him just that much different from his English contemporaries.

One can add that it was knowing Sickert and Hartrick that opened David Jones' eyes in that direction too. For a painting such echoes are as important in mediating meaning as any literary ones. But the artist himself may so completely have absorbed them as to have forgotten them. I had been struck by the similarity in composition which some of David Jones' window pictures have with paintings made by Matisse in 1905 and later in 1912. I mentioned this to him and asked whether such works had influenced him towards painting landscape or seascape as seen through a window. He answered: "I hate being out of doors."

The very look of the inscription "Cara Wallia Derelicta" seems to say, "Here is treasure!" It is arresting in its formal dignity and there is movement in it. There is rhythm in the relationship of the letters and words like that which one sees in standing wheat. David Jones in his *Introduction to the Rime of the Ancient Mariner* writes of the "visual artist for whom the supposed words of Galileo, *Eppur si muove* apply to any decent painting however static its content." Usually letters stay put. But here they sway and rise with the moving content of which he seems to say, "here is treasure, but you've got to dig for it." He himself gives the following account:

> Title: *Cara Wallia derelicta.* Inscription in opaque water color on thick Chinese white ground on paper. Date 1959 (Used as Frontispiece to *Wales through the Ages* Vol. I.) Six lines and a half from *Brenhinedd y Saesson.* Three lines and a half from Vergil's *Aeneid* Bk II. Six lines, including line at left margin, from *Marwnad Llywelyn ap Gruffydd*, e.g. Gruffydd, ab yr Ynad Coch. Lines at top and bottom: *Cara Wallia Derelicta/ab hieme anni 1282* added by D.J. size 23" x 14 1/4" unmounted and unframed.

Since, even when I had read this, the treasure lay for me mostly hidden I asked David Jones what the inscription meant and he started translating: "Dear Wales all buggered up," and then pointing to the last line: "Since the winter of 1282." He continued by translating the words of the second line which he had taken from a Welsh Chronicle, *The Kings of the English*. "On the feast of Pope Damaseus on the 11th of the month of December on the day of Venus (there follows a cross for this is Friday), then was cast down All Wales (the two words taking the whole of the middle line) to the ground." At this point the language changes from Welsh to Vergil's Latin: "and the end of the days and the ineluctible time of Troy has come." The continuation in Welsh is taken from the Elegy for Llywelyn. "A leader's head, a dragon's head was on him." And the color of the letters is warmer for "the head of fair, stubborn Llywelyn. It shocks the world that an iron stake should go through it." Alongside are words written by Gruffydd, son of the Red Judge: "There is no council, no lock nor opening."

The translation unfolds further meanings to be explored. How, for instance, does Vergil fit here? Not that it is unlikely that David Jones should take a lead from the Latin poet whom Dante addressed as, *"Tu duca, tu segnore e tu maestro."* He is here suggesting that the death of Hector and the consequent fall of Troy is comparable for Wales with the death of "Fair Llywelyn" and furthermore it is recalled that from "Aeneas, our great ancestor" who fled from the flames of Troy, are also descended the Welsh. So thought Geoffrey of Monmouth. Concerning Llywelyn, David Jones has much to say of importance to people of this Island in his essay "Wales and the Crown," included in the collection of essays, *Epoch and Artist*:

> The *princeps Walliae* who died that day, at unequal odds with his overlord, the King of England, had dominion over a small, somewhat loosely knit society, comprising groups of semi-tribal, semi-feudal Celts and others. He was, none the less, the last bodily representative, the visible sign or sacrament of a tradition of rulers that were already established when Augustine of Hippo began on *The Confessions* in A.D. 397, that is to say, exactly two centuries before the *other* Augustine came to Canterbury. What came to its term in 1282 was unique as far as this island is concerned.... Nowhere else in this Island was there a line of mediaeval princes that stemmed straight from Roman Britain. (*E&A*, 41)

Evidences of this David Jones then sets out, and one wonders how far to follow him. There is nectar in the honey jar of this inscription brought from very far in space and time.

A consideration of *Manawydan's Glass Door* and the inscription makes us aware that David Jones is concerned to awaken our consciousness of the relationships which deepen our understanding of the meaning to be found in things and events. His works of art in their variety of

media are to him "corporeal metaphors of spiritual things--
spiritualia sub metaphoris corporalium" (St. Thomas
Aquinas [*Summa Theologiae*, 1, qu. 1, art. 9, c]). With eager
patience he uses every art at his disposal as mediator. When
he makes his inscription he has in mind not only elegiac
thoughts but also the fact that, because native dynasties
resisted foreign domination in Wales nearly to the end of
the 13th century, there can now be a growth of national
consciousness and a concern for the living and ancient
language of Wales. Thoughts of Llywelyn link readily with
thoughts of Brân. When it was recognized that it was
Llywelyn, Prince of Wales, who had been slain in that
confused encounter in a wood his head was taken and "set
up at the White Tower in London above the site where,
according to the myth, the blessed head of Bran was buried,
with his face towards the Channel, for the protection of the
whole island" (*E&A*, 42).

But what if these matters are allowed to be
forgotten? Why should David Jones make things that cause
us to go digging into the scarcely remembered past? I think
he might reply: "If I forget thee O Jerusalem, let my right
hand forget its cunning." This is *our* past.

In *Manawydan's Glass Door* of 1931 a painting of
the sea at Hove becomes involved in the Matter of Britain,
which is also called to mind in the Lament for Wales
inscription. From Malory's retelling of the Matter of Britain
David Jones takes one of the oldest tales in the Celtic
tradition, "Trystan ac Essyllt."

David Jones' own account in conversation about this
watercolor drawing went something like this:

> They're sailing into a headwind and so are having to furl the mainsail.
> The only sail you'd use is a foresail, which has slipped and the chap
> in the cabin is wondering what the hell has happened to the thing. The
> little figure a trifle aft and to the right of Essyllt is labouring to
> belay the cordage. The lovers have been larking about in the cabin and are
> in their dressing gowns, so to speak. I wanted them on deck because I
> wouldn't have known what to do about that confined space in the cabin.
> Essyllt is triumphant, in line with and at one with the vessel itself.
> Trystan is letting his hawk fly off. 'He means business'. So the
> kinsmen of the Earl had said when he let free from his wrist his most
> beloved falcon before he stepped forward into the battle line at Maldon.
> The wolf hounds are a present to King Mark from Trystan, master of
> all that pertains to venery, knowing the track ways of the stag desirous
> of water brooks or how from a coracle to use a fish spear, and so on; also I
> think a perfect harpist. The hounds are howling for a hunt, but today
> they will be disappointed.

Trystan and Essyllt have just drunk, mistakenly, the love
potion made by Essyllt's mother for King Mark of Cornwall

and her daughter, his bride to be, for their wedding night. As
he peers into the goblet Trystan becomes aware of all the
misery which is to befall them and that finally they will
reach and eternally remain in a place where the spirits of
the damned are blown hither and thither like flocks of
starlings in a winter storm which bellows like the sea.
There Dante is to find them and be overcome and
bewildered with pity. But we in this picture see them

> where Mor Iwerddon meets
> Mare Gallicum,
> where the seas of the islands war with the ocean, to white
> the horse-king's *insulae*
> to blanch
> main and Ushant. (*A,* 97-98)

It is day *and* night, for we see both flying gulls and
the Pole star. From the position of the constellation of
Arcturus on the skyline we know it is February 1st, St.
Brigit's day, a patron saint of Ireland, from where the ship
has come, but also a goddess who presided over the three
chief professions known in Erinn, of poetry, healing and
Smith works.

In the *Morte d'Arthur* Malory recounts what "the
French book tells." Said Sir Tristram (to King Anguish of
Ireland)--

> this is my desire, that ye will give me La Beale Isoud to go with me
> into Cornwall for to be wedded to King Mark mine uncle .... So to make
> short conclusion, La Beale Isoud was made ready to go with Sir
> Tristram.... Then the queen, Isoud's mother, gave to her and Dame
> Bragwaine, her daughter's gentlewoman, ... a drink and charged them
> that what day King Mark should wed, that same day they should give
> him that drink, so that King Mark should drink to La Beale Isoud, and
> then, said the queen, I undertake that either shall love other the days
> of their life.... And then anon Sir Tristram took the sea, and La Beale
> Isoud, and when they were in their cabin, it happened so that they were
> thirsty, and they saw a little flacket of gold stand by them and it
> seemed by the color and the taste that it was a noble wine. Then Sir
> Tristram took the flacket in his hand, and said, Madam Isoud, here is
> the best drink that ever ye drank. ... Then they laughed and made good
> cheer, and either drank to other freely, and they thought never drink
> that ever they drank to other was so sweet nor so good. But by that their
> drink was in their bodies, they loved each other so well that never
> their love departed for weale neither for woe. And thus it happed the
> love first betwixt Sir Tristram and La Beale Isoud, the which love
> never departed the days of their life.[1]

It is in support of the validity of what he writes that Malory
periodically says: "as the French book tells." And likewise
the French author Béroul, possibly a travelling jongleur,

---

1. Sir Thomas Malory, *Le Morte d'Arthur* (London: Dent, 1927), pp. 179-80.

makes no claim to originality but rather is recounting what he has heard and is known. Similarly David Jones is retelling a timeless tale. And when he is showing the picture he explains how he found out how things actually were when these things happened: "I rang up a nice man in Greenwich to find out about the ship, and for some time I have taken the *Mariners' Mirror*. Even so the damned thing kept looking like the Death of Nelson." His letter written on the 9th and 11th August, 1963, records him studying astronomy and navigation in the times of Arthur. He was interested in ships when he was a boy because his grandfather Ebenezer Bradshaw was a master block and mast maker of Rotherhithe, London. The art of David Jones is a seamless garment woven of his own experience of history and myth.

When in describing the picture David Jones said: "They are in their dressing gowns so to speak"; this may reasonably fit the gorgeous robe worn by Essyllt. But, it will hardly do for Trystan's garb. Essyllt stands in her time of triumph as she must have looked when she sent a knight to King Arthur's court to recommend her to Queen Guenever and say: "I send her word that there be within this land but four lovers, that is Sir Lancelot du Lake and Queen Guenever and Sir Tristram de Liones and Queen Isoud."

Of Trystan David Jones said: "He's had it!" The artist himself seems to be in awe of Essyllt, but for Trystan it seems rather a fellow-feeling that he entertains. Not only is he featured like the soldier portrayed as frontispiece to his *In Parenthesis* but like him also he is half shod. For this condition David Jones offers explanations which confirm the notion that he is at one with Trystan. When he was in the front line of the trenches there was a strict order in force not to take off one's boots when asleep in the dug out. One night Jerry, whose front line was very near, started shelling and David Jones could only find one boot. The terror of his search in the pitch blackness and roar of gunfire taught him in future to obey the order: "Keep yer boots on!" An earlier experience takes us back to the artist's boyhood and mediaeval Welsh history. When he was ten years old his brother fell ill with tuberculosis, and so, to save him from catching the illness David was sent to stay with an uncle. There he found Green's *History of England* and in it saw the drawing used to distinguish MSS concerning Edwardian Welsh wars from others. It was of a Welsh spearman or bowman who had one boot on and one off. Presumably, says David Jones, this was to show that he was some poor bogman, as it were, perhaps because a bare foot could better grip the earth while the soldier was aiming and shooting his missile.

In a letter of September 29, 1966, David Jones was commenting on a technical matter and added:

> It's so often the 'finishing touch' (as they say) that does the trick, or doesn't as the case may be--at least, again, that's so often been my impression with my stuff--as for example the deck boards of the 'quarter deck' between the heads of Essyllt and Trystan in that confounded water colour. I put them in with, to quote Blake, 'fear and trembling' not knowing if it would mess the thing up or what, but actually it pulled the whole thing together--at least I think so.

Indeed; and it does furthermore rivet the lovers together. The picture is the result of a very few rough try-outs of which one is the same size as the final version, which also he called unfinished. In what sense could it be finished? True, there are some sketched in passages, while others are painted so that they come to mind like lines of poetry which one never forgets: for instance, to use Jones' own words about the sword in the letter already quoted: The "straight bright steel length of Tristan's sword, its tempered point *all but* in contact with the proud step forward of Essyllt's bare right foot"; then there are the restless dogs and the "ship's cat walking with forelegs splayed and not giving a damn for slant of deck," Essyllt's arm and ribbons streaming from it in the wind, and the yard whose tilt tells of the lurching of the ship. But it is just such varying of emphasis which serves to articulate the narrative and guide our thought and feeling to what must engage the mind and touch the heart.

The water color drawing *Y Cyfarchiad i Fair* ("The Greeting to Mary,") brings us to what for David Jones is the the heart of things. The reproduction of this picture cannot convey the effect of shafts of light from the cadmium yellow of the stars which gleam on the goldfinch and which is found again in Mary's auburn hair (she is a Welsh girl), some strands of which take up the crimson of the lining of the white tunics which she and Gabriel have on. Only in the original can one see the hot brown of the hawk's feathers, of the pelt of the stag, the red of the bramble stems, the green of the hills and the brighter green of the leaves and grasses, the white steel of the sword, the other white of the blackberry blossom and the purple of the spotted foxglove. In general effect the picture conveys the cloudy, moist atmosphere of the Black Mountains through which silver

light glows and sometimes pierces, and in which the colors
of things are clear.

I got some insight into the practical problems
involved in making so complete and rich a thing when
David Jones told me that he had made between a hundred
and fifty and two hundred drawings for the ten engravings of
the Ancient Mariner and also when he showed me one of
the very few small studies he made in preparation for the
Trystan ac Essyllt. I turn aside for a brief consideration of
this drawing because it seems to show the very birth of an
idea, the seed from which a final work springs. Out of a
swirl of lines, sea birds fly swooping round the lovers.
Trystan looks down into the cup for there in it he can
already see what the future holds for them both. His hair is
already enmeshed by the swirl of Essyllt's hair. The cup,
Trystan's sword and his arm linking with that of Essyllt
emerge as though out of chaos.

Turning again to the Annunciation we find Mary
sitting in a field by a stream under a tump of the Daren
Llwyd range where David Jones walked when he was
working with Eric Gill. She is a crowned queen. It is she to
whom Villon's mother prayed as

Dame du ciel, regente terrienne
Emperiere des infernaux palus.

She is also Eve, the mother of all living, for she still holds
in her hand the apple whose eating brought us knowledge of
good and evil. Beside her on the fence sits the owl, for she
is also Minerva, the seat of, and as she was for Botticelli,
the embodiment of Divine Wisdom, *Sedes Sapientiae*.
Furthermore, in less time than it takes to write one word we
can, looking at the imagery of the painting, know that this
Queen has her place in Celtic myth under yet other names.
Rhiannon may originally have meant Great Queen. We are
told that the singing birds of Rhiannon, who here surround
her on the wing or sit perched on the wattle fence, would
bring sleep to the living and awaken the dead. The wattle
fence is the *bangor* which in olden times was put round
religious communities in Wales and also, as sign of Mary's
virginity, the enclosure of the garden, the *hortus conclusus*.
When Manawydan and Pryderi were staying at Harlech with
the head of Bran, on their way to the White Mount in
London, the birds of Rhiannon sang to them. Concerning the
foxglove which Rhiannon/Mary holds in her hand--"as near
as you could find to a lily in the top end of a valley in the

Black Mountains"--David Jones has much to say in a letter
of 14 October 1972:

> ...as this Annunciation is in an upland setting in Wales, I thought,
> well, the fleur-de-luce or lis, what you will, would hardly seem to fit
> that wild tir-y-blaenau and certainly not lend aid to my idea of what
> was most typic of the site intended yet sufficiently 'lily-like in
> form to keep within the iconographic tradition.'

This then is one reason why he gives her a foxglove and in
his poem "The Sleeping Lord" he describes the very place
where the Virgin Mary must have picked the flower:

<pre>
                              in the leafy hollow
                              below the bare *rhiw*
        where the sparse hill-flora
                              begins to thicken
        by the rushing *nant* where the elders grow
        and the talled-stemmed *ffion*
                              put on the purple
        to outbright the green gossamer fronds
        of the spume-born maiden's hair. *(SL, 73)*
</pre>

Searching further concerning this foxglove-*ffion*, we
find that in the oldest story concerning Arthur in the
Mabinogion the girl whose cheek was redder than the
reddest foxglove is Olwen. So she too is here recalled, no
doubt because to win her Culhwch had difficulties far
beyond the thorns through which another hero broke to
reach his bride. Culhwch was a cousin of Arthur and asked
the King for his help and that of his warriors to obtain
Olwen, whose father, Yspaddaden Penkawr, told Culhwch
that he could have Olwen if he could accomplish tasks
culminating in getting the comb and scissors which were
between the ears of the Twrch Trwyth, the hog who laid
waste lands in Ireland, Wales and Cornwall. Of each task
Culhwch is told: "Though thou get this there is yet that
which thou wilt not get." It is only the hunter Mabon who
can tell how to hunt Twrch Trwyth; so to find Mabon they
ask first the Ousel of Cilgwri who, for the sake of Arthur,
guides them to the stag of Rhedynfre, who sends them to the
place where is the Owl of Cwm Cawlwyd, who has never
heard of the man for whom they are enquiring but guides
them to the oldest animal in the world, the Eagle of
Gwernabwy, who has heard once of the man when he struck
his claws into the Salmon of Llyn Llyw. This salmon takes
two of them, Arthur's knights, on his shoulders to Gloucester
where they find Mabon in prison. Arthur returns home and
Mabon the hunter with him at liberty. In the poem "The
Hunt" in *The Sleeping Lord*, David Jones tells how Arthur

opposed the Hog "life for life." But in this picture it is enough for us to know that after they had accomplished all the marvels, and had got the comb and scissors, Yspaddaden Penkawr said to Culhwch, "She is thine." In the picture, surrounding her, we find the animals assembled because of the part they had played.

On the sides of the hills behind Mary there are remains of Druidic association, but behind Gabriel there is such a broken column as to tell us that the bearer of the sword is Roman. Of the sword Simeon the priest had said to Mary, "Yea, a sword shall pierce through thine own soul also." The wolf who lies at Mary's feet, she too is Roman. She is the ravaging beast who, finding the baby sons of Mars, Romulus and Remus, abandoned, took them to her den on the Palatine. In the painting she, who suckles the sons of the god of war, lies still at Mary's feet. The bearer of the sword is the guide to souls and messenger of the god Mercury, for there are birds about his head and feet, and along his sword runs the light from the planet Jupiter.

Concerning the constellations of Virgo and Libra seen in the sky above Gabriel and Mary it is well to quote what David Jones himself writes in his *Introduction to the Rime of the Ancient Mariner*. After explaining that the word *statera* is used of the beam of the Cross, but is primarily a "steelyard" and so a *libra* or "scales," he goes on:

> Should we so choose we can regard as a Sign of the Cross the Constellation of Libra which is in fixed juxtaposition next the Constellation of Virgo,... which... can hardly fail to remind us that according to the Fourth Gospel there stood, next the Cross, the Mother. (*DG*, 221-22)

He further explains that while *statera* was primarily used of that weighing instrument, it was also used of the value or worth of anything, so "the word evokes the beam that made possible the restoration of the equilibrium of all creation and also the price, paid once for all" (*DG*, 222).

Memory gets sadly diluted with time so that, even if one has at one time known the events mythical or historical to which David Jones refers, they nevertheless act with fresh vigor when they are told again in these pictures and inscription. Moreover, although the words "sheepfold," "hawk" or "heron" may evoke in the mind's eye a vague image of the thing named, the bird, stream, animal or grassy hill that David Jones makes with pencil and pigment stands forth for us with extraordinary clarity and meaning. The clarity is of a thing seen in a state of wrapt awareness, the meaning is that by which all things are related and, as it were, tied up. Words cannot convey what one sees by looking at this meeting of angel and woman.

David Jones in *Epoch and Artist* reminds us that, "For the artist the thing called 'the past' is very much what the thing called 'nature' is for him, viz--something which he 'recalls', 'represents' and 'discovers' " (*E&A*, 139). We who meditate on a story or event which he has recalled in one of his works find further that no story is the same for us after a lapse of time, for we who read it are not the same interpreter. The interpreting is often difficult. He makes us dig for the treasure. But perhaps it is not only the painter and poet, but also we who think about their works, who may claim, "difficulty is our plough."

PAUL HILLS

"THE PIERCED HERMAPHRODITE":
DAVID JONES' IMAGERY OF THE CRUCIFIXION

The reenactment of Christ's sacrifice on Calvary in the ritual of the Mass was the essential mystery of which, ultimately, all David Jones' art was a celebration and reconnaissance. To readers of his poetry this is well known. What
is less often acknowledged is that his preoccupations as a
poet were nearly all adumbrated in his visual art, usually
two or three decades in advance.

The crux of history is the Crucifixion: the crux of
David Jones' life, his service in the Great War. To the soldiers who fought in that war the Passion of Christ was frequently brought to mind, not least by the wayside Calvaries
of Flanders, which, as Robert Graves testifies, aroused "a
sympathetic reverence for Jesus our fellow-sufferer."[1] To
those who advanced into No-man's-land, it must have
seemed as if they had shared in the harrowing of Hell. Yet
though David Jones knew intimately the sacrifices made by
the front fighters, British and German, and although he him-
self--like Aphrodite--was wounded in the leg, he understood
things differently. He did not presume to draw an exact
parallel between the pains he and his fellows suffered, and
those endured by Christ in his Passion.

It was on the Western Front, place of perturbation
and enchantment, that he first saw, through a chink in the
wall of a byre, a Roman Catholic Mass. Other witnesses
might have been attracted only by the priest and the ritual
at the altar, whereas Private Jones' eye encompassed the
soldiers too. And from soldiers attending Mass his thoughts
were to turn--time and again in succeeding decades--to
those soldiers of mixed recruitment who, nearly two millennia earlier, were detailed to carry out the orders of Pontius
Pilate on the hill of Golgotha.

---

1. See Paul Fussell, *The Great War and Modern Memory* (Oxford: Oxford University
Press, 1975), p. 119.

Soon after demobilization he started work on a Crucifixion. To judge from several oil sketches and squared
drawings, all of which remained in his possession until his
death and are now in the archives of the Tate Gallery, this
was to have been an ambitious work. The best preserved of
the squared drawings (fig. 11) is painstakingly drawn in the
rather unprepossessing manner of illustrators to Henty. The
artist has envisaged the Crucifixion from the matter-of-fact
perspective of an infantryman with a job to do. In this
modern-dress execution there is no sign of angels, and the
front stage is dominated by tin-helmeted soldiers who dice
for the robe of Christ. (I suspect that David Jones had
already taken to heart the Crucifixion by Tintoretto in the
Scuola di San Rocco. In that vast work the dice playing and
the physical exertions of the soldiers are given great promi-
nence. Since I well remember how David Jones' face would
light up at the mention of Tintoretto, it was no surprise to
find a photograph of the Venetian Crucifixion tucked
amongst his early portfolios. Another early and sustained
influence was surely Mantegna. Jones would have admired
Mantegna's historical imagination, in particular his attention to the role of Roman soldiers in the Gospel narratives.)

It is not hard to see why the first project for a Crucifixion was abandoned. Jones' borrowed illlustrator's style is
too prosaic to accommodate ambiguity. Though the
infantryman's perspective foreshadows the meditations on
the Passion of twenty to forty years later, notably "The
Fatigue," the irony that sustains the written works is missing
here. Yet one detail is prophetic: the two soldiers closest to
us, far from being silent witnesses, are engaged in animated
discussion. Their words will take shape as the monologues
and dialogues of the "Roman" poems.

When David Jones went to work with Eric Gill at
Ditchling in 1921 his style was purged of its disturbingly literal quality. He continued to draw scenes from the Passion,
such as *Christ before Pilate* and *Jesus Mocked*, but the
allusions to modern dress are contained within a radically
simplified style akin to the idiom of Gill's contemporary
reliefs of the Stations of the Cross for Westminster Cathedral. Jones' interpretations differ from Gill's in the accent
he gives to the soldiers. Often they wear the tin helmet of
the Tommy. In the panel painted for the chapel at Ditchling, *Jesus Mocked*, soldiers dance around the Man of Sor-
rows, and one, the Longinus of the scene, drops on one knee

as if his mocking had turned to reverent genuflection.[2] The one image speaks of aggression and of love, contraries we shall meet again in David Jones' mature work. By means of such ambivalence we come to understand that the soldiers who inflict pain on their victim, and finally execute him, are typical of all mankind--responsible through their sins for the Passion yet given the hope thereby of redemption. In these early studies we discern the germ of an intuition, developed more fully later, that the soldiers who officiate at Calvary are akin to the very first priests officiating at Mass, and that soldiers, like priests, by participating in the sacrifice are identified with the victim. Where roles are interchangeable, the saucer helmet may take on a halo's gleam.

In 1924 Jones followed Gill and his family to Capel-y-ffin in the Black Mountains of Wales. There he painted several Crucifixes; one as a mural on the walls of the former monastery in which they lived, now sadly flaked, and another as a tiny gouache, which he inscribed *Sanctus Christus de Capel-y-ffin* (fig. 13). The gouache presents an image of wooden simplicity, not so much a picture of the Crucifixion as a rough-hewn wayside shrine. By distancing his work from realism, Jones uncovers signs: the limbs of Christ are like the branches of the Cross, and both are evidently lopped from the trees on the mountainsides. To one who had walked between the splintered boughs of No-man's-land, trees were to become a potent sign. Many years later he will put into the mouth of a legionary who had served in the northern borders of Roman Britain this reminiscence in which the shivering of timber is likened to the breaking of the Host in the Mass:

> Once, after a night of tempest, of wind of gale strength, my cohort was held up for many hours, for right across the *agger* that carried a half-laid *via*, a great *ulmus*, rotten within, had tangled in its fall a fair flexing fraxinus, and snapped it right at the middle bole, as though some still small voice unheard for the crowing of wind and weather had from outside time quietly commanded, *frangit per medium*. The sound of that rending is with me yet: the gods alone know why, for often enough I have heard the curious cleavage-cry of breaking living timber. (*RQ*, 66)

Rather than wearing the traditionl loin cloth, the Christ of Capel is swathed in a long skirt, as in certain Romanesque crucifixes, such as the Volto Santo at Lucca. Perhaps this was chosen to give him greater dignity and so

---

2. Illustrated in *David Jones*, Catalogue of the Exhibition at the Tate Gallery, London, 1981, p. 80.

as to remind us of the garb of the priest who will take his place at the altar. Our poet will refer to priests as "the men in skirts."

David Jones loved the tumbling streams, freshets and waterfalls of Capel. When he set his Crucifix not on a hill, as would be appropriate to Golgotha, but in the valley, lapped by the rushing waters of the Honddu brook, he was following instincts that will run deep. In Part VI of *The Anathemata* he will meditate on how the wood of the Cross will furnish the principal timbers--keel, ram and stauros--of the vessel of salvation, the universal church: already at Capel he points to this metamorphosis by siting a chapel near the Crucifix, as a local and visible token of the spiritual Church, come to rest here like an ark, or upturned *navis*, on the Welsh hillside. Lest we miss the link between Crucifix and Church, the chapel is topped by a large cross.

In the mid to late 1920s water pervaded David Jones' art. He painted the sea when he stayed on Caldy Island (Ynys Byr) in Wales, and again at Portslade, near Brighton. Water flows through the narrative and symbolism of the books he chose to illustrate: in 1927, the *Book of Jonah* and the *Chester Play of the Deluge*; in 1928-9, Coleridge's *Rime of the Ancient Mariner*. In the second of the Ancient Mariner engravings (fig. 16) he likened the death of the immaculate Albatross to the sacrifice of Christ by showing the bird impaled by the Mariner's arrow to the crossing of the yard and mast. The act of wounding is engraved with precision and beauty: the arrow, central to the design, pierces the bird's breast and provokes a spurt of blood. To the pointed instruments of wounding, the makers of stigmata, whether arrows or spears--or the graver, burin or pencil wielded by the artist--I shall have cause to return.

Coleridge's mariners, becalmed when the Albatross was crucified, were set free by the rebirth of love. The same theme of release from becalment and sterility is treated in David Jones' unfinished wood-engraving, *He Frees the Waters* (fig. 18). A glance back at *Sanctus Christus* reveals that the Unicorn is kin to the pony that grazes to the right of the Crucifix, and that this pony, like the chapel on the left, may be read as in some way Christ in sign. It is characteristic of Jones' imagination to reconcile such oppositions as nature and culture, the world of creatures and of artefacts. For Freud the horse is a preeminent symbol of male sexuality, while for Jung it symbolizes psychic energy in general. Both readings find some support in the myth of the Unicorn, the fabulous beast that could only be tamed by

a virgin. Since the Middle Ages, the Unicorn had been
taken as a type for the Messiah born of a Virgin. In Jones'
haunting engraving the Unicorn is seen against the wasted
land of broken walls, trees that bear no fruit, and cattle
without calf. Over this darkened world a bright star has
risen, its rays beaming down the horn with which the Unicorn stirs the waters and so fructifies the land. To the right,
flowers bloom. Below the Unicorn a large chalice or grail
stands on what may be a ruckled cloth, a reference to the
linen corporal. Two of the instruments of Christ's Passion,
the spear and sponge, stand aslant within the chalice; this
recalls the scene in Book XVII of *Morte d'Arthur* where
Galahad and his companions saw "the holy spear even
upright upon the vessel."[3] According to Jessie Weston, whose
From Ritual to Romance Jones had read shortly before he
started his engraving, the lance of the Grail story originally
had nothing to do with the lance with which Longinus
pierced Christ's side, but was an emblem of phallic potency,
just as the cup originally signified the uterine resources of
the female. We know from Jones' annotations to Weston--his
copy is in the National Library of Wales--that he disagreed
with this separation of meanings, therefore we can presume
he had the sexual archetypes *and* the Christian symbols in
mind when he replicated the virile thrust of the horn in that
of the lance. Like the poet's rhyme, the artist's design sparks
connections that reach beyond his conscious intent, yet in
which he realizes his meaning. Time and again in Jones'
art, instruments of procreation and instruments of wounding
--guns, stick bombs, knives, lances, nails and fluked spears--
appear interchangeable in a kind of visual naming of parts.
Of *He Frees the Waters* it might be said that both the horn
and the lance induce, eventually, a freeing or breaking of
waters, the one of the waters that first support life, the
waters of the womb, the other of the waters essential to
rebirth into eternal life, the water and blood that flowed
from the wound in Christ's side. To state the parallel so
boldly may be to distort the artist's intent. It was only in
1943 that he wrote to a friend, "I've only just tumbled to the
simple scientific fact that 'water' is the womb of all life--
and of the simplest organisms--well that thrilled me no end
--no wonder baptism is by water. . ." (*DGC*, 122).
    In the engraving of the Unicorn the lance is crossed
by the stick bearing a sponge. Some twenty years after it

3. Thomas Malory, *Le Morte d'Arthur*, Bk XVII, Ch. xx. Jones used the Everyman edition, ed. J. Rhys, London, 1906; his annotated copy in the National Library of Wales is
inscribed "1929."

was engraved, *He Frees the Waters* was inserted in the final
part of *The Anathemata*, "Sherthursdaye and Venus Day." In
this meditation on the events of Maundy Thursday and Good
Friday the poet circles round the symbolism of water as
primary sign of the Redeemer, alternately recalling Christ
as divine maker of signs, their *fons et origo*, and Christ as
incarnate man, involved in the very substance of signs, as
when in his mother's womb--

> her federal waters ark'd him. (*A*, 235).

At its climax, the imagery of the psalmist prepares us for
Christ's ejaculation on the Cross, "I thirst":

> As the bleat of the spent stag
> > toward the river-course
> he, the *fons*-head
> > pleading, *ad fontes*
> his desiderate cry:
> > SITIO. (*A*, 237)

The same word, *Sitio*, dominates an inscription which is
reproduced in this section of *The Anathemata*. The sponge
soaked in vinegar, which would hardly quench the
Redeemer's thirst, is then one of the meaningful signs of our
artist and poet.

Substitute Christ for the Unicorn, candles for stars,
and *He Frees the Waters* is transposed into *Tywysog Cariad*
(fig. 15). Here only the pencilled ghost of the sponge on a
stick remains to foil the lance, for this Christ is more the
Lord who feeds than the man who thirsts. In the artist's
words, *Tywysog Cariad* is an "unfinished study for a proposed work illustrating the Oblation and Immolation of the
Cross and of the Altar in a Welsh hill-setting." The title is
Welsh for "Prince of Love," and the superscription on the
Cross reads *Brenhnu Cariad*, "King of Love." This is the
young king, prince or hero who reigns from the Tree, as
described in *The Dream of the Rood*, the great Anglo-Saxon
poem of which Jones will write, "It's glorious . . . when the
Cross speaks about the weight of the hero and how the hero
and the wood were bound together" (*DGC*, 122). Beyond the
Dream, the source for the intertwining of Crucified and
Cross in nuptial embrace is to be found in the scriptural
images of Christ as bridegroom, such as that of Psalm 19:15.
"He is as a bridegroom coming out of his chamber, and
rejoiceth as a strongman to run his race."

The prince and bridegroom of *Tywysog Cariad* is
alive, his fingers raised in blessing. His stigmata are radiant

like the jewels that stud mediaeval roods, and they call to
mind the imagery of the *Dream*--

> Gems gleamed
> Fair at the earth's four corners, and five there were
> High on the cross-beam.[4]

As in Jones' wood-engraving, *The Bride*,[5] candles are lit
(three for the Trinity?), for this is a marriage feast, and
there needs must be--in the words of the title of one of his
watercolors--a candle for the cup. Many times will our poet
contrast the darkness of Calvary, the tenebrae of the Good
Friday office, with the "lit board" that first furnished the
Upper Room, and later every apse and chancel. And in *The
Sleeping Lord*, a poem set in the same Welsh hill-country
as *Tywysog Cariad*, a paean will be sung to the candle--

> that flames upward
> in perfection of form
> like the leaf-shaped war-heads
> that gleam from the long-hafted spears
> of the lord's body-guard--

as "One of the Three Primary Signa of the Son of Mary"
(*SL*, 77). Note, incidentally, how the poet's simile of spear-
point and candle-flame depends upon the draughtsman's
delight in analogies of shape. I suspect that few Christians
have imagined any parallel between candles and an instrument of wounding such as a lance or nail, yet when David
Jones kissed a votive candle and impaled it on a spiked
hearse or harrow, with which Roman Catholic churches are
furnished, the action, intimate and tender yet with a hint of
violence, tangibly recalled the impaling of the Son of Mary
on the Cross. In *Tywysog Cariad*, Mary the Bride--who also
will be gladius-pierced--is present as the crescent moon that
appears to move, as if drawn towards Christ, the Sun.

   In the 1920s David Jones was exposed to the sculpture and engravings of Eric Gill. Their erotic blend of carnal and religious feeling did not go unnoticed. Like Gill,
Jones loved to describe the roundness of a mother's breast as
a dominant shape in his designs. In a number of his drawings, engravings, and miniature boxwood carvings, the
Madonna bares her breast to feed her child. Jean Fouquet's
Madonna of Etienne Chevalier, in which the fulness of the
breast was revealed in all its splendour, was ever one of his
favourite paintings. Referring to it by the name of the

4. Translation by J. A. W. Bennett, *Poetry of the Passion* (Oxford: Oxford University Press, 1982), p. 27.
5. Illustrated in *David Jones* (Tate Gallery), p. 76.

artist's model--as if to accent the synthesis of portrait and icon--he observed

> In Fouquet's *Agnes Sorel as Our Lady* ... he does somehow manage to make of the French king's mistress a *theotokos.* And certainly not by muting the superficial attractiveness of the physical and bodily, that is there, candid enough and almost overpowering, but more powerful still, he gets the solemnity and nobility of the 'subject' in its more profound sense, and all in terms of the painter's art and unified by splendour of form" (*DG*, 141).

An altogether more risqué fusion of the spiritual and sexual than Fouquet's was made by Gill in his engraving of 1923, *The Nuptials of God.* In this a naked woman is shown embracing--and apparently at one with--Christ on the Cross. Compared to this, Jones' engraving of the *Crucifixion* (fig. 14), of 1926, may appear unexceptionable, yet I believe it shows that, like Gill, he was embarking on a quest for an image of the wounded God that would adequately encompass the feminine as well as the masculine. Thanks to an unusually short cross, the Virgin and Mary Magdalen get close to Christ's body and embrace it ardently. Instead of kissing his feet, Mary Magdalen throws her head right into his lap. Her passion is as uninhibited here as in a *Lamentation* (fig. 12), drawn by Jones in the early 1920s, in which she presses her face against the body of her Lord to kiss the wound in his side. As for the Virgin in the Crucifixion, the breast that once fed the child is now pressed against the man. Her hand is raised to caress, and her eyes meet Christ's in a mutual gaze that leaves no doubt that--in the words that open "Sherthursdaye and Venus Day"--

> He that was her son
> is now her lover .... (*A*, 224)

On the right, the pelican in her piety pecks her breast to feed her young, a traditional figure for Christ's sacrificial offering of himself. David Jones used this image as tail-piece to the Ancient Mariner. In the context of this Crucifixion it reminds us of the mother/child bond now so poignantly transformed.

On the left, pendant to the pelican, a tree grows sinuously, in contrast to the rectilinear carpentry of the Cross. To tie down its meaning would be a mistake; it is not attached to it like a label; it wells up from its place in the composition. It is eloquent of organic life, especially of the issue of trunk from roots, and of branch from trunk. Whether an allusion to the messianic prophecy of Isaiah 11:1, "And there shall come forth a rod out of the stem of Jesse, and a Branch shall grow out of his roots," is intended, I cannot

tell. Certainly, the tree echoes and substantiates the joining
of the Lovers with their Beloved: its lopped branches speak
of the pain of separation, the drooping, of death and sorrow.
Yet as branch grows from trunk, Son and Mother are dependent one upon the other. So the single image comprehends
birth and death, a Blakean marriage of contraries which
only a great and humble artist achieves.

The engraving displays a text, UBI CARITAS ET
AMOR DEUS IBI EST, "Where there is Charity and Love,
God is there." In a conventional Crucifixion this would refer
exclusively to the Son of God's love in laying down his life
for mankind. Here it suggests that love between human
beings is also an incarnation of divine love.

In 1927 David Jones' engagement to Eric Gill's
daughter Petra was broken. In the following years, through
his thirties and forties, he made many images of bride and
groom, feeder and fed, wounder and wounded. The relationships of lover to beloved became more troubled, the symbolism more recondite. From 1932 onwards he was plagued
by nervous illness. In 1937 his mother died. Increasingly, he
lived on his own--in the late 1930s embattled in his seaside
retreat, the Fort Hotel in Sidmouth.

It was at Sidmouth in Devon, in the difficult years of
the late 1930s, that Jones' imagination fastened upon the
Arthurian figure of Launcelot. Through that most paradoxical of Grail heroes, flawed by his adultery yet marked as a
type for Christ, he reached a deeper understanding of the
Crucifixion. In his writings at this time, particularly those
only published posthumously in *The Roman Quarry*, sexual
and Christian imagery are frankly entwined. As a poet and
an artist he was searching, and he realized that to succeed
in his quest he would have to forsake the known paths. He
could not trust even the hard-won disciplines of his art; he
had to enter the labyrinth:

> No Lancelot no! you must be lost before you find the cornucopia, the
> lamb that bleeds beyond the double guard of Guenever within the vaginal
> traverses ... You must be lost, and the Roman way is to be certain of
> one's bearings. (*RQ*, 182)

From the sexual allegory of *Morte d'Arthur* grew
the major work of 1940, *Aphrodite in Aulis* (fig. 4). At first
sight this drawing baffles by its complexity: once we recognize the inherent clue that its format is that of a Crucifixion we are on the road to understanding. We soon realize
that the Tommy on the left bears the lance of Longinus, and
that Aphrodite, like Christ on the Cross, is at once victim of

sacrifice and object of worship. Like Christ, she draws all men unto her. The necessary theological connection between the institution of the Eucharist and the Passion of Christ, upon which Jones laid such emphasis, is expressed in bodily image by the juxtaposition of the *Agnus Dei* beneath the goddess. That a Mass is in progress is implied by the presence of the vested priest who censes the altar.

Yet this priest takes second place to the soldiers in an inversion of functions that recalls the Welsh proverb cited by Jones in his essay "Art in Relation to War"--

> Here is a mystery which never shall cease
> The priest promotes war and the soldier, peace. (*DG*, 147)

The soldier's warlike art is converted into a parade of lovers, in which the man in the skirt can only play a minor part. The British soldier on the left, and the German on the right, identified by his helmet, the stick bombs tucked into his belt and the *fasces*--the Roman insignia of the fascist-- upon his arm, are united as suppliants of the goddess. Their love is at once sacred and profane, for Aphrodite, like the Romans' Flora, is both goddess and courtesan.

From the artist's letters we know her first profession was courtesan. In June 1940 he wrote, "I'm doing a picture of Phryne the hetaira and the sum of all beauty, who showed her splendours to the Court . . . and so impressed them that they said she was innocent" (*DGC*, 98). Two months later he reported: "Still trying to do my picture of Phryne--hope it gets done. I've made her a nice girl--it is an interesting picture to do" (*DGC*, 106).

Though--according to Lemprière--the Phryne who unveiled her bosom to her judges was a different courtesan from the Phryne who was model and mistress to the sculptor Praxiteles, David Jones almost certainly had both in mind. Praxiteles' statue of Phryne was set up in the temple at Delphi; Apelles, it is said, painted his Venus Anadyomene after he had seen Phryne naked on the sea shore, her hair dishevelled. David Jones would have been attracted to these stories for the same reason that he was fascinated by Fouquet's painting of the French king's mistress as Our Lady: they exemplified the lesson that our apprehension of the sacred and universal is mediated by the bodily and particu- lar. In our quest for the sacred we do not leave the bodily behind. That carnal and spiritual desires are not opposed is the theme of the section of *The Anathemata* entitled, "The Lady of the Pool." The reason that David Jones found *Aphrodite* "an interesting picture to do" was that in the process of its making--in the relation of the artist to his model --a quest for redemption was enacted. Unlike Fouquet, Apelles and Praxiteles, Jones did not work directly from a model or a mistress, but his drawing is autobiographical in its exploration of his own perplexities with regard to women. The Tommy on the left stands, in a sense, for the artist himself. His helmet is camouflaged with flowers, a bouquet for Aphrodite; his lance, so threateningly sharp, carries the potency of the sexual archetype--its point thrusting close to the *Agelastos Petra*, the cleft stone set in the hillside as symbol of the female organ. Once again, Jones' obsessive equation of weapon and phallus is unavoidable, and demands explanation.

Our best starting point is Freud's *Totem and Taboo*.[6] Taking our cue from this classic study, we may begin to understand why Jones replaced the male on the Cross by the female Aphrodite. Freud argues that a child's relations to its parents are dominated by incestuous longings, and so for the male child the father is an obstacle to the fulfillment of his desire and the attainment of his manhood. In primitive societies the ritual sacrifice of a totem animal is a substitute for the murder of the father. Freud explains how the introduction of agriculture transformed the mythic relation of the male to his mother:

> He ventured upon new demonstrations of his incestuos libido, which found symbolic satisfaction in his cultivation of Mother Earth. Divine figures such as Attis, Adonis and Tammuz emerged, spirits of vegetation and at the same time youthful divinities enjoying the favors of the mother goddesses and committing incest with their mother in defiance of their father. But the sense of guilt, which was not allayed by these creations, found expression in myths which granted only short lives to these youthful favorites of the mother godesses and decreed their punishment by emasculation or by the wrath of the father in the form of an animal. Adonis was killed by a wild boar, the sacred animal of Aphrodite; Attis, beloved of Cybele, perished by castration. The mourning for these gods and the rejoicings over their resurrection passed over into the ritual of another son-deity who was destined to lasting success.[7]

Jones did not read *Totem and Taboo* until some years after he had drawn *Aphrodite in Aulis*,[8] but he was well versed in Freud's major source on myth and ritual, Frazer's *Golden Bough*. So it may not be too far-fetched to suggest that the young ram beneath Aphrodite's feet, while

6. First published in 1913; reissued in *The Complete Psychological Works*, XIII, (London, 1953).
7. *Ibid.*, pp. 152-3.
8. Thomas Dilworth, "Sex and the Goddess in the Poetry of David Jones," *University of Toronto Quarterly*, 54 (1985), p. 261.

ostensibly the Agnus Dei of Christian iconography--the
innocent son whose foretype was Isaac--as totem animal,
stands, in psychological terms, for the father. This father,
ritually slain, allows the sons to become lovers of their
mother. Yet so strong is the original force of the incest
taboo that an emotional ambivalence endures. What is
remarkable about *Aphrodite in Aulis* is that the artist has
embraced and offered up this ambivalence. There is no
shame, and no attempt to disguise. The ambivalence is
integral to the subject and to the emotions of the draughtsman. Certainly the artist intended to indicate that the soldiers are the lovers--or would-be-lovers--of Aprhrodite or
Phryne; how far he realized that their gestures and weapons
imply that their desire is bedfellow to aggression and fear is
open to conjecture. If it is the artist's *alter ego* who carries
the lance that doubles as cupid's arrow, the implications are
reminiscent of the myth of Pygmalion.

Ovid tells the story of the sculptor who had resolved
never to marry. One day he fell in love with his own statue
of a woman, and Venus answered his prayers by transforming
it into flesh and blood. David Jones' *Aphrodite* is both
statue, cracked like marble, and living flesh. Praxiteles
transformed Phryne into a marble goddess fit for a temple:
this goddess may be transformed into a courtesan. Which
way the metamorphosis--the transubstantiation--may go is
open, and the artist evidently relished this state of flux.
Jones made frequent play in his writings of such surrealist
metamorphoses as flesh into marble, and marble into flesh:
in *The Dream of Private Clitus*, a prose poem, which, like
Aphrodite was conceived in the aftermath of his mother's
death, a statue of a mother goddess, *Tellus Mater*, comes to
life in a soldier's dream. The change from marble into flesh
may be a metaphor, perhaps subliminal, for bringing the
dead back to life, the resurrection of the body.

The artistic significance of the story of Pygmalion
has been elucidated by E.H. Gombrich in his study of the
psychology of pictorial representation. "Without the underlying promise of this myth, the secret hopes and fears that
accompany the act of creation, there might be no art as we
know it." And later in the same chapter of *Art and Illusion*
Gombrich reminds us: "There are stories all over the world
of images that had to be chained to prevent their moving of
their own accord and of artists who had to refrain from
putting the finishing touch to their painting to prevent the

images coming to life."[9] Seen in this light, the mighty
chain that belays the goddess to the altar of sacrifice seems
doubly necessary. Unlike Pygmalion, David Jones, one may
intuit, fears as well as desires that this all-powerful, fecund
mother-goddess may burst into life. This Aphrodite, towering over the puny soldiers, drawn from no mortal viewpoint,
is dangerous. We get a clue as to the reason why in the
final pages of *In Parenthesis*. There the poet describes the
slaughter on the fields of Flanders in terms of an ironic
equation between violent death and the sexual act:

> But sweet sister death has gone debauched today and stalks on this high
> ground with strumpet confidence, makes no coy veiling of her appetite
> but leers from you to me with all her parts discovered.
> By one and one the line gaps, where her fancy will--howsoever they
> may howl for their virginity
> she holds them--who impinge less on space.... (*IP*, 162)

To enjoy the goddess' embraces is to be received
into the bosom of mother earth and to share in the redemptive sacrifice of the sacred victim. At the close of *In
Parenthesis*, when battle is done, the Queen of the Woods
"has cut bright boughs of various flowering" which she
awards to the soldiers who strew the field. Doubtless these
bright boughs are the Golden Bough of Vergilian fame, that
will see them safely across the waters of death. In
Aphrodite in Aulis, the German's rifle is bursting into leaf--
his rod, like Aaron's, is budding--and in that bough, sacred
wood of the Redeemer's Cross, lies his hope of salvation.

At one level, then, the drawing commemorates the
soldiers of Britain and Germany who were at that moment
dying in battle. At another level it reveals the primal anxi-
eties of the artist. In 1947, soon after he had read *Totem and
Taboo*, Jones reported, in a note for his doctor, that his
painting of *Aphrodite* was "considered not psychologically
balanced"; and later in the same note he admitted that as a
result of psychotherapy, "I understand far better the ramifications of the sexual impulse and how the fear of assuming
the 'father figure' position works in the most unexpected
conjunctions, and I see how all my life I've avoided such a
position in innumerable and subtle ways" (*DGC*,
140).Though the ram beneath Aphrodite may be slain, the
soldiers are doomed to remain suppliants rather than attain-
ing to fatherhood.

We may add here an insight derived from Melanie
Klein's analysis of the psychology of children. Every infant

9. London, 1959, pp. 80 and 94.

loves to play Bo-peep. For the adult such games of concealing and revealing are ritualized in the theatre, or at least
they were until directors and designers decided that we
must leave behind such childish tricks as proscenium arches,
flats and curtains. Klein argues that the first performance
we ever attended was, in a sense, parental coitus, and that
our voyeuristic fascination with curtains goes back to our
infantile experience of bedclothes, not only our own but
also those of our parents. But since that first performance is
attended illicitly, barely glimpsed and half-concealed, it
deposits a primal anxiety in the psyche of the child. To
look behind the curtain is fraught with danger.

In all his art, whether painting or poetry, David
Jones loved the theatrical play of concealing and revealing. Time and again, from the weather of Britain, its mists,
showers, sudden shafts of sunlight, the spray of its seas and
the waves of its rivers, he weaves similes of curtains, veils,
clothes and hair. Curtains, as light and gauzy as petticoats,
flutter and dance at the margins of his watercolors. Like the
veil of the temple that was rent in twain when Christ died
on the Cross, these curtains appear strangely agitated. They
are animated by the breath of a spirit, a *pneuma*. In *Curtained Outlook*, a watercolor of 1932, one diaphanous curtain
drifts across the center of the window, veiling the distance
and drawing it mysteriously close within its folds.

Aphrodite in Aulis is a theatrical performance with
spectators included in the show:

> The salutary spectacle is, in the first instance, seen of the soldiers,
> as is proper.
> Beggar man,
>   thief,
>   rich man, and if
> priests dare look, for them also beauty on five hooks discovers herself,
> the sum of Aphrodite and the wounded Eros, the pierced
> Hermaphrodite. (*RQ*, 175)

What the priests barely dare look at, and the soldiers only
by a furtive sideways glance, is the tabernacle of the living
god with its curtain blown aside--the shift of Aphrodite/
Phryne in disarray, leaving "all her parts discovered."

A metamorphosis far more strange than that worked
on Phryne by Praxiteles may be perceived in David Jones'
Aphrodite: in the buxom lineaments of the goddess of love
we may discern the figure of the chaste Virgin. In the
engraved *Crucifixion* of 1926 the Virgin was identified with
Christ as co-redemptress by means of the embrace and
mutual lovers' gaze. In this disguised Crucifixion of 1940,

David Jones refers back to the first union of male and female in God's scheme for the redemption of the world, namely the moment of Christ's conception in the Virgin's womb. The moon above the goddess' head and the stars in her hair are attributes of the Madonna of the Apocalypse. Though the birds may allude to the doves sacred to Aphrodite, from one a radiance shines down in token of Annunciation. And it was at that first moment of the Incarnation that Mary became *Ecclesia*, the House of the Lord, even as here Aphrodite is properly identified with the sacred enclosure, the *temenos*, of which she is the central column of breathing marble. Once again we see the recurring patterns in Jones' images: the ionic temple to the left of Aphrodite has taken the place of the chapel of *Sanctus Christus de Capel-y-ffin.*

The identification of the cult figure and the sacred building is rephrased in David Jones' greatest drawing on the mystery of the Crucifixion, *Vexilla Regis* of 1947 (fig. 5). Whereas in the earlier works Christ was likened to the tree, Aphrodite to the column, now the Prince and his Rood have become one, a mighty tree, which, like the Yggdrasil of Northern mythology, reaches from earth to heaven. And just as Aphrodite was encircled by the columns of the temple, the Vexilla Regis is set within a grove. This wood foretokens the Gothic churches of the north, like the wood in which Private Clitus dreamed of the mother goddess:

> And where we lay it was as if we lay in a kind of peristyle, builded of the tall trees, deep within the shadowy labyrinth of those woods. Long corridors of arches stretched all ways. Smooth, straight boles those trees had, and no low growth with the sward beneath each as it were like a pavement. And it was as if the rounded arches of our basilicas were suddenly to bestir themselves and the genius of each column to exert itself and reach across toward the numen of the column opposite. For all is thrusting and directional in the labyrinth of those parts and each swaying limb of each tree struggles for the mastery, high up. (*SL*, 16)

What Clitus prophetically envisages is a transubstantiation of tree into pier and arch, wood into stone--the reverse of the transubstantiation of the marble of *Tellus Mater* into a mother's flesh and blood.

Some critics, particularly literary ones, have laid stress on David Jones' theological and philosophical reading, notably of the works of Maritain and Maurice de la Taille. Important as these intellectual sources may be, we must never forget that David Jones' habitual activity from his earliest childhood was to draw. He shared the instinct of all great draughtsmen which is to show slightly more than two sides of whatever he was drawing, and also, as it were, to open up the guts of a thing, to pierce inside it. Thus he loved to show the cut stems of flowers, the section across the courses of a broken wall, the end of wattled fence where the withies are sliced across, the edge of a knife, or the upturned paw of a dog. It was through drawing that he discovered a pervading sense of "metamorphosis and mutability," and it was because he spent all his life probing with his pencil that he would express his devotion to Christ Crucified with the tactile image, "I have felt for his wounds in nozzles and containers" (*SL*, 9). All his art, not just the engravings and watercolors we have been looking at, was an act of worship and a quest for "the pierced Hermaphrodite."

Plate Numbers of Works Discussed.

(All by David Jones)

11. *Crucifixion*, c.1920 Chalk, watercolor and ink 30 x 22 Tate Gallery Archive Collection.

13. *Sanctus Christus de Capel-y-ffin*, 1925 Watercolor and gouache 7 1/2 x 5 1/8 Tate Gallery.

16. *The Albatross*, 1929 Engraving on copper, illustrating "The Rime of the Ancient Mariner" 7 x 5 1/4 Douglas Cleverdon.

18. *He Frees the Waters in Helyon*, 1932 Unfinished wood-engraving 6 x 9 1/2 Douglas Cleverdon.

15. *Tywysog Cariad*, c.1929 Pencil and watercolor 12 1/4 x 9 3/4 Anthony d'Offay.

14. *Crucifixion*, 1926 Engraving on copper 5 7/8 x 4 3/4.

12. *Lamentation*, c.1925 Watercolor 8 1/2 x 4 5/8 Private collection.

4. *Aphrodite in Aulis*, 1940 but signed 1941 Pencil, ink and watercolor 24 1/2 x 19 1/2 Tate Gallery.

5. *Vexilla Regis*, 1947 Pencil and watercolor 29 7/8 x 22 Kettle's Yard, Cambridge.

All measurements are given in inches.

THE THINKER

KATHLEEN HENDERSON STAUDT

THE DECLINE OF THE WEST AND THE OPTIMISM OF THE SAINTS: DAVID JONES' READING OF OSWALD SPENGLER

In a letter to Harman Grisewood dated 26 February 1942, David Jones describes his struggles with Oswald Spengler's *The Decline of the West*:

> I've been immersed in Spengler, I'm battling with him. I've not mea-
> sured him up yet! (if I may say so without appalling presumption).
> He's *so right*, and, as I think, also *so wrong*.... A lot of it one just reads
> as if one were reading one's own exact thoughts for the past twenty
> years put down by someone who could think clearly and who had the
> power of expression and elucidation. One just recognizes the "truth,"
> but it is far other with large tracts of it. So far I've only been able to
> ascertain that what I disagree with, and resent, is his insensitivity and
> scorn at certain important junctures, his schoolmaster's laying-down-
> the-law tendency, his cheapness and brutality and inhumanity, and
> something very like bluster when he really is on a sore-ish point.
> (*DGC*, 115)

Jones' appreciation for Spengler puzzled and even embar-
rassed many of his friends and early commentators. Certainly the poet and the German philosopher-historian differ
radically in their allegiances and personalities. Spengler's
philosophical orientation, influenced by German Idealism
and the Romantic traditions of Goethe and Nietzsche, often
conflicts with Jones' orthodox Roman Catholic sacramentalism. Moreover, Spengler's positivistic insistence on the
"facts" of history dismisses as futile any pursuit of an artistic
or religious vocation in an age which has replaced art and
religion with military and technological might. This
clearly puts him at odds with Jones, the advocate of "man-
the-artist" in all times.

Probably because of such clear incongruities, Jones'
friend and commentator René Hague repeatedly minimizes
Spengler's influence on Jones, often dismissing it as an irri-
tating eccentricity in Jones' work. He refers somewhat
patronizingly, for example, to Jones' "magpie-like borrow-

ings" from "the loquacious German"[1] and to the poet's use of
Spengler as an "endless supply of gold bricks" (*DGC*, 115).
Hague is particularly eager to dissociate Jones from the
racism implicit in Spengler, which such commentators as
Christopher Dawson and W. T. Albright have criticized
vehemently (Hague, 18). Hague is right, of course, that the
aspects of Spengler that most appealed to Jones were
"abstracted from a background that is fundamentally abhor-
rent to the poet" (Hague, 18). A conversation recalled by
William Blissett attests to the poet's distress regarding
Spengler's possible role in the subsequent rise of the Nazis in
Germany.[2] Unfortunately, however, Hague's effort to absolve
Jones of objectionable views inevitably undervalues the
fundamental role of Spengler's cyclic model of history in
Jones' vision; more seriously, it overlooks the challenges to
Spenglerian ideology that inform Jones' poetry and thought,
often in the places where the poet seems to be adopting
most faithfully Spengler's terms and models.

   The annotations which appear in Jones' copy of *The
Decline of the West*, now housed with the rest of Jones' personal library at the National Library of Wales in Aberystwyth, confirm and amplify the account given to Grisewood
of Jones "taking the measure" of Spengler. These notes
reveal in composite form a more articulate and consistent
response to Spengler than Jones seems to have been able to
give at the time of this letter or indeed in the other passing
references to Spengler which appear in his published essays.
Jones marked some 240 pages of this well-thumbed volume
with marginal lines, asterisks, underscorings, question marks,
"N.B.s" and "very goods." In addition, he covered the five
blank pages at the beginning of the volume with notes,
scribbling on the front cover, front end paper and flyleaf
and also on the back cover. Other books in his personal
library testify to Jones' habit of making notes on the cover,
flyleaf and other blank pages, but his copy of *The Decline of
the West* contains more such notes than most volumes in the
library. The cover and flyleaf notes, together with a number
of longer annotations which Jones made in the margins,
show him engaged in an intense and thoughtful dialogue
with Spengler, now amplifying, now challenging, now re-
forming an argument which clearly appealed to him despite

---

1. René Hague, *A Commentary on* The Anathemata *of David Jones* (Toronto: University of Toronto Press, 1977), p. 46.
2. William Blissett, *The Long Conversation: A Memoir of David Jones* (Oxford: Oxford
University Press, 1981), p. 12.

an inevitable antipathy for the author's temperament and ideology.

The original of Spengler's *Das Untergang des Abend-landes* was first published in Germany in 1918, and the first English translation appeared in 1926. Jones may have been familiar with the argument of Spengler's work as early as the 1930s through his reading of other writers who had read Spengler, notably Christopher Dawson, whose *Age of the Gods* (1929) significantly influenced Jones and other promi-nent writers and thinkers of his circle.[3] Jones' earliest thor-ough reading of Spengler, however, appears to date from the early 1940s. His copy of the work, a one-volume edition published by George Allen and Unwin of London, has inscribed on the flyleaf, in the poet's hand, *"David Jones, August 19th, 1941."*[4]

Jones' acquisition of his own copy of Spengler coin-cides with a crucial period in the development of his work. His letters to friends in the early 1940s indicate that at that period he was abandoning the manuscript of "The Book of Balaam's Ass," begun shortly after the publication of *In Parenthesis*, and taking up seriously the composition of what became *The Anathemata*. In October 1941, he moved into lodgings in 12 Sheffield Terrace, and it was probably here that he did most of the intensive reading of Spengler recorded in his letter to Grisewood. (An annotation on p. 211 of Volume II identifies a smudge on the page as a "cat-paw at Sheffield Terrace.") Though most of the annotations probably date from this period, one Jones note on p. 213 of Volume I, referring to Christopher Dawson's *Religion and the Rise of Western Culture* (1949), shows that he returned to Spengler later in his career as well. This is confirmed by unpublished letters to Grisewood written in 1951, while Jones was revising the typescript of *The Anathemata*, and in 1968, when he was lamenting the results of the Second Vatican Council and revising the poems of *The Sleeping Lord*.

Taken together, the markings and annotations that I shall discuss here show that Jones' reading of Spengler goes beyond the objections to style or to "the *way* he expresses

---

3. See Hague, p. 18. Blissett notes that Jones "read Spengler quite early but was com-pletely saturated in him during the early years of the war--1940-2. He got no support or encouragement from his friends here--probably because of the Englishman's com-plete lack of sympathy with metahistory. . . ." Blissett goes on to record Jones' admi-ration for Christopher Dawson (p. 65). See also Elizabeth Ward's account of Jones' "Chelsea Period" in *David Jones: Mythmaker* (Manchester: University of Manchester Press, 1983), pp. 42-63.

4. Oswald Spengler, *The Decline of the West* (complete in one volume) (London: George Allen and Unwin, 1926). Quotations from this volume will be labeled "DW"; Jones' anno-tations will be given in italics and labeled "DJ on *DW*."

it" described in the letter to Grisewood (*DGC*, 117), to articulate a new version of Spengler's historical vision which
would become an essential part of Jones' own poetic myth.

   The Decline of the West argues that the history of
civilization has always followed a cyclical pattern, beginning with the first stirrings of "Culture" as they emerge from
a primitive peasant society and evolving through a golden
age in the arts, political structures, architecture and religious life of a people. Ultimately this lively culture
declines into what Spengler calls a "megalopolitan" civilization, where the power struggles of imperialist rulers take
precedence over all other concerns. In this period, the arts,
religion, and social structures from the past decline into
mere lifeless shells, recalling but no longer recapturing the
achievements of the past culture. They become, in Jones'
words, the "cramped repeats" (*A*, 49) or the "dead limbs"
(*SL*, 64) of a once lively culture. Ultimately, in Spengler's
account, the rigid hierarchies of late civilization give way
to a chaotic, almost tribal or feudal military order, the
period of "caesarism," led by the "soldier-emperors." Amid
the disorder of this last phase of civilization, a new culture
emerges out of the primitive life of the peasantry, whose
"plantlike" existence has heretofore resisted the cycles of
historical change (See *DW* I, 435).

   Spengler's cycles follow a seasonal pattern, beginning with the springtime of Culture, when arts and institutions remain closely tied to the rhythms of the earth and
the artistic instincts of a particular people, blossoming into
the summer of a mature culture, and waning into the
autumn and winter of "civilization," cultural decadence, and
the "megalopolis." Spengler portrays the Europe of 1918 as
entering the late autumn and early winter of a civilization
which began with the emergence of Gothic culture in the
twelfth century. The springtime of this culture is reflected
not only in what Jones calls the "living floriations" of
Gothic architecture (*A*, 49), but also in the dominance of a
fully realized Catholic Christendom and in the ordered
hierarchies of feudal society and court life. This Culture
waned into late summer in the Renaissance and Reformation. For Spengler, it entered its late phase in what he calls
the "Faustian" era, which began after the Reformation and
extended to the early twentieth century. In Faustian culture,
intellect and the scientific method replace the old religion,
and men become conscious of history and destiny for the

first time.[5] Spengler sees this Faustian phase giving way, in his own time, to an age of imperialism dominated by political pragmatism and by moral and cultural bankruptcy.

Though Spengler was not himself a supporter of Adolf Hitler, much of *The Decline of the West* appears to prophesy the rise of the Third Reich in Germany, and the Nazis could easily have found support for their programs in many of the racial and national stereotypes that Spengler outlines in *The Decline of the West*, especially in its portrayals of the "Magian" nation of the Jews. A later work by Spengler, entitled *Hour of Decision* and published in 1932, advocates conformity to the National Socialist program, though without explicitly supporting Hitler or the Nazis. The letter to Grisewood shows that Jones was repelled by the propagandistic and brutal style of this work, which he describes as "less concerned with an analysis of history than with hinting as to how chaps better behave now and in the future if they are to be worth anything." As with *The Decline of the West*, he still felt drawn by its account of the inevitable decline of western culture, and in that sense called it "enormously interesting and full of true things," but he objected to its overall tone, "cheap and a little sixth-form" (*DGC*, 116).

A Spenglerian atmosphere of civilizational "lateness" pervades much of Jones' later work. It is implicit in the setting of *The Anathemata*, at "the sagging end and chapter's close" of the West. It is even more pronounced in the poems of *The Sleeping Lord*, where a Roman Tribune declares to his men, "We are men of now and must strip as the facts of now would have it. Step from the caul of fantasy even if it be the fantasy of sweet Italy" (*SL*, 51-2), and where a representative of waning "Culture" prays for protection "in all times of *Gleichschaltung*, in the days of the central economies" (*SL*, 63).[6] And yet Jones' poetry and the myth informing it show no sympathy for Spengler's conclusion that "true men" of the time must submit themselves to the inevitable destiny of the coming civilizational phase. Nor does Jones subscribe to the racial stereotypes or to the often

5. When Spengler writes "men," he usually means to refer to masculine history-makers, for in his view, the kind of history that he is discussing is the kind made by males and ruled by the "masculine principle." (*DW* II, 327). Hence I have not attempted to use more gender-neutral terms in describing his account of human history. Jones uses the terms "man the artist" or "man the sign-maker" so frequently that it seemed awkward to alter his terms, so I have usually let his terminology stand, though it is not always clear that he intends to exclude female sign-makers from his definition.
6. See my "At the Turn of a Civilization: Spenglerian Vision and Re-Vision in David Jones's *The Sleeping Lord*." *Contemporary Poetry* (now *Poiesis*) 5:2 (Spring 1983), pp. 51-71.

crude aesthetic and moral oppositions which pervade Spengler's work, despite his adoption of many of the German's terms.

Northrop Frye has pointed out that Spengler's vision in *The Decline of the West* is not strictly "cyclical"; unlike Yeats' *A Vision*, where history returns and repeats itself inexorably, Spengler's model is organic, allowing room for the randomness of historical accidents and cultural cross-fertilizations.[7] Nonetheless, Spengler's scheme shares with other Modernist historical myths—including Yeats' *A Vision*, Toynbee's *A Study of History*, and the series of thunder-claps and resurrections in Joyce's *Finnegans Wake*—a keen sense of the "lateness" of twentieth century civilization. Though many of its "facts" and analyses may be questionable from a historian's point of view, *The Decline of the West* remains an important work of twentieth century mythmaking. As Frye puts it, "What Spengler has produced is a vision of history which is very close to being a work of literature. . . . If *The Decline of the West* were nothing else, it would still be one of the world's great Romantic poems."[8]

David Jones seems to have recognized in Spengler a mythic imagination equal to his own, and it is as poetic myth that Spengler's formulations enter Jones' work. In particular, the poet adapts for his own purposes Spengler's account of the "lateness" of contemporary civilization, his parallels between late imperial Rome and mid-twentieth century Europe, and the oppositions he discerns between Culture and Civilization, between "truth men" and "fact men." The annotations to these portions of Spengler's argument, taken together with scattered published remarks about Spengler, help to explain the attraction that so absolute and deterministic an argument could have held for the far more catholic and flexible temperament of David Jones.

Jones' myth intersects most obviously with Spengler's in its development of a parallel between the world of first century Rome and the civilization of his own time. A note on the flyleaf which reads "p. 26, Greeks-Romans" refers to Spengler's italicized comment, *"The break of destiny that we express by hyphening the words Greeks=Romans is occurring for us also, separating that which is already fulfilled from that which is to come"* (*DW* I, 26. Spengler's emphasis). According to Spengler, the "Classical" civilizational cycle had its springtime in the Attic culture

7. Northrop Frye, "Spengler Revisited," in *Spiritus Mundi: Essays on Literature, Myth and Society* (Bloomington: Indiana University press, 1976), pp. 179-98.
8. Ibid., p. 187.

of the fourth and fifth centuries B.C. By the time of Christ, under Roman rule, it had begun to harden into a civilization which would ultimately give way a few centuries later to early Latin Christian culture--the first phase of the Faustian west. A Spenglerian view of first century Rome as a civilization parallel to that of the mid-twentieth century is evident in *The Anathemata*, particularly at the beginning of "Mabinog's Liturgy," where the short-lived Pax Augustae of the Romans is connected to Europe of the thirties through an allusion to Neville Chamberlain's "Peace for our Time" speech (*A*, 186). It is also clear in a well known letter to Saunders Lewis written in April 1971, in which Jones recalls his trip to British-occupied Palestine in 1934 and conflates the British troops of that period with the Roman soldiers who occupied Jerusalem at the time of Christ. The same letter insists on the obvious importance of this insight for both *The Anathemata* and *The Sleeping Lord* (*DGC*, 57).

The letter to Grisewood remarks in passing that Spengler shows "enormous sympathy and understanding of greatness in both religion and art no less than in political and military achievement" (*DGC*, 115). Yet Jones' annotations to Spengler's chapters on art and religion point to many disagreements with the details of Spengler's discussion, as Jones struggles to reconcile what he sees as Spengler's inaccuracies of artistic perception with the chapter's general account of the civilizational "lateness" displayed in the arts, a concept which Jones clearly finds appealing.

Spengler's chapter distinguishes carefully between the limited, closed-in feeling pervading the "Classical" art and architecture of Greece and Rome, the soaring use of space in the Gothic and "Faustian" art of the west, and the brooding, cavernous feeling of the "Magian" architecture of the Arab world. Within this framework, he classifies The Hagia Sophia in Constantinople, a typically "Magian" building, as "an introverted Gothic striving under a closed outer casing" (*DW* I, 185). Jones' note on p. 184 weighs Spengler's statement about space in the Hagia Sophia against his friend Prudence Pelham's firsthand account of the same building. *"Prudence said that of all the buildings in the world which she had seen Sancta Sophia was the most hugely spacious in feeling & in going in one felt one was coming outside"* (DJ on *DW* I, 185). This insight contradicts Spengler's account of the same building as "introverted" and closed. Later, Jones objects more definitely to this chapter's overall account of the Classical as limited and uninterested in "space":

> *The trouble with this, otherwise accurate, theory as to the antithesis of*
> *the Classic and the Faustian, is that actually <u>there is vast</u> space in good*
> *classic art. There is 'distance' round limbs and torsos as 'immaterial'*
> *as that in the paintings of the Masters of the West, & in a way no great*
> *art is "here-and-now"--all is, of a 'living course' it seems to me--and*
> *if one tries to copy a good classic nude figure one finds this out--the*
> *circumference of a thigh is somehow made as extensive as a landscape*
> *and the difference between original and copy is usually in this. The*
> *'copy' loses that extension and space-sense.* (DJ on DW I, 250-1)

Jones' experience as a practicing artist makes him uneasy with the neat dichotomies controlling Spengler's argument. This sort of reservation also leads Jones to question Spengler's evaluations of specific artists and styles. For example, when Spengler gives Beethoven and Rembrandt as typical examples of artists who captured the mystical "darkness" of the Faustian's infinite striving, Jones writes *"I wonder very much about this Rembrant [sic] business. The night & storm of the Eddic stuff, yes--but Rembrant's deep tones are utterly removed from it & belong to some quite other and much less satisfactory & less profound darkness"* (DJ on DW I, 187). He also takes issue with the distinction between the style of the West and what Spengler calls "the Byzantine-Islamic style (hitherto called Lombard, Frankish, Celtic or old-Nordic)." Here Spengler distinguishes sharply between the aesthetic of the dominant civilization of the West and these more peripheral styles; Jones, on the other hand, insists on influences and fusions. He writes in the lower margin *"true but it must not be altogether forgotten that certain prehistoric 'Celtic' art forms were fused in the Dark Age art of the West--it was a fusion of many sorts"* (DJ on DW I, 214-15).

Jones also questions Spengler's canon of art works and his portrayals of individual artists. When Rubens is called "a brilliant performer, but no thinker" (*DW* I, 253), Jones writes in the margin *"damned unfair."* Later, at the end of Spengler's account of the decline of oil painting since Rembrandt, Jones remarks, *"Curious that <u>Turner</u> is not given--he of all painters gave expression to Faustian infinity"* (DJ on *DW* I, 289). Here Jones accepts the concept of "Faustian infinity," but he can see that Spengler lacks the expertise in the arts to make his point as well as Jones might be able to make it for him. A few pages later, his superior authority as an artist shows more clearly. Spengler points out here that in the earlier culture-phases, artists have an easier time because they work within a context that values and appreciates their enterprise. Artists working in the later phases, on the other hand, must struggle to complete their works because art in their time has become a matter of "intellectual operations . . . a poor substitute for the trained instinct that has died out." The same discussion continues, "Cézanne and Renoir left work of the best quality unfinished because, strive as they would, they could do no more. Manet was exhausted after he had painted thirty pictures, and his *Shooting of the Emperor Maximilian*, in spite of the immense care that is visible in every item of the picture and the studies for it, hardly achieved as much as Goya managed without effort in its prototype the *Shootings of the Third of May* (*DW* I, 292). Jones writes "*good**" in the left margin next to this paragraph. The asterisk refers to his note at the foot of the page: "*except that the 'unfinished' Cézanne has a 'completion' that is only found in the greatest painting*" (DJ on *DW* I, 292).

The note about Cezanne reflects a sense of the limitations of Spengler's artistic appreciation which becomes clearer in two subsequent annotations to the same chapter. Spengler continues on the next page, "What is practised as art to-day--be it music after Wagner or painting after Cézanne, Leibl and Menzel--is impotence and falsehood." Here Jones underscores the names of the painters and writes "*This is a curious trio. The first unlocked a door for a remarkable development of painting--the other two are of comparatively little consequence*" (DJ on *DW* I, 293). Jones summarizes his reactions to Spengler's canon and judgments at the end of the chapter "Act and Portrait," where Spengler characterizes the art of all "late" phases as necessarily derivative and devoid of originality or innovation. To conclude this chapter, Spengler illustrates with German examples his contention that his own age, like the age of the Romans, marks the beginning of a late civilization: "The famous statue of Augustus in armour, for example, is based on the Spearman of Polycletus, just as--to name the first harbingers of the same phase in our own world--Lenbach rests upon Rembrandt and Makart upon Rubens" (*DW* I, 295). Jones marks this sentence with an * in the right hand margin, commenting at the foot of the page,

> *It is a pity the examples chosen are Germans, because the contemporary, however temporary, vitality in W.E. painting is to be found more in France & England. It does not of course invalidate his main argument as to the general eclecticism & decay--but it is a foolish mistake & lack of understanding not to admit the real vitality of some painting in the last 50 years--however doomed to fruitlessness the movement may be. & however much it is a hot-house growth. "Contemporary" painting has produced some quite "new" beauties which could only*

belong to this particular "late" stage. But the main argument stands.
(DJ on *DW* I, 295).

Taken together, Jones' annotations to Spengler on
the arts typify his objections to *The Decline of the West* as a
whole. In areas where he knows as much as or more than
Spengler, he discerns easily the simplistic character of
Spengler's distinctions, insisting, for example, on the continuing vitality evident in modern painting by Turner and
more recent French and British artists. Yet while these
examples might seem to contradict Spengler's account of
contemporary cultural decadence, the mythmaker in Jones
remains fascinated by "the overall argument"--the cyclical
structure of Spengler's view of history, with its account of
his own time as a "late" period. Rather than question the
Spenglerian model of history, he consents to describe the
freshest art of his own time as "doomed to fruitlessness," a
"hot-house growth."

Jones similarly objects to aspects of Spengler's
account of western religion--especially when it comes to
matters of Christian doctrine. Yet as with the chapter on
the arts, he clings to the basic structure of Spengler's argument, despite fundamental differences in belief and sensibility. This is particularly significant if we consider that
Spengler explicitly excludes a man like Jones--a religious
man living in a late civilization--from the "history" that
matters. He insists that men must abandon the religion of
the early phases of Culture in the progress toward civilization; those who fail to do so will necessarily find themselves
doomed to futility, encumbrances to the course of high history. On p. 185 of Volume II, Jones marks with two sets of
parallel lines a rather harsh paragraph about what Spengler
calls the "fellaheen"--intellectual and spiritual leaders with
"world-improving theories." Part of this passage seems worth
quoting, for it illustrates one of Jones' primary objections to
Spengler's overall argument and ideology. Spengler writes
of the "fellaheen" tendency:

> It begins with the everlastingly fearful who withdraw themselves out
> of actuality into cells and study-chambers and spiritual communities,
> and proclaim the nullity of the world's doings, and it ends in every Cul-
> ture with the apostles of world-peace. Every people has such
> (historically speaking) waste-products. Even their heads constitute
> physiognomically a group by themselves. In the "history of intel-
> lect" they stand high--and many illustrious names are numbered
> amongst them--but regarded from the point of view of actual history,
> they are inefficients. (*DW* II, 185).

Jones makes no comment on this particular instance of Spengler's inclination to make outrageous racial and cultural generalizations. But we know that in his own view, all people who embrace the world of sacrament and sign, in preference to the technocracy's orientation toward the "utile," share with Spengler's "fellaheen" a refusal to assent to a historical destiny. In his essay "Wales and Visual Form," written in 1944 but unpublished during his lifetime, Jones blames the anglicization of Wales, and the consequent loss of a genuinely Welsh material culture, on the leaders who denied their roots and allowed themselves to be co-opted by an alien culture--in this case by Tudor English culture. When folk leaders thus ally themselves with the oppressor, he continues ". . . the delicately balanced corporate way of life, the liturgy and syncretism of the tribal ecclesia, become meaningless, as we see in many 'backward' and 'primitive' peoples in our time; it is then that the 'folk' become 'fellaheen.' And the folk-leaders become identified with the alien cultures and are 'pensioned off' " (*DG*, 83).

Jones does agree with Spengler's contention that the course of civilization contradicts the religious impulse, but he balks at the inferences Spengler draws from this. His assent is summarized in a flyleaf note which reads *"The essence of all 'civilization' is irreligion; the two words are synonymous."* As a summary of Spengler's argument, this is accurate; it also indicates the distance that Jones feels between his own vocation and the concerns of the civilization that surrounds him. The flyleaf note refers to Spengler's statement, marked and underscored by Jones, that "Atheism comes not with the evening of the Culture but with the dawn of the Civilization. It belongs to the great city, to the 'educated man' *of the great city who acquires mechanistically what his forefathers the creators of the Culture had lived organically"* (*DW* I, 409 [DJ's underscoring]). A few pages later, in the same vein, Spengler writes "the megalopolitan *is* irreligious; this is a part of his being." It is significant that Jones chooses the word "irreligion" rather than "Atheism" as a synonym for "civilization" in his summary. Unlike the more neutral term, "irreligion" connotes the abandonment of something of value, and it is this aspect of Spengler's argument which appeals to Jones--its account of a genuine loss that accompanies the progress of history, a loss which for Jones threatens the very nature of humanity. Spengler views this loss as the inevitable consequence of historic "destiny," and he urges his readers to abandon out-

dated beliefs and to collaborate with this inevitable
approach of the atheistic megalopolis.

Perhaps as a consequence of Spengler's sympathy for
the deliberate irreligion of the megalopolis, Jones questions
aspects of his account of religion in the West. This is especially evident when Spengler attempts to describe the
"Magian" view of the world, shared, in his account, by Christians, Jews and Moslems and finally alien to the spirit of
the Faustian west, despite the importance of the institu-
tional church in western history. The Magian, according to
Spengler, sees the truth as "substance," and this is why the
Sacred Book--the Torah, the Bible, the Koran--is so important in these religions; it is seen as a "Word made Flesh"
(*DW* II, 224). Jones wonders, in a marginal note, whether
this reflects *"a confusion between the word of God i.e. the
Scriptures & the Word of God i.e. our Lord?"* (DJ on *DW*
II, 244). Here we see the orthodox Roman Catholic Jones
questioning Spengler's theological expertise. Later in the
same chapter, Spengler asserts, with apparent sympathy for
the sects he is discussing, that the early Christians saw
Nestorians, Mazdaists and Manichaeans as belonging to a
single Persian religion, and that the Western church based
in Rome could not distinguish between Mithras and Christ
as defined in these sects. In the margin here, Jones writes
"evidence?" (DJ on *DW* II, 260). Elsewhere, Jones wonders
about a Spenglerian parallel between the religious life of
the Roman and late Faustian civilizations. In his chapter on
"Nature Knowledge" in Volume I, Spengler recalls that the
cult of the emperor as god was taken very seriously in the
first century A.D., even at a time when most Romans did
not seriously believe in the gods or the mythologies that
had nourished Classical culture. He compares this to the
religion of Enlightenment thinkers who had rejected the
authority of the church. Jones marks Spengler's summary
statement that "The Roman Stoic, who without faith in the
mythology piously observed the ritual forms, has his counterpart in those men of the Age of Enlightenment, like Less-
ing and Goethe, who disregarded the rites of the Church but
never doubted the 'fundamental truths of faith.'" Jones
comments at the foot of the page, "not utterly convinced
that the comparison works here" (DJ on *DW* I, 411).

Other annotations to Spengler on the history of religion in the West show Jones engaged in a lively conversation with the German author, adding information from his
own store to question or to amplify Spengler's conclusions.
These annotations suggest the excitement with which Jones

followed and grasped the argument of *The Decline of the West*. For example, when Spengler compares the Christian hymnology of southern Europe, especially the *Dies Irae*, to the Eddas of the North, arguing that both are typically "Faustian," and writes that "they are alike in the implicit space-endlessness of prosody and rhythmic syntax and imagery," Jones adds the following gloss: "*Is not the* Dies Irae *thought to be in fact derived from a marching-song of the Roman Army? & if so of 'Classical' derivation--or perhaps S. would argue that at that late date the legions were already largely Germanic*" (DJ on *DW* I, 185). He also adds a long note on Spengler's passing reference to the beginnings of A.D. dating in the sixth century. Spengler gives the Christian system of dating as one of several examples in the West of the adoption of the Arabian Culture's use of "time-reckonings that begin at some event felt as a peculiarly significant act of Providence. . . ." Jones underscores Spengler's reference to the system "of the Christians, introduced shortly after 500 and beginning with the birth of Jesus." He places an asterisk next to this sentence and writes "*the beginning of A.D.*" next to it. At the foot of the page, and running up into the side margin, Jones continues Spengler's sentence as follows: "*by Dionysius Exiguus in 525 AD at Rome (A Scythian living in Rome in the Compilation of the Easter Table).* Bede *is one of the earliest users of the A.D. dating & from him it spread to most of Europe. At the Synod Whitby 664 its use was suggested by Wilfred* (DJ on *DW* II, 239). Elsewhere Jones draws on his own eclectic fund of information to challenge Spengler. For example, to illustrate the contrast between the Faustian and Classical views of history, Spengler writes, "Every Greek knew his *Iliad* but not one ever thought of digging up the hill of Troy" (*DW* I, 254). Jones insists on one example of the Romans' ability to recall actual history, in a comment which foreshadows part of *The Anathemata*'s sequence on "oreogenesis," the creation of hills, including the hill of Hissarlik or Troy (see *A*, 55-57). Following Spengler's statement, he comments "*but Augustus built a Roman City on the Hissarlik site out of antiquarian and patriotic veneration for the site of Priam's Troy*" (DJ on *DW* I, 254).

Annotations of this sort, where Jones draws from his own reading to amplify and correct details of Spengler, show him engaged actively in a kind of dialogue with Spengler, testing where his own knowledge fits the German historian's conceptions, how far Spengler's argument can be taken, and what details Spengler omits. Even when they

challenge specific points of detail or judgment, these annotations show Jones' respect for and lively interest in the
argument of *The Decline of the West*. But in other annotations, Jones disputes Spengler's categories more sharply.
Probably the most important arguments of this sort center
on the often simplistic dichotomies which structure much of
Spengler's argument, particularly the oppositions he draws
between "fact-men" and "truth-men," "heroes" and "saints."

For Spengler, a crucial moment in history occurs
with the confrontation between Jesus and Pilate. For him
this meeting demonstrates the absolute conflict between
men of "fact," represented by Pilate, and men of "truth,"
exemplified by Jesus, who claims that his kingdom is "not
of this world." Jones alludes to this discussion when he
refers to Pilate as "the fact-man, Europa's vicar" (*A*, 239).
On the front end paper of *DW*, Jones writes "*216 Jesus and
Pilate etc.*"--underscoring and starring this note as if to set it
off from others on that page. His note refers to the following passage in Spengler:

> But when Jesus was taken before Pilate, then *the world of facts and the
> world of truths were face to face in implacable hostility...* (Spengler's
> emphasis). In the famous question of the Roman Procurator; what is
> truth?... lies *the entire meaning of history*, the exclusive validity of
> the deed, the prestige of the State and war and blood, the all-powerful-
> ness of success and the pride of eminent fitness.... For [Pilate] actual-
> ity was all; for [Jesus] nothing. Were it anything, indeed, pure reli-
> giousness could never stand up against history and the powers of his-
> tory, or sit in judgement on active life: or if it does, it ceases to be
> religion and is subjected itself to the spirit of history. (*DW* II, 216)

Spengler explicitly allies himself to Pilate's side of this
confrontation in a footnote which Jones marks with an
asterisk. Here Spengler insists "the method of the present
work is historical. It therefore recognizes the anti-historical
as well as the historical as a *fact*. The religious method, on
the contrary, necessarily looks upon itself as the true and
the opposite as *false*. This difference is quite insuperable"
(*DW* II, 216, n.1).

Jones will not agree that Spengler, or indeed anyone,
is purely a man of fact. The preface to "Epoch and Artist,"
where Jones disputes Edward Caird's approval of the modern
tendency to "take particular facts for no more than they
are" summarizes his recognition of the "factual" or "utile"
view of human activity as a threat to sacramental or "extra-
utile" creations and activities which for him determine the
identity of humanity as a sign-making species (*E&A*, 14).
But unlike Spengler, Jones does not see the conflict
between fact and truth as ultimately "insuperable." In other

annotations to volume II of *The Decline of the West,* Jones exposes the internal inconsistencies in Spengler's account of this dichotomy. A few pages after the account of Jesus and Pilate, for example, Spengler praises St. Paul as "the first great personality of the new movement and the first who had the sense not only of truths, but of facts (*DW* II, 220). Jones' comment points to the contradiction between this statement and Spengler's assertion earlier on that the religious and factual views of the world are mutually exclusive. Alluding to the statement about St. Paul, Jones writes at the foot of p. 220, *"Was P. then a true 'fact man' or 'truth-man' (see p. 216)?"* (DJ on *DW* II, 220).

Jones explains his own more complex view of the fact v. truth dichotomy in a longer annotation, where he accuses Spengler of the same rigidity and dogmatism which Spengler condemns in the religious man. Here Jones underscores Spengler's statement "But in the historical world, there are no ideals, but only facts--no truths, but only facts." An asterisk in the margin refers to the following annotation at the foot of the page:

> *These reiterated and vital distinctions which S., makes* so clearly *are in all men so merged--I feel he himself is "doctrinaire" and "theoretic" in speaking of* any *given man as wholly of one or the other. Not even the Cecil Rhodes of this world are only men of "facts" and not even St. John of the X only a man of "truths"--but he's right enough in saying that in our "contemporary" world and more so in the future the top boys will be those of the "fact" world.* (DJ on *DW* II, 368)

The merging of "fact-man" and "truth-man" that Jones describes here is characteristic of his most memorable Roman speakers in *The Sleeping Lord.* The speaker in "The Tribune's Visitation" exhorts his men to abandon "everything presuming difference/and all the sweet remembered demarcations" in favor of "the fact of empire" (*SL,* 50-51); yet this same tribune pauses at the end of his stern monologue to pray to Juno. The narrator of "The Dream of Private Clitus" is similarly torn between his loyalty to the empire of Rome and his roots in the earlier traditions of the Roman people, which the empire is deliberately obliterating. Yet though Spengler's "doctrinaire" and "theoretic" categories repel him, Jones remains willing to concede that the leadership of the immediate future belongs to the "those most of the fact world." He accepts Spengler's account of history, but his interpretation comes from the opposite side of the fact-truth dichotomy.

From this alternate perspective, Jones recognizes Spengler himself as a "fact-man" who nonetheless sympa-

thizes with aspects of the world of ideals. Many portions of
The Decline of the West do betray a degree of nostalgia for
the great moments in the history of culture, and a sensitivity to the pathos of civilizational decline that belies the
German's stated allegiance to "no ideals, but only facts." A
perceptive note earlier in *DW* shows Jones discerning this
blind spot in Spengler. In Volume I, Spengler is criticizing
the philosophy of Nietzsche, as being inadequately scientific, commenting that "he tried to be at once sceptic *and*
prophet, moral critic *and* moral gospeller. It cannot be
done. One cannot be a first-class psychologist as long as one
is still a Romantic." In a marginal note to this passage,
Jones comments wryly, *"I think perhaps this is also true
of the author"* (DJ on *DW* I, 346).

Though he accepts Spengler's prediction regarding
the increasing ascendancy of the "fact-men" in his own
time, Jones emphatically rejects the conclusions that Spengler draws from this, especially his belief that the only reasonable course for "true men" to follow is fatalistic conformity. This is clearest in his notes to the introduction, where
Spengler excludes from the course of high history any who
are unwilling to accept their destiny as technocrats: "We
cannot help it if we are born as men of the early winter of
full Civilization, instead of on the golden summit of a ripe
Culture, in a Phidias or a Mozart time. Everything depends
on our seeing our own position, our *destiny*, clearly, on our
realizing that though we may lie to ourselves about it we
cannot evade it. He who does not acknowledge this in his
heart, ceases to be counted among the men of his generation, and remains either a simpleton, a charlatan or a
pedant." Jones' brief note to this passage objects to the dismissal of the nonconformist as "a simpleton, a charlatan or
a pedant," countering, *"He might be merely an intelligent
person who knows he is living in a kind of hell* (DJ on *DW*
I, 44). This terse comment reflects the most fundamental
conflict between Jones' view of history and Spengler's, a
conflict based finally on contrasting views of what it means
to be human. Perhaps the most important of his annotations
show him weighing Spengler's overall thesis against his own
view of man as sign-maker, and, in the process, formulating
his own alternative to Spengler's determinism.

This alternate vision emerges in a vivid passage
from "Art in Relation to War," another long essay written in
1944 but unpublished during Jones' lifetime:

> When Spengler, with a kind of satisfaction at the grimness of our des-
> tiny, advised young men, if they would excel, to abandon the muses for

technics, ... he too was showing a prophetic astuteness, even if we think it was the astuteness of an evil genius. He, so to say, bid the devils believe, but not tremble, for he believed it to be the devils' hour. The hour of the daemons of power that take possession of the Waste Land when true cultural life is at its lowest ebb and the "young hero" has not yet restored "the maimed king" and the time of resuscitation is not yet. When all is "doing" and there is no "making." When the end is all, and the means nothing. When there is no organic growth, but only organization and extension of dead forms.

The artist, however, in whatever age, and whatever the determined destiny, has both to believe and to tremble and somehow or other to affirm delight.[9] (*DG*, 129)

Jones' evocation of the waste land myth here enables him to emphasize the inevitability of restoration and revival, even in the darkest times. The artist, by implication, is always allied to the young hero who restores the waste land; he must pursue this vocation "in whatever age, and whatever the determined destiny." Though the plots of history and myth move forward in linear fashion, the role of humanity as sign-maker and the consequent importance of the artist remain constant. Spengler, on the other hand, recognizes no such constancy in human nature; rather, he appears to see the "true men" of any historical phase as those who are most willing to submit themselves to the discipline and patterns of thought demanded by the age, whatever their true feelings might be.

Jones recognizes the earliest phases of Spenglerian Culture as most congenial to the nature of "man-the-artist." Thus in his view, the social and political world becomes increasingly alien as the Spenglerian historical cycle progresses. The consequences of this are suggested in two annotations to *The Decline of the West*, in Spengler's account of the irreconcilable conflict between "Culture" and "Civilization." Jones underscores and marks with an asterisk Spengler's statement, "Culture and Civilization: the living body of a soul and the mummy of it." At the bottom of the page he writes, "*If this is true & I think it is, it seems to follow than* [sic] *'man' will be nostalgic and wretched in any 'civilization'--yet S. urges in the introduction and elsewhere that one is a third-rate person if one has such nostalgia for a 'culture.' He can't have it both ways*" (DJ on *DW* I, 353). The comment continues on the next page, where Spengler, using Goethe's *Faust* to illustrate the ethical evolution of Faustian humanity, has been arguing that the instinctive morality or "morale" of primitive man becomes

9. Remember William Blake's question to another artist, which ran something like: "Do you, sir, paint in fear and trembling?" (Jones' note).

increasingly intellectual and abstract in later civilizational phases. Jones writes at the bottom of this page, "*All this again seems to show plainly that men must be nostalgic in a 'civilization'--only the bastards could feel otherwise. You can't have 'morale' if you are living a 'mumified' existence-- except the will to see the end of it--to hope for its collapse. It seems to be his main contradiction. but see 363-4*" (DJ on *DW* I, 354). In the passage on I, 363-4 referred to here, Spengler admits that late Faustian man has lost his sense of purpose and his capacity to hope. "Nothing remains," he writes, "but the mere pressure, the passionate yearning to create, the form without the content." Jones underscores this sentence and writes "*good*" next to the paragraph which contains it. Perhaps he sees in this sentence a concession to his own view of "man-as-artist." Deprived of anything positive to hope for, "Faustian" man, in this account, takes a kind of refuge in his own creative powers, in what Jones would call his true nature as "man-the-artist."

But Spengler's contempt for those who fail to conform to their destiny remains inescapable. *The Decline of the West* concludes, in fact, by exhorting Spengler's contemporaries to embrace the inevitable destiny that their late phase of civilization is bringing upon them. My italicizing here indicates the portion of this paragraph that Jones has marked with two sets of parallel lines in the margin. Spengler concludes:

> For us, however, whom a Destiny has placed in this Culture and at this moment of its development--the moment when money is celebrating its last victories, *and the Caesarism that is to succeed approaches with quiet, firm step, our direction, willed and obligatory at once, is set for us within narrow limits, and on any other terms life is not worth the living.* We have not the freedom to reach to this or to that, but the freedom to do the necessary or to do nothing. And a task that historic destiny has set *will* be accomplished with the individual or against him. (*DW* II, 507)

Jones must have been thinking of passages like this when he complained to Grisewood of "this German jack-boot thing" in Spengler (*DGC*, 115). Both as a thinking individual and as a representative of man-the-artist, Jones sees that he is effectively excluded from Spengler's vision of history, and his annotations show him looking for an alternative response from within the Spenglerian system, some kind of recourse for his "intelligent person who knows he is living in a kind of hell" (DJ on *DW* I, 44). He appears to be moving toward this kind of constructive response when Spengler writes with characteristic absolutism, "Let a man be either a hero or a saint. In between lies, not wisdom, but banality" (II, 274). Jones underscores this sentence and writes at the foot of the page, *"There is the third condition of the great artists detached from 'the-world-as-history,' but not in the same mode as the saint, but not 'making history' like the hero"* (DJ on *DW* II, 274).

Jones places a question mark to the left of his own note here, perhaps to indicate his uncertainty about this formulation, but the depiction of the natural artist and the sacramental order as offering a "third way" within the Spenglerian scheme becomes an important theme in Jones' later poetry. Both *The Anathemata* and *The Sleeping Lord* depict vividly the deepening shadows of Spengler's declining west, yet the poetry itself strives to reveal ways in which man, living in the "kind of hell" which is civilization, nonetheless remains aware of his roots in a Culture, and affirms the persistence of a sacramental mode of being. The opening setting of *The Anathemata*, at "the sagging end and chapter's close" of the west, is vividly Spenglerian in its lament for "the young-time, the sap-years" of medieval Latin Christendom (*A*, 49), and yet in the poem as a whole, the makers of anathemata persistently resist the "utile infiltration" which threatens their activities.[10] In *The Sleeping Lord* the mood is darker, especially in the increasingly "Caesarist" world of "The Tribune's Visitation," in the gathering storm of encroaching civilization which threatens the primitive hearth in "The Tutelar of the Place," and in the wasted land of "The Sleeping Lord." Yet the volume as a whole embodies the hopefulness of the poet's outlook on history, the faith that the quickening impulses of the "young world" will somehow return. This is implicit in the vigil of the candlebearer and the immanence of the Sleeping Lord in the landscape of the title poem, and it is given voice at the end of "The Tutelar of the Place," in the appeal to the "Womb of the Lamb the spoiler of the Ram" (*SL*, 64). Jones' later poetry thus challenges Spengler's determinism by giving voice to elements within the late Civilization which refuse either to conform to or to be crushed by the "quiet, firm step" of Spenglerian destiny.

Jones comes closest to articulating this challenge to Spenglerian determinism in another passage from "Art in Relation to War," where he concedes that Spengler's primary purpose in *The Decline of the West* was "to steel the wills of

---

10. See my "Incarnation Re-considered: The Poem as Sacramental Act in *The Anathemata* of David Jones," *Contemporary Literature*, 26:1 (Spring 1985), pp. 1-25.

his German readers to resist this quite inevitable and proper
rebellion of human nature against the monstrous regiment
of the power-age." He goes on to offer an alternative conclusion from Spengler's data, from the perspective of man-
as-artist:

> It is indeed "human nature" that is rebelling--it is man-as-artist that
> is in rebellion, and it is men-as-artists who are casualties in the strug-
> gle.
>   Had Spengler had a different metaphysics, his analysis, at least of
> this particular subject, might have remained unaltered--but his
> inferences from the evidence might have been different. His realism as
> to the this-world facts is here most salutary. His "pessimism," as
> far as this subject is concerned, can be attacked only on other grounds, and
> those are metaphysical ones, that is to say, in the last resort, by the
> "optimism" of the Saints, which optimism, human nature in all men
> recognizes as valid, and which is notably *reflected* for man in his
> "intransitive activity" called art, for to "make anything" pre-
> supposes that such activity is "worthwhile." (*DG*, 159)

Though Jones will not accept Spengler's determinism, he
does adopt his uncompromisingly grim description of contemporary civilization. The "optimism" Jones offers in resistance to this stems, not from a naive or despairing will to
escape, but from a lucid realism about the cultural decay
which surrounds the artist in Spengler's "megalopolis." But
this realism does not lead Jones to despair. Rather, his
characteristic response is implied in the working title of his
manuscript "The Book of Balaam's Ass," which he abandoned in the early forties in favor of *The Anathemata*. A
letter to Jim and Helen Ede dating from 11 April 1939
explains the title: "it is really about how when you start saying in a kind of way how *bloody* everything is you end up in
a kind of *praise--inevitably* (*DGC*, 91). Jones' "optimism of
the saints" resides in the act of making, which persists in all
civilizational phases, quietly affirming the autonomy of
"man the artist" against the pressures of Spengler's history
and destiny.

     Viewed with the optimism of the saints, the Spengle-
rian cycle becomes a pattern in which the worst of times is
ultimately redeemed, through a sign-making impulse in
humankind which somehow survives to resist the darker
moments of civilizational decline, reemerging in a new culture. Though Jones' poetry is filled with anguish at what is
being destroyed by the advancing technocracy, his myth
nonetheless insists that the impulses which govern the
sacramental order and which define human nature must also
persist. Along with the hero and the saint, the fact-man and
the truth-man, there remains the consciousness of "man the

artist," and this consciousness is embodied in the work of the poet, who writes blessings when he means to curse, who knows, as Jones' Elen Monica knows, that "what's under works up" (*A*, 164).

Spengler, contemplating the subjugated cultures and hardening political orders of the early twentieth century, advises resignation to their inevitable conquest. There is no place in his scheme for any who would question the course of destiny. Jones, speaking for "man-the-artist," views Spengler's late civilization as a dark era that must ultimately run its course; thus he insists on challenging the Spenglerian view of destiny. At the end of his essay "Use and Sign," he recalls how "the hero in the ancient tale (Peredur, better known as Perceval) was blamed, not only for not 'asking the question' concerning the Waste Land, but for actually causing the land to be waste by failing to ask the question" (*DG*, 185). Against the willed passivity that Spengler counsels, Jones' poetry persists in questioning the dominion of the waste land. Working from within Spengler's model, it invokes the romance tradition to recall how even the darkest moments of "civilization" have been followed by cultural resuscitation in some form. Hence even the bleakest of Jones' late poems ends with a question which at once recognizes the contemporary power of Spengler's late civilization and looks forward to its eventual overthrow by forces hidden within the subjugated landscape:

Does the land wait the sleeping lord
         or is the wasted land
that very lord who sleeps? (*SL*, 96)

THOMAS R. WHITAKER

HOMO FABER, HOMO SAPIENS

Like the significantly unnamed Wanderer whose Gest and sign-making inform *The Anathemata*, David Jones was "signed with the quest-sign" (*A*, 224). His thought in every medium was interrogative, digressive, committed to love, and inseparable from the signs through which it sought and found itself. On his own assumptions, such thought is not idiosyncratic but normal and necessary. He came to see that every artist or "maker" is essentially a "sign-maker" (*A*, 23) and that every person is essentially an artist. Man is "man-the-maker." This means that *poiesis* is not only his defining activity but also "his native and authentic mode of apperception and in the end his only mode." (*E&A*, 13) According to that bold statement, which David Jones characteristically embedded in a question, our knowing is enabled and mediated by our sign-making. "We were then *homo faber, homo sapiens* before Lascaux and we shall be *homo faber, homo sapiens* after the last atomic bomb has fallen" (*E&A*, 184).

Nearly three decades after the publication of *Epoch and Artist*, we have hardly begun to describe and assess the interrogative complexity of this understanding of man. David Jones' epistemology is strikingly modern. In recognizing that linguistic and non-linguistic signs shape our meanings and mediate our apperception, he avoided the traps of a naive rationalism or an objective realism. He understood that we interpret the world and ourselves through a signifying power native to our species, and that our signs are heuristic acts of some indeterminacy, historically conditioned, far from transparent, and open to elucidation only through yet more signs. Ever since Vico said that we can know only what we make, philosophers in several traditions --idealist, pragmatist, analytic, and phenomenological--have proposed doctrines in roughly this direction. Kantians have held that our apprehension of objects must conform to our ideas. Nietzsche and his heirs have variously proclaimed

that the structures of our language determine what seem the
structures of reality. And it was Henri Bergson who, in *Creative Evolution*, argued that "we should say not *Homo sapiens*, but *Homo faber*."[1] Other modern philosophers who have
remained open to ontology have not been far, in certain
respects, from David Jones' position. An American absolute
pragmatist could say in 1913: "The universe consists of real
Signs and their interpretation." And a French phenomenolo-
gist could say in 1960: A speaker "does not express just for
others, but also to know himself what he intends . . . . The
significative intention gives itself a body and knows itself
by looking for an equivalent in the system of available sig-
nifications represented by the language I speak and the
whole of the writings and culture I inherit."[2]

Though modern in its reliance on mediating signs,
David Jones' quest for meaning led him toward a Christian
orthodoxy that approximates what Ananda K. Coomaraswamy, Eric Gill's most immediate intellectual master,
called the *philosophia perennis*.[3] The result was an apparent tension between epistemology and ontology at the center of his thinking about man-the-maker. He could propose
that the thought we discover through our inductive making
must be incarnational in mode and transcendental in final
reference (*E&A*, 12-16, 156-57, 166-67). No skeptic or agnos-
tic would accept that yoking of the empirical to the theological. Nor would Gill or Coomaraswamy have put the
matter in that way: though seekers themselves, they preferred the clarity of axioms and deductive consequences.
But when David Jones stated an "axiom" in an "essay of
inquiry" (*E&A*, 173, 179), he usually phrased it as a crystal-
lization of experience, a traditional deposit or "saying" (*DG*,
134) that, when held to "even if, to all appearance, it
seemed without meaning," would "sooner or later be seen to
cast light" on a new situation (*E&A*, 173) Unlike philosophical first principles, such axioms do not set the world in
order. Though steadier than working hypotheses, and sometimes hard to distinguish from articles of faith or love, they

1. Henri Bergson, *Creative Evolution*, tr. Arthur Mitchell (Westport, Conn.: Greenwood, 1975) p. 153.
2. Josiah Royce, *The Problem of Christianity* (Chicago: University of Chicago Press,
1968), p. 345; Maurice Merleau-Ponty, *Signs* (Evanston: Northwestern University
Press, 1964), p. 90.
3. See Eric Gill, *Autobiography* (London: Jonathan Cape, 1940), p. 174, for a tribute to
Coomaraswamy. For their relation, and for the *philosophia perennis*, see Roger Lipsey,
Coomaraswamy: His Life and Work (Princeton: Princeton University Press, 1977), pp.
117-22, 265-79. For a placing of this aspect of David Jones' thought in the context of
what Coomaraswamy called "the traditional doctrine of art," see Brian Keeble,
"Epoch, Art and Utility," *Anglo-Welsh Review*, 25 (Summer 1975), pp. 39-54.

are open to temporary disconfirmation. Like a carpenter's
bench-marks, a navigator's compass-bearings, or a painter's
"line of beauty," they orient the maker and allow him to
apprehend imperfectly, through the approximations of temporal signs, the claims of some final geometry. It is not surprising that David Jones' essays, letters, and annotations
could so often shuttle disconcertingly between the absolute
and the relative.

That apparent tension between an epistemology of
mediating signs and an ontology employing the signs of
Christian orthodoxy may partly account for our tardiness in
describing and assessing what David Jones meant by *homo
faber, homo sapiens*. Critics have often ignored epistemological questions, assumed his thought to be more simply
deductive than it was, and written as if he had just absorbed
or adapted certain concepts that then dictated his views.
They have explicated "*poiesis*" and "*anamnesis*," "sign" and
"sacrament," the "gratuitous" and the "utile," and have shown
their ancestry in the work of Gill, Thomas Aquinas, Jacques
Maritain, Maurice de la Taille, and Gregory Dix. They have
shown the derivation of certain historical and mythopoeic
patterns from Jessie Weston, Christopher Dawson, T. S.
Eliot, W. F. Jackson Knight, and Oswald Spengler. Sometimes they have conducted probing inquiries into the paradoxes of David Jones' incarnational aesthetics.[4] But the
major studies have often reduced his thought to strands in
the history of ideas or fended it off with a generous condescension, an anxious orthodoxy, or a dismissive rationalism.
They have therefore distorted some central issues or suggested that they might be of real interest only to a rather
quirky and alienated English-and-Welsh artist of Roman
Catholic subscription.

In his pioneering book of 1971, for example, David
Blamires warned that the papers in *Epoch and Artist* "are
not the writings of a philosopher" and that "it would do
David Jones a disservice if one tried to make out that they
should be taken as philosophical essays."[5] Both David Jones

4. Among the most helpful of these inquiries: Jeremy Hooker, *David Jones: An
Exploratory Study of the Writings* (London: Enitharmon Press, 1975); Thomas Dilworth, *The Liturgical Parenthesis of David Jones* (London: Golgonooza Press, 1979)
and "The Anagogical Form of *The Anathemata*," *Mosaic*, 12 (Winter 1979), pp. 183-95;
and Kathleen Henderson Staudt, "The Text as Material and Sign: Poetry and Incarnation in William Blake, Arthur Rimbaud, and David Jones," *Modern Language Studies*, 14
(Summer 1984), pp. 13-30, and "Incarnation Re-Considered: Poetry as Sacramental Act
in *The Anathemata* of David Jones," *Contemporary Literature*, 26 (Spring 1985), pp. 1-
25.
5. David Blamires, *David Jones: Artist and Writer* (Manchester: Manchester University Press, 1971), p. 16.

and his editor seem to have been vexed by this kindly
retreat from serious discussion. "As you say in your letter,"
David Jones wrote to Harman Grisewood in the same year,
"it's not much good saying that it must be remembered that
David Jones is not a philosopher--of course not--but that
implies that 'a philosopher' would find the answer to this
extremely difficult question concerning man's innate and
million-years' habit of making inutile acts . . . ." What he
wanted was an engagement with the questions he raised:
"They are or are not real questions" (*DGC*, 232) But that
task could not be much advanced by taking his answers as
"a helpful background to his poetry" and then quoting W. H.
Auden's bright remark: "I am always interested in hearing
what a poet has to say about the nature of poetry, though I
do not take it too seriously."[6]

No doubt René Hague took what David Jones said
about poetry with great seriousness. Hague assumed, however, that "poetic form" must actualize a prior "thesis" or
"argument"[7]--a position quite opposed to the claim that
poiesis itself is our "native and authentic mode of apperception." Hague's respect for certain theological formulations, as distinct from signs of faith that might always
require further elucidation, often led him to try to bring his
friend's thinking within bounds. In the early pages of his
valuable commentary on *The Anathemata* he suggests that
David Jones confused "effective" (or sacramental) and
"hieroglyphic" signs, warns that his "idiosyncratic" use of the
term "myth" "blurs the essential distinction (to which he was
fully alive) between pagan myth and Christian *revelation*,"
and tells us to read the term "cult-man" as a periphrasis for
"priest."[8] At issue in each instance is the problematic relation between Christianity and a *poiesis* that mediates
analogies among all signs, sacraments, rites, and myths.
Hague usually resolved that issue by declaring that David
Jones' language deviates for rhetorical or poetic purposes
from the rightly intended concept. It would follow, of
course, that "signed with the quest-sign" is just a periphrasis
for "baptized"--as defined, say, by the Council of Trent--and
not an exploratory naming of a universal that shines through
those acts in the river Jordan. But David Jones' comment
on the term "anathemata"--to say nothing of such adjacent
poetic strategies as "He that was her son / is now her lover"

6. Ibid., pp. 28, 31.
7. René Hague, *David Jones* (Cardiff: University of Wales Press, 1975), pp. 56-57.
8. René Hague, *A Commentary on "The Anathemata" of David Jones* (Toronto: University of Toronto Press, 1977), pp. 7, 8, 11, 12.

(*A*, 224)--points to a more open and heuristic mode of interpretation: ". . . I mean by my title as much as it can be
made to mean, or can evoke or suggest, however
obliquely . . ." (*A*, 28). Such emergent meaning is a central
phenomenon as we explore the world through our "native
and authentic mode of apperception." It helps to explain
why, despite Hague's distinctions, David Jones can say that
the "myth" linking "our tradition" with the line of Aeneas,
Venus, and Jove "proposes for our acceptance a truth more
real than the historic facts alone discover" (*A*, 124n).

Hague's procedure could therefore bring to questions
of theology and typology a set of answers partly at odds
with David Jones' own language. There is a passage of
Keatsian eloquence in "The Myth of Arthur" that speaks of
our apprehending, in "unplumbed deeps and recessions below
and beyond the medievalised and Christianised" romances
of Chrétien de Troyes and Malory, the "weight of what lies
hidden." Sensory intimations lead us toward an imagined
vision: "Gusts drive down upon us through sudden rifts in the
feudal vaulting, up through the Angevin floor; we stumble
upon twisted roots of primeval growth . . . . Behind the
contemporary 'sets' . . . we scent things of another order."
Could we remove the Gothic attire of some "passing meek
gentlewoman," we might behold "the ageless, powerful,
vaticinal, mistress of magic, daubed with ochre, in the shift
of divination, at the gate of the labyrinth" (*E&A*, 234-35).
Hague read that passage (which, as he did not happen to
note, partly derives from Jackson Knight's *Cumaean Gates*)
as a statement about the "Celtic imagination" but avoided
its visionary urgency by removing the details from the
realm of conceptual truth: "Sliding, as he often does when
the pressure builds up, into poetry, David puts the matter in
a form that is more cogent than argument."[9] The compli-
ment is disarming, but we must ask: Do we apprehend
through the romances an "ageless" archetype? Is something
like "divination" then a universal possibility? And is this
pagan "labyrinth" cognate with the "megaron" of *The Anathemata* (*A*, 244) and that world-center about which David
Jones could say that "the by-ways, the meanders, even the
culs-de-sac, all roads, lead to the omphalos" (*DG*, 148)? The
very next paragraph in "The Myth of Arthur" suggests the
importance of those questions and the likelihood of affirmative answers, for it indicates that, as in Keats' odes, "Poesy"

9. Hague, *David Jones*, pp. 79-80. See W. F. Jackson Knight, *Vergil: Epic and Anthropology*, ed. John D. Christie (London: Allen & Unwin, 1967), p. 257.

has truth-bearing powers beyond the dull brain's perplexities. "The Chapel of the Grail," we read, "discloses a symbolism and ritual which a Sacred Congregation of Rites
would find hard to define in purely Christian terms, but
twelfth-century allegory and French genius made superb use
of the material. Never was the unicorn more subtly tamed,
seldom a more fruitful baptism" (*E&A*, 235). Here, at least,
"baptism" is an effective act of *poiesis* that eludes theological definitions.

Hague could elsewhere claim David Jones' support
for his own retreat from the primary signifying force of
poiesis. He quoted, in response to Thomas Dilworth's
demonstration that *In Parenthesis* employs many analogies
between the soldiers and Christ, David Jones' statement that
". . . in writing 'In Paren.' I had no intention whatever in
presuming to compare the varied maims, death-strokes, miseries, acts of courage etc. of the two contending
forces . . . with the Passion, Self-Oblation & subsequent
Immolation & death of the cult-hero of our Xtian tradition
for that is a unique and profound Mystery of Faith." That,
said Hague, ignoring the strangely relativizing flavor of "the
cult hero of our Xtian tradition," is "an illumination of *In
Parenthesis*" and "has even more force as a commentary on
The Anathemata."[10] Was David Jones retracting his poetic
analogies? So it might seem if we did not recognize that he
was using "compare" in its narrow and etymological sense of
"declare to be equal." Hague was content to safeguard the
uniqueness of the Incarnation and ignore the difficult question of participatory analogy, which is no less central to
David Jones' *poiesis* than to the arguments of Aquinas.
Dilworth, however, in expanding his essay, quoted a quite
different statement from David Jones to Hague: " 'I think
that all our miseries and sufferings can be seen as in some
way part of the whole anabasis and passion' of Christ." And
he reaffirmed his view not only that the soldiers' suffering
"finds its archetype in the suffering of Christ" but also that
"because of the spiritual communion initiated by the
redemption, archetype here gives way to anagogue, or mystical assimilation."[11]

We can further generalize that insight, for mystical
theology provides a language through which we may
describe the world of participatory analogy that opens itself
to *homo faber, homo sapiens* in sign-making. And here

10. Hague, *David Jones*, p. 48.
11. Dilworth, *The Liturgical Parenthesis of David Jones*, p. 22.

David Jones' epistemology and ontology turn out in certain respects to be not at odds but mutually supportive. The world we discover through sign-making must be structured by the perception of similarity-in-difference or analogy. But all analogies, even if they are no more than provisionally valid, must be founded on some real participation of our signifying acts in a world that itself involves some real participation of all individuals in each other and in their common source. Otherwise sign-making is arbitrary, and meaning is a baseless illusion--as some post-structuralists appear self-contradictorily to maintain. All signs must therefore lead us through analogical discriminations toward all other possible signs and toward the universal ground or act that inheres in them, calls them into being, and can be known imperfectly through them. That is one reason why all roads, even the culs-de-sac, must lead to the omphalos. Taken to its limit, this understanding of sign-making implies a non-dualist world of translucency and mutual interpenetration--indeed, the "total harmony" of Plotinus, in which "analogy will make every part a Sign."[12]

Just such a world is evident in the signs of Christian orthodoxy as David Jones repeatedly understood them. The economy of grace allows all persons, and indeed what St. Paul in *Romans* 8:22 called the "whole of creation," to participate in divine archetypes and be assimilated into the Logos as members of one body. This conclusion is evident in David Jones' note describing how the Mass offers to the Trinity the "argosy or voyage of the Redeemer" (" 'Myself to myself' as in the *Havamal* is said of Odin") on behalf of "the whole argosy of mankind, and, in some sense, of all sentient being, and, perhaps, of insentient too" (*A*, 106n)--especially if we gloss that note with yet another statement to Hague: "Of course in what I think is called an ontological sense there is only one voyage."[13] Our "quest" or "argosy" as *homo faber, homo sapiens* discovers that *one* voyage as its ontological ground.

In David Jones' view, each "made" work moves toward a realization of that harmony. "It must be understood," he could say, "that 'art' *as such* is 'heaven,' it has out-

12. Plotinus, *The Enneads*, tr. Stephen MacKenna, 2nd ed. rev. by B. S. Page (New York: Pantheon Books, n.d.), p. 95. For one of several Thomist accounts of analogy that David Jones knew (*A*, 19), see Thomas Gilby, *Barbara Celarent* (London: Longmans, Green, 1949), pp. 77-95.
13. Hague, *A Commentary*, p. 32. David Jones often insisted on the distinction between human beings and other animals. But he could speak of the "dignity" of animals as resulting from "God-in-them" (*E&A*, 89) and could accept the possibility of baboons' ceremonial mourning for their dead as having a bearing on St. Paul's statement about the "whole of creation" (*DG*, 183).

flanked 'the fall'--it is analogous not to faith but to charity"
(*DG*, 164). But against such participation in "heaven" or
what Plotinus called "There," both an anxious orthodoxy and
a this-worldly realism will always insist on the distinctions
appropriate to a fallen "here" in which *this* is emphatically
not *that*. David Jones understood such objections very well.
After a careful discussion of Aquinas' identification of the
Good and the Real, he could conclude with a frankly speculative response to a mediating sign: "we guess what is meant
by those vivid and measured words: *Bonum et ens convertuntur*" (*E&A*, 157). And elsewhere he could yet more emphatically recognize our immersion in a fallen world:

> The apparent realness and effectual triumph of what is inimical (and
> to that extent deficient of reality), obscures for most of us, most of
> the time, for some of us all the time, that Reality upon which fixed
> lode philosophers *cyn Cred* and Christian theologians alike would have
> us take our bearings.
>   What has the majority of us ever made of a Reality in which it is
> said that the good and the real are interchangeable terms? (*DG*, 200-
> 201)

Sign-making discloses form, which "is a good in itself." But
"for a thing to be good in itself it must be part of the whole
good and that good is clearly not 'of this world.' For here
'goods' do not fulfil each other, they cancel out as often as
not" (*DG*, 135). Art, therefore, in seeking "of its nature to
evade the consequences of the 'fall,' . . . only makes the
'fall' more obvious." And yet it does succeed "in 'reminding'
man, in keeping before his eyes, that perfection which is
unity" (*DG*, 156).

For David Jones sign-making is a cognitive and aesthetic action that requires an assumption of transcendent
harmony, leads us toward a vision of that harmony, and also
heightens our awareness of the disharmonies in our fallen
experience. That is why, shuttling between mediated
glimpses of the Real and gropings in the relative, he could
acknowledge in the same breath the claims of a "unique
and profound Mystery of Faith" and those of an anthropological and historical perspective on "the cult hero of our
Xtian tradition." If René Hague was prevented by a somewhat rationalist version of Christian orthodoxy from recognizing this understanding of the power and predicament of
homo faber, homo sapiens as a "creative creature" (*DG*,
161), a more recent critic, Elizabeth Ward, has been led by a
secular rationalism to reject it.

More alert than any other critic to the apparent tensions in David Jones' thought, Ward described his

"mythopoeic sensibility" as a "Manichaean style of imagination" based on a "firmly dualistic mode of thinking."[14] Setting art against utility, the past against the present, the primitive against the technological, and the local community against the empire, that imagination seemed to Ward merely to use a Christian orthodoxy for its own purposes. David Jones' "interest in Catholicism," she said, was "less a spiritual quest than an extension of that fascination with 'significance' " instilled in him at art school. His interest in Thomism was a "life-long alliance of expediency." And Maurice de la Taille's doctrine of the Sacrifice carried for him "an aesthetic rather than a theological appeal."[15] In her view, *The Anathemata* itself is "not primarily a Catholic or even a Christian poem" but to some degree "the disconfirmation of unique revelation," for in it the "Christian myth" is "but a partial and interchangeable component."[16] The "almost Manichaean simplicity" of David Jones' convictions, she argued, shaped a "complex aesthetic primitivism, self-contained and apparently apolitical, but in fact integrally related to the political extremism whose intellectual sources it shared." His poetry "emerged from and contributed to a 'pre-fascist' consciousness in inter-war English Catholic circles." Ward concluded that we should judge his "strain of obsessive nostalgia" in the light of Stephen Spender's remark that, "when applied through action to contemporary history," such nostalgia is "Fascism."[17]

We must certainly grant that David Jones' thought was sometimes weakened by an abstract dualism, and that his understanding of *poiesis* involves a problematic relation to Christianity. We must also grant that he let his Christian optimism be dangerously clouded by Spenglerian despair, even though he recognized that Spengler lacked "the humour of true disinterestedness" (*DGC*, 117) and seemed to exhibit "the astuteness of an evil genius" (*DG*, 129). Finally, we must grant that, partly because he had incorporated into his own more complex views Eric Gill's belief that "capitalism is robbery, industrialism is blasphemy and war is murder,"[18] he could underestimate the political and ethical differences between democracy and fascism. But Spender had actually summarized his own impressions of David Jones in a much friendlier and more generous way: "He was

14. Elizabeth Ward, *David Jones Mythmaker* (Manchester: Manchester University Press, 1983), pp. 40, 42.
15. Ibid., pp. 35, 39, 131.
16. Ibid., pp. 126, 133.
17. Ibid., pp. 206, 59, 222.
18. Gill, *Autobiography*, p. 257.

doubtless an artist who entered into, almost obsessively, the
suffering of a century which has produced the most terrible
wars in history, yet the memory of him that remains in my
mind is that of a man loving and happy."[19] And in fact each
of Ward's main assertions is quite wrong or at best a half-
truth. A look at the nature of her distortions will help us to
understand more fully what David Jones meant by *homo
faber, homo sapiens.*

Her account of his "dualism," in the first place,
relied very heavily on reductive readings of the poetry. She
overlooked complicating ironies, as when she read a statement in "The Wall"--"they used to say we marched for Dea
Roma behind the wolf sign to eat up the world" (*SL*, 14)--as
an "allegory" for the "supersession of the noble goals of
war."[20] She could oversimplify an entire poem by neglect-
ing its scriptural language, as when she called "The Tribune's Visitation" fatalistic and "essentially Spenglerian."[21]
Just as the proleptic allusions in Eliot's "Journey of the
Magi" place its speaker in a context beyond his understanding, so the Tribune's Pauline references to a "second birth,"
to "members / of the Strider's body," and to being if not "of
one hope then of one necessity" cast him as an ironically
unknowing agent of an empire that will prove to be not just
the embodiment of the "gnosis of necessity" but also, after
Constantine's baptism, a vessel of faith, hope, and love--a
historical development already potential in the "mutilated
signa" (*SL*, 58) of the Tribune's proto-Eucharistic celebration. Despite Ward's claim that David Jones always pits the
local community against the empire, this poem--like *The
Anathemata*--combines the Augustinian recognition that
empire is a robbery with the equally Augustinian recognition that the city is a central sign for our actual and our
redeemed life. That is one reason why the frontispiece for
Epoch and Artist can quote *Ecclesiasticus* 38:22--without
these sign-makers, at whatever moment of history, *"non aed-
ificatur civitas."*

The dualism Ward claimed to find is also usually
denied or overcome by the complex and interrogative texture of David Jones' essays. She said, for example, that the
"symbolic" and the "utilitarian" are for him "permanently
incompatible ways of knowing."[22] But "The Utile" begins by

19. Stephen Spender, "Preface," in *Introducing David Jones*, ed. by John Matthias
(London: Faber and Faber, 1980), p. 11.
20. Ward, op. cit., pp. 53-54.
21. Ibid., p. 174.
22. Ibid., p. 208.

admitting that no human works "can, in strict, literal fact, be wholly and exclusively ordered toward mere utility" (*E&A*, 180). "Art and Democracy" recognizes that the "habit of art" cannot be lost but only crippled (*E&A*, 90-91). "Art and Sacrament" argues that military strategy, a making "at all points governed by urgent, hard, practical, this-world necessities," discloses forms that are typical of the "archetypal form-making" of the Logos (*E&A*, 159-60). "Art in Relation to War" and "Use and Sign" are tissues of such complications, punctuated by an insistence on an "interrogatory attitude" (*DG*, 123, 184). Nor can Ward's account of a Manichaean imagination begin to cope with the awareness of ethical complexity ("This goodness for that badness--each qualified") that led David Jones to write in "The Roland Epic and Ourselves" this shocking but carefully qualified statement: "It is, conceivably, for a baptized Führership that we may yet have cause to pray, if only in the sense that a sophisticated Roman of The Province would have asked heaven's prevenience for the difficult barbarian invested with The Purple . . ." (*DG*, 100). Was he flirting with fascism, yielding to despair, recognizing the ironies of history, or relying on Christian hope? In answering that question, we should not forget all that he could mean by "baptized."

Ward's reduction of his theological interests to expediency and aesthetics, and her denial that his quest was primarily "spiritual," followed not from the evidence but from her own assumptions. Never did she grant that the human appetite for meaning or beauty must explain or justify itself through signs that point toward the metaphysical. David Jones clearly saw such a need. If there is a creature whose "informing principle" is "rational," a creature "having a measure of freedom of will," what are the pre-conditions for its existence? Those "who believe there is such a creature as man," said David Jones, "may find it hard to continue in that belief without coming to the opinion that the proper end of that creature is God" (*E&A*, 148). He granted that we may self-contradictorily deny the ground of our reason, freedom, and potential virtue by boasting "a fidelity to the world of fact." The "virtues practised have ends and explanations which may be, and often are, repudiated by the men who practise them most" (*DG*, 155, 156). But he was clear that intellectual consistency required an ontology and a faith. Not only must we "take our bearings" from those vivid and measured words: *"Bonum et ens convertuntur."* Another of Aquinas' propositions--*"Ex divina pulchritudine esse omnium derivatur*"--was for him "that best of sayings" (*DG*, 134).[23] He thought it necessary, moreover, that the realm of spirit subsume and justify not only the good, the significant, and the beautiful but also the whole gamut of love, from the boldest *eros* (as in "The Lady of the Pool" and *Aphrodite in Aulis*) through the most tender *philia* (as in "The Tribune's Visitation" and *In Parenthesis*) to the *agape* with which he held art to be analogous (as in the tailpieces for *The Rime of the Ancient Mariner* and *In Parenthesis* or, by implication, any of his re-presentations of life's dappled things). His most complex signs fold together all these modes of love, including, as he knew, the Oedipal: "He that was her son / is now her lover" (*A*, 224). In its aesthetic, social, psychological, ritual, and metaphysical implications, the Body of Christ was for him a real Sign. To judge otherwise is to dismiss as "expediency" the entire Western tradition of ontological speculation and religious belief.

It is conceivable that, despite his intentions, David Jones' most elaborate manifold of signs might be "not primarily a Catholic or even a Christian poem." Ward's reading of *The Anathemata*, however, was based on a reductive view of Christian doctrine and a simplistic notion of analogy. Ignoring Irenaeus and other patristic writers who regarded pagan as well as Old Testament figures as anticipations of Christian revelation, and whose typologies meant much to David Jones (*DG*, 215-16; *SL*, 83-84)[24] she said that he was "more profoundly influenced by nineteenth-century Protestant theology, matrix of the modern 'mythologisation' of religion, than fully accords with adherence to the Church's teachings." She understood the nineteenth century to have replaced a "literal and exclusive consent to the central Christian dogmas by the notion of Christianity as 'the evolved summary of all mythological revelations from the beginning of experienced time.' "[25] We need not attend

23. He had long known the saying as expounded by Maritain--see *Art and Scholasticism and The Frontiers of Poetry*, tr., Joseph W. Evans (Notre Dame: University of Notre Dame Press, 1974), p. 31--but had probably met it again in 1943 as the epigraph to Coomaraswamy's "Beauty and Truth" in *Why Exhibit Works of Art?*--for which see Coomaraswamy, *Christian and Oriental Philosophy of Art* (New York: Dover Publications, 1956), p. 102.
24. For David Jones' further praise of Irenaeus, see Hague, *A Commentary*, p. 49. For Irenaeus' doctrine of the divine education of man, see F. R. Montgomery Hitchcock, *Irenaeus of Lugdunum* (Cambridge: Cambridge University Press, 1914), and for his theme of *recapitulatio* see also Jean Danielou, *From Shadows to Reality* (London: Burns and Oates, 1960), pp. 30-47.
25. Ward, op. cit., p. 121. The quotation is from E. S. Shaffer, *"Kubla Khan" and "The Fall of Jerusalem": The Mythological School in Biblical Criticism and Secular Literature, 1770-1880* (Cambridge: Cambridge University Press, 1975), p. 187. Ward later (p.

to the fact that Aquinas, for example, could quote Ambrose as saying, "All that is true, by whomsoever it has been said, has its origin in the Spirit."[26] This collapsing of a long historical development Ward posited as the precedent, mediated through such poets as Blake and Coleridge, for a move in *The Anathemata* to make Christianity depend on a merely human imagination: "The 'symbol producing' imagination which on this view defines humanity is a *sine qua non* of Christianity, not vice versa, even though Christianity, which believes that from the beginning 'the Word was with God and the Word was God,' might be acknowledged as the repository of the ultimate symbol."[27] *The Anathemata* does far more, of course, than acknowledge such a travesty of the Logos doctrine. As its references to the "New Light" and "his perpetual light" (*A*, 73, 81) make clear, and as its opening and closing passages also imply, *The Anathemata* finds not that Christianity is a "repository" of a "symbol" but that it reveals in its still incompletely interpreted and therefore open signs the full meaning of a Logos that, before and after the Incarnation, enables and informs all making. Mistakenly attributing to the poem a merely human imagination and a "cyclic" view of history,[28] Ward set them against a "literal and exclusive" Christian doctrine that would preclude typology and deny the gradual unfolding of the faith.

If *The Anathemata* is on that score not primarily Catholic or even Christian, what must we say of one of the Church's great thinkers in this century? In his *Theological Investigations*, Karl Rahner argued that to make the Incarnation appear "merely as something subsequent, a particular event *in* a world already *finished*," would indeed make revelation "mythological":

> The Incarnation of the Logos ... appears as the *ontologically* ... unambiguous goal of the movement of creation as a whole, in relation to which everything prior is merely a preparation of the scene. It appears as orientated from the very first to this point in which God achieves once and for all both the greatest proximity to and distance from what is other than he (while at the same time giving it being) .... Here we must remember that the world is something in which everything is related to everything else, and that consequently anyone who makes some portion of it into his own history, takes for himself the world as a whole for his personal environment. Consequently it is

139) recognized the concept of "accommodation" but without placing it in its early historical context.
26. Cited by Coomaraswamy in "A Figure of Speech or a Figure of Thought," an essay David Jones probably read. See *Coomaraswamy: 1: Selected Papers, Traditional Art and Symbolism*, ed. Roger Lipsey (Princeton: Princeton University Press, 1977), p. 33.
27. Ward, op. cit., pp. 126-27.
28. Ibid., p. 136.

not pure fantasy (though the attempt must be made with caution) to
conceive of the 'evolution' of the world *towards* Christ, and to show how
there is a gradual assent which reaches a peak in him. Only we must
reject the idea that this 'evolution' could be a striving upward of what
is below by its own powers.[29]

That might serve to summarize one aim of "Rite and Fore-
Time," which never suggests that the sign-making on which
Christianity depends is other than a gift of the Logos "whose
name is called HE-WITH-US" (*A*, 75, with capitalization as
corrected in *IN*, 29). David Jones agreed here with Eric
Gill: "the meaning of the Universe is Emmanuel, God with
us. . . . And it applies in all times and places. It is not only
the Christians who have lived with God."[30]

Ward also claimed, however, that the analogies in
The Anathemata reduce Christianity to a "partial and interchangeable component" in an ahistorical reciprocity of
signs. That argument rested on Elinor Shaffer's account of
syncretic mythology as the "unity of meaning of all apparently dissimilar myths."[31] But Shaffer had uncritically
adopted Northrop Frye's model of "a world of total
metaphor, in which everything is potentially identical with
everything else."[32] In *The Anathemata* neither Dea Roma
and the Virgin Mary nor Hector and Christ are "functionally
interchangeable."[33] That would be to travesty both typology
and analogy. Whether for Plotinus, Aquinas, or David Jones,
the structure of analogy is a harmony of similarities-in-dif-
ference that assumes no interchangeability of parts. The
Thomist analogy of being was phrased by Gilby in this way:

> Behind the variety we experience, there is not one exclusive, com-
> plete, and monotonous reality, but a richness of perfection to which
> the mind can respond with many and different notes. Nor is there a
> diversity of fundamentally different and independent units, for the uni-
> verse is a planned order, composed of multiple systems all closely
> intermeshed, and none of them closed. Tapeworms illustrate the doc-
> trine of the image of God and even illusory desire is warmed by divine
> happiness.[34]

David Jones used one of Gilby's phrases to describe "The
Rime of the Ancient Mariner," where "what is natural and
within the range of our five senses . . . is closely inter-

29. Karl Rahner, *Theological Investigations* (Vol. I: *God, Christ, Mary and Grace*), tr.,
Cornelius Ernst (Baltimore: Helicon Press, 1961), pp. 164-65.
30. Gill, *Last Essays* (London: Jonathan Cape, 1942), p. 17.
31. Ward, op. cit., p. 133; Shaffer, op. cit., p. 184.
32. Shaffer, op. cit., p. 185, quoting Northrop Frye, *The Anatomy of Criticism*
(Princeton: Princeton University Press, 1957), p. 146.
33. Ward, op. cit., p. 133.
34. Gilby, op. cit., p. 89. The passage has been illuminatingly emphasized by Patrick
Deane, "Raising a Valid Sign: A Defence of the Form of David Jones' *Anathemata*,"
diss., Univ. of Western Ontario, 1986.

meshed with the supra-mundane, very often with the unearthly . . . , sometimes with fantasy of a delectable nature, sometimes with celestial vision . . ." (*DG*, 196). When sign making operates within such an order, some signs must be more complex, central, and adequate reflections of the world's transcendent meaning than others. Every system of analogy therefore requires what David Tracy has called a "focal meaning" or "prime analogue" in accord with which the entire system is interpreted.[35] For David Jones that prime analogue was revealed when, in de la Taille's phrase, "He placed himself in the order of signs" (*E&A*, 5, 179).[36] A succinct and comprehensive designation of that analogue as "prime" occurs in "A Christmas Message 1960":

> The mewling babe in the ox-stall, the quasi-artefacts of bread and wine ... are to be regarded, so our religion demands, not as signs only but signs which are also the Thing signified, namely the Eternally Begotten Word, the Logos which gave *poiesis* to the expanding or contracting (whichever it should turn out to be) cosmos.
>
> (*DG*, 171-72)

But here we encounter another difficulty. Ward also claimed that *The Anathemata* "renders all its allusions profoundly ambiguous" through its "focus on the sacramental nature of *all* ritual activity."[37] And indeed David Jones regarded not only all ritual activity but all *poiesis* as sacramental: "sign and sacrament are to be predicated not of *some* men and their practices but of *all* men and their practices." We find "sacrament at every turn and all levels of the 'profane' and 'sacred,' in the trivial and the profound" (*E&A*, 166, 167). That must be so because sign-making always involves the "re-presenting" or, in some sense, the "real presence," of the signified. Hence, despite Hague, even what Augustine called "hieroglyphic" signs must have "effective" power. The practice of depth psychology, as David Jones knew, supports this idea. He could speak in Jungian terms of "ancient and archetypal images" in the "collective unconscious" becoming attached to historical figures. (*E&A*, 45-46) He could speak "from experience and with feeling" of the truth of Hilaire Belloc's statement that "names have power to bind and loose material things" (*DG*, 37). And he could say that in a poem to one's love "the 'sacramental' will pile up by a positively geometric progres-

---

35. David Tracy, *The Analogical Imagination* (New York: Crossroad, 1981).
36. See Maurice de la Taille, *The Mystery of Faith and Human Opinion Contrasted and Defined* (London: Sheed and Ward, 1930), p. 212: "He placed himself in the order of signs, in the order of symbols, to have the joy of symbolising and, by symbolising it, of building up the mystical Body of which we are the members."
37. Ward, op. cit., p. 139.

sion," so that "what was Miss Flora Smith may turn out to be
Flora Dea and Venus too and the First Eve and the Second
also and other and darker figures, among them, no doubt,
Jocasta" (*E&A*, 167). Jung and Freud there join hands with
patristic typology. But the practice of art, as David Jones
understood it, also supports this idea. The artist is "an invet-
erate believer in 'transubstantiations' of some sort. The sign
must *be* the thing signified under forms of his particular art"
(*DG*, 136). Every good painter must therefore say, "This is
not a representation of a mountain, it is 'mountain' under
the form of paint" (*E&A*, 170). That conviction is hard to
explicate, however, because every sign opens up a network
of analogy that reaches beyond the horizon of the known. In
commenting on Hogarth's "Shrimp Girl," David Jones was
careful to acknowledge the complexity and partial
unknowability of what is "really present under the form of
paint," and also careful to state that he used the phrase
"really present" not in "the particular sense used by the theologians, but in a certain analogous sense" (*E&A*, 175).

Had he been a philosopher, of course, he might have
defined that sense with greater precision. But at least he
had clearly argued that the "sacredness" of a sign results
from its participation in a "being" that is interchangeable
with the "good" (*E&A*, 157). In any case, the sacramentality
of all *poiesis*, though requiring a capacious understanding
of Christian signs, need not imply a de-Christianizing ambiguity. The real presence of the signified in the sign is subject to complex gradations of kind and importance--"all
levels of the 'profane' and 'sacred,' . . . the trivial and the
profound"--even as analogy itself is a graded manifold. For
that very reason, to speak of David Jones' "application of
the sacramental metaphor to poetry"[38] may reduce to an
allegedly non-metaphysical account of figuration a pan-
sacramentalism that he rightly believed to require the
"emphasis" of theological language (*E&A*, 175).

The world of analogy that is mediated by the gift of
sign-making requires that each sign participate in the forms
it discloses and to some degree in all other forms, known
and unknown, with which these are "closely intermeshed."
Hence the necessary openness of a sign, and its power of
leading us on to yet undiscovered meanings, whether
brighter or darker figures. The complex, graded, never completely definable, but real presence of the signified in the

38. Kathleen Henderson Staudt, "Incarnation Re-Considered: Poetry as Sacramental
Act in *The Anathemata* of David Jones," loc. cit., p. 25.

sign is a logical corollary. In more fully articulating that corollary--which he had already clearly stated, for example, in the autobiographical notes prepared for H. S. Ede in 1935--David Jones was helped by the notion of "re-presentation" that he found in Gregory Dix's discussion of the Eucharist.[39] But he probably found the same notion, developed with respect to art itself, in Coomaraswamy's volume of 1946, *Figures of Speech and Figures of Thought*. Every work of art, Coomaraswamy said, contains "something like a real presence of its theme." Even an imperfect likeness " 'participates' in that which it resembles." Nor does such "imitation or re-presentation" depend on verisimilitude, for all things participate "in their formal causes." Because each work enters this order of participation, Coomaraswamy could speak of "the fundamental identity of all the arts."[40] In the same way David Jones could speak of "the unity of all made things" (*E&A*, 171). The two men, one inside and the other outside the visible Church, explored much the same world of signs. Just as for David Jones "all roads . . . lead to the omphalos," which is also the "high cave" of *The Anathemata* (*A*, 52), so for Coomaraswamy the main paths, at least, lead to the same summit, the site of sacrifice that is "always theoretically both on a high place and at the center or navel of the earth."[41] And just as Coomaraswamy could say, "Never let us approach another believer to ask him to become 'one of *us*,' but approach him with respect as one who is already 'one of *His*,' who *is*, and from whose invariable beauty all contingent being depends,"[42] so *The Anathemata* can say:

> For all WHOSE WORKS FOLLOW THEM
> among any of these or them
> *dona eis requiem.*
> (He would lose, not any one
> from among them.
> Of all those given him
> he would lose none.) (*A*, 65)

But here we must ask: Does not *The Anathemata*, by using the ambiguous pronoun "he" as a sign for all agency, whether apparently human or apparently divine, dissolve what must be for Christianity a necessary theological dis-

39. See Gregory Dix, *The Shape of the Liturgy* (Westminster: Dacre Press, 1945), especially pp. 245, 256. David Jones' notes of 1935, reproduced only in part in *DGC*, 19-21, and John Rothenstein, *Modern English Painters* (New York: St. Martin's Press, 1976), II, 292-297, are held by the Library of the Tate Gallery.
40. Coomaraswamy, *Coomaraswamy: 1: Selected Papers*, pp. 279, 281, 21, 296n, 15-16.
41. Ibid., p. 4.
42. Coomaraswamy, "Paths That Lead to the Same Summit," in *Am I My Brother's Keeper?* (New York: John Day, 1947), p. 50.

tinction between the unnamed Wanderer and *homo faber, homo sapiens*? On this point David Jones could be elliptical enough in straight prose: "The artist is anthropomorphic to the core; so that unless his *anthropos* is also the Unbegotten, he must be an idolater" (*DG*, 142). But this virtual identification of the species with the Logos, perhaps the strongest indication of mystic assimilation or the "one voyage," does not result from nineteenth-century Protestant theology as mediated by liberalizing poets. It is true that John Livingston Lowes, in a study admired by David Jones (*A*, 37), gave a secularized and psychologized account of the *"true inward creatrix"* that Coleridge himself had called a "repetition in the finite mind of the eternal act of creation in the infinite I AM." But even Lowes acknowledged Coleridge's immersion in Neo-Platonized Christianity and noted that his definition of the imagination's power to "see all things in one" was drawn from a noble sentence in Jeremy Taylor's *Via Pacis*.[43] It is also true that Blake said, "Therefore God becomes as we are, that we may be as he is."[44] But he was rephrasing the most widely quoted statement by Irenaeus: "The Son of God became the Son of Man, that man . . . might become the son of God."[45] And it was no Protestant theologian but Gerard Manley Hopkins who could say, in "As kingfishers catch fire," that the "just man"

Acts in God's eye what in God's eye he is--
Christ--for Christ plays in ten thousand places...

and could effectively gloss those lines in a sermon: "It is as if a man said: That is Christ playing at me and me playing at Christ, only that is no play but truth: That is Christ *being me* and me being Christ."[46]

Hopkins, who was one of David Jones' major antecedents, had been helped by the work of Duns Scotus to find Christ immanent in all things. And behind Scotus we can discern the non-dualist vision of Dionysius the Areopagite, who (as Maritain's *Art and Scholasticism* would have made clear to David Jones) also heavily influenced

43. John Livingstone Lowes, *The Road to Xanadu* (Boston: Houghton Mifflin, 1930), pp. 56, 603. For the definition of the "primary imagination" see Samuel T. Coleridge, *Biographia Literaria*, ed. J. Shawcross (Oxford: Clarendon Press, 1907), I, 202.
44. William Blake, *There Is No Natural Religion*, in *The Poetry and Prose of William Blake*, ed., David V. Erdman (Garden City: Doubleday, 1965), p. 2.
45. Irenaeus, *Adversus Haereses*, Book II, Chap. 19, par. 1.
46. Gerard Manley Hopkins, *The Sermons and Devotional Writings of Gerard Manley Hopkins*, ed., Christopher Devlin (London: Oxford University Press, 1959), p. 154. Hopkins' sacramental vision also merged empiricism and faith: see Daniel Harris, *Inspirations Unbidden* (Berkeley: University of California Press, 1982), pp. 39-44. David Jones, who frequently echoed Hopkins, had read W. H. Gardner, *Gerard Manley Hopkins* (2 vols.) (London: Secker and Warburg, 1944) (*E&A*, 54) and found important the "haecceity" of Scotus (*E&A*, 46; *A*, 148n; *DGC*, 207.)

Aquinas.[47] According to Dionysius, "in divine things the undifferenced Unities are of more might than the Differentiations and hold the foremost place and retain their state of Undifference even after the One has, without departing from Its oneness, entered into Differentiation."[48] Of the unnamable God who is in and above all the divine names, Dionysius could say:

> He *is* all things as being the Cause of them all, and as holding together and anticipating in Himself all the beginnings and all the fulfilments of all things; and He is above them all in that He, anterior to their existence, super-essentially transcends them all. Hence all attributes may be affirmed at once of Him, and yet He is No Thing.[49]

We can understand why David Jones, when reading *The Divine Names* in 1940, said, "it's the cat's whiskers" (*DGC*, 104). And we can also understand why, when writing an appreciation of Eric Gill a few months later, he could speak of "that peculiar lightness of heart which some experience when they come upon a definition of St. Thomas, or a sentence from *The Divine Names* for the first time. For a while, at all events, the labyrinth is illuminated, the muddle shakes out into a discernible figure" (*E&A*, 296).

Only in this context can we begin to acknowledge without distortion David Jones' relations to nineteenth-century theology as mediated, for example, by his childhood world. Elizabeth Ward said that "there is no evidence of David Jones' having been acquainted with such currents of thought at their contemporary sources."[50] In fact, one of the books in the household of James Jones was "Keble's *Christian Year* with illustrations by Johann Friedrich Overbeck" (*E&A*, 135). In the poems of that volume John Keble blended allusions to classical poetry and pagan religion with certain of the ideas of typology and divine immanence that he laid out in "On the Mysticism Attributed to the Early Fathers of the Church," No. 89 of *Tracts for the Times*--a series, of course, that was often suspected of being Catholic rather than Protestant in tendency. Perhaps we should imagine the child who would some day make *The Anathemata* perusing on the third Sunday in Lent a poem celebrating the "consecration of classical literature to Christ" ("thoughts beyond their thought to those high Bards were given"), or on a Septuagesima Sunday immersing him-

47. See W. J. Sparrow-Simpson, "The Influence of Dionysius in Religious History," in Dionysius the Areopagite, *The Divine Names and The Mystical Theology*, tr., C. E. Rolt (London: Society for Promoting Christian Knowledge, 1940), pp. 202-19.
48. Dionysius the Areopagite, *The Divine Names*, p. 80.
49. Ibid., pp. 139-40.
50. Ward, op. cit., p. 131.

self in a poem that glosses *Romans* 1:20--"The invisible
things of Him from the creation of the world are clearly
seen, being understood by the things that are made"--and
that ends: "Give me a heart to find out Thee, / And read
Thee everywhere."[51]

David Jones was no obsessive dualist of doubtful
Christianity but an empirical artist who approached the
paradoxes of Christian non-dualism through the medium of
the things that *homo faber, homo sapiens* is enabled to
make. What then must we say of Ward's attempt, roughly
following Frank Kermode, to place David Jones' thought
with that of Ernst Cassirer and Susanne Langer as a
"complex aesthetic primitivism" that depends on "a rejection of the rational or scientific intellect"?[52] We must say
first that, although the post-Kantian philosophical context
that includes Cassirer's theory of symbolic forms can certainly shed light on David Jones, Ward's description of it is
astonishingly reductive. When Cassirer defined man not as
"animal rationale" but *"animal symbolicum,"* he was not
rejecting the rational intellect but providing an epistemological account of its empirical basis--and doing so in a
more rigorous manner than Bergson had employed when
displacing *homo sapiens* by *homo faber.* Cassirer maintained that all relational thought must depend on symbolic
thought, and that naming is fundamental to our construction
of a world of objects. But he also acknowledged science as
the latest stage in "the process of man's progressive self-lib-
eration."[53] It seems likely that David Jones knew of Cassirer
through a book by an acquaintance of many years, the art
critic and man of letters Herbert Read. In *Icon and Idea*
(1954), Read argued with Cassirer's help for the psychological and epistemological priority of the image over the word
in the history of what, following Bergson, he called *"homo
faber."* Read took a strong position: "It is only in so far as
the artist establishes symbols for the representation of reality that mind, as a structure of thought, can take shape."[54]
That statement may well lie immediately behind David
Jones' formulation of 1958 that *poiesis* is man's "native and
authentic mode of apperception and in the end his only
mode" (*E&A,* 13). Even before completing *The Anathemata,*

51. John Keble, *The Christian Year* (London: Methuen, 1895), pp. 82-85, 64-66. See also
"On the Mysticism Attributed to the Early Fathers of the Church," in *Tracts for the
Times* (London: Rivington, 1833-41), VI, No. 89, pp. 1-186.
52. Ward, op. cit., p. 36.
53. Ernst Cassirer, *An Essay on Man* (Garden City: Doubleday, 1953), pp. 44, 58, 171,
286.
54. Herbert Read, *Icon and Idea* (New York: Schocken Books, 1965), pp. 19, 53.

however, he had admired (*A,* 37) the work of another author-
ity on whom Read would rely: the archaeologist Rachel
Levy, who traced in *The Gate of Horn* the emergence of
Greek thought from the ritual signs of neolithic culture.[55]

   We must also say that Ward's description of such
thought as "primitivist" results from a more simplistic dualism than any attributable to David Jones, and from assumptions that could not, without self-contradiction, sustain her
readings of his work. Against a primitivism that she
described as valuing "image-making powers," an "intuitive
perceptive process," a "non-rational perception," the
"instinctive life of the imagination," and an "unconscious
harmony between man and the natural world," Ward set
what she variously called the "Western values of rationalism
and materialism," the "scientific or materialist intellect,"
the "pure reason" that produces technology, and "the rationalist consciousness which derides the symbol, thinks
sequentially," and "speaks through 'facts,' logic and technology."[56] That dualism, which distorts C. G. Jung as much as
Cassirer or David Jones, offers as the only alternative to
"primitivism" a late nineteenth-century materialism that
can explain or justify neither the possibility of its own ideas
nor their assumed harmony with a posited objective world.
Since Ward proposed no *via media,* she could not recognize
any of David Jones' artistic successes or important perceptions without tacitly relying on all that she had dismissed as
primitivism. She admired in the "total metaphor" of *In
Parenthesis,* for example, its "creative tension between
'myth' and the unassimilable ambiguities of 'ordinary human
experience.' " She said that myth, "objectively defined, . . .
embodies a permanent and universal psychic truth." She
could speak of "the force of a symbol working at its most
complex level," of "the free exercise of the imagination,"
and of the "integrity" of "response." She could even speak of
"a genuinely visionary experience," and say that the language in a poem "activates one's sensitivity to equivalent
spiritual qualities."[57] But her stark alternative between
"primitivism" and the "scientific or materialist intellect"
had left her no possible ground for any of those observations.

   David Jones would have been dismayed but not surprised. He knew that "neither in 1900 nor now is it possible
for human beings effectively to take the particular for no

55. Gertrude Rachel Levy, *The Gate of Horn* (London: Faber and Faber, 1948).
56. Ward, op. cit., pp. 221, 36, 136, 126, 190, 82, 56, 39, 135.
57. Ibid., pp. 106-107, 117, 128, 180, 195, 194.

more than it is, or to be emancipated wholly from the tendency to in some sense make sacral, or give otherness to, the particular" (*E&A*, 14). He faced up to this question: Is there a creature whose "informing principle" is "rational," whose powers include "a measure of free will" (*E&A*, 148), and whose "mode of apperception" is *poiesis*--or is there not? If not, who are we who claim to make or understand this statement and how can we do so? But if *homo faber, homo sapiens* exists, David Jones rightly inferred that members of this community-creature would find themselves called to shape, through the signs they make and find, as coherent and inclusive an account as possible of their "argosy" in this world. Working through "what is known by a kind of touch" (*E&A*, 244), hoping that they may speak of "a committed love of the Muse," (*DG*, 37) they would engage a "sign-stream" or "sign-world" (*A*, 236) of indefinite metamorphic range, which mediates what they must posit as an ontological "order of signs" (*E&A*, 5, 179). Such a creature would have to acknowledge that "man's form-making has in itself the nature of a sign" (*E&A*, 159). He would have to admit that when he asserts that "the Word makes the Flesh," "as though this thesis were true," he does so "by a kind of 'unity of indirect reference'" or confluence of signs that enables all roads to lead to the omphalos (*DG*, 148).[58] For that reason he might agree with Aquinas that analogy provides a *via media* between anthropomorphism and agnosticism.[59] And, because of this empirical mysticism, he might list among his "formative" works not only the "pseudo-Denis" who wrote *The Divine Names* but also Friedrich von Hügel (*DGC*, 188), who expounded in *The Mystical Element of Religion* our necessary transcendence of all pragmatic but intermediate dualisms, in various modes of thought and stages of civilization, as we move toward a vision of the living Unity that is constituted in Multiplicity.[60]

Such a member of *homo faber, homo sapiens* might also be uncomfortably aware--despite his insistence on the second term of his double name--that the artist who deals in "the contactual and the particular" must find all "generalizations" to be "useless" (*DG*, 31), and might himself

---

58. The "unity of indirect reference," expounded by H. S. V. Bickford in his privately published *Certainty*, was important also to Gill and to Martin D'Arcy. See D'Arcy, *The Nature of Belief* (London: Sheed and Ward, 1931), pp. 186, 191-200. As D'Arcy put it, "we perceive evidence of an infinite complex consistency by means of indirect reference in terms of unity" (p. 314).
59. Martin D'Arcy, *Thomas Aquinas* (London: Ernest Benn, 1930), pp. 168-69.
60. Friedrich von Hugel, *The Mystical Element of Religion* (2 vols.) (London: J. M. Dent, 1908), I, 3-82; II, 259-396.

"find exposition excruciatingly difficult" and, "in the main," be "doubtful of the value of the effort" (*E&A*, 17). Considering himself therefore no "philosopher"--and perhaps requiring the services of an expositor to put his thoughts in a somewhat more coherent order--he might nevertheless be in his digressive and interrogative essays a more precise thinker than any of his critics. But he would also know that his most accurate, coherent, and adequate thinking-through-signs must occur not in such essays but in a "made work" (*E&A*, 17)--whether it be a writing, engraving, or painting--in which, as Picasso had said, seeking has yielded to finding. That is "not a bad affirmation," said David Jones, "of the differing ways of love and knowledge, of the receptive and measuring processes" (*E&A*, 99). And with that remark he had come around once more--perhaps through a misleading dualism--to the recognition confirmed again and again in his experience that the final goal of *homo faber, homo sapiens* must be the receptive knowledge of love.

THE TESTAMENT

SAMUEL REES

DAVID JONES BIBLIOGRAPHY

INTRODUCTION

First the *addenda*, or the news. As of August, 1988, new on the bookshop shelves are Thomas Dilworth's *The Shape of Meaning in the Poetry of David Jones* (University of Toronto Press) and Christine Pagnoulle's *David Jones: A Commentary on Some Poetic Fragments* (University of Wales Press). Imminent is Nicolete Gray's *The Paintings of David Jones* (Lund Humphries); also in press, and likely to be published in the spring of 1989, is a *festschrifft* titled *Craft and Tradition: Essays in Honour of William Blissett*, edited by H. B. deGroot and Alexander Leggatt, to include essays on Jones by Guy Davenport, Thomas Dilworth, W. J. Keith, and Vincent B. Sherry (University of Calgary Press). A biography commissioned by Secker & Warburg is being written by Thomas Dilworth with the full cooperation of the Trustees of Jones' estate; it is to be published in the centenary year of Jones' birth. To the present listings, let me also add Dilworth's "David Jones' 'The Hunt'" in *The Anglo-Welsh Review* 85 (1987): 93-102; and Vincent B. Sherry, Jr., "Current Critical Models of the Long Poem and David Jones' *The Anathemata*," *ELH* 52 (Spring, 1985): 239-255. No doubt there are other works in process and/or already in print of which I know nothing and hence cannot mention.

A word about what *is* here contained. The listing is not complete, definitive, or exhaustive; this is a selected bibliography, selectively annotated. It concentrates on writings on the writings; it concentrates on work published after 1976. Were it to be otherwise, these fifty pages would expand and multiply and so distend this volume in the *Man and Poet* series as to make it unbindable.

Part I provides a chronology of the writings of David Jones: the published works (including letters) in their major, most accessible editions (brief annotations expand, in some instances, the range of reference). As have all volumes in this series, Part II lists, in alphabetical order by author, the contributors whose work is further listed in chronological order, and in many instances annotated, in Part III. The numbers given parenthetically allow for easy cross-access between authors and their works. Or such is the intention. Part III lists first those works published before 1976 (the last date of entries in the earlier Rees Bibliography--see item 101), and selects from such work that which I have deemed to be the most indicative, the most interesting, the most essential. (One can note in passing that Jones' work is by now almost routinely included in anthologies and standard literary reference books. 'Twas not always thus.) What follows in Part III is a year-by-year bibliography of writings about David Jones, arranged within each year alphabetically by name of author.

The annotations allow for the occasional outburst of enthusiasm, but in the main they are intended to be descriptive and illustrative, by way of quotation, of the contents of the books, essays, and articles listed. They are, I hope, fairly and responsibly made; annotation is a reductionist art at best, and few essayists would applaud another's reducing of their meditated utterances to a few lines of summary. The bare bibliographical description will endure, however, and those who make use of this work are enjoined to read the works so pointed and not rely on the annotations as being in any sense definitive.

The question of whether or not David Jones' work is merely the venerated object of a narrowly self-defined band of cultish admirers vexes some critics and commentators. Without engaging the question here, I note only that this bibliography includes criticism in five languages other than English (Welsh, German, Italian, French, Japanese) published in at least eight different countries on four continents. And by both sexes. And by persons of a wide variety of religious and political persuasions, the precise coloring of which it is irrelevant and unwise (and also against the law) to enquire into.

It is customary to offer thanks where it is most due, and in that spirit and more, much more, I thank Vince Ambrock, graduate student in English at the University of Alberta, for his assiduous and always cheerful labors. I shall also see to it that he receives a fair measure of blame for any errors of commission or omission that may be spotted in this bibliography.

Samuel Rees
University of Alberta
August, 1988

Part I

In Parenthesis: seinnyessit e gledyf ym penn mameu.
London: Faber and Faber, 1937. New edition 1961, with
"A Note of Introduction" by T.S. Eliot; American
edition, New York: Chilmark Press, 1962; paperback
editions by the Viking Press (Compass Books), and
Faber and Faber in 1963.

The Anathemata: fragments of an attempted writing.
London: Faber and Faber, 1952; second edition, 1955.
American edition, New York: Chilmark Press, 1963; also
paperback editions by Viking Press (Compass Books)
1965, and Faber and Faber, 1972.

Epoch and Artist: Selected Writings. Ed. Harman
Grisewood. London: Faber and Faber, 1959. American
edition, New York: Chilmark Press, 1963; paperback
edition by Faber and Faber, 1973.

An Introduction to "The Rime of the Ancient Mariner."
London: Clover Hill Editions, 1972. Separate
publication of the full text intended for the Clover
Hill edition of *The Rime* published in 1964 but deemed
too long. See the 1964 volume for Jones' abbreviated
"Foreword."

The Sleeping Lord: and other fragments. London:
Faber and Faber, 1974. Comprises the text of the title
poem plus "A, a, a, Domine Deus," "The Wall," "The
Dream of Private Clitus," "The Fatigue," "The Tribune's
Visitation," "The Tutelar of the Place," "The Hunt," and
a fragment from "The Book of Balaam's Ass," the latter
here printed for the first time.

David Jones: Letters to Vernon Watkins. Ed. with
notes by Ruth Pryor; foreword by Gwen Watkins.
Cardiff: Univ. of Wales Press, 1976. See item 85.

The Dying Gaul: and other Writings. Ed. with
introduction by Harman Grisewood. London and Boston:
Faber and Faber, 1978. A collection of 15 "prose pieces"
which are not included in *Epoch and Artist*; the seven
listed below appear in this volume for the first time:
"On the Difficulties of One Writer of Welsh Affinity
Whose Language is English," "An Aspect of the Art of
England," "Wales and Visual Form," "The Death of

Harold," "The Welsh Dragon," "Welsh Culture," and "Art in Relation to War." See item 105.

David Jones: Letters to William Hayward. Ed. Colin Wilcockson. London: Agenda Editions, 1979. See item 126.

Dai Greatcoat: A Self-Portrait of David Jones in his Letters. Ed. René Hague. London and Boston: Faber and Faber, 1980. See item 134.

David Jones: Letters to a Friend. Ed. Aneirin Talfan Davies. Swansea: Christopher Davies Ltd., 1980. See item 129.

The Roman Quarry: and other sequences. Ed. Harman Grisewood and René Hague. London: Agenda Editions, and New York: The Sheep Meadow Press, 1981. See item 154.

Inner Necessities: The Letters of David Jones to Desmond Chute. Ed. Thomas Dilworth. Toronto: Anson-Cartwright Editions, 1984. See item 203.

Part II

Alexander, Michael. "David Jones, An Introduction: The Unknown Modernist." (201)

Alexander, Michael. "On David Jones' Letters, Man, Poetry and the BBC." (144)

Allchin, A. M. "The Discovery of David Jones." (49)

Archard, Cary, ed. *Poetry Wales.* (165)

Auden, W. H. "Adam as a Welshman." (19)

Auden, W. H. "A Contemporary Epic." (7)

Auden, W. H. "The Geste Says This..." (13)

Austin, Diana. *A Study of "In Parenthesis" by David Jones.* (190)

Bard, Glenn. "Corrigenda to *The Sleeping Lord.*" (127)

Bard, Glenn. *An Elucidation of "The Sleeping Lord."* (104)

Barnard, John. "The Murder of Falstaff, David Jones, and the 'Disciplines of War.'" (113)

Bartlett, Neil. "'Cara Wallia Derelicta.'" (166)

Bennett, J. A. W. *Poetry of the Passion.* (167)

Bergonzi, Bernard. *Heroes' Twilight.* (27)

Berryman, John. "Epics from Outer Space and Wales." (20)

Blamires, David. *David Jones: Artist and Writer.* (40)

Blamires, David. *David Jones and the Nativity.* (168)

Blamires, David. "The Ordered World: *The Anathemata*..." (28)

Blamires, David. "The Medieval Inspiration of David Jones." (73)

Blamires, David, ed. "Corrigenda to *The Anathemata.*" (71)

Blamires, David, ed. *The David Jones Newsletter.* (72)

Blissett, William. *The Long Conversation.* (145)

Blissett, William. "Corrigenda to *In Parenthesis.*" (74)

Blissett, William. "David Jones: 'Himself at the Cavemouth.'" (32)

Blissett, William. "The Efficacious Word." (75)

Blissett, William. "*In Parenthesis* Among the War Books." (50)

Blissett, William. "To Make a Shape in Words." (212)

Bonnerot, Louis. "*The Anathemata* de David Jones: Poème Epique et Eucharistique. (37)

Bonnerot, Louis. "David Jones, Poète du Sacré." (51)

Bonnerot, Louis. *"Ulysses" Cinquante Ans Après*... (55)

Bouyssou, Roland. *Les Poètes-Combattants Anglais de la Grand Guerre.* (56)

Breslin, John B. "David Jones: A Christian Poet for a Secular Age." (146)

Breslin, John B. *David Jones: The Making of a Sacramental Poetic.* (191)

Breslin, John B. (S.J.). "The Shaping of a Poet's Mind." (213)

Bunting, Basil. From "A Conversation with Basil Bunting." (90)

Butler, Arthur T. *Armageddon in Perspective.* (57)

Castay, Marie-Thérèse. "A propos de *l'Anathemata.*" (76)

Cleverdon, Douglas, comp. *Word and Image IV.* (48)

Cleverdon, Douglas. "David Jones and Broadcasting." (41)

Cleverdon, Douglas. "The Dating of *Guenever, Aphrodite in Aulis,* and *The Four Queens.*" (202)

Cleverdon, Douglas. *The Engravings of David Jones.* (147)

Coffey, Warren. [Review of *In Parenthesis.*] (21)

Cohen, Joseph. "Depth and Control in... *In Parenthesis.*" (169)

Cook, Diane DeBell. *Poetry and Religion in the Major Writings*... (148)

Cookson, William, ed. *Agenda* (David Jones Special Issue), 1967. (33)
Cookson, William, ed. *Agenda* (David Jones Special Issue), 1973-74. (54)
Cooper, John X. "The Writing of the Seen World." (114)
Corcoran, Neil. *The Song of Deeds: A Study of "The Anathemata"* ... (170)
Corcoran, Neil. *David Jones' "The Anathemata": A Study of Its Background and Significance.* (115)
Daly, Carson. *The Amphibolic Structure of "The Anathemata."* (128)
Daly, Carson. "The Amphibolic Title of *The Anathemata.*" (171)
Daly, Carson. "*The Anathemata*: A Brilliant Modernist Poem." (172)
Daly, Carson. "Hills as the Sacramental Landscape in *The Anathemata.*" (214)
Daly, Carson. "Transubstantiation and Technology in the Work of David Jones." (173)
Davie, Donald. "Editorial." (149)
Davies, Aneirin Talfan, ed. *David Jones: Letters to a Friend.* (129)
Davies, Aneirin Talfan. "Ar ymyl y ddalon." (52)
Davies, Aneirin Talfan. "Corrigenda to *The Anathemata.*" (77)
Davies, Philip W. *A List of the Papers...Deposited by the Executors of [David Jones'] Estate in 1978.* (150)
DeBell, Diane. "Strategies of Survival: David Jones...and Robert Graves..." (78)
Dilworth, Thomas. *The Liturgical Parenthesis of David Jones.* (117)
Dilworth, Thomas. *The Technique of Allusion in the Major Poems* ... (92)
Dilworth, Thomas, ed. *Inner Necessities: The Letters...to Desmond Chute.* (203)
Dilworth, Thomas. "The Anagogical Form of *The Anathemata.*" (116)
Dilworth, Thomas. "Arthur's Wake: The Shape of Meaning in...*The Sleeping Lord.*" (204)
Dilworth, Thomas. "The Arts of David Jones." (207)
Dilworth, Thomas. "A Book to Remember By: David Jones' Glosses on a History of the Great War." (130)
Dilworth, Thomas. "David Jones and Fascism." (215)
Dilworth, Thomas. "David Jones' Glosses on *The Anathemata.*" (131)
Dilworth, Thomas. "David Jones' Use of a Geology Text for *The Anathemata.*" (91)
Dilworth, Thomas. "Form versus Content in David Jones' 'The Tribune's Visitation.'" (216)
Dilworth, Thomas. "*In Parenthesis* as Chronicle." (174)
Dilworth, Thomas. [Review of *Introducing David Jones.*] (151)
Dilworth, Thomas. "Sex and the Goddess in the Poetry of David Jones." (208)
Dilworth, Thomas. "Threading the Labyrinth." (132)
Dilworth, Thomas. "Wales and the Imagination of David Jones." (152)
Dorenkamp, Angela G. D. "*In the Order of Signs*": An Introduction to the Poetry... (58)
Ede, H. S. "David Jones." (2)
Ede, H. S. "David Jones, 1895-1974." (62)
Eliot, T. S. "A Note of Introduction" to *In Parenthesis.* (12)
Eliot, T. S. "A Note on *In Parenthesis* and *The Anathemata.*" (9)

Feaver, William. "Private Jones." (63)

Fowkes, Robert. "Helaethrwydd locer Dafydd Jones/The Abundance of David Jones' Locker." (118)

Friedman, Barton. "Tolkien and David Jones: The Great War and the War of the Ring." (175)

Funato, Hideo. "England no soto no Bungaku: David Jones o Chushin ni." (93)

Fussell, Paul. *The Great War and Modern Memory.* (64)

Gallagher, Elizabeth Joan. *The Mythopoetic Impulse in the Poetry* ... (133)

Garlick, Raymond, ed. *Dock Leaves* (A David Jones Number, 1955). (10)

Gemmill, Janet P. *"In Parenthesis*: A Study of Narrative Technique." (38)

Giardelli, Arthur. "Another Meeting with David Jones." (176)

Giardelli, Arthur. "The Artist David Jones." (79)

Gill, Eric. "David Jones." (1)

Grant, Patrick. *Six Modern Authors and Problems of Belief.* (119)

Gray, Nicolete. *The Painted Inscriptions of David Jones.* (153)

Grisewood, Harman. *David Jones: Writer and Artist.* (29)

Grisewood, Harman, ed. *The Dying Gaul: and Other Writings.* (105)

Grisewood, Harman and René Hague, eds. *David Jones: The Roman Quarry and other sequences.* (154)

Grisewood, Harman. "A Poem of Power and Originality." (4)

Hague, René. *A Commentary on "The Anathemata" of David Jones.* (94)

Hague, René. *David Jones* (Writers of Wales Series). (65)

Hague, René, ed. *Dai Greatcoat: A Self-Portrait of David Jones in His Letters.* (134)

Hague, René. "Myth and Mystery in the Poetry of David Jones." (95)

Halsall, T. *"Then-ness" and "Now-ness": A Study of Modern and Historical Elements in the Major Works of David Jones.* (96)

Hamilton, Alex. "From David Jones' Locker." (42)

Heaney, Seamus. "Now and in England." (59)

Hills, Paul. *David Jones.* (155)

Hills, Paul. "The Romantic Tradition in David Jones." (53)

Hinchcliffe, Michael. "David Jones et la guerre de 1914-1918: le heros entre parentheses." (177)

Hinchcliffe, Michael. "Welsh and Foreign Words in David Jones' *The Sleeping Lord.*" (156)

Hirst, Désirée. "Fragility and Force: A Theme in the Later Poems." (80)

Holland, Stephen, comp. of catalogue. *David Jones: Poet and Artist.* (135)

Hollander, John. "A Raid on the Inarticulate." (14)

Holloway, John. *The Colours of Clarity.* (23)

Holloway, Watson L. *Alone in Pellam's Land: A Prolegomenon to ... "The Anathemata."* (192)

Holloway, Watson L. "Apocalypse and Moment in the Poetry of David Jones." (205)

Holloway, Watson L. "The Pagan Liturgy of David Jones." (193)

Hooker, Jeremy. *David Jones: An Exploratory Study of the Writings.* (66)

Hooker, Jeremy. *John Cowper Powys and David Jones: A Comparative Study.* (120)
Hooker, Jeremy. "Brut's Albion." (81)
Hughes, Colin. *David Jones: The Man Who Was on the Field: "In Parenthesis" as Straight Reporting.* (121)
Ironside, Robin. *David Jones* (Modern Painters Series). (3)
Ivainer, Catherine. [Thesis] (11)
Jacobs, Nicolas. "David Jones a'r Traddodiad Cymraeg." (43)
James, M. Ingli. "Relating to David Jones." (209)
Jennings, Elizabeth. *Reaching into Silence: A Study of Eight Twentieth Century Visionaries.* (60)
Johnston, John H. *English Poetry of the First World War.* (24)
Jones, Bedwyr Lewis. "David Jones." (44)
Jones, Malcolm. *Lament for a Maker.* (67)
Keeble, Brian. "Art Decadence and a Small Press." (97)
Keith, W. J. "'The Carpentry of Song.'" (106)
Keith, W. J. "Encounters with Otherness." (157)
Kenner, Hugh. "Seedless Fruit." (8)
Kermode, Frank. *Puzzles and Epiphanies.* (15)
Klawitter, Brother George, C.S.C. "A New David Jones Letter." (178)
Kranz, Gisbert. "Die Tellus der Ara Pacis Augustae und andere Bildwerke in den dichtungen von David Jones." (179)
Kranz, Gisbert. "Walisisches Erbe. Erster Blick auf David Jones." (180)
Lehmann, John. *The English Poets of the First World War.* (158)
Levi, Peter, S.J. *In Memory of David Jones.* (68)
Levy, Edward. "David Jones: 'Life-out-there' and the limits of love." (107)
Li, Victor P. H. *The Inward Continuities: Aesthetics, Anxiety, and "The Anathemata" of David Jones.* (69)
Littlewood, J. C. F. "Joyce-Eliot-Tradition." (6)
Lochhead, Douglas, ed. *Word Index of "In Parenthesis" by David Jones.* (194)
Manglaviti, Leo M. J. "David Jones and *The Anathemata*: Life as Art." (181)
Mathias, Roland, ed. *David Jones: Eight Essays on His Work as Writer and Artist.* (82)
Mathias, Roland, ed. *The Narrows.* (160)
Mathias, Roland, ed. "David Jones: Three Letters." (108)
Mathias, Roland. "David Jones: Towards the 'Holy Diversities.'" (159)
Matthews, Caitlin and John. "David Jones: Alchemist of Images." (182)
Matthias, John. "Robert Duncan & David Jones: Some Affinities." (195)
Matthias, John, ed. *Introducing David Jones: A Selection of His Writings.* (136)
Matthias, John, ed. "David Jones: Letters to H.S. Ede." (161)
McArthur, Kathleen. "A Vision of Desolation: An Examination of the Passchendaele Section from the Abandoned *Book of Balaam's Ass*." (210)
McKay, Jan. "David Jones, Eric Gill, and Other Good Men." (162)
McPhilemy, K. M. *Towards Open Form: A Study of Process Poetics in Relation to Four Long Poems ...* (137)

Miles, Jonathan. *Coherent Eclecticism: Intellectual Disposition, Content and Form in the Work of David Jones.* (206)

Muir, Edwin. "Correspondences." (5)

Murray, A. C. C. *Mediaevalism in the Works of David Jones and Charles Williams.* (36)

Nemerov, Howard. *Poetry and Fiction.* (22)

Noon, William T., S.J. *Poetry and Prayer.* (34)

Orr, Peter. *The Poet Speaks: Interviews with Contemporary Poets.* (30)

Orr, Peter. "David Jones and His Recorded Readings." (83)

Orr, Peter. "David Jones the Artist." (84)

Orr, Peter. " 'Mr. Jones, your legs are crossed': A Memoir." (98)

Pacey, Philip. *David Jones and Other Wonder Voyagers.* (183)

Pacey, Philip. *Hugh MacDiarmid and David Jones: Celtic Wonder-Voyagers.* (99)

Pagnoulle, Christine. *David Jones: A Commentary on the Poetic Fragments.* (122)

Peck, John. "Our Politics and 'The Dream of Private Clitus.' " (163)

Phelps, Teresa Godwin. *Empress of the Labyrinth: The Feminine in David Jones' Poetry.* (138)

Phelps, Teresa Godwin. "David Jones' 'The Hunt' and 'The Sleeping Lord': The Once and Future Wales." (184)

Phillips, Robert Kenney. *The Literary Art of David Jones.* (100)

Press, John. *Poets of World War I.* (196)

Pryor, Ruth, ed. *David Jones: Letters to Vernon Watkins.* (85)

Raine, Kathleen. *David Jones and the "actually loved and known."* (109)

Raine, Kathleen. *David Jones: Solitary Perfectionist.* (61)

Raine, Kathleen. "David Jones." (185)

Rees, Samuel. *The Achievement of David Jones, Anglo-Welsh Poet.* (35)

Rees, Samuel. *David Jones* (Twayne Series). (110)

Rees, Samuel. *David Jones: An Annotated Bibliography and Guide to Research.* (101)

Richards, Frances. *Remembering David Jones.* (139)

Rosenberg, Harold. "Aesthetics of Crisis." (25)

Sandars, N. K. "The Present Past in *The Anathemata* and Roman Poems." (86)

Sanesi, Roberto. "Il 'genius loci' di David Jones." (140)

Savoia, Dianella. "Gerusalemme 'signum' di *The Anathemata.*" (142)

Savoia, Dianella. "*In Parenthesis*: 'art and sacrament' nella poesia di guerra." (111)

Savoia, Dianella. "L'Ultimo Jones: l'universalizzazione dei 'Fragments.' " (141)

Schwartz, Joseph, ed. *Renascence (The Poetry of David Jones).* (217)

Scott, Winfield Townley. "Delayed Shock of Recognition." (16)

Sherry, Vincent B. Jr. *The Habit of Monologue: Poetic Voices and Literary Tradition in David Jones' "In Parenthesis."* (123)

Sherry, Vincent B. Jr. "David Jones' *In Parenthesis*: New Measure." (186)

Sherry, Vincent B. Jr. "A New Boast for *In Parenthesis*: The Dramatic Monologue of David Jones." (187)

Sherry, Vincent B. Jr. "'Unmistakable marks': Symbols and Voices in David Jones' *In Parenthesis.*" (197)

Silkin, Jon. *Out of Battle: The Poetry of the Great War.* (45)

Spears, Monroe K. "Shapes and Surfaces: David Jones, with a Glance at Charles Tomlinson." (39)

Spender, Stephen. "Comradeship is Shared." (17)

Stallworthy, Jon. "Surviviors' Songs in Welsh Poetry." (164)

Stancliffe, Michael. "David Jones and the Liturgy." (188)

Staudt, Kathleen H. *Metaphor, Sign and Sacrament: The Problem of Transcendence in Shelley, Mallarmé, and David Jones.* (143)

Staudt, Kathleen H. "The Language of T.S. Eliot's *Four Quartets* and David Jones' *The Anathemata.*" (218)

Staudt, Kathleen H. "'At the turn of a civilization': Spenglerian Vision and Revision in David Jones' *The Sleeping Lord.*" (198)

Steele, Peter. "David Jones: Precision as Presence." (26)

Stephens, Meic, ed. *Poetry Wales* (A David Jones Number 1972). (46)

Stoneburner, Charles J. [Tony]. *The Regimen of the Ship-Star: A Handbook for "The Anathemata" of David Jones.* (31)

Stoneburner, Tony, comp. *A List of Letters by David Jones.* (102)

Stoneburner, Tony. "Notes on Prophecy and Apocalypse in a Time of Anarchy and Revolution: A Trying Out." (47)

Stoneburner, Tony. "Triad from Great Britain: Introduction to Three Recent Longer Poems and a Trying-Out to Discover if Faith Coinheres There." (112)

Summerfield, Henry. *An Introductory Guide to "The Anathemata" and "The Sleeping Lord" Sequence of David Jones.* (124)

Terpstra, John. "'Bedad He Revives! See How He Raises!': An Introduction to David Jones' 'The Sleeping Lord.'" (189)

Thwaite, Anthony. *Poetry Today: A Critical Guide to British Poetry, 1960-1984.* (211)

Tomlinson, Charles. *The Sense of the Past: Three Twentieth-Century British Poets.* (199)

Wald, Richard C. "'I Don't Think I'm Modern.'" (18)

Walker, Roy. "The Work of David Jones." (125)

Ward, Elizabeth. *David Jones: Mythmaker.* (200)

Watson, Julian. *Style and Imagination in the Art of David Jones.* (70)

Whitaker, Thomas R. "Since We Have Been a Conversation..." (87)

Wilborn, William Francis. *Sign and Form in the Poetry of David Jones.* (88)

Wilcockson, Colin, ed. *David Jones: Letters to William Hayward.* (126)

Wilcockson, Colin. "David Jones and 'The Break.'" (103)

Wilcockson, Colin. "Notes on Some Letters of David Jones." (89)

Part III

Pre-1976

1. Gill, Eric. "David Jones." *Artwork* 6.23 (Autumn, 1930): 171-177. Repeated, revised, in *It All Goes Together: Selected Essays,* and *Essays: Last Essays and In a Strange Land.*

2. Ede, H. S. "David Jones." *Horizon* 8.44 (August, 1943): 125-136.

3. Ironside, Robin. *David Jones.* Harmondsworth: Penguin Books (Modern Painters Series), 1949.

4. Grisewood, Harman. "A Poem of Power and Originality." *The Dublin Review* 226.458 (Fourth Quarter, 1952): 80-85.

5. Muir, Edwin. "Correspondences." *The Observer,* 2 November 1952: 9.

6. Littlewood, J. C. F. "Joyce-Eliot-Tradition." *Scrutiny* 19.4 (October, 1953): 336-340.

7. Auden, W. H. "A Contemporary Epic." *Encounter* 2.2 (February, 1954): 67-71. Excerpts appear in the present volume.

8. Kenner, Hugh. "Seedless Fruit." *Poetry* 83.5 (February, 1954): 296-298.

9. Eliot, T. S. "A Note on *In Parenthesis* and *The Anathemata.*" *Dock Leaves* 6.16 (Spring, 1955): 21-23. Included in the present volume.

10. Garlick, Raymond, ed. *Dock Leaves* (A David Jones Number) 6.16 (Spring, 1955), 32 pp.

11. Ivainer, Catherine. [Thesis] L'Institut D'Etudes Anglaises et Américaines, Sorbonne, 1960.

12. Eliot, T. S. "A Note of Introduction" in David Jones, *In Parenthesis*. London: Faber & Faber, 1961.

13. Auden, W. H. "The Geste Says This . . ." *The Mid-Century* 39 (May, 1962): 9, 14. Excerpts appear in the present volume.

14. Hollander, John. "A Raid on the Inarticulate." *Partisan Review* 39.3 (Summer, 1962): 451-453.

15. Kermode, Frank. *Puzzles and Epiphanies: Essays and Reviews 1958-1961*. London: Routledge and Kegan, 1962. See Chapter II, "On David Jones."

16. Scott, Winfield Townley. "Delayed Shock of Recognition." *New York Herald Tribune Books*, 8 July 1962. 3, 11.

17. Spender, Stephen. "Comradeship is Shared." *New York Times Book Review*, 15 April 1962: 4, 39.

18. Wald, Richard C. " 'I Don't Think I'm Modern.' " *New York Herald Tribune Books*, 8 July 1962: 3, 11.

19. Auden, W. H. "Adam as a Welshman." *New York Review of Books*, March, 1963: 12.

20. Berryman, John. "Epics from Outer Space and Wales." *New York Times Book Review*, 21 July 1963: 4-5.

21. Coffey, Warren. [Review of *In Parenthesis*.] *Ramparts* 2.2 (Autumn, 1963): 90-91.

22. Nemerov, Howard. *Poetry and Fiction*. New Brunswick, N.J.: Rutgers University Press, 1963. See "Seven Poets and the Language," pp. 200-214. Reprinted from *Sewanee Review* 62 (Spring, 1954): 305-319.

23. Holloway, John. *The Colours of Clarity: Essays on Contemporary Literature and Education*. London: Routledge and Kegan Paul, 1964.

24. Johnston, John H. *English Poetry of the First World War*. London: Oxford University Press; and Princeton: Princeton University Press, 1964.

25. Rosenberg, Harold. "Aesthetics of Crisis." *The New Yorker*, 22 August 1964: 114-122.

26. Steele, Peter. "David Jones: Precision as Presence." *Twentieth Century* (Australia) 18 (Winter, 1964): 335-345.

27. Bergonzi, Bernard. *Heroes' Twilight: A Study of the Literature of the Great War*. London: Constable; and New York: Coward-McCann, 1965. See Chapter 10, "Remythologizing: David Jones' *In Parenthesis*." Second edition (London: Macmillan, 1980).

28. Blamires, David. "The Ordered World: *The Anathemata* of David Jones." *Review of English Literature* 7.2 (April, 1966): 75-86. Revised in *Agenda* (David Jones Special Issue) 5.1-3 (Spring-Summer, 1967): 101-111.

29. Grisewood, Harman. *David Jones: Writer and Artist*. London: BBC Publications, 1966.

30. Orr, Peter. *The Poet Speaks: Interviews with Contemporary Poets*. London: Routledge and Kegan Paul, 1966. See "David Jones," pp. 97-104.

31. Stoneburner, Charles Joseph [Tony]. *The Regimen of the Ship-Star: A Handbook for "The Anathemata" of David Jones*. Ph.D. diss., University of Michigan, 1966.

32. Blissett, William. "David Jones: 'Himself at the Cave-mouth.' " *University of Toronto Quarterly* 36.3 (April, 1967): 259-273.

33. Cookson, William, ed. *Agenda* (David Jones Special Issue) 5.1-3 (Spring-Summer, 1967), 176 pp.

34. Noon, William T., S.J. *Poetry and Prayer.* New Brunswick, N.J.: Rutgers University Press, 1967.

35. Rees, Samuel. *The Achievement of David Jones, Anglo-Welsh Poet.* Ph.D. diss. University of Washington, 1969.

36. Murray, A. C. C. *Mediaevalism in the Works of David Jones and Charles Williams.* M. Litt. diss. Glasgow U, 1970-71.

37. Bonnerot, Louis. "*The Anathemata* de David Jones: Poème Epique et Eucharistique." *Etudes Anglaises* 24.3 (Juillet-Septembre, 1971): 233-256.

38. Gemmill, Janet Powers. "*In Parenthesis*: A Study of Narrative Technique." *Journal of Modern Literature* 1.3 (March, 1971): 311-328.

39. Spears, Monroe K. "Shapes and Surfaces: David Jones, With a Glance at Charles Tomlinson." *Contemporary Literature* 12.4 (Autumn, 1971): 402-419.

40. Blamires, David. *David Jones: Artist and Writer.* Manchester: Manchester University Press, 1971; Toronto: University of Toronto Press, 1972. Second edition with new preface, Manchester University Press, 1978.

41. Cleverdon, Douglas. "David Jones and Broadcasting." *Poetry Wales* 8.3 (Winter, 1972): 72-81.

42. Hamilton, Alex. "From David Jones' Locker." *The Manchester Guardian Weekly*, 26 February, 1972: 21.

43. Jacobs, Nicolas. "David Jones a'r Traddodiad Cymraeg." (David Jones and the Welsh Tradition.) *Taliesin* 25 (Dec. 1972): 12-25.

44. Jones, Bedwyr Lewis. "David Jones." *Taliesin* 25 (Dec. 1972): 27-34.

45. Silkin, Jon. *Out of Battle: The Poetry of the Great War*. London: Oxford University Press, 1972. Paperback reprint 1978.

46. Stephens, Meic, ed. *Poetry Wales* (A David Jones Number) 8.3 (Winter, 1972), 114 pp.

47. Stoneburner, Tony. "Notes on Prophecy and Apocalypse in a Time of Anarchy and Revolution: A Trying Out." In *Literature in Revolution*, eds. George A. White and Charles Newman. New York: Holt, Rinehart & Winston, 1972.

48. Cleverdon, Douglas, comp. *Word and Image IV: David Jones, b. 1895*. Catalogue of the National Book League Exhibition, 1972.

49. Allchin, A. M. "The Discovery of David Jones." *Theology* 76.636 (June, 1973): 283-291. Reprinted as Chapter 10 in *The World is a Wedding: Explorations in Christian Spirituality*. London: Darton, Longman, and Todd, 1978.

50. Blissett, William. "*In Parenthesis* Among the War Books." *University of Toronto Quarterly* 42.3 (Spring, 1973): 258-288.

51. Bonnerot, Louis. "David Jones, Poète du Sacré." *Etudes* (Avril, 1973): 575-588.

52. Davies, Aneirin Talfan. "Ar ymyl y ddalon." *Barn* 131 (Sept. 1973): 496-498.

53. Hills, Paul. "The Romantic Tradition in David Jones." *The Malahat Review* 27 (July 1973): 39-80.

54. Cookson, William, ed. *Agenda* (David Jones Special Issue) 11.4/12.1 (Autumn-Winter, 1973/74), 159 pp.

55. Bonnerot, Louis, ed. *"Ulysses": Cinquante Ans Après: Témoignages Franco-Anglais sur le Chef-d'Oeuvre de*

James Joyce. Paris: Librarie Marcel Didier, 1974. See pp. 223-242.

56. Bouyssou, Roland. *Les Poètes-Combattants Anglais de la Grand Guerre*. University of Toulouse, 1974. See Chapter VII, "La Geste de David Jones."

57. Butler, Arthur T. *Armageddon in Perspective: A Study of the Responses of Six Writers to the First World War*. Ph.D. diss. Claremont Graduate School, 1974.

58. Dorenkamp, Angela Gloria Donati. *"In the Order of Signs": An Introduction to the Poetry of David Jones*. Ph.D. diss. University of Connecticut, 1974.

59. Heaney, Seamus. "Now and in England." *The Spectator*, 4 May 1974: 547.

60. Jennings, Elizabeth. *Reaching into Silence: A Study of Eight Twentieth Century Visionaries*. New York: Barnes and Noble, 1974.

61. Raine, Kathleen. *David Jones: Solitary Perfectionist*. Ipswich: Golgonooza Press, 1974. See also enlarged edition, 1974-75.

62. Ede, H.S. "David Jones, 1895-1974." In catalogue, *A Memorial Exhibition*, Kettle's Yard Gallery, ed. Paul Clough, February, 1975.

63. Feaver, William. "Private Jones." *The Sunday Times Magazine*, 1 June 1975: 29-34.

64. Fussell, Paul. *The Great War and Modern Memory*. London and New York: Oxford University Press, 1975. See esp. pp. 144-154, "The Honorable Miscarriage of *In Parenthesis*."

65. Hague, René. *David Jones*. Cardiff: University of Wales Press (Writers of Wales Series), 1975.

66. Hooker, Jeremy. *David Jones: An Exploratory Study of the Writings*. London: Enitharmon Press, 1975.

67. Jones, Malcolm. *Lament for a Maker*. B.A. thesis, Cambridge University, 1975.

68. Levi, Peter, S.J. *In Memory of David Jones:* The text of a sermon delivered in Westminster Cathedral at the Solemn Requiem . . . 13 December 1974. London: The Tablet, 1975.

69. Li, Victor P.H. *The Inward Continuities: Aesthetics, Anxiety, and "The Anathemata" of David Jones*. M. A. thesis, University of British Columbia, 1975.

70. Watson, Julian. *Style and Imagination in the Art of David Jones (1895-1974)*. B.A. thesis, University of Leeds, 1975.

1976

71. Blamires, David, ed. "Corrigenda to *The Anathemata*." *David Jones Society Newsletter* 4 (Sept. 1976): 4.

    Brief contributions by René Hague, Colin Wilcockson, and Henry Summerfield on the question of errors and/or misprints in various editions of *A.*

72. Blamires, David, ed. *The David Jones Society Newsletter*. 1976-1984.

    A labor of scholarship and love by the society's first and only secretary, who wrote, edited, collated, stapled and mailed 38 issues over a period dating March, 1976 to November, 1984. No one, apparently, volunteered to take over the work at that date and so, in Blamires' closing words, "it may be...that the newsletter has served its purpose and lived its natural life." The David Jones society was founded in 1975, and numbered around 130 members at its peak. The newsletters contain a wealth of material: notices of new books by, or about, or tangentially concerned with Jones; notices of exhibitions, recordings, conferences, broadcasts; reviews of such works, and occasional correspondence touching on *corrigenda* and matters textual and otherwise--the number of Joneses to be found in *IP*, the propriety of using the name "David" in scholarly articles, the propriety/relevance of discussing perceived "homoerotic" aspects in Jones' work, etc. The newsletter serves also as a continuing *addendum* to and corrector of the Rees *Bibliography* (1977). See Nos. 8 (Aug. 1977) and 32 (Sept. 1982) for lists of subscribers' names and addresses; I give here those libraries listed: Fine Arts Department, British Council, London; Poetry Library, Arts Council of Great Britain, London; Tate Gallery, London; John Rylands University Library of Manchester; Poetry Collection, SUNY, Buffalo (Lockwood Library); the Library, University College of North Wales, Bangor; the Library, University of Kent; the Library, Memorial University of Newfoundland; the Library, Open University, Milton Keynes, England. No doubt there are others.

73. Blamires, David. "The Medieval Inspiration of David Jones," in *David Jones: Eight Essays*, ed. Roland Mathias (Gomer, 1976): 73-87.

A wide-ranging account of Jones' allusions to medieval literature, especially Chaucer, Wyatt, Malory, Dunbar, and medieval lyrics: also to earlier sources in the Anglo Saxon Chronicle and Old English heroic poetry. Blamires discusses Jones' passion for etymology ("the field of linguistics most shunned by modern linguists yet of most interest to the ordinary person") and for words as signs whose power resides in "the layers of meaning residing... through their previous use."

74. Blissett, William F. "Corrigenda to *In Parenthesis*." *David Jones Society Newsletter* 1 (March, 1976): 4.

"Corrections entered by David Jones in [Blissett's] copy of *IP*, 1959." Widely reprinted. See also, in *DJSNL* No. 5 (Nov./Dec. 1976) Blissett's *corrigenda* to *The Sleeping Lord*, "approved by David Jones in May, 1974."

75. Blissett, William F. "The Efficacious Word," in *David Jones: Eight Essays*, ed. Roland Mathias (Gomer, 1976): 22-49.

A highly informative and, indeed, entertaining account of the four-letter-word language in *IP*. Blissett's treatment of the subject both within and without the text (he draws attention to Eric Partridge's *Songs and Slang of the British Soldier 1914-1918* (pub. 1930 and 1965)) helps focus attention on a less-noticed and less "literary" source in Jones' word hoard than most commentators have dwelt on-- that is, Jones' "strictest accuracy of diction" drawn from the personal and communal experience of the soldiers in the war.

76. Castay, Marie-Thérèse. "A propos de *l'Anathemata* de David Jones." *Annales de l'Université de Toulouse-Le Mirail* 12 (1976): 113-123.

77. Davies, Aneirin Talfan. "Corrigenda to *The Anathemata*." *David Jones Society Newsletter* 3 (July, 1976): 2-3.

A list of corrections made in Davies' copy of *A* by David Jones on 13 October 1954. "These corrections are almost all incorporated in the second edition (1955)"--Blamires.

78. DeBell, Diane. "Strategies of Survival: David Jones, *In Parenthesis*, and Robert Graves, *Goodbye to All That.*" Chapter 15 in *The First World War in Fiction*, ed. Holger Klein. London and Basingstoke: Macmillan, 1976; and New York: Harper & Row, 1977: 160-173.

> DeBell notes the outward parallels (Graves and Jones both served in the Royal Welch; both works were published long after the war), and holds that "the task of writing about that experience becomes, for both of them, a means of making personal sense of it." She argues further that the common autobiographical element, which is present in widely differing degrees in the poems, is reflected both in the manner and content of these writings; the poets "struggled to avoid acknowledging the full horror ... of the war experience." Both works are seen to be "conditioned by a tradition of romantic conservatism and a history of solitary suffering." The theme and images of sacrifice in *IP* are explored fully.

79. Giardelli, Arthur. "The Artist David Jones," in *David Jones: Eight Essays*, ed. Roland Mathias (Gomer, 1976): 88-100.

> Primarily an account of three major paintings ("Manawydan's Glass Door," "Trystan ac Esyllt," and "Y Cyfarchiad i Fair") and the inscription "Cara Wallia Derelicta," and their sources in Celtic, Christian, and Classical mythology. Revised in the present volume.

80. Hirst, Désirée. "Fragility and Force: A Theme in the Later Poems of David Jones," in *David Jones: Eight Essays*, ed. Roland Mathias (Gomer, 1976): 101-122.

> An essay which is provocative in its raising of questions relating to feminism and the Female Principle in Jones' life and work. Asserting his "extra-ordinary devotion to the Feminine," Hirst notes Jones' connection with the "complete masculinist" Eric Gill, whose influence Jones was capable in large part of resisting. Nonetheless, for all Jones' "strivings towards the resolution of the basic confrontation of fragility with force, his admiration for the strength of the conqueror comes through, his respect for the man of authority." It is finally in the figure of Arthur in "The Sleeping Lord" in which "the union of strenuous effort in ordeal and saving sacrifice is effected. Fragility triumphs over force, or is sustained by it."

81. Hooker, Jeremy. "Brut's Albion," in *David Jones: Eight Essays*, ed. Roland Mathias (Gomer, 1976): 123-138.

In a discussion which touches on the "ship as metaphor for the poetic imagination.... the *David Jones*, we might say, is, more consciously than any other, a sign-bearing craft." The essay delves into Jones' exploration of the "Island as a corporate inheritance" (see *IP* notes, p. 192), and the paradox that Jones' concern with the ancient Matter of Britain "may even seem to condemn him as eccentric precisely because it is traditional." Hooker argues that Jones is "a supremely confident poet" in his language(s), imagination, and themes despite the querying tone of much of his writings. What he believes and what his writings show forth is contrary to the "generally accepted ideas of Britain in the twentieth century"; and Hooker sees Jones' attitude towards Welsh culture in particular as becoming increasingly "defensive, and yet offensive." And it is proper, Hooker writes, at least to raise the question of whether or not Jones "ever looked steadily at what a total resurgence of the Celtic cultures in this island might mean for the kind of unity in which he believed."

82. Mathias, Roland, ed. *David Jones: Eight Essays on His Work as Writer and Artist*. Llandysul, Wales: Gomer Press, 1976.

The first published transactions of *Yr Academi Gymreig* (English Section); with slight exceptions, these are "substantially the papers that the respective contributors gave to the David Jones Weekend School at Aberystwyth early in September 1975." Contributors were Peter Orr (2), William Blissett, N. K. Sandars, David Blamires, Arthur Giardelli, Désirée Hirst, and Jeremy Hooker. See entries under those names for annotations.

83. Orr, Peter. "David Jones and His Recorded Readings," in *David Jones: Eight Essays*, ed. Roland Mathias (Gomer, 1976): 13-21.

An account of Jones' submission "frequently and willingly to ordeal by tape-recorder" by Orr, who first met Jones on 15 October 1964 and recorded much of Jones reading his poetry over the next eight years. See also *The Poet Speaks: Interviews with Contemporary Poets*... (London: Routledge & Kegan Paul, 1966, pp. 97-104) for a transcript of the interview recorded 24 November 1964.

84. Orr, Peter. "David Jones the Artist," in *David Jones: Eight Essays*, ed. Roland Mathias (Gomer, 1976): 9-12.

A very brief autobiography collated and edited from recorded interviews.

85. Pryor, Ruth, ed. *David Jones: Letters to Vernon Watkins*. Cardiff: University of Wales Press, 1976.

A carefully edited and annotated volume of 23 letters, variously dated from 1953 to 1964, to Jones' fellow Welshman, fellow poet, and friend. Watkins was highly instrumental in bringing about the first publication, in the United States and subsequently in Britain, of

"The Wall." Much of this correspondence deals with matters textual, from word choice to page layout; in *Landmarks and Voyages* (1957), edited by Watkins, "the typographical lay-out was *absolutely perfect*" [Jones' emphasis]. The single most important letter is probably that of 11 April 1962, characteristically (but not accurately) described by Jones as "14 pages of a lot of tedious stuff apropos of this confounded Welsh-English thing." Boston College, Massachusetts, has eight long letters to Watkins dated between April 1960 and March 1963 which fall chronologically among the letters in Pryor's volume. Boston College also has the holograph letters printed in this work.

86. Sandars, N. K. "The Present Past in *The Anathemata* and Roman poems," in *David Jones: Eight Essays*, ed. Roland Mathias (Gomer, 1976): 50-72.

An essay which ranges widely through Jones' poetry, prefaces, and letters, written by an archaeologist and student of history and ancient literatures and pre-history. Revised in the present volume.

87. Whitaker, Thomas R. "Since We Have Been a Conversation . . ." *CLIO* 6.1 (Fall, 1976): 43-69.

The title is part of a phrase from Hölderlin: "Much has man learned... Since we have been a conversation." The essay is itself written as a series of diary entries, in which Whitaker asks: "Suppose I re-question four texts" as a way of examining this position: that the historian or literary critic "speaks *toward* truth, within the horizon of conversation.... And he will understand his own utterance to be a speculative *trouvaille*, an attentive fiction." The four works are Conrad Aiken's *Ushant* (1952), André Malraux's *The Voices of Silence* (1951), C. J. Jung's *Answer to Job* (1952), and *The Anathemata*. "Each, because it enacts its own conversation with history through its verbal form, also tends to become a kind of late romantic poem." The essay is itself labyrinthine, engaging self-consciously and reflexively the questions of language, self, phenomena, identity. *A*, like the other books under re-examination, "is necessarily a complex hermeneutical spiral.... Does the poem have a pattern? Certainly. It is an *anamnesis* in behalf of all who have fallen asleep, during which all that is wrongly thought dead, profane, or *anathema* is by intention lifted up as living and sacred, as *anathemata*."

88. Wilborn, William Francis. *Sign and Form in the Poetry of David Jones: A Study in the Poetics of the Image*. Ph.D. diss. Cornell University, 1976.

89. Wilcockson, Colin. "Notes on Some Letters of David Jones." *Agenda* 14.2 (Summer, 1976): 67-87.

Extracts from letters, and commentary, by one who knew Jones for a brief time at Northwick Lodge and corresponded with him over the years 1955 to 1974.

1977

90. Bunting, Basil. Quoted by Roland Nord in "A Bibliography of Works about Basil Bunting" (Item 50, p. 412), from "A Conversation with Basil Bunting," *St. Andrews Review* (Spring/Summer, 1977): 21-32. In *Basil Bunting: Man and Poet*, ed. Carroll F. Terrell. Orono, Maine: The National Poetry Foundation, 1980.

> "I should say Yeats and Pound and Eliot, with David Jones, the Welshman, Hugh MacDiarmid, the Scotsman, and Louis Zukofsky, the son of an immigrant Jew in New York, provide a galaxy of poets as splendid as any century can show, and I hope that when things get filtered down by time they will all be clearly visible still."

91. Dilworth, Thomas. "David Jones' Use of a Geology Text for *The Anathemata*." *English Language Notes* 15.2 (December, 1977): 115-119.

> The text is William Whitehead Watts' *Geology for Beginners* (London, 1929), which is not acknowledged by Jones in his preface or annotation to *A*. The book was in Jones' personal library (now deposited at the National Library of Wales, Aberystwyth), and Dilworth shows "beyond doubt" (in his words, and I'm convinced) that Jones used the textbook, especially in adapting "terms and categories" in Part I of *A*. "Jones' use of the scientific terms found in Watts' charts is striking in that he took over so much so nearly as he found it.... The changes he did make indicate the poetic values to which he was willing to sacrifice categorical inclusiveness."

92. Dilworth, Thomas. *The Technique of Allusion in the Major Poems of David Jones*. Ph.D. diss. University of Toronto, 1977.

93. Funato, Hideo. "England no soto no Bungaku: David Jones o Chushin ni." *Eigo Seinen* (Tokyo) 124: 449-450.

94. Hague, René. *A Commentary on The Anathemata of David Jones*. Wellingborough, England: Christopher Skelton, 1977; also Toronto and Buffalo: University of Toronto Press, 1977.

> A comprehensive and systematic annotation of *The Anathemata*, written by Jones' friend and collaborator of fifty years, and blessed further by Hague's having had "the good fortune to be able to send him a first draft of the first three sections, on which he wrote his comments"; Jones was "later to elucidate many points in conversation and correspondence." Hague addresses his book to his "friends (to all, that is, who delight in this great poem)," and in his brief discussion of the difficulty of deciding just how much commentary or explanation was needed, declares that "in the end I had to write as

though simply for myself, with a friend reading over my shoulder."
The work is far more than a gloss of "difficult" words in the poem,
and is not un-critical of Jones, especially with regard to Spengler. It
is particularly useful, both within the running commentary of the
text and in the bibliography appended, as a pointer to Jones' sources.
An essential source itself is this *Commentary*, which will not
likely be surpassed in scope and authority until the future yields a
Variorum edition of the poem.

95. Hague, René. "Myth and Mystery in the Poetry of
David Jones." *Agenda* (Special Issue on Myth) 15.2-3
(Summer- Autumn, 1977): 37-79.

> A lengthy (but unfinished, see p. 78) essay on the meanings of the
> word "myth"; on what Jones meant by myth and mythos or mythus;
> on what part myth plays in his work; and on "to what extent his
> work [can] be regarded as a making of myth." Hague quotes extensively
> from Jones correspondence and published work to elaborate further on
> Jones' understanding and use of the words "sign," "sacrament," and
> "mystery," and their application apropos of *IP* and *A*. The essay
> concludes with notes toward its completion "which any reader with a
> knowledge of the text can fill out."

96. Halsall, T. *"Then-ness" and "Now-ness": A Study of
Modern and Historical Elements in the Major Works
of David Jones.* M. Phil. thesis. University of
Warwick, 1977.

97. Keeble, Brian. "Art Decadence and a Small Press."
Art Libraries Journal (Winter, 1977): 16-23.

> Includes mention of the Golgonooza Press and its publication of works
> by and about David Jones.

98. Orr, Peter. " 'Mr. Jones, your legs are crossed': A
Memoir." *Agenda* 15.2-3 (Summer-Autumn, 1977): 110-
125.

> A personal, anecdotal memoir and tribute by one who first met and
> interviewed Jones in 1964, who recorded Jones' readings, and who became
> a personal friend over the remaining 10 years of Jones' life.

99. Pacey, Philip. *Hugh MacDiarmid and David Jones:
Celtic Wonder-Voyagers.* Preston: Akros Publications,
1977.

> This "reconnaissance into the common ground inhabited by David
> Jones and Hugh MacDiarmid" begins with a comparison of *E & A* and
> *Lucky Poet* (1943), and argues that these works reveal "that their
> authors hold far more in common than their enormous difference of
> temperament could lead one to guess." Pacey also points out that
> MacDiarmid quotes generously from Jones' Preface to *IP*. The

monograph compares the poets on three fronts: (1) "Fact and Sacrament," (2) "The 'Celtic Front,'" and (3) "Wonder Voyagings"; the latter section drawing on the ship as object, image, and metaphor in both poets' work. "There can be no doubt that David Jones and Hugh MacDiarmid would agree that it is in the ship of our art... that we must launch into the unknown... that in so doing we will partake in and renew the tradition of the 'Celtic wonder-voyagings.'" The essay also appears in Pacey's *David Jones and Other Wonder Voyagers* (see item 183).

100. Phillips, Robert Kenney. *The Literary Art of David Jones*. Ph.D. diss. University of Virginia, 1977.

101. Rees, Samuel. *David Jones: An Annotated Bibliography and Guide to Research*. New York and London: Garland Publishing, 1977.

An indexed bibliography of over 500 items, most of which are (briefly) annotated. The attempt was to be comprehensive, and a number of the works itemized include only brief mention of Jones. Part I provides a combined chronology and publishing history of Jones' works, including letters, printed to that time. Part II annotates writings about Jones, with particular attention to those which deal "in whole or substantial part" with the subject. Part III gathers periodical essays, articles, notes, and reviews; Part IV is a miscellany of broadcasts, recordings, conferences, translations, etc., and notes on work in progress. Not without error and, of course, omission. Has been found useful, but now out-dated. Should be supplemented by reference to *DJSNL* (1976-1984), later dissertations, Ward's *David Jones: Mythmaker*, and the present volume.

102. Stoneburner, Tony, comp. *A List of Letters by David Jones*. Granville, Ohio: Limekiln Press, 1977.

A list of "about 700 items addressed to about 75 persons" including letters to editors, and letters cited or included in published books. The work is arranged alphabetically by name of recipient, and within that ordering by date of letter. The longest list is of letters to Helen Sutherland (some 6 pages of entries); other longish lists note letters to W. F. Jackson Knight and H. S. Ede. The listings are not, of course, complete, and there are but brief references, say, to René Hague and Aneirin T. Davies, each of whom has published a separate collection. Some useful references to letters to be found at University of Texas (Austin), SUNY (Buffalo), McPherson Library (University of Victoria), University College of North Wales (Bangor), Kettle's Yard, the Bodleian, and the B.B.C.

103. Wilcockson, Colin. "David Jones and 'The Break.'" *Agenda* 15.2-3 (Summer-Autumn, 1977): 126-131.

A brief essay noting some parallels in theme and vocabulary between David Jones and William Morris. "It seems very likely that the 'something we christened The Break' was in fact a half-forgotten memory of Morris' 'this break in the continuity of the golden chain.' "

1978

104. Bard, Glenn. *An Elucidation of "The Sleeping Lord" by David Jones*. M. A. thesis, University of Wales, 1978.

105. Grisewood, Harman, ed. *The Dying Gaul: and Other Writings*. London and Boston: Faber and Faber, 1978.

> Described in Grisewood's Introduction as "a companion volume or sequel to *Epoch and Artist* .... a collection of nearly all the prose pieces found among David's papers which were not included" in *E & A.* The editor elaborates further on the considerations which affected decisions on what to include; also on his purposeful arrangement of the material in this posthumous volume. Seven of the pieces are previously unpublished anywhere; others of the fifteen are altered, amplified, with reference to tapes or manuscript (see the chronology of Jones' writings for specific titles).

106. Keith, W. J. " 'The Carpentry of Song': New Approaches to David Jones." *University of Toronto Quarterly* 47.3 (Spring, 1978): 277-282.

> A review article of *The Kensington Mass* and six recently published books on David Jones: Pryor, ed., *Letters to Vernon Watkins*; Rees, *Bibliography*; Hague, *David Jones* and *A Commentary*; Hooker, *An Exploratory Study*; Mathias, ed., *Eight Essays.*

107. Levy, Edward. "David Jones: 'Life-out-there' and the limits of love." *Anglo-Welsh Review* 61 (1978): 66-88.

> A long essay which outlines the major works and ideas and asks the question, "What are the radical and basic meanings attached to the recognition of David Jones?" Levy starts with the non-recognition of Jones, "the ignorance of the majority of literate and even culturally concerned people as to who he was and what he did," and contrasts Jones' example as an artist with those who exemplify "the selfish hogging of individual reputation, the conceited flaunting of or superficial preoccupation with 'talent,' " in recent years. The essay's title borrows from Auden's "The Cave of Making," a memoriam to Louis MacNeice, and Levy includes MacNeice with Hopkins, Joyce, and Jones among those who "affirm a world-out-there of which they are a part." By contrast, much in Pound, Auden, and Larkin is seen to reflect a destructive tone of "diffidence" or "defeatism."

108. Mathias, Roland, ed. "David Jones: Three Letters." *Anglo-Welsh Review* 61 (1978): 53-65.

The first two letters, dated 12 Medi [Sept.] 1964 and 19 Awst [Aug.] 1967 are addressed to Wyn Griffith, a fellow Welshman, soldier (an officer in "C" company) and author (*Up to Mametz*, 1931). The letters "reflect two facts: first, that David and Wyn, though they had an experience of war which was locationally and socially almost common and yet separate ... did not know each other very well ... [and] second, that David ... had reached that last gentle slope of slowly diminishing powers upon which ... the same complaints are made and the same difficulties engross the mind." The third letter, dated 7 September 1974, is to a Mr. Diffey of the Royal Welch Fusiliers, in which David Jones declines, on grounds of health, an invitation to a regimental reunion dinner.

109. Raine, Kathleen. *David Jones and the "actually loved and known."* Ipswich: Golgonooza Press, 1978.

A monograph which argues to the centrality of Jones' concerns which, for all their apparent otherness to modern readers--as in Jones' use of Welsh mythology, the Latin liturgy, the trench experience of the First World War--nonetheless speak to the fact that "everyman has his own unique place in a total mythus." Excerpts appear in the present volume.

110. Rees, Samuel. *David Jones*. Boston: Twayne Publishers, 1978.

The author's stated intention is to provide "an introduction to, and critical assessment of" David Jones' poetry and thought. To that end the book moves fairly systematically through a brief biography to study of *Epoch and Artist* (with particular attention to the essays "The Myth of Arthur," "Wales and the Crown," and "Art and Sacrament"), and then to outline and analysis of the major works *IP*, *A* and *SL*. The final chapter, titled "The Modern Context," attempts, in a series of brief comparative notes, to link Jones with other writers of World War I, with Welsh writers Dylan Thomas, R. S. Thomas, and Vernon Watkins, and with "modernists" Hopkins, Eliot and Pound.

111. Savoia, Dianella. *"In Parenthesis*: 'art and sacrament' nella poesia di guerra." *Università degli studi di Padova, Quaderni di lingue et letterature* (1978-79): 87-112.

112. Stoneburner, Tony. "Triad from Great Britain: Introduction to Three Recent Longer Poems and a Trying-Out to Discover if Faith Coinheres There." *Semeia* 13 (1978): 93-129.

The poems under discussion are Geoffrey Hill's *Mercian Hymns*, John Heath-Stubbs' *Artorius*, and "The Sleeping Lord." I quote from the conclusion to the author's abstract of his long and unconventionally organized essay: "*Mercian Hymns* presents a world in which Christianity is patron of arts and of empty-of-meaning and demonic actuality and in which faith verges on a possibility only at the margins of the world; *Artorius* presents a world in which faith is possible and actual in both private and public life; 'The Sleeping Lord' presents a world in which faith is possible and actual, and the work itself, as a kind of prayer, is an expression of faith."

1979

113. Barnard, John. "The Murder of Falstaff, David Jones, and the 'Disciplines of War.' " In *Evidence in Literary Scholarship: Essays in Memory of James Marshall Osborn*, ed. René Wellek and Alvara Ribeiro. Oxford: Clarendon Press, 1979.

> An essay very different in kind from most writing on Jones. Much of it deals with textual questions arising from Shakespeare's *Henry V* and its perceived inadequacies ("an intriguing failure, the root cause of which lies in its inability to maintain the heroi-comical mode of *1-2 Henry IV*"). Barnard's "accidental re-reading" of *IP* for a lecture led to ideas that go far beyond noting the allusions to *Henry V* in *IP*. He suggests that *IP* "adds a dimension to the play.... David Jones' intuition is right. The mock soldiers [of the First Quarto] were meant as a humanizing gesture. Shakespeare's murder of Falstaff came about, I would guess, because the fat knight could not fit into a national epic without destroying the whole enterprise."

114. Cooper, John X. "The Writing of the Seen World: David Jones' *In Parenthesis*." *University of Toronto Quarterly* 48.4 (Summer, 1979): 303-312.

> Much recent writing on Jones has sought to amplify and elucidate the mythic/liturgical aspects of his work. Cooper chooses to concentrate on "a particular aspect of [*IP*'s] realism: Jones' consummate skill in visual imaging." While acknowledging the presence of other modes of ordering both the experience of war and Jones' poem, Cooper holds that "the visual ... forms the first mode in a hierarchy of modes that, acting as a whole, gives meaning in the widest sense to the war experience." Cooper draws attention to the allusions to painters and paintings within the text, also to the visual detail that attends the soldiers' perception of their alien space. He dwells particularly on Jones' use of light sources to illuminate the landscape (both external and internal) from the natural sources of moon, stars, and sun to the man-made star-shells and candles. "Jones' particular descriptive talent lies, I believe, in representing, with extraordinary verisimilitude, the world in continuous transformation, the world, in short, as process."

115. Corcoran, C. Neil. *David Jones' "The Anathemata": A Study of Its Background and Significance.* M. Litt. thesis. Oxford University, 1979.

116. Dilworth, Thomas. "The Anagogical Form of *The Anathemata.*" *Mosaic* 12.2 (Winter, 1978-79): 183-195.

> A part-by-part "simplified account" of the poem is included in this essay, not as self-sufficient but to illustrate the formal unity of the poem in which "narrative time is instantaneous. Narrated time forms a circle that opens in prehistory and rounds to completion at the birth of Christ, on Holy Thursday and Good Friday, in every celebration of the Eucharist. Time ends in eternity even before the end of time." The poem in its archetypes, typological interrelationships, symbolism rises to "the anagogic phase of symbolism [after Northrop Frye], where meaning is universal." That is, while the Eucharist might be primarily a Christian metaphor for the making present of Christ, "because Christ is also God, present to all space and contemporary with all time, the metaphor is literalized and expanded." Jones' narrative form and interrelated themes are truly anagogic.

117. Dilworth, Thomas. *The Liturgical Parenthesis of David Jones.* Ipswich: Golgonooza Press, 1979.

> A monograph which incorporates material from Dilworth's *UTQ* article (Spring, 1973), but which is revised in "several important respects." It is an examination of *IP* that consists largely in drawing analogies and parallels between language, syntax, actions in the poem and their sources in the Roman Catholic liturgy, the Bible, Greek mythology (Eleusinian mysteries, the descent into Hades), and other literary and mythological referents. The treatment is not wholly literary/textual, however, and Dilworth's conclusion is that *IP* "is ultimately about human life, finite and possibly meaningless. Of life in general, war--in this poem--is an efficacious sign, and this is true partly because liturgical allusions universalize the acts and events that evoke them. But for anyone capable of sharing the poem's analogical vision, war need not signify that life is ultimately meaningless, because in war the apparent absurdity of life is magnified to become its own sign of contradiction."

118. Fowkes, Robert. "Helaethrwydd locer Dafydd Jones./The Abundance of David Jones' Locker." *Ninnau* 4.5 (March, 1979).

> Brief account in Welsh, printed in *The North American Welsh Newspaper*, published in Basking Ridge, New Jersey.

119. Grant, Patrick. *Six Modern Authors and Problems of Belief.* London and Basingstoke: Macmillan, 1979.

> David Jones is treated in Chapter IV as representative of Belief in Religion; other "beliefs" are in Mysticism (Aldous Huxley), Anarchy (Robert Graves), Fantasy (J. R. R. Tolkien), Thinking (Owen Barfield and Michael Polanyi). There is some comparison of Jones with Joyce, but the most important comparison is with William Empson: "the anti-Christian abhors the cross, welcomes scientific skepticism and material progress.... He and Jones clearly

believe utterly different things, and yet, as soon as we begin to look even at their opinions on language, this convenient distinctiveness begins to blur." Grant discusses Jones' and Empson's ideas in some detail, and compares briefly "Arachne" to *A:* "when we look at their poems, even acknowledging the contribution of personal idiom, the importance of the authors' beliefs dwindles before their compassionate sense of the perplexity of man striving to know." All the authors treated in this book are "distinguished in their own right.... Also they conform to a set of criteria having to do with epistemological problems occasioned by the rise of science and given paradigmatic modern form during the seventeenth century, and with the symbol of the cross."

120. Hooker, Jeremy. *John Cowper Powys and David Jones: A Comparative Study.* London: Enitharmon Press, 1979.

A tentative comparative study of two writers of Welsh connection and affinity, but with little else self-evidently in common. Jones had read Powys (but not Powys, Jones), and "made it quite clear that the form of the novels did not interest him.... He found the Powys 'romance' an old-fashioned form." What the two writers have most in common is "the aim of reconciliation on many levels, not least of present with past, where past embraces both childhood and the past of man." Hooker is declaredly "uncomfortable" with the comparison insofar as it might seem to suggest "an adversely critical evaluation" of Powys. One conclusion he draws is that the experience of reading each author is "different"; what the critic "admires in each writer, equally, is his uniqueness."

121. Hughes, A. Colin. *David Jones: The Man Who Was on the Field: "In Parenthesis" as Straight Reporting.* Manchester: The David Jones Society (German Department, The University), 1979.

Appears in the present volume. A study of *IP* that sets out to link events and characters depicted therein with material from war/regimental records and Hughes' visit to Mametz Wood. See also Hughes' *The Capture of Mametz Wood.* M.Phil. thesis, The Open University, 1975; and *Mametz: Lloyd George's "Welsh Army" at the Battle of the Somme.* Orion Press, 1982.

122. Pagnoulle, Christine. *David Jones: A Commentary on the Poetic Fragments.* Ph.D. diss., University of Liège, 1979.

123. Sherry, Vincent B. Jr. *The Habit of Monologue: Poetic Voices and Literary Tradition in David Jones' "In Parenthesis."* Ph.D. diss., University of Toronto, 1979.

124. Summerfield, Henry. *An Introductory Guide to "The Anathemata" and "The Sleeping Lord" Sequence of David Jones.* Victoria, B.C.: Sono Nis Press, 1979.

> The guide includes maps, chronology, selected bibliography, a synopsis of each book of *A* and of seven poems or fragments in *SL*, plus "The Narrows." The commentary and glosses are based in part on responses given by Jones in a letter to the author; glossed are "difficult words and proper names together with notes on such quotations as I have been able to detect and identify."

125. Walker, Roy. "The Work of David Jones." *The Friend* 137.18 (4 May 1979): 536-537.

126. Wilcockson, Colin, ed. *David Jones: Letters to William Hayward.* London: Agenda Editions, 1979.

> Includes Foreword, introductions to, and text of, six letters, and notes. An appendix reprints "with one or two minor alterations" the editor's essay on David Jones as a letter writer from *Agenda* 14:2 (Summer, 1976). The correspondence here collected dates from December, 1957 to July, 1961.

1980

127. Bard, Glenn. "Corrigenda to *The Sleeping Lord*." *David Jones Society Newsletter* 21 (Feb. 1980): 6.

> Six emendations of Welsh spelling in the Faber (1974) edition.

128. Daly, Carson. *The Amphibolic Structure of "The Anathemata": David Jones' Rhetoric of Anamnesis.* Ph.D. diss. Johns Hopkins University, 1980.

129. Davies, Aneirin Talfan, ed. *David Jones: Letters to a Friend.* Swansea: Christopher Davies (Triskele Books), 1980.

> A collection of 31 letters on a wide range of topics, dating from 14 October 1954 to 16 December 1971. The longest and perhaps most important is that of 27 November 1962. Davies' book includes introduction and three appendices: (1) Saunders Lewis, "An Introduction to David Jones' 'Dream of Private Clitus'"; (2) a list of broadcasts by and about David Jones produced by the editor; and (3) Jones' introductions to readings of "The Wall" and "The Tutelar of the Place" recorded in Northwick Lodge and broadcast on B.B.C. 18 December 1956. The letters cover topics such as Jones' health; his grasp, or lack of it, of the Welsh language (but always urging its preservation and use); Joyce, Dylan Thomas, and Hopkins; the intricacies of Celtic writing and art-making; the oneness of form and content; visitors (students from the Sorbonne); the bardic voice as contrary to technic.

130. Dilworth, Thomas. "A Book to Remember By: David Jones' Glosses on a History of the Great War." *Papers of the Bibliographical Society of America* 74.3 (1980): 221-234.

> The book referred to in the title is *A History of the 38th (Welsh) Division by the G.S.O.s of the Division*, ed. Lt. Col. J. E. Munby (London: H. Rees, Ltd., 1929), which Jones read in 1929 and which he frequently underlined and glossed. (The book is on deposit at the National Library of Wales.) Dilworth reproduces passages marked by Jones, also some of Jones' marginalia. Example: where the *History* records that a "slight drizzle somewhat marred the day, which was otherwise a great success," Jones notes that "actually it rained bloody hard & was an exceedingly depressing experience in all respects." The glossed *History* is important as a biographical source (Jones may have consulted it when he began to write *IP* in 1932); it is of further importance "for literary reasons. It provides a basis for interpreting the interplay, in his poem, of memory and imagination. In particular it demonstrates the importance of memory in the imaginative expansion and enrichment of the poem's seven-month period, upon which the full range and variety of Jones' military experience is brought to bear."

131. Dilworth, Thomas. "David Jones' Glosses on *The Anathemata*." *Studies in Bibliography* 33 (1980): 239-253.

> A listing, with further annotation and interpretation by Dilworth, of Jones' handwritten marginal glosses to *A* in two of Jones' own copies of the first edition (now on deposit in the National Library of Wales). Some of these glosses derive from Jones' listening to the B.B.C. broadcast of portions of *A* on 5 May 1953; they include comments on the actors' readings of particular lines and passages. While the glosses "vary in kind and importance," in sum they "constitute an authoritative commentary" on the poem.

132. Dilworth, Thomas. "Threading the Labyrinth." *The Southern Review* 16 (Spring, 1980): 512-515.

> A review of René Hague's *Commentary*, of special value because of Dilworth's correcting of Hague's occasional inaccuracies and misreadings: Hague "is not a completely trustworthy guide.... He is nevertheless the best we have to date; that is to say, he is often very good."

133. Gallagher, Elizabeth Joan. *The Mythopoetic Impulse in the Poetry of David Jones*. Ph.D. diss. University of Manchester, 1980.

134. Hague, René, ed. *Dai Greatcoat: A Self-Portrait of David Jones in His Letters*. London and Boston: Faber and Faber, 1980.

Preface and "Introductory" by René Hague, plus connecting notes, glosses, elucidations, translations, etc. This is a collection of dozens of letters, chiefly to Jim Ede, Tom Burns, Harman Grisewood, and of course Hague, plus one each to Eliot and Auden and to others. Note that the letters are "edited" frequently, not printed in full. Included are biographical details about Jones' health; his love life (if one is to call it that--strong emotional attachments to Petra Gill, Prudence Pelham, and later Valerie Wynne-Williams); his drinking habits (some affection for Scotch, though Hague insists that Jones never knew from experience what a hangover was); his financial affairs. These kinds of details help to ground Jones autobiographically in a way not previously accessible. There is a lot of recounting of the experience of the War, especially in later letters to Colin Hughes, and wide-ranging discussion of the ideas behind Jones' poetry and paintings. There is a wealth of material from the Gill years, and a host of references to other literati--Eliot, Auden, Sassoon, Graves, Owen, Dylan Thomas. Many of the letters convey a gruff tone, with much use of "balls," "bugger," and "damn," plus the occasional "fucking." Some despair that the modern world was not as appreciative as it might have been is expressed; Jones felt that Americans were more sympathetic to the aims and intricacies of *A* than were the English; there is considerable muttering about the changes in the Catholic liturgy. As to just why the letters are edited as much as they are, see "Preface." Hague also says occasionally that "it would not be fair to David" to include a certain passage, so the aim is not total disclosure. Hague is critical of Jones on the subject of Spengler and Hitler, and of Jones' studied Welshness, which Hague finds to be archaic and Romantic. An absolutely indispensable book for the student of Jones' life and work; choice excerpts appear in the present volume.

135. Holland, Stephen. Compiler of catalogue, *David Jones: Poet and Artist*. Kent University Library, 1980.

Includes illustrations and four photographs of Jones, a brief introduction, and an appendix by Canon A. M. Allchin describing two letters to him written by Jones on 3 September 1967 and 28 February 1968.

136. Matthias, John, ed. *Introducing David Jones: A Selection of His Writings*. London and Boston: Faber and Faber, 1980.

The short "Preface" by Stephen Spender, based in part on memories and impressions of Jones dating back to the mid-1930's, when they first met, is reprinted in the present volume. Matthias' "Introduction" makes plain that this selection is intended to introduce and encourage readers new to the work of David Jones; to that end the volume includes selections from *IP*, *A*, and *SL*, together with Jones' notes. Specifically, the volume includes "A, a, a, Domine Deus," Part 3 of *IP*, and selections from Parts 4 and 7; almost entire the Preface to *A*, plus selections from I and VII, and II entire; from *SL*, "The Tribune's Visitation," "The Tutelar of the Place," "The Hunt," and a selection from "The Sleeping Lord." Matthias' "Introduction" seeks to place each selection in the context of the particular poem and in the larger frame of Jones' life work and recurring major themes; and while it is clearly and declaredly advocatory, it eschews "stridency." "One of the great lessons we can derive from David Jones' career will come from the thought of his nearly infinite patience." Matthias further emphasizes Jones' craftsmanship, his care and determination "to use a word as a *thing*, as an object to be moved here or there, to be seen in relationship to this or that. But his willingness so often to think out his music in terms of the nominative, of the word-as-a-noun, produces a texture which is wonderfully knitted with the stuff of otherness: we want to run our finger over the page."

137. McPhilemy, K. M. *Towards Open Form: A Study of Process Poetics in Relation to Four Long Poems: "The Anathemata" by David Jones, "In Memoriam James Joyce" by Hugh MacDiarmid, "Passages" by Robert Duncan, "Gunslinger" by Edward Dorn.* Ph.D. diss. University of Edinburgh, 1980.

138. Phelps, Teresa Godwin. *Empress of the Labyrinth: The Feminine in David Jones' Poetry.* Ph.D. diss. University of Notre Dame, 1980.

139. Richards, Frances. *Remembering David Jones.* London: Enitharmon Press, 1980.

   A private printing of 105 copies. The briefest (4 pages) of biographical notes/remembrances, by the wife of the artist Ceri Richards.

140. Sanesi, Roberto. "Il 'genius loci' di David Jones." *Annali dell' Instituto di lingue e letterature germaniche, Università di Parma, Facolta di magistero* 6 (1980-81): 9-43.

141. Savoia, Dianella. "L'Ultimo Jones: l'universalizzazione dei 'Fragments,'" *Studi di letteratura inglese e americana* (1980): 127-146.

142. Savoia, Dianella. "Gerusalemme 'signum' di *The Anathemata.*" *Università degli studi di Padova, Quaderni di lingue e letterature* 5 (1980): 5-17.

143. Staudt, Kathleen H. *Metaphor, Sign and Sacrament: The Problem of Transcendence in Shelley, Mallarmé, and David Jones.* Ph.D. diss. Yale University, 1980.

1981

144. Alexander, Michael. "On David Jones' Letters, Man, Poetry and the BBC." *Agenda* 18.4/19.1 (Winter-Spring, 1981): 162-169.

> A review of *Dai Greatcoat* and four other books on Jones. See also, in the same issue, Harman Grisewood's brief address at the Requiem Mass for René Hague in Westminster Cathedral, given 13 March 1981 (pp. 191-192).

145. Blissett, William. *The Long Conversation: A Memoir of David Jones*. Oxford University Press, 1981.

> The genesis of this "memoir" is in the notes written by the author after thirty or so visits to David Jones over the years 1959 to 1974. Blissett and Jones became close friends, and this memoir (the only serviceable title, really, for the contents, which also include *corrigenda* to texts, reprints of letters, and miscellany of various sorts), reads almost like a novel at times: the account of how contact was made and how friendship grew, and how old age and ill-health also grew on David Jones, leading to his death in 1974. The memoir is laden with details of biography, references to other friends of Jones, artists, authors; it's an essential book for biographer and textual scholar alike. Appendix A reprints Blissett's review of *A* (UTQ 24 (1955): 212-215; Appendix B reprints from *The Times*, 6 July 1971, an "Appeal to Preserve Mass Sent to Vatican," to which Jones was one of numerous literary signatories. Excerpts appear in the present volume.

146. Breslin, John B. "David Jones: A Christian Poet for a Secular Age." *America* 145.20 (19 December 1981): 394-396.

> A short, essentially introductory essay in a North American Jesuit publication on Jones' ideas, particularly in relation to the sacramental nature of art and sign-making. "What makes this enterprise...especially important for Christians is the synthesis he attempts between the aims of art and religion, two powerful cultural forces that have seldom in this century laid credible claim to the mutual nourishment that was once taken for granted in the West (*Ars fovet fidem. Fides fovet artem*)."

147. Cleverdon, Douglas. *The Engravings of David Jones: A Survey*. London: Clover Hill Editions, 1981.

> A limited edition consisting of "A Survey of the Engravings of David Jones" (pp. 1-22), "A List of Engravings by David Jones" (pp. 23-39), a "List of Books and Ephemera: Containing Engravings by David Jones" (pp. 41-58), and Plates, 1-96. Cleverdon had first come to know Jones and Eric Gill in the spring- of 1926, and biographical details abound in his introductory survey, as does quotation from correspondence. An intriguing biographical note: "After his breakdown in 1933, David did no painting for several years.... He was

much under the influence of a friend with (as it has been called) a 'destructive intelligence,' who considered that the modern world was so awful that no Catholic artist could or should work in it."

148. Cook, Diane DeBell. *Poetry and Religion in the Major Writings of David Jones.* Ph.D. diss. University of East Anglia, 1981.

149. Davie, Donald. "Editorial." *PN Review* 24 (Autumn, 1981): 1.

Some of the most stringent criticism of Jones yet to appear. Davie's reflections arise out of consideration of the publication of *Dai Greatcoat* and of Matthias' presentation of a selection of Jones' letters to H. S. Ede (see *PNR*, No. 22). Davie argues that it is time to recognize, and not excuse, Jones' sometimes "silly and irresponsible" utterances; to give credit to his "moving and tough-minded achievements" while challenging the highly Romantic, anti-intellectual image of Jones as one who "certainly in his life, and often in his art, [is] getting mileage out of this notion that the artist has the right to be muddle-headed, muzzy and ineffectual so long as he is strenuously well-intentioned." Davie's tone and content is, of course, sharply at variance with that of Matthias in *PNR* 22 and also with Nicholas Tredell's review of David Jones at the Tate (*PNR* 23) or Peter Levi's review of *The Roman Quarry* (*PNR* 24).

150. Davies, Philip W., compiler. *David Jones Papers (1978 Deposit): A List of the Papers of David Jones (1895-1974) Deposited by the Executors of His Estate in 1978.* The National Library of Wales, 1981.

A 53-page description of the contents of six boxes of assorted material which are made up largely of "drafts" of letters to friends and acquaintances and the press, plus numerous drafts of prose writings and mss. and typescript and page proofs. See also the National Library of Wales *Annual Report*, 1978-79, pp. 79-80, where a brief list of the contents of the 1978 *Deposit* first appeared. See also page 62 of that report for a brief list of the contents (3 boxes) of the NLW's *Purchase*. In total these make up a mass of material ranging from (yes) a laundry list and a statement of Jones' income for the year 1966 to worksheets, manuscripts, typescripts, proofs, lists of corrections, etc., for poetry, prose, and correspondence. The National Library of Wales also holds David Jones' personal library and various other related items.

151. Dilworth, Thomas. [Review of John Matthias' *Introducing David Jones*.] *The Georgia Review* 35.2 (Summer, 1981): 437-441.

The review serves itself as a brief introduction to Jones' major works. A printer's devil has surely misdated the anecdote of the opening paragraph, in which it is related that Yeats (in 1927?) declaims: "I salute the author of *In Parenthesis*."

152. Dilworth, Thomas. "Wales and the Imagination of David Jones." *Anglo-Welsh Review* 69 (1981): 41-52.

> An essay which cites biographical information recorded by Dilworth in conversation with Jones regarding his earliest identification with the Welsh language and Welsh self-identity. There is further material relating to Jones' earliest attempts to study Welsh from a pocket dictionary; and the observation that in Jones' library (on deposit at the National Library of Wales, Aberystwyth) "of the approximately 1500 books belonging to him... only twelve books and pamphlets are in Welsh. About 190 more, however, are Welsh in subject matter." Dilworth goes on to discuss the Welsh aspects of character and language in *IP, A* (especially "Mabinog's Liturgy") and "The Sleeping Lord" and of Jones' conversion to Catholicism. Dilworth writes that "For many Welsh converts, the Catholic faith is partly a means to recovering a spiritual heritage progressively denied to the Welsh, first by Anglicanism and its attendant English imperialism, then by a Methodism more Calvinist than the English variety, and finally by a spreading agnosticism in which religious sensibility is reduced, as Jones once put it, to membership in the Labour Party." Dilworth argues that the importance of Wales as landscape, history, and imagination in Jones' poetry must be wholly apprehended; for Jones and reader, whether Welsh or not, "Welshness extends back to the cultural origins of our world."

153. Gray, Nicolete. *The Painted Inscriptions of David Jones*. London and Bedford: Gordon Fraser Gallery, 1981.

> A handsome folio volume of virtually all of Jones' inscriptions, many reproduced in color, all annotated. Introduction (pp. 9-26) includes a brief discussion of lettering as an art, and a critical account of Jones as a lettering artist. See also extracts from letters by Jones to Nicolete Gray, Helen Sutherland, and Vernon Watkins.

154. Grisewood, Harman and René Hague, eds. *David Jones: The Roman Quarry and other sequences*. London: Agenda Editions, and New York: The Sheep Meadow Press, 1981.

> In the Foreword, Grisewood notes the death of his co-editor on 19 January 1981. In 1975 Grisewood was asked by the heirs of Jones' estate "to examine his papers and sort them into categories"; the prose pieces, previously unpublished at least in book form, came to make up *The Dying Gaul* (1978). The Introduction by Grisewood and Hague is dated July, 1980, and tells of their difficulties in disentangling some 1300 sheets of foolscap. After *IP* was "more or less finished--that is, some time about 1935--all that he [Jones] produced, whether printed or unprinted, may be regarded as a draft for a wide-ranging poem which he was never able to complete." The editors caution that "it will, we hope, be understood that we are reading the pages that follow in confidence, so to speak--a confidence that the poet is unable to withhold. So fastidious a writer would not have published these

pieces unrevised." Necessarily, then, the status of this collection as an authentic addition to the Jones canon is in some doubt. It forms a wealth of new material indeed, but just how to treat it will remain a vexing question for scholars. The volume is divided into four main sections: Part I includes "The Roman Quarry," "The Narrows," and "Under Arcturus"; Part II includes "The Kensington Mass," "Caillech," and "The Grail Mass"; Part III includes "The Old Quarry, Part One," "The Agent," and "The Old Quarry, Part Two"; Part IV is "The Book of Balaam's Ass." The volume concludes with an extended "Commentary" by René Hague; this material, essentially compiled from Hague's letters, memoranda, and running commentary as he worked upon the poems given in this volume, was not intended, Grisewood notes, for publication.

155. Hills, Paul. *David Jones*. London: The Tate Gallery, 1981.

Published for the retrospective exhibition of 21 July to 6 September 1981, "the first major exhibition of the work of David Jones since his death in 1974" and his second at the Tate Gallery (the first was in 1954-55). Includes Chronology; an essay on "The Art of David Jones" by Paul Hills (pp. 19-71); an essay on the inscriptions by Nicolete Gray (pp. 127-128); 17 color plates of paintings and inscriptions; a thoroughly annotated and illustrated catalogue of engravings, illustrations, drawings, paintings, and inscriptions; a list of lenders. It is a magnificent volume, indispensable as a source depicting Jones' work, which is widely scattered in galleries and private collections; and for Hills' essay, which discusses Jones' art works in relation to his life, his written works, and his relations within and without the British art world of the 1920's through 1950's.

156. Hinchcliffe, Michael. "Welsh and Foreign Words in David Jones' *The Sleeping Lord.*" *Annales de l'Université de Toulouse-Le Mirail* 17 (1981): 33-43.

157. Keith, W. J. "Encounters with Otherness: Readings of David Jones." *University of Toronto Quarterly* 50.3 (Spring, 1981): 330-335.

A review-article of six recently published books on David Jones. As Keith notes, *UTQ* has been, for many years, "especially hospitable to scholarly writing about David Jones," in part because of the ongoing interest of its previous editor, William Blissett. Keith is correct, and this review is itself supplementary to a previous "round-up" of seven Jones books (*UTQ*, Spring, 1978). The treatment of each work is, necessarily, brief, and is lightly judgmental. It is in *Dai Greatcoat* that Keith finds the truest introduction to Jones: "I doubt if there is a single page in the book which does not add a new dimension to our knowledge of a great poet and painter and an intensely lovable man."

158. Lehmann, John. *The English Poets of the First World War*. London: Thames and Hudson, 1981.

> See especially (of the 58 illustrations) Nos. 37-41 by David Jones. Twenty-one poets are discussed in this work; Jones is treated in Chapter 7, where he is included (but given pride of place and most of the attention) with Laurence Binyon, Wilfred Gibson, Richard Aldington, Edgell Rickword, Arthur Graeme West, and T. P. Cameron Wilson. Lehmann introduces Jones' life and, in particular, *IP*, which he describes as "difficult of access." Whether or not its method "is simply an unique (and perhaps eccentric) phenomenon, or is fertile for the literature of the future, it is still too soon to say."

159. Mathias, Roland. "David Jones: Towards the 'Holy Diversities.' " *Transactions of the Honourable Society of Cymmrodorion* (1981): 137-178. See also *A Ride Through the Wood: Essays on Anglo-Welsh Literature*. Bridgend: Poetry Wales Press, 1985.

> An important and lengthy essay, difficult of access but well worth the tracking down. The occasion for the essay was the first Llewelyn Wyn Griffith Memorial Lecture to the Honourable Society of Cymmrodorion, 20 May 1981, and there is brief initial attention to the connections between Jones and Wyn Griffith (a common experience of the trenches in Mametz Wood, their authorship of books based upon that experience; the two Welsh soldier-writers did not, however, meet until 1940). The first half of Mathias' essay is largely biographical; it is, however, interpretive biography, characterizing Jones as "an extreme example of the creative intelligence that jibs at and refuses all other kinds of order than the one it can and does itself create from its own beginnings and its own ancillary likings"; and as an "agglomerator, digressive, magpie-like, searching for what *he* wanted." There is further investigation of what the institutions of the army and the Church provided for Jones; Mathias' declared thesis is, however, "that Wales, after many vicissitudes, won a great battle for him. It became, so to speak, the shibboleth with which he could put away fear." The second half of the essay examines, not un-critically, the major works in an "attempt now to show how Wales and the idea of Wales plays a part in" Jones' work. Mathias argues that "in the later years of [Jones'] better health" the poet moved closer toward Wales, which "spoke to him constantly of freedom and a separate tradition," and away from the *imperium*, which earlier "had been the emblem of his own need for strength and reassurance." See also *Spirit* 41 (Fall-Winter, 1974/75) and 48 (1982) for other (brief) writings on Jones by the same author.

160. Mathias, Roland, ed. *The Narrows*, by David Jones. Budleigh Salterton, Devon: Interim Press, 1981.

> I borrow from David Blamires' review of this new edition of *The Narrows* (*DJSNL* No. 29, October-November, 1981: 1-2). "The introduction by Roland Mathias provides fascinating material about the original presentation and meaning of the poem, since his

editorial queries and attempts to understand what it was that David Jones had provided him with for the fiftieth celebratory number of the *Anglo-Welsh Review* [Autumn, 1973] drew from the poet a lot of comments on what he considered important and why." This publication also includes an essay by Eric Ratcliffe titled " 'The Narrows' and the Western Empire," which Blamires describes as "extremely helpful on the historical context." See also review by Greg Hill in *Anglo-Welsh Review* 71 (1982): 87.

161. Matthias, John, ed. "David Jones: Letters to H. S. Ede." *PN Review* 22 (1981): 10-16.

First see, in the same issue, Matthias' " 'Speak that I may see thee' " (pp. 17-21) for a very substantial review of *Dai Greatcoat*. The review serves also as an introduction to the preceding selection of letters and excerpts from over 100 letters collected at Kettle's Yard, Cambridge. Matthias provides introduction to, and continuity between, these selections, which are not included in *Dai Greatcoat* and which cover the period from c. 1934 to 1971. They deal in topics ranging from contemporary British art to European politics of 1936, to Jones' financial situation (much alleviated through the good offices of Jim Ede), to his psychotherapy (1947-1948), to his surprise and delight at being awarded the Midsummer Prize of the City of London (1968). And there's more. An essential supplement to *Dai Greatcoat* and other collections of letters. The selected letters are also presented in *Notre Dame English Journal* 14:2 (Spring, 1982): 129-144, with altered prefatory material; and in the present volume.

162. McKay, Jan. "David Jones, Eric Gill, and Other Good Men." *Antiques Trade Gazette*, 21 Nov. 1981.

Not seen. Described in *DJSNL* nos. 29 and 30 as an account of prices fetched at Sotheby's sale.

163. Peck, John. "Our Politics and 'The Dream of Private Clitus.' " *Ploughshares* 6.4 (1981): 208-227.

Peck's is an intense and detailed study of the poem's dream frame, its setting in time and place, its allusions or "rhyming," with particular attention to "the conjugations of Clitus' dream--its grammar and also its marriages--[which] in fact demand that we hear the poem's several cries as a fragmentation, or choral analysis, of its form." The study of this dream poem, written by a poet who is both Catholic and modernist, allows us to "begin to respecify for a politics that undersense which is spiritual, and below, and tends toward the enactments of art."

164. Stallworthy, Jon. "Survivors' Songs in Welsh Poetry." *Times Literary Supplement*, 4 Sept. 1981: 1015-1016.

A "slightly edited version" of the author's Gwyn Jones Lecture, given at University College, Cardiff, earlier in 1981. The essay is largely a study of *IP*'s narration, action, allusions, but Stallworthy sets the poem in the context of other "survivors' songs" by Aneirin, Taliesin,

Wilfred Owen, and Alun Lewis--with further pertinent reference to the *Chanson de Roland* and the book of *Job*. The unifying theme asserted (if somewhat tentatively) is that "the work of Celtic poets in general, and that of Welsh poets in particular, is generated, animated by, a stronger sense of kinship with the dead than you find in English or American poetry."

1982

165. Archard, Cary, ed. *Poetry Wales* 17.4 (Spring, 1982).

Pages 35-71 are titled "The Achievement of David Jones" and present five short essays arising from a special session at the MLA convention in New York, December, 1981. Brief introduction by Michael Collins. See separate entries under Cohen, Daly, Dilworth, Manglaviti, and Phelps.

166. Bartlett, Neil. " 'Cara Wallia Derelicta,' " in *The Celtic Consciousness*, ed. Robert O'Driscoll. New York: George Braziller, 1982. Volume first published in a limited edition of 500 copies by McClelland and Stewart and the Dolmen Press, Canada, 1981.

One of the papers first presented at a "Symposium on the Celtic Consciousness" in February, 1978, at the University of Toronto. An essay both sympathetic and critical (Bartlett wants to "touch and test" Jones' ideas), treating Jones and his work after "The Break." Bartlett argues that a Welsh or Celtic tradition, "a continuity[,] is being invented, in order that the function of the maker may be maintained. If the poet is to retain the garb of the *sacerdos*, then his 'history,' like that of the priest (like that of Joyce) must be converted, transmuted by the invocation of extra-historical continuities, authorities."

167. Bennett, J. A. W. *Poetry of the Passion: Studies in Twelve Centuries of English Verse*. Oxford: Clarendon Press, 1982.

See Chapter VIII, "From *Adam Bede* to *Anathemata* [sic]." Discussion of the twelve centuries ends with fairly detailed study of Jones' works, written and visual, but especially *A* and its relation to "The Dream of the Rood." In Jones' work, "we are drawn beyond consideration of literary genres, even as we are drawn beyond theological formulas.... We apprehend [the crucifixion] afresh in the light of two thousand years of human suffering. The deepening and revivifying of Christian belief ... is sometimes entrusted to poets: to a Dante, a Langland, a David Jones."

168. Blamires, David. *David Jones and the Nativity: A Christmas Essay*. Manchester: David Blamires, 1982.

A privately printed, illustrated monograph noting that in *IP*, *A*, *SL*, and Jones' inscriptions, one can trace Jones' "life-long fascination with the meaning and iconography of the Nativity."

169. Cohen, Joseph. "Depth and Control in David Jones' *In Parenthesis*." *Poetry Wales* 17.4 (Spring, 1982): 46-52.

> A rebuttal of Paul Fussell's position that *IP* is "curiously ambiguous and indecisive." Cohen argues from the term "simultaneity" as used in relativity theory, in which "simultaneous occurrence is the key to structural coherence." *IP* "is, in fact, structured coherently by virtue of its adherence to the principles by which we now understand the universe to operate: the primacy of simultaneity, the uncertainty of measurement, and the invalidation of causality."

170. Corcoran, Neil. *The Song of Deeds: A Study of "The Anathemata" of David Jones*. Cardiff: University of Wales Press, 1982.

> A substantial study of *A* which serves as both an introduction to the work and a critical engagement of its methods and ideas. Corcoran raises some objections and takes some exceptions on matters of style and of intent / performance; nonetheless, he perceives the poem as striving for "epic inclusiveness" and achieving it. The discussion ranges from glosses on particular passages, to noting Jones' debt to (and diversions from) Spengler, to perceiving the possible influence of Jones' work in John Montague's *The Rough Field*, Seamus Heaney's *North*, and Geoffrey Hill's *Mercian Hymns*. There is further consideration of how "the world in *The Anathemata* seems to be discovered in the process of generating names for itself, of bringing itself to birth through language"; and Corcoran holds that "the essential structural unit... is not the line, or even the phrase, but the word itself." The union of Welsh culture and Roman Catholicism, while it may not be central to the experience of many of Jones' readers, nonetheless is a "unified and coherent... world in which the human imagination has lived and found enriching satisfactions."

171. Daly, Carson. "The Amphibolic Title of *The Anathemata*: A Key to the Structure of the Poem." *Renascence: Essays on Values in Literature* 35.1 (Autumn, 1982): 49-63.

> An extended discussion of the rhetorical term "amphibole," defined as a word that has "two meanings and two levels of meaning," which starts with Jones' choice of, and *apologia* for, his term "anathemata" (see Preface to *A*). The essay is not then a reading of the poem, or an interpretation of its setting, allusions, etc., but a directive on how to read the poem. Critics who belong to either the "pro-fragments" or "pro-unity" factions are both right, "as far as they go." Multiple or diverse interpretations are "not only possible, but necessary.... The fact that critics who argue exclusively for the unity or the fragmentation of the work end by inadvertently demonstrating both, indicates that the poem is structured amphibolically."

172. Daly, Anne Carson. *"The Anathemata*: A Brilliant Modernist Poem." *Poetry Wales* 17.4 (Spring, 1982): 53-58.

> A brief essay, essentially introductory in nature: "the final test of the poem's greatness, however, lies not just in its scope, subject, profundity, pathos, intellectual interest, visual appeal, varied style, sensitivity to sound, or technical virtuosity, but also in the beauty and resonance of the images and thoughts evoked by its language."

173. Daly, Carson. "Transubstantiation and Technology in the Work of David Jones." *Notre Dame English Journal* 14.3 (Summer, 1982): 217-230.

> Primarily a study of Jones' prose writings on the title's subject, framed by a consideration of how, in the twentieth century, it is technology, not the nature of the Eucharist, "which is the subject of impassioned debate, national wars, philosophical controversy, and common interest." For David Jones, however, transubstantiation is "the focal point of his life and his art"; it is "the only possible remedy for the menace of technocracy."

174. Dilworth, Thomas. *"In Parenthesis* as Chronicle." *Poetry Wales* 17.4 (Spring, 1982): 37-45.

> A brief essay detailing the historical, biographical, and autobiographical accuracy of persons and events in *IP*, while also noting the variances in chronology, etc. Jones, says Dilworth, is being over-careful and perhaps misleading when he writes in his Preface that "none of the characters in this writing are real persons, nor is any sequence of events historically accurate" (*IP*, p. ix). Dilworth argues that Jones excludes personal anecdotes and deliberately writes "flat" characters. "As chronicle [*IP*] maintains an objectivity to match that of the work's multi-layered allusions.... In these allusions, but perhaps more clearly in the underlying chronicle, Jones bases his aesthesis on the Aristotelean reality-principle."

175. Friedman, Barton. "Tolkien and David Jones: The Great War and the War of the Ring." *CLIO* 11.2 (Winter, 1982): 115-136.

> The essay ranges widely in war literature to include mention of Blunden, Sassoon, Kipling, Barbusse, et al. and makes frequent reference to Fussell's *The Great War and Modern Memory*. Tolkien, an officer in the Lancashire Fusiliers, fought at the Somme; also, like David Jones, he was a Roman Catholic. Friedman sees the two writers (in Tolkien's *Lord of the Rings* and Jones' "Art in Relation to War") as "celebrating the delight of war rather than deprecating its slaughter.... Resurrection is essential to Jones and Tolkien. As Christians, they must believe that the sacrifices of men have meaning; that soldiers too imitate Christ; that, despite whatever evidence, there is order in history." Tolkien is seen by Friedman to put a "romancer's ... construction on history"; Jones "fashions myth

from history; operates on the premise that both are of the same stuff." That there is "order in history is the principle informing [Christopher] Dawson's argument in *The Making of Europe* ... and Dawson is implementing the thesis of an even more famous Catholic historian, Lord Acton."

176. Giardelli, Arthur. "Another Meeting with David Jones." *Anglo-Welsh Review* 71 (1982): 75-79.

A review of the David Jones exhibition at the National Museum of Wales, 31 October to 13 December 1981.

177. Hinchcliffe, Michael. "David Jones et la guerre de 1914-1918: le heros entre parentheses." In N. J. Rigaud, ed., *Le Mythe du heros: Actes du colloque interdisciplinaire, Centre Aixois de recherches anglaises, 12-13-14 Mars 1982.* Aix-en-Provence: Publications Université de Provence (1982): 165-183.

178. Klawitter, Brother George, CSC. "A New David Jones Letter." *Notre Dame English Journal* 14.2 (Spring, 1982): 145-146.

Text of a very brief letter dated 29 August 1938 by David Jones to Douglas and Mea Woodruff, which is now in the Special Collections of the Notre Dame Memorial Library.

179. Kranz, Gisbert. "Die Tellus der Ara Pacis Augustae und andere Bildwerke in den dichtungen von David Jones." *Anglia* 100 (1982): 92-102.

180. Kranz, Gisbert. "Walisisches Erbe. Erster Blick auf David Jones." *Stimmen der Zeit* 197.6 (June, 1979): 394-402.

181. Manglaviti, Leo M. J. "David Jones and *The Anathemata*: Life as Art." *Poetry Wales* 17.4 (Spring, 1982): 59-63.

A brief article which introduces Jones' life and the poem and then draws them together, observing that in the accidents of his birth Jones shared the traditions of both Roman and Celtic Britain, and that in his conversion to Roman Catholicism those traditions were joined to Christianity. "Poetic materials, from personal life and preserved history, mirror the life's search for fulfillment and attempt for definition of self."

182. Matthews, Caitlin and John. "David Jones: Alchemist of Images." *Temenos* 2 (1982): 243-251.

A short review/article covering 10 books on Jones published from 1978
to 1980. The authors decry the "already rampant preciousness
surrounding Jones' memory," and are most appreciative of Hague's *Dai
Greatcoat* as a corrective: "a single reading of this collection will be
enough to balance the adulation which threatens to swamp the real
David Jones." Among the critical or interpretive works, the writers
value most highly the work of Kathleen Raine, "a critic whose own
understanding of the numinous is as great as that of her subject."

183. Pacey, Philip. *David Jones and Other Wonder
Voyagers*. Bridgend: Poetry Wales Press, 1982.

In his Introduction, Pacey declares that his "primary purpose of
collecting these essays from the last ten years is to pay tribute to
David Jones, whose own work both as poet and in the visual arts
marvellously illustrates the proposition of a lifetime's art as one
work, one wonder-voyage." Three of the essays deal more or less
exclusively with Jones (see, for example, "Why David Jones is not a
Household Name," pp. 49-61). The remainder treat him in the
company of other poets such as Basil Bunting, John Heath-Stubbs,
Geoffrey Hill, and Jeremy Hooker, fellow "navigants of the obscure
passage," and Paul Nash, George Mackay Brown, and Ian Hamilton
Finlay.

184. Phelps, Teresa Godwin. "David Jones' 'The Hunt' and
'The Sleeping Lord': The Once and Future Wales."
Poetry Wales 17.4 (Spring, 1982): 64-71.

A brief introductory essay which "explores Jones' connection to his
Welsh heritage and how his Welsh affinities are manifested in his
art" (in particular, in these two poems).

185. Raine, Kathleen. "David Jones" in *The Celtic
Consciousness*, ed. Robert O'Driscoll. New York:
Braziller, 1982. (See entry under Bartlett, Neil, for full
bibliographical information.)

A brief essay, largely introductory, relating how David Jones "has
given continuity to the supporting imaginative structure of the
whole Island." His subject might be, indeed is, Wales, whose
Arthurian material is part of the larger Matter of Britain;
however, Jones leads us into the "living present" of Wales and finally
to "the sleeping presence of the King, who is the very-life-spirit
of the Island of Britain, whose past secures the future."

186. Sherry, Vincent B. Jr. "David Jones' *In Parenthesis*:
New Measure." *Twentieth Century Literature* 28.4
(Winter, 1982): 375-380.

A brief article engaging Fussell's criticism of Jones. Sherry,
dwelling on the allusions to Mars, Pandora, and the chivalric code,
shows that Jones invokes in his imagery, characters, and settings,
"mesure" or the "heroic motif of restraint." He wants the careful
reader to perceive that Jones is indeed "making a recondite and precise

judgment on the unheroic nature of technological war, and conveying this judgment in controlled, imaginative artistry."

187. Sherry, Vincent B. Jr. "A New Boast for *In Parenthesis*: The Dramatic Monologue of David Jones." *Notre Dame English Journal* 14.2 (Spring, 1982): 113-128.

A close reading of Dai Greatcoat's boast, its context, voice, allusions, meaning, with particular reference to "related forms of antiquity: the dramatic flyting and the riddle." A second and complementary frame is that of the dramatic monologue, in which (see Robert Langbaum, *The Poetry of Experience*), "forced to set aside moral categories and 'external' systems of judgment, we must, instead, project ourselves sympathetically into the speaker to grasp the meaning of the poem." The latter mode enables the reader to resolve the riddles explicit and implicit: "Christ is indeed the analogue and archetype of the agent-victim Dai." A revised version appears in the present volume.

188. Stancliffe, Michael. "David Jones and the Liturgy." *Temenos* 3 (1982): 13-25.

Stancliffe uses the word "Liturgy" in both its narrow and broad sense: in the first, as "the service of the Holy Eucharist" as performed in the various Christian churches; in the latter, as "the whole of the Church's prescribed public worship--the forms of all its services; the fixed patterns ... movements ... actions ... rubrics ... Calendar." The essay treats *IP* and *A* in some detail, and makes passing reference to the liturgical language and modes in "The Sleeping Lord" and "The Tutelar of the Place." The "influence that [the Liturgy] had on David Jones--both upon the substance and the form of his poetry--" is more extensive than can be found in the works of Dante, George Herbert, Herrick, Wordsworth, Eliot, Auden, or other poets.

189. Terpstra, John. " 'Bedad He Revives! See How He Raises!': An Introduction to David Jones' 'The Sleeping Lord.' " *University of Toronto Quarterly* 52.1 (Fall, 1982): 94-105.

The title is derived from a Dublin street-ballad (see *The Dying Gaul*, p. 58). Terpstra provides a close sequential reading, paraphrase, interpretation of "The Sleeping Lord," which is seen as being "in the nature of a summary of David Jones' thought and feeling, as if it was composed over his entire lifetime, before it was finally written down, close to life's end." There is particular attention to Jones' relationship to Wales; treatment also of the relation between the central figure of the sleeping lord, Arthur, and the Dying Gaul, and Christ.

1983

190. Austin, Diana. *A Study of "In Parenthesis" by David Jones*. D. Phil. diss. Oxford University, 1983.

191. Breslin, John Bernard. *David Jones: The Making of a Sacramental Poetic*. Ph.D. diss. Yale University, 1983.

192. Holloway, Watson L. *Alone in Pellam's Land: A Prolegomenon to David Jones' "The Anathemata."* Ph.D. diss. Emory University, 1983.

193. Holloway, Watson L. "The Pagan Liturgy of David Jones." *Antigonish Review* 53 (Spring, 1983): 47-53.

> An essay largely introductory in nature, drawing attention to those passages and words in *A* that "resonate with 'pagan' as well as Christian ritual intensity." There are times, as in the "vine-juice skipper" passage (*A*, p. 182), borrowed from the sea ditty "Shallow Brown," when "it seems that Jones, in his constant interplay between the exalted and the vulgar, skates on thin ice; the tension between styles (as in Dante) propels him dangerously close to the brink of blasphemy." However, Jones' "humility," perhaps "naivete," "self-effacing seriousness," and "high reverence" rescue him from this charge; his mission and achievement, like that of all "sacramental 'makers,'" is "the consecration of the profane (making it numinous), the drawing forth of the divine from the purely material."

194. Lochhead, Douglas, ed. and comp. *Word Index of "In Parenthesis" by David Jones*. Sackville, New Brunswick: Harrier Editions, 1983. Limited edition of 100 copies.

> The editor/compiler takes pains to describe his work as a "preliminary attempt to provide access to the immense arsenal of words" which make up *IP*. He describes his methods of compilation (primarily a labor of hand, using 3" x 5" slips) and cautions the reader against the possibility of errors. Yes, there are errors (e.g., Chinest for Chinese, p. 44); the user should observe also Lochhead's note that "upper case letters are placed first in each alphabetical section." Thus the name "Christ" (capitalized) is listed for six occurrences (p. 45), and for four lower-case occurrences nine pages later (p. 54). To be used with care, yes, but to be used. Blissett's *Corrigenda* to the text of *IP* is given in an appendix.

195. Matthias, John. "Robert Duncan & David Jones: Some Affinities." *Ironwood* 22 (1983): 140-157.

> As the title itself indicates, Matthias' linking of the two poets is offered tentatively, modestly, suggestively, as a "kind of experiment." "The purpose of these notes is simply to suggest some

of the pleasures--as well as the critical difficulties--of . . . reading Jones and Duncan together." In fact the essay, subdivided into three major categories--(1) The Actually Loved and Known; (2) The Feminine, Man-the-maker, and their Sign; and (3) Sign, Hearth, Meadow, Cave, and "Requisite Nowness"--draws widely on the poets' writings in both poetry and prose to show that the affinities are indeed pervasive and demonstrable. It is a lengthy and detailed essay whose main theme is that the poets (whatever their differences, a subject for another occasion, Matthias hints) share most profoundly a common "sacramental ethos." For both, "man is *homo faber* and art a gratuitous and intransitive activity which, embodied fully in a work, implies also an element of transitivity or sign that is sacramental in its nature and incarnational in its affirmations."

196. Press, John. *Poets of World War I*. Windsor (Berks.): Profile Books, 1983.

> See Chapter VIII: "The Aftermath: Herbert Read and David Jones." A very brief treatment in which the poets are linked as later writers who "attempt to assimilate certain qualities of modern prose fiction" in their move away from the "impressionistic" and "lyrical" modes. Jones' "The geste says this..." phrasing at the conclusion of *IP* "may serve as an epitaph for the poets of 1914-1918... and as a commemoration of all who suffered and bore witness on the battlefields of World War I."

197. Sherry, Vincent B. Jr. " 'Unmistakable marks': Symbols and Voices in David Jones' *In Parenthesis*." *Critical Quarterly* 25.4 (Winter, 1983): 63-73.

> The essay's title comes, of course, from Part 7 of *IP* and before that from Lewis Carroll's "The Hunting of the Snark." Sherry notes its origin, and further notes that it, like many other allusions and symbols in the work, also poses a riddle, as the reader will likely want to identify the phrase with Christ's wounds. In short, it might be a "mistakable mark" (Sherry's phrase). If, however, the reader perceives these problematic riddles in the spirit of participatory reading and engages sympathetically as respondent in the dramatic monologue mode of the speaker John Ball, then he can reconcile the perplexing or apparently contradictory symbols. Jones "authenticates his symbols by joining his persona and reader in the very process of symbol making. Reading in this active and creative fashion will solve the problem of the riddling symbol."

198. Staudt, Kathleen H. " 'At the turn of a civilisation': Spenglerian Vision and Revision in David Jones' *The Sleeping Lord*." *Contemporary Poetry* 5 (1983): 51-70.

> Staudt first outlines the cycles described by Spengler as typifying the movements of world "Cultures" in their springtime to their inevitable evolution and decline into imperialist "Civilization." The poems of *SL* are seen as falling essentially into two opposing groups: "the first depicting the Civilization of the late Roman empire, the second celebrating the Culture represented by the ancient customs and

legends of the Celtic people." While Jones' later works can be seen to
"echo and rework Spengler explicitly," what critics have not noted
is the challenge to Spengler that is to be seen in Jones' poetry, "often
in the places where the poet seems to be adopting most faithfully
Spengler's terms and models." The essay concentrates on "The
Tribune's Visitation" and "The Tutelar of the Place," the latter of
which affirms most strongly Jones' belief that in the sign-making
activity of the artist lies the possibility of the renewal of Culture
and the preservation of "some remnant of a persistent and humane
creative order."

199. Tomlinson, Charles. *The Sense of the Past: Three
Twentieth-Century British Poets.* (The Kenneth Allott
Lectures, No. 3.) Liverpool University Press, 1983.

> The text of a lecture given on 21 October 1982 on Jones in the company
> of Basil Bunting and Geoffrey Hill. For Tomlinson, Jones' *IP* is
> "surely his finest book," but "one is always left in two minds by
> Jones--one admires the range ... yet one remains uncomfortably aware
> that any given insight is likely to be crushed by imaginative over-
> crowding, by relentless typological parallels." What these three
> poets have in common is that they serve to revive English poetry;
> this revival "helps to rectify a loss of cultural memory and reminds
> us that under the dull new suburb the altar stone of the mother
> goddesses and the spirit of place may well still exist."

200. Ward, Elizabeth. *David Jones: Mythmaker.* Manchester: Manchester University Press, 1983.

> A study of Jones' life and works that is decidedly critical and un-
> adulatory ("most existing critical studies of his work ... see things
> through David Jones' eyes"). Ward's central argument is that
> "although David Jones' mythopoeic impulse proved at first to be a
> creative catalyst of the most fruitful kind, it later hardened into an
> obsession with the abstract features of the myths haunting his
> imagination, to the point of causing severe creative blockages." It
> follows then, and Ward is unambiguous in her ordering of the works,
> that *IP* is the major achievement, that *A* is "markedly inferior,"
> that the prose essays are polemical and repetitious, that the
> fragments of *SL* (with the exception of "The Book of Balaam's Ass"
> excerpt and to a lesser degree "The Sleeping Lord") are characterized
> by Jones' "commonest stylistic faults: repetitiveness,
> sententiousness, and over-simplification." That last word leads to, or
> derives from, in Ward's book, her analysis of Jones' life and thought:
> how to reconcile the paradox implicit in one whose impulses and
> ideas are nostalgic, primitivist, dualistic, dogmatic, reductive but
> whose works are highly original, experimental, and difficult. Ward
> is not content to let the paradox lie (and I'm not going to summarize
> her conclusions); suffice it to say that her study of Jones' life in the
> context of contemporary ideas in politics, aesthetics, and ideology
> (especially with reference to Eric Gill, Maurice de la Taille,
> Jacques Maritain, Bernard Wall, and Christopher Dawson) is
> original and essential; that her rebuttals of Paul Fussell on *IP* are
> sound; that her reading of individual passages and works is always
> pointed and relevant to her stated intentions; that her critique is

wide-ranging, is seriously and responsibly rendered, and must be engaged.

201. Alexander, Michael. "David Jones, An Introduction: The Unknown Modernist." *Scripsi* (University of Melbourne) 2.4 (1984): 257-298.

> An edited transcript of a radio program first broadcast on Radio Helicon in 1979; it was commissioned by Richard Connolly of the Australian Broadcasting Corporation. The script ranges widely through Jones' life and works, and includes Alexander's recorded interviews with William Cookson, editor of *Agenda*, Lord Kenneth Clark, and Dr. Ieuan Williams, philosopher at the University College of Swansea. Also included are portions of a recorded conversation between Jones and Saunders Lewis ("The Writer's World," BBC-2, 15 March, 1965), and a lengthy reply by René Hague to Alexander's question, "What is *The Anathemata* about?"

202. Cleverdon, Douglas. "The Dating of *Guenever*, *Aphrodite in Aulis*, and *The Four Queens*." *David Jones Society Newsletter* 38 (November, 1984): 6-10.

> A personal account of difficulties arising from the author's compilation of the Catalogue for the National Book League exhibition in 1972 (see *Word and Image*); and a reasoned re-dating of these three paintings based on correspondence and manuscripts in Cleverdon's possession.

203. Dilworth, Thomas, ed. *Inner Necessities: The Letters of David Jones to Desmond Chute*. Toronto: Anson-Cartwright Editions, 1984.

> A collection of 15 letters and two fragments, virtually all written in the months following publication of *A.* The letters are carefully edited and annotated by Dilworth, who presents them in his introduction as having their "chief value [in] their elucidation of *The Anathemata*." An appendix reprints Desmond Chute's review of *A* in *Downside Review* 71 (Summer, 1953): 339-344; the letters here printed indicate that Chute consulted Jones at some frequency before writing the review, and that Jones replied at length to his enquiries. Jones liked the review so much that he arranged for T. S. Eliot to read it--and regretted later having done so. The letters include occasional references to Pound, Eliot, Emyr Humphreys, and even Dylan Thomas (who had been held up as a model of intelligibility and discipline by one Jones reviewer, to Jones' bemusement).

204. Dilworth, Thomas. "Arthur's Wake: The Shape of Meaning in David Jones' *The Sleeping Lord*." *Anglo-Welsh Review* 76 (1984): 59-71.

> A detailed study of the poem's rhetoric, allusions, imagery, structure, modes, and movements. That is, the poem is "about" Arthur, but it is "also about the meaning of its own imaginative expansion. It is, in other words, a poem about itself, but without

being obviously self-referential." Dilworth notes the division of the
poem into three parts, the first and last of which are informed by a
series of questions that one can identify with (or ascribe to) the
poet. The central third is the chief focus of Dilworth's essay; the
interior monologue-prayer of the priest is observed to occupy
"considerable narrative or subjective time but very little narrated,
chronological time." Nonetheless, it is truly "central" to the
experience of the poem; it is "not only the work's spatial centre but
also its primary focus of meaning... its ultimate and all-
encompassing symbol."

205. Holloway, Watson L. "Apocalypse and Moment in the
     Poetry of David Jones." *Faith and Reason* 10.3 (Fall,
     1984): 191-199.

> An enquiry into the reasons behind the apparent "unexpected
> effusion of enthusiasm for an unabashedly Christian poet" in the
> world of secular literary scholarship. Holloway points to Jones'
> "apocalyptic orientation" as the cause for this phenomenon, and
> cautions that he is using "apocalyptic" in its biblical sense, not as
> re-defined by Frank Kermode and Northrop Frye. From a study of *A*
> and *IP*, the latter seen as more "personally apocalyptic," Holloway
> concludes that "the intensity of the present, forced by an erosive
> past and a threatening future, drives the apocalyptic community to
> look fervently for the redemption and the security offered by the
> ending and to glimpse in a fleeting moment of insight (which doom
> offers) the fundamentally spiritual nature of the world.... David
> Jones' poetry revolves around this interplay of ritual and apocalypse
> and apparently strikes a chord in the thinking of contemporary
> readers whether religious or secular in outlook."

206. Miles, Jonathan. *Coherent Eclecticism: Intellectual
     Disposition, Content and Form in the Work of David
     Jones*. D. Phil. diss. Oxford University, 1984.

1985

207. Dilworth, Thomas. "The Arts of David Jones." *Religion
     and Literature* (formerly *The Notre Dame English
     Journal*) 17.1 (Spring, 1985): 87-98.

> This is a review-article dealing but briefly with *The Dying Gaul* and
> *The Roman Quarry*, and more extensively and critically with five
> other works on Jones published in 1981 and 1982. Dilworth concludes
> that Corcoran's *The Song of Deeds*, "despite its errors and what I take
> to be its mistaken emphases... is certainly the best work of
> literary criticism on David Jones." One third of the article is given
> to evaluation of Elizabeth Ward's *David Jones: Mythmaker*, itself a
> highly critical treatment of Jones' work and ideas; it is a study to
> which Dilworth directs substantial and sustained criticism. He
> finds, for example, that Ward is "weakest... where other reviewers
> have said she is strong, in her attempted refutation of Paul Fussell's
> negative judgment of [*IP*] in *The Great War and Modern Memory*."

The other books given briefer attention are Blissett's *The Long Conversation*, Pacey's *David Jones and Other Wonder Voyagers*, and Nicolete Gray's *The Painted Inscriptions*.

208. Dilworth, Thomas. "Sex and the Goddess in the Poetry of David Jones." *University of Toronto Quarterly* 54.3 (Spring, 1985): 251-264.

> A closely detailed study of the female figure in Jones' work, dwelling in particular on the Queen of the Woods from *IP*, Elen Monica and Gwenhwyfar in *A*, and the goddess who is "The Tutelar of the Place" and who is embodied in the Tellus Mater of "The Dream of Private Clitus." Dilworth compares Jones' female figures/goddesses with those of Joyce, Pound, and Graves, for whom the goddess is "theologically or ontologically, merely the ghost of a dead mythology." With "a certain amount of conjecture," Dilworth discusses, apropos of Jones' celibate life, his relations with the three women with whom he had once been in love (Petra Gill, Prudence Pelham, and Valerie Price), also his neurosis, breakdowns, and psychotherapy. The main focus is, however, on the literary goddess: "Prominent throughout his work, the goddess is always a vestige of primitive religion, but for David Jones, Catholic Christianity is the fulfilment of pagan religion, and validates it even as it alters its meaning.... She is, in short, the pagan personification of the Christian mystery of redemption, and in a form that any man, in the sexual depths of his humanity, can well appreciate."

209. James, M. Ingli. "Relating to David Jones." *Anglo-Welsh Review* 80 (1985): 64-75.

> At the heart of James' essay is a study of the two versions of "Trystan ac Esyllt," approached "in a way one might approach any of Jones' works, written or pictorial." The study illustrates that the principle by which Jones' work lives for the reader or viewer is in the "conscious *engaged detachment* [James' emphasis] induced in the viewer by the work's conspicuous artifice, its palpable made-ness. For all Jones' later work is in this sense rhetorical, it announces its nature as art: it is, as he might have put it, art *qua* art." The essay serves both as an explanation of, and defense of, the alleged "obscurity" of Jones' works.

210. McArthur, Kathleen. "A Vision of Desolation: An Examination of the Passchendaele Section from the Abandoned *Book of Balaam's Ass*." *Poetry Wales* 20.3 (1985): 67-77.

> One of the few studies of this fragment from the *SL* volume. McArthur views it first as a "transition piece" between *IP* and *A*, but is primarily concerned to study it as a "war poem" and to raise the question of "whether David Jones was able to come to terms in his poetry with the later period of the war." The critic holds that this work, in whose form "one sees a bold movement away from the progressive linear structure of *In Parenthesis* towards the freer

form of *The Anathemata*," is "an ill-balanced piece." She concludes
that Jones "saw clearly the spiritual and physical desolation and
destruction of the Great War, but as these were so recalcitrant to his
deeply religious and essentially optimistic view of life, he was
unable to sustain such a vision poetically."

211. Thwaite, Anthony. *Poetry Today: A Critical Guide to
British Poetry, 1960-1984.* London and New York:
Longman, 1985.

A "revised and expanded version" of *Poetry Today: 1960-1973*, with
little revision in respect to David Jones who, in a chapter titled
"Robert Graves and David Jones," is described as " 'difficult' in a way
that Graves never is." Jones "has attracted a cult-following rather
than general affection and admiration." A brief comparison to Pound
suggests that Jones' Christianity provides a unifying force for his
fragments. The achievement is, finally, seen as "puzzling and not
always apparently coherent," but "impressive" nonetheless.

1986

212. Blissett, William. "To Make a Shape in Words."
Renascence 38.2 (Winter, 1986): 67-81.

Noting that Jones omits from his preface to *IP* any mention of
"plot line" in his narrative fiction, Blissett poses first a series of
questions such as: "Will his characters 'do' anything or merely
suffer? Will the sequence of events have any meaning beyond mere
succession?" The answer is immediately forthcoming, and includes
the observation that "generally speaking... in epic and mythic
narrative and even in realistic prose fiction there is likely to be an
appreciable element of the known shape, the foregone conclusion, the
plot that goes without saying." Certain ordering shapes are, as it
were, received or inferred by the reader, whether they be the routine
passage of a day or the routines of a military unit going up to war or
into battle. For readers of *IP*, who may indeed be removed in time
from the experience of the Great War, it remains true that that
event provides "the principal known shape." *IP* is in a sense "the
typical [my emphasis] war book, using every conceivable device to
evoke the experience of the Great War, whose historical-narrative
succession is everywhere assumed." Blissett documents his argument
in a part-by-part treatment of *IP*, and concludes that "from *In
Parenthesis* (and *In Parenthesis* alone, I am confident in saying) the
Great War on the Western Front could be reconstructed--in substance,
language, feeling, and meaning--as the Dublin of 16 June, 1904, could be
reconstructed from *Ulysses*."

213. Breslin, John B., S.J. "David Jones: The Shaping of a
Poet's Mind." *Renascence* 38.2 (Winter, 1986): 83-102.

A long essay given in the first part to a study of "three epiphanies,
drawn from Jones' own letters and essays, [which] give us a rather
clear picture of the way his imagination and memory worked--or, at
least, of the way he saw them working." The incidents treated are,

first, Jones' recollection from age five of "a troop of horses, moving in column to the tarantara of bugles" (*DG*, 19-21); the second, Jones' recounting of his "spying unintentionally on the Mass in Flanders in the Forward Zone" after the Somme (*Dai Greatcoat*, 248-250); the third, Jones' musings on the presence of soldiers in Jerusalem in 1934 (letter to Saunders Lewis, December, 1971). The latter half of the essay relates the discoveries of the first part to, in particular, the influence of Maurice de la Taille.

214. Daly, Carson. "Hills as the Sacramental Landscape in *The Anathemata*." *Renascence* 38.2 (Winter, 1986): 131-139.

An article which first sketches the impulses of the "religion and regionalism" which inspire Jones' poetic in all his works (Daly cites the evident affection for hills in details from Jones' life in Wales and on Harrow Hill, also in his paintings), and then concentrates on *A* to show specifically how Jones transforms "the hill-country he describes into a truly sacramental landscape." The process moves through several stages from recognition of the realistic presence and characteristics of hills, the hill as, literally, a hill, to "hill-ness," to the archetypal hill in which "one quickly recognizes the importance of this geological form in art and in ritual, as well as its cultural, historical and religious significance." It is finally in perceiving the hill form and its "role... in the events of the Incarnation, Crucifixion and Resurrection" that the metamorphosis is completed.

215. Dilworth, Thomas. "David Jones and Fascism." *Journal of Modern Literature* 13.1 (March, 1986): 149-162.

To the ongoing debate about Jones' attitudes, as expressed in life and poetry, towards Hitler and Fascism (see *Dai Greatcoat* and Ward, *David Jones: Mythmaker*), Dilworth introduces two new and exceedingly interesting documents: (1) a previously unpublished "Hitler" essay typescript, dated 11 May 1939; (2) a letter to Dilworth from Harman Grisewood dated 10 August 1984. An expanded version of this essential piece is included in the present volume.

216. Dilworth, Thomas. "Form versus Content in David Jones' *The Tribune's Visitation.*" *Renascence* 38.2 (Winter, 1986): 103-116.

Dilworth quotes Jones' own assessment of the poem as "the best thing I've done... the best thing I've managed to make" of all the poems in *SL*. The study focuses closely on the shifting moods and modes of address of the Tribune, whose monologue Dilworth describes as "the most subtle and ambiguous of the poems" in *SL*; "certainly it is the darkest poem David Jones ever wrote." Dilworth charts four rhetorical movements in the poem: the first prefatory, liturgically referential, and establishing a "symbolic resonance" that will sound throughout; the second, "a routine word" of military command; the third, "a more necessary word" which constitutes an attack on "myth, ritual, folklore, and domestic attachments"; and the fourth, a return to ritual. This outline is, however, merely a starting place, for this most "elusive and disturbing of David Jones' personae ... so often and so subtly changes his point of view, and reveals various and conflicting levels of personality, [that] one cannot be sure that he has him figured out."

217. Schwartz, Joseph, ed. *Renascence: Essays on Values in Literature (The Poetry of David Jones)* 38.2 (Winter, 1986). 76 pages.

This special issue devoted to Jones' poetry includes essays by William Blissett, John B. Breslin, S.J., Carson Daly, Thomas Dilworth, and Kathleen Staudt. See annotations under individual names.

218. Staudt, Kathleen H. "The Language of T. S. Eliot's *Four Quartets* and David Jones' *The Anathemata.*" *Renascence* 38.2 (Winter, 1986): 118-130.

An examination of the poems' differing modes of discourse, which "reflect the complementary traditions within Christianity on which the two poets are drawing: the *via negativa* of St. John of the Cross and other mystics, whom Eliot read and admired, and the more temporally oriented way of sacramental theology which forms the basis for Jones' poetics." Staudt avoids the "temptingly neat" formula that would assign to Eliot the "negative way" and to Jones "the affirmative way," cautioning that Jones' concept of the "incarnation" as he explores it and exemplifies it in *A* renders a formulaic division impossible. Both poems ultimately lead the reader to, in Eliot's words, "arrive where we started / and know the place for the first time."

PAUL HILLS

*A LIST OF DRAWINGS, PAINTINGS, CARVINGS,
AND INSCRIPTIONS BY DAVID JONES
IN PUBLIC COLLECTIONS*

(a) Great Britain

Aberdeen, Art Gallery
"Landscape" 1941 (?) Watercolor

Aberystwyth, National Library of Wales
"Tregaron" 1913 Oil
"Tir y Blaenau" 1924-25 Watercolor
"Capel-y-ffin" 1925 Watercolor
"Llys Ceimiad: La Bassée Front 1916" 1937
    Watercolor
"PWY YWR GWR" 1956 Inscription
"BEIRD BYT BARNANT" 1958 Inscription
"CLOELIA CORNELIA" 1959 Inscription
"CARA WALLIA DERELICTA" 1959 Inscription
"OPTIMA MUSA VERITAS" 1948 or earlier
    Inscription
"ACCENDAT IN NOBIS" 1961 Inscription
"TALIESIN" 1961 Cover design for periodical

Bangor, University College of North Wales
"The Park" 1932 Watercolor
"Musical Instrument and Flowers" 1932 Watercolor

Barnsley, Yorks, Cooper Art Gallery
"Jaguar" 1931 Pencil and watercolor

Bedford, Cecil Higgins Art Gallery
"Pigotts Farm" c. 1930 Watercolor
"Cumberland" 1946 Watercolor

Belfast, Ulster Museum
   "Seascape" 1927 Watercolor

Birmingham, City Art Gallery
   "Tangled Cup" 1949 Watercolor and chalk

Bristol, City Art Gallery
   "Still life with Gladioli" 1927 Watercolor

Caernarfon, Regimental Museum of Royal Welsh Fusiliers
   A number of drawings done in the trenches

Cambridge, Fitzwilliam Museum
   "Head of a Negro Girl" c. 1919 Watercolor
   "The Shepherdess" 1930 Watercolor

Cambridge, Kettle's Yard, University of Cambridge
   "Lourdes" 1928 Gouache
   "Sea from a terrace" 1929 Watercolor
   "Vexilla Regis" 1947 Pencil and Watercolor
   "Flora in Calix-light" 1950 Pencil, chalk, watercolor
   "The Fox" Pencil
   "QUIA PER INCARNATI" 1949-50 Inscription
   Also numerous engravings and hand-colored photographs of inscriptions.

Cardiff, National Museum of Wales
   "Pilate Washing his Hands" 1922 Pencil
   "Saint Hilary raising a man from the dead" 1922 Pencil
   "Crucifixion" 1925 Boxwood carving
   "The Dog on the Sofa" 1926 Watercolor
   "The Maid at No. 37" 1926 Watercolor
   "Tenby from Caldy Island" 1925 Watercolor
   "Balcony and sea" 1927 Watercolor
   "Roman Land" 1928 Watercolor
   "Eric Gill" 1930 Watercolor
   "The Old Animal from Tibet" 1930 Watercolor
   "Herbaged Landscape, Ynys Byr" 1931 Watercolor

"The Translator of the Chanson de Roland" 1932
Watercolor

"Edwart: Tywyson Cymru" 1936-7 Pencil

Frontispiece for *In Parenthesis* 1937 Pencil, ink
and watercolor

Tailpiece for *In Parenthesis* 1937 Pencil, ink and
watercolor

"Female Nude" Pencil and watercolor

"Dwynwen Deg in Livia's Frock" 1948 Chalk

"Major Hall's Bothy" 1949 Watercolor

"MABINOGI IESUCRIST" 1955 Inscription

"Mehefin" c. 1950 Watercolor

"Trystan ac Essyllt" c. 1962 Watercolor

Study for "Trystan ac Essyllt" c. 1959-60
Watercolor

Study for constellations in "Trystan ac Essyllt"
Pencil

"Y Cyfarchiad I Fair" c. 1963 Watercolor

Cardiff, Welsh Arts Council

"Putting out the Washing" 1926 Watercolor

"Bristol Docks" 1927 Watercolor

"Vessels Sheltering" 1927 Watercolor

"In the Pyrenees" 1928 Watercolor

"Jug of Wild Flowers" 1929 Watercolor

"Eisteddfa Calupso" 1931 Watercolor

"Sidmouth" 1940 Watercolor

"Chalice with Flowers and Seal" c. 1950 Watercolor

"Girl in a hat" c. 1950 Crayon

"CUM LUCIA" 1950s Inscription

Edinburgh, Scottish National Gallery of Modern Art

"Northumberland Fields" Watercolor

"Princess with Long-boats" c. 1948-49 Pencil and
crayons

"Chalice with Flowers and China Mug" c. 1950
Watercolor

"IN PRINCIPIO" c. 1951 Inscription

548 *Paul Hills*

Huddersfield, Art Gallery

"Portrait of Desmond Chute" 1932 Pencil and watercolor

Leeds, City Art Gallery

"The Sitting Room, Howson Road" 1926 Watercolor

"Portrait of René Hague" 1930 Pencil and watercolor

"The Open Bay" 1931 Watercolor

Leeds University

"Martha's Cup" 1932 Watercolor

Leicester Museum and Art Gallery

"La Bonne Bergere" 1951 Pencil and watercolor

"Window at Sidmouth" Watercolor

London, Arts Council Collection

"Female Nude" Watercolor

"Passing Sail" 1929 Watercolor

"Tree trunks and shed" 1948 Watercolor

"Still Life" Watercolor

London, Bethnal Green, Museum of Childhood

Four puppets 1920s Carved and painted wood

Toy village c. 1922 Carved and painted wood

London, British Museum

"Gill's house at Ditchling" 1922 Watercolor

"The Ship off Ynys Byr" 1927 Watercolor

London, British Council Collection

"Curtained Outlook" 1932 Watercolor

"The Lord of Venedotia" 1948 Pencil and chalk

"Brief record of bird on bough" 1948 Pencil and chalk

"The Storm Tree" 1948 Watercolor

The Museum of London

"St John's Wood" 1928 Watercolor

London, Tate Gallery

"Standing Nude" 1921 Pencil

"The Garden Enclosed" 1924 Oil

"Sanctus Christus de Capel-y-ffin" 1925 Gouache and watercolor

"The Terrace" 1929 Watercolor

"The Chapel in the Park" 1932 Watercolor

"Guenever" 1938 Pencil, ink and watercolor

"Aphrodite in Aulis" 1940 Pencil and watercolor

Study for "Aphrodite in Aulis" Pencil

"The Four Queens" 1941 Ink and watercolor

"Chalice with Flowers and Pepperpot" 1950s Pencil and watercolor

"EXIIT EDICTUM" 1949 Inscription

London, Tate Gallery Archive Collection

This consists of over ninety items from the estate of David Jones. Most of them are slight, unfinished drawings or diagrams; the more significant works are listed in the *David Jones Society Newsletter* no. 38, pp. 4-5, Nov. 1984. The collection can only be visited by appointment.

London, Victoria and Albert Museum

"Male Nude" 1926 Pencil

"Portrait of a Woman" 1926 Pencil and watercolor

"Number One Elm Row" 1927 Watercolor

"The Table Top" 1928 Watercolor

"The Violin" 1932 Watercolor

Manchester, City Art Gallery

"Out Tide" c. 1931 Oil

"Leafless Tree" 1948 Crayon and pencil

Manchester, Whitworth Art Gallery

"The Waterfall, Afon Honddu Fach" 1926 Watercolor

"Surf" 1927 Watercolor

"Portrait of a Boy" 1928 Pencil and watercolor

"Montes et omnes colles" 1928 Watercolor

"The Winter Solstice" 1928 Pencil, ink and watercolor

Newark-on-Trent, Gilstrap Municipal Museum

"Seascape, Ynys Byr" 1925 Watercolor

Newcastle-upon-Tyne, Laing Art Gallery
"The Mother of the West" c. 1942 Pencil, ink and
watercolor

Newport, Gwent, Museum and Art Gallery
"Lynx" 1929 Pencil and watercolor

Oxford, Ashmolean Museum
"Ship off Ynys Byr" 1925 Watercolor
"French Hillside" 1928 Watercolor

Portsmouth, City Museums and Art Gallery
"The Suburban Order" 1926 Watercolor

Salford, Lancashire City Art Gallery
"Back Gardens, London" 1926 Watercolor

Sheffield, Graves Art Gallery
"Streams and Trees" 1932 Watercolor

Swansea, Glynn Vivian
"The Vulgate and Flowers" 1929 Watercolor
"Petra" 1929 Watercolor

(b) Outside the United Kingdom

Sydney, Art Gallery of New South Wales
"Self-portrait" 1928 Oil
"The Candle for the Cup" 1932 Watercolor

Melbourne, National Gallery of Victoria
"Mr Carlile's Acacia" 1948 Watercolor
"Sitting Room Table" Watercolor

Adelaide, Art Gallery of South Australia
"Vase on Sill" 1931 Watercolor

Fredericton, New Brunswick, Beaverbrook Art Gallery
"Welsh Ponies" 1926 Watercolor
"Welsh Goats" Watercolor

Ottawa, National Gallery of Canada
"Pigotts Farm" 1932 Watercolor
"Carr's Splint" 1932 Watercolor

Toronto, Art Gallery
"Evening by the Sea" 1931 Watercolor

Vancouver, Art Gallery

"The Gentle Bird" or "Flower piece with yellow bird"
1950 Watercolor

"Resting" 1928 Oil

Chicago, Art Institute

"Meadow Gate" 1937 Watercolor

Dunedin, New Zealand, Art Gallery

"Dorset Coast near Lulworth" 1926 Watercolor

"The Park, Cumberland" c. 1932 Watercolor

"Still Life with Jug" 1932 Watercolor

INDEX

Like the index of the George Oppen volume in this series, this index is divided into two parts. The first part lists chiefly the names of people, places and things. It lists historical figures, people who knew or wrote about David Jones and people David Jones knew or wrote about, the names of literary, artistic, cultural and religious movements or organizations, certain military terms, battles and battle-sites of the First World War, figures from myth and legend, some technical geological, archeological and anthropological terms, and, as Carroll F. Terrell has said in his index to the Zukofsky and Bunting volumes in the series, "most . . . capitalized words . . . except for the names of cities and publishing companies or other routine names used in bibliographical notes." In indexing the bibliography, we have followed the lead of the H.D. volume in the series. Because authors of articles are listed alphabetically in Part II, we do not index the item citations themselves. An author's name is indexed only if it appears somewhere in the bibliography other than in the citation or annotation of his or her own article. Neither the brief chronology of David Jones' life nor Paul Hills' list of art works in public collections has been indexed. Since it was felt that the table of contents gives a clear enough guide to the main subjects discussed by contributors, there is no entry for David Jones himself subdivided either alphabetically or in accordance with the chronological development of his life and work.

The second part of the index lists the titles of books, poems, essays and works of visual art by David Jones. It also indicates on which pages quotations from, or references to, his published letters may be found, whether these are published individually in journals or collected in groups in *Dai Greatcoat, Letters to Vernon Watkins, Letters to a Friend* and *Inner Necessities*. In the interest of economy, the chief book publications of David Jones are listed with inclusive pagination for those essays in the volume which are grouped in the table of contents under a section heading indicating that they focus specifically upon the text in question. For example, the initial such listing for *The Anathemata* is p. 243 to p. 262, the full length of N. K. Sandars' essay. Otherwise, the index lists individually all references to *The Anathemata* in essays which are *not* grouped in the table of contents under the section heading indicating that they focus specifically upon that book. The same principle is maintained for *In Parenthesis, The Sleeping Lord, The Roman Quarry, Epoch and Artist*, and *The Dying Gaul*. Subdivisions of the major book publications of David Jones--the titles of the seven parts of *In Parenthesis* and the eight parts of *The Anathemata*, the individual poems of *The Sleeping Lord* and *The Roman Quarry*, and the titles of essays in *Epoch and Artist* and *The Dying Gaul*--are indexed separately, both for those sections of the volume dealing specifically with the books in which they appear, and elsewhere.

*   *   *   *   *

Part I: Index of People, Places and Things

A

Aachen, 156
Aaron, 437
Abbot Extraordinary, 135
Abel, 227, 233, 234, 245
Aberystwyth, 175, 444
Abraham, 44, 175
Absalom, 398
Achieux, 172
Achilles, 154
Acid (Drop) Copse, 163
Acropolis, 294
Acton, Lord, 533
Adam, 233
Adam Bede, 530
Adams brothers, 111
Adams, Henry, 48
Adonis, 344n, 374, 376, 377, 435
Adversus Haereses, Book II, 482n
Aegean culture, 303
"Aegis," 296
Aeneas, 382, 390, 400, 416, 469
Aeneid, 273, 300, 415
Aeron, 376
Agamemnon, 154

Age of the Gods, 445
Agelastos Petra, 292, 435
Agenda, 19, 66, 243, 247, 273, 342n, 409n, 539
Agenda Editions, 30, 32
Agnes Sorel as Our Lady, 432
Agnus Dei, 434, 436
agon, dilemma of, 241
Agony [in the Garden] (El Greco), 88
Agravaine, Lord, 216
Aiken, Conrad, 511
Albatross, 428
Albert (France), 173
Albert, Prince, 141
Albright, W. T., 444
Aldasa, 243
Aldington, Richard, 528
Alexander the Great, 56, 304
Alexander, Michael, 65, 251
Alfred, King, 55, 304
Alice Books, the, 111
Allchin, Canon A. M., 522
Allen, Reggie, 92
Alpert, Marie McCosh, 31
Alps, 193
Am I My Brother's Keeper?, 481

Index

Dai Greatcoat, Boast of, 30, 216, 224, 227, 228, 229, 230, 231, 232, 236, 239, 241, 535
Daly, Ann Carson, 288n, 327, 327n, 328, 544
Dalriada, 243
Damaseus, Pope, 416
Danielou, Jean, 476n
Dante, 47, 219, 388, 416, 418, 530, 535, 536
D'Arcy, Fr. Martin, 51, 140, 486, 486n
Daren Llwyd range, 421
Darius the Mede, 47
Dark Ages, 288, 289, 290, 302
Darwin, Charles, 268
Darwinians, 287
Das Untergang des Abendlandes, 445
Davenport, Guy, 17, 19, 73, 491
David, King, 234, 235, 398
David Jones (Hague), 468n, 469n, 470n, 515
David Jones (Ironside), 97n
David Jones (Tate Gallery Catalogue), 427n, 431n
David Jones: A Commentary on Some Poetic Fragments (Pagnoulle), 491
David Jones: An Annotated Bibliography and Guide to Research (Rees), 17n
David Jones: An Exploratory Study of the Writings (Hooker), 285n, 332n, 334n, 467n, 515
"David Jones and Broadcasting" (Cleverdon), 23
David Jones and Other Wonder Voyagers (Pacey), 541
"David Jones and the Actually Loved and Known" (Raine), 59
David Jones: Artist and Writer (Blamires), 19, 120, 467n
David Jones: Eight Essays on His Work as Writer and Artist (Mathias), 19, 515
David Jones: Mythmaker (Ward), 20, 21, 143, 371n, 445n, 473n, 540, 543
"David Jones: The Man Who Was on the Field. *In Parenthesis* as Straight Reporting" (Hughes), 93n
"David Jones: Towards the Holy Diversities" (Mathias), 332n, 344n, 385n
David Jones Weekend School, 510
Davies, Aneirin Talfan, 328, 370n, 514

Davies, David (Lord Davies of Llandinam), 167
Davies, John, 385
Davies, Dom Raphael, 98, 100
Davy, Derek, 206n
Dawn in Britain, The, 200
Dawson, Christopher, 55, 140, 279, 444, 445, 445n, 467, 533, 538
De Defecta Oraculorum (Plutarch), 56
de la Mare, Richard, 112, 198
de la Taille, Maurice, 338n, 439, 467, 473, 479, 479n, 538, 543
"De Mundi Universitate" (Bernardus Silvestris), 73
Dea Roma, 335, 474, 478
Deae Matres, 349
Deane, Patrick, 19, 30, 478n
Deborah, 167
Decline of the West, 30, 154, 270n, 286, 287, 297, 300n, 443-464
Degas, Edgar, 126, 415
deGroot, H. B., 491
Dell, Colonel, 164, 221, 222
Delphi, 434
dene, 68
Derby, Lord, 165
Derbyshire, 56
Derfel Gadarn, 235
Derfel Gatheren, 234, 235
"Derfel the Mighty," 235
Des Pres, Terence, 392n
Descartes, Rene, 388, 389n
Devlin, Christopher, 482n
Devon, 433
Diary of a Nobody (Grossmith), 92
Diaspora, 145, 298, 298n
Dies Irae, 254, 305, 455
Dillon, Myles, 282n
Dilworth, Thomas, 19, 20, 21, 23, 25, 26, 27, 30, 143, 215n, 325, 325n, 435n, 467n, 470, 470n, 491, 544
Dionysius Exiguus, 455
Dionysius the Areopagite, 482n, 483, 483n
Dionysus, 49
Ditchling Common, 95, 96, 97, 98, 136, 426
Ditchling Common Guild of Craftsmen, 97, 98, 98n
Divine Comedy, 45
Divine Names and The Mystical Theology, The, 483, 483n, 486
Divine Wisdom, 421
Dix, Gregory, 266, 467, 481, 481n

Holderlin, Friedrich, 511
Hollander, John, 17
Holloway, 92
Holy Communion, Office of, 397
Holy Spirit, 295
Holy Thursday, 338, 338n
Holywell, 87
Homer, 44, 57, 291, 379
homoerotic (poetry), 217
Homosexual (ambience of *IP*), 217
Honddu, 354, 355, 428
Honeyman, Stanley, 153, 153n, 156n
Hooker, Jeremy, 19, 30, 79, 254, 285n, 332n, 333, 334n, 344, 344n, 467n, 510, 515, 534
Hopkins, Gerard Manley, 118, 222, 379, 482, 482n, 515, 516, 520
Horse's Mouth, The, 130
Hough, Graham, 197n
Hour of Decision, 447
Hove, 104, 406, 414, 417
Hove Seaside Villas, 413
Howson Road, 89
Hugel, Friedrich von, 486, 486n
Hughes, Colin, 29, 93, 93n, 163, 522
Hughes, Daniel, 95
Hughes, Ted, 159
Huk, Romana, 31
Human Age, The, 130
Humphreys, Emyr, 539
Hunt, Holman, 411
Hunting of the boar Trwyth, 110
"Hunting of the Snark, The," 110, 224, 537
Hutchins, Patricia, 286n
Huxley, Aldous, 518
"Hymn on the Morning of Christ's Nativity" (Milton), 91
Hyne, Alice Mary ("Cissie"), 87
Hyne, Tony, 87

I

I Ching, 230
Iberian, 81
Ichthus, 368, 370
Ichthus-Son, 370
Icon and Idea, 484, 484n
Ignatius, Fr., 98
Ilia, 295, 296, 334n
Iliad, 455
"Image and Presence" (Bonnefoy), 391n
Imitation and Design, 134, 134n
Imperator, 259

Impressionism, 406, 415
"In der Nacht" (Schumann), 414
"In Memoriam James Joyce" (MacDiarmid), 523
In Paradisum, 353
Incarnation, 273, 281, 288, 291, 302, 305, 321, 329, 439, 470, 543
India, 164
Indian myths, 48
Industrial Revolution, 290n
"Influence of Dionysius in Religious History, The," 483n
Inns of Court, 94
Inspirations Unbidden (Harris), 482n
Institute for Scholarship in the Liberal Arts, University of Notre Dame, 31
"Intentional Fallacy, The," 231n
Introducing David Jones, 109; "Preface" in, 474n, 522
Invention of the Cross (Vernal Festival of), 321n
Investigating English Style, 206n
Ireland, 56, 81, 84, 126, 138, 151, 414, 418, 422
Irenaeus of Lugdunum, 476n
Irenaeus, St., 62, 331n, 476, 476n, 482, 482n
Irene, 335
Iron Age, 289
Ironside, Robin, 18, 97n, 115
Isaiah, 432
Isaias, Book of, 119, 212
Iscoed oaks, 354
Iseult (Isolde, Isoud; see also Essyllt), 409, 410, 412, 418, 419
Isis, 287
Islington, 44, 175
Israelite mythology, 261
Italian Army, 168
Itinerarium Joannis de Hese, 232

J

Jacobeans, 111
James the Apostle, St., 207
James Joyce's World, 286n
Jeffers, Robinson, 268, 357
Jenkins, Lt., 63, 170, 177, 199
Jeremiah, 372
Jerusalem, 24, 103, 248, 258, 394, 395, 400; Roman, 393, 395, 397
Jesse, 432
Jesuits, 135, 136

*   *   *   *   *

Part II: Index of Books, Poems, Essays, Letters, Art Works and Annotations by David Jones